Comparative Management and Economic Progress

# THE IRWIN SERIES IN MANAGEMENT

Consulting Editor  JOHN F. MEE  *Indiana University*

# Comparative Management
# and
# Economic Progress

**Richard N. Farmer**
Associate Professor of
International Business Administration
Indiana University

**Barry M. Richman**
Associate Professor of
Management and Industrial Organization
University of California, Los Angeles

1965

RICHARD D. IRWIN, INC.

Homewood, Illinois

To Jean and Vivian
who in their own gracious ways
have made a unique contribution to this book

# PREFACE

This study was begun as an attempt to answer the general question of why industrial managerial activity and the effectiveness of management in terms of economic progress seemed to vary sharply between different countries. Both authors had fairly extensive research, academic and managerial experience in various countries, and it seemed clear that the usual techniques of exploring management problems and firm efficiency, as well as economic growth, were inadequate to explain all such variations.

It first appeared that the key to this question might be in the internal management of productive enterprises, and the initial explorations of the problem were in this direction. However, it soon became clear that management theory, in all of its present forms, could not explain many significant deviations in managerial effectiveness and behavior between different countries. Most of management theory tends to assume that the external environment is basically the same for all productive enterprises and proceeds from there, and yet, in examining various economic and social systems, it is abundantly clear that external environments vary enormously between countries and cultures. Differences in the external environments within which productive enterprises must function clearly have a crucial impact on the performance of enterprise management.

A second approach was to examine the various theories of economic development. This also appeared inadequate, mainly because most economists tend either to assume that managers are efficient or virtually to ignore managerial problems completely. If, for example, "X" million dollars are invested, it is possible to discuss the proper place for the investment, the impact this investment will have—at least on paper—on various economic sectors, and so on. But little is said about how the actual management of the investment spending, by either a public or private agency, will be accomplished. Who draws up and implements the detailed investment plans? Who buys the machines? Who organizes and directs human activity so that investment will produce desired results? Which individuals will become responsible for what business situations, and how will they be chosen, motivated, and controlled? Such management questions are usually not considered.

Further difficulties exist. We have been aware for some time that legal, political, educational, sociological and cultural variables bear heavily on firm performance and managerial activity. However, management theory does not adequately take into account such variables and their impact on management in different countries. With few exceptions, political scientists, lawyers, educators, sociologists, psychologists, and anthropologists concerned with economic progress tend to ignore the problems of management, and concentrate their attention primarily on the transformation of social, political, legal and/or educational institutions. No one discipline seemed capable of explaining in any operational manner the significant deviations between managerial performance in various countries.

The result of these explorations into comparative management situations and the rationale of effective management is this book. Here we attempt to interrelate in a systematized framework all relevant disciplines which bear significantly on managerial performance. Since we view this book as a pioneer work in this newly emerging field of comparative management, much of it is highly suggestive rather than conclusive.

One result of this study is that we have been able to explain, to our own satisfaction, many of the large deviations in managerial performance and productive efficiency throughout the industrial world. A second result is that we have been made keenly aware of the rich complexity of the management process in involved cultural situations. Given the large number of variables relevant even in a relatively simple managerial problem, no one theory of management can hope to explain everything—our hope is that this volume will encourage others to attempt to evaluate the performance of management in various countries in a total systems manner. Management is not something that takes place in a black box isolated from all other activities in the country—it is complexly interrelated with a variety of economic, political, legal, social, educational and cultural activities.

We regard management as the one most critical factor in economic progress. The expectations revolution now raging in the world has led citizens of virtually every country, whether capitalist or marxist, to expect a better material life in the foreseeable future than he now enjoys; but such increases in material well-being will not occur automatically. The key factor in such material gains will be the manner in which the management of productive enterprise is handled.

A central thesis here is that effective enterprise management is the key to expanding per capita incomes in any country. If a country has a stated or implied goal of such income expansion, it can most easily be achieved by concentrating on those internal and external factors, which bear most heavily on the practice of management in productive firms.

Our analyses focus primarily on industrial management, particularly the management of complex industrial establishments employing at least a dozen persons. Such organizations generate the bulk of a nation's production and wealth. In these organizations the managerial job becomes extremely significant, since a great number of interdependent activities must be coordinated, if desired economic results are to be forthcoming. It will, however, be necessary to take cognizance of various nonindustrial organizations—financial, commercial, governmental, agricultural, and so forth—as important institutions which shape the general industrial environment.

It is our hope that this book will prove valuable to persons interested in a variety of fields in addition to general and comparative management or economic development. Students and practitioners of international business operations, governmental officials, and a wide variety of academicians and intelligent laymen may find this treatise, or at least substantial parts of it, both useful and enlightening. We risk sacrificing depth for breadth in many facets of this study, but we feel that this is the only way that an operational, total systems concept of management can evolve. We are convinced that such a concept of management is urgently needed in our complex industrial world.

This is the first of a two volume study dealing with comparative management and economic progress. In this volume our major aim is to develop a general theory of comparative management, although much use will be made of country examples in order to illustrate how the theory applies to the real industrial and managerial world. The second volume, to be published at a later date, deals with comprehensive studies of a number of diverse countries.

The general theory presented here is based on several phases and types of research activity. They include:

(a) Our own firsthand research and/or work experience in ten foreign countries—Canada, Mexico, Great Britain, the Soviet Union, Czechoslavakia, Poland, Lebanon, Egypt, Kuwait and Saudi Arabia. We have also had the opportunity to observe for shorter periods of time industrial firms in more than a dozen other foreign countries.

(b) A comprehensive study of numerous written sources (including many unpublished United Nations studies) many of which are foreign language publications.

(c) Extensive research conducted and insights provided by our research assistants. Several of them have been doctoral students from various foreign countries, and some of them have had considerable business experience in their homelands.

(d) Interviews and discussions with numerous educators in different fields who are experts on different countries, and with foreign and local business executives, government and United Nations officials and graduate students who are highly interested in and knowledgable about various aspects of industrial management in different foreign countries. In several cases written questionnaires and informal personal letters have been used to obtain useful information from persons of the above types.

Through the above activities we have acquired some significant insights into the problems and process of industrial management in several countries in addition to those that we have studied firsthand. In part, these countries include India, Indonesia, Turkey, Japan, Brazil, Argentina, Chile, Syria, Ghana, the Sudan, Union of South Africa, Germany, Italy, France, Sweden, Belgium, the Netherlands and Yugoslavia.

In view of our exploratory research activity in the field of comparative management to date, we feel that the general theory to be presented in this volume can prove uesful in analyzing comparative management situations and economic progress in any country.

This book has evolved through several years of intensive study in the United States and abroad. Since it is not possible to acknowledge here all those persons and organizations who aided us in this study, we have limited our list to those parties who have most significantly and directly contributed to the preparation of this book. All errors, omissions, distortions, and interpretations are, of course, the authors' responsibility entirely.

We are particularly indebted to our research assistants and graduate students who have contributed significantly through their insights and by taking a serious interest in and conscientiously applying themselves to our study. They include Armin Schafler, Vishvanath Phatek, Loren Raymond, David Hitchin, Abdallah Abou-Aish, Mohamed Khalil, and Bernard Estafen at the University of California, Los Angeles, and M. Michael Moorman of Indiana University.

We are also indebted to Dean Neil Jacoby and Professors George Steiner and Anant Negandhi of the Graduate School of Business Administration, UCLA, for their encouragement, support, constructive criticism and advice in the preparation of this study. Our appreciation is also extended to Professor John Mee of Indiana University for his thoughtful and extremely helpful review of our manuscript.

We wish to thank Dr. Benjamin Barg of the United Nations for his time and effort in helping us search out and obtain pertinent U.N. sources for our study.

Three business managers deserve a special word of thanks for their insights and contributions which are reflected in this study. They are S. S. Olayan, president and owner of Olayanco, Beirut, Lebanon and General Contracting Company, Saudi Arabia; Ghalib Aidi, assistant manager, General Contracting Company, Saudi Arabia; and Harry H. Walker, executive (now retired) of Trans-Arabian Pipeline Company. Finally we wish to acknowledge our primary financial benefactor during the last three years, the Division of Research of the Graduate School of Business Administration, University of California, Los Angeles.

RICHARD N. FARMER
BARRY M. RICHMAN

June, 1965

# TABLE OF CONTENTS

# Chapter 1

# Economic Progress,

# Management Theory and

# Comparative Management

Comparative management deals with problems of managerial performance in various countries. The emphasis is on the management of local enterprises in different cultures; however, the conceptual framework and analysis to be presented have significant implications not only for local firms and managements in a given country but also for international firms engaged in business operations in foreign countries and for governments involved in the economic development of a given nation.

Our focus is on the role and significance of management in any country's economic progress, and of major concern are the environmental factors which have a significant bearing on managerial activity and effectiveness in any society. The factors under study are essentially external constraints within which firm managements must operate. These constraints are classified into four broad categories—educational, sociological, political-legal, and economic—and each one may either aid or hinder managerial performance in a particular country.

We view management as the single most critical social activity in connection with economic progress. Physical, financial, and manpower resources are by themselves but passive agents; they must be effectively combined and coordinated through sound, active management if a country is to experience a substantial level of economic growth and development. A country can have sizable natural and manpower resources including plentiful skilled labor, and substantial capital but still be relatively poor because very few competent managers are available to put these resources efficiently together in the production and distribution of useful goods and services.

As will be shown later, the degree of managerial effectiveness and productive efficiency achieved in any society is determined by a sizable number of interrelated educational, sociological, political-legal, and economic factors. The factors to be considered have a significant effect on economic progress through their direct impact on managerial effectiveness; management is seen as the crucial intermediate link between the overall environment and tangible economic results in a given country.

## LIMITATIONS OF ECONOMIC GROWTH AND DEVELOPMENT STUDIES

Unfortunately, the role of management in economic growth has been either ignored or underestimated by most economists, political scientists, legal experts, behavioral scientists, educators, and other scholars concerned with economic progress. For example, a study of educational effectiveness might compare (qualitatively or quantitatively) the levels of education in a culture with per capita gross national product, or an economic study might compare the amount of capital per worker with per capita national income. The implications here are that if a country achieves a certain educational level, or a certain supply of capital, economic progress will be enhanced, and consequently income per capita will be higher. In both of the above cases, it is true that more education and more capital per worker may well result in somewhat higher levels of per capita income.[1]

It is tempting to conclude at this point that all a country needs to become wealthier, in the material sense, is to expand education or save more; however, this is only a part of the problem, since the increase in per capita income is likely to be substantially greater if managerial problems are also given proper attention.

The major defect in the above type of analysis is that it implicitly assumes that what persons do with their better education or their increased capital stock is the right thing in terms of economic progress. A country with a large number of educated persons is not necessarily a well managed country, and it is possible that its income will be considerably lower than it might be if this education were focused more sharply on the managerial problems involved in operating complex enterprises and a complex economy. The fact that *usually* a country able and willing to expend large sums on education is also a well managed country does not lead to the inevitability of *any* educated population having *good* management (but management would undoubtedly be better with an educated as compared to an illiterate population, regardless of the type of education).

Similarly, the fact that a country has a large per capita capital stock does not necessarily lead to its efficient use. One familiar pattern in the underde-

---

[1] See Benjamin Higgins, *Economic Development* (New York: W. W. Norton & Company, Inc., 1959), pp. 85–213, for summaries of the more important economic growth theories.

veloped countries is capital wastage caused by inadequate management of assets.[2] One must explore behind the obvious façade of physical assets or educational accomplishments to determine under what conditions such features result in reasonably efficient and well managed economies and firms.

A real danger here is that a country may be led down a perilous path by such oversimplification. An economist may claim, "Save more, and accumulate capital, and you will be rich"; but there is no single, straight road to economic progress.[3] The country following the above advice with limited resources will surely neglect other factors relevant to productive efficiency, such as sound enterprise management, the creation of a sound economic system, a good legal-political framework, a cultural environment conducive to increased productivity, and possibly an adequate educational system, in order to accumulate capital. When and if the capital is obtained, however, nothing much happens, because the necessary components of a well managed system have not been created to supplement the capital stocks. Machines rust because no one knows how to plan maintenance; they operate at much less than capacity because no one is able to market output effectively, or because skilled labor cannot be obtained to run them; firms go bankrupt for lack of sound financial planning; and so on.

Even in relatively advanced countries such misuse of capital continues, though certainly not as extensively as in less well managed economies. While much management may appear simple and obvious, particularly in small, single product firms, it does not automatically follow that sound management results from *more* capital or *more* education per se.

It is true that some recent works on economic growth have attempted to explore the problems of management and enterpreneurship to some extent, since economists, particularly those with practical experience in administration and management, have realized for some time that these critical factors cannot be ignored in any meaningful discussion of economic progress.[4] Such discussions, however, tend to focus more on the critical need for management than on how management is actually practiced in a variety of cultural situations. One who has experienced operations under bad management is clearly aware of the need for better management, but this is not the same

---

[2] For one example, see Lee C. Nehrt, *A Pre-Investment Study of the Flat Glass Industry* (Washington: International Bank for Reconstruction & Development, 1964), p. 38. Nehrt notes that in small new glass plants in underdeveloped countries 20 to 40 percent of glass produced in the first year is unusable. In developed countries 85 to 90 percent is usable.

[3] In fairness to a sizable number of perceptive economists, it should be noted that many of them recognize clearly the complexity of the development process, including the need for better management. See Stefan H. Robock, *Brazil's Developing Northeast* (Washington, D.C.: The Brookings Institution, 1963), pp. 146–176, and particularly pp. 164–165, for one good example of this thinking.

[4] Robock, *op. cit.*, pp. 103–176.

thing as giving clear guides to how better management might be achieved.

It should be noted that management science has been slow to develop. Only in the twentieth century have scholars worked seriously in this area, and the attitude of many scholars in other fields even now is that this type of theorizing is not intellectually respectable. Perhaps this follows from the fact that most scholars in the economic growth and development field are, or were, trained as economists.

In economics, the managerial and entrepreneurial functions are recognized, but typically it is assumed that internal firm management is done efficiently—that is, that management always makes the correct economic decisions. For this we can probably blame Ricardo. In his early analyses of firm behavior, Ricardo (a very successful nineteenth century stockbroker) implicitly saw a productive firm as a type of stockbroking operation. Costs and prices were known—hence the one man firm could intuitively adjust his sales and purchases immediately to the point of maximum productive efficiency; this led to the economic assumption that any firm management, given costs and prices, would always be efficient.[5] While many one man firms may still attempt to operate this way, a General Motors, or for that matter most any complex modern firm, cannot be run out of the owners' hats, and the management problems of this type of large enterprise are significantly different from the simple one man operation of Ricardo's era. Yet many economists still react to such enterprises as if they were always managed by wise, competent, and seemingly automatic individuals who always do the right thing economically.

Those who follow the teaching of Marx (who was a keen student of Ricardo), frequently have an even more naive view of managerial efficiency—primarily because in most parts of the world the first time a Marxist sees a realistic management problem is immediately after the revolution.

The result of this assumption about managerial efficiency is that the practice of management has not received the attention it deserves, outside of business schools. Increasingly, however, as scholars and practical men trained in other disciplines encounter serious managerial defects, both at home and abroad, there has been more interest in the practice of management. Anyone who has managed or closely observed a productive enterprise is keenly aware of the results in a firm without management—if management is truly absent, the enterprise stops operating. The combination of inputs to obtain useful outputs cannot occur without some management being performed, and the levels of managerial effectiveness in various enterprises and countries have an extraordinary range. Probably more than anything else, this factor explains why some countries and firms produce more efficiently than others.

---

[5] Philip Charles Newman, *The Development of Economic Thought* (New York: Prentice-Hall, Inc., 1952), pp. 78–88.

## LIMITATIONS OF CONVENTIONAL MANAGEMENT AND ORGANIZATION THEORY

In the past few decades scholars and management practitioners with surprisingly heterogeneous backgrounds have contributed significantly to the development of management and organization theory. It is becoming widely accepted, in the more advanced countries at least, that a systematized body of management theory is essential for improving the practice of management. Yet in exploring the existing bodies of management theory to determine what useful concepts and tools might be utilized in the area of comparative management, it becomes clear that such theory has some serious drawbacks in terms of its orientation and applicability to different types of cultures and economies.

### Inadequate Attention Given to the External Environment

Explorations into the field of management reveal that, with very few exceptions, existing theories approach management as an internal problem within a given organization. The impact of external constraints on internal management is treated peripherally, if at all. In fact, external constraints are assumed constant in most formulations.

In effect, most studies of management have taken place in a "black box" labeled "management," without much concern for the external environment in which the firm and its management may operate. As long as this external environment is basically the same for all firms the approach is valid; however, in cases where the environment differs significantly, present theory fails to describe, explain, or predict comparative differentials in managerial performance.

In addition, existing management theory falls short of defining efficiency in operational terms, and the existing concept of efficiency has little, if any, meaning in comparative management situations. In making comparisons of managerial efficiency and effectiveness between countries with widely different social and cultural environments, difficulties soon arise when traditional types of analysis are applied.

We observe two firm managements in the same sector, and we note that in country A managers seem far superior to their counterparts in country B; however, we cannot then state categorically that managers in A do their internal managing job better than those in B, since the nature of the external environment facing the two managements may be completely different. A may be a country with ample supplies of high skill labor, while B may have serious shortages of this important factor. A may also have a good, low cost transportation system, while B is faced with transport shortages, high cost freight movements, and the need to build far larger inventories than in A. A may have an excellent credit system, which allows a competent firm to obtain adequate funds, while *B* may have no organized capital markets. The result could well be that the presumably inept managers in *B* are actually doing better than their counterparts in *A*, given their external constraints.

In such a case it is fruitless to argue that the firm in country *B* should improve its internal management. This is clearly possible in most cases, but the gains from urging change in external constraints might prove much larger. The point here is that comparisons between internal managements in different countries may prove rather useless unless the external environment is also studied carefully. With this point in mind, let us briefly explore the various conventional approaches to management and organization theory.[6]

## The Management Process or Universalist Approach

In the universalist or management process approach to management theory attention is focused on the functions, principles, and techniques of internal management applicable to any productive enterprise, in a given environment, seeking to determine how the enterprise might gain more efficient operations. It is true that the management of any complex organization is called upon to perform similar basic functions—for example, planning and decision making, control, organization, staffing, direction and leadership. It is also true that there are a number of principles, techniques, and criteria expounded that serve as guidelines for carrying out the managerial functions efficiently anywhere; however, how and how well management actually performs its functions, and the adaptability of various principles and techniques, depend largely on the external environment of the enterprise in a particular country.

## The Empirical and Policy Approach

A second approach to management theory is sometimes referred to as the empirical school. In this approach management is identified as a study of experience, sometimes with the intent to draw pertinent generalizations but often merely as a means of transferring this experience to students and practitioners. The emphasis is largely on business policy, problem solving, and the study and analysis of cases. The major limitation here, with regard to the field of comparative management, is that the experiences and activities of managers vary substantially in firms operating in different environ-

---

[6] For a comprehensive treatment and analysis of the various conventional approaches, as well as extensive documentation regarding leading authorities and their works, see: Harold Koontz, ed., *Toward a Unified Theory of Management* (New York: McGraw-Hill Book Company, 1964); J. March and H. Simon, *Organizations* (New York: John Wiley & Sons, Inc., 1958); M. Haire, ed., *Modern Organization Theory* (New York: John Wiley & Sons, Inc., 1959); J. Litterer, *Organizations: Structure and Behavior* (New York: John Wiley & Sons, Inc., 1963); P. Gordon, "Transcend the Current Debate on Administrative Theory," *Academy of Management Journal*, Vol. VI, No. 4, December, 1963, pp. 290–302.

mental settings. To date, this approach has not developed an operational, conceptual framework which sets forth the major environmental factors which have a significant bearing on managerial performance in any country.

## Behavioralist Approaches

The various behavioralist and human relations theories of organization and management—developed largely in the United States—focus primarily on the persons in a given organization, in a given environment, trying to determine how the organization might function better. The chief aim here has been to describe and explain human motivation and behavior in organized groups. It is felt (rightly) that by acquiring greater understanding of human beings in a going organization the manager will be in a better position to motivate subordinates effectively, to predict their behavior, and to direct them toward the accomplishment of organizational objectives.

Within the overall behavioral science approach to organizational management theory there has been a wide range of research studies. Many scholars have focused on interpersonal or human relations, bringing to bear existing and newly developed theories, techniques, and methods of the relevant social sciences upon the study of inter- and intrapersonal phenomena. Some behavioral studies look upon management and organization as a social system—that is, a system of cultural interrelationships. They identify the nature of the cultural relationships of various groups and attempt to show these as related and, usually, integrated systems.

A few prominent scholars have been chiefly concerned with the concept of organizational equilibrium and have focused on the organization as a cooperative system. This ecological approach, as it is sometimes called, deals with both internal and external organizational relationships and is concerned with those forces—mainly psychological and partially economic—which regulate interdependent adaptation, innovation, and change. While this approach certainly contributes to an understanding of the mutual relations between organisms and their environments, it is highly abstract and rather nonoperational. Any limited application it may have to the real world would be confined primarily to a competitive economic environment such as that in the United States.

Many behavioral scientists have been concerned with theories of bureaucracy and/or the impact of various elements of the formal organization on human behavior. In this connection, there have been numerous studies dealing with the interaction between the formal and informal organization in a given environment. Some scholars have focused their attentions on the manager as a leader in an attempt to depict key leadership traits; others have been concerned with the most effective leadership and direction techniques to utilize in a given situation.

With few exceptions, all of the behavioral theories of management and organization view the productive organization as essentially fixed in space and time. It may prove fatal to apply various theories of this type developed in one culture to other cultures. Human motivation and behavior, as well as organizational and cultural interrelationships, in productive enterprises are a function of various complex environmental factors, many of them beyond the control of enterprise management. Direction and leadership techniques which prove effective in the American firm may prove inadequate, or even disastrous, when applied to firms in Saudi Arabia, Japan, or India.

## The Decisional Approach

A group of theorists with diverse backgrounds are expanding our understanding of organizational decision making and human problem solving. But the decisional approach to management theory also fails to provide an adequate conceptual framework for comparative management analysis.

The descriptive decision theorists are primarily concerned with describing how organizational decisions are actually made. In this approach researchers may deal with the pertinent steps in decision making, with the decision itself, with the individuals or organizational groups who make the decision, or with an analysis of the entire decision process. Some scholars in this field expand decision theory so it covers the psychological and sociological aspects of decisions and decision making. The normative decision theorists, or management scientists, as they are sometimes called, view decision making as a highly rational process entailing a series of logical steps and are concerned with how optimum decisions ought to be made. They draw heavily on mathematics, statistics, economics, logic, and engineering and use as their chief tools computers, operations research, mathematical models, and econometrics.

The major limitation of the decisional approach, with regard to comparative management studies, is that the actual decision making process, the attitudes and goals of the decision makers, and—perhaps most importantly—the types of decisions actually made tend to vary between organizations in substantially different environmental settings.

## Concluding Remarks on Conventional Management and Organization Theory

The various approaches to management and organization theory can undoubtedly help an individual firm achieve higher levels of efficiency. No organization is perfect; and close study of its functions, operations, and personnel will often yield insights which will increase productive efficiency and improve performance. Existing management theory does not, however, attempt to deal with the problem of relative efficiencies between firms in different environments; nor does it consider significant differences in managerial behavior and performance in different countries. If, for example, a competent manager of a machine tool company in Boston were to be placed in charge of a similar firm in Bombay, he might well appear less efficient and effective than he was in his American job. Moreover, the way in which he actually performs his managerial functions would probably also differ substantially in the two different environments. The man has not changed but the environment has.

Where environments do vary, as is the case between countries, it is extremely important to examine the external pressures, or constraints, upon internal enterprise management. A manager may perform competently in his internal activities, given his constraints; but he is influenced substantially by various external constraints in his country, which directly react on and influence his performance. For example, during the depression of the 1930's even the most competent firm managements in America achieved relatively poor economic results because of environmental factors beyond their control. The same could be said about competent managers presently operating in many countries, particularly newly developing countries, having environments which significantly hinder managerial performance.

It is true that firm management may at times influence, control, and even shape various elements of its external environment. The management of a given enterprise is not, however, in a position to exert extensive independent direction or control over the external constraints considered in this study; this is a matter of collective action on a large scale.

## LIMITATION OF EXISTING STUDIES ON INTERNATIONAL AND COMPARATIVE MANAGEMENT

The growing number of studies in the newly emerging field of international management have failed to provide us with the type of systematized, operational framework which comparative management analysis calls for. Many studies in this area tend to be too narrow. For example, a paper on the ten best ways for a firm to advertise in Japan may be useful to a particular firm, but it fails to give much insight into the many crucial environmental factors bearing on management activity in this (or any other) country.

Most studies which do deal with environmental factors do so in an unsystematic way. It may be pointed out, for instance, that legal problems in various foreign countries are critically important, but no weighting is given to this factor relative to other key factors which may also directly affect the firm and its management. A number of environmental factors may be noted without any evaluation of relative importance, or without regard to how they directly affect managerial performance. Some works labeled as studies in international management, and particularly international business, really do not deal in any depth with management and managing per se. Managers engaged in international operations are seen as passive agents who automatically respond (properly) to economic or political stimuli—for example, tax, tariff, and foreign trade policies. Just how they actually respond, or whether or not the response is efficient management, is left unexplained.

Certain available studies in international management do, however, provide some valuable data and concepts for our comparative analysis; but none appear to provide the type of conceptual framework that is needed. One notable work on international business policy deals with various important factors that an American (or other) firm should take into account when considering or engaging in foreign business operations.[7] While some significant environmental factors are considered, many others which directly bear on firm results are not. Moreover, no attempt is made to consider variations in managerial performance in different countries.

A leading study on comparative management—covering twelve countries—discusses management as an economic resource, a system of authority, and a class or elite.[8] While this is certainly a commendable study—proving useful to us in our own work—it does not shed much light on the actual process of managing, or on differences in managerial performance, in different countries. In general, this volume is highly descriptive and rather nonoperational in nature; it does not attempt to deal with, explain or predict the impact of a wide range of environmental factors which directly bear on managerial effectiveness and behavior.

## CONCLUSION

We are convinced that when comparative management situations involving different countries are considered, existing management theory in effect assumes away many of the crucial variables. As a result, existing theory is rather inadequate to use as a conceptual framework or research foundation in the area of comparative management. Available studies on international and comparative management also fail to provide the type of operational structured framework that is needed. Neither management theory nor international management is much concerned with the problems of economic growth and development in a given country. On the other hand, economics, political science, and various other disciplines concerned with economic growth and development tend to ignore, or at best underestimate, the role and significance of management in economic progress.

Our aim is to develop an operational conceptual framework, using a comprehensive systems approach, which will prove useful in the analysis of critical comparative management problems and in understanding the complex problems involved in economic progress.

---

[7] See Richard D. Robinson, *International Business Policy* (New York: Holt, Rinehart & Winston, Inc., 1964).

[8] See F. Harbison and C. Myers, *Management in the Industrial World* (New York: McGraw-Hill Book Company, 1959).

# Chapter 2

# Management and Economic Activity

## UNIVERSAL ECONOMIC GOALS

As a beginning for our comparative analysis it is useful to consider the question of what general economic goals most societies have. In virtually all contemporary societies the paramount economic goal is to obtain more useful goods and services, and a higher level of per capita real income is preferred to less.[1] In economic terms, what is wanted is steady—and, if possible, rapid—economic growth in the gross national product of the country concerned. To be really effective, such growth should be in terms of increases in productivity per employee, although growth caused by expansion of the labor force is also accepted.

Regardless of what type of output is wanted by a society, be it atomic bombs, highways, consumer goods, steel mills, farm produce, or even art objects, the goal can be reached more easily if productivity growth is sustained and an increasing level of economic efficiency is achieved. To date, no modern country has expressed a serious desire to reduce the total flow of goods or services, no matter what the precise goals may be.

Poorer countries are striving mightily to expand outputs; and development economics, almost unknown twenty years ago, is a thriving branch of general economic analysis. Governments uninterested in economic development have been overthrown, to be replaced by those that are interested. International commissions, agencies, and bureaucracies have been organized to deal mainly with rapid economic progress. Wealthy countries worry about their rates of growth, while poorer ones steadily push for improvements in this sphere. There are few countries in the world which fail to give serious attention to economic progress; and many nations, rich and poor, set national plans of achievement for the next five, ten, or twenty years—always with some large per capita income growth indicated.

---

[1] For a related discussion see J. Galbraith, *The Affluent Society* (Boston: Houghton Mifflin Company, 1958), chap. ix.

11

One important limitation on this economic growth process is that the goods and services be in usable form. It is not enough to produce things generally: production must be desired or needed by some person or organization. If output does not serve to fulfill the end or functional use intended but, rather, rots in warehouses and stores, even though such output may enter into national economic growth statistics, it represents no real gain.

A second possible limitation might be that the work force be fully employed. Full employment does not necessarily mean that every person seeking work is always fully occupied; rather, a reasonable level of "full" employment is desired. Hence inputs should be used in a way which does not lead to extensive unemployment (for example, through automation), since most societies would probably opt for a slower rate of growth (but not an absolute decline in income) in order to keep most persons gainfully employed.

There may also be other restraints placed on the rate of economic growth because of various noneconomic goals, such as more leisure time for the population. However, the evidence is overwhelming that the hypothesis that economic progress through increased productive efficiency, is desired by virtually all countries and is a good working beginning for our analysis. The way to such increase lies in the direction of making the individual productive enterprises in each country more efficient—and, if necessary, creating new productive enterprises.

It should be kept in mind, however, that economic and business activities are not the ultimate goal of human societies. It is pleasant to have a high income, with its concomitant level of goods and services. It is also pleasant to live in a wealthy society, with its implied environment of capable physicians, good dentists, clean and sanitary cities, and the host of amenities that accompany such an environment. But man's goals seldom are limited to the goods and services that a country provides—and if they are, the culture may indeed be impoverished. One of the major problems in all economic systems is the tendency of critics to demand more results from the system than it is able to give. We insist that our economies give us "culture," proper religious attitudes, architectural beauty, and complete souls, as well as the grubby details of more goods and services. No economic system, however good or bad, can really perform noneconomic activities of this sort. To expect too much is to court perpetual disillusion.

What a relatively efficient economic system *can* do, however, is to generate the wealth necessary to create and accomplish such noneconomic goals. If we want more churches, a wealthy country finds it easier to provide the resources to construct them than a poor country; if we want more artistic beauty, a wealthy country can easily support more (though not necessarily better) artists to create such beauty; if we want more parks, a wealthy country has the available land to divert to this purpose; if we want more leisure for creative pursuits, a wealthy country can provide more time for its citizens, plus more income for books, libraries, and schools; if we want better cities, a wealthy country can divert resources to city planning, and so on.

A further advantage to being wealthy, not unnoticed by political leaders, is that military power is basically dependent on income. The wealthier countries have the necessary resources to devote to building up complex military machines, and many dictators have for this reason favored the maximum economic growth possible. Prestige among nations also is a factor. A man from a poor country typically is intensely conscious of this fact, particularly if he is one of the ruling elite, while a man from a wealthy country need never apologize for the economic conditions at home. The passion with which citizens of backward areas defend noneconomic goals suggests that they indeed protest too much.

Hence, we come full circle. It seems clear that in the modern world the prime motivation of nations is toward increasing wealth through economic progress, and we can adopt this assumption without further qualification (although keeping the above discussion in mind). If nations and peoples desire economic progress, the next question is how this might be achieved. Let us now turn to the role and significance of industrial management in any nation's economic progress.

## MANAGEMENT AND ECONOMIC PROGRESS

Management of industrial enterprise involves the coordination of human effort and material resources toward the achievement of organizational objectives. The basic objectives of industrial organizations in any country are economic in nature and ultimately reflect the desires of society for useful goods and services. This is true whether the enterprise is a private corporation attempting to achieve a desired level of profitability or a public entity attempting to fulfill a production plan established by state authorities. In the final analysis, all industrial enterprises are social organizations, and their survival is directly linked to their ability to provide useful goods and services, regardless of whether these goods and services are consumed by other organizations, the government, or the public at large.

The basic problem of industrial management, from society's point of view, is to become steadily more efficient over time. Increasing productive efficiency is generally considered a desirable goal for enterprise managers in most societies. In fact, increasing productive efficiency may be regarded as the basic inherent social desideratum of virtually every managerial job. In capitalistic countries, improved efficiency generally means higher profits and greater rewards for firm owners and managers; at the same time the public benefits from more useful goods and services. In Marxist countries, the planners stress enterprise efficiency so that the country can produce more useful output with the same inputs. Since a country's total production will be the sum of output of component productive enterprises, the more efficient each enterprise is, the more efficient the country will be. In a later chapter we shall explore in depth the concept of efficiency.

Since comparative management deals with the performance and problems of industrial managers and their enterprises in different countries, it is necessary to provide a common denominator or classification scheme which can be used for comparing the management process and managerial performance in different countries. In other words, one must have some useful description of the things that industrial firms and their managements do virtually anywhere in the world in order to undertake a meaningful comparative analysis. A first approximation of such an operational classification scheme is presented in the balance of this chapter.

Attention will first be given to the types of basic economic decisions that must be made and executed and to types of productive enterprise functions that must be organized and performed in any society if it is to survive through time. The emphasis will be on the role of management and industrial firms in the economic decision making process and in the organization and performance of the productive functions.

Then attention will be given to common basic managerial functions performed by the managements of industrial enterprises throughout the world. This will be followed by a brief outline of common types of policy decisions pertaining to the productive functions which are also applicable to industrial firms everywhere. After the managerial functions and the policy decision areas corresponding to the productive functions have been presented in the form of a broad classification scheme, the critical elements of the overall management process—as we define them—will be broken down, and classified in greater detail. Each element to be presented depicts a specific type of variable or pattern of managerial or firm behavior.

In this study, management is thought of as the hierarchy of individuals who play a direct and major role in the performance of the basic managerial functions, economic decision making, and/or the organization of the productive functions. In most cases a manager will be a person having subordinates, but this need not always be the case. A so-called staff man may also fit into our conception of the managerial hierarchy, and we have for this reason carefully avoided differentiating between line and staff personnel in our definition of management.

## MANAGEMENT, BASIC ECONOMIC DECISIONS, AND THE CRITICAL PRODUCTIVE FUNCTIONS

In any type of economy certain basic economic decisions must be made and certain critical economic or productive functions must be performed, if the economy is to survive. The critical productive functions will also be referred to in this study as enterprise functions.

In all societies human beings make the necessary economic decisions and human beings carry them out. Human beings also organize and per-form the critical productive functions essential to survival. Since human beings do not react solely according to biological instincts, they must somehow be induced to do the right thing at the right time if the basic economic decisions and the critical productive functions are to be carried out in a manner consistent with economic progress. Economic decision making and the effective and efficient performance of the critical productive functions are the task of management in all of its forms.

The first problem is production. Land (including natural resources), labor, and capital must be combined to produce usable goods and services. Production can range from combining factors in the most automated factories to handicraft production in peasant huts; but unless a society can produce some minimum amount of goods to house, feed, and clothe its population, it cannot survive. A modern industrial state must produce far more than the minimum in order to maintain its advanced status.

In all cases it must somehow be decided what is going to be produced and how much of each item is needed. It must also be decided how to produce the commodities we have decided to produce. Since production can be combined in unending variations, particularly in advanced econo-mies, our choice is great, especially in the long run. For any given period, however, total production is limited. Increased production of one commod-ity means decreased production of another. Hence, directly related to the critical function of production is the problem of procurement and the allocation of scarce resources among competing ends for the achievement of maximum desired output. The proper quantity and quality of resources must be directed to those productive sectors which can deliver the needed goods and services.

The second critical productive function is distribution. While the production function is concerned with the problems of what to produce and how much of each item to produce, these problems are intimately linked to the distribution problem of for whom to produce. An economy must somehow distribute the commodities it produces to their intended destina-tions, regardless of whether the goods in question are processed materials, parts, components, machines, or consumer goods. Distribution, or market-ing, is concerned with both the organization of distribution channels, involving the interrelationships between buyers and sellers, and physical distribution of goods, which involves warehousing, transportation, and inventory planning. Such distributive organization and facilities can range from the most primitive barter systems to elaborate worldwide networks of trade.

Third, an economy must finance its production and distribution activi-ties, and here too resource allocation in the form of capital is essential. This goes deeper than mere money financing, although such activity is extremely important. Real savings must somehow to accumulated in the form of stocks and capital if there is to be economic expansion in the future.

Fourth, a progressive society must do research and development to obtain new and improved products and processes. This can range from activities in elaborate laboratories of the most advanced type to mere observation and adoption of simple innovations emerging in the next village, but no society can make substantial advances without innovation in the product and process sense.

In addition to the above critical functions, any economy, as well as each complex enterprise within a given economy, must keep track of its economic activities in order to plan effectively and make decisions for tomorrow. Statistics of every type perform this function, as do various systems of accounting. Without any knowledge of what is going on at present, no meaningful or efficient pattern can be planned for the future. In most societies there are many integrated firms performing all of the above productive functions, and there are also numerous organizations performing only one or a few. In capitalist countries the productive functions are typically diffused in all sorts of complex ways through the economy. The American businessman who sets about establishing a new enterprise is limited only by his imagination of the advantages of the different types of organizations open to him. By contrast, in Marxist states the various types of productive enterprises are usually assigned one or more of the productive functions, and the state consciously fashions their basic forms of organization.

In most economies the bulk of the nation's industrial wealth is the result of the work of integrated enterprises engaged in varying degrees in all of the critical productive functions. It is the integrated type of enterprise that is of major concern here.

## THE FUNCTIONS OF MANAGEMENT

While the tangible economic results of the industrial enterprise are achieved through the various productive functions, the coordination and execution of these functions is only part of the managerial job. In complex business organizations management coordinates and executes the productive functions by engaging in certain basic managerial functions. In reality, the productive functions and the managerial functions are closely and intricately interwoven, with the conscious or unconscious aim of coordinating human effort and material resources toward the achievement of organizational objectives. The manner in which the managerial and productive functions are actually performed has a direct and significant bearing on the productive efficiency of the enterprise.

If a complex productive enterprise is to continue operating, certain common functions of management must generally be performed regardless of whether the enterprise is state or privately owned and regardless of whether resources are allocated through state planning or a competitive market price system. In this regard, at least some objectives and plans must be formulated, operations must be controlled, and organization structures must be established; at least some authority must be delegated and responsibility exacted; and personnel must be recruited, selected, trained, appraised, motivated, led, and supervised. Moreover, firm managers are generally expected to improve operations and results through innovation where feasible, particularly where ownership and control are separated. In addition, at least some administrators of each enterprise engage in negotiations of various sorts with external parties and organizations.

In this study the basic functions of management are classified as planning (including decision making and innovation), control, organization, staffing, and direction (including supervision, motivation, and leadership). These functions are defined as follows:[2]

The planning function determines organizational objectives and the policies, programs, schedules, procedures, and methods for achieving them. Planning is essentially decision making since it involves choosing among alternatives, and it also encompasses innovation. Thus, planning is the process of making decisions on any phase of organized activity.

The control function includes those activities which are designed to compel events to conform to plans. It is thus the measurement and, if necessary, the correction of activities of subordinates to assure the accomplishment of plans. It involves the establishment of control standards and the gathering of information required for evaluating performance, and it forms the basis for subsequent planning.

The organization function of management involves the determination and enumeration of the activities necessary to carry out the plan, the grouping of these activities, the assignment of such groups of activities to units headed by managers, and the delegation of authority to carry them out. Sometimes all these factors are included in the single term *organization structure*; sometimes they are referred to as authority relationships. In any case it is the totality of such activities and relationships that make up the organization function.

The staffing function comprises those activities that are essential in manning, and keeping manned, the positions provided by the organization structure. It thus encompasses the activities of defining the human requirements for the jobs to be done and includes, among other things, the activities of inventorying, recruiting, appraising, and selecting candidates for positions and the activities of training and developing both candidates and incumbents to accomplish their tasks as effectively and efficiently as possible. It also includes the provision of adequate basic inducements to attract and maintain needed personnel.

---

[2] We have been greatly influenced in their classification of managerial functions by the following works: H. Koontz and C. O'Donnell, *Principles of Management* (3d ed.; New York: McGraw-Hill Book Company, 1964); W. Newman and C. Summer, *The Process of Management* (Englewood Cliffs, N.J.: Prentice-Hall, Inc., 1961); W. Newman, *Administrative Action* (2d ed.; Englewood Cliffs, N.J.: Prentice-Hall, Inc., 1963).

The managerial function of direction embraces those activities which are related to leading, guiding, supervising, and motivating subordinates so that they will perform their tasks effectively and efficiently. This function entails personal communication, man to man relationships, and the use of rewards and/or penalties to motivate personnel in desired directions. It is at the heart of getting things done through people. While clear plans, sound organizations, and proper staffing set the stage for coordinated efforts, a manager must also provide direction and leadership if the people in his organization are to work together to achieve its objectives. It is the job of effective management to maintain a good balance between individual motivation and cooperative efficiency.

We could add to our category of functions that of assembling the nonhuman resources which are required to keep the enterprise functioning; however, such activity is implicit in the productive functions of procurement and finance as well as in the managerial function of planning.

Even in poorly managed business firms in underdeveloped countries such as Saudi Arabia,[3] or in Soviet industrial enterprises,[4] managements engage in the above basic functions—at least to some extent—although this may not be very evident to an outsider. However, the ways in which these functions tend to be performed in different countries vary strikingly in many cases. Since managerial effectiveness and productive efficiency are so largely dependent on how and how well the managerial functions are performed, much of our analysis of management in different countries will deal with this problem.

## COMMON POLICY DECISIONS

It appears that in addition to performing common managerial functions industrial firms and their managements virtually everywhere operate—either consciously, unconsciously, or by default—in accordance with a common framework of policy decisions pertaining to the different productive functions that they engage in.[5] The common policy decision areas pertain to marketing, production, procurement, research and development, and finance.

We have chosen to deal with personnel policies under the managerial function of staffing, and we have also chosen not to present as a separate classification those policies pertaining to other functions such as accounting and data processing. We shall, however, consider policies pertaining to the

---

[3] This statement is based on the experiences of one of the authors, who managed a Saudi owned business firm in that country for two years.

[4] See B. Richman, *Soviet Management: With Significant American Comparisons* (Englewood Cliffs, N.J., Prentice-Hall, Inc., 1965), particularly Chaps. iii and iv.

[5] For a classification of business policies having universal application see W. Newman and J. Logan, *Business Policies and Central Management* (Cincinnati: Southwestern Publishing Co., 1965).

relationships that enterprise managements have with external agents and organizations.

## CRITICAL ELEMENTS OF THE MANAGEMENT PROCESS[6]

The overall management process in this study includes critical elements pertaining to the managerial functions and the critical policy decision areas. While we are interested in both classes of elements throughout this book, somewhat greater attention will be given to those corresponding to the managerial functions. The elements that have been identified as being most critical are presented in Table 2–1 below in our comprehensive classification scheme. The list is far from exhaustive or conclusive, but we feel that it is adequate at this stage of our research in comparative management.

Each element presented in the table is a variable corresponding to a specific type or pattern of managerial or firm behavior and is coded as a B with appropriate subscripts. The majority of the B's are basically structural elements of the management process. The others are essentially dynamic, problem oriented variables which are present in varying degrees in the management process in different firms and countries.[7] The latter are indicated by an asterisk in the table. More will be said about the distinction between these two general types of variables in Chapter 4.

It is theoretically possible to measure with reasonable accuracy significant differences in the management process among firms in different countries by using our classification scheme. Accurate measurement involving many of the elements would, however, require much more intensive and extensive empirical research in the field of comparative management than has taken place to date; therefore, as indicated earlier, the analysis presented throughout this book is highly suggestive and far from conclusive. Moreover, no attempt is made to deal in depth with all of the variables presented

---

[6] Our selection and classification of these critical elements are based on our own analyses and experiences and on the sources cited in Footnotes 2 and 7 of this chapter, as well as on many personal interviews and questionnaire surveys involving experts in different areas of management and business administration. Use has been made of the "Delphi" Technique, to be discussed in Chapter 11, in obtaining the opinions of experts.

[7] In our selection and classification of problem oriented variables we have been influenced by many of the leading behavioral studies of management and organization. These include in part: C. Argyris, *Integrating the Individual and the Organization* (New York: John Wiley & Sons, Inc., 1964); L. Sayles, *Managerial Behavior* (New York: McGraw-Hill Book Company, 1964); R. Cyert and J. March, *A Behavioral Theory of the Firm* (Englewood Cliffs, N.J.: Prentice-Hall, Inc., 1963); W. Scott, *Human Relations in Management* (Homewood, Ill.: Richard D. Irwin, Inc., 1962); R. Likert, *New Patterns of Management* (New York: McGraw-Hill Book Company, 1961); R. Dubin, *Human Relations in Administration: The Sociology of Organization* (Englewood Cliffs, N.J.: Prentice-Hall, Inc., 1961); R. Tannenbaum, I. Weschler, and F. Massarik, *Leadership and Organization* (New York: McGraw-Hill Book Company, 1961).

## TABLE 2–1

### CRITICAL ELEMENTS OF THE MANAGEMENT PROCESS

#### $B_1$:   *Planning and Innovation*

$B_{1.1}$   Basic organizational objectives pursued and the form of their operational expression
$B_{1.2}$   Types of plans utilized
$B_{1.3}$   Time horizon of plans and planning
$B_{1.4}$   Degree and extent to which enterprise operations are spelled out in plans (i.e. preprogrammed)
$B_{1.5}$   Flexibility of plans
$B_{1.6}$   Methodologies, techniques, and tools used in planning and decision making
*$B_{1.7}$   Extent and effectiveness of employee participation in planning
*$B_{1.8}$   Managerial behavior in the planning process
*$B_{1.9}$   Degree and extent of information distortion in planning
*$B_{1.10}$  Degree and extent to which scientific method is effectively applied by enterprise personnel—both managers and nonmanagers—in dealing with causation and futurity problems
*$B_{1.11}$  Nature, extent and rate of innovation and risk taking in enterprise operations over a given period of time
*$B_{1.12}$  Ease or difficulty of introducing changes and innovations in enterprise operations

#### $B_2$:   *Control*

$B_{2.1}$   Types of strategic performance and control standards used in different areas (e.g., production, marketing, finance, personnel)
$B_{2.2}$   Types of control techniques used
$B_{2.3}$   Nature and structure of information feedback systems used for control purposes
$B_{2.4}$   Timing and procedures for corrective action
$B_{2.5}$   Degree of looseness or tightness of control over personnel
*$B_{2.6}$   Extent and nature of unintended effects resulting from the overall control system employed
*$B_{2.7}$   Effectiveness of the control system in compelling events to conform to plans

#### $B_3$:   *Organization*

$B_{3.1}$   Size of representative enterprise and its major subunits
$B_{3.2}$   Degree of centralization or decentralization of authority
$B_{3.3}$   Degree of work specialization (division of labor)
$B_{3.4}$   Spans of control
$B_{3.5}$   Basic departmentation and grouping of activities
     Extent and uses of service departments
$B_{3.6}$   Extent and uses of staff generalists and specialists
$B_{3.7}$   Extent and uses of functional authority
*$B_{3.8}$   Extent and degree of organizational confusion and friction regarding authority and responsibility relationships
$B_{3.9}$   Extent and uses of committees and group decision making
$B_{3.10}$  Nature, extent, and uses of the informal organization
*$B_{3.11}$  Degree and extent to which the organization structure (i.e., the formal organization) is mechanical or flexible with regard to causing and/or adapting to changing conditions

#### $B_4$:   *Staffing*

$B_{4.1}$   Methods used in recruiting personnel
$B_{4.2}$   Criteria used in selecting and promoting personnel
$B_{4.3}$   Techniques and criteria used in appraising personnel
$B_{4.4}$   Nature and uses of job descriptions
$B_{4.5}$   Levels of compensation and nature and extent of fringe benefits and employee services
$B_{4.6}$   Nature, extent, and time absorbed in enterprise training programs and activities
$B_{4.7}$   Extent of informal individual development
$B_{4.8}$   Policies and procedures regarding the layoff and dismissal of personnel
*$B_{4.9}$   Ease or difficulty in dismissing personnel no longer required or desired
*$B_{4.10}$  Ease or difficulty of obtaining and maintaining personnel of all types with desired skills and abilities

#### $B_5$:   *Direction, Leadership and Motivation*

$B_{5.1}$   Degree and extent of authoritarian vs. participative management
     (This relates to autocratic vs. consultative direction.)

$B_{5.2}$  Techniques and methods used for motivating managerial personnel
$B_{5.3}$  Techniques and methods used for motivating nonmanagerial personnel
$B_{5.4}$  Supervisory techniques used
$B_{5.5}$  Communication structure and techniques
*$B_{5.6}$  Degree and extent to which communication is ineffective among personnel of all types
*$B_{5.7}$  Ease or difficulty of motivating personnel to perform efficiently, and to improve their performance and abilities over time (irrespective of the types of incentives that may be utilized for this purpose)
*$B_{5.8}$  Degree and extent of identification that exists between the interests and objectives of individuals, work groups, and departments and the enterprise as a whole
*$B_{5.9}$  Degree and extent of trust and cooperation or conflict and distrust among personnel of all types
*$B_{5.10}$  Degree and extent of frustration, absenteeism, and turnover among personnel
*$B_{5.11}$  Degree and extent of wasteful time and effort resulting from restrictive work practices, unproductive bargaining, conflicts, etc.

### $B_6$:  *Marketing (Policies Pursued)*

$B_{6.1}$  Product line (degree of diversification vs. specialization, rate of change, product quality)
$B_{6.2}$  Channels of distribution and types and location of customers
$B_{6.3}$  Pricing (for key items, in relation to costs, profit margins, quantity and trade discount structure)
$B_{6.4}$  Sales promotion and key sales appeals (types used and degree of aggressiveness in sales promotion)

### $B_7$:  *Production and Procurement*

$B_{7.1}$  Make or buy (components, supplies, facilities, services, extent to which subcontracting is used, etc.)
$B_{7.2}$  Number, types, and location of major suppliers
$B_{7.3}$  Timing of procurement of major supplies
$B_{7.4}$  Average inventory levels (major supplies, goods in process, completed output)
$B_{7.5}$  Minimum, maximum, and average size of production runs
$B_{7.6}$  Degree to which production operations are stabilized
$B_{7.7}$  Combination of factor inputs used in major products produced
$B_{7.8}$  Basic production processes used
$B_{7.9}$  Extent of automation and mechanization in enterprise operations

### $B_8$:  *Research and Development*

$B_{8.1}$  Nature and extent of $R \& D$ activity (e.g., product development and improvement, new material usages, new production processes and technology)

### $B_9$:  *Finance*

$B_{9.1}$  Types and costs of financing (e.g., equity, debt, short term, long term)
$B_{9.2}$  Sources of capital
$B_{9.3}$  Major uses of capital
$B_{9.4}$  Protection of capital
$B_{9.5}$  Distribution of earnings

### $B_{10}$:  *Public and External Relations*

(*The relationships, attitudes, and policies of enterprise management regarding major types of external agents and organizations*)

$B_{10.1}$  Customer and consumer relations (e.g., does firm management regard consumer loyalty and satisfaction as being important; or is it chiefly interested in short run results, quick profits, etc.?)
$B_{10.2}$  Supplier relations
$B_{10.3}$  Investor and creditor relations
$B_{10.4}$  Union relations
$B_{10.5}$  Government relations
$B_{10.6}$  Community relations (e.g., educational institutions, chambers of commerce, business and professional associations, community welfare activities)

in this section. This would be an impossible task to handle in one or even ten books, but it is our hope that many other persons will take up the challenge.

From our research thus far, it appears that there are dominant patterns of managerial and firm behavior in different countries, which can be depicted by analyzing the critical elements of the management process as we define them. In this study our primary interest is in such dominant patterns and trends rather than in the exceptions, and we shall make use of hypothetical representative firms in our explorations of industrial management in different countries. This approach is obviously subject to considerable overgeneralization, since many exceptions to dominant patterns may be found in various countries. There may be some significant differences in the management process in different branches of industry, in different regions, and even within the same branch of industry within a particular country; however, at this stage of our research, and because of limited data to work with, overgeneralization seems to be the only fruitful course to follow. We intend to go into greater depth in a future volume which will deal with comprehensive country studies.

Of major concern throughout this study are relationships between the environmental variables or constraints (C's), to be presented in Chapter 3, and the elements of the management process presented above. It is our aim to explain significant differences in both the management process and managerial effectiveness in different countries as caused by the environmental constraints that we have identified as being important.

## MICROMANAGEMENT AND MACROMANAGEMENT[8]

In discussing management in any country it is useful to distinguish between micromanagement and macromanagement. Micromanagement is the management of individual productive enterprises on the lower operating levels of the economy, from whence production and wealth actually come. In any fairly large country there are typically thousands of productive units which contribute to and largely determine overall national economic performance. Managers at this level engage in the basic managerial functions and various productive functions within their respective enterprises.

On the micromanagement level are found the production managers in factories, sales directors, vice presidents of finance, and all other persons concerned with the management of individual enterprises, large and small. Such managers may be working in public or private organizations. A plant superintendent and a company sales manager are clearly micromanagers— as is a steel company president, until one steel company, as is common in some smaller countries, is the only firm in the industry. In Communist

---

[8] This concept of micro- and macromanagement was initially presented in B. Richman and R. Farmer, "Ownership and Management; The Real Issues," *Management International*, Vol. 5, No. 1, 1965; and Richman, *Soviet Management*, chap. i.

countries micro- and macromanagement clearly represent a continuum of control. It is difficult to determine at times where one stops and the other begins.

Macromanagement deals with the management of an entire economy. Here the problem of interpretation can be quite vexing. In some countries, particularly Communist states, this type of management is pervasive and detailed. All significant phases of economic activity are regulated through comprehensive national economic plans, and virtually all productive organizations and assets are owned by the state. In other countries, most typically those considered capitalistic, such management is often by law, tradition, or custom rather than by comprehensive design. In this type of system the key economic regulations are competitive market prices and the profit motive; another distinguishing feature is widespread private property ownership of productive assets. In either case, however, macromanagerial activity imposes various restraints on micromanagers. The United States Federal Reserve Board is producing macromanagement when it alters interest rates; so is the United States government when it approves changes in corporate tax rates or antitrust laws. So, for that matter, is a Soviet central planner who makes investment or resources allocation for the steel industry.

Macromanagement is not normally considered management in the sense in which the word is used in business administration; but it in fact is, since it involves economic decision making and policy formulation. Macro-managerial organizations include the entire government economic, regulatory, and administrative apparatus apart from productive enterprises per se—for example, central banking and budgetary organizations, regulatory and planning agencies, and various other governmental departments. In all Communist states, and in many other countries as well, various macroagencies play a significant and direct role in planning, controlling, staffing, directing, and/or organizing the activities of virtually all or at least many of the productive enterprises in the system. This is far from true in privately owned American firms.

This study is basically concerned with micromanagement; but macro-management will also be given due consideration, since the manner in which various macroagencies are managed and perform their activities has a direct bearing on micromanagerial performance and the productive efficiency of firms.

In general, societies have endless ways of organizing and performing the productive and managerial functions. In theoretical political terms, the possible range is from laissez-faire capitalism through monolithic totalitarian communism; but regardless of how a particular economy is organized, the ultimate economic objective is generally more useful goods and services, resulting in increased per capita gross national product, and the basic desideratum of the managerial job is to increase productive efficiency.

How efficiently the productive and managerial functions are performed in a given country depends largely on the *overall* macromanagerial structure within which enterprise managers much operate. In this study *macromanagerial structure* includes more than the types of macromanagement activity discussed above. The macromanagerial structure is defined as that portion of the overall economic, political, legal, sociological, educational, and cultural environment of a given country which significantly bears on and influences the activities of productive enterprise managers. We shall explore in greater depth this concept and the relevant environmental factors in the following chapter.

# Chapter 3

# Enterprise Management and the External Environment

While much of the management process is concerned with internal enterprise operations exclusively, it is also true that overall managerial performance depends in large part on factors external to the firm. A productive enterprise necessarily forms a part of a complex educational-sociological-cultural-political-legal-economic whole. No industrial enterprise or individual can exist entirely divorced from its environment, and firms both influence and are significantly influenced by the nature of the total environment. The major purpose of this chapter is to identify—at least in rough outline—those environmental factors which in virtually every country tend to have a significant and direct bearing on the management process and the performance of industrial firms.

## THE CONCEPT OF MANAGERIAL EFFECTIVENESS

It is important to bring up the concept of managerial effectiveness at this point, although this concept will be treated more fully in later chapters. Managerial effectiveness is defined as the degree or level of efficiency, from society's point of view, with which the overall management process is performed in a given enterprise. Microefficiency indicators which would enable one to estimate the level of managerial effectiveness in a given situation will be developed in later chapters. In this connection, we are interested in determining what environmental factors tend to have a significant impact on managerial effectiveness.

## THE SIGNIFICANCE OF ENVIRONMENTAL FACTORS

If it is true that the external environment directly influences managerial effectiveness, and if the critical environmental factors can be identified and isolated, it may be possible to alter the environment in order to improve the efficiency of many or most firms in a particular country. Since it may be much easier in the political sense to alter environmental conditions rather than the internal affairs of numerous individual firms in order to obtain greater economic progress, such knowledge could be most useful to political leaders, economic planners, and other macrotechnicians in all sorts of countries.

If it were known, for example, that in the United States changing a certain law would probably enable a substantial number of business firms to improve their efficiency by roughly 5 percent to 10 percent, it might be relatively easy to change the law. If, on the other hand, this efficiency gain could be made only by interfering with the internal operations of the firms, such changes would tend to be much more difficult, time consuming, and perhaps much more costly.

One of the authors recently published a comprehensive study dealing with the impact of various external environmental factors on the performance of industrial enterprise managers in the Soviet Union. A major, general conclusion of this study is reflected in the following quotation:

> The major emphasis in this book has deliberately been on the environmental constraints of the Soviet industrial enterprise to clearly show that in the Soviet Union major gains could best be achieved by changing the external environment of the enterprise. Some marginal gains could be achieved by working within the enterprise: improving the qualifications of personnel, bettering the performance of managerial functions, and so on. But such internal gains are obviously small compared to possibilities inherent in properly reforming the external structure of control, regulation and guidance of enterprise managers.[1]

Hence, it seems extremely important to try to determine what environmental factors tend to have a significant impact on managerial effectiveness generally and in specific situations, and the nature of such impacts.

Throughout this study we use the terms *environmental* or *external factors, characteristics, variables,* and *constraints* synonomously unless otherwise noted; however, we prefer the term *constraint* and use it with a twofold meaning. When *constraint* is used in relation to managerial effectiveness the connotation is typically negative. A given environmental variable may limit or serve as a *constraint* upon managerial effectiveness in varying degrees, depending on the particular country in question (and in some cases the particular region or industry). In some cases, a given environmental constraint may have an extremely negative impact on managerial effectiveness; in others the impact may be negligible. More will be said in later chapters about the actual weighting of various constraints in terms of managerial effectiveness and the ranking of countries.

The term *environmental constraint* is also used when we describe and

---

[1] B. Richman, *Soviet Management: With Significant American Comparisons* (Englewood Cliffs, N.J.: Prentice-Hall, Inc., 1965), p. 256.

explain specific elements in the overall management process, but here the term does not necessarily have a negative connotation. In this context we are interested in how environmental constraints tend to produce dominant patterns of managerial and firm behavior in different countries; these relationships are depicted by focusing on the elements of the management process. It does not necessarily follow that a given dominant behavior pattern, which is largely the product of a particular environmental constraint or set of constraints, is negative in terms of management effectiveness. In many instances dominant behavior patterns may have a positive impact on managerial effectiveness. In any event, the word *constraint* is used in this connection since environmental factors frequently tend to confine behavior in certain directions, at least in a majority of cases in a given country.

One intuitively expects that the external environments in which industrial enterprises and their managements must function vary greatly among different countries—particularly between underdeveloped and advanced nations. This situation is clearly reflected in the following direct quotation which appears in a recent United Nations report based on data provided by teams of experts in different fields:

The manager of an enterprise in a developing country generally has a more difficult task than his counterpart in a developed country. As a rule, the operation of industry in the more advanced countries takes for granted the existence of the so-called external economies; that is, of a complex of economic overhead, including transportation, power and water supply, repair facilities, and availability of spare parts, and of a variety of skills ranging from highly complex managerial skills to a labor force brought up in an industrial tradition and possessing at least a minimum of general and professional education. The entire institutional framework, which has gradually evolved throughout the course of economic development, provides a favorable climate for the operation and growth of the industrial sector, or at least does not interfere with it.

In the developing countries, economic and social changes brought about by industrialization are relatively recent phenomena and are accompanied by a number of frictions and maladjustments; many and varied obstacles have still to be overcome. The manager cannot always recruit workers with the necessary understanding of the functions of the enterprise and of such matters as administrative discipline. Moreover, there is no body of managerial colleagues who can help him solve his problems and correct his mistakes when necessary. He has to be highly self-reliant and must constantly help other members of the staff to do their work properly.[2]

While the above quotation is probably applicable in varying degrees to most or virtually all underdeveloped and newly developing nations, there are significant differences in the environments of various developing countries. The significance of different environmental constraints often varies among such countries. For example, the legal system and various educa-

---

[2] United Nations, Economic and Social Council, *Training of National Technical Personnel for Accelerated Industrialization of Developing Countries* (Report No. E/3901 [New York, 1964]), Part I, Add. 1, p. 85.

tional factors may be more significant negative constraints upon managerial effectiveness in Saudi Arabia as compared to India, while India may fare worse than Saudi Arabia with regard to certain sociological and economic factors; various political constraints and inflationary pressures may be more significant in Indonesia than in Thailand; and so forth.

Among more advanced countries also there are substantial differences in environmental conditions which tend to result in different dominant patterns of management and different levels of management effectiveness. For example, it appears that managerial effectiveness in the Soviet Union is hindered primarily by the general economic framework of the country; in Great Britain various sociological and educational factors seem to be having a more negative impact than in the U.S., but Britain may fare better than the U.S. on some legal factors; Japan is faced with extremely scarce natural resources; Brazil has been confronted with serious inflationary problems and political instability.

## IDENTIFICATION AND CLASSIFICATION OF CRITICAL ENVIRONMENTAL CONSTRAINTS

When one accepts the apparent fact that the external environment has a significant impact on the management process and managerial effectiveness in productive enterprises virtually everywhere, it seems very important that the critical environmental factors be identified and defined. An initial step in our comparative management research has been tentatively to identify, isolate, and classify what seem to be the most critical external constraints bearing on industrial management. We have hypothesized that these constraints tend to have direct and significant influence on managerial and firm performance in general.

The environmental factors that we have chosen for analysis have been derived initially from (*a*) numerous available studies which point to certain environmental factors as being important in different countries and situations; (*b*) our own firsthand research and experiences in a number of different countries; (*c*) research conducted and insights provided by our research assistants, several of whom are doctoral students from foreign countries; (*d*) interviews, discussions, and correspondence with numerous educators in different fields who are experts on different countries and with foreign and local executives, government and United Nations officials, and graduate students; (*e*) intuition and deductive reasoning. Through this phase of our research a number of refinements have been made in our selection and classification of critical environmental constraints,[3] and at this point the analysis can proceed at a reasonable level of confidence.

Table 3–1 presents the environmental constraints identified as being

---

[3] As a reflection of such refinements, compare our list of constraints presented in an earlier paper with those presented here; see R. Farmer and B. Richman, "A Model for Research in Comparative Management," *California Management Review*, winter, 1964, pp. 59–60.

## TABLE 3–1

### CRITICAL ENVIRONMENTAL CONSTRAINTS

#### $C_1$:  *Educational–Cultural Variables*

$C_{1.1}$:  Literacy level:  The percentage of the total population and those presently employed in industry who can read, write, and do simple arithmetic calculations, and the average years of schooling of adults.

$C_{1.2}$:  Specialized vocational and technical training and general secondary education:  Extent, types, and quality of education and training of this kind not directly under the control or direction of industrial enterprises; the type, quantity, and quality of persons obtaining such education or training and the proportion of those employed in industry who have such education and training.

$C_{1.3}$:  Higher education:  The percentage of the total population and those employed in industry with post-high school education, plus the types and quality of such education; the types of persons obtaining higher education.

$C_{1.4}$:  Special management development programs:  The extent and quality of management development programs which are not run internally by productive enterprises and which are aimed at improving the skills and abilities of managers and/or potential managers; the quantity and quality of managers and potential managers of different types and levels attending or having completed such programs.

$C_{1.5}$:  Attitude toward education:  The general or dominant cultural attitude toward education and the acquisition of knowledge, in terms of their presumed desirability; the general attitude toward different types of education.

$C_{1.6}$:  Educational match with requirements:  The extent and degree to which the types of formal education and training available in a given country fit the needs of productive enterprises on all levels of skill and achievement. This is essentially a summary category; depending on the type of job involved, different educational constraints indicated above would be more important.

#### $C_2$:  *Sociological-Cultural Variables*

$C_{2.1}$:  Attitude toward industrial managers and management:  The general or dominant social attitude toward industrial and business managers of all sorts, and the way that such managers tend to view their managerial jobs.

$C_{2.2}$:  View of authority and subordinates:  The general or dominant cultural attitude toward authority and persons in subordinate positions, and the way that industrial managers tend to view their authority and their subordinates.

$C_{2.3}$:  Interorganizational cooperation:  Extent and degree to which business enterprises, government agencies, labor unions, educational institutions, and other relevant organizations cooperate with one another in ways conducive to industrial efficiency and general economic progress.

$C_{2.4}$:  Attitude toward achievement and work:  The general or dominant cultural attitude toward individual or collective achievement and productive work in industry.

$C_{2.5}$:  Class structure and individual mobility:  The extent of opportunities for social class and individual mobility, both vertical and horizontal, in a given country, and the means by which it can be achieved.

$C_{2.6}$:  Attitude toward wealth and material gain:  Whether or not the acquisition of wealth from different sources is generally considered socially desirable, and the way that persons employed in industry tend to view material gain.

$C_{2.7}$:  Attitude toward scientific method:  The general social and dominant individual attitude toward the use of rational, predictive techniques in solving various types of business, technical, economic and social problems.

$C_{2.8}$:  Attitude toward risk taking:  Whether or not the taking of various types of personal, collective, or national risks is generally considered acceptable, as well as the dominant view toward specific types of risk taking in business and industry; the degree and extent to which risk taking tends to be a rational process in a particular country.

$C_{2.9}$:  Attitude toward change:  The general cultural attitude toward social changes of all types which bear directly on industrial performance in a given country, and the dominant attitude among persons employed in industry toward all types of significant changes in enterprise operations.

TABLE 3–1—*Continued*

$C_3$:  *Political and Legal Variables*

$C_{3.1}$:  Relevant legal rules of the game:  Quality, efficiency, and effectiveness of the legal structure in terms of general business law, labor law, tax law, and general law relevant to business, degree of enforcement, reliability, and so on.

$C_{3.2}$:  Defense and military policy:  Impact of defense policy on industrial enterprises in terms of trading with potential enemies, purchasing policies, strategic industry development, labor and other resource competition, and similar factors.

$C_{3.3}$:  Foreign policy:  Impact of policy on industrial enterprise in terms of trading restrictions, quotas, tariffs, customs, unions, foreign exchange, foreign aid, and so on.

$C_{3.4}$:  Political stability:  Influence on industrial enterprises of revolutions, changes in regime, stability or instability over protracted periods, and so on.

$C_{3.5}$:  Political organization:  Types of organization in constitutional terms; degrees of centralization or decentralization; degree and extent of red tape, delays, uncertainty and confusion in industry-government dealings; pressure groups and their effectiveness; political parties and their philosophies; and so on.

$C_{3.6}$:  Flexibility of law and legal changes:  Degree to which relevant barriers to the efficient management of industrial enterprises can be changed and the timeliness of such changes, predictability and certainty of legal actions, and so on.

$C_4$:  *Economic Variables*

$C_{4.1}$:  General economic framework:  Including such factors as the overall economic organization of the country (i.e., capitalistic, Marxist, mixed), property rights, and similar factors.

$C_{4.2}$:  Central banking system and monetary policy:  The organization and operations of the central banking system, including the controls over commerical banks, the ability and willingness to control the money supply, the effectiveness of government policies regarding price stability, commercial bank reserves, discounting, credit controls, and similar factors.

$C_{4.3}$:  Fiscal policy:  General policies concerning government expenditures, their timing, and their impact; the general level of deficit, surplus, or balance; total share of government expenditures in gross national product.

$C_{4.4}$:  Economic stability:  The vulnerability of the economy to economic fluctuations of depression and boom, price stability, and overall economic growth stability.

$C_{4.5}$:  Organization of capital markets:  The existence of such markets as stock and bond exchanges, their honesty, effectiveness, and total impact; the size and role of commercial banking, including loan policies and availability of credit to businessmen; the existence of other capital sources, such as savings and loan associations, government sponsored credit agencies, insurance company loan activities, and so on.

$C_{4.6}$:  Factor endowment:  Relative supply of capital and land (agricultural and raw materials) per capita; size and general health of the work force.

$C_{4.7}$:  Market size:  Total effective purchasing power within the country, plus relevant export markets.

$C_{4.8}$:  Social overhead capital and external economies:  Availability and quality of power supplies, water, communications systems, transportation, public warehousing, physical transfer facilities, housing, and so on.

most critical. They have been classified into four broad categories: educational, sociological-cultural, political-legal, and economic. The variables presented are obviously very complex, and detailed study of even a few could take a lifetime; however, if only the portion of each constraint directly bearing on industrial management is considered, the task becomes much simpler and more manageable. Hence, we are interested not in all of laws and legal theory but only in the portions of law which bear directly and significantly on the management process and managerial effectiveness in industrial enterprises. Similarly, our concern with education includes not all pedagogy but only the portion which directly concerns industrial management. By focusing our attention in this way, it may be possible to gain meaningful insights into how these constraints actually do affect managerial performance in different countries. We refer to those aspects of the overall external environment bearing directly on enterprise management as the macromanagerial structure.

It is evident from Table 3–1 that many of the constraints are closely interrelated, and this makes our task ahead even more difficult. The dominant attitude toward industrial managers and management in a given country may be closely connected with interorganizational cooperation and with various educational and legal factors; the view of achievement may be closely connected with class structure, the attitude toward wealth, and various educational and political variables; basic literacy may have a significant bearing on many if not most of the economic, political-legal, and sociological constraints; the nature and effectiveness of central banking and monetary policy may depend at least in part on various legal-political factors; and so forth. The result is an extremely complex set of interrelationships which determine in large part how efficiently individual firms and an entire country perform economically.

## CONCLUSION

The basic hypothesis presented here is that management of productive enterprises is directly related to the external environment in which this management operates. In turn, management may affect its environment as well. The overall management process and managerial effectiveness in industrial firms depend largely on the external educational, sociological-cultural, political-legal, and economic characteristics of the society in question; and these characteristics can be identified and in time, one hopes, measured with a reasonable degree of accuracy. If a paramount goal of society is to achieve greater economic progress through higher levels of productive efficiency, it is necessary not only to directly change productive firms internally but also to consider seriously proper and effective changes in the external environment. Such changes should be considered in terms of their impact on the internal management process and managerial effectiveness in industrial enterprises, if this goal is to be achieved.

# Chapter 4

# Toward a General Theory

## INTRODUCTION

Previous chapters have identified the critical elements of the management process (B's) and the critical environmental constraints affecting the firm's internal operations (C's). Also considered were the universal economic goals that most contemporary societies have, either consciously or unconsciously. The concept of managerial effectiveness has also been defined. This chapter is intended to bring all of these factors and concepts together to form a general theory of comparative management and economic progress.

Of major concern here and throughout the remainder of this book are the significant relationships that tend to exist between environmental constraints, elements of the overall management process, and managerial effectiveness. Significant differences in both the management process and managerial effectiveness will be explained in terms of the impact of external environmental constraints. It is theoretically possible to measure with reasonable accuracy such differences among firms in different countries.

As noted earlier, the primary concern of this study is with dominant patterns and trends of managerial and firm performance rather than with substantially deviant patterns within a given country. Hence, a hypothetical representative industrial enterprise will be used here to evaluate management processes and managerial effectiveness. This leads in many cases to considerable overgeneralization, but this technique does allow us to focus on the more critical environmental impacts on the average firm within a given country.

The personality, motivation, and capabilities of individual managers are ignored here; "ideal types" are used instead. These serve as rather crude norms for the entire industrial managerial class and the firm management process in a given country. The overall character attributed to our hypothetical manager and firm is in fact the product of the external environment, particularly of the educational and sociological factors. This means that little attention is given to the controllable aspects of the internal management process and managerial effectiveness within a given real firm.

Whereas conventional management theory tends to assume away the external environment or hold it constant, we can rightfully be accused of partially assuming away the controllable aspects of internal management. Internal management is held constant since the focus is on the way in which the external environment influences internal firm behavior.

It is recognized that various aspects of the management process can be changed and managerial effectiveness can be improved in a particular firm in a relatively short period of time. This can even happen in a relatively underdeveloped country if, for example, top management undergoes an effective training program and has the basic motivation to improve performance. But primary attention is devoted here to extensive collective action, change, and improvement involving the majority of industrial firms in a given country. This would usually entail substantial changes in the external environment and is likely to occur over long periods of time.

The nature of the impact on the enterprise and its management of environmental constraints which make up the macromanagerial structure is shown in Figure 4–1. The productive enterprise, in this case an industrial firm, is taking available inputs of various types and creating usable outputs. The external constraints act on the firm and its management in different ways in different countries, resulting in different behavioral patterns in the management process and varying degrees of managerial effectiveness.

What is wanted is an evaluation of the external constraints upon internal management. How much would a legal change, such as a tax cut, affect the firm's internal operations, and in which way? Or if the number of college trained engineers increased substantially over a decade, what effects would this have on the firm? Each external constraint was initially selected with this type of interrelationship in mind. Our problem now is to develop more precisely the ways in which such interrelationships occur and what their effect on firms and societies may be.

## CONSTRAINT QUANTIFICATION AND TIME PROBLEMS

It is obvious that some of the external constraints can be measured and quantified more easily than others, in terms of their direct impact on the internal operations of firms. For example, it would be easier to quantify some of the educational and economic factors for a given country than to quantify most of the sociological or legal constraints. It is, however, theoretically possible to measure with reasonable accuracy even the attitudinal or sociological factors by focussing on dominant values, beliefs, and behaviors of the populations, particularly that portion employed in industry. A growing amount of fruitful work is being done in this area by various types of social scientists. Many sources cited in Chapters 6–11 provide data that point to the measurement of the constraints for various countries. A growing amount of pertinent data can also be obtained from data and information "banks" located at various educational and research institutions in the United States and elsewhere.[1] Considerable use will be made of such data in following chapters and in our forthcoming volume dealing with comprehensive country studies. The problems involved in quantifying and weighting the environmental constraints and in ranking different countries in terms of managerial effectiveness are dealt with in Chapter 12.

FIGURE 4–1

EXTERNAL CONSTRAINTS ON THE ENTERPRISE AND ITS MANAGEMENT

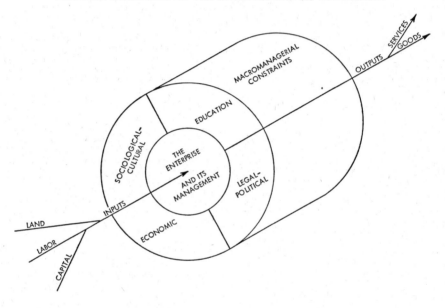

Our evaluation of the external constraints is essentially static, taken at a given moment in time. It is conceptually possible to examine any country or firm; evaluate as of the moment its constraints; and attempt to discover how these constraints affect current management processes, managerial effectiveness, and productive efficiency. It is clear, however, that the factors presented in Table 3–1 are dynamic, in that they tend to change over time at different rates. Populations typically become more educated; certain laws and economic conditions may change; and sociological attitudes may shift under various pressures within the culture. This type of dynamic shift over time will be considered in Chapter 12. In our analysis of environmental constraints in Chapters 6–11, the emphasis is on what the environment has

---

[1] Among the leading information centers of this type are the International Data Library and Reference Service located at the University of California, Berkeley, and the Cross-National Data Archive Holdings at Indiana University in Bloomington.

been over the past several years; this permits meaningful current comparisons between and within countries.

## CENTRAL ISSUES

Analysis of the environmental constraints reveals a number of closely interrelated phases, as shown in Figure 4-2. In this figure, all the interrelationships presented in this chapter are shown. The first relationship is that

FIGURE 4-2

CONSTRAINT-MANAGEMENT PROCESS—MANAGERIAL EFFECTIVENESS–
EFFICIENCY RELATIONSHIPS

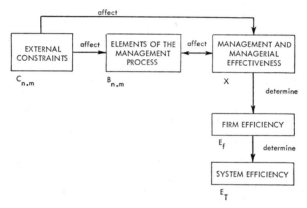

between the external constraints and elements of the management process. In the cases presented some constraints in effect give the management of the firm little or no choice in the way in which it performs the managerial function. Thus, a country with a population holding a negative attitude toward education presents firms with staffing difficulties, if educational achievements are important in proper fulfilment of some of the elements of the managerial process. Attempts to hire men who want to educate themselves more fully will be fruitless or very difficult. Or if the population has an unfavorable view of scientific method, it may prove difficult to staff the firm with persons who do have a favorable view in this important area. The result can be losses and inefficiencies within various departments of the firm. There may be a law against pollution of streams by industrial firms; and this may cause readjustments, at some cost to the firm, of their production activities. A lack of social overhead capital such as an adequate telephone network leads to communications problems and to inability to control and organize the firm efficiently. All of these constraints may be at least partially overcome by the firm, although all will cost something to correct. The result can be less efficient operation of various departments of the firm and less efficient overall operation.

A second impact of the external constraints is directly on the firm's management or managers, themselves. This in part interrelates with the staffing function, since factors such as higher education, educational match with requirements, attitude toward industrial managers, and class structure may determine in large part what kinds of managers are available. Such questions as "Why do managers behave as they do?" are determined largely by external constraints. A manager's view of achievement, risk taking, or change, for example, may determine deportment. In many cultures, firms have different kinds of goals and managers have different types of values. Such differences may depend on various external constraints.

Also important is the impact of environmental constraints on managerial effectiveness, where managerial effectiveness has been defined as the degree or level of efficiency, from society's point of view, with which the overall management process is performed in a given firm. By exploring the impact of the constraints on the management process, we may gain considerable insight into their impact on managerial effectiveness; however, it appears that the total impact of the external constraints on managerial effectiveness cannot be determined by studying only their impact on the critical elements of the management process, since in many instances they may influence managerial effectiveness directly, through their impact on managers themselves.

For example, managers may want to improve firm efficiency, but they may not know how; here the educational constraints are relevant. If managers do not *care* about improving enterprise operations and results, sociological constraints may be important. Many other examples of this type of direct constraint–managerial effectiveness relationships, as well as examples of direct constraint–critical element interactions, will be covered in Chapters 6–11 below.

These two types of relationships between constraints and the productive enterprise are both relevant in determining how well the firm operates, although specific interactions may be different. In Figure 4–2, these two relationships are indicated by the lines drawn from the $C_{n.m}$ box to the $B_{n.m}$ box and from the $C_{n.m}$ box to the X box.

## THE CONSTRAINT-BEHAVIOR MATRIX

Table 4–1 presents a constraint-behavior matrix which indicates tentative relationships between the environmental constraints and the elements of the managerial process. The external factors, following the notation of Table 3–1, are placed horizontally across the page, while the elements of the management process, following the notation of Table 2–1, are listed vertically. Not all the constraints affect all the managerial elements; the x's in Table 4–1 indicate which constraints and managerial elements might be related.

The relationships in Table 4–1 include both the direct $C$ to $B$ relationships and the $C$ to $X$ relationships noted above. In many cases, both

TABLE 4–1

CRITICAL MANAGERIAL ELEMENTS AND EXTERNAL CONSTRAINTS

| | $C_1$ Educational | | | | | | $C_2$ Sociological | | | | | | | | | $C_3$ Political-Legal | | | | | | $C_4$ Economic | | | | | | | |
|---|---|---|---|---|---|---|---|---|---|---|---|---|---|---|---|---|---|---|---|---|---|---|---|---|---|---|---|---|---|
| | 1 | 2 | 3 | 4 | 5 | 6 | 1 | 2 | 3 | 4 | 5 | 6 | 7 | 8 | 9 | 1 | 2 | 3 | 4 | 5 | 6 | 1 | 2 | 3 | 4 | 5 | 6 | 7 | 8 |
| $B_1$ 1 | | | x | | | | x | | x | x | x | x | x | x | | x | x | x | x | x | x | x | x | x | x | x | x | x | x |
| 2 | x | x | x | x | | x | x | x | x | | | | x | x | x | x | x | x | x | x | x | x | x | x | x | x | x | x | x |
| 3 | x | x | x | | | | | x | x | | | | x | x | x | x | x | x | x | x | x | x | x | x | x | x | | | |
| 4 | x | x | x | | x | | x | x | x | | | x | x | x | x | x | x | x | x | x | x | x | | | | | x | x | |
| 5 | x | x | x | | | | x | | | | | | x | x | x | x | x | x | x | | x | x | x | x | x | x | | | |
| 6 | x | x | x | | | | x | | x | | x | x | x | x | | x | x | x | | | x | x | | | | | x | | |
| 7 | x | x | x | x | x | x | x | x | x | x | x | x | x | x | x | x | | | | | | x | | | | | x | | |
| 8 | x | x | x | x | x | | x | x | | x | x | x | x | x | x | | | | | | | | | | | | | | |
| 9 | x | x | x | x | x | x | x | x | x | x | x | x | x | x | x | | | x | x | | | | | | | | | | |
| 10 | x | x | x | x | x | x | x | | x | x | | x | x | x | | | | | | | | | | | | | | | |
| 11 | x | x | x | x | x | x | x | x | | x | x | x | x | x | x | x | x | x | x | x | x | x | x | x | x | x | x | x | x |
| 12 | x | x | x | x | x | x | x | x | x | x | x | x | x | x | x | x | x | x | x | x | x | x | x | x | x | x | x | x | x |
| $B_2$ 1 | x | x | x | x | x | x | x | x | | x | x | x | x | x | x | x | x | x | | | | x | | | x | x | | | |
| 2 | x | x | x | x | | x | x | x | | x | | | x | x | x | x | x | x | | | | x | | | x | x | | | |
| 3 | x | x | x | x | | x | x | x | | x | | | x | x | x | x | | | | | | x | | | | x | | | |
| 4 | x | x | x | x | | x | x | | x | | | | x | x | x | x | | | | | | x | | | | x | | | |
| 5 | x | x | x | x | x | x | x | x | x | x | x | x | x | | x | x | | | x | x | | x | | | | | x | | |
| 6 | x | x | x | x | x | x | x | x | | x | x | x | x | x | x | x | | | x | x | x | x | | | | | | | |
| 7 | x | x | x | x | | x | x | x | x | x | x | x | x | | x | x | x | x | x | x | x | x | x | x | x | x | | | |
| $B_3$ 1 | x | x | x | x | | x | x | x | x | x | x | x | x | x | x | x | x | x | x | x | x | x | x | x | x | x | x | x | x |
| 2 | x | x | x | x | x | x | x | x | | x | x | x | x | | | x | | | | | | x | | | | | x | | x |
| 3 | x | x | x | x | | x | x | x | x | x | x | x | x | | | x | | | | | | x | | | | | x | x | x |
| 4 | x | x | x | x | | x | x | x | | x | x | | x | | | | | | | | | | | | | | | | x |
| 5 | x | x | x | x | | x | x | x | x | x | x | | x | | | | | | | | | | | | | | | | x |
| 6 | | x | x | x | | x | x | x | x | x | x | | x | | | x | | | | | | x | | | x | | x | | x |
| 7 | x | x | x | x | | x | x | x | | x | x | | x | | | x | | | | | | | | | | | | | |
| 8 | x | x | x | x | x | x | x | x | | x | x | | x | | | x | | | x | | | x | | | | | | | x |
| 9 | x | x | x | | | x | x | x | | x | x | | x | | x | | | | | | | | | | | | | | |
| 10 | x | x | x | x | | x | x | x | | x | x | | | | | | | | | | | | | | | | | | |
| 11 | x | x | x | x | x | | x | x | | x | x | | x | x | x | x | | | | | | x | | | | | | | |
| $B_4$ 1 | x | x | x | x | x | x | x | x | | x | x | x | x | | | x | x | | | | | | | | | | | x | x |
| 2 | x | | x | x | x | | x | x | | x | x | x | x | | | x | | | | | | | | | | | | x | x |
| 3 | x | x | x | x | x | | x | x | | x | x | x | x | | | x | | | | | | | | | | | | | |
| 4 | x | x | x | | x | | x | x | | x | x | | x | | | x | | | | | | | | | | | | | |
| 5 | | | | | | | x | x | | x | x | x | x | | | x | | | | | | x | | | x | x | x | | |
| 6 | x | x | x | x | x | x | x | x | | x | x | x | x | | x | x | | | | | | | | | | | | x | |
| 7 | x | x | x | x | x | x | x | x | | x | x | x | | x | | x | | | | | | | | | | | | x | |
| 8 | | | | x | | | x | | | x | x | x | | x | | x | | | | | | | | | | | | x | x |
| 9 | | | | | | | x | x | | x | x | | | | | x | | x | x | | | | | | | | | | |
| 10 | x | x | x | x | x | x | x | x | | x | x | x | x | | | x | x | | | | | x | x | x | x | | x | | x |
| $B_5$ 1 | x | x | x | x | | | x | x | | x | x | | | | | | | | | | | | | | | | | | |
| 2 | | x | x | x | | x | x | x | | x | x | x | x | | | x | | | | | | | | | | | | | |
| 3 | x | x | | | x | x | x | x | | x | x | x | x | | | x | | | | | | | | | | | | | |
| 4 | x | x | x | x | x | x | x | x | | x | x | x | x | | | | | | | | | | | | | | | | |
| 5 | x | x | x | x | | x | x | x | | x | | x | x | | | x | | | | | | | | | | | | | |
| 6 | x | x | x | x | x | x | x | x | | x | x | x | | | | | | | | | | | | | | | | x | |
| 7 | x | x | x | x | x | x | x | x | | x | x | x | x | | | | | | | | | | | | | | | x | |
| 8 | x | | | | | x | x | x | | x | x | x | | x | x | x | | | | | | | | | | | | x | |
| 9 | | | | | | | x | x | x | x | x | x | | | | | | | | | | x | | | | | | | |
| 10 | x | x | x | x | x | x | x | x | x | x | x | x | | x | x | x | | | | | | | | | | | x | | x |
| 11 | | | | | | | x | x | x | x | x | x | | | | x | | | x | x | | x | | | x | | x | | x |

TABLE 4–1—*Continued*

| | | Col 1 | Col 2 | Col 3 | Col 4 |
|---|---|---|---|---|---|
| $B_6$.......... | 1 | | x     x x x | x x x | x x x x x x x x |
| | 2 | | x     x | x x x | x x x x x x x x |
| | 3 | | x     x | x x x | x x x x x x x x |
| | 4 | x | x x x x | x | x     x     x x |
| $B_7$.......... | 1 | | x     x | x x x | x     x x x x x |
| | 2 | | x     x | x x x | x     x x x x x |
| | 3 | | x     x | x | x     x x     x x |
| | 4 | | x     x x | x x | x     x x x x x |
| | 5 | | x     x x | x x | x     x x x x x |
| | 6 | | x     x x | x x x x x | x x x x x x x x |
| | 7 | x x x x   x | x x   x x x x | x x x | x x x x x x x x |
| | 8 | x x x   x | x   x | x x x x | x     x x x x x |
| | 9 | x x x   x | x | x x x x | x     x x x x x |
| $B_8$.......... | 1 | x x x x x x | | x x x | x x x | x     x x x x x |
| $B_9$.......... | 1 | | x x x | x     x x | x x x x x x x |
| | 2 | | | | |
| | 3 | | x     x x x | x     x x | x x x x x x x |
| | 4 | | x     x x x x | x x x | x x x x x x x x |
| | 5 | | x x x x | x x x x | x x x x x |
| | 6 | | x     x x x x x x | x | x     x x |
| $B_{10}$.......... | 1 | | x x x x x | x     x x | x     x     x |
| | 2 | | x x x x x x x | x x x x | x     x x x     x |
| | 3 | | x x x x x x x x | x     x x | x x x x x x |
| | 4 | x x x   x | x x x x x x x | x     x x x x | x x x x   x |
| | 5 | | x x x x x x x x x | x x x x x x | x |
| | 6 | x x x x x | x x x x x x x x x | x     x x x | x |

relationships are present to some extent. Thus, the antipollution law (constraint) noted above does directly affect several $B$'s, but it also may cause changes by working through management. For example, as a result of the law the firm's management may decide to buy another type of equipment. Here, in addition to other impacts coming directly from the constraint to the element of the management process, the impact on planning, financial factors, and future production operations is transmitted through management activity.

These hypothesized relationships can be presented in the form of equations. For example, following Table 4–1, we have:

$$B_{3.2} = f\,(C_{1.1}, C_{1.2}, C_{1.3}, C_{1.4}, C_{1.5}, C_{1.6}, C_{2.1}, C_{2.2}, C_{2.4}, C_{2.5},$$
$$C_{2.6}, C_{2.7}, C_{3.1}, C_{4.1}, C_{4.6}, C_{4.8}) \tag{4-1}$$

where $C_{1.1}$, $C_{1.2}$, $C_{1.3}$, $C_{1.4}$, $C_{2.1}$, $C_{2.2}$, $C_{2.5}$, and $C_{4.8}$ might be the most significant variables.

$$B_{7.4} = f\,(C_{2.3}, C_{2.7}, C_{2.8}, C_{3.2}, C_{3.3}, C_{4.1}, C_{4.4}, C_{4.5}, C_{4.6}, C_{4.7}, C_{4.8}) \tag{4-2}$$

where $C_{2.3}$, $C_{2.7}$, $C_{2.8}$, $C_{4.4}$, $C_{4.7}$, and $C_{4.8}$ might be the most significant variables.

In words, Equation 4–1 says that the degree of centralization or decentralization of authority depends significantly on literacy level, specialized vocational and technical training and secondary education, higher education, special management development programs, attitude toward education, view of industrial managers and management, view of authority and subordinates, attitude toward achievement and work, class structure and individual mobility, attitude toward wealth and material gain, view of scientific method, relevant legal rules, general economic framework, factor endowment, and social overhead capital. Of these factors, literacy level, specialized vocational and technical training and general secondary education, higher education, special management development programs, view of industrial managers and management, view of authority and subordinates, class structure and individual mobility, and social overhead capital might be most important.

Equation 4–2 states that average inventory levels (major supplies, goods in process, completed output) depend on interorganizational cooperation, view of scientific method, attitude toward risk taking, defense policy, foreign policy, general economic framework, economic stability, organization of capital markets, factor endowment, market size, and social overhead capital. Of these, interorganizational cooperation, view of scientific method, attitude toward risk taking, economic stability, market size, and social overhead capital would be the most significant constraints.

If nothing else, Table 4–1 permits the statement of a large number of suggestive interrelationships in a very small space. What it does not indicate, however, is exactly what quantitative relationships are indicated by the C to B relationships.

In general, the total interrelationships of the variables presented in Tables 4–1 are extremely complex. Only intensive empirical research can help us to verify these hypotheses with a high degree of confidence and only extensive research can enable us to determine the relative significance of different constraints in terms of their impact on a given element of the management process in a given situation. Chapters 6–11 explore in some depth what seem to be significant relationships between external constraints and the management process. Appendix 1, which deals with a typical day in the life of an American manager of a Saudi Arabian business firm, also gives some insights into pertinent relationships of this type.

Table 4–1 presents the authors' hypothesis of the interrelationships between external constraints and critical behavioral elements. It is possible that everything depends on everything else to some extent and that x's should be placed in every square of the matrix; however, the concern here was to suggest only the most significant relationships, which at a later date could, by empirical research, be verified with a higher degree of confidence.

## MANAGERIAL EFFECTIVENESS AND PRODUCTIVE EFFICIENCY

The basic problem of industrial management from society's point of view is to become steadily more efficient over time. This follows from the goal of most societies to obtain more useful goods and services in the future. Increases in productive efficiency are generally considered the basic social desiderata of industrial enterprise management, since a country's total useful industrial output will be the sum of the value added to production by component enterprises. The more efficient each firm is, the more efficient and wealthy the country will be.

The notion of productive or economic efficiency, which is explored in some detail in Chapter 5 below, is essentially a relative concept. One can never be quite sure what truly optimum economic efficiency would be, but it is possible to evaluate and rank firms and countries in terms of their relative levels of productive efficiency.

One goal here is to determine, in a tentative manner, the impact of the environmental constraints on managerial effectiveness, both directly and through the various elements of the management process. The aim is to assign a value to each constraint for each country studied. This should indicate the extent to which each constraint inhibits managerial effectiveness. This quantification of the constraint matrix is attempted in Chapter 12 for several countries. The constraint scores assigned for each country are added to give a total "constraint–managerial effectiveness" score or index. The scores for various countries can be used to rank countries.

The ratings assigned to countries by use of the external constraints must be verified by other meaningful measures, however, in order to determine whether the constraint scores are valid. Thus a country might be scored low on its constraints, yet by some other measure of productivity it might be rated high. This would suggest error in the constraint selection or ratings.

Figure 4–2 indicates that system efficiency is determined by firm efficiency $(E_f)$. That is, the level of general efficiency in any system is determined by what happens in every productive enterprise within the system; but this firm efficiency is in turn determined by managerial effectiveness. Thus system efficiency serves as a rough cross check on the validity of the constraint ratings.

Measures of system efficiency are such factors as gross national product per capita, rate of growth of gross national product per capita, rate of utilization of inputs, and other factors discussed in detail in Chapter 5 below. Low constraint ratings would suggest that these macroefficiency ratings should also be low. If there is a close rank order correlation between the constraint–managerial effectiveness indices and the total system efficiency indicators for different countries, this would suggest that an approximate measure of total system efficiency in any country could be obtained directly by evaluating the critical environmental constraints in terms of their impact on managerial effectiveness.

If aggregate measures of firm efficiency can be evolved, these will also serve as a useful cross check of the external constraint ratings, since the ratings in effect evaluate how well the firms' managements perform. Such efficiency indicators as general profitability, usable output per man hour, exports, and others, are developed in Chapter 5 to serve as this type of cross check.

The aggregate indicators pertain to concrete results achieved by the firm as a whole. It should be noted that in each case the indicator would have to be measured either in roughly comparable physical or time units or in converted standard units of money if meaningful comparisons are to be made among firms in different countries. For this reason, it may be more feasible to study and compare entire branches of industry rather than miscellaneous firms. Once the various aggregate efficiency indicators for an entire industry in given countries are known, the indicators for hypothetical representative or average firms in the industry can be determined.

One difficulty with using firm efficiency indicators is that in some cases the efficiency of a firm or an industrial sector may reflect subsystem optimization. That is, the sector may be very efficient at the expense of other sectors' efficiency. This problem is discussed in Chapter 5. Such subsystem optimizations can also in part be cross checked by use of the total system efficiency indicators.

There is still one missing link in this conceptual approach. It may be generally true that a low literacy level, a negative view of scientific method, political and economic instability, and so on, tend to inhibit significantly managerial effectiveness, and this may be verified by an independently determined low score for $E_f$; but why is this so, and how can one check even roughly the extent to which internal management effectiveness is negatively influenced by *each* constraint? Another type of efficiency cross check is required for this purpose.

This necessary check can be obtained by observing the way in which each critical element of the managerial process is performed. An efficient firm would necessarily be efficient in its performance of critical elements, in some general way. One cannot merely evaluate each $B_{n.m}$ in efficiency terms and add the evaluations to determine managerial effectiveness, since the $B$'s are interconnected in various complex ways and their relative importance may differ. For example, the firm may be quite efficient in its production activities, but only at the expense of being highly inefficient in marketing; or the level of planning efficiency may determine in large part how efficiently financial and organizational problems are handled. The lack of equal weighting and linear relationships among the $B$ efficiency indicators means that independent evaluation of the efficiency of such factors will not indicate the total efficiency of the firm. A precise measure of internal managerial effectiveness must take into account the degree of optimization of all the firm's operations in an extremely complex, and often very subtle, manner. A basic problem here, often found in modern firms, is avoiding subsystem optimization of the type noted above.

We can use $e_{n.m}$ to indicate the efficiency with which any critical element will be performed. It is clear that the problems involved in accurately measuring the efficiency indicators are enormous, but there is no conceptual reason why this cannot be done. Some combined score of the $e_{n.m}$'s will be helpful in evaluating firm efficiency, but care must be exercised to avoid errors caused by subsystem optimizations. The equation $E_f = \Sigma se/\Sigma s$, where $s$ is the weight assigned to each indicator, is not precisely correct, although it may be possible to use it as a rough working guide for the determination of internal managerial effectiveness.

As was pointed out earlier, there are two basic types of $B$'s making up the overall internal management process. The majority of the $B$'s are essentially structural variables; the others (indicated by asterisks in Table 2–1) are essentially dynamic, problem oriented variables. It would generally be easier to evaluate the latter type of $B$ in efficiency terms; however, there is no conceptual reason why all the $B$'s cannot be evaluated in terms of relative degrees of efficiency. If it can be determined with reasonable confidence what the significant relationships between the $B$'s are in a given situation, it will be possible to estimate the approximate impact of the constraints on internal managerial effectiveness.

It will also be possible to study a given firm to determine what types of intrafirm inefficiencies are critical in this regard. Thus if one finds considerable information distortion in a firm's planning, this suggests that some phases of the firm's operations (i.e., the critical elements) are being performed inefficiently. Or if product quality is very poor, this is evidence that one or more production elements are being handled inefficiently. This type of evidence is not specifically an inefficiency, but it points to types of firm inefficiencies which might be evaluated by actually computing the relevant $e_{n.m}$ for the given $B_{n.m}$.

The list below is made up of examples of this type of evidence which might be found in a given firm and which would lead to deducible inefficiencies. Actual measures of the $e$'s will be covered in Chapter 5. Here, the problem is to identify where potential inefficiencies, caused largely by various external constraints, might exist.

### Examples of Intrafirm Inefficiency Indicators

1. Considerable information distortion in planning—$B_{1.9}$
2. Highly inflexible plans that cannot be effectively adjusted to changing conditions—$B_{1.5}$
3. Deficient planning techniques and methodologies—$B_{1.6}$
4. Ineffective information feedback and control systems—$B_{2.3}$
5. Ineffective corrective action in the control process—$B_{2.4}$
6. Overburdened spans of control—$B_{3.4}$
7. Overcentralization resulting in serious delays and red tape in decision making—$B_{3.2}$
8. A very low degree of work specialization—$B_{3.3}$
9. A high degree of organizational confusion and inefficiency regarding authority relationships—$B_{3.8}$
10. Unclear job descriptions leading to considerable conflict and confusion among personnel—$B_{4.4}$
11. Use of selection and promotion criteria which lead to inefficient staffing—$B_{4.2}$
12. Great difficulties in motivating personnel to improve performance—$B_{5.7}$

13. Ineffective communication among personnel—$B_{5.6}$
14. Inadequate supervisory techniques—$B_{5.4}$
15. Products of extremely poor quality—$B_{6.1}$
16. Extensively restrictive work practices—$B_{5.11}$
17. Relatively uneconomical channels of distribution—$B_{6.2}$
18. Ineffective sales promotion techniques—$B_{6.4}$
19. Uneconomical subsidiary production operations—$B_{7.1}$
20. Unstable production operations—$B_{7.6}$
21. A relatively low level of automation and mechanization—$B_{7.9}$
22. Exceptionally large inventories relative to reasonable requirements—$B_{7.4}$
23. Little or no research and development activity—$B_{8.1}$
24. Relatively high cost of capital—$B_{9.1}$
25. Considerable union-management conflict—$B_{10.4}$
26. Serious difficulties with suppliers—$B_{10.2}$

It is not our intention in this volume to deal in any detail with the various efficiency indicators noted here or to present related quantitative data for specific firms and countries. Chapter 5 will, however, deal with more precise definitions of efficiency. This type of analysis will be undertaken in greater depth in the volume dealing with comprehensive country studies. Our aim here is to set up a conceptual framework that can be used for intensive empirical comparative studies of firm efficiency and managerial effectiveness.

At this point, it is useful to refer back to Figure 4-2 to note that the two boxes labeled "elements of the management process" and "management and managerial effectiveness" are in effect the internal core of Figure 4-1, labeled "Enterprise and its Management." That is, the use of the complex X:B relationship is an effort to unlock the "black box" of management by exploring the way in which external constraints force firms and/or managers to behave the way they do internally. This also explains why we use the concept of managerial effectiveness, instead of merely moving from the external constraints to firm efficiency. Firm efficiency merely states how efficient a firm is, relative to other firms—it does not indicate *why* it has this level of efficiency. The use of the X:B relationships should allow detailed analysis of the *why*, as well as the how, of efficiency, in terms of the environmental constraints.

## THE GENERAL THEORY IN SUMMARY AND EQUATION FORM

The following variables have been introduced to this point:

$E_T$: Total system or country efficiency

$E_f$: Overall efficiency of a single firm

$E_f$: Overall efficiency of an average firm in a given country

$X$: Managerial effectiveness

$e_n$: Microefficiency indicators for critical elements of the management process

$B_{n.m}$: Given critical elements of the managerial process

$C_{n.m}$: Given environmental constraints

The basic hypothesis presented here can be summarized as follows:

1. Total system efficiency depends on firm efficiency. If we are measuring the efficiency with which the total flow of goods and services is created, the required figure can be obtained by aggregating the total performance of every productive enterprise in the country, subject to subsystem optimization qualifications.

2. The performance of an average representative industrial firm could serve as an approximate measure of total system efficiency.

3. Overall firm efficiency depends on managerial effectiveness. The way in which firm management performs in total determines how efficient each firm or hypothetical representative firm will be. There are two potential measures of managerial effectiveness. One can be derived from the values assigned to the environmental constraints. The other can be determined theoretically by obtaining a combined weighted score for selected critical microefficiency indicators $(e_n)$. We shall exclude this latter measure of managerial effectiveness from the equations presented below, since the values of the $e$'s are implicit in $E_f$ and the $B$'s.

4. Managerial effectiveness will depend on how efficiently each critical element in the management process is performed.

5. In what manner and how efficiently the overall management process is performed will depend on the environmental constraints in a given country.

6. A final consideration remains in order to close this system. The level of managerial effectiveness for a given actual or hypothetical firm is likely to depend on the direct impact of the environmental constraints, as well as on their less direct impact through the existing internal management process.

This system can be indicated notationally as follows:

1. $E_T \cong \dfrac{\Sigma\, w\, E_f}{W}$ , where $w$ is a weight indicating the value of

output of each firm converted to standard comparable units of money and $W$ is the total output of all firms. A firm producing a million dollars of output might have an efficiency level of 0.5, while one producing a thousand dollars of output might have an efficiency level of 0.2. Both efficiencies would have to be weighed properly to avoid distortion.

2. $E_f \cong \dfrac{\Sigma\, w\, E_f}{W}$

3. $E_{\bar{f}} = f(X)$

4. $X = f(B_{1.1} \ldots B_{n.m})$

5. $B_{n.m} = f(C_{1.1} \ldots C_{n.m})$. Here, not all the $C$'s may be included for any given $B$.

6. In order to close the system, we must include $X = f(C_{1.1} \ldots C_{n.m})$.

From the above, the following relationships can be derived:

7. $E_T = f(X)$

8. $E_T = f(C_{1.1} \ldots C_{n.m})$

Figure 4–2 indicated diagramatically the general hypothesis presented above. The external constraints affect the critical elements of the management process, which affect managerial effectiveness, which determines firm efficiency, which determines total system efficiency; but external constraints also affect managerial effectiveness directly.

## CONCLUSION

While it is relatively easy to indicate the general theoretical schema in this way, the actual number of measurement and quantification problems suggested by it is tremendous. The environmental constraints are interrelated; the elements of the management process are interrelated; firm efficiencies may also be interrelated in that one firm's efficiency may depend in part on what other firms do; and intrafirm efficiencies are interrelated.

Meaningful insights and conclusions may be forthcoming, however, by explaining the elements of the management process and their relationships with the environmental constraints. Study of the various complex relationships indicated in the general theoretical schema suggests that the key to explaining differences in the management process and managerial effectiveness in firms in different countries is in the environmental constraints. If the constraints can be adequately analyzed and evaluated in terms of how they interact with the management process and managerial effectiveness, it should be possible to explain much of the reason why firm and total system efficiencies differ between countries.

In spite of the great difficulties and complexities involved, there is no conceptual reason why the measurement problem cannot be dealt with in a meaningful manner by analyzing a limited number of the most critical variables at a time.[2] By breaking down the total problem into its most critical parts, intensive empirical research in conjunction with a large number of well reasoned qualitative and quantified judgment can lead to a meaningful, albeit rough, cross check and justification of the managerial effectiveness index.

There are three levels of efficiency which are relevant in this problem. They are total system efficiency, firm efficiency in the aggregate sense, and intrafirm efficiency. We have referred to these efficiencies in this chapter without detailed analysis of what the terms mean, and it is to this problem that we now turn.

---

[2] For an intensive analysis of the impact of a small number of environmental factors on industrial managerial performance in a single country see B. Richman, *Soviet Management: With Significant American Comparisons*, (Englewood Cliffs, N.J.: Prentice-Hall, Inc., 1965). The Soviet study suggests the amount of work that would be involved in analyzing in depth the impact of all the environmental factors indicated in the present study on managerial performance in a large number of countries.

# Chapter 5

# Efficiency of Firms and Countries

## INTRODUCTION

I n Chapter 4 we discussed three efficiencies which need definition. We have assumed that societies want to become more efficient, in the sense of expanding usable outputs with available inputs. To achieve this goal, it is necessary that productive enterprises also become more efficient; and in order to achieve this improvement in firm efficiency, it is necessary that firms improve the efficiency with which they perform the key elements of the management process. The problem in this chapter is to develop usable definitions of these efficiencies and to indicate the types of problems inherent in any discussion of economic efficiency. For both the firm and the economy, the problem of definitions of efficiency are extremely difficult; but a careful evaluation of the efficiency of the society and the managers of productive enterprises is necessary if meaningful evaluations of comparative management are to be made. The emphasis here is on empirical measures which will prove workable in practice.[1]

## EFFICIENCY DEFINITIONS

The level of efficiency of any type of system may be defined as $E = O/I$, where $E$ is efficiency, $O$ is output, and $I$ is input. If outputs and inputs can be measured in the same units, such as some energy measure, it is a fairly straightforward process to measure efficiency directly. $E$ will always be less than 1.0, since it is impossible, in the physical sense, to get more out of a system than was put in.[2] $E$ can range from 0.0 (no output at all) to a theoretical 1.0.

---

[1] For a more theoretical discussion of efficiency problems, see Appendix 2.

[2] In economics and business, the same flow analogy is used for efficiency; but since inputs are not energy, but value units, the precise formulation used in engineering is invalid. Given economic definitions, what goes in equals what comes out, since the balancing factor is profit; but if profit is excluded, the definition that efficiency is at a maximum when profits are maximized can be used. See Tibor Scitovsky, *Welfare and Competition* (Homewood, Ill.: Richard D. Irwin, Inc., 1951), particularly pp. 51–187 and pp. 338–372, for further discussion of this point. See also Appendix 2.

The concept of efficiency was initially used in engineering and the natural sciences, where inputs and outputs can be converted to the same units. Some amount of energy is put into a mechanical or electrical system, and some useful output is obtained; the ratio of these is $E$. In economics and business, the efficiency measurement process is complicated by the fact that the inputs consist of productive factors, such as land (including minerals and climate), labor, capital, and management. Outputs consist of useful goods and services. Each productive enterprise is engaged in taking such inputs, including components or semifinished goods and services from other firms, and converting them into useful outputs, as shown in Figure 5–1. If the inputs and outputs can be converted to similar units (such as money values), the efficiency definition noted above can be used; however, one of the major difficulties in economics is the problem of rational unit conversion. This problem will be discussed at length below.

### FIGURE 5–1

#### FACTOR TRANSFORMATION PROCESS

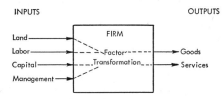

A second consideration in economic efficiency is that all firms are interrelated to some extent; what happens in a steel mill will influence what happens in an automobile assembly plant. Countries are interrelated, in that economic and political events in Europe may directly affect the American economy. Intrafirm efficiencies also are interrelated, in that a marketing change will affect production, finance, and personnel. Thus the definition of efficiency has to be expanded to include the provision that improvements in efficiency in one part of the total economic system are considered efficiency gains only if they have no negative impact on efficiencies in other parts of the system, or that aggregate efficiency gains must be positive. To be considered more efficient, a firm must either produce more output with the same inputs or produce the same output with fewer inputs; but if these changes result in larger negative efficiency changes elsewhere in the system, they will not be considered a general efficiency gain. This type of difficulty pervades every economy, and it is discussed below at some length under the problem of subsystem optimization.

Conceptually, the definition of economic efficiency is clear cut, and the problem is to determine how efficient the total system or any of its basic components may be; but in practice the concept bogs down in many problems, which will be discussed below.

## BASIC EFFICIENCY PROBLEMS

Any macro- or microeconomic efficiency problem presents a series of difficulties which are extremely hard to resolve. They appear, in various guises, in any discussion of efficiency; and resolution in some cases is impossible. Since they tend to affect all of the efficiency measurements discussed later in this chapter, they are considered as a group here. They are as follows:

### Problems of Measurement[3]

Unlike the systems considered in engineering, economies and firms use different kinds of inputs to create many kinds of outputs. A steel mill will take labor of various sorts, land (including raw materials such as coal and iron ore), capital, and management and will generate outputs of various types of steel products. Not only are the inputs diverse, but outputs also fall into different categories. Steel rails will not be sold in the same markets as tinplate for can manufacture. The quality of inputs will differ significantly also, since some ores have higher iron content than others, some workers are more capable than others, and so on. If efficiency of the firm is to be measured, these different inputs and outputs must be converted into some standard units.

Since the total production of a country is the sum of its firms' production, any measure of national output is even more complex. A modern industrial country may produce 10,000 to 15,000 different items, subdivided into millions of particular goods. How can ten-millimeter bolts be added to Size 8 shoes, a certain grade of plywood, or one issue of a weekly newsmagazine? Unless this can be done, no general output measure can be found, and no efficiency value can be determined.

The common measuring rod is money. It is possible to price any input or output and evaluate different firms by observing what the dollar value of inputs is as compared to the dollar value of inputs used by other firms producing the same items. One major difficulty is that the prices of inputs and outputs become important. If there is some competition in both items, prices will presumably reflect the true value of inputs and outputs; but even a casual observation of any society shows that many prices are artificial in some sense. Wages may be set arbitrarily by governments; or monopolists may hold the price of raw materials above competitive levels. Marxist states often set prices that are seemingly based on whim rather than on careful analysis of true value. On the output side, firms frequently have some power over pricing, and they may set artificially high prices for some products and

---

[3] See Oskar Morgenstern, "Qui Numerare Incipit Errare Incipit," *Fortune*, Vol. LXVIII (October, 1963), No. 4, p. 142, for a discussion of the types of measurement problems typical in business and economics.

services. Governments may also have some price controls which keep prices below equilibrium levels.

Firm managers do have information about both input and output prices[4] which they can use as data for decision making; but, given the above problems, they may not have the right ones. They may also be unable in some complex cases to determine the costs of doing some operations. Problems of cost allocation can prevent adequate determination of true costs. When using money measures of values, one must proceed with caution, given the difficulties of determining actual, as compared to stated, value.

### The Problem of Knowledge[5]

Economists assume that government officials and firm managers know enough about costs and prices to make meaningful decisions. Such knowledge is not obviously determined in a complex industrial situation. Thus, it may be that the cost of operating a legal department is known but whether or not this cost is optimal is unknown. Should the manager add lawyers to his staff, hoping for cost reductions; or should he dismiss some of his legal personnel? Extensive investigation of such a department would be necessary before such an issue could rationally be decided, and the search for information also entails a cost.[6] It is common in business to find such issues decided according to some rule of thumb—such as a rule that legal expenses for a given type of firm should be around 0.5 percent of gross revenues—yet further analysis may reveal that no manager really knows whether or not this rule is correct.[7] As a firm gains more experience in its business, it typically acquires more relevant knowledge about its operations; but even in the most progressive firms more is unknown than known.

A firm or an economy can hardly make decisions about efficiency if it is unable to determine what the factors in the problem are, but the typical company or country anywhere is forced to operate in ignorance because relevant knowledge is not available. In so far as such ignorance exists, no firm can be highly efficient, since it does not know whether or not it is being efficient. One student of business activities in less developed countries puts it this way:

---

[4] Managers may not even know this much in complex situations. It has been estimated that there are 33 trillion railroad rates alone in the United States, and it is doubtful that all prices are really known in very complicated situations. See George Wilson, "The Effect of Rate Regulation on Resource Allocation in Transportation," *American Economic Review*, Vol. LIV (May, 1964), No. 3, p. 171.

[5] See G. B. Richardson, *Information and Investment* (Oxford: Oxford University Press, 1960), for a more nearly complete discussion of this point.

[6] Richard W. Cyert and James G. March, *A Behavioral Theory of the Firm* (Englewood Cliffs, N.J.: Prentice-Hall, Inc., 1963), pp. 10–13 and pp. 120–122.

[7] Robert Dorfman, "Operations Research," *American Economic Review*, Vol. L. (September, 1960), No. 4, pp. 574–579.

The dearth of data on output, prices, products, and employment means that a manager has little or nothing to go on. One of the major blocks to managerial efficiency is the absence of comprehensive, reliable, and current information. Given two equivalent decision-making situations, one before a manager in the United States and one before a manager in Khartoum [Sudan], a very poor manager in the United States might stumble almost automatically onto a correct decision because he has at his hand the appropriate body of information or people from whom he can get it. His opposite number in Khartoum needs to be of first class caliber, thoroughly and personally aware of all aspects of the business and the industry, and possessed of a sixth sense which tells him where events are leading to come up with the proper decision. It has often been observed that managers and entrepreneurs in underdeveloped nations are more conservative than managers and entrepreneurs in Western Europe or North America. It is little wonder: it is the difference between flying with instruments and flying "by the seats of the pants."[8]

## The Problem of Uncertainty[9]

Uncertainty may be defined as the possibility of unforeseen changes in the future. It should not be confused with *risk*, which is defined as unexpected events which can be predicted, in the actuarial sense, and hence covered by some form of insurance for the group experiencing the risk.[10] Thus, fires in factories cannot be predicted for any one factory, but for all factories some reasonable prediction can be made as to fire frequency and loss, and an insurance company can collect enough premium income from all risk bearers to cover losses.

An unexpected change in consumer tastes, on the other hand, cannot be predicted in the same manner; and no insurance is available for manufacturers of coonskin caps and Hula Hoops to prevent loss because of this factor. Nor can a petroleum company buy insurance against the possibility that some new source of energy will make petroleum obsolete and will cause this industry to become unprofitable. Countries as well as firms face such uncertainties; and on the national level no one can insure against war, drought, or other natural or manmade catastrophes which may afflict them. Nor can a country foresee that some exceptional good fortune will make the country wealthy beyond its dreams, as has happened on occasion when some unexpected resources were discovered.

Firms and countries are forward oriented in time. Decisions made today have impact some time in the future. Thus, if a company decides to produce a new product, preparations for production are made now and

---

[8] Peter F. M. McLoughlin, "Business and Its Managers in the Sudan," *California Management Review*, Vol. VI (fall, 1963), No. 1, pp. 86–87.

[9] See Milton H. Spencer and Louis Siegelman, *Managerial Economics* (rev. ed.; Homewood, Ill.: Richard D. Irwin, Inc., 1964), pp. 1–73, for further discussion of this point.

[10] *Ibid.*, p. 3.

expenses incurred, although sales will occur only in the future. The implication here is that the managers are able to predict with reasonable accuracy what demand will be; but demand in a capitalist economy depends on a number of factors which are presently unknown, such as prices of competing products next year, levels of income next year, future tastes of consumers, and similar matters. Moreover, sharp changes may occur, such as the beginning of a war, a depression, some act of God such as an earthquake, or other possibilities. The firm can attempt to minimize uncertainties of this sort, but it can never escape them. A decision which seems rational now, based on sound knowledge and excellent business judgment, may turn sour quickly in the future because of unforeseen changes. On the other hand, decisions that seem poor now may later prove to be brilliant. Since no one can correctly foretell all of the future, the manager is faced with the problem of not only performing well today but making decisions for tomorrow which may be impossible to reverse. In many cases, a decision locks the firm into a pattern which is difficult or expensive to change. A railroad which digs a tunnel or a power company which builds a dam is making a commitment which may last for decades. A country may make a decision to build a highway net into a region which for unforseen reasons is unproductive, and most of the investment may be lost.

The uncertainties of any productive operation make evaluations of firms in the present quite difficult. A company which appears to be efficient may, after a decade, prove to be hopelessly inefficient because its managers failed to foresee relevant and critical changes. Business history is full of firms which failed because they could not cope with the uncertainties of the future. In at least one American case (the electric interurban railway industry), an entire industry failed because it improperly evaluated the impact of the automobile. Within this group of firms were many which operated with excellent efficiency in the technical sense, yet history's evaluation of this efficiency is that it was completely irrelevant.[11]

## The Problem of Goals

The question, "Efficiency toward what?" may be legitimately raised. If a firm has goals which are different from those of others, it is difficult to compare its results with those of other firms. A company may want to be profitable, pay out a given sum per quarter to its stockholders, and be known as the firm which pays its employees more than other firms in its industry. A second firm in the same industry may want to maximize sales. Problems of comparison in such cases are difficult. Country goals are even more complicated, and they will be discussed in more detail in the following section on national efficiency.

A common assumption about firms made in capitalist countries is that

---

[11] George W. Hilton and John F. Due, *The Electric Interurban Railways in America* (Stanford, Calif.: Stanford University Press, 1960), pp. 208–251.

they want to maximize profits.[12] In many cases firms are interested in other goals, but profitability for a privately owned firm is a necessary condition for survival.

The concept of profit maximization has been attacked violently by scholars and men of affairs for over a century. It is argued, first, that managers would not maximize even if they could and, second, that maximization of this sort is immoral, in that it implies some sort of exploitation. Much of the debate is semantic, since classical economic analysis is timeless, and maximization clearly has some time dimension. If a capitalist firm maximizes today by exploiting its workers and suppliers unmercifully, it may not be around tomorrow. A company which does not appear to be maximizing in the short run may be doing so in the long run, since its present actions help guarantee its survival later.

It has been suggested that the firm usually is *satisficing* rather than maximizing, which means that it tries to perform satisfactorily, rather than optimally.[13] The question is again semantic, since satisficing in the short run can well be profit maximizing in the long run.

Inasmuch as the goals of firms are not the same, the problem of comparing efficiency bogs down in a mass of incompatible data. The use of profit maximization as a working assumption for any capitalist firm has the major advantage of forcing the observer to consider all firms as seeking the same goal; however, if firms do not try to maximize profits, few if any comparisons are possible. It would be tempting at this point to note that empirically goals *are* different and that hence no meaningful discussion of relative managerial efficiency can be made. This has the advantage of allowing any manager, no matter what he does, to be considered efficient. It also allows any social system, regardless of its economic situation, to be considered efficient, since it may well be optimizing in some uneconomic direction. If we can assume that the goal of profitability is reasonably widespread and general, it is possible to proceed with the analysis.

### The Problem of Subsystem Optimization[14]

In any complex economy, many types of productive organizations exist, each with its own management and its own interpretation of the goals it seeks to achieve. Such goals, as well as the manner in which they are achieved, may conflict with the overall goals of the total socio-economic system. In such a case, it is possible for various subsystems to be extremely efficient yet for the total system to be quite inefficient.

---

[12] George S. Stigler, *The Theory of Price* (New York: The Macmillan Company, 1949), p. 4.

[13] Herbert A. Simon, *Administrative Behavior* (New York: The Macmillan Company, 1961), p. xxv.

[14] R. McKean and Charles Hitch, "Suboptimization in Operations Problems," in McCloskey and Trefethen, eds., *Operations Research for Management* (Baltimore: The John Hopkins Press, 1954).

For example, consider a monopoly firm whose sole goal is profit maximization. The firm may achieve this goal by raising prices and selling less (that is, by equating marginal cost and marginal revenue in the economic sense[15]); but even if the firm is making the maximum amount of profit possible, it is not helping to achieve the general social goals of rapid growth, higher outputs of useful goods and services, improvements in technology, and economically fair prices for other firms needing the output of the monopolist. These goals may be quite valid in achieving higher incomes and increased efficiency in the society as a whole, but the monopolist may resist them all on the correct grounds that to cooperate in achieving them would result in poorer profit results for the monopoly.

Examples of subsystem optimization at the expense of the total system are also common in Marxist countries. A firm manager may be given the goal of maximizing production of bolts and be rewarded by bonuses if he achieves or exceeds the goal. An implicit goal might be that the bolts be manufactured in usable sizes. The manager, his eyes fixed on the potential bonus, may optimize production of the bolts easiest to produce, not those most needed. His production may be optimized, but it may also be largely unusable, since the sizes he made are not the sizes needed. The Soviet press for years has carried accounts of such subsystem optimization resulting in lower total system efficiency.

Subsystem optimization occurs often within enterprises. The sales manager, seeing as his goal the maximization of dollar sales, fights with the credit manager, who is unwilling to allow more dubious credit risks. Sales could rise, but the losses stemming from failures to pay for the goods could more than offset profits made. Production managers whose major goal is production of goods at the lowest possible unit cost conflict with marketing personnel who want frequent product design changes in order to have the latest and best designs available for improving sales. In such cases, it is quite possible that the maximization of any subsystem goal will result in less overall system efficiency.

### The Problem of Resource Mobility

Mistakes occur in every society, and a frequent problem faced by national planners and productive enterprises is how to correct such errors. Plants may be built in the wrong location, changes in demand may make certain equipment obsolete, or new technology can make workers' skills unnecessary, to name a few examples.

In such cases, the question of how easily and rapidly inputs, particularly labor and real capital, can be shifted from relatively less profitable employments to more productive work becomes quite relevant. Such shifts depend on factors such as the types of capital assets employed, the relative

---

[15] John F. Due and Robert W. Clower, *Intermediate Economics Analysis* (4th ed.; Homewood, Ill.: Richard D. Irwin, Inc., 1961), pp. 185–289.

mobility of workers and managers, and rapid recognition by the society and its members that shifts are necessary. Failure to move inputs rapidly out of low productivity uses into ones of higher productivity can lead to extensive system inefficiencies.

Such movements may depend on the kind of inputs utilized. If a country or firm builds a dam or a railroad erroneously, it is quite difficult to shift assets rapidly; but an aircraft, a general purpose machine tool, or a motor truck can easily be shifted from one purpose to another, or from one location to another. Highly specialized assets can become a drag on system efficiency.

Labor may present similar problems.[16] A man trained in electronics or medicine can practice his profession in a variety of ways and locations, assuming that he is willing to move. A glass blower or a diamond cutter might find it more difficult to shift easily to other trades. Also serious is the question of mobility when entire regions are declining, as is now the case in American coal areas. Mines decline, either through loss of demand or through depletion, and workers and families are unwilling to move to other areas. The ghost towns all over the world are mute testimony to the necessity of moving when resources are exhausted and workers must shift their location and possibly their trade.

It is common in many countries to find that employment rates, both of men and of capital, vary from region to region. Thus northern England frequently has unemployment rates of over 3 percent, while the South and Midlands have rates of less than 1 percent. Variations between American cities are common, too. Plants also show large variations, particularly when the capital is long lived. Decaying textile towns in New England in 1965 had a rate of unused capacity of over 50 percent, while color television factories in other regions expanded rapidly trying to meet demand.

Much of the problem here is in terms of what kinds of skills and capital are required to meet demand. The problem interrelates considerably with uncertainty and knowledge, since choice of investments and assets determines in part the flexibility of the firm and the economy. Hence, a mine may use a railroad or trucks, of which the former is quite inflexible and immobile. If unforseen changes in demand result in abandonment, the loss and inefficiency will be greater if the less flexible assets are utilized. Choices can become quite complicated in such cases though, since the railroad could be more efficient if demand does not decline.

These efficiency difficulties apply to countries in the aggregate sense as well as to intrafirm issues. Countries as well as firms must struggle with problems of goals, measurements, subsystem optimizations, and the rest of the problems. It is not always true that a country knows, for example, just what its gross national product might be, since this figure is aggregated from

---

[16] See G. S. Tollez and B. M. Farmer, "Factor Market Efficiency for Agriculture," *American Economic Review*, Vol. LIV (May, 1964), No. 9, pp. 107–119, for a discussion of this problem in American agriculture.

a large number of subreports, many of which are not particularly accurate. Attempting to fulfill national goals when it is not clear where the country is at the moment can be extremely difficult. This problem is made more complicated by the tendency of many economic agents to conceal information. Firms or individuals, fearing higher taxes, may not report incomes or outputs correctly. National planners, attempting to arrive at consensus goals, may not realize where they are at present.

## THE CONCEPT OF NATIONAL EFFICIENCY

The efficiency of a country is measured by the output it manages to get from its inputs. The greater the output is with given inputs, the more efficient the country will be.

To be precise, all inputs should be considered. The productivity (or efficiency) of land, labor, and capital can be measured, with the difficulties noted above taken into account, and total efficiency computed. In practice, however, the measure is usually taken to be output per person. It may be true that the country is extremely productive in terms of its capital or land; but these are not human elements, and the usual interest in efficiency is whether or not the country provides more or less income per person. Thus the usual measure of country efficiency is some measure of output per person, not output per production factor. This distorts efficiency measures for countries like Kuwait, where enormous petroleum reserves are very productive but the average Kuwaiti is not. Income per capita in this country is among the highest in the world, but the Kuwaitis have little to do with how it is generated. For a fairly wide range of resource endowment, however, the person efficiency measure is probably valid.

**Problems of National Goals.** A difficulty which arises here is that the goals of a society may be quite complex and diverse. The goal of a design engineer is (presumably) to develop a more efficient machine, and this goal is quite clear cut. But the economic goals of countries may be quite diffuse, and precise notions of what is wanted may be lacking. Hence, it is difficult to discuss the question of more efficiency, since it is not clear what *more efficiency* might mean to various persons.

One country may be interested in maximizing productive efficiency in order to be able to build larger and better churches. Another may have as a general economic goal the maximization of consumers' present standards of living. A third may see its destiny as fulfilled when it builds up the largest possible military system. If such diverse goals can be spelled out and agreed upon generally by those persons who make aggregate decisions for the society, it is possible to design an economic system which achieves the goals; but efficient operation of the three societies noted above would be quite different. All might function well; but firms within each would be operating in quite different ways, producing different products.

At this point, value systems and economics coincide. A person may feel strongly that consumer sovereignty is right and proper, while another may feel equally strongly that the role of a government is to have a large military force. The observer can only note the feelings, attempt to evaluate them for a society, and proceed. It is impossible to rationalize ethics in such cases.

Another difficulty is that countries typically have a variety of goals, some of which conflict with others. The United States seems to want a high and rising gross national product, which is basically a desire for more efficient production; but it also wants price stability, an adequately strong defense force, full employment, and the preservation of "The American Way of Life" (however defined). It is not clear that these other goals necessarily lead to greater efficiency. The full employment of all persons wanting work could lead to less productive efficiency, as could the draining off of valuable resources into nonproductive defense installations. Since no one in this society is able to speak for all, the goals and subgoals tend to become quite diffuse, and it is difficult to determine whether the country is actually achieving what it seemingly wants to achieve.

A major goal problem for all countries is to decide which portion of output should be enjoyed by future generations and which portion should be consumed now. In a dynamic, growing economy, a country must invest to become more efficient, since the usual means of getting more income is to build the necessary capital equipment which will make workers and managers more productive; but if this investment takes place, consumption must be reduced so that real goods and services can be devoted to investment. The range of investment as a percent of GNP is from about 5 to 40 in modern countries, reflecting diverse views about how the future and the present should share in total wealth being created now. Such differences in attitude are reflected on the firm level in terms of which sorts of firms prosper and which are squeezed.

**Empirical Measures of Country Efficiency.** A few general measures exist for evaluating the productive efficiency of a given country. While there is no all-inclusive, completely accurate measure available, the following suggest how such an evaluation might take place:

1. *Level of Real per Capita Gross National Product* (*GNP*). The higher this figure is, the more efficient a country presumably is. It is possible of course that a few countries will be so blessed with natural resources (e.g., Kuwait) that this measure is not particularly useful. Problems of measuring national income also may lead to distortions, particularly when different countries are compared.[17] Changes in tastes and price levels may make year to year comparisons somewhat tenuous; but in spite of these difficulties, this measure is the best single evaluation of overall system efficiency. It is recognized implicitly as such by most political and economic

---

[17] Analysis of how national income accounts are constructed reveals this point clearly. See Paul Samuelson, *Economics* (6th ed.; New York: McGraw-Hill Book Company, 1964), pp. 179–202, particularly pp. 197–199.

leaders in most countries, and the question of how to maintain and increase per capita GNP is a subject of constant debate in most societies.

It must be emphasized that intercountry GNP comparisons are extremely tenuous, given data collection and processing problems. Even the most advanced countries with elaborate statistical organizations are forced to make a series of estimates about some key data going into GNP. In some cases, particularly when comparing Marxist and capitalist countries, the techniques of counting GNP are different, and it is not even clear that the same things are being measured. For a country like India or Egypt, where peasants consume a great deal of what they produce, much output never enters the money sector of the economy and hence never gets counted accurately as a part of GNP.[18]

Further difficulties emerge when differences in culture and demand arise. The Egyptian middle class uses servants and pays them, whereas American families on similar income levels utilize the unpaid (and hence uncounted) work of housewives for similar services. Tenants' rent becomes a part of GNP, but owned houses are either not counted or made subject to estimates with large potential error. Much income is generated in urban economies in such sectors as local passenger transportation and sanitation services which are not needed in rural environments. Many difficulties of this sort tend to make measurements difficult and comparisons even more difficult.

**2. *Rate of Growth of Real per Capita GNP.*** Since no country feels it has enough of the world's wealth and income, virtually all countries are concerned not only with absolute levels of per capita GNP but also with the way in which it might be increased. In effect, this is a measure of the growing productivity (or efficiency) of the aggregate economy, since a rapid growth rate suggests that a country is getting more output with about the same inputs.[19]

This measure, along with the absolute level of per capita GNP, forms a good general measure of the efficiency with which an entire economy operates; however, the two do not indicate how well the economy might be doing if it really utilized all its resources efficiently, and further measures can be used to develop at least a partial evaluation of this factor.

Table 5–1 shows some available data for selected countries on GNP per capita and rates of growth in recent years. This sort of intercountry comparison must be used with extreme caution, because of the numerous statistical discrepancies and varying statistical methodologies used by various countries; but the data is presented to indicate that some comparative measures between countries are available. Also to be emphasized is that data of this

---

[18] *Ibid.,* pp. 528–535.

[19] Benjamin Higgins, *Economic Development* (New York: W. W. Norton & Company, Inc., 1959), pp. 3–24.

TABLE 5–1

Estimated GNP/Capita and Growth per Capita: Selected Countries

| | GNP per Capita, in U.S. Dollars | | |
|---|---|---|---|
| Country | GNP/Capita | | |
| | 1953 | 1958 | 1961 |
| U.S.A........ | $2083 | $2324 | $2572 |
| U.K......... | 814 | 1084 | 1244 |
| U.A.R....... | 95 | 116 | N.A. |
| India........ | 62 | 67 | 73 |
| Japan....... | 196 | 285 | 464 |

Source: United Nations, *Yearbook of National
Accounts*, 1962 (New York, 1963), pp. 315–317.

| Average Annual per Capita Rates of Growth in Real GNP, Percent | | | |
|---|---|---|---|
| Country | Period | Growth in Total GNP* | Per Capita GNP |
| U.S.A........ | 1952–60 | 2.6 | 0.9 |
| U.K......... | 1952–60 | 2.7 | 2.2 |
| U.S.S.R...... | 1952–60 | 9.9 | 8.0 |
| India........ | 1954–60 | 3.0 | 1.3 |
| Japan....... | 1952–60 | 9.5 | 8.4 |

* Before adjustment for population growth.
Source: United Nations, *op. cit.*, pp. 311–313.

sort tell only what is—they do not explain *why* it is. The basic purpose of obtaining such efficiency indications is to assist in obtaining the $E_T$ values for various countries, to be used as a cross check on the external constraint values.

**3. *Rate of Utilization of Inputs.*** Data may exist on the utilization of inputs of land, labor, and capital. If unemployment rates are quite high, this suggests that the economy might do better than it is in fact doing. A country with a 2 percent unemployment rate is probably coming closer to its full potential than one whose unemployment rate is 10 percent. Relevant here is not only the rate for persons formally unemployed but also that for persons suffering from disguised unemployment. It is often difficult to obtain completely valid data for such subtle types of unemployment, but typically some information is available. Also important here is the rate of utilization of plant and equipment. If a country has 20 percent of its capital stock unutilized, this is evidence that the country could be doing considerably better than it is.

Overutilization of labor and capital may be as inefficient as underutilization. Overemployment, leading to wage-price inflation; possibly increased turnover of employees; and the use of manpower which is unqualified may prove as inefficient as moderate levels of unemployment. Plants operated at 100 percent or more of capacity may be using very inefficient, old facilities.

Various bottleneck problems can also lead to substantial under- or overutilization of inputs. Social overhead capital facilities which are inadequate at critical points—such as in key transport terminals, power supplies at given industrial centers, or overloaded communications systems on important routes—can result in other types of capacity being underutilized. Firms may be willing to produce more goods, but they may find themselves unable to ship in raw materials or to ship out finished product. A firm may want to hire new workers, only to find that housing shortages prevent recruitment. Rarely is an economy so adept at long run planning that all necessary facilities expand at exactly the proper rates in all regions and cities; and the inevitable result of unequal expansion rates is underutilization of some inputs and overutilization of others.

The fabled American executive who works eighty hours per week is reflecting the inability of the society to produce enough of this highly skilled manpower; and even while the American economy suffers a 5 percent unemployment rate, many types of jobs go begging for lack of qualified applicants. Less than 1 percent of skilled professionals and technicians were

### TABLE 5–2

#### UNEMPLOYMENT DATA

| Country | Labor Unemployment Rate: Percent |
|---------|----------------------------------|
| U.S.A. | 5.6 (1962) |
| U.K. | 2.1 (1962) |
| U.A.R. | 3.2 (1961) |
| Japan | 0.9 (1962) |

Source: United Nations, *op. cit.*, pp. 60 61.

unemployed in 1964, while over 20 percent of unskilled teenage workers were without work.[20] This suggests that labor inputs are not being produced in the proper proportions. A familiar pattern in many countries is the surplus of university graduates, coupled with large surpluses of illiterate, unskilled peasants and extreme shortages of skilled craftsmen and technicians.[21]

Some data are ordinarily available on employment, although the usual statistical disclaimers must be made. Table 5–2 presents some data from selected countries.

Data on land utilization are impossible to obtain, although some subjective evidence exists. The United States, as a part of its agricultural policy, has kept millions of acres of potentially fertile land out of cultivation, while much land in countries like Egypt is not cultivated because of water shortages. A major difficulty here in evaluation is to decide what *out of use* means for land. Most of Egypt is desert; and land actually utilized for agri-

---

[20] American Bankers Association, *Proceedings of a Symposium on Unemployment* (New York, 1964), p. 15.

[21] Frederick Harbison and Charles A. Meyers, *Education, Manpower, and Economic Growth* (New York: McGraw-Hill Book Company, 1964), pp. 174–177.

culture, industry, trade, or homes is a very small percentage of total area. A more relevant measure here would be the percentage of potentially irrigated land not used. American land which might grow corn but which has been converted to forest wood-lots for long run use presents another kind of evaluation problem, as does idle urban land being held for future use. Conceptual and measurement problems make land utilization figures very dubious, even when they are available.[22]

Available data suggest that the United States tends to utilize its capital and labor less intensively than many other countries, implying that American efficiency is reduced by this measure. If the American economy could better utilize its existing plant, labor, and land, without major adverse effects such as price inflation, it could be much richer. Estimates indicate that 1964 U.S. GNP could have been as much as $40 billion per year higher than it was if utilization rates were higher.[23]

**4. *Usability of Outputs.*** This factor is in part the reciprocal of Point 3 above. If a country has manpower and plant unsuited for the production of needed and wanted goods and services yet insists on producing them, the result may be the piling up of inventories. In the case of services such as transportation passenger or ton miles, the unneeded production shows up as low load factors.

Capitalist countries are typically organized in a manner which tends to throw this burden into the unemployed resource position, since profit seeking firms usually do not pile up inventories if there are no current sales prospects. Instead, they stop production, which leads to unemployment as noted above. Only where government action either forces service industries to operate (as in transportation) or buys up surpluses (as in agriculture) do capitalist countries usually show any major unsold or unusable inventory accumulation.

Marxist countries typically push adjustments in the opposite direction. If errors in past planning have led to plants and manpower in sectors where the output is unneeded, the plants may produce anyhow. The result is less unemployment of factors but more unusable goods and services. Considerable inflexibility may occur here as well. The costs of unemployment may be high, but it does force both men and owners of land and capital to seek new needed outlets for their services.

**5. *Degree of Competition.*[24]** Among capitalist countries, the level of actual competition varies widely from industry to industry and from country to country. The notion here is that the more competitive firms are, the more likely it will be that they will be forced to become efficient.

---

[22] Some of the extremely complex problems in this area are analyzed by F. Stuart Chapin, Jr., *Urban Land Use Problems* (New York: Harper & Brothers, 1957), 397 pp.

[23] *Economic Report of the President,* 1964 (Washington: U.S. Government Printing Office, 1964), pp. 7, 38.

[24] This is considered the critical point in economic analysis. See Joe Bain, *Industrial Organization* (New York, John Wiley & Sons, Inc., 1959), particularly pp. 1–43.

Nothing can be as inefficient as protected monopoly, far removed from the rigors of the marketplace. The degree of competition is influenced by such factors as market size, legal arrangements regarding cartels, entry controls, price fixing agreements, and similar matters which determine in part how many competitors a firm may have and to what extent firms compete. It is also determined by tariff protection granted by governments, and by public utility controls in force. Competition should be measured in terms of the relevant market, which may be worldwide. Some smaller countries have single firm monopolies in given economic sectors which are kept very competitive by allowing the import of competing items.

A variation of the infant industry argument may make temporary monopoly a means of achieving rapid development from low levels.[25] Temporary protection of initially inefficient industries may allow them to get under way and follow a learning procedure which, it is hoped, will lead to efficiency in time. It does take considerable time to train both workers and managers, and protection from excess competition may make an industry initially feasible; but if after fifty years the same protection is applied, one can be reasonably sure that the protected firm or industry is complacent and inefficient.

Competition rarely exists in any Marxist state, since such behavior is regarded as antisocial. Capitalist states sanction several degrees of competitiveness. The United States has long tried to develop adequate antitrust laws to deal with monopoly problems;[26] but where pure monopoly clearly was desirable, as in electric power generation, this country has pressed for public utility commissions to control firms directly.[27]

It is also possible that excess competition will tend to be destructive. Firms may be subject to cutthroat price competition, attempted market penetration by discriminatory pricing below marginal cost, and similar destructive tactics. In such cases, competitive pressures could lead to less efficiency. Some evidence exists to suggest that such competitive warfare has taken place in the past.

A country as a whole may gain by becoming a monopolist in a product which is extensively exported. Here the entire country gains the monopoly income, at the expense of the rest of the world. The local monopoly may be inefficient; but it is able, in the short run at least, to overcome its inefficiencies through its monopoly pricing power. Such situations have probably existed in the past—with Chilean nitrates, Peruvian guano, and South

---

[25] This argument for protection goes back 200 years. See Charles P. Kindleberger, *International Economics* (3d ed.; Homewood, Ill.: Richard D. Irwin, Inc., 1963), pp. 221–223.

[26] See William Lee Baldwin, *Antitrust and the Changing Corporation* (Durham, N.C.: Duke University Press, 1961), 307 pp.

[27] This type of public utility control is a long and complex story in itself. See Stuart Daggett, *Principles of Inland Transportation* (4th ed.; New York: Harper & Brothers, 1955), pp. 569–763, for analysis and discussion of the problem in transportation.

African diamonds as historic examples—but high monopoly prices lead to searches for substitutes and the eventual breakdown of the monopoly. Measurements of potential country monopoly gains, because of the many possible alternatives involved, are very difficult to make.

6. *Planning Efficiency.* In Marxist countries, competition is not typically a major factor in the economy. Instead, firms follow plans developed at higher levels by the senior bureaucracy. This system requires an enormously increased amount of data and information, as compared to the simpler capitalist system.[28] Planning is quite complex, and difficulties increase as the number of productive enterprises and goods and services produced expand. As the economy develops, the problem of planning efficiently increases. Each output of the system is interrelated to some extent with every other output, and an efficient plan must take this into account. If one stated goal of the economy is to increase the production of clothing, plans must include expanded cotton production, which requires more steel, which requires more coal, and so on. Such interrelationships are often subtle and not foreseen.[29] The increase in coal demand may increase the incomes of miners and lead to increased demand for clothing by miners, which is above the initial plan as stated.

Marxist countries are perpetually trying to correct planning errors caused by this sort of interrelationship. The usual result of defective planning is to produce unwanted and unneeded items in some sectors, while creating shortages in others. While it is typically impossible to evaluate an entire plan for even a small Marxist country, such defects can be evaluated subjectively by considering carefully the comments, evaluations, and criticisms made in the country. Objective foreign evaluation by disinterested experts is also available at times.

**Uses of System Efficiency Measures.** The six measures of system efficiency discussed above can be used to evaluate the general level of efficiency ($E_T$) for any economy. Given the difficulties of measurement and analysis, it is unlikely that a precise efficiency number can be found; but usually any country can be placed in rank order of efficiency with other countries. Where differences are large, the measures of GNP per capita and GNP growth per capita over the past decade usually are enough to indicate relative positions. A comparison of France with Iraq would present this simpler kind of evaluation. Where countries are quite close in terms of these two measures, however, the other system efficiency indicators could be used. A comparison of West Germany with England would be an example of this sort of problem.

---

[28] B. Richman, *Soviet Management* (Englewood Cliffs, N.J.: Prentice-Hall, Inc., 1965), especially chapters 5, 6 and 12.

[29] This is the input-output analysis first explored by Leontieff. See W. W. Leontieff, *The Structure of the American Economy, 1919–39* (New York: Oxford University Press, 1951). See also C. E. Ferguson and J. M. Kreps, *Principles of Economics* (New York: Holt, Rinehart & Winston, Inc., 1962), pp. 157–170.

## THE CONCEPT OF FIRM EFFICIENCY

Most of the work on economic efficiency has been done by economists rather than business specialists.[30] It is necessary to explore the economic work in this area in order to achieve workable efficiency concepts. In analyzing the activities of firms, economists have been concerned with the way in which given firms will select inputs and choose products and services to produce in order to maximize their profits. The fact that one firm may be making more money than another implies that it is doing something better than the other, which suggests immediately some rank ordering of efficiency among firms.

The major reason for economic interest in efficiency comes from welfare economics, which deals with the question of whether or not the economic system yields results which are "desirable," given general economic goals.[31] The notion that one set of results may be considered more desirable than another suggests that some measure of efficiency is useful in evaluating economic systems. Since productive economies are made up of productive firms, it is also relevant to consider the efficiency of individual firms in the system.

The economist, however, seldom explores the internal operations of the firm.[32] Management activities are in a sealed box labeled "management," as shown in Figure 5-1. The usual assumption is that managers are capable and know their jobs. If it can be determined, given a set of inputs and desired outputs, what the best combination of these might be, then managers will perform in this manner. The intrafirm efficiency problems discussed below are usually not of interest to economists but rather fall in the province of business administration proper.

Any firm is a subsystem within the economic system, and subsystem optimization problems abound in this area. One firm can become extremely efficient if all other firms are forced to provide it with exactly the inputs it needs when it needs them; but the result here might be a loss of total system efficiency, as the other firms' efficiencies declined. Managers of any single firm tend to see their own problems as most important, and they press for measures which will enable them to ease their difficulties and become more efficient. The cost, in total system efficiency terms, can be high.

**Empirical Measures of Firm Efficiency.** Regardless of the economy's general level of efficiency, it is usually true that not all firms operate at the

---

[30] E. J. Misham, "A Survey of Welfare Economics," *Economic Journal*, LXX (June, 1960), 197–265. See also I. P. M. Little, *A Critique of Welfare Economics* (2nd ed.; Oxford: Oxford University Press, 1957).

[31] Due and Clower, *op. cit.*, pp. 510–512.

[32] The typical microeconomists' concern is with decision making in view of price variations for inputs or outputs. Problems of planning, organizing, controlling, and so on are rarely considered. See Joel Dean, *Managerial Economics* (New York: Prentice-Hall, Inc., 1951), for a classic treatment of business problems in the economic manner.

same level of efficiency. Some companies will be quite efficient; others will show moderate effectiveness; still others will literally be in the dark ages of operational efficiency. It is commonly noted that in a country such as England or the United States the better firms are two to ten times as efficient as the worst. Such a statement suggests that individual productive enterprise evaluation would also prove useful, both for internal and external comparison with other companies. Intersectoral comparisons also may prove useful, since total system efficiency may be adversely affected by a few inefficient sectors.

General measures of firm efficiency are discussed below. Like the measures of system efficiency, they all suffer from serious conceptual drawbacks; but at present these are the best measures available.

**1. *Profitability*.**    In capitalist countries, the most direct measure of firm efficiency is profitability. The rate of return on net worth can be compared to firms in this industry at home and abroad. This measure of profitability suffers from a series of defects, summarized below:

A) The firm may operate in an imperfect market characterized by overt or tacit collusion or by pure monopoly. In the absence of effective competition between firms, it is easy to rig market prices, and possibly input prices, so that the firm appears very profitable.[33]

B) Profitability in the short run may prove to be inadequate, as the company is in effect borrowing against the future. An oil company which shows very high returns for a few years but which is depleting its assets in the process has this type of problem. When the oil in the ground is gone, the company goes bankrupt. Some of the profits here should have been expended for developing and maintaining depleting assets. One way to avoid this type of problem is to consider profitability over time, rather than for only a few years. Averages over several decades would be more meaningful than short term results. Long run profitability also tacitly measures the ability of managers to replace themselves with new, equally competent men, which is one critical problem not always foreseen by presently profitable firms.

C) Potentially very profitable firms may be subject to government price controls (or restrictions on input prices) which prevent "normal" profitability. Thus, public utilities are often restricted to a "reasonable" rate of return by regulatory commissions.[34] Publicly owned companies frequently underprice their product to obtain only a nominal return.[35] In this case, the firm has other goals than profit maximization.

This problem is made more complex by the fact that regulatory commissions rarely have enough information to know whether or not a utility is being managed efficiently. Hence, two similarly placed electric

---

[33] See Due and Clower, *op. cit.*, pp. 242–254.

[34] Daggett, *op. cit.*, pp. 648–649 particularly.

[35] M. Einaudi, M. Bye, and E. Rossi, *Nationalization in France and Italy* (Ithaca, N.Y.: Cornell University Press, 1955), pp. 122–134.

power companies may both be earning a statutory 6 percent on net worth. Without controls, the maximum rate of return might be 50 percent, but firm A, operating inefficiently, would earn only 8 percent, even without controls. Firm B, better managed, could easily earn the 50 percent. Since the control is typically asymmetrical, applying only to profit restrictions, both firms earn their 6 percent, and both appear equally efficient superficially.[36] Public utility commissions do try to eliminate the obviously inefficient expenditures of poorly managed firms, but few regulators have enough knowledge to eliminate all inefficiencies. The administrative efficiency of the regulatory body is also obviously relevant here, and variations in such efficiency tend to be extreme.[37]

D) Accounting conventions vary strikingly within and between countries. One result is that profitability can be varied widely by using the "proper" accounting techniques. One major external pressure here is tax law. In countries such as the United States, where firms pay up to 50 percent of their net profits in income taxes, there is pressure for firms to reduce stated profitability by expanding noncash expenses (mainly depreciation) to increase net cash flow. Success in doing this depends in part on the efficiency of tax lawyers and accountants, as well as on the law as written and interpreted.[38] In a country where taxes are levied in a different manner, the pressure may be to make profits as high as possible by reducing noncash expenses to the minimum. Thus, if textile firm A in the United States shows a rate of return of 5 percent, while textile firm B in another country shows a rate of return of 20 percent, evaluation of the accounting techniques used must be made before any efficiency conclusions can be drawn.[39]

E) Some firms may be subsidized by governments, mainly to achieve noneconomic goals. It is common to find subsidies paid to airlines and ocean shipping companies.[40] Indirect subsidies of all sorts also may make profits a poor measure of performance. In the United States, such indirect subsidies range from municipal construction of plants for free use of firms, to various types of entry control applied against competitors, to special tax advantages. The rate of return of a subsidized American international ocean shipping firm may be high, but this return is not comparable to that

---

[36] Roger C. Crampton, "The Effectiveness of Economic Regulation: A Legal View," *American Economic Review*, Vol. LIV (May, 1964), No. 3, pp. 182–191.

[37] Wilson, *op. cit.*, pp. 160–171. See also Marver H. Bernstein, *Regulating Business by Independent Commission* (Princeton, N.J.: Princeton University Press, 1955).

[38] William L. Raby, *The Income Tax and Business Decisions* (Englewood Cliffs, N.J.: Prentice-Hall, Inc., 1964), 438 pp.

[39] See T. A. Wise, "The Auditors Have Arrived," *Fortune*, Vol. XLII (November and December, 1960), No. 5, p. 151 and No. 6, p. 144, for a discussion of the types of accounting issues which directly affect corporate profits.

[40] Carl E. McDowell and Helen M. Gibbs, *Ocean Transportation* (New York: McGraw-Hill Book Company, 1954), pp. 247–273. See also Stephen Wheatcraft, *The Economics of European Air Transport* (Cambridge, Mass.: Harvard University Press, 1956), pp. 203–230.

achieved by a steel company. A motor trucking firm may make high profits, but these may result from the inability of competitors to gain entry to compete on lucrative routes. Or an oil company may have a high rate of return because of special tax advantages on depletion. Such special privileges mean that profitability as a relative measure must be analyzed with care.

*F*) Variations in risk and uncertainty may cause profits to vary sharply between firms in different industries. A baker of bread, where demand is quite stable and risks low, would tend to have a lower rate of return than a maker of fashion clothing, where demand is volatile and risk is very high. Where risk is high, some firms may earn nothing, while others consistently earn high returns. A measure of profitability over long periods of time may indicate which firms are best able to handle uncertainty problems; but a high rate of return in a few consecutive years may indicate only that the management was lucky, not that it was competent.

**2. *Exports.*** A manufacturing firm may be a monopoly at home, because of the size of its domestic market; however, one measure of its relative efficiency internationally is how well it competes in export markets. If the firm is able to sell effectively in competition with other international firms, in third country markets, or even in the competitors' home markets, this implies relative efficiency. Its selling prices and/or product quality are such as to make its products salable overseas.

This measure, like others to be noted below, is interrelated with profitability. It is possible to export at a loss, or at no profit, merely to gain revenues to satisfy government requirements. Governments often subsidize, directly or indirectly, such export sales. Clearly, some evaluation must be made of this export process. A reverse evaluation can be made if the firm requires heavy government protection for imports in competition with the home product. If the domestic price for a radio of a given quality is $50.00, when they can be obtained in other countries for $8.00, this suggests that the local manufacturer is not a particularly efficient producer, regardless of his level of profitability.

Also important here, particularly in developed countries, is the tendency for countries to export and import the same commodity. This follows from the general complexity of industrial goods. Steel is found in a variety of sizes, shapes, and grades; and it is common to find a West European country exporting some types of steel and importing others. In such cases consideration of net imports or exports may prove useful. A second reason for dual trade, particularly in larger countries, is that it is cheaper to obtain supplies from nearby regions of a foreign country than from more distant or inaccessible areas of the same country. In countries such as Pakistan, it is often easier to trade with foreigners than to trade within a country divided into two distant parts.

When this dual export-import situation is common, careful study of individual cases is necessary. Is the country importing because it may be economical to buy less-used grades of steel from foreigners, or are imports a reflection of local firms' inefficiencies? Style problems in such goods as automobiles are important. The United States imports Volkswagens, while Germans import Dodges. Here the question of relative efficiency hardly arises, since the two kinds of vehicles are so dissimilar. Textile imports, particularly of style goods, may show similar cross trading. This type of problem also illustrates the dangers of drawing hasty efficiency conclusions from single pieces of evidence which might be available.

3. *Usable Output per Man.* If output can be valued in dollars, such evaluation suggests efficient utilization of employees. In making inter-country comparisons of the same industry, real output measures, such as tons of steel per employee, can also be useful. One major difficulty here is in international comparisons where wage-capital costs are substantially different. A firm in a country where capital is worth 10 percent and wages are a dollar a day would not utilize labor (if the firm were rationally managed) in the same way as a firm in a country where wages are $25.00 a day and capital costs 6 percent.[41] Corrections for such discrepancies can be made, however, since wages and capital costs are generally known. If usable output per man per year was $3,000 for firm A and $40,000 for firm B, yet capital-labor price ratios were such as to suggest that firm A should have at least an output of $6,000 per man, there is some evidence to indicate inefficiency.

4. *Plant Utilization Rates.* A firm which operates at an average capacity utilization rate of 30 percent, when its industry operates at 80 percent, is probably less efficient. The implication here is that the managers made bad decisions in investment, and that these resulted in excess capacity. Some excess capacity may be desirable in order to handle unexpected demand fluctuations, but most managers prefer to operate at least at 90 percent of capacity.

Definitional problems here are particularly severe, since the word *capacity* is subject to many interpretations. It may be for a twenty-four hour per day, seven day per week production schedule, or for an eight hour per day, five day per week basis. Obsolete equipment not yet scrapped may be ignored or included in the calculations. As with many other firm measures of efficiency, such evaluations must be used with care.

Firms may also operate for years without expanding capacity where needed; and a company which operates at 100 percent of capacity for years, with large backlogs of orders, is not particularly efficient. In this case, profits are probably being foregone by failure to expand. The profitability of the company may be excellent, but it could be still better.

5. *Prices Relative to Foreign Firms.* Some types of goods and services are rarely exported. Local transportation services and electric power used are examples. It is possible to obtain unit prices of such items and compare them regionally or internationally to determine if prices are un-

---

[41] See Joe Bain, *Pricing, Distribution and Employment* (New York: Henry Holt & Company, 1948), pp. 269–310, for the economic theory here. See also Samuelson, *op. cit.,* pp. 528–535.

usually high or low. Variations may reflect differing efficiencies of the firms involved. Care must be exercised here, since various economic and technical constraints may yield substantially different costs between firms. An electric power company producing its electricity in an area characterized by dense population, a good supply of high grade coal, and a good transportation system may look good when compared to a relatively efficient firm operating without these advantages; however, some evaluation is possible, particularly in cases where large deviations occur.

6. *Long Run Innovation Effectiveness.*    The problem of short run as compared to long run efficiency is also relevant here. Short term or immediate enterprise activities and decisions should not be detrimental or lead to adverse consequences in the more distant future, but rather they should lead to improvements in enterprise results and serve more effectively the future needs of society. The basic problem is how much in the way of output, sales, profits, productivity, and so on should be foregone at present in order to obtain even more in the future by undertaking innovations of both the product and process types today.

For capitalist firms, the long run profitability measure discussed earlier provides one evaluation of this factor, particularly when the necessary adjustments to profitability have been made. Measurement of the rates of change of exports, usable output per man, plant utilization rate, and relative prices would also evaluate this factor.

If data were available, it would be possible to determine firm efficiency levels in at least a rough way. What would be measured here would be the $E_f$'s of Chapter 4, just as relevant measures of system efficiency discussed above would be measures of $E_T$. Knowing approximately what these efficiency levels were would serve as a good cross check on the basic hypothesis in Chapter 4. The methodology of the remaining part of this book is to evaluate the environmental constraints and their impact on managerial effectiveness, either directly or through the critical elements of the managerial process. If the constraints indicate that managerial effectiveness is low, this implies that the $E_f$'s and $E_T$ should also be low. The empirical measures of efficiency noted here could serve to verify the basic hypothesis.

A major problem here is that of aggregation. It is possible to compare per capita gross national products of various countries, although it may not be very clear what the comparisons mean. It would prove more difficult, because of data problems, to analyze a steel company and compare it, as noted above, to other firms. At this level of aggregation some data usually exist, and such factors as average output per man hour possibly could be obtained; however, this type of comparison might not prove very useful, in view of the tremendous variety and diversity of both steel production techniques and products. Average productivity figures may conceal the fact that in tinplate production the firm is quite efficient, while in steel rails it is hopelessly inefficient. If various categories of important products are averaged in this case, the final efficiency figure may not indicate much.

To obtain meaningful efficiency data, it may prove necessary to dis-aggregate problems down to the single firm or even plant level within the firm. Production efficiency can conceptually be regarded as an average; but the various problems of production are worked out, and efficiencies changed, at the plant floor level for each product in the firm's product mix. Market channel design may again be some composite average in computing distribution costs, but specific channels must be designed for each product. At this level, firm efficiency is directly affected. Working with aggregate data in such cases may lead to various sorts of subsystem optimizations, since studies reveal relatively little about the detailed practices taking place within firms.

## THE CONCEPT OF INTRAFIRM EFFICIENCY

The complexities of even moderately sized industrial firms lead to difficulties of analysis for students of business. Granted that a firm should be efficient, what should happen within the firm to achieve this result? For a company with several plants, hundreds or even thousands of employees, geographically scattered personnel, and many middle managers concerned with small parts of the total firm operation, the answer is not immediately obvious.

The problem is complicated by the interrelationship of the various segments of the firm. Production efficiency depends in part on how well finance and marketing officials do their jobs, and vice versa. Each critical element in Table 4–1 can be evaluated independently in terms of how efficiently it is performed in a given firm. Since firms are run by many people with different interests and aptitudes for different jobs, the usual result is that some of the critical elements of the management process are accomplished much more efficiently than others. Some firms are known for their financial acumen, others for their production prowess; while still others are noted for marketing brilliance. These intrafirm efficiencies, often achieved at the expense of other firm functions, reflect the views of senior managers as to what is important, as well as what the society appears to see as important. The usual result is some form of subsystem optimization.

The usual overemphasis historically has been on production, although overemphasis of every enterprise function has occurred on occasion; but production has long been regarded as the most difficult part of a firm's activities, particularly since 1800, when modern methods of mechanized production came into active and steadily growing use. Even today, many Marxist states and underdeveloped countries tend to regard production of goods as critical, while other enterprise functions are considered relatively unimportant.[42] The usual result is that production gets overemphasized within the firm at the cost of less efficiency in the overall operations of the

---

[42] A. A. Sherlime, "Marketing in the Industrialization of Underdeveloped Countries," *Journal of Marketing*, Vol. XXIX (January, 1956), No. 1, pp. 28–32.

company. Only in very advanced and developed countries do other enterprise functions tend to get steadily overrated by firm managements.

### Intrafirm Efficiency Measures

The general goal of divisions or departments within the firm is assumed to be the efficient achievement of goals with a minimum of unsought consequences. If the general goal of the company is to become efficient, then the firm divisions will be most efficient when they help achieve this firm goal. The unsought consequences often are the subsystem optimizations which would have the effect of making the department more efficient at the cost of a decline in total firm efficiency.

The basic problem here is to measure $e_n$, or efficiency of the critical elements of the management process, discussed in Chapter 4. Figure 5–2 indicates some suggestive microefficiency indicators which might be used for this purpose. Note that some of them are similar to the aggregate firm indicators. Thus, labor productivity can be utilized for the entire firm, as noted above, or it can be used for any part of the firm, such as the production department. One measure of $e$ in this department might be the productivity of men working here, excluding other divisions. Similarly, the sales division might be interested in some productivity figures for salesmen, accounting in such figures for clerks and accountants, and so on.

With the exception of Item 12 in Figure 5–2, each indicator would represent average short run performance for a limited period of time. Either physical or monetary units of measure could be used for each indicator; however, in all cases the physical units used would have to be at least roughly comparable when divisions of firms, total firms, or industries are being compared. When monetary values are used they must be converted to standard units of money to permit meaningful comparisons.

The items in Figure 5–2 are intended to be suggestive of the kinds of intrafirm efficiency measures which can be used to evaluate internal efficiency. Such measures could be used within one firm, or between various kinds of firms, in the same manner as the interfirm comparisons discussed above. The usual warnings about statistical inconsistencies apply here, since many of the accounting and measurement conventions of firms in different environments are quite different.

The way in which the measures in Figure 5–2 can be used is as follows: Consider a need to evaluate the relative $e$'s of two comparable firms in different countries in the area of production $(B_7)$. Here a measure of the $e_7$'s could be the output of the department per man per hour, which would be Measure 1 in Figure 5–2. Firm A might have an output of 400 units per man hour, while firm B might have an output of 600 units per man hour. This measure (400 units compared to 600) is of course not $e$ itself but an indication of what $e$ might be, since $e$ theoretically represents some measure from zero to one.

The immediate implication is that $e_7$ of firm B is better than $e_7$ of firm A. Note that this merely measures relative efficiencies in one depart-

FIGURE 5–2

SAMPLE MEASURES OF INTRAFIRM EFFICIENCY

| *B Elements Evaluated* | *Measure* |
|---|---|
| 1. $B_4, B_6, B_7, B_8, B_9$ | $\dfrac{Q}{P}$, where $P$ = relevant personnel; $Q$ = some output measure |
| 2. $B_1, B_2, B_6$ | $\dfrac{Q_s}{Q_t}$, where $Q_s$ = output sold; $Q_p$ = total production |
| 3. $B_1, B_2, B_6, B_7, B_9, B_{10}$ | $\dfrac{\Delta Q_s}{\Delta I}$, where $\Delta Q_s$ = change in sales; $I$ = incremental increase in investment |
| 4. $B_1, B_2, B_3, B_6$ | $\dfrac{TC}{QT}$, where $TC$ = total production costs; $QT$ = total output |
| 5. $B_1, B_2, B_6$ | $\dfrac{S}{QT}$, where $S$ = total spoilage |
| 6. $B_1, B_2, B_3, B_6, B_9$ | $\dfrac{TDC}{Q_s}$, where $TDC$ = total distribution costs |
| 7. $B_1, B_2, B_7, B_9$ | $\dfrac{Q_s}{K}$, where $Q_s$ = total output sold; $K$ = total fixed capital |
| 8. $B_3, B_4, B_5, B_{10}$ | $\dfrac{NQ}{NT}$, where $NQ$ = number of personnel leaving; $NT$ = total personnel |
| 9. $B_1, B_2, B_6, B_7, B_{10}$ | $\dfrac{KW}{KF}$, where $KW$ = working capital; $KF$ = fixed capital |
| 10. $B_1, B_2, B_6, B_7, B_9$ | $\dfrac{KW}{QT}$ |
| 11. $B_1, B_2, B_6, B_7, B_9$ | $\dfrac{KW}{Q_s}$ |

12. Rate of change of above measures over time

ment of the firms. It is entirely possible that the reason for the discrepancy is that some marketing activity in firm A causes it to have lower production efficiency. It is also possible that planning, staffing, research and development, or finance inefficiency might be indicated by a low $e$ in production. The measure used here in effect measures the combined $e$'s of these critical elements. A perpetual difficulty of working with any $e$ measure is that all of the possible internal interrelationships between critical elements of the management process must be constantly evaluated.

While it may be difficult initially to determine which critical element has the worst $e$ value, analysis, either qualitative or quantitative, can be used to evaluate the efficiency of the critical elements. Thus, a finance expert can evaluate the problem noted above to determine if financial factors do directly influence this low productivity. His evidence may be qualitative; but if he is an expert, he will be able to disassociate the $e_9$'s from the $e_7$'s. The difficulty is that no $e$ stands alone—all are interrelated to some extent. Any measure of an $e$, as presented in Figure 5–2, will necessarily measure several $e$'s in at least two critical element categories. Further analysis by experts in the various areas of critical firm elements is required to break out more accurately (even if more qualitatively) the precise $e$ being measured.

The $e$ values determined in this relative way would be used to verify the predictions indicated by the relevant external constraints. Thus, if a low educational constraint in higher education indicated that planning methodology ($B_{1.6}$) would be poor, it would be expected that $e_{1.6}$ would be low as well. Note that there is no direct quantitative measure of $e_{1.6}$ available, although several measures of intrafirm efficiency noted in Figure 5–2 (Items 2, 4, 5, and 6) would measure this in part. It would probably require still more detailed analysis and study, including qualitative judgment, to determine even in a general way what this particular $e$ would be.

It would be possible to extend Figure 5–2 by including various other measures utilized in conventional business analysis. Thus, there are available many kinds of financial ratios used in financial analysis which serve as evaluations of efficiency in the financial, planning, and control elements.[43] Similar measures exist for other parts of the firm.[44]

Data of the sort needed for computation of the ratios in Figure 5–2 normally are available only within the firm itself. Only a few large corporations make public enough information to allow even partial completion of the lists. Precise evaluations of intrafirm efficiency would require access to firm records, although in a few advanced countries enough data are available from government sources on an aggregate basis to allow for some calculations of a few $e$'s.

## CONCLUSION

This chapter began with the problem of determining system, firm, and intrafirm efficiency definitions, with the idea of both defining and measur-

---

[43] J. Fred Weston, *Managerial Finance* (New York: Holt, Rinehart & Winston, Inc., 1962), pp. 53–96.

[44] Many of them are not so precise, however. See J. B. Kernan and J. U. McNeal, "The Closest Thing to Measuring Advertising Effectiveness," *Business Horizons*, Vol VII, (winter, 1964), No. 4, pp. 73–80, for a marketing example.

ing efficiency independently of the implied results obtained from considering the external environmental constraints. Thus we have three efficiencies—$E_T$, $E_f$, and $e_n$—to determine independently.

Unfortunately, there is no easy way to obtain these efficiencies, nor can they even be defined very precisely when inputs and outputs consist of variegated items and when goals of countries differ. Hence, this chapter discussed at length the kinds of problems faced in determining what economic efficiency might be in given situations. No simple answers were derived, and the question of what efficiency actually is in any given situation must remain in part a subjective evaluation rather than a precise figure.

A skilled investigator, however, can evaluate efficiency levels for a country, a firm, or an intrafirm situation, utilizing the various analyses and data noted here and in Chapter 4. The evaluation can more easily be done as a rank order problem than as a precise quantitative evaluation. One can study two countries and, by applying the macroefficiency criteria noted, reach tentative conclusions about which country is more efficient; or he can observe two textile firms in different countries and evaluate their relative efficiencies. Such evaluations will often be more suggestive than precise, but some meaningful evaluation can be made. If the various efficiencies can be determined, the next step is to evaluate countries and firms by use of the external environmental constraints and predict what sort of efficiencies could be expected with given constraints. The efficiency values found serve as a cross check of the theory pertaining to the environmental constraints.

Measuring efficiency is not the same as explaining it. The purpose of the theory is to explain and predict what sorts of inefficiency may be found and how they might be corrected. If these efficiency cross checks verify predicted levels of efficiency, it is suggestive evidence that the theory is serving to focus on the kinds of problems which must be solved if the society, and its industrial firms, are to become more efficient. Hence, we now turn to the chapters covering the external environmental constraints and their impact on country, firm, and intrafirm efficiency.

# Chapter 6

# Environmental Constraints:

# Education

## INTRODUCTION

The quality, efficiency, and structure of any industrial enterprise depend largely on the types and overall quality of the persons in the organization. Hence, the nature and quality of the educational process within a country is a critical factor in determining the level of managerial effectiveness and the nature of managerial activity. One intuitively expects that a firm able to recruit high school and college graduates in the United States will be quite a different type of organization than one which must depend largely on illiterate or barely literate human resources. Our problem in this chapter is to explore the manner in which the education of the manpower and management in an industrial enterprise affects the internal operations of the enterprise.

Education is not monolithic. To say that a man graduated from college does not make him a perfect substitute for a second man who also completed a higher education. Educators spend a great deal of time evaluating the quality of school systems and educational practices on all levels of education, and it is clear that Harvard is not to be equaled with Mississippi State, nor is a high school in Boston quite the same thing as a secondary school in Bangkok. The fact that a person has completed a given number of school years may indicate a great deal, or very little; and not to be overlooked are the possibilities of self-education of determined individuals. There is a danger here that one becomes bemused with data showing massive aggregates of school attendance statistics, while forgetting the qualitative implications of education. Business management cannot afford to make this mistake, since to assume uniformity in education can be disastrous for productivity.

It is true that any kind of education imparts some knowledge, and knowledge is a key determinant of managerial performance and productive efficiency; but it is the *type* and *depth* of knowledge that is crucial in this connection. Knowledge about music, Latin, or even literature is not very important in running an industrial enterprise; while knowledge about economics, human behavior, mathematics, engineering, the techniques and functions of management, and machine operations is of utmost importance. The types of education and knowledge possessed by those persons employed in various nonindustrial organizations—for example governmental economic, legal and regulatory agencies, banking institutions—which have a significant influence on the activities of industrial enterprises are also important to industrial management.

The problems of both qualitative and quantitative effects in education also are compounded by the nature of written information contained in the language in which the person is literate. If a man is well educated in Tagalog, but his basic needed information is only available in French, Russian, and English, he is probably less able to perform efficiently than a more fortunate person educated in one of the more usable languages. The information of relevance to industry tends to be written largely in European languages, which imposes a handicap to those unable to read or write these tongues. In any case, however, it is clear that education does have a great impact on the individuals working in industry.

The overall educational system in any country affects virtually every spect of managerial and industrial life. In particular, it has a great bearing on the entire staffing function, the size of industrial enterprises and their overall organization structures, degrees of centralization or decentralization, degrees of specialization, types of processes, techniques and technology used, costs of production, and the overall productivity of firms and their managements.

It is possible for a country to import foreign manpower to staff its enterprises, and/or to send promising students abroad for study; but there are limits to how far a given country will go in this direction; in the final analysis, the local educational system tends to play the paramount role in determining the types and quality of human resources available for industry.

There is substantial evidence that there are large discrepancies in the number, types, and quality of personnel employed in similar types of industrial enterprises, producing a given level of output, in developed as compared to less developed countries. These discrepancies appear evident not only among unskilled workers but through the entire vertical skill and occupational structures.[1] Such discrepancies are due primarily to differences in the overall educational systems found in different countries. In those countries where educational and training systems are not properly geared to the needs of modern industry, the number of personnel required to produce a given level of output, even with the same technology, tends to be

---

[1] Many data of this type can be found in United Nations, Economic and Social Council, *Training of National Technical Personnel for Accelerated Industrialization of Developing Countries* (E/3901 [New York, June 3, 1964]), Part III, Add. 2.

substantially greater than in a more advanced economy which has a high quality, diversified system. Often three, four, and in some cases more than ten times as many personnel are required in a less developed as compared to a developed country. In numerous cases more productive technology cannot even be employed because of the lack of suitable skilled manpower. Even among the more developed countries there are often significant differences in the organization structures of similar types of firms, which are due in large part to differences in their educational systems.

Differences of the types noted above obviously have a significant impact on managerial performance and productive efficiency.

## LITERACY LEVEL

The term *literacy* implies the ability to read and write with reasonable accuracy. Again the qualitative evaluation becomes important, since pedagogs have pointed out that some high school graduates in the United States are functionally illiterate—while a few two year olds have taught themselves to read; however, for working purposes, the completion of about six years of formal schooling can be taken to indicate that a person should be able to read simple instructions and books and to write enough to convey information.

The literacy level of most countries is available statistically, although the statistics themselves are often suspected. Ranges of literacy in the sense defined above run from over 99 percent in places like Japan and Scandinavia to about 10 percent in some underdeveloped African and Asian nations. No modern, developed industrial state has a literacy level lower than 90 percent, while most fall in the 95–99 percent range. High illiteracy levels virtually define underdeveloped countries, and the correlation between literacy and per capita income levels is striking in nearly all cases. It appears to be impossible to develop a modern economy without educating most of the population at the same time.

It is true that in countries which have a high rate of illiteracy the proportion of literate persons employed in industry tends to be well above the national average; however, most industrial firms in such a country find that they must employ a substantial number of illiterate or barely literate personnel. Moreover, management must deal with many barely literate or illiterate people outside of the firm. This tends to have a significant impact on managerial effectiveness and behavior, as has been experienced firsthand by one of the authors who was general manager of a locally owned motor trucking firm in Saudi Arabia for two years.

Even in a more developed country such as Brazil, illiteracy poses a significant problem for industrial enterprises. The state of Rio Grande do Sul boasts the highest literacy rate in Brazil; yet one-third of its adult citizens cannot read or write, and there is a great lack of good, compulsory primary education. Only 18 percent of the inhabitants of this state have finished four grades of primary school. (The figures for high school and university education are 2.5 percent and 0.5 percent respectively.)

Some of the implications of this situation in Brazil for industrial enterprises are expressed in the statements of a number of Brazilian managers:

> The basic problem in Brazil is the weakness of primary education. It is difficult to get good help. Workers are willing and intelligent, but they have had only four years of schooling and they can't do simple arithmetic problems.

> One big problem is the low quality of primary schools in Brazil. Workers can't understand technical orders.

> The level of people is very low. They lack ability to understand mathematics, designs, or drawings.[2]

In considering the impact of the educational constraints on industrial management, it is useful to consider the extremes of the literacy spectrum—on the one hand a firm operating in a modern, fully literate industrial state, and on the other a firm operating in a country where perhaps 10 percent to 20 percent of the population is literate.[3] In examining the issue in this way, it is possible to see most clearly the differences in the manner in which such firms would perform and operate.

The organization of a literate firm would tend to be very different from one using a large proportion of illiterates, mainly because the possibilities open to an enterprise with literate personnel are so much greater than one operating with illiterates. It is common for management theorists to advocate that in devising an organization structure, one should begin with the ideal structure, then try to get the men with the necessary qualifications to fill this structure. In fitting the man to the job it is realized that at times modifications must be made in the structure because of the unavailability of suitable personnel.

In countries having a severe shortage of high talent manpower and many barely literate persons, it is frequently necessary to build the entire organization structure around relatively few competent, literate personnel. That is, the qualifications of personnel take precedence in organizing activities, and the number of alternatives possible in devising the organization structure are severely limited. So is the amount of specialization that is possible.

The possibilities of a high degree of decentralization in the enterprise organization are virtually impossible for the illiterate-staffed firm. Because

---

[2] W. Oberg, "Cross Cultural Perspectives on Management Principles," *Journal of the Academy of Management*, Vol. VI, No. 2, June, 1963, pp. 135–136.

[3] Many of the following examples are based on the firsthand experiences of one of the authors, who managed a Saudi firm. See also the discussions in: United Nations, *Management of Industrial Enterprises in Underdeveloped Countries* (New York, 1958); U.N. *Public Industrial Management in Asia and the Far East* (New York, 1960); "Some Problems of Industrial Management Reported by Technical Assistance Experts," *Industrialization and Productivity*, No. 2, 1959, pp. 53–57.

there are few literate persons available, the idea of breaking down a large firm into smaller, semiautonomous units is usually impossible. The precious few educated managers and technicians available must be carefully husbanded in the organization. One immediate effect here is on spans of control. The most common organization in an illiterate environment would be a quite horizontal firm, with few layers of management and large, frequently overburdened spans of control. Even here the chain of command is often circumvented because top management finds it necessary to delve into the detailed affairs of the lowest levels because of incompetent lower level supervisors.

Another point is that it is difficult to organize large enterprises at all in an illiterate society. The cement which holds a big organization together is usually the tremendous mass of horizontal, upward, and downward communication in the organization. Much of this communication must necessarily be written, particularly if the firm is scattered geographically; but who performs this communication function if few can read or write? The familiar, depressing examples of incompetence and inefficiency in large government enterprises and departments of underdeveloped nations stems in part from this problem. If the workers, foremen, and supervisors are illiterate, they must be instructed orally—which is an extremely difficult and time consuming job for senior men. While illiterates may have more keenly developed memories than literates, no instructions, particularly complex ones, can be remembered completely, which means that errors and inefficiencies crop up all over the enterprise.

The usual consequence is that firms tend to be quite small, and frequently family operated, in the more illiterate societies, often restricting themselves to sizes which can be managed by one or two people. (Private firms with over 100 employees are strikingly rare all over the underdeveloped world—unless they are managed by foreigners.) With small firms, many of the potential advantages derived from economies of scale are not obtained. This tendency to small size also influences the type of governmental organization which has to deal with the firms. Instead of a few large firms to police, authorities have many small, secretive operations to watch. Since the authorities also have serious organizational problems caused by illiteracy and incompetence in their staffs, they typically do not bother to perform their job—which creates another familiar pattern of tax evasion, lack of business law enforcement, and similar problems in many countries.

Illiteracy also creates striking planning and control problems for industrial enterprises. Planning tends to be conducted on a very short term—often day to day—fire fighting basis. It is extremely difficult to make use of written policies, procedures, or methods. Management tends to be so absorbed in staffing, direction, and control problems that there is little time left for even simple planning, and even less time for creative planning, market forecasting, and demand analysis, or innovation activities. The idea of having comprehensive plans, well integrated horizontally and vertically throughout the organization structure, is extremely difficult to apply in an illiterate environment.

The typical modern business control system has at its heart a series of interrelated reporting documents—but who fills out the documents when few can write? A firm may have a warehouse full of inventory, and no one can go through the warehouse and even count the materials and write down a list of items in long or short supply; or a firm may have a job order report form which is not made out because the foreman cannot write. Such examples could be multiplied endlessly, but the result is usually the same—the large firm trying to operate in such an environment runs out of control most of the time. In countries where large firms are government owned, the deficits may be covered, but the inefficiency of operations are striking. Where control is a well studied and thoroughly explored problem, such simple activities as filling out forms are taken for granted—but where much of the work force is illiterate, this cannot be considered a simple problem.

The control problem is compounded by the fact that illiterate societies, without exception, are poor societies, and typically more controls are needed in them than in societies where workers are less in need. Problems of petty thievery can become overwhelming in such a situation, but short of educating the work force there is little which management can do about it. Even when the work force is diligent and cooperative, the inability to handle even simple control devices, such as oil pressure gauges, air pressure readings, and rulers, leads to serious control problems. Again the pressure is to make the firm small and easily controlled. If the owner cannot obtain staff to help him with his managerial problems, the enterprise will not grow beyond the point where he alone (or perhaps he and a few close relatives) can handle the control problems of the firm.

The staffing problem is virtually overwhelming in a highly illiterate society. Even where there are a few educated persons, the difficulty of filling routine positions, to say nothing of key management jobs, is extremely difficult. A literate clerk becomes valuable; and if he can type and do routine filing, he becomes extremely valuable. Even the problem of informing the potential workers about jobs open is difficult in such a society, since want ads are quite out of the question. One must orally inform people of what opportunities exist.

In such a society much time is spent in training. Such training often has to start from the very beginning, since the typical worker will have had no experience to speak of in modern industry. Even where the management is extremely well educated and competent, this training problem is complex. American and European oil companies in the Mid-East operating with senior staffs composed largely of skilled men have discovered that such training programs absorb tremendous amounts of expensive manpower. One cannot simply pass on an instruction book to a worker or give him a set of rules to follow—he must be taught orally and visually every possible step of his job, including all necessary exception routines. Driving a truck or operating a lathe seems simple enough—until one tries to train illiterates to do the jobs. It is incredible how many supposedly simple, relatively unskilled industrial jobs require large amounts of reading, calculating, rechecking, and evaluating before they are done properly. Training in many such cases starts with a basic literacy program, since this skill is so essential to rapid progress later on. Management staffing is even more complex. The inability to read his own or other languages cuts off the manager from much of the information available to him, and he must learn by observation and example alone; companies with such management tend to be highly static —and inefficient.

The more illiterate the work force, the more time managers must spend on directing and supervising personnel. As was pointed out above, when workers are illiterate, management must give oral instructions exclusively. Written rules are useless. The result is that managers must spend far more time than they would in literate companies instructing workers on how to do their jobs. If the job does have written rules or instructions (such as how to rebuild a motor), the literate supervisor must read the material to the workman as he proceeds. Where measurements or arithmetic calculation are important (as in operating a screw cutting lathe), the supervisor must make the necessary calculations and measurements.

In effect, the presence of mass illiteracy suggests that the firm has to run without paper. While firms buried in red tape may at times wish that they could move to such a state of affairs, the facts are that the operation of such a company on a large scale is virtually impossible. The company runs out of control, and its harassed managers are unable to plan and direct company affairs properly. If the firm is subject to competitive discipline (for example, from foreign companies), in the sense that losses will lead to bankruptcy and discontinuance of operations, the firm may well die. If it is supported from tax revenues as a public concern, costs will be unrelated to output, and the drain on the public purse will tend to become strikingly large.

Marketing in an illiterate culture is organized in a completely different manner from that in a literate society. Written ads are useless; the firm must make oral or pictorial contact with its clients. Westerners have almost forgotten that not too long ago shops had to have signs bearing symbols rather than words (what remains is the pawnshop emblem of three balls); in illiterate cultures the older pattern still prevails. Salesmen must have a much more intimate contact with customers than would be necessary in a literate society.

Production problems tend to become severe when workers cannot read.

The usual patterns of quality control are based on relevant feedback and adjustment of discrepancies in the production process; but when your drivers cannot read their instruction manuals and are unable to tell when a vehicle needs to be greased, when a filter is to be changed, or what to do when the ammeter reads −30, you are in trouble quickly. It is common in such situations that machinery is ruined before it ever goes to work because no one can follow the often complicated instructions regarding breaking-in and initial preparation.

It is common also to find in such situations that production costs are extremely high, even though labor costs are quite low. The workers may be paid a dollar a day or less, but their gross output per man is so low that a $25.00 a day American or European actually is more valuable. This type of problem is closely connected to the type of equipment a man can use. The trained, literate employee is able to handle efficiently more valuable equipment than his illiterate counterpart, which raises his output. Many types of capital equipment simply cannot be handled properly by illiterates, and as a result the production system has to be simple. A chemical plant or an oil refinery, for example, will close down in weeks unless highly trained personnel are on hand to correct deviations. Even apparently simple activities such as repair work on vehicles, selling, office work, and manual manufacturing require some skills and, equally important, some ability to learn, before a fairly high level of efficiency can be achieved.

The importance of basic literacy, at least among a substantial part of the working population, must not be underestimated. The greater the rate of illiteracy, the more serious will be the managerial problems discussed in this section. In the same vein, greater illiteracy means greater waste and spoilage in production and distribution, less innovation and progress, and lower overall human productivity.

As we shall see later, basic literacy is interconnected with other constraints in a very direct way. Modern societies rely heavily on literacy in all phases of their operations, from industrial production, to law, to police protection, to governments, and so on through the fabric of modern life. Not only are illiterates a relatively low grade work force in the productive sense, but they also are low grade in the social sense generally. Illiterates tend to be sick more often, to be unable to support sound government, to fail to support such policies as overall development of the population in terms of more schooling, and so on. An illiterate society is an unproductive society, which is another way of saying that it is a badly managed society. Management in the modern sense of the word is almost impossible to perform adequately. One of the major tasks of a country faced with a large literacy problem is to improve the quality of future workers and managers by instituting large scale educational programs. Unfortunately, even the management of a major educational effort is quite complex, and countries tend to have great difficulties in planning and carrying out such an effort.

## SPECIALIZED VOCATIONAL AND TECHNICAL TRAINING AND GENERAL SECONDARY EDUCATION

In this section we are interested in all types of secondary educational programs, as well as vocational, technical and apprenticeship training programs, which are not under the direct control of industrial enterprises. These programs are taken as given by the enterprises in a given country and in large part determine the types and quality of personnel available to them, as well as the amount of training that enterprises must undertake independently to carry out their activities.

The extent, quality, and diversity of vocational and technical training and general secondary education in a given country has a significant bearing on the organization structures, degrees of work specialization, managerial performance, and overall productivity in industrial enterprises. Education and training of this type would prove significantly less of a constraint on work specialization and managerial effectiveness in American as compared to Indian industry, while India would fare better than the Sudan.

There are data available on the content and extent of vocational, technical, apprenticeship, and secondary education and training for many countries. Often such data indicate the number of persons employed in industry who have had training of this type. A rough estimate of the quality of such training can be made by analyzing student-instructor ratios in these programs, as well as the qualifications of the instructors.[4]

In the United States various vocational, apprenticeship, and special technical training programs provide industrial firms with the bulk of their semiskilled and skilled labor, technicians, foremen, and other lower level technical supervisors. General secondary education provides industry with clerical staffs, salesmen, and white collar supervisory personnel. In addition, the large majority of unskilled workers of all types are now recipients of at least some education and training beyond elementary schooling. In recent years the equivalent of a secondary education has become a necessary minimum requirement for most good jobs. Most teachers in the secondary school system have college degrees, and this is reflected in the relatively high quality of secondary education in the United States. The U.S. has the largest per capita enrollment in secondary education in the world; however, all of the industrial advanced nations have extensive systems of secondary education, as well as a variety of vocational, technical, and apprenticeship

---

[4] For data of this type see *Training of National Technical Personnel for Accelerated Industrialization of Developing Countries*, Parts I, II, and III. Various other U.N. groups and the ministries of education in most countries issue reports containing relevant data of this type. The most comprehensive book to date on all types and levels of education throughout the world is F. Harbison and C. Myers, *Education, Manpower and Economic Growth* (New York: McGraw-Hill Book Company, 1964). See also F. Harbison and C. Myers, *Manpower and Education* (New York: McGraw-Hill Book Company, 1965).

programs of fairly high quality.[5] The Soviet Union, in particular, has made great progress in this sphere in the past four decades; and in Japan about 75 percent of all persons in the fifteen to nineteen age bracket are now enrolled in secondary educational programs. The Netherlands and Sweden have developed very extensive systems of vocational, technical, and secondary education which turn out large numbers of persons well suited for a wide range of industrial careers.[6]

Some of the western European nations—Britain, for example—have traditionally underemphasized technical secondary education, but the pressures of industrial expansion are changing this emphasis somewhat. While the British have long had a well developed apprenticeship training system, it has not kept pace with the needs of modern industry. This is clearly reflected in a recent report of the British National Development Economic Council:

> There are considerable doubts whether the existing apprenticeship system with its traditional craft divisions, quota systems; and the lack of standards and tests, can meet the needs of an expanding economy characterized by the more rapid introduction of new techniques, materials, and methods. A thorough overhaul of the apprenticeship system is vital for expansion in the long run.[7]

This report points out that not only are there growing shortages of qualified skilled craftsmen and workers—particularly in engineering and construction industries—but better education and training is needed for office personnel, front line supervisors, and various types of technicians. Even in the U.S. the system of vocational and technical training is far from perfect. For example, in 1964 an acute shortage of skilled toolmakers forced many manufacturers into expensive overtime operations and also extended the delivery dates of shipments to customers by several months.[8] It is true that this and similar manpower shortage situations may be due in part to general economic conditions, but they are often due to inadequacies in the system of vocational and semiprofessional technical training.[9]

In most of the advanced industrial nations many responsible managerial, scientific, technical, and white collar positions in industry are filled by persons having at least some higher education. (A summary of some of these positions is presented in the next section.) This is especially true in the U.S. and U.S.S.R.

---

[5] See Harbison and Myers, *op. cit.*, 1964, chap. vii.

[6] Cf. United Nations, *Questionnaire on Industrial Planning and Development* (E/C.5/24 [New York, March, 1963]), responses of Japan, Netherlands, Sweden, and many other advanced and newly developing countries. For a comprehensive study of Soviet education at this level see N. Dewitt, *Education and Professional Employment in the U.S.S.R.* (Washington, D.C.: U.S. Government Printing Office, 1961), chap. iii.

[7] National Development Economic Council, *Conditions Favourable to Faster Growth* (London: Her Majesty's Stationery Office, 1963), p. 9.

[8] *Business Week*, October 3, 1964, p. 19.

[9] Cf. H. David, ed., *Education and Manpower* (New York: Columbia University Press, 1960), chaps. vii and viii.

At the other end of the spectrum, in the more underdeveloped countries—for example, Sudan, Saudi Arabia, Niger, Ethiopia, Haiti—nationals having the equivalent of a secondary education constitute between .1 percent and 1.0 percent of the entire local population. Such persons fill the key positions in the country which are not occupied by foreigners, and in most cases these are governmental or educational rather than industrial jobs.[10] Hence, it is obvious that industrial enterprises, particularly private firms, are faced with very severe shortages of educated and formally trained manpower. In the majority of cases, skilled workers, technicians, foremen, and even higher level managers are illiterate or little more than barely literate. The exceptions are found chiefly in foreign owned firms or where foreigners are employed by local enterprises.

In the Saudi firm managed by one of the authors, the number two man—a non-Saudi Arab—did not have the equivalent of a secondary education, nor did he have any formal vocational or technical training; therefore, the author personally had to engage in detailed supervisory training and to control activities even at the lowest level in the enterprise. Decision making was very highly centralized. In many underdeveloped countries there is no effective legislation regarding apprenticeship training, and there are no public technical training programs which provide manpower for industry. In such an environment the managerial problems discussed in the last section are vivid realities.

Even in partially developed and semiadvanced countries—such as Brazil, Colombia, Mexico, India, Indonesia, Turkey, Pakistan and Egypt—there are critical shortages of technically trained people and skilled labor of all types.[11] These shortages persist in spite of efforts in recent years by many of these countries to expand vocational, apprenticeship, technical, and general secondary educational and training programs. With the expansion of such programs, the bulk of the qualified graduates continue to enter governmental or educational careers rather than industrial employment. The majority of them who go into industry are assigned to or prefer government operated enterprises and, to a lesser extent, foreign rather than locally owned firms. The consequences of this dilemma are reflected in the words of two Brazilian industrial managers:[12]

We can buy machinery easier than we can get good men to run the machinery. It takes up to two years to train a good lathe man. There is a real shortage of good technical people in the shop and office.

We have to train our mechanics. We can't hire any. Then we have the problem that when you train a man you often lose him. Other companies hire him away from you after you've spent the time and money to train him.

---

[10] See the related discussion in Harbison and Myers, *op. cit.*, chap. iv, on underdeveloped countries. See also United Nations, *Economic Bulletin for Africa* (Addis Ababa), Vol. II, No. 2, June, 1962, especially pp. 18–20.

[11] Harbison and Myers, *op. cit.*, chaps. v and vi.

[12] The statements that follow are taken from Oberg, *op. cit.*, pp. 133, 135,

The shortage of qualified human resources pertains not only to workers and technicians but also to lower level managers, particularly foremen. This is reflected in the words of another Brazilian manager: "This is a family company so we don't have much trouble at the top, but the people below this level—the foremen and sub-foremen—give trouble." In such an environment both the efficiency and size of firms tend to be severely constrained by educational factors largely beyond the control of management.

In India during the 1951–59 period, secondary education enrollment doubled; but deficiencies in the quality and content of secondary education are still resulting in serious bottlenecks for industrial development. One Indian authority has made this statement about secondary education in India.

It is rightly pointed out that secondary education in India suffers from aimlessness, its primary aim being to prepare children for entrance into the universities or for clerical jobs. Colleges are being clogged with undeserving students, and unemployed matriculates are running amuck for getting a job on a couple of rupees a day. Unfortunately secondary education is a victim of its own traditions.[13]

These traditions evolved under British colonial rule, and have resulted in little diversity and in the lack of technical emphasis in secondary education.

Egypt has done better than India with regard to the expansion of technical education, although the Egyptians started from a much lower base. During the 1954–61 period, general secondary education in Egypt increased by 43 percent, while secondary technical education increased by 400 percent. This policy has been pursued in an attempt to provide large numbers of technical and supervisory personnel for industry, commerce, and agriculture;[14] however, industry is still faced with critical shortages of skilled workers, mechanics, technicians, and foremen. Private firms fare much worse than government owned enterprises, since most of the trained manpower is assigned to the rapidly extending nationalized sector. Given such shortages of manpower resources, job specialization has been greatly retarded, particularly in the chemical, mechanical engineering, and textile industries.[15]

In general, even in those newly developing countries where there has been a great expansion with regard to the quantitative aspects of secondary education and technical, vocational, and apprenticeship training programs, quality looms as a paramount problem. Many of the instructors used in these programs do not even have the equivalent of an adequate secondary

---

[13] Harbison and Myers, *op. cit.*, p. 112, from S. Mukerji, *Education in India Today and Tomorrow* (Baroda, India: Archarya Book Depot, 1960), p. 140.

[14] *Comparative Statistics of Education: 1953–60* (Cairo: Department of Statistics, United Arab Republic, 1961), pp. 28 ff.; Harbison and Myers, *op. cit.*, p. 114.

[15] Cf. *The Development of Manufacturing Industries in Egypt, Israel and Turkey* (New York: United Nations, 1959), pp. 83 ff.

education—at least by American or western European standards—very few have college educations, and many are employed on a part time basis. There is also the very real problem of adequate teaching materials.

In many of the newly developing nations where industrial managers desire to train enterprise workers and improve their skills, there are frequently great limitations arising from the lack of knowledge and of staff who have the necessary qualifications to train others. Hence, in countries where few persons are formally trained as welders, machine maintenance men, computer technicians, and so on, such positions are extremely difficult to fill with qualified people, and often the positions do not even exist. There are many operations and activities performed in various types of industrial enterprises in the advanced countries which are not found in most of the similar types of enterprises in many less developed countries. The result is different types of organization structures and different levels of productivity among the enterprises of different countries. Such differences can be at least partially explained by significant differences in vocational, apprenticeship, technical, and general secondary education and training programs.

It seems evident that the types of educational and training programs discussed in this section have a significant impact on managerial performance in any country. In America we tend to take such education and training for granted, but in the large majority of the countries of the world it serves as a significant negative constraint upon managerial effectiveness.

## HIGHER EDUCATION

Higher education here means formal training beyond the secondary school level. Like the other types of education discussed in this chapter, higher education is statistically measurable. Most countries know how many citizens have taken advanced work in colleges, universities, and technical institutes. The qualitative evaluation, as noted earlier, is difficult, since not all advanced education is at the same level. Variation in standards and programs between schools, and particularly between countries, tends to be extreme; and it is not uncommon for professors and instructors to discover that seemingly technically qualified students are in fact incapable of doing the type of advanced work their degrees would indicate that they are capable of doing. This also holds true for graduates who become business managers and public administrators.

Modern industries are voracious consumers of high grade manpower. Even cursory examinations of the types of managerial and technical tasks to be done in a relatively modern industrial enterprise suggest that this type of high skill manpower is critical to efficient production and distribution of the firm's products. The list of manpower skills to be presented below is far from complete, but it does suggest the kinds of manpower required in a not very large and fairly simply organized modern manufacturing firm in the United States. The availability and utilization of such skills have a significant bearing on managerial performance. Most of the activities outlined call for well educated persons, if they are to be carried out in a reasonably efficient manner; and in the U.S. probably a large majority of these people will possess at least some formal education and training beyond the secondary school level. In countries where there is a shortage of people with the indicated skills, the activities will either be carried out poorly, in many cases, or not performed at all. This would mean that many of the modern techniques and tools of management, as found in American industry, would not be found on any sizable scale, if at all, in various other countries. The list of manpower skills follows.

### Marketing and Distribution

Skills in this category are: market research capabilities, including knowledge of economic and psychological factors influencing demand; statistical abilities, including knowledge of sampling techniques, ability for rational and logical compilation of sales information, considerable knowledge of product prices and costs; complex report writing; sales promotion techniques, including knowledge of packaging and purchasing of ad space in various media, channel design abilities, mastery of inventory planning techniques, familiarity with product line additions and deletions, and so on.

Firms may operate without detailed knowledge in these areas only at their peril. It is clear that the kinds of knowledge required to handle these types of operations are not taught in the primary schools; nor are they taught in the required depth, if at all, in most secondary level educational and training programs. Even many higher educational institutions do not cover the types of advanced statistics, mathematics, economics, and psychology often used routinely by modern marketing departments and organizations. While self-taught, capable individuals may do quite well in such activities, the availability of persons with at least some of the basic skills required for a specific job in this area tends to cut short the training time required and increases overall managerial effectiveness.

### Production, Procurement, and Research and Development

These skills are: engineering and possibly scientific skills of all sorts, including ability for product development and design, process planning and design, and evaluation of changes in product lines or processes; ability to purchase materials and capital equipment logically and efficiently, as well as abilities to integrate new equipment into older processes properly; quality control analytical ability, including ability to conduct statistical analysis of existing outputs in terms of production norms; knowledge of plant and layout planning for optimum efficiency; ability to conduct time and motion studies of personnel activities to determine most efficient operations; knowledge of value engineering, including analyses of present utilizations of materials and operations to obtain greater efficiencies; ability to manage design, operations, and changes in materials handling systems such as conveyors, fork lifts, and manpower; ability to manage maintenance of machinery and plant; costing and preparation of cost effectiveness studies; knowledge of inventory control; and so on.

Again, firms can survive (at times) without this type of skilled manpower, but usually they cannot operate very efficiently. Most of the skills noted above are typically taught in a systematic fashion at the college or university level, and some of the more advanced techniques of production management and control are not encountered by students until they are in graduate schools of engineering or business. Persons can teach themselves such skills, but only at considerable cost and effort; and firms may suffer if the proper trained personnel are not available.

## Personnel

Besides being able to handle the typical routine of payrolls, leaves, illnesses, and similar factors, personnel specialists must often deal with complex problems of statistics, including such items as the construction of interrelated, intricate pay structures. They must be able to describe positions in the firm—a practice which requires more skill than is immediately apparent—and they often must have considerable knowledge relating to the recruiting, selecting, appraisal, and training of personnel. In addition, they must often be effective practitioners in the field of labor law, which may call for a specialized knowledge of complex law rivaling that of a practicing attorney. Qualified personnel specialists must frequently know a great deal about behavioral sciences, particularly psychology, in order to perform their functions adequately.

Even this brief description of a few personnel duties suggests the need for advanced training of all sorts for competent people. Lacking such specialists, a firm may perpetually be in difficulty with governments, their own employees, trade unions, and individuals. The larger and more complex the firm, the more likely it will be that this function becomes a specialized part of the firm, staffed by professionals in the field. Inability to obtain such persons results in inefficiencies which can only help defeat the major goals of the firm.

## Finance

Skills in this category include: knowledge of operations of money markets, including technicalities of bank loans and similar factors; ability to analyze interest rate changes, find credit, prepare financial feasibility reports, develop projected profit and loss and balance sheets, cash flow analysis, and similar data for use by firm management and credit suppliers; ability to prepare financial projections of all sorts for the firm, in light of cost and revenue predictions. Ability to analyze the company's liquidity position now and in the future; capability for managing the firm's available cash through planned uses and investments; and so on.

As is typical in business situations, such persons do not emerge fully trained from a country's educational system; however, such men can be prepared for a firm apprenticeship in finance through extensive university training in money and banking and finance, often through some years of postgraduate study. Such a candidate is clearly superior, other things being equal, to a man who must learn, at company expense, the kinds of basic economic, monetary, and financial theory needed in such a job.

## Accounting and Data Processing

Skills of this kind are: ability to prepare profit and loss and income statements; ability to analyze reporting systems in light of possible improvements; capability to evaluate the firm's cost and financial position now, historically, and in the future; ability to effect refinement and improvement of reporting systems in light of requirements for information, safety of company funds, and cost of reporting; ability to explore the theory of accounting in terms of effects of various accepted systems on tax liabilities, accurate reporting, and information required by management; skill in maintenance of accurate records required by company officials, governments, tax authorities, and others. If the firm finds it feasible to use electronic computers in the accounting or any other function, a variety of additional special skills is entailed.

In this area, many countries have an organized professional group (in the U.S., certified public accountants) who are qualified by examination by their peers. A vast and intricate body of received theory and practical knowledge must be mastered by candidates before they can expect to become practitioners in this field. The complexity of knowledge in this area is suggested by the usual requirement that a candidate have extensive accounting work in a university before he even qualifies to take the examination. Noncollege graduates can occasionally qualify, but only after many years of practical experience with a qualified accounting firm. Lack of such trained men often means that a firm runs out of financial control. Since no one is able to document and analyze the financial position of the company, no one is in a position to manage effectively.

There are numerous examples available of the impact of shortages of qualified people in all of the above functions on managerial effectiveness. For illustrative purposes let us look at the accounting function in many newly developing countries. One team of experts which has made a comprehensive study of accounting in the industrial firms of a number of newly developing nations had this to report.

The absence of good cost accounting often leads managements to attach too much importance to economizing on labor, causing unrest and impaired relations, when a good analysis of costs would reveal that savings in other sectors such as raw materials or better machine utilization would reduce costs considerably more. Good costing would also reveal the cost of labor turnover, an item that most managements in a country where there is a surplus of labor completely fail to understand.[16]

This situation is attributed not only to critical shortages of qualified accounting specialists but also to managements' lack of basic knowledge regarding the accounting function.

## Management

To our list of categories we should add management, since it contains its own unique functions, as discussed in earlier chapters. Whether a manager is involved in one of the above enterprise functions, or whether he is part of general or top management, he will—even if in a very unsophisticated way—engage in the functions of planning and decision making, controlling, organizing, staffing, and directing. His behavior and effectiveness depend in large part on his knowledge of the techniques, tools, criteria, and principles which can be used in performing these functions. While only relatively few countries have long recognized management as an independent field of research, education and application, the number has been increasing rapidly in recent years.[17]

When additional skilled types of professional talent and various other high skilled persons required in performing subfunctions of the above categories are included in a firm's requirements, it is easy to see why complex industrial firms all over the world turn increasingly to schools of higher education to obtain the men they need. In this search for manpower, they must compete energetically with government bureacracies; the desire of many professionals to practice independently; the colleges, schools, and universities themselves; and various international and nonprofit organizations. Seldom are there enough really capable, well educated persons to fill all requirements. The greater the shortfall of well educated persons, the more likely it will be that the productive enterprises in an economy will perform less efficiently than they might.

Lacking such trained men, enterprises are forced to perform complicated tasks with inadequate personnel—or the jobs do not get done at all. Here is another reason why in countries with inadequately educated people firms tend to be quite small. Many of the problems noted above can be handled by an owner-manager, if the firm is small enough; but as it grows, trained specialists are required. It should be noted that these jobs have to be done regardless of the ownership of the firm—enterprises in Marxist socie-

---

[16] G. Ronson, "Use of Accounting as an Aid to Management in Industrial Enterprises in Underdeveloped Countries," *Industrialization and Productivity*, No. 1, 1958, p. 62.

[17] Cf. the comprehensive study of management education and development in sixty countries, *Organized Efforts to Advance the Art and Science of Managing in Selected Countries* (Sydney, Australia: International Committee of Scientific Management, 1960).

ties, owned by governments, have the same types of duties to perform. The problem is more one of firm size and complexity than of ownership, although duties will differ somewhat—mainly in their distribution—as ownership shifts. Thus, a privately owned firm's financial planning or market forecasting might be somewhat different from that of a similar firm owned by a government—although in either case *some* sort of financial planning and market forecasting would be critical. To expect an untrained, unskilled individual to handle properly such complicated matters is unsound and can result only in confusion and inefficiency.

One major area in which the supply of skilled and highly trained people affects a firm is in its ability to decentralize. If capable persons are available in abundant quantity, decentralization of a large firm is quite feasible and often economic. Suborganizations can be established as semi-independent units, and top level managers can be reasonably certain that the overall objectives of the firm will be met; but if such people do not exist in sufficient quantity, a high degree of centralization is a necessity. Key men must be centralized, since no one in the field can handle their problems. This centralization tendency in larger firms limits somewhat the potential efficiency of the firm, in that in some cases firms using thousands of men and millions of dollars of capital simply cannot operate efficiently from one central office. A familiar pattern in many large, and even medium sized, public and private firms around the world is the pattern of a harassed, overworked central office, which feels, perhaps logically, that it must handle every detail of management and administration for the entire operation. Executives must sign requisitions for the purchase of minor items in a distant branch office, while subordinates in the field relax and wait. Such patterns are partial evidence of inadequate control systems and insufficient decentralization, caused often by the inability of firms to find competent middle managers to operate their distant offices and factories.

Large and/or complex productive enterprises cannot operate efficiently without substantial numbers of highly skilled, highly trained men. Their absence will have a significant impact on the efficiency of firms, and a country fortunate enough to possess large numbers of such men is in a position to develop much more easily desired levels of productive efficiency. Hence, the overall system of higher education in a given country has a crucial and direct bearing on the activities and effectiveness of industrial enterprise managements.

The United States is the world leader in per capita higher education. The Soviet Union has closed the gap significantly in the past few decades. In both the U.S. and U.S.S.R. about 25 percent of all higher education graduates are employed in industrial activities, and a substantial portion of the more responsible managerial, administrative, and technical positions in industrial enterprises are filled by persons having the equivalent of a higher education. For example, in Soviet industry more than 25 percent of all managers have the equivalent of a college degree, while more than two-

thirds have at least the equivalent of a semiprofessional, specialized secondary education or junior college training.[18]

The performances of a number of the other advanced nations are also
fairly impressive in this connection. The United States is way ahead of the
entire field with regard to the employment of persons with postgraduate
training—at the masters' or doctorate level or in the professions—in industry.

At the other end of the scale, a number of underdeveloped
nations—for example, Niger, Nyasaland, Saudi Arabia—do not even have
any local colleges or universities. Promising students must go abroad if they
are to receive a higher education, and most of them who do this enter the
government when and if they return. In the case of Saudi Arabia,
Aramco—the large American oil company—does offer some fairly advanced
technical training for nationals whom they employ—and in some cases for
their sons. While much of the training is oriented specifically to the oil
industry, a good part of it is transferable to other activities, and many
trained Saudi in both public and private life are Aramco alumni. The
company has never seriously tried to hold on to good Saudi men with better
prospects elsewhere in the country, perhaps recognizing the inevitability of
this transfer process; but the extent of higher level training offered by
Aramco does not provide nearly a sufficient supply of highly talented
manpower for local Saudi industry, even though this sector is not especially
large.

Many of the partially developed and semiadvanced countries have
greatly expanded their higher education facilities in the past decade. In a
few of these countries, such as India, Mexico, and Egypt, the total number
of graduates turned out would perhaps be reasonably sufficient in terms of
the existing needs of industrial enterprises, *but* the *quality* of their higher
educational systems, and particularly the match of education with the
actual requirements of industry, leaves much to be desired.[19] As a result,
there are still critical shortages of highly talented scientific, engineering,
technical, and managerial personnel in these and numerous other countries.
We shall deal at greater length with the problems of "educational match"
later, but a few words on this subject are in order in this section.

Probably the majority of the countries of the world overemphasize the
humanities, arts, law, and possibly medicine at the expense of engineering,
science, technical, business administration, and management education, for
various social and cultural reasons and because of the costs involved,
particularly regarding engineering and the sciences.[20] Most of the Commu-

---

[18] These and other pertinent U.S.–U.S.S.R. data can be found in N. Dewitt,
1961, *op. cit.*, p. 501, table VI–52, and chap. 4; N. Dewitt, "Education and the
Development of Human Resources: Soviet and American Effort," in *Dimensions of
Soviet Economic Power* (Washington, D.C.: U.S. Government Printing Office, 1962),
pp. 252 ff.; S. Rosen, "Higher Education in the U.S.S.R.," in *Dimensions, op. cit.*,
pp. 295 ff.; D. Gronick, *The Red Executive* (Garden City, N.Y.: Anchor Books, 1961),
chap. 4.

[19] Harbison and Myers, *op. cit.*, chaps. 5 and 6.

[20] *Ibid.*

nist nations are notable exceptions, with their great emphasis on scientific, engineering, and advanced technical education. In fact, there is much evidence that the Soviet Union is now suffering from emphasis and specialization in scientific engineering and advanced technical training in excess of the requirements of industry.[21]

A pretty good balance in higher education can be found in several of the more advanced countries—for example the U.S., Canada, Sweden, Netherlands, and more recently Japan.[22] The U.S. has gone the farthest in providing industry with scientific, engineering, and high talent technical personnel who are capable of engaging in both basic and applied research and who undertake research, development, and innovation activities on a broad plain. This is the reason that there are large research and development (R&D) departments in numerous U.S. firms. By contrast, in the less developed countries there are frequently no R&D activities and little if any product or process innovation, even in larger enterprises.

The U.S. is clearly the leader in professional management education, business administration, and the social sciences, at both the undergraduate and graduate levels.[23] With the great emphasis on research and teaching in these fields, new techniques, tools, methods, and concepts are continually discovered and applied in industry, often yielding substantial increases in productivity. Some of the other advanced economies—particularly Sweden, Belgium, and, to a somewhat lesser extent, the Netherlands—have also made considerable strides in management and business education. Japan has also made great strides in the past decade; however, the application of many Western management concepts, principles, and practices is still limited by Japanese cultural tradition. Of the less developed countries, Mexico is a leader in business education.

In the great majority of countries—both developed and underdeveloped, Communist and capitalist—where there are business administration programs, there tends to be little if any emphasis on management per se, human relations, or the behavioral sciences. The stress tends to be on the specialized aspects of accounting, finance, production, economics, and, to a

---

[21] See the sources cited in footnote 18, above. See also V. Elyutin, "The Higher School at a New Stage," *Soviet Education*, January, 1962, pp. 28 ff.; *Izvestia*, March 14, 1963, p. 3.

[22] This statement is based on a comprehensive survey of unpublished United Nations reports and questionnaires. See also Harbison and Myers, *op. cit.*, chap. 7. Canada benefits greatly from the U.S. higher educational system, since many students go to the U.S. for their education, particularly at the postgraduate level. On the other hand, Canada loses a significant portion of its high-talent manpower to U.S. industry.

[23] See the comprehensive study of the International Committee on Scientific Management, *Organized Efforts to Advance the Art and Science of Management, op. cit.*; F. Harbison and C. Myers, *Management in the Industrial World*, (New York: McGraw-Hill, 1959); D. Granick, *The European Executive* (New York: Doubleday, 1962); S. Reksodihardjo, *Skills Investment in a Developing Country* (unpublished doctoral dissertation, University of California, Los Angeles, 1964). This dissertation contains an in-depth analysis of management education and training programs in several countries. See also *European Guide to General Courses in Business Management* (European Productivity Agency, June, 1960).

lesser degree, marketing. In the majority of the western European countries higher educational institutions still resist adding courses and programs in business administration and management.

While the British have an extensive network of technical and commercial colleges there is very little in the way of courses dealing specifically with management or human relations. This is also true of the three universities offering graduate programs in business administration. Business and management education has traditionally been taboo at Oxford and Cambridge. Only a few engineering schools offer a smattering of industrial administration. A recent report issued by the British National Economic Development Council stresses that inadequate attention has been given in higher education to "new techniques in decision-making, planning and forecasting, human relations, communication, and marketing."[24] A decision has recently been made to expand professional management education, and it appears that one or two high powered postgraduate schools of business administration (along the lines of Harvard) are to be established.[25]

The Soviet Union offers narrow specialties in a number of business administration and economic fields in their system of higher education; but in that country management has not been considered an independent field of research, teaching or application with its own body of theory. Only now are the Soviets calling for the introduction of management courses and the establishment of professional management educational programs.[26]

In both Britain and the Soviet Union, as well as in a growing number of countries, the absence of management education is now recognized as a serious constraint upon managerial effectiveness.

It is evident that a manager who has had good formal training in the field of management through a higher educational program, or in some other way, is likely to perform his job in a somewhat different manner than a similar type of manager who has had no such training. There is also a greater likelihood that he will perform his job more effectively.

## MANAGEMENT DEVELOPMENT PROGRAMS[27]

In this section we are interested in special management development programs which are not part of the regular undergraduate or postgraduate

---

[24] *Conditions Favorable to Faster Growth, op. cit.,* p. 4.

[25] "B-Schools for Britain," *Business Week,* December 7, 1963, pp. 84–86.

[26] N. Adfelt, "Management Personnel and the Science of Administration," translated in *Current Digest of the Soviet Press (CDSP),* Vol. XIV, No. 40, 1962, pp. 3–4; V. Gvishiani, "Administration is Above All a Science," *Izvestia,* May 19, 1963, p. 2; partially translated in *CDSP,* Vol. XIV, No. 20, 1963, pp. 25 ff; K. Plotnikov, "E. Liberman: Right or Wrong," translated in *Problems of Economics,* April, 1963, pp. 25–26; Editorial, *Planovoe Khoziaistvo,* November, 1962; V. Lisitzin in *Ekonomicheskaya Gazeta,* October 26, 1963, pp. 7–8.

[27] Much of the discussion in this section is based on data presented in the sources cited in Footnote 23 above. See also Council for International Progress in Management (USA) Inc., *Proceedings of the International Management Congress (CIOS),* September 16–20, 1963, New York City (New York, 1963), Vol. IV.

higher educational system and which are not undertaken internally by industrial enterprises. They include part time or live-in programs that are offered by various educational institutions, associations, or government organizations with the aim of developing and improving the abilities and skills of existing managers or potential managers who are sponsored by their enterprises. Owner-managers attending such programs would also fit into this category.

This type of training, if properly organized and conducted, can do much to raise managerial effectiveness by providing participants with new information and knowledge about research findings, techniques, methods, and tools which are applicable to their present or future jobs. It can obviously result in changes in the manner in which they perform their jobs.

The extent and, particularly, the content of management development programs in the majority of countries correlate fairly closely with the content and extent of management training offered in the system of higher education. In those countries where management has for some time been regarded as a profession and as an independent field of research, teaching, and application, there are a sizable number of programs focusing on managerial skills and aimed at all types and levels of management. This is most evident in the U.S. and more recently in Japan. Canada benefits not only from its own programs but also from various U.S. programs. While many countries now offer management development programs—also called executive development or training programs—in the great majority of cases they do not stress the development of managerial skills per se. They tend to stress such fields as economics, finance, accounting, business law, production, or various other technical aspects of enterprise operations.

In France, for example, most programs are aimed at top executives, and the university programs are strongly oriented toward law and economics. Some even require that participants have a law background. In Britain there are only a few management development programs, and even these do not have much support or recognition from the leaders of industry. In western Europe, the programs offered in Sweden, Germany, Belgium, and the Netherlands seem to come closest to those offered in the U.S.; however, there does appear to be some convergence toward the U.S. philosophy and approach to management development in most of the advanced European nations.

In eastern Europe the emphasis is primarily on technical training and the enterprise functions rather than on managerial functions or human relations. Programs offered in Yugoslavia seem to resemble those in the U.S. more closely than do those in the other countries, although Russia and a few other Communist states appear to be on the threshold of greater convergence.

In many of the newly developing nations—for example, India, Indonesia, and Egypt—various types of management development programs have been organized in the past decade; however, in most of these countries there are facilities available for training only a very small number of managers and potential managers. Often the great majority of the participants are employed by large government enterprises or departments. Another problem is that in most newly developing countries the vast majority of industrial enterprises are small, and few facilities exist for training managerial and other personnel of small firms. Japan has gone the farthest of any country in providing training and management development facilities for smaller firms.

In newly developing countries it is usually more important to focus on improving the quality of existing managers rather than on substantially expanding the quantity of managers; however, the quality of management training is in many cases greatly hindered by inadequate instructors and course materials. While the great expansion of management development programs in the U.S. has resulted in large part from increased and more complex industrial activity, such programs in newly developing countries have as a chief aim the bringing about of a higher level of industrial activity. In many of the more underdeveloped nations—for example, Saudi Arabia, Kenya, Uganda—there are as yet no special management development programs. In such countries it is extremely difficult, if not impossible, for local managers to acquire information or knowledge which can improve their performance.

## ATTITUDE TOWARD EDUCATION

The prevailing attitude toward education in a given country is a product of various sociological and political factors. The problem is further complicated by historic and institutional views of what constitutes an educated man. Many societies still see law, liberal arts, and/or religion as being the only suitable fields of study for a "gentleman." As long as only a small elite was educated, such an outlook had relatively little impact on the economy; but as the society shifts to mass educational system with the aim of modernizing the economy, such attitudes can be very costly. Status seekers and the better students take to law, the classics, and the arts or to political science, ignoring engineering, science, economics, and administration; and the result is a critical shortage of such important skills.

Attitude toward education is of interest in this study for a number of reasons. First, it has a great bearing on the extent, quality, and content of the overall educational and training system within a given country; and this in turn in large part determines the types of persons found in industrial enterprises and in other organizations which influence the operations of industrial enterprises. Secondly, it has a significant bearing on the fields that attract the better students. Thirdly, it tends to be a determinant of how much effort and sacrifice people are willing to undertake in educational and training pursuits. Finally, it has a bearing on whether or not people are inclined to want to improve their skills and abilities through education, training, and self-development. Little can be done until people really want education.

A leading study on education points out that the choices made in the strategies of human resource development are greatly influenced by the orientation of the dominant elites of a given country.[28] In traditional societies dominated by a dynastic elite or tribal chiefs, or in countries dominated by malevolent dictatorships usually of the military type, the educational systems tend to be the worst in terms of the human resource requirements of productive enterprises and economic progress. The goal is to maintain the status quo, to preserve the traditional class structure, discrimination, and values as much as possible, while modernization takes place slowly if at all. The rulers tend to oppose mass literacy and extensive education in order to avoid revolutions and the stirring up of the masses. Secondary and higher education—if available locally—is reserved for the select few; and it stresses rigid classical lines with religion, humanities, and law—in some cases religious law—as avenues to positions of prestige. Scientific and technical training is largely ignored, as is business education. Saudi Arabia is a country falling in this educational-elite category, as are various other countries in Africa, Asia, and Latin America.

A second class of elites is referred to as the revolutionary intellectuals. They have given an ideology to the Communist countries and have presented a clear strategy for human resource development. Man is developed for his service to the state, not educated for his own sake. An attempt is made to achieve a perfect match between the educational system and the human requirements of productive enterprises—and in fact with the economy as a whole. This is done through comprehensive national planning.

Education in such a system tends to be functional and highly specialized; much of it is related to employment through evening or correspondence courses and through other types of combined work and study programs undertaken by employed personnel of all types. In fact more than half of the students currently enrolled in Soviet higher education are studying on a part time basis. Scientific, engineering, and technical education has top priority and prestige, while broad education in the social sciences and humanities is given relatively little attention. Marxism-Leninism dominates all nontechnical education. In a fairly advanced industrial economy, intensive educational specialization, dogmatism, lack of emphasis on the social sciences and humanities, and the absence of adequate numbers of well rounded generalists are handicaps in achieving the flexibility and adaptability which is increasingly needed in a scientific and

---

[28] Our discussion of dominant elites and educational strategies is based primarily on Harbison and Myers, *op cit.*, pp. 178–181, and C. Kerr, J. Dunlop, F. Harbison, and C. Myers, *Industrialism and Industrial Man* (Cambridge, Mass: Harvard University Press, 1961), chap. iii, pp. 47–76, also pp. 118–119.

technological age. This is most evident from the present day experiences of the Soviet Union where there is a growing gap between their system of education and training and the requirements of productive enterprises.

A third class of elites is the nationalist leaders, found most frequently in the newly independent nations such as India, Egypt, Indonesia, and Ghana. Such leaders attempt first to free their educational systems from the pattern established by the colonial administrators. The latter usually adopted an educational system similar to that of the home country or geared to the local human requirements of colonial rule. The new nationalist leaders are in a great hurry; they see education as the road to modernization, and urge reforms and expansion as rapidly as possible. Large expenditures tend to be made on education, international agencies are consulted, teams of experts are invited to the country, and many students may be sent abroad for training; but such countries have generally not thought through the complex policy choices between universal schooling for the masses and more selective qualitative improvement in education, particularly at the secondary and higher levels. In many of these countries the traditionally elite educational fields and occupations—for example, law, the humanities, religion, the arts and classics, political science, medicine—continue to be favored by educators and the more able students alike, while scientific, technical, engineering, and business education are not held in very high repute. As a result, the educational system does not turn out adequate numbers of qualified people for productive enterprises.

India is a good example of such a country. In Egypt there is still a strong tendency for secondary schools to direct their best students to law, language, and the arts at the college level, while shortages of good students persist in most engineering and business administration fields.[29] In Nigeria the new University of Ife had openings for eighty students in the Faculty of Science in October, 1962; but only forty-one out of 109 students offered admission enrolled. On the other hand, the Nigerian government observed in 1962 that each of four new universities was opening a law school, despite the fact that 50 percent of Nigeria's 1,213 lawyers were underemployed.[30]

Finally there are countries characterized by rising middle class elites. The middle class society tends to be quite affluent and democratic and believes in widespread public education. While some countries of this type do have more rigid class structures than others—for example, Britain compared to the U.S.—class structures tend to become more blurred over time. Educational systems in such countries grow out of the needs of the broader society and its values, rather than evolving through conscious, comprehensive educational planning. Education in this type of society is regarded more as a human right than as a functionally oriented training system for the

---

[29] I. Abdel-Rahman, "Manpower Planning in the U.A.R." (Geneva: International Institute for Labour Studies, 1962), p. 14; see also Harbeson and Meyers, *op. cit.*, p. 106.

[30] Cited in Harbeson and Meyers, *Education, Manpower and Economic Growth*, p. 85.

economy. Faculties and students, particularly in higher education, have been generally free to pursue their own interests and careers, as influenced by their individual goals in relation to society and its needs. Education is the principal avenue for mobility, and there tends to be a wide range of respectable occupations. A diversified system of education tends to evolve since the typical middle class society needs many kinds of talents.

In spite of these broad similarities among the economically advanced middle class countries, there are also significant differences in the proportion of the population that receives secondary and higher educations in different fields, the actual curricula offered in various fields, and the prestige ranking of different fields. While it is true that countries in this category are usually characterized by high quality education on a broad scale, some achieve a substantially better match between their system of education and training and the requirements of modern productive enterprises.

The above classification of societies in terms of dominant elite types does not correspond perfectly in reality to any particular country. Many countries are mixtures of several types, although most countries are more accurately characterized as one type or another by their attitude toward education and their educational strategies. It is true, however, that Japan patterned much of its educational system after the U.S. system before it had a sizable middle class population. There are also countries characterized by traditional monarchies, dictatorships, and/or military rule which pattern parts or much of their systems after various developed countries; and there are essentially democratic, but relatively poor, nations which have highly inadequate educational systems.

The amount of effort and sacrifice that people in a given country are inclined to undertake for the sake of education and training is not necessarily related to the educational strategies pursued by the country. It is often dependent on various nonrelated sociological and cultural factors—for example, parental encouragement and rearing of promising young people, general respect or disrespect for education.

In many of the newly developing countries where an educational revolution is taking place, much of the population fails to recognize or identify with the kind of social and economic revolution their country is undergoing and also fails to stress to their children the need for literacy, education, and acquiring skills. Parents, not being literate, do not realize the advantages of education, particularly in the more traditional rural cultures.[31]

On the other hand, in some of the more underdeveloped countries the masses tend to view education quite favorably. In Saudi Arabia, for example, education and educated people of all types tend to be highly regarded by the common man, in spite of this country's extremely sparse educational system. A young Saudi with a foreign university education is

---

[31] Cf. *Economic Bulletin for Africa*, 1962, chap. vii.

very highly regarded, and families constantly make enormous financial sacrifices to send their promising sons to secondary schools or colleges at home or abroad. Even a literate clerk is a man of considerable prestige, recognized as one cut above the common man.

In many countries where education is highly regarded people are willing to enroll in part time education and training programs while working full time, in spite of the great overall work load this may entail. This is clearly the case in Russia. The extent of adult education, extension and correspondence programs, and various other types of part time education and training in a given country serves as an indicator of society's attitude toward education. This type of education and training has increased greatly in recent years in the U.S. and various other countries. If persons employed full time in industry undertake effective part time education and training with the aim of improving their occupational skills and abilities, this would tend to have a favorable effect on the staffing function of management. This would also tend to be the case if they educate and further develop themselves informally by reading journals and books and by attending various extracurricular meetings and conferences pertaining to their occupations. Such informal education and self-development is pervasive throughout Soviet industry and fairly widespread among managers and specialists in American industry, while in British industry managers are less inclined to undertake such self-development.[32]

In general, if workers and managers are eager and willing to expend substantial effort on education, training, and self-development—either formally or informally, within or outside the enterprise—this would tend to have a favorable bearing on managerial effectiveness and productive efficiency. Even if there are severe shortages of highly talented manpower in a given country, it may be possible for an enterprise to employ primary school graduates and train them upwards into more responsible positions, if the trainees themselves are willing to devote considerable time and effort of their own to such improvement.[33] This is evident from the experiences and observations of one of the authors in Saudi Arabia; whereas visits to some other Mideastern countries indicated substantially less desire for education, training, and self-improvement on the part of industrial personnel.

It is important to point out here that the attitude of individuals in a given society toward education, training, and self-improvement depends largely on the opportunities for career advancement and/or greater material gain, as well as on their own view of achievement and material gain.[34] If

---

[32] Cf.: R. Lewis and R. Stewart, *The Managers* (New York: New American Library, 1961), pp. 189 ff, 285 ff; The National Development Economic Council, *Growth of the U.K. Economy to 1966* (London: Her Majesty's Stationery Office, 1963), especially p. 31.

[33] See the related discussion in *Public Industrial Management in Asia and the Far East*, pp. 26 ff.

[34] See D. McClelland, *The Achieving Society* (New York: D. Van Nostrand Co., Inc., 1961), especially pp. 412 ff.

there is a rigid class structure which prevents much of the population from getting ahead because of race, religion, caste, sex, wrong family background, and the like, there will be little or no incentive for those actively and acutely discriminated against to improve their skills and abilities. At the other extreme, if advancement in society is desired and is based on qualification to do the job properly, and new opportunities for advancement frequently arise, this would serve as a widespread and patent incentive to improve one's abilities through education and training. The latter situation would clearly be much more conducive of a high degree of managerial effectiveness and productive efficiency than the former.

## EDUCATIONAL MATCH WITH REQUIREMENTS

Basic general education, of the type normally presented in primary schools, has a universal value to persons and countries; however, as a person moves through the educational system, he tends to specialize in various subjects of interest to him or in which he is talented. Hence, we find the typical higher educational institution offering majors in various fields, while secondary schools may present technical curricula or programs intended as preparation for college.

Highly skilled people are needed not generally but specifically by industrial enterprises and society. One desires an electrical engineer, a financial specialist, a marketing researcher, a computer programer, or a manager with a background in particular fields, not a college graduate in general. Or a firm may want to recruit potential machinist apprentices who already have learned some algebra and trigonometry, since this is important in their future work. The usual desire—and the more efficient course of action—is to train a basically qualified candidate to fill his role and future roles in the firm, not to take a completely unsuited individual and make him do as well as possible. In addition, *ideally* all of the industrial skills of a given person will be used in performing his job. That is, there should be a perfect fit between the man's qualifications and the requirements of his job. If he is substantially overqualified there is much waste of talent, and if he is underqualified the job won't get done efficiently and effectively.

In reality, a person who has received a secondary and/or higher education in almost any field may be better suited to the needs of industry than one who has had no education at these levels. In other words, substitutability of nonspecialists and nonprofessionals in specialist and professional jobs would be greater where persons have a good education in almost any field, rather than an inadequate education in total—in the former case at least some trade-offs of knowledge and skill would usually be possible.

For example, other things being equal, a university graduate in law or liberal arts could, in most cases, perform marketing, financial, or general management functions better than someone without any higher education, but probably not as competently as persons formally trained in these fields.

Eventually, of course, he could become a very competent specialist or general manager, through company training, which may entail substantial time, costs, and effort, and/or through self-education. In U.S. industry, many lawyers and liberal arts graduates do in fact turn out to be competent performers in various business fields in which they have not received a formal education—but the fact that they did have a quality higher education in some field was of great benefit. Similarly, technicians with high quality secondary educations in countries like Sweden often successfully serve as good substitutes in various industrial jobs calling for college trained engineers and scientists.

In spite of the possibilities for trade-offs and substitutability of educated people in various jobs, the way in which education meshes with the needs of productive enterprises is a problem of great importance in any country. Unfortunately, this is not recognized or stressed in many societies that are obsessed with the quantitative aspects of education. A leading study on education throughout the world clearly points out this dilemma: "The balance in any program of human resource development may be fully as important as the amount of investment in education. This is a crucial point, and is often neglected by purely quantitative measures of educational investment."[35] Too many lawyers may be produced, and too few engineers, resulting in discrepancies in job opportunities and pay. At worst, such discrepancies can produce a large number of unemployed intellectuals sitting idly around coffee houses plotting revolutions. At best, such problems can be resolved only by firms exerting considerable effort to retrain persons who have in effect wasted much of their time and their country's resources by studying the wrong subjects.

Because of poor educational matches and shortages of highly talented manpower for industry, in many countries sales personnel must perform procurement and legal functions; financial executives must perform industrial relations, personnel, and selling functions; and top level managers must undertake detailed production, engineering, maintenance, and marketing activities, even in medium sized and large enterprises.[36] In numerous countries industrial managers are recruited from the civil service, and the intrusion of civil service procedures, practices, and routines tend to yield substantial inefficiencies when applied to industrial firms. In Sovet industry, numerous engineers and technologists perform complex accounting, financial, marketing, and economic duties—often at the expense of efficiency—while in other countries engineering, production, and other purely technical jobs must often be performed by lawyers and graduates in the arts and humanities.

Other parts of the constraint matrix are also relevant in determining

---

[35] Harbison and Myers, *Education, Manpower and Economic Growth*, p. 185.

[36] Cf.: "Some Problems of Industrial Management Reported by Technical Assistance Experts," especially pp. 53–57; *Management of Industrial Enterprises in Underdeveloped Countries*, pp. 16 ff.: K. Nougaim, *Standard Refrigeration Company* (case material ICH 76205 [Cairo: National Institute of Management Development, 1962]).

how well the educational system will produce needed persons. It may be traditional that lawyers get more money than managers and engineers, even though lawyers are in excess supply and engineers and managers are impossible to find; but tradition may maintain wage differentials long after such differentials have any meaning. While this typically is more true in government service than in private business, examples of such inefficient pricing may be found all over the world.

There is also the problem of static vs. dynamic match. There tend to be time lags between education and application. A person who graduates this year will probably be working for about thirty or forty more years, and it is impossible to predict accurately the changes which may occur in personnel requirements in that time. Skills and knowledge which now seem important may become obsolete, while still newer requirements cannot be foreseen with any certainty. This is as true for an advanced country as for an underdeveloped one in today's rapidly changing world. It is easier to cope with this problem if industrial personnel have broad, high quality educations in their particular fields than if they received highly specialized, narrow training. This is evident from the current Soviet experience.

The problem of statics vs. dynamics can be dealt with by refresher courses, part time education, management development programs, and various other retraining programs for all types of industrial personnel. In many countries—for example, the U.S., Sweden, Japan, Netherlands— there are many facilities and much government support for such programs. To deal with this problem of the dynamics of educational match the U.S. Manpower Development and Training Act of 1962 will provide training for 750,000 workers over a three year period.[37] Sweden in particular has already made great progress in this direction.[38]

Further complications regarding the educational match are added when a country lacks an adequate job announcement system. Vacancies may exist and persist, but few potential applicants may know about them. The problem is further compounded if much of the population is illiterate. Even in the most advanced countries there is a lack of knowledge of jobs and recruits available—although Russia and some of the other Communist countries probably come the closest to perfect knowledge in this connection. There are also inadequacies in career advice, counseling, and exchanges of information between industry and educational institutions regarding human resource development and requirements. In the U.S., and most other advanced nations, employment agency systems are weakest in connection with professional jobs.[39]

---

[37] *Conditions Favourable to Faster Growth*, p. 8; *Manpower Report of the President* (transmitted to Congress March 1963 [Washington, D.C., 1963]).

[38] *Conditions Favourable to Faster Growth, p.* 8. This report condemns Britain's shortcomings in this area.

[39] See the related discussions in: H. David, *op. cit.*, chap. ix; R. Barry and B. Wolf, *Epitaph for Vocational Guidance* (New York: Bureau of Publications, Teachers College, Columbia University, 1962); *Training of National Technical Personnel*, Part I, pp. 10 ff. and Part II, pp. 45 ff.

As a result of the above problems, countries do fail to match the requirements of productive enterprises in varying degrees. The larger the discrepancies in this regard, the greater the constraint on managerial effectiveness and productive efficiency. Some examples and consequences of educational mismatches in various countries were presented earlier. Further elaboration and a few more concrete examples are warranted here in order to drive home the point forcefully.

In many of the newly developing countries which have expended large sums on education, there is still a great shortage of technical training programs. A major problem is the shortage of supporting technicians. Engineers, also frequently in scarce supply, often outweigh technicians in industrial enterprises by a ratio of three to one, while the desirable ratio may be one to three.[40] As a result, talented engineers must frequently perform activities beneath their skills and abilities. This problem is clearly stated in a recent report of the Pakistan Planning Commission.

The talents of engineers have been dissipated by assigning them duties for which they have not been specifically trained. Engineers have been used as technicians at a lower level, thereby creating shortages at higher levels while failing to provide efficient operators at the supervisory stage.[41]

The underemphasis in numerous countries on scientific, engineering, social science, business administration, and management education serves as a significant constraint on managerial effectiveness and productive efficiency. India is a country with a rather poor match in its overall educational system, as noted earlier. For example, in 1959, 3.3 percent of all graduates of Delhi University—a very prestigious university in India—from 1950 and 7.2 percent from 1954 were unemployed. Many honor graduates in arts and science and law, as well as many with M.A. degrees, were working as clerks even eight years after graduating. About 25 percent of all 1950 graduates and 40 percent of 1954 graduates were working as clerks, while numerous enterprises were faced with shortages of qualified technicians, engineers, and administrators of all types.[42] In 1964 the most critical shortages were felt at the level of qualified engineering and technical experts in higher supervisory and plant maintenance jobs.[43]

In Egypt it was estimated that in 1962 there would be a surplus of

---

[40] Harbison and Myers, *Education, Manpower and Economic Growth*, pp. 60 ff., and 86 ff.

[41] *The Second Five Year Plan, 1960–65* (Karachi, November, 1961), p. 370.

[42] V. Rao, *University Education and Employment: A Case Study of Delhi Graduates* (Occasional Papers, No. 3, Institute of Economic Growth, Delhi [Bombay: Asia Publishing House, 1961]).

[43] United Nations, *Trade in Manufacture and Semi-Manufacture—India* Conference on Trade and Development, Geneva, March 23–June 15, 1964, E/Conf.46/76 [New York, 1964]).

4,338 law graduates and of 5,247 graduates in language and arts but a shortage of 1,165 in mechanical engineering, of 348 in civil engineering, of 169 in chemical engineering, and of 1,443 in commercial and business fields.[44] Such shortages in any newly developing country are obviously very critical in terms of managerial effectiveness and productive efficiency.

Even some of the advanced industrial economies experience serious shortages of high talent scientific, engineering, and technical manpower. For example, in recent years British industry has been faced with such shortages. This country has been producing about five times fewer university trained engineers per capita than the U.S., and even fewer if compared to the Soviet Union.[45]

A few years ago, one of the authors visited a large British firm which was trying to recruit a person trained in both economics and psychology to head its newly established marketing research department. In the U.S. such high talent people can usually be found if the firm is willing to pay the price, but in Britain this company could not obtain such a person even after an extensive and lengthy search. A less qualified man was finally selected, and top management is convinced that the job is not being carried out as efficiently or effectively as it could be. A similar problem was experienced by another British corporation that tried in vain to recruit a well qualified man to head its data processing and electronic computer operation. This second company also experienced great difficulties in obtaining the services of competent computer programers and operations research experts.

The U.S.S.R., while strong in the physical sciences, engineering, technology, and mathematics, is weak in economics, marketing, behavioral science, personnel, general management, and various other fields in higher education which have a bearing on industry. As pointed out earlier, even much of their purely technical, engineering, and scientific education is too narrow and overspecialized at their present stage of industrial development.

Even the U.S. is not without educational mismatches and shortages.[46] For example, there appear to be shortages of various kinds of technicians as indicated by very low ratios of subprofessionals to professionals in the research and development departments of many firms. At the same time there are shortages of persons with postgraduate degrees in some scientific, engineering, and mathematical fields. As a result many companies are inclined to hoard such high talent employees, often using them on subpro-

---

[44] I. Abdel-Rahman, *op. cit.*, p. 14.

[45] *The New York Times*, January 5, 1962, p. 32; see also G. Payne, *Britain's Scientific and Technological Manpower* (Stanford, Calif.: Stanford University Press, 1960). Other shortages of high skilled manpower in British industry are discussed in National Development Economic Council, *The Growth of the Economy* (London, 1964).

[46] Harbison and Myers, *Education, Manpower and Economic Growth*, pp. 145, 157, 160–165.

fessional work; this may account in part for the low ratios discussed above.[47] In general, many firms are critical about the extent, content, and quality of vocational and technical secondary education, and have found it necessary to develop their own costly training programs in order to develop qualified skilled workers and technicians of various types.[48] At the same time a fairly substantial portion of the labor force remains unemployed, even though shortages of various types of skilled workers, craftsmen, and technicians persist. Canada is faced with similar educational and manpower problems.[49]

In numerous countries of all types there are serious shortages of qualified managerial personnel at all levels.[50] As discussed earlier, even such advanced economies as Great Britain and the Soviet Union are experiencing growing shortages of high talent managerial resources. In fact there appear to be but few exceptions regarding this problem. The U.S., Belgium, Netherlands, Sweden, Japan and Canada apparently fare best in terms of highly talented managerial manpower.[51]

As an example of a less developed country faced with critical shortages of managerial manpower let us take Brazil. The problem of finding and training high talent executives and supervisory personnel is a serious one for numerous Brazilian firms, as is indicated in the words of a number of Brazilian managers:

Our businessmen have had no training. In many cases, a man gets to be director because he's the only man available, not because he's well qualified or the best man for the job.

We can't get good management trainees. The universities don't produce them. We tried to get good men from the university. They haven't worked out. The people here who are managers have all started as clerks.

We've grown but our people have not. We've grown too fast for our management.

We need to decentralize but we can't. We don't have any people to give the responsibility to.[52]

---

[47] Cf.: G. Henning, *The Technical Institute in American Education* (New York, McGraw-Hill Book Company, 1959), especially pp. 130 ff; The White House, *Meeting Manpower Needs in Science and Technology* (Washington, D.C., December 12, 1962); OECD, *Country Reviews: Scientific Manpower and Higher Education in the U.S.A.*, (Paris, 1963). A close look at the want ads of the newspapers in large cities such as Los Angeles and New York also confirm these points.

[48] See: H. David, *op. cit.*, chaps. vii and viii; J. Conant, *The American High School Today* (New York, McGraw-Hill Book Company, 1959), pp. 127 ff; *New York Times* (Western Edition), November 28, 1962, p. 9.

[49] Cf. Ontario Legislative Assembly, *Report of the Select Committee on Manpower Training* (Toronto, February, 1963).

[50] Cf.: *Training of National Technical Personnel, op. cit.* Parts I, II, and III; Harbison and Myers, 1959, *op. cit.*

[51] Cf. sources cited in Footnote 23 above. Canada has a great advantage in this regard, being a neighbor of the U.S.A.

[52] Oberg, *op. cit.*, pp. 132–133.

The problem of competent managers at all levels in industry is even more serious in other partially developed countries—for example, Pakistan, Iran, Indonesia, and Turkey—since their educational and training systems are even more poorly geared to turning out such human resources.[53] In most African nations the supply of adequately educated managerial personnel is even more meager. In fact, it is usually far less expensive—in terms of productivity and efficiency—to import much more highly paid foreign managers for industry.[54]

Before concluding this chapter, a brief summary analysis of how educational mismatches directly affect industrial enterprise management is in order. Realistic examples of this condition are easy to develop.

Firms unable to find the proper candidates for existing or new positions must usually either make do with less capable persons or leave the positions unfilled. The entire staffing function tends to become much more time consuming and costly given this type of problem. Costly training programs may have to be devised to bring personnel up to requirements, and much time and effort may have to be expended on recruiting adequate personnel. If management does not have adequate knowledge about the types of skills needed for efficient performance, this further compounds the problem.

The organization of the firm may have to be altered to adjust to less qualified personnel than are required for various jobs and activities; typically the adjustment will be in the direction of less specialization and more centralization, as authority tends to concentrate in the hands of the relatively few key persons in the firm. Direction and control will be affected, since persons lacking the necessary qualifications will have to be more closely supervised and controlled than those with proper training and qualifications. The firm may also lack managers who are qualified or have the time to undertake planning activities which are conducive to greater operating efficiency.

It is often difficult to rectify mismatches of education with requirements of productive enterprises. Educational authorities must fight tradition, dynamic change, and the inevitable problem that resources available to education are never sufficient to fully accomplish all tasks at once. Newly developing countries struggle with such issues as whether it would be more desirable to place limited funds in primary education or in selected types of advanced education obviously needed, while advanced countries attempt to forecast work force needs twenty or thirty years in the future and plan accordingly.

---

[53] Cf.: International Committee of Scientific Management, *op. cit.*; *The Development of Manufacturing Industries in Egypt, Israel and Turkey*, pp. 83 ff; C. Skinner, "A Test Case in Turkey," *California Management Review*, spring, 1964, pp. 57 ff; Reksodihardjo, *op. cit.*

[54] P. McLaughlin, "Business and its Managers in Africa," *California Management Review*, summer, 1963, pp. 43–56.

It is clear that any country must orient its educational system to the types of skills needed not only today but also in the future; however, it is still far from clear how this might be accomplished in a given case, although some countries are clearly much more successful than others in this regard. With greater success, managerial effectiveness and productive efficiency are enhanced.

## CONCLUSION

A country is no better, in economic terms, than the skills, education, and training of the persons in it. The educational constraints discussed are closely interrelated with other types of constraints, in the sense that if a country suffers from poor educational standards, the entire productive organization of the country will be sadly deficient. Not only will productive enterprises suffer because of internal deficiencies, but quite probably the economic, political, and legal systems also will be poor. In the general absence of qualified persons, nothing works well. In this connection, the first task of any country interested in making economic gains is to consider what must be done to improve the quality of the persons who will be directly responsible for such gains on the operational level. Without a literate, skilled, education oriented population, all other reforms are doomed to less than mediocre results at best. At worst, literally nothing can be done, since there are no persons capable of doing anything. Productive enterprise remains small, static, and inefficient, if the firms are privately owned. If they are publically owned, they are large, conservative, and even more inefficient, since large scale production of almost anything requires large numbers of capable persons who can keep the organization going.

A familiar picture in the less developed societies in the past decade has been that of the poor country trying to make major gains by establishing industrial enterprises of large size, typically owned by the state. The hope is that such firms will be able to skip a generation of effort in reaching higher production levels. More commonly, the result is near chaos—the plant remains unfinished, much plant capacity is unused, the organization runs out of control, much spoilage results, costs are often so high, and quality is so low as to make the product unsalable even on the domestic market. The difficulty here is in the implicit assumption that well educated and trained persons are really unnecessary for sound and effective management. Until these people are produced, the outlook for the society is dim indeed.

In advanced countries, no society really ever has enough well educated people, even if the educational match with requirements criterion is reasonably met. Advanced industrial societies consume more brainpower, and need it more, than any raw materials or capital; therefore, there is a continual educational revolution in these countries on both the secondary and college levels, and most countries realize that they must do far more about education than they have done in the past, if they expect to progress rapidly in the future.

# Chapter 7

# Environmental Constraints:

# Sociological-Cultural

## INTRODUCTION

E very productive enterprise is part of a more nearly complete and more complex society. No firm can demand and obtain complete allegiance of its managers and workers twenty-four hours a day; much of employees' attitudes, philosophies, abilities, and motivations are developed before they work for the firm, or during their nonworking hours.

Our basic contention here is that the sociological or cultural environment of a given country has a considerable impact on the ways in which industrial enterprises and their personnel carry out their functions. We use the terms *sociological* and *cultural* synonomously unless otherwise noted, although both these terms defy precise definition. We agree with the eminent scholar Clyde Kluckhohn who has pointed out that a universal definition of culture does not exist: "While virtually all students of man agree upon the indispensable importance of culture, no single definition has yet won universal acceptance, and it must be acknowledged that none is completely clear edged."[1]

For operational purposes, sociological-cultural factors or constraints in this study correspond to the *dominant* human attitudes, values, and beliefs

---

[1] "Culture," *Collier's Encyclopedia* (New York: The Crowell-Collier Publishing Co., 1963), VII, 554. For a detailed analysis of the concept of culture see A. Kroeber and C. Kluckhohn, *Culture, a Critical Review of Concepts and Definitions* (Papers of the Peabody Museum of American Archaeology and Ethnology [Cambridge, Mass.: Harvard University, Peabody Museum, 1952]), Vol. XLVII, No. 1. See also the relevant discussion and sources cited in B. Berelson and G. Steiner, *Human Behavior: An Inventory of Scientific Findings* (New York: Harcourt, Brace & World, Inc., 1964), chap. xvi. Much use is made in our present chapter of the scientific findings summarized in the Berelson and Steiner book.

Considerable use has also been made of the following journals in shaping our ideas and analysis of the impact of culture and sociological factors on management and economic progress: *Economic Development and Cultural Change, Sociometry, International Journal of Sociometrics, Behavioral Science, Journal of Social Issues, American Sociological Review, American Journal of Sociology, British Journal of Sociology, Journal of Abnormal Social Psychology,* and *Human Organization,* among others.

in a given society or country and the way they tend to influence the motivation, behavior, and performance of individuals working in productive enterprises. Since there may be various subcultures in a particular country, research in this area can be very complex; and overgeneralization can lead to a false view of industrial reality. With such problems and potential dangers in mind, we shall proceed cautiously with our presentation in this chapter.

In general, the prevailing culture in a given country or region and the industrial enterprise interact constantly, and no enterprise operates in a vacuum. Neither does any culture. The activities of work centered institutions have their impact on the culture as well. The United States, to take one example, is clearly influenced by its large corporations; the type of culture which exists in this country has evolved over many decades and is much different than it might be if productive enterprises were organized and operated in a different manner.

For any point in time the sociological-cultural environment produces various constraints—factors taken as given—for the large majority of enterprises operating in a given country. Widespread and sudden disregard for certain prevailing sociological-cultural factors by firm managements in a particular country may well bring chaos, and probably greater inefficiency than might exist even under relatively unfavorable sociological conditions. Extensive and effective change in the sociological-cultural environment in any society is usually a slow evolutionary process, often taking years or even generations. To be sure, some firms—particularly foreign operated companies—and their managers may not be significantly affected by or behave in accordance with various sociological constraints prevailing in a given culture, but this would tend to be the exception rather than the rule at any point in time.

The impact of certain aspects of the sociological-cultural environment on American management is clearly reflected in the report of sixty British businessmen who visited the United States for nine months: "If there is one secret above all of the American achievements in productivity, then it is to be found in the attitude of American management." The Britishers were impressed with an attitude that, "seems to engender an aggressive management which believes that methodological planning, energetic training, and enthusiastic work can solve any problem in business . . ." The visitors attribute this viewpoint to four sociological-cultural factors:

(1) The legacy of the frontier; a spirit that has fostered a sense of opportunity pervading American industrial and community life.

(2) Faith in business and the individual; a faith reflected in the high esteem with which the businessman is regarded in the American national community.

(3) Belief in change; a belief whereby a successful experiment is not allowed to crystallize into accepted custom, whereas an unsuccessful experiment is accepted as an occupational risk and is set against the experience that has been gained.

(4) The ideal of competition; an ideal that leads "even those companies which are not operating in a highly competitive market to run their enterprises as though they were . . . (American managers) know that their firms must maintain their competitive position if they are to provide their people with a continuing career." [2]

The above statements in effect reflect part of the American management philosophy which, in turn, is shaped by various sociological-cultural attitudes and values prevailing in the country as a whole. It is true that American industrial managers adhere and respond to this philosophy in varying degrees; some are not even constrained in their behaviors by this philosophy. In the large majority of cases, however, the philosophies, attitudes, and actions of firm managements, at a given point in time, are undoubtedly conditioned in large part by the general sociological-cultural environment of the country. In fact, close examination of several countries strongly suggests that the prevailing sociological-cultural environment has a significant bearing on the philosophies, attitudes, and behaviors of probably the large majority of firms and their managements.

It is now being realized by a growing number of management theorists and practitioners that many of the principles, techniques, and practices of management which prove quite effective in one culture cannot always be transplanted effectively in another culture. For example, a comprehensive study dealing with management in sixty countries had this to say about management in two of these countries, Japan and India:

To some management thinkers in Europe and the U.S.A., the overwhelming need of Japanese managers is for management principles and knowledge applicable to Oriental cultural tradition. There are few who would today seek major changes in Japanese culture to adapt the culture to known management principles. . . . In industrial relations, organization structure, delegation, and definitions of authority, many Japanese feel an impending need of guidance. The labor movement and growing competition appear to be the chief factors inciting recognition of these needs. From the Western industrialized nations such guidance is sought, but the Westerners themselves, having developed knowhow suitable to Western organizations, are able only to teach them Western management principles. According to some Japanese managers, these principles are effective when applied in Japanese organizations but only to the extent that they can be applied without running counter to basic tradition. A U.S. trained Japanese management consultant estimates that only about two-thirds of American organization principles are safely applicable to Japanese organizations, but that 90% of American and European industrial management methods can be applied without major modification in Japanese factories.

As in most countries where the cultural environment differs sharply from those in which management principles have been most intensely developed, research is needed to determine how to apply known management principles most

---

[2] From *Advanced Management*, Vol. XX, No. 10, p. 30, as cited in W. Newman and C. Summer, *The Process of Management* (Englewood Cliffs, N.J.: Prentice-Hall, Inc., 1961), p. 5. See also, O. Nowotny, "American vs. European Management Philosophy," *Harvard Business Review*, March-April, 1964, pp. 101–108.

effectively in India, or to develop management principles suitable to India's cultural environment.[3]

A major problem here is that sociological-cultural constraints which apparently have a significant bearing on managerial performance are difficult to measure and quantify. While the variables to be discussed in this chapter are clearly relevant, it is even difficult at times to determine precisely how they affect the operations of industrial enterprises. This is always a problem when one wishes to deal with human attitudes and values. It is often hard to distinguish popular misconceptions and myths from the realities of the situation.

More accurate measurements of cause and effect relationships can generally be determined by scientifically studying what people do and why they do it, rather than what they say; this generally entails costly and time consuming research if accurate results are to be forthcoming. There has not been a large number of scientific studies of this type, and many more empirical and experimental studies are needed before we can explain and predict managerial performance in terms of sociological constrains with a high degree of accuracy and confidence; therefore our present analysis is suggestive rather than conclusive, although we hope that, at least, a number of significant, operational hypotheses that warrant further testing will result from our efforts.

Although we may be on somewhat shaky ground in this chapter, we are convinced that the sociological-cultural constraints to be considered do have a significant bearing on managerial performance and enterprise operations. The staffing, direction, and organization functions of management are clearly affected, since various sociological factors determine in large part the attitudes, types and quality of people who work for and manage industrial enterprises, the relationships between people in enterprises, their motivation, status and performance, and so on. Certain sociological variables also clearly have an impact on planning and control, as well as on the various productive functions of enterprises such as research development, production, marketing, and finance. In total, the sociological constraints have a substantial impact on managerial effectiveness and productive efficiency, even though the extent of this impact cannot be precisely measured in a given instance.

## VIEW OF INDUSTRIAL MANAGERS AND MANAGEMENT

Every society has its heroes and high prestige careers. Some professions and occupations are always considered better than others and are held up to the young as examples of what they might become if they try hard to succeed. Usually, though not always, such occupations are better rewarded

---

[3] *International Committee of Scientific Management* (Project Reports on Management Development in Japan and India [Sydney, Australia, 1960]).

economically than other, less esteemed jobs. Thus in the United States, such occupations as Supreme Court justice, medical doctor, and, more recently, professor and physical scientist rank among the highest in terms of prestige, while jobs such as garbageman, bootblack, busboy, and the like are regarded as extremely low prestige occupations. There are some scientific studies available which indicate the preference and prestige ranking of various occupations in different countries.[4] The educational system, as well as popular folklore in a particular country, also reflects this attitude.

The place of business managers in the prestige hierarchy of a particular country is quite relevant in determining managerial effectiveness and the efficiency of productive enterprises. Closely connected to this point is the way in which alternative elite groups are viewed in the culture. If traditional elite occupations of the central government bureaucracy, the clergy, the military, and law are regarded so highly and rewarded so well as to drain off the great majority of the talented and well educated persons from management, business enterprise will suffer accordingly. The impact of such status rankings will be reflected not only in the recruiting of competent people for management and industrial firms but also in the way in which managers see themselves and in their influence in the society.

A recent authoritative report on the world social situation has this to say about the status of various occupations in numerous countries:

A common psychological obstacle to economic achievement is the fact that much higher status tends to be associated with land ownership or government position or professional or intellectual activity than is enjoyed by the business-man, engineer, mechanic, agronomist, or some other person concerned directly with material production.[5]

The importance of prestige rating and general attitude toward industrial managers is not restricted to capitalist countries. Communist nations also have managers in productive enterprises; and if these jobs are highly regarded, industry will gain from being able to recruit the always scarce,

---

[4] Cf.: the findings and other studies cited in A. Inkeles and P. Rossi, "National Comparisons of Occupational Prestige," *American Journal of Sociology*, LXI (January, 1956) 329–339; Rossi and Inkeles, "Multidimensional Ratings of Occupations," *Sociometry*, September, 1957, pp. 241 ff; Berelson and Steiner, *op. cit.*, chap. xi, contains an excellent summary of major findings and sources in this area of research. Another important recent study dealing with occupational prestige is R. Hodge, P. Siegel, and P. Rossi, "Occupational Prestige in the United States," *The American Journal of Sociology*, Vol. LXX, No. 3, November, 1964, pp. 286–302.

See also the findings and studies presented in: D. McClelland, *The Achieving Society* (New York: D. Van Nostrand Co., Inc., 1961), pp. 239–257; R. Avery, *Orientations Toward Careers in Business* (unpublished doctoral dissertation, Cambridge, Mass., Harvard University, 1959); G. Litwin, *Achievement Motivation, Social Class, and the Slope of Occupational Preferences in the United States and Japan* (mimeographed paper, Department of Social Relations, Harvard University, 1959).

[5] UNESCO, *Report on the World Social Situation* (Paris, March 9, 1961), p. 79; see also E. Shils, "The Intellectuals in the Political Development of the New States," *World Politics*, April, 1960, pp. 336 ff.

truly competent men and women. In the Communist countries the Communist party and the central government play the key, conscious role in determining the attitude, preferability, and prestige ranking regarding various careers and occupations through their control over education, ideaology, and remuneration and other rewards. In the Soviet Union and most other Marxist states, managerial and various other industrial jobs are viewed favorably and are filled by much of the high talent manpower of the country.

Capitalist states have a two-fold problem. On the one hand, there is a clear need for professional management types, men who are trained as managers for medium sized and large scale enterprises. On the other hand, there may be need for the more purely entrepreneurial types, men who are willing and able to take substantial risks in business, particularly in terms of establishing new types of enterprises. Social approval may not regard the two types as similar.

A society may admire the poised professional and regard with contempt the "wheeler dealer" or owner-manager. For example, in various Latin American countries, such as Chile, the long established large family firms are respected, but new entrepreneurs tend to be frowned upon and regarded as social upstarts, particularly by the old landed and commercial aristocracy. Attitudes of this sort have implications for the development of new and growing firms. At times the general attitudes may be reversed, and the dynamic entrepreneurs may be the admired group. In Germany, for example, industrial managers do not even consider themselves as professionals, while the owner-manager or top manager of a large firm is considered an entrepreneur; and he tends to be highly regarded by society at large. In the United States, both the professional manager and the entrepreneur are recognized for their contributions to society, and they tend to be viewed favorably. In general, society's view toward managers and entrepreneurs tends to have a significant effect on the types and quality of firms and managements a country has.

There may be significant differences in the status of managers of public enterprise as compared to private enterprise, and there also may be differences among different branches of industry in a particular country; however, at the risk of overgeneralizing, we shall focus, for the most part, on all industrial managers as a single class in a particular society. Our major concern is with higher level and middle managers, but where it is appropriate we shall discuss lower level managers as well.

It does not necessarily follow that industrial managers and management will be viewed more favorably in more advanced as compared to less developed countries, although this may be true in the majority of cases. Economic progress can be partially a result of a favorable view of managers and management, as well as a cause of such a view. For example, industrial managers were viewed favorably in Japan even before that country's great leap forward in industrial activity. In the Soviet Union, the view toward management and other industrial careers probably increased in status somewhat more rapidly than the economy developed. Saudi Arabia, a substantially underdeveloped country, tends to view all authoritarian figures favorably and with respect, including industrial managers. On the other hand, in France and Great Britain, as compared to the United States, Japan or the Soviet Union, a less favorable view of industrial managers and business careers has probably been a barrier to managerial effectiveness and economic progress, in spite of these countries' advanced stages of industrialism.

With a vast amount of scientific research, every country could perhaps be accurately ranked on a continuum indicating the degree of favorability or unfavorability of each society's view of industrial managers and management. At one extreme, managers may be seen as highly respected professionals, capable of performing very worthy feats that enrich the culture and the economy. At the opposite pole, they may be seen as cynical exploiters of humanity, concerned only with a short run, narrow view of profits and crass business activities.

The more favorably a particular society views industrial managers and management, the less likely it is that the profession will lack capable recruits; and in a favorably inclined society it would also be easier to attract competent persons to work under and with the managers of industrial enterprises. The on-going managerial task would obviously be made more effective and easier by the availability of capable individuals who are eager to spend their careers as productive enterprise managers, or as persons working for and with them. In an environment where managers are respected and highly regarded, there would tend to be greater cooperation and trust, and less conflict, between managers and employees, and also less unproductive time and greater overall efficiency. Moreover, stringent direction and control could be replaced by greater reliance on self-control and individual initiative. If desired, authority could more readily be decentralized in order to achieve greater efficiency and growth; however, decentralization depends not only on a favorable view of managers but also on various other cultural factors such as the view of authority and subordinates, as will be discussed later.

With a high prestige rating for managers and management, it is more likely that educational institutions such as schools of business and industrial administration would also be highly regarded, and one can expect that formal training for managerial and business careers would be of high caliber, making staffing still easier and more efficient. Many highly capable individuals in each generation would be drawn into this sphere of activity.

At the other extreme, the closer the society comes to viewing industrial managers as only slightly better than mad dogs or vicious exploiters—justly or unjustly—the more likely the profession and the overall staffing function would suffer greatly. So, for that matter, would the leadership effectiveness of managers and productivity. The more unfavorable this view, the more closely subordinates would have to be supervised and controlled, since it is likely that there would be considerable distrust, antagonism, and conflict between managers and workers. Hence, there would also tend to be a very high degree of centralization, little creative planning or innovation, relatively small firms, poor interorganizational communication, considerable unproductive time, and a rather destructive informal organization, even where employees are fairly competent and reasonably well educated.

Negative social attitudes regarding managers are likely to interact with other types of constraints that industrial enterprises face. A country which has small regard for management and business activity is not likely to have a government, or labor organizations, or potential investors who are sympathetic to business problems. Hence, constraints such as tax law, interorganizational cooperation, business codes, labor legislation, foreign policy, monetary and fiscal policy, availability of capital, and similar factors will reflect prevailing attitudes.

There is probably no country in the world today where managers are truly regarded as heroes; however, there are countries where managers have considerable respect and status—particularly higher level managers—and where managerial and business careers are chosen by a substantial proportion of highly talented and competent persons. We have already commented on the Soviet Union in this regard. In Japanese industry, where paternalistic management is dominant and enterprises tend to operate in a family type environment, society tends to view Japanese managers with considerable trust, gratitude, and confidence.

An Anglo-American productivity team report on management reflects the high regard for American managers, although the following statement may be somewhat strong and exaggerated:

To be a high industrial executive in America is considered not only eminently respectable, but also socially desirable. It is a prevailing opinion that business attracts the best talents from educational institutions, whereas in Britain there is a strong tendency for the best students to find their way into the civil service and traditional professions.[6]

It is true that in several western European countries, such as Britain, France, Spain, and Italy, there is still much skepticism about management as a profession, and managerial careers are probably not as high on the preferability or prestige scale as in the United States. Government service,[7]

---

[6] R. Lewis and R. Stewart, *The Managers* (New York: New American Library, 1961), p. 65.

[7] Some of the sources dealing with attitude toward managers and management in various western European countries are: Lewis and Stewart, *op. cit.*; D. Granick, *The European Executive* (New York: Doubleday & Company, Inc., 1962); F. Harbison and C. Myers, *Management in the Industrial World* (New York: McGraw-Hill Book Company, 1959), particularly chaps. xi, xii, and xvi; National Economic Development Council, *Conditions Favorable to Faster Growth* (London: Her Majesty's Stationery Office, 1963), pp. 4 ff.; United Nations, *Questionnaire on Industrial Planning and*

law, the clergy, medicine, and other traditional elite occupations still rate substantially higher than industrial management; however, higher income, widespread education, and a rapidly growing middle class has attracted an increasing number of competent young people into managerial and business careers. Several European countries have large landed estates once owned by the traditional elite groups but now serving as residences for the previously downgraded managerial class. This, too, tends to raise the status and desirability of managerial careers. In some countries of western Europe—notably Belgium, the Netherlands, Sweden, and West Germany —industrial management is generally viewed as a very favorable and respected career.

There are still countries in Africa, Asia and Latin America where enterprise owners and managers are seen as a corrupt, contemptible group, whose main activities consist of scheming and the systematic exploitation of people. Marxist propaganda often assists in creating this image, as do the activities of many of the businessmen. In such an environment it is extremely difficult for firms to recruit reasonably competent managers and workers; as a result they tend to remain small, static, inefficient, and under rigid family control. The capable young persons who do exist are attracted to the law, the military, the government bureaucracy, and various other high prestige occupations. While these and other occupations also need capable men in order to function properly, their virtual monopolization of talent in various countries can only have a detrimental effect on productive enterprises generally. There is a vicious circle working here which may tend to keep business at the bottom indefinitely, in both efficiency and status. Because business is despised, few capable, moral persons are attracted to business careers, which in turn leads to unfortunate results in business, which again leads to failure to attract capable people. A society can—and in many cases does—stagnate in this manner for generations, or even centuries in some extreme cases.

Even in many newly developing countries that are striving for industrial expansion and economic progress, the high prestige occupations continue to be law, medicine, landowning, and the government, while the status of managers and other types of industrial personnel continue to be downgraded.[8] This situation was discussed briefly in the chapter on educa-

---

*Development* (E/c.5/54 [New York, March, 1963]), responses of Sweden and the Netherlands. The statements in the present study are also based on opinions derived from discussions and interviews with many European executives, managers of U.S. international companies with subsidiaries in Europe, and European graduate students studying in the U.S.

[8] Cf. Harbison and Myers, *Education, Manpower and Economic Growth* (New York: McGraw-Hill Book Company, 1964), pp. 92 ff; R. Naschese, (a Brazilian industrialist), "Ideology and Formation of the Manager for Private Industry," *Proceedings of the International Management Congress* (CIOS), September 16–20, 1963, New York: McGraw-Hill Book Company, 1964), pp. 92 ff; R. Naschese (a Brazilian 1963), pp. 314–315.

tion (Chapter 6).[9] Hence, in Nigeria, Ghana, Indonesia, Pakistan, and various other countries, industrial firms continue to be plagued by critical shortages of competent managers and staffs in spite of substantial expansions of their educational systems in recent years. Overcentralization, overburdened spans of control, extremely close supervision and control, lack of trust and cooperation between workers and managers, and general inefficiency are common features of probably the large majority of industrial enterprises in such countries.[10]

In a number of the partially developed and semiadvanced nations—for example, India, Mexico, and particularly Egypt—management is gradually being regarded as a favorable occupation.[11] In Egypt, the resurgent wave of Arab nationalism and the desire for rapid economic progress has placed increasing social value on efficient management. Managers in the rapidly growing public enterprise sector are now being viewed as professionals with considerable status, and they are drawn in growing numbers from the military, the civil service, and the universities. At the same time, the role of the small, privately owned firm is rapidly diminishing in importance.

While the view toward industrial managers in India is somewhat more favorable than in the past, only the managers of large public enterprises and a few large privately owned progressive firms are highly respected. The managements of most of the privately owned and family controlled firms still tend to be regarded with considerable distrust. One authoritative source sums up the situation in India's private sector thusly:

Widespread criticism and suspicion of the activities of businessmen have been a striking feature of public debate on economic affairs in India since 1947. It has almost been a matter of habit with literate Indians to blame the commercial classes and the financial interests for the country's economic backwardness.[12]

In many countries, including India, only higher level executives are regarded as managers. Lower level supervisors, and particularly foremen, are not viewed as part of the managerial hierarchy; and they are given little

---

[9] See the sources cited in footnotes 10, 11, 12, 42, 53 and 54 of chapter 6.

[10] Much evidence to this effect can be found in the sources referred to in Footnote 9 above. See also A. Raza, "Management Ideologies and Resources in Pakistan," *Journal of Industrial Relations*, March, 1965; S. Reksodihardjo, *Skills Investment in a Developing Country* (unpublished doctoral dissertation, University of California, Los Angeles, 1964), especially chap. vii; United Nations, *Management of Industrial Enterprises in Underdeveloped Countries* (New York, 1958); "Some Problems of Industrial Management Reported by Technical Assistance Experts," *Industrialization and Productivity*, No. 2, 1959, pp. 53 ff.

[11] See Harbison and Myers, *Education, Manpower and Economic Growth*, chaps. vii, viii. This statement is also based on information obtained from recent personal interviews and discussions with business executives, educators, and graduate students from these countries.

[12] R. Bhambri, "Myth and Reality About Private Enterprise in India," *World Politics*, January, 1960, p. 186.

status or authority. Consequently, even where higher level executives are regarded favorably, the lower level managerial and supervisory positions tend to rate low on the occupational preference scale. This situation is most pervasive in underdeveloped and newly developing countries, but even in advanced nations the role of labor unions has tended to decrease the status and authority of lower level production supervisors and foremen. It appears that front line supervisors and foremen may be more highly regarded in Soviet industry than in most other countries.[13]

Before concluding this section, we should emphasize again that a given society's general view toward industrial managers and management may be determined not only by various environmental factors over which managers have little or no control but also by the actions and attitudes of industrial managers themselves. In many, if not most, countries, there are dominant managerial philosophies or ideologies which have a significant bearing on how the majority of managers behave in running their enterprises and on how they view the managerial job. For example, one authority on Turkish industrial management has this to say about the managerial job in that country; he points out that his statement is also applicable to other underdeveloped countries:

Local national managers, even those with a "good education and experience" tend to think that managers do no more than keep people happy and under control, sign papers, and make compromises. Their concept of management is as underdeveloped as is their economy. They do not perceive the dynamic nature of management responsibility or the critical factor of time . . .[14]

It is true that the dominant managerial philosophy in a given country is in large part the product of the external environment, but the environment need not indefinitely serve as a rigid straitjacket which prevents a break from traditional philosophy. Industrial managers do not necessarily have to wait for extreme social pressures, collective action, or government intervention to cause changes in their basic philosophy; they can often independently change certain aspects of their philosophy, which, in turn, may gradually lead to favorable changes in the environment. In a country where industrial managers and management are not viewed favorably, a few progressive firms might adopt a new philosophy which, if successful, other

---

[13] This is the conviction of one of the authors who had the opportunity to interview and observe many industrial managers of all types and at all levels who are employed in Soviet enterprises. During research trips to the U.S.S.R. in 1960 and 1961, many Soviet economists, planners, government officials, educators, and Communist party and trade union officials were also interviewed by this author. See B. Richman, *Soviet Management: With Significant American Comparisons* (Englewood Cliffs, N.J.: Prentice-Hall, Inc., 1965), App. I. See also the data on foremen in Soviet industry in Rossi and Inkeles, "Multidimensional Ratings of Occupations."

[14] C. Skinner, "A Test Case in Turkey," *California Management Review*, spring, 1964, pp. 64–65.

firms will gradually follow; and this could eventually lead to a higher regard for the management profession in general.

Unfortunately, in many countries most industrial managers do tend to pursue a highly egocentric philosophy which breeds considerable antagonism and distrust. They emphasize quick turnover on capital and high profit margins on limited output. They may operate and even grow rich in a sellers' market, under government patronage and protection, and/or in an environment of cheap surplus labor, while their firms remain static and highly inefficient. Such managers tend to have little interest in economic progress and no conception of social responsibility. If competition, government control, and other forms of countervailing power are not very effective, they continue to exploit labor, take advantage of customers, and so on.

A major constraint connected with changing a dominant managerial philosophy is education; but once a few responsible, progressive enterprise managements acquire knowledge about, and implement, a different, potentially better long range philosophy, the path is open for others to follow, and the chances of achieving a more favorable view toward industrial managers are enhanced. In general, where the majority of industrial managers in a particular country tend to act in accordance with the values and goals of society at large, they are much more likely to be favorably regarded. Moreover, if industrial managers tend to view management as a responsible professional activity with its own body of theory and criteria for objectively judging managerial competence, and if they can convince society that management is a worthy profession, this will promote a more favorable view toward industrial managers and management. Unfortunately, in many countries the personal goals and material gain of industrial managers are not conducive to, but are in conflict with, economic progress, social responsibility, fair treatment, and national achievement and prestige. In many countries the managers themselves do not view management as a profession; in fact, the dominant view of society and of managers in probably the large majority of countries is still that management requires no special qualifications or skills, only authority and power, and that managerial jobs need not be filled on the basis of personal ability or objective criteria.

Progress and widespread action along the lines indicated above are generally a long range matter. Distrust of industrial managers and skepticism about management as a worthy profession often linger on, even long after a more positive managerial philosophy emerges on a fairly widespread basis. Moreover, a basic and widely adopted change in a dominant managerial philosophy often takes many years. Nevertheless, through education and the dissemination of knowledge, further progress along these lines is gradually being made in many parts of the world—not only in less developed countries such as Mexico, India, and Egypt but even in some advanced countries like Great Britain. In the short run, however, the dominant managerial philosophy and society's view of industrial managers and management do serve as constraints upon managerial performance in probably the large majority of cases.

## VIEW OF AUTHORITY AND SUBORDINATES

We are interested here in the dominant views of authority and subordinates in different societies and in the impact of such views on managerial behavior and effectiveness. Our present analysis not only involves sociological and cultural factors but is also interconnected with various political, legal, and economic factors, including certain constraints considered elsewhere in this study; therefore, some repetition is unavoidable. We feel, however, that the topic of authority and relations with subordinates is important enough to warrant a separate section, and this section fits best in our sociological chapter since the subject matter is primarily concerned with individual and group interaction.

Much of our discussion in this section relates closely to the previous section, since both deal with dominant managerial philosophies and practices. Moreover, the ways in which managers exercise their authority and deal with subordinates tend to have a significant bearing on the way in which society at large views industrial managers and management.

In general, the sociological-cultural-institutional environment tends to form dominant views of authority and subordinates in a given society. In turn, such dominant views tend to result in dominant patterns of managerial authority and superior-subordinate relationships which are reflected in the behavior of industrial managers. In most countries some or many exceptions could probably be found to the dominant views and to customary managerial behavior patterns, because of differences in the convictions and personalities of individual managers; but here again we are interested in the representative majority of cases rather than the substantially deviant ones. It does appear, however, that in some countries such dominant views and behavior patterns are much more "culture bound" than in others. In such cases the environment serves as a much more potent and pervasive constraint upon industrial enterprise managements in their exertion of authority and in their relations with subordinates, and it would generally be much more difficult and risky to go against tradition.

In Japan, for instance, managerial effectiveness and productive efficiency may suffer greatly if the enterprise deviates substantially and abruptly from the traditional Japanese practice of paternalistic management. Similarly, it is likely to be much more costly, time consuming, and risky to introduce substantially greater participative management effectively in industry in Peru, Saudi Arabia, India, or even Germany, as compared to the U.S., Canada, Great Britain, Russia, or Yugoslavia. In fact, empirical research studies based on questionnaire surveys conducted in electric utility companies in Peru and the United States strongly suggest that authoritarian management and close supervision tend to be more acceptable and effective in Peru, as compared to the U.S.[15] The Peruvian employees (both white collar and blue collar) also tend to favor emphasis on short term productivity more than their American counterparts, and participative management is generally viewed less favorably by the Peruvians. If participative management were to be applied quite extensively in a fairly short period of time in a firm in Peru it is likely that productivity would decline and employees would tend to lose respect for their superiors.

The discussion and analysis which follows has a number of dimensions.[16] We shall examine the alternative ways that authority may be viewed in society, and the effect of these views on dominant authority patterns within the industrial managerial hierarchy by using concepts which can be represented on a continuum. The major environmental conditions which appear to be responsible for each dominant view of authority will also be considered briefly. Our analysis of authority pertains directly to the organizational function of management and the delegation of authority. We shall follow the same procedure with regard to dominant views toward subordinates and resulting dominant patterns of superior-subordinate relationships. Here we are concerned with both workers and subordinate managers, and our analysis pertains to the directional and supervisory function of management. The dominant philosophies and practices regarding authority and subordinates, as well as the underlying environmental conditions in a given society, tend to have much in common, as will be seen shortly.

In our theoretical discussion we shall deal only with "ideal" types which represent the extreme points on each continuum. If enough research were to be conducted, each country could perhaps be ranked with reasonable accuracy on the various continua in terms of its dominant views and resulting behavior patterns of managerial authority and superior-subordinate relationships.

In this section we shall also deal briefly with the restraints on managerial authority with regard to employee welfare matters, and for the sake of convenience this topic will be considered when we discuss attitude toward subordinates. An analysis of the possible effects that the various dominant

---

[15] W. Whyte, and L. Williams, "Supervisory Leadership—An International Comparison," *Proceedings of the International Management Congress*, 1963, pp. 481–488.

[16] The theoretical concepts to be presented here are based upon a synthesis of data and ideas derived from many of the sources cited throughout this section which pertain to different countries and cultures, as well as our own research and firsthand observations in several diverse countries. A few of the written sources which we have found to be most useful and helpful warrant citation at this point: Harbison and Myers, *Management in the Industrial World*; M. Haire, E. Ghiselli, and L. Porter, "An International Study of Management Attitudes and Democratic Leadership," *Proceedings of the International Management Congress*, 1963, pp. 101 ff; this study is based on data collected by means of a questionnaire administered to some 3,000 managers in fourteen different countries throughout the world. The samples of managers encompassed a wide range of business and industrial firms in these countries, and at least 200 managers were interviewed in each country; R. Bendix, *Work and Authority in Industry; Ideologies of Management in the Course of Industrialization* (New York: John Wiley & Sons, Inc., 1959).

patterns of managerial authority and superior-subordinate relationships can have on managerial effectiveness will also be undertaken. Finally, some country examples will be presented for illustrative purposes.

Our theoretical schema of analysis can best be summarized as follows:

A. Critical environmental conditions
B. Dominant views toward authority and subordinates
C. Dominant patterns of managerial authority and superior-subordinate relationships as reflected by managerial behavior
D. Impact on managerial effectiveness

## Relationships among Attitudes toward Authority, the Environment, and Managerial Behavior

We shall consider view toward authority by examining the views that would prevail at each end of a hypothetical continuum. The resulting dominant behavior pattern with regard to authority within the industrial managerial hierarchy in each case would also represent the extremes of a continuum.

*View I.* Authority is viewed as an absolute natural right of management or other types of formal leaders. Top level managers in particular feel that they are born to manage and rule others and that their authority is based on some type of natural law and/or charismatic endowment, rather than on a clearly defined role in the organization or specific skills and knowledge.

The effect of this view of authority in terms of managerial behavior would typically be a high degree of centralization and little delegation of authority within industrial enterprises. This view tends to be dominant to the extent that the following environmental conditions exist:

1. Where the economy is characterized by a preponderance of privately owned enterprises, typically operated under a system of patrimonial management and rigid family control. While industrial firms in such an environment tend to be quite small, medium sized and even some large firms may be found under this type of system.
2. Where management is not viewed as a profession based at least in part on theoretical concepts and principles, and where it is believed that managerial competence cannot be evaluated on the basis of objective criteria.
3. Where subordinates tend to respect and obey a strong domineering type of formal leader.
4. Where there is a considerable feeling of dependency on top management by subordinate managers and employees.

*View II* The extent and degree of authority that a given manager should possess should and can be based on objective criteria and careful evaluation of the requirements of the managerial job in question and the qualifications of the incumbent or candidate. This view would tend to be accompanied by a belief that delegation of authority is conducive to industrial growth, effective management development, and productive efficiency.

The effect of this view of authority upon managerial behavior would be a tendency toward decentralization and delegation of authority. This view would tend to be dominant to the degree that the following environmental conditions exist:

1. Where the economy is characterized by a substantial number of large and/or rapidly growing enterprises in which ownership and control are generally separated.
2. Where management is regarded as a profession having an operational, theoretical underpinning.
3. Where there is a sizable professional managerial class consisting of well educated and trained personnel throughout the industrial managerial hierarchy and where subordinate managers are trusted by top management.
4. Where social values place considerable emphasis on individual freedom, initiative, and achievement.

Most Communist countries represent special cases, since there is a high degree of centralization in their industrial systems even though some of the environmental conditions conducive to decentralization are present to a high degree. More will be said about this situation later in this section.

In general, each country could theoretically be ranked along a continuum with regard to the prevailing dominant pattern of managerial authority as reflected by relative degrees of centralization or decentralization in industry. It is true that there may be considerable variation regarding degrees of centralization and decentralization among various industrial enterprises within a particular country; however, the dominant pattern within a given country, as it relates to the relative rankings among different countries, could be discerned by carefully analyzing samples of representative, comparable enterprises in different branches of industry for the various countries under study. Depending on the specific countries chosen for such an analysis, there could be very significant or negligible differences in the relative rankings that evolve. It is unlikely that any country would fall at either extreme of the centralization-decentralization continuum.

### Relationships among Views of Subordinates, the Environment, and Managerial Behavior

*View A.* Subordinates are expected to be unquestioningly obedient and totally subservient in executing the orders and instructions issued by their superiors.

The effect of this view of subordinates would be a high degree of autocratic direction and authoritarian management in superior-subordinate dealings. Here, managers would tend to issue orders and make decisions without any concern for the wishes or opinions of subordinates. At the ultimate extreme, we would have dictatorial management under a system of forced labor or concentration camps, but it is not likely that such a system would be very durable in time.

This view would tend to be dominant to the extent that the following environmental conditions exist:

1. Where management views its authority as a natural right.
2. Where there is little or no concern for individual dignity, freedom, or initiative, particularly where this is accompanied by an environment of cheap surplus labor.
3. Where employees are highly dependent on the enterprise and its management because top management is the major unilateral supplier of welfare benefits which are urgently needed.
4. Where subordinates are inclined to prefer, respect and obey a strong, domineering leader.
5. Where the working population is in large part poorly educated and trained.
6. Where there is little or no countervailing power over personnel matters exerted by the government and/or labor organizations.

*View B.* All subordinates should have a direct voice in all decisions that significantly affect them and their working lives.

The effect of this view of subordinates would be a high degree of participative (democratic) management and consultative direction in superior-subordinate dealings. Here, the advice, opinions, and suggestions of subordinates—whether they be managers or workers—would be sought before any final decision was made that significantly affects them; however, the superior manager would not necessarily relinquish his authority or decision making powers. This view would tend to be dominant to the extent that the following environmental conditions are present:

1. Where the society places high value through its educational system, religious ethics, and other cultural channels on individual dignity and initiative and on the freedom of the individual to have a voice through direct democratic means in determining his own present or future.
2. Where there is a widespread conviction that people respond best when they can participate in decisions that directly affect them and their work and that they have something worthwhile to contribute. This would typically be accompanied by a belief that people are not basically lazy, need not be pushed in their work, and don't respond only to money or penalties.
3. Where personnel become increasingly less dependent on a particular enterprise because of greater opportunities through mobility, growing labor shortages, and/or rising living standards.

4. Where there is little emphasis on status and class distinctions.
5. Where much of the labor force is fairly well educated and trained and possesses a high level of skill in their respective jobs.

Here again, various Communist countries (and Yugoslavia) represent a special case. Widespread participative management and consultative direction is a matter of state policy and decree rather than choice, although this policy is based largely on some of the above environmental conditions. More will be said about this situation later.

In general, authoritarian management in conjunction with autocratic direction tends to go hand in hand with centralization of authority, since there are several similar underlying environmental conditions in both cases. For the same reason participative management and consultative direction are more likely to be found where there is also a tendency to decentralize authority; however, it is possible to have a high degree of centralization with participative management and consultative direction or, conversely, decentralization of authority regarding various types of decisions under a system of basically authoritarian management and autocratic direction.

Here again each country could theoretically be ranked along a continuum in terms of its dominant pattern of superior-subordinate relationships as reflected by degree of autocratic or consultative direction. It is unlikely that any present day country would fall at either extreme of the continuum.

Two other aspects of superior-subordinate relationships and authority which can also be represented by continua are worth discussing briefly in this section. They shall be referred to as views X and Y. Here we need only deal with one end of each continuum, since the conditions conducive to the opposite ends are implicit in our discussion.

**View X.** It is natural, proper and desirable for enterprise management independently to assume responsibility for the overall welfare of employees.

The effect of this view is a high degree of paternalism in industry. This view tends to be dominant to the extent that the following environmental conditions exist:

1. When the transition to industrialization in a particular society does not involve a major break from feudalistic tradition
2. Where enterprise management is a major supplier of a wide range of welfare benefits, services and facilities either by necessity and default—as where the government, labor unions, or society at large does not perform this function adequately—or by choice—in cases where employees prefer this type of arrangement and favor being dependent on management because of cultural attitudes and/or tradition

Since a high degree of paternalistic management typically involves a father-son or master-servant relationship, and hence considerable dependence on the part of subordinates, it is generally conductive to a high degree of centralization, authoritarian management, and autocratic direction; however, it is possible to have elements of participative management and consultative direction under certain conditions.

*View Y.* Managerial authority regarding all important personnel welfare matters such as dismissals, promotions, pay scales, safety and working conditions, and so on should be shared and, if deemed necessary, restrained by representatives of labor and the government.

The effect of this view is typically a high degree of countervailing power over management's authority and prerogatives as a rule maker in employee welfare issues and as an enforcer of discipline. This type of authority shared with or restrained by other institutions is referred to by some writers as constitutional management. Most countries today have, as a minimum, some laws pertaining to the physical treatment, safety, and dismissal of personnel—many also have minimum wage laws—but in many cases such laws are not effectively enforced.

This view would tend to prevail to the extent that the following environmental conditions exist:

1. As a given economy develops and becomes more complex and as a pluralistic society evolves
2. Where the expectations of industrial personnel are rising and strong, united organized labor or employee unions emerge
3. Where the government plays an increasingly large and active welfare role

Again, Communist nations represent a special case, since the state is the supreme power in all personnel matters; however, within the limits of his authority, the Communist enterprise manager does act as a type of constitutional manager.

The following page presents a highly tentative, hypothetical ranking of several countries on the three continua which correspond to views *A*, *B*, *X*, and *Y* and the resulting dominant patterns of managerial behavior.

## Impacts of Views of Authority and Subordinates and Resulting Behavior Patterns on Management Effectiveness

It is difficult and somewhat speculative to generalize about whether the dominant patterns of managerial authority and superior-subordinate relationships in a particular country are the best in terms of managerial effectiveness and productive efficiency, since they are in large part culture bound. A given pattern may work effectively in one society, but if it is transplanted suddenly and extensively to a second society a substantial decline in managerial effectiveness might well result. As will be discussed shortly, under strikingly different dominant patterns of managerial authority and superior-subordinate relationships Japan, West Germany, and Yugoslavia have achieved very impressive economic growth rates—among the highest in the world—during the past fifteen years.

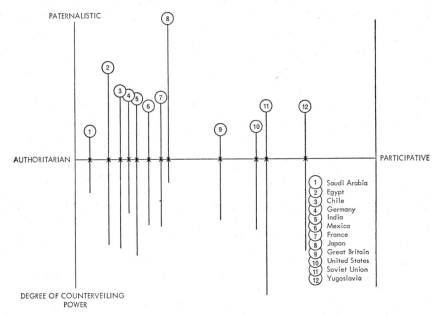

FIGURE 7–1

It is apparent, however, that in many countries the prevailing dominant patterns do serve as significant constraints not only upon managerial behavior but also upon managerial effectiveness and productive efficiency.

In countries characterized by highly centralized patrimonial enterprise managements, such firms tend to be noninnovating, static, and quite small, while potential economies of scale in operations through growth are not derived. If such enterprises do grow larger, we are likely to find overburdened spans of control, frequent short circuits in the chain of command, ineffective delegation of authority, wasted talents at lower levels, considerable frustration, possibly much personnel turnover and absenteeism, and a variety of other serious inefficiencies. Highly centralized patrimonial enterprises are likely to expand effectively and achieve a fairly high level of productive efficiency only where top management is extremely competent, well trained, and energetic. Overcentralization is also a critical problem in noncapitalistic industry. In the Soviet Union, and other extensively socialistic economies, inefficiency, waste, and opposition to innovation have become increasingly serious and pervasive problems because of overcentralization of authority in industrial administration.[17]

Autocratic management—even a high degree—can be conducive to a favorable level of managerial effectiveness and productive efficiency where

---

[17] Richman, *Soviet Management*, especially chaps. 8, 9, and 12.

enterprise managers are competent, well trained men and where subordinates respect and perform best under a strong, domineering type of leader. On the other hand, in large firms in particular, a high degree of autocratic direction can lead to serious communication and information gaps among the various levels within the enterprise. Moreover, it tends to curb individual initiative, and it can stifle the development of lower level managers which may be crucial in an expanding firm.

Under proper conditions, participative management and extensive use of consultative direction can serve as a potent and effective motivational, educational and training device. It can also lead to greater mutual trust and more effective communication between superiors and subordinates. Moreover, consultative direction and participation can yield worthwhile suggestions and advice from subordinate managers and workers, particularly when they are engaged in fairly complex jobs involving a high level of skill. On the other hand, this pattern of superior-subordinate relationships may lead to various problems such as information distortion; conflicting interests and objectives resulting in much unproductive bargaining and bickering; excessive time spent in meetings, conferences, and committees; and job insecurity. In general, for consultative direction and participation to be effective, both managers and their subordinates must be or become culturally, socially, and psychologically adjusted to such a system. In many societies this type of adjustment, on a widespread scale, could take considerable time— even decades or generations in some cases.

Paternalistic management can produce stability and individual security, which, in turn, may yield loyalty, hard work, and identification with the goals and problems of the enterprise on the part of employees. Such a system can be conducive to a favorable level of managerial effectiveness and productive efficiency, particularly if the higher echelons of management are staffed by highly competent and energetic people and if employees place high value on a paternalistic relationship. As industry and firms expand and grow more complex, however, and as competition, living standards, and the expectations of employees continue to increase, a number of significant problems are likely to arise eventually; for a high degree of paternalistic management tends to substantially limit individual initiative and mobility, the development of lower level managers, and overall company flexibility.

A system of effective countervailing power and constitutional management can be conducive to economic progress if all the parties involved are seriously concerned about economic progress and cooperate with this end in mind. On the other hand, widespread antagonism, conflict, and distrust are likely to result in significant barriers to managerial effectiveness and productive efficiency.

### Some Country Examples

In underdeveloped and newly developing countries, the private sector is characterized by patrimonial enterprise management, rigid centralization, and a high degree of autocratic direction. This generally holds true as well for the fairly large family owned firms that might exist, although there are some notable exceptions in various countries. Autocratic management and a high degree of centralization of authority are the dominant patterns in most of the public enterprises as well. In many of these countries a growing amount of countervailing power over employee welfare matters is being exerted by the government and, to a lesser degree, the labor unions. There is also a fairly high degree of paternalistic management in many underdeveloped and newly developing countries—in some cases by choice or necessity, in others by law.

One source clearly reflects the dominant view of subordinates in underdeveloped countries: "What enterprises in underdeveloped countries most urgently need is a new conception of the role a subordinate should play. They are regarded as potentially undisciplined creatures who have to be watched in the manner of a warden watching a prisoner."[18] This source goes on to point out that subordinates are usually seen as passive instruments, completely lacking in initiative, and that management spends most of its time in trying to "catch" and rigidly control subordinates rather than in trying to improve their abilities and increase productivity.

An expert on industrial management in Pakistan points out that because of rigid centralization and autocratic direction in his native country, the initiative of subordinates is severely stifled, the talents of middle managers are wasted, and a big gap in communication and information typically exists between the top and lower rungs of industrial enterprises. Because subordinates are generally distrusted, management spends much of its time in detecting and controlling trouble, frequently by using a spy system. Often firms even employ internal "secret service" checks on other secret service members. As one top executive of a Pakistani company stated in an interview: "It is a sort of FBI, what you have in the U.S."[19]

In India, patrimonial management and autocratic direction are entrenched in the private sector, even in most of the large companies operated through the managing agency (holding company) system.[20] Even a low

---

[18] United Nations, *Public Industrial Management in Asia and the Far East* (New York, 1960), p. 23.

[19] Raza, *op. cit.*, 1965.

[20] Our statements on authority and subordinates in Indian industry are based on written sources, as well as on the experiences of several of our research assistants, faculty colleagues, and foreign students who have worked or done firsthand research in Indian industry and the experiences of a number of top level Indian executives who are personal friends of one of the authors. For pertinent secondary sources see: Harbison and Myers, *Management in the Industrial World*, chap. vii, A. Agariwala, "Management of Big Business in India," *The Indian Journal of Public Administration*, April-June, 1962, pp. 178 ff; R. Lambert, *Workers, Factories and Social Change in India* (Princeton, N.J.: Princeton University Press, 1963); S. Mead, "Management in Developing Countries," *Proceedings* (CIOS), 1963, pp. 428–30; C. Ram (Chairman of a large Indian engineering company), "Management Development in the Developing Economy," *ibid.*, pp. 306–309; R. Likert, "Trends Toward a World-Wide Theory of Management," *ibid.*, pp. 110–114.

level employee or supervisor is often summoned to the highest seats of power for a command or reprimand, thus violating the principle of unity of command and the authority level principle and circumventing the chain of command. Since authority is highly centralized and personal, there is little management development at lower levels. As in many other countries, lower level supervisors, particularly foremen, are not usually considered part of management and have virtually no decision making powers in Indian industry. This often has unfavorable consequences in terms of control, supervision, and leadership at the operating level.

Even in the large privately owned Indian firms—except for a few progressive ones—there is a strong tendency for the head of the family to maintain virtually complete authority on all major issues even when there are other well educated and potentially effective family members in the managerial hierarchy. There is also typically a high degree of centralization accompanied by autocratic direction in the larger public enterprises, since they are staffed largely by managers with a civil service background who are accustomed to this type of administration.

Probably a large majority of Indian managers still adhere to a cheap labor mentality. Participative management is still very rare and can be found only in a small number of progressive firms; however, greater labor legislation and trade union pressures, as well as growing labor expectations, are restricting managerial authority over various personnel matters. Since democratic values have been increasingly stressed in this country, direction over subordinates may become less autocratic and more participative over time, particularly as the educational level of the population continues to rise.[21]

A recent study on industrial management in Turkey points out that even American firms operating there feel compelled to abide by certain prevailing local attitudes and values with regard to managerial authority and superior-subordinate relationships. In Turkey, paternalistic management is pervasive, evolving from the landlord or village head relationship with subordinates and workers in the preindustrial era. As a result of this social relationship:

Neither American nor Turkish production managers showed concern that labor becomes a fixed production cost when employees become wedded to the company through the cultural characteristics that placed value on the company's obligation to provide security and steady employment.[22]

---

[21] The Indian Ministry of Labor has been publicizing extensively the potential gains in productivity that may be derived through participative management. It is interesting to note that this ministry has recently reproduced for widespread distribution an article by one of the authors dealing with participative management in Soviet industry. This article is B. Richman, "Increasing Worker Productivity; How the Soviets Do It," *Personnel*, January, 1964, pp. 7–18. See also the comments on participative management practice in India in Likert, *op. cit.*, and P. Mills, "General Management Progress Report," *Proceedings* (CIOS), 1963, p. 22.

[22] Skinner, *op. cit.*, pp. 56–57.

Turkish industry is also characterized by a high degree of centralization and autocratic—often harsh—direction over subordinates, as well as rigid control. This situation is reflected in the words of two Turkish managers:

We must treat the workers as a schoolmaster who loves his children but is strict with them.

My main problem is checking on the work. When you turn your back they do nothing. . . . I trust the foreman, but still I must check on the work all the time.[23]

Industrial management in Egypt and Chile have much in common with Turkey.[24] While paternalism appears to be more extensive in Chile, in both countries the tendency in industrial firms is toward a high degree of centralization of authority and autocratic direction. This is also true in the growing Egyptian public industrial sector as well. In Chile, necessity, as well as various government incentives and growing labor union demands, encourages paternalistic management. Many of the larger firms in Egypt are quite paternalistic, but they are so more often by law than by choice. In Egypt in recent years the government, and to a lesser degree the unions, have restricted industrial management's unilateral authority over personnel matters.

High degrees of paternalism, centralization of authority, and autocratic direction can also be found as dominant patterns in some of the more advanced nations. Nowhere is paternalism more pervasive than in Japanese industry—in both small and very large enterprises.[25] Japanese management's view of authority and subordinates is closely tied in with the Japanese concept of society, which is based on hierarchy, paternalism, loyalty to superiors, and integration of the individual into the social struc-

---

[23] *Ibid.*

[24] Cf. Harbison and Myers, *Management in the Industrial World*, chaps. viii, ix. The findings presented in this source are still generally applicable today in view of the recent experiences of one of the authors in Egypt and the recent firsthand observations and experiences in Egypt and Chile by a number of research assistants, faculty colleagues, and graduate students.

[25] Among the important studies of management, authority, and superior-subordinate relations in Japan are: A. Whitehill and S. Takezawa, *Cultural Values in Management-Worker Relations in Japan: Gimu in Transition* (Research Paper 5 [Chapel Hill, N.C.: University of North Carolina, School of Business Administration, March, 1961]) (this study is based on extensive interviews with a broad cross section of Japanese workers and managers); J. Bennet and I. Ishino, *Paternalism in the Japanese Economy* (Minneapolis: University of Minnesota Press, 1963); Japanese Productivity Center, *Organization and Management in Japanese Industry* (Tokyo, June 1964); "Who Has Total Security," *Business Week*, October 17, 1964, pp. 45–46. Much valuable information has been obtained by one of the authors from interviews with visiting Japanese executives and business school educators, as well as with Japanese faculty colleagues and graduate students in the U.S. Professor Fred Massarik of UCLA has also provided the authors with some valuable data obtained during his research trip to Japan in 1964. On the basis of interviews and questionnaires he predicts a convergence of Japanese management practice in the direction of American practice, although such convergence will undoubtedly be a long range matter.

ture. The emphasis is on the group, family or company, rather than the individual. Japanese paternalism entails a life commitment of employment to personnel in return for loyalty, dedication to job and company, subordination to superiors, and respect for elders. Management is typically responsible for the whole employee—including such matters as health, medical care, and even shelter—and direct superior-subordinate relationships tend to be much more personal than in the West. These values are derived from traditional Japanese feudalism, and they have been preserved to date throughout industry.

Japanese management is generally highly centralized and quite autocratic. At the highest levels it is still largely patrimonial, while at lower levels there has been a definite growing trend toward professional management; however, authority is seldom delegated below the top three or four rungs of management even in large firms. Middle managers, by American standards, are considered as foremen or first line supervisors, and below this level decision making powers are rarely delegated. Even in the largest companies with product divisions there is typically little decentralization of authority; and, in order to preserve the family concept, such divisions often are not considered as independent profit centers. As a result of these conditions, Japanese enterprise organization structures tend to be substantially taller than in a comparable American firm.

While direction is typically autocratic in Japanese industry, there are often elements of participative management and consultative direction, particularly within the managerial hierarchy at the higher levels. Participation at different levels is conducted only through representation and indirect consultation. Supervisors are viewed as part of their work group and as its representative to higher management. Participation is carried out through group discussion and agreement at each level on various matters and grievances. In this way, social harmony may be achieved through mediation and compromise rather than mute acceptance of higher management's formal authority. Under this group concept there is virtually no individual responsibility, blame, or praise. At the same time, there is usually a very big communication gap between higher management and the lower rungs of the organization, and much time is spent in meetings, committees, and conferences throughout the enterprise, but to a much greater degree at the higher levels, in an effort to maintain social harmony. Under this system there has been little union power and not much government regulation over personnel matters. Japanese management has maintained its prerogatives and authority over most employee issues.

On the whole, paternalistic management in Japanese industry has proved highly effective in mobilizing Japanese society for rapid industrial progress while maintaining stability and individual security in a drastic social and economic revolution. Employees have generally been willing to identify with the company and to subordinate individual objectives to group and company objectives. In fact they have been inclined to consider their work lives at least equal in importance to their personal lives; however, growing foreign and domestic competition, stronger labor unions, and greater awareness of management practices in the United States are causing pressures for change in this paternalistic system, as well as in the other aspects of managerial authority. Management, employees, and unions are beginning to express dissatisfaction with the overall system because of its deadening effect on versatility, flexibility, employee mobility, and individual initiative; but any extensive changes will probably only come about very gradually.

French industrial enterprise is still strongly marked by family origins and patrimonial management, as is the case in many other countries of feudalistic lineage. French industry is characterized by a preponderance of relatively small, privately owned firms looked on by the family as a source of personal security.[26] Authority tends to be highly centralized; and a fairly high degree of autocratic direction is typically used, even in the larger firms. There is frequently a considerable feeling of underlying antagonism and distrust between management and employees, and there tends to be a gulf between them which grows greater if and as the enterprise expands. This can and does often lead to considerable inefficiency. In most cases front line supervisors are not considered part of management. In this type of environment it is not surprising that the great majority of enterprises remain quite small, conservative, static, and restrictive; however, in recent years a growing number of large progressive firms have evolved which recognize the need for professional management, and they have gone in the direction of greater decentralization of authority and participative management.

In West German industry, the top executive (*Unternehmer*) is the dominant industrial leader and traces his authority to value systems and/or charismatic endowment, rather than knowledge, special qualifications, or skill subject to objective evaluation.[27] He claims the obedience of subordinates—and generally receives it—because he considers himself a trustee of private property, an individual of extraordinary powers, and one called to his position by a divine or otherwise transcendent force. There tends to be considerable centralization of authority even in most larger companies, and in fact there are not very many large privately owned corporations in Germany. German managers also tend to be highly auto-

---

[26] The following are related and relevant sources on industrial management in France: Harbison and Myers. *Management in the Industrial World*, chap. xi; Reksodinardjo, *op. cit.*, pp. 96 ff; Lewis and Stewart, *op. cit.*, pp. 183 ff; Granick, *op. cit.*, chaps. iv, xiv, and xix.

[27] Cf.: H. Hartman, *Authority and Organization in German Management* (Princeton, N.J.: Princeton University Press, 1959); Harbison and Myers, *Management in the Industrial World*, chap. xiv; Granick, *op. cit.*, chaps. v, xii, and xvi; Reksodihardjo, *op. cit.*, pp. 71 ff; Lewis and Stewart, *op. cit.*, pp. 166 ff; A. Sturmthal, *Workers Councils* (Cambridge, Mass: Harvard University Press, 1964), chap. iii.

cratic, and extensive use of consultative direction would probably be viewed as a sign of weakness by many subordinates.

The dominant pattern of authority in West German industry has proved quite effective, since top level managers are generally well trained, competent men; and in family controlled firms they are also inclined to make sure that their sons obtain a good education and adequate training in order that they may effectively help operate and eventually take over the business. In this regard, German industry fares better than industry in France.

Countervailing power over managerial authority regarding personnel matters is still rather limited in German industry. There is a fairly high degree of paternalism exerted through sizable voluntary welfare and social service investments by many firms. In spite of significant labor shortages and a skilled labor force there has been a relatively low rate of personnel turnover in West German industry.

British management has been described by one leading expert as being less authoritarian and patriarchal than in France, less paternalistic than in Germany, and less constitutional than in the United States;[28] however, except for a relatively small number of progressive firms, managerial authority is still typically fairly centralized, and there is not a very high degree of consultative direction or participative management even within the managerial hierarchy. It seems that in many enterprises lower level managers do not even get relevant information for control purposes, and this tends to hinder timely corrective action when needed.[29]

There is probably a higher degree of decentralization of authority in United States industry than in any other country. Extensive decentralization is not only an effect of the many large scale firms which have evolved in American industry, it has also done much to bring about this situation. Even in smaller firms there is probably a greater tendency to decentralize and delegate authority than in other countries, because of cultural attitudes, social values, and various other prevailing environmental conditions.

There is generally little or no need for American management to be paternalistic; however, in recent years a growing number of corporations have been spending sizable sums on welfare and recreational services and facilities in an effort to achieve greater employee satisfaction, loyalty and identification with the company.[30]

The use of participative management and consultative direction has

---

[28] Harbison and Myers, *Management in the Industrial World*, p. 313 and chap. xvi. One of the authors of the present study did research in British industry in 1961, and his views correspond quite closely to those contained in the sources cited in this and the following footnote.

[29] Cf. Granick, *op. cit.*, especially pp. 249 ff.

[30] Cf. *Business Week*, April 11, 1964, pp. 98–100.

increased substantially in American industry during the past few decades, particularly within the managerial hierarchy; however, worker participation in management, while apparently on the increase largely because of various cultural attitudes and social values, is still far from pervasive. It is likely that in the majority of cases autocratic direction of workers is still the dominant practice, and in many cases where participative management is used it is conducted in an insincere manner.[31] Yet few nations practice true participative management and consultative direction in industry as extensively as the United States.

One indication of the extent of participative management and consultative direction in a given country is the time spent by enterprise personnel at various levels in meetings, conferences, and committees. In numerous American firms—large and small—considerable time is spent in such activities. Another indication is the extent to which staff advisors and specialists are used in industry. In this regard, considerably more use is made of staff men in American industry than in most if not all other countries, including such advanced nations as Sweden, Great Britain, France, and West Germany.[32]

A rough indication of both the extent and effectiveness of participative management and consultative direction in industry in a particular country is the number of worthwhile employee suggestions—in terms of company economies, increased revenues, and so on—made and adopted by management through the use of various channels of participation. The National Association of Suggestion Systems (NASS) was founded in 1942 to assist member enterprises and agencies in United States and Canadian industry, commerce, and government in the improvement of their suggestion programs and in their efforts to obtain widespread employee participation. The association has grown from the original group of thirty-five members in 1942 to a membership of over 1,200 in 1963. The number of suggestions submitted per 100 eligible employees in NASS member organizations has shown an upward trend, increasing from 25.6 in 1955 to 30.5 in 1960. About 25 percent of all suggestions submitted have been implemented by management.[33]

There are associations similar to NASS in Great Britain and West

---

[31] See the empirical evidence discussed in Haire, Ghiselli, and Porter, *op. cit.*, pp. 101–107. While the trend is in the direction of greater participative management in American industry, a number of prominent scholars in the field of management and organization theory feel that not enough progress has been made to date; see, for example, C. Argyris, *Integrating the Individual and the Organization* (New York: John Wiley & Sons, Inc., 1964); R. Likert, *New Patterns of Management* (New York: McGraw-Hill Book Company, 1961); D. McGregor, *The Human Side of Enterprise* (New York: McGraw-Hill Book Company, 1960).

[32] Cf., Harbison and Myers, *Management in the Industrial World*, chaps. xi, xiv, xv, and xvi; Granick, *op. cit.*, Part V.

[33] The data cited have been obtained from the annual statistical reports issued by the NASS head office in Chicago. Other pertinent information regarding suggestion systems can also be obtained from NASS.

Germany, although they have substantially fewer member organizations. It is significant to note that data submitted by the associations in these countries indicate considerably poorer per capita suggestion system performance than in North American industry. The German results, in turn, lag substantially behind the British results. These differences can probably be attributed largely to a higher degree of autocratic management in Germany as compared to Britain and in Britain as compared to the United States.[34]

In the Soviet Union—and various other Communist countries—as was indicated earlier, widespread participation and the use of consultative direction is a matter of state decree rather than independent choice. There are many available channels for both managerial and worker participation in decision making, and there is a standardized suggestion system within every industrial enterprise. While many, if not a majority, of Soviet industrial managers may be inclined to be autocratic and not to take employee participation very seriously, there is much evidence that the number of employee suggestions made and implemented have been substantial both on a national scale and within individual enterprises. In addition, the economies and improvements in operations resulting from implemented employee proposals have been quite substantial to date. On the other hand, there is also much evidence that a great deal of unproductive time is expended on employee participation in Soviet industry through numerous meetings, conferences, and committees.[35]

When discussing centralization or decentralization of authority within the managerial hierarchy in Communist countries, one must include the entire industrial structure which extends from the highest Communist party and central government level right down through the enterprise hierarchy, since the entire system is interlocked. In planned economies of the Communist type, where all significant phases of economic activity are planned, controlled, and directed through one comprehensive national plan, it has been necessary to restrict greatly the authority and autonomy of enterprise management in order to coordinate the literally billions of interdependent and interrelated decisions and activities that are made and performed throughout the economy. This type of system has been building significant barriers to managerial effectiveness and productive efficiency in the USSR and other Communist countries.

The degree of industrial centralization and the authority extended to enterprise managers do vary somewhat among various Marxist nations. The Soviet Union has maintained a somewhat higher degree of centralization than some other Communist countries—for example, Poland, Hungary,

---

[34] *Ibid.*

[35] Evidence of this type and quantitative data pertaining to suggestion system results in Soviet industry can be found in Richman, *Soviet Management*, chap. x; "Employee Motivation in Soviet Industry," *Annals of Collective Economy*, Vol. XXXIV, No. 4, October-December, 1963, pp. 551–571.

and Czechoslovakia.[36] Yet even within the limited degree of authority that Soviet enterprise directors possess, there appears to be somewhat greater decentralization of authority within Soviet enterprise as compared to industrial firms in many "mixed" or essentially capitalistic economies. Even front line supervisors, including foremen, have some decision making powers within the framework of the enterprise operating plan in Soviet industry; but because of constant pressure on the top management of the Soviet enterprise to fulfill short run plans, decentralization of authority even within a large firm is quite limited. It is also because of such pressure that managers, for the sake of expediency, must often resort to autocratic direction when dealing with subordinates.

In most Communist countries industrial enterprises provide a wide range of welfare services and facilities by law, and employee welfare, social and personal problems are primarily the concern of the local Communist party committee and, to a lesser extent, the trade union committee, rather than management.

Yugoslav industry is characterized by a highly unique and interesting pattern of managerial authority and superior-subordinate relationships.[37] Since 1950, widespread participative management and substantially greater decentralization has evolved under Yugoslavia's system of "market socialism." This country, through its impressive economic growth and rising living standards, has proved that competition, a market price system, and a meaningful profit motive in industry can work quite effectively under a system of state ownership.

A 1950 law established a system of elected workers' councils and governing management boards as executive bodies at all industrial enterprises. Each enterprise, through a process of essentially democratic and universal annual elections, forms a workers' council composed of from fifteen to 120 members, depending on the size of the firm. This council acts as a decision making body on various matters and elects a managing board of three to eleven members. The board decides on managerial appointments; various policy matters; and, in the area of industrial relations,

---

[36] Cf.: Richman, *Soviet Management*, pp. 235–241; B. Richman and R. Farmer, "Ownership and Management: The Real Issues," *Management International*. No. 1, 1965; W. Grampp, "New Directions in the Communist Economics," *Business Horizons*, fall, 1963, pp. 32 ff; R. Vicker, "Marxists Inc.," *The Wall Street Journal*, April 3, 1964, p. 1; B. Richman, "Managerial Motivation in Soviet and Czechoslovak Industries: A Comparison," *Journal of the Academy of Management*, June, 1963, pp. 107 ff; J. Montias, *Central Planning in Poland* (New Haven, Conn.: Yale University Press, 1962); J. Michal, *Central Planning in Czechoslovakia* (Stanford, Calif.: Stanford University Press, 1962); J. Kornai, *Overcentralization in Economic Administration* (London: Oxford University Press, 1959); B. Balassa, *The Hungarian Experience in Economic Planning* (New Haven, Conn.; Yale University Press, 1959).

[37] For a related and comprehensive discussion of the Yugoslav system, see Sturmthal, *op. cit.*, chap. iv; A. Waterson, *Planning in Yugoslavia* (Baltimore: The Johns Hopkins Press, 1962), especially chap. vi; International Labor Organization, *Management and Labor Relations in Yugoslavia* (Labor-Management Relations Series, No. 5 [Geneva, 1958]).

individual complaints against the enterprise director. The director is appointed on the basis of a public, open competition in the local district, and he is the top executive of the firm. He can hire and fire—except for those executive positions which are under the control of the management board—and he assigns duties and delegates authority within the enterprise. In general, the director maintains authority over a wide variety of day-to-day decisions.

A large number of workers in Yugoslav industry have served as members on workers' councils, and many have served on managing boards. There are considerable regional variations in the effectiveness of participative management in Yugoslav industry. These variations apparently correspond to the level of the working population's industrial skill, experience, and education in different parts of the country. In general, however, the system of workers' councils and managing boards has undoubtedly served as an effective educational and training device with regard to industrial problems and has greatly facilitated the transition of Yugoslavia's rural agricultural economy to a relatively modern urban and industrial society.

# INTERORGANIZATIONAL COOPERATION

## Cooperation and Conflict

The extent to which various groups, organizations, and industrial enterprises in any culture cooperate voluntarily with one another determines in part how efficiently the productive system of the country will function. A society marked by extensive labor-management conflicts, suspicion between government and firms, and mistrust of motives between intellectuals and businessmen will not normally be as productive a country as one in which such frictions are minimized.

Every human society needs some cooperation between its members in order to survive. Man is a gregarious animal, and few hermits are able to survive and prosper entirely alone; however, the range and degree of such cooperation can vary enormously. All members of the culture are subject to varying pressures to conform and cooperate, and the general pressures faced are as follows:

1. *Economic Pressures.* In order to survive and maintain their income, persons and organizations must cooperate to some extent. In capitalistic societies, where buyers normally have various options to purchase, this type of pressure is clearly seen. Failure to help a purchaser, in terms of assisting him in getting what he wants, can mean sales losses in the future and lower profits. Employees doing the selling are usually well aware that sales declines mean loss of jobs. Some modern corporations in effect argue that their entire marketing effort be oriented to the consumers' needs and desires. Failing in this aim means eventual destruction for the firm.

Buyers with some monopsony power, such as governments, also usually recognize the need to cooperate with sellers. A strong buyer, such as the

United States government as an obtainer of missile systems, clearly sees that if the sellers are pressed too hard, there will be few or no sellers at a later date.

Trade unions also may recognize that their pay and jobs are related to their degree of cooperation with employers. It does little good for a union to price itself completely out of the market. It is not uncommon for unions in advanced capitalist countries to forgo pay increases in crisis situations—such as when a firm becomes unable to compete in normal times. In some cases, as in the American clothing trades, the union has tried to develop for a large number of fragmented firms a semblance of unity in the face of government and economic pressures, recognizing clearly that the welfare of its members is closely tied to the welfare of the firms in the industry.[3]

Where diverse groups recognize that each has something the other can use, cooperation proceeds apace. American firms work closely with professors and universities, seeing here potential usable knowledge and analysis, while the professors gain income and knowledge about firms' internal operations.

Such gains from cooperation are in part economic, representing pressures on firms and individuals to cooperate with each other. They also are interconnected with educational constraints, in that much of the cooperation described above requires a longer run time dimension than is immediately obvious. Some sellers cheat customers as often as possible, unconcerned about tomorrow's loss of business; some unions strike even when it is fairly obvious that higher wages will lead to their firm's quick demise; and some monopsony sellers squeeze suppliers unmercifully, even when this can mean the loss of key supplies in the future. In some cases, such short run attitudes seem stupid to an impartial observer, and they often represent the inability or unwillingness of the party in a powerful position to look any further than the immediate present. In this sense, failure to be educated to appreciate longer run situations is very relevant.

Economic pressures can also have negative effects on cooperation. Marxist countries, lacking effective price systems and competitive supplier situations, have great difficulty here. The seller has no incentive to be nice to his buyer, since the buyer usually has no immediate alternatives.[39] This, incidentally, is also often a problem in capitalist states under monopoly conditions. One can be furious with the telephone service he gets, but aside from futile protests in letters to editors and unsympathetic public utility commissions, there is little he can do about it. It is not surprising that much of the antagonism to monopoly in countries like the United States stems from this inability to realize a cooperative relationship—unless the monopolist forces himself to be cooperative.

---

[38] Cf. M. Danish, *The World of David Dubinsky* (Cleveland: The World Publishing Company, 1957); M. Danish and L. Stein, eds., *ILGWU News—History, 1900-1950* (New York: International Ladies Garment Workers Union, 1950); D. Dubinsky, "Rift and Realignment in World Labor," *Foreign Affairs*, January, 1959, pp. 232 ff.

[39] Cf. Richman, *Soviet Management*, especially chaps. vi, viii.

Sellers' markets which persist for long periods also lead to lack of cooperation. Americans who suffered through the 1941–45 war period are well aware of how difficult it was to secure cooperation from many suppliers of goods and services.

**2. Legal Pressures.**   Most societies provide penalties for failure to cooperate in many kinds of matters. Contracts typically are enforced, and failure to observe prior agreements carry penalties. Certain types of behavior, both collective and individual, are outlawed, and violators are punished. An individual would not normally throw his garbage on his neighbor's lawn, nor would he appear drunk and disorderly on public streets. Innumerable examples of such legal personal pressures exist. Firms are also constrained—sellers must cooperate with buyers by not selling them poisonous substances as food, by not organizing illegal price fixing cartels to exploit customers, and so on. A very large amount of individual and firm behavior is at least technically illegal, and fear of punishment can be a powerful factor on occasion in forcing cooperation.

Firms often cooperate with governments, unions, and individuals not because laws exist but because they fear punitive legislation. No law requires Bell Telephone operators to be polite, but surly employees might cost the firm very much in terms of future legal sanctions. A given type of cartel might be legal, but may not be formed because the resulting public objections might lead to still tighter law. Some firms, at least, try to label their products honestly, fearing more stringent pure food and honest marking laws than now exist. Failure to cooperate in this way can be very costly—American drug firms successfully blocked more stringent labeling and safety legislation in the drug industry, until the thalidomide scandal in 1962 almost immediately led to even more drastic legislation than had been initially contemplated.

**3. Sociological Pressures.**   Persons cooperate because social pressures, custom, and tradition lead to certain types of cooperation. Thus in some countries, extended family cooperation is regarded as the norm. If a firm trusts anyone, it is the cousins, brothers, sons, and other relatives—and outsiders are greeted with suspicion. In most countries, cooperation with religious leaders is taken for granted. Some prestige figures, such as judges, senior civil servants, military leaders, industrialists, and so on, are considered with great respect, and their requests for cooperation, if not greatly in conflict with other pressures, are usually honored.

Such sociological factors can also lead to considerable lack of cooperation in terms of productive efficiency. The family cooperation noted above may lead to nepotism and lack of cooperation with outsiders, creating less efficiency than might otherwise be the case. An important factor here is the nature of the class structure in the society and the way in which it is viewed by participants. If the structure is fairly flexible and open, as in the United States, Australia, or Canada, considerable cooperation toward mutual goals can be expected. Individuals, for economic, prestige, or political reasons, may be convinced that cooperation is more desirable than conflict. The

Soviet Union and other Marxist countries also have this advantage in some spheres of economic activity.

If, on the other hand, class structures are rigid, and capable individuals find that avenues of advance are completely blocked, considerable conflict is possible. This point is the one Marx seized on in his analysis of class warfare. If the proletariat can never rise, while at the same time generating some extremely capable individuals, conflict is very likely. It may take the form of political trade unionism, as in France and England, or revolutionary ferment, as occurs in many of the less developed countries. Wise is the country which develops some sort of escape hatch for competent members of lower classes, for their conflicts will be minimized.

If a country has a class structure which is truly believed in by the majority of the people, for religious, dogmatic, or other reasons, such conflicts may be minimized even if class barriers are rigid. Japan probably represents this sort of culture—and a rather unusual case it is. Few countries in the modern world have been able to maintain rigid class structures and minimal conflict through protracted periods of time.

It seems clear that interorganizational cooperation, or lack of it, stems from all of the above factors. In a given situation involving industrial enterprises, economic, legal, and sociological pressures will tend to push the situation to more or less conflict—with corresponding impacts on managerial effectiveness and productive efficiency. In most cases, all three pressures will be present to some extent, plus the usual individual psychological factors of the persons making key decisions in potential conflict situations; however, this constraint—interorganizational cooperation—is placed under sociological variables because it appears that these pressures are often more important, in terms of productivity, than the other two. Moreover, legal and economic aspects of interorganizational cooperation will be treated more fully at appropriate points in later chapters.

Not all conflict situations are relevant in this study. The focus here is on cooperation between factions in the society which tend to have a significant bearing on the productivity or efficiency of the industrial firms of the country in question. Hence, it is useful to spell out in some detail the kinds of institutions, organizations, and situations in the productive portion of the society which do directly influence such efficiency.

The balance of this section is concerned with the extent of cooperation that exists among industrial enterprises and other relevant related organizations in connection with endeavors that are basically voluntary rather than purely legal or contractual. Within this context we are particularly concerned with the relationships that firms and their managements in different countries have among themselves directly or through various associations, and with labor unions, government agencies, and educational institutions.

While the extent of voluntary cooperation that the management of a specific enterprise has with other organizations may be partly under its control and an expression of company policy, in most countries there appear to be dominant patterns with regard to the different categories of organizations involved. Such dominant patterns of interorganizational cooperation —or lack of it—are shaped largely by tradition, in conjunction with a variety of historical, cultural, and sociological factors, including society's view of industrial management and management's view of itself.

Interorganizational relationships of the type under study here can have a significant bearing on managerial performance, productive efficiency, and hence general economic progress. We shall briefly explore a number of significant aspects of cooperative relationships, indicating how the degree of cooperative effectiveness is revealed, and in some cases how it might even be measured with reasonable accuracy through further research.

### Union-Management Cooperation

Union-Management relationships are considered first. At one extreme there may be a basic, deepseated conflict between management and labor organizations in a given country, or at the other extreme there may be a very high degree of cooperation. In the former situation one is likely to find widespread and rather frequent strikes, both official and unofficial; extensive informal restrictive labor practices and featherbedding; and probably a great amount of unproductive time, effort, and expense absorbed in politiking and bargaining. The nature of union-management relations is also likely to have a significant bearing on the rate and extent to which more productive technology is developed and introduced by industrial firms.

In Sweden there has for several decades been a high degree of cooperation between management and labor unions regarding industrial relations issues and colllective bargaining. Consequently, there have been few major strikes during this period—the last one taking place in the early 1950's. This situation has certainly been conducive to managerial effectiveness and productive efficiency.

Under the system of paternalism in Japanese industry there had been very little management-labor union conflict, although such conflict has been increasing somewhat in recent years.[40] Traditionally, Japan's industrial managers have viewed union affairs as employee affairs; therefore, unions have not had a distinct, separate identity. They have frequently been allowed, even encouraged, to use company time and facilities for their activities. In general, Japanese management has been favorably disposed to unions, and for the most part labor unions have been organized on an enterprise rather than on a national basis. In recent years, however, efforts have been made in a number of cases to organize strong national unions, and this has been resulting in greater conflict in management-union relations.

In Soviet industry strikes have long been outlawed, and there is little

---

[40] Cf. "Who Has Total Security," *Business Week*, October 17, 1964 p. 46; see also the discussion of unions in Japanese industry in Whitehill, *op. cit.*, pp. 59 ff.

basic conflict between trade unions and industrial management, since the state has maintained and exercised ultimate authority and power over industrial relations matters. The absence of strikes in the Soviet Union has undoubtedly been a plus factor in terms of managerial effectiveness; however, informal restrictive practices on the part of industrial employees, as well as extensive bargaining and politicking regarding industrial relations problems have been and still are quite pervasive under the Soviet industrial system.[41]

In the U.S. industry union-management conflicts resulting in strikes, work stoppages, slowdowns, various other restrictive practices, extensive and costly bargaining, and politicking have been, and still are, fairly significant barriers to managerial effectiveness—but in some industries more than others. The U.S., however, fares considerably better in this regard than some advanced western European countries—most notably Britain and France—and this shows up in labor productivity performance in various industries such as railroading, automobiles, and aluminum.

In these European countries there has been a historical, deepseated conflict between labor and management which is based to a higher degree than in the U.S. on political identification, ideology, and class struggle.[42] The European unions want to change society, not merely get more for the worker; and it is generally more difficult to reach a compromise on ideological as compared to economic issues. This situation is further aggravated since there are more government laws and regulations over social security, wages, and working conditions than in the U.S.; and hence the unions feel that they must justify their existence by turning to politics and ideology. Industrial managers, particularly in Britain, also contribute to union-management conflict, since they tend to be adamant in their prerogatives and rights and will not cooperate beyond legally defined rules. Hence, stubbornly held moral principles are often upheld at the expense of work stoppages, inefficiency, and profits.[43]

The way that labor unions are organized in Britain and various other countries also results in considerable conflict and inefficiency.[44] British

---

[41] Cf.: E. Brown, "Interests and Rights of Soviet Industrial Workers and the Resolution of Conflicts," *Industrial and Labor Relations Review*, January, 1963, pp. 254 ff; "The Local Union in Soviet Industry," *Industrial and Labor Relations Review*, January 1960, pp. 195 ff; V. Grishin (Chairman of the Central Council of Soviet Trade Unions), in *Current Digest of the Soviet Press*, Vol. XV, No. 44, 1963, pp. 5 ff; Richman, *Soviet Management*, pp. 200–204, 225–226.

[42] Cf. the comprehensive discussion and analysis in Granick, *op. cit.*, chaps. xiii–xvii, and the sources cited in the bibliographies to these chapters.

[43] *Ibid.*, especially pp. 234 ff.

[44] *Ibid.*; D. Robertson, *Factory Wage Structures and National Agreements* (Cambridge; Cambridge University Press, 1960); E. Phelps Brown, *The Growth of British Industrial Relations* (London: Macmillan, 1959); National Economic Development Council (U.K.), *op. cit.*, pp. 52 ff; "American Business Looks at Britain," *The Manager*, July, 1964, p. 28. Specific data on union-management conflicts and work stoppages in British industry can be found in most issues of the *Ministry of Labour Gazette* (London); see, for example, the July, 1964 issue. See also, "Britain's Crisis in Efficiency," *Business Week*, December 26, 1964, p. 83.

unions have a national rather than a company orientation in virtually all matters, since they represent an entire class. Under this type of system little or no attention is given to local conditions or company differences in collective bargaining, and this results in serious conflicts at the local level. In the U.S., national bargaining typically deals with minimum standards, while details are worked out by local representatives at individual companies. British industry is plagued with the unofficial "wildcat" strike under their system of national bargaining, while U.S. industry is in large part protected against this type of activity because local conditions are taken into account in labor-management agreements.

Another aggravating factor in British industry is the intra-union rivalries that arise because there are more labor unions than in the U.S. and hence more union representatives in most factories. Conflicts also arise frequently between shop stewards and the central union agencies, and the unofficial strike is often resorted to as a technique for settling local material issues. British managers typically have local union representatives to deal with who will usually support them when they live up to national agreements, and this situation also contributes to unofficial strikes and to informal restrictive practices. In general, British workers are subject to attacks not only by management but also by national union representatives, and this tends to breed insecurity and rigid enforcement of informal restrictive practices, as well as unofficial strikes.

While unions in the U.S. do have some control over dismissals and layoffs, they are still accepted because of the unions' acceptance of a market economy; but in Britain, and many other countries, layoffs due to business conditions are viewed as morally wrong virtually any time and are interpreted as an attack on the working classes. Hence, there is a strong tendency to fight every layoff and dismissal.

In numerous underdeveloped and newly developing nations, particularly those characterized by political and/or economic instability and growing union power, management-union conflicts are pervasive and very serious. Labor union unrest and bargaining are frequently based on noneconomic grounds, and sympathy strikes based on remote events or political moves in other countries tend to be frequent. In many cases there is constant pressure to raise wages without any concern for the economics of the situation, and seniority and political favoritism lead to the creation of many unneeded jobs.[45]

## Cooperation between Industry and Government

The extent of voluntary cooperation between government and industry in a particular country also tends to have a significant bearing on managerial performance and productive efficiency. If there is considerable antagonism between government agencies and industrial management there would tend to be little cooperation, consultation, or communication regarding eco-

---

[45] Cf.: Reksodinardjo, *op. cit.*, pp. 219 ff; C. Ram, in *Proceedings* (CIOS), 1963, pp. 307–308.

nomic or technical problems of common concern. Government organizations would not be inclined to collect and disseminate statistics and other data that could be very useful for micromanagerial decision making in industry; and management may also be reluctant to supply the government with pertinent, accurate information it may need for effective macrodecision making. Government agencies would be inclined to design and attempt to implement economic plans and policies and to undertake various economic activities without first seeking the advice, opinions, or knowledge of industrial leaders, while industrial managers, in turn, might be reluctant to cooperate in the achievement of national plans and objectives. In this type of environment it is also unlikely that the government would render much if anything in the way of economic or technical assistance to industry.

When considering the topic of voluntary cooperation between industry and government a distinction should be made between private industry and state-run and -controlled industry. In the case of private or capitalistic industry, there is considerable conflict and antagonism between industrial managers and the government apparatus in numerous countries, for a variety of historical, cultural, sociological, and political reasons. One may be inclined to assume that in public industry such friction would not exist and that the degree of cooperation would tend to be high, since the government or state controls the public enterprises and would be fighting against itself, so to speak. Yet in many countries there is in fact considerable conflict and rather ineffective cooperation between public enterprise managers and the state. This situation is generally based more on economic and political grounds rather than on historical or cultural factors per se, but it still can serve as a significant negative constraint on managerial effectiveness and productive efficiency. This is particularly true in various Communist and highly socialistic economies.

In the Soviet Union, for example, there is a basic conflict of objective between the highest state planners and industrial enterprise managers, which greatly hinders effective cooperation and communication. The former attempt to establish tight industrial operating plans calling for maximum production with estimated available resources, while the latter strive for modest or easy plans because of deficiencies in the resource allocation and incentive systems within which they must operate. More will be said about this situation in later chapters; but the point here is that this type of conflict of interest in state controlled industry leads to ineffective cooperation, poor communication, and information distortion involving a wide range of technical and economic matters.[46]

In many newly developing countries which formulate national economic plans there is little cooperation and communication between the government planners and private industry—and even, in some cases, be-

---

[46] Cf.: Richman, *Soviet Management*, chaps. vi, viii, and ix.

tween government planners and the public industrial sector in some cases.[47] The government formulates fiscal, monetary, and foreign trade policies and makes major investment decisions, without any representation from industry. The government also offers little if any technical or economic assistance to private firms, large or small, while industry in turn tends to have little interest in the economic objectives being pursued by the government.

In some countries characterized by political instability, such as Brazil, the government does not pay its bills—often extremely large bills—to private firms for several years, if at all.[48] Where there are frequent changes in government, the new regime is often very reluctant to pay the debts to industry incurred by the former regime. Such lack of cooperation or concern for the needs of industry clearly has a highly negative impact on managerial effectiveness and productive efficiency.

In several of the more advanced, essentially capitalistic nations there has been growing cooperation between industry and government in the past few decades. This has undoubtedly contributed substantially to sustained economic progress. In the United States there is considerable dissemination of information, communication, and representation between government and industry. There has also been growing government financial, technical, and educational assistance, particularly for smaller firms. For example, the Small Business Administration has been playing a significant role in this connection. U.S. business and industry also provides the government with pertinent information, advice and assistance through such bodies as the Committee on Economic Development (CED) and by having prominent business leaders in key government positions.

In most western European countries voluntary cooperation between government and industry has grown and become more effective since the end of World War II. For example, France has a national economic plan—*Le Plan*—which is carried out in a spirit of essentially voluntary cooperation between industry and government. In the Netherlands there are many government departments providing relevant information, research facilities, and various other types of assistance to industry. For smaller

---

[47] Cf.: United Nations, *Management of Industrial Enterprises in Underdeveloped Countries* (New York, 1958); U.N., *Public Industrial Management in Asia and the Far East* (New York, 1960); U.N., *Economic Bulletin for Africa* (Addis Ababa), June, 1962. While cooperation and communication between government and industry has been improving somewhat in recent years in various newly developing nations, it still remains a serious problem in many cases. This is evident not only from information contained in available written sources but also from the firsthand experiences of one of the authors in a number of less developed countries, as well as the information obtained from interviews with many United Nations officials and businessmen and educators from several newly developing countries.

[48] Cf. W. Oberg, "Cross Cultural Perspectives on Management Principles," *Journal of the Academy of Management*, June, 1963, p. 132. It would be surprising if the government pays its bills promptly to private industry in a country like Syria where there have been some fifteen changes in the government in the past eighteen years. The same could be said about South Vietnam and several other countries.

enterprises there is much in the way of free technical, educational, and economic assistance.[49]

Japan, probably more than any other capitalist nation, has gone the farthest with regard to cooperation between the government and private industry, particularly in the case of medium sized and small firms.[50] The Smaller Enterprise Agency was established in 1958 under the Ministry of Internal Trade and Industry with the primary objective of aiding and improving the efficiency of industrial enterprises employing fewer than 300 persons. These small firms play a major role in Japan's exports because of their relatively low wage rates and labor costs. In general, there is considerable cooperation between the government and firms of all sizes with regard to export promotion and facilities, research and development, training, technical and financial assistance, and so forth. There is also extensive communication and exchange of information between government and business leaders, and Japan has an effective Joint Economic Council composed of governmental and industrial representatives. Moreover, there is a network of some 442 state operated public employment offices throughout the country which have much liaison with industry and educational institutions regarding the requirements, placement, and relocation of personnel. This environment of cooperation between industry and government in Japan has undoubtedly contributed substantially to managerial effectiveness and general economic progress.

## Educational Institutions and Industry

The extent and quality of voluntary cooperation between educational institutions and industry is also likely to have an important bearing on managerial performance and productive efficiency. Where there is a great deal of cooperation and communication involving joint consultation and research projects, and where there is extensive exchange and dissemination of information and ideas on problems of common concern, managerial effectiveness would tend to increase. Moreover, a better educational match with the requirements of industry, and more effective placement of graduates would also be likely.

The extent of voluntary cooperation between industry and educational institutions is likely to correlate quite closely with the extent of and general regard for formal business and management education in a particular country. In probably the great majority of countries educators and "intellectuals" are still inclined to spurn business and its managers, while in many countries numerous industrial managers are basically anti-intellectual and anti–higher education.

---

[49] Cf. *Questionnaire on Industrial Planning and Development*, response of the Netherlands.

[50] *Ibid.*, response of Japan; A. Toyoroku, "Interrelations Between Large and Small Scale Industries in Japan," *Industrialization and Productivity*, No. 2, 1959, pp. 27 ff; "Organization and Operation of Cottage and Small Industries," *Industrialization and Productivity*, No. 2, 1959, pp. 37–42.

It appears that voluntary cooperation between educators and industry is greatest in the United States. Japan and the Soviet Union would also rate quite high in this area. In the U.S. a sizable proportion of faculty members from universities and colleges engage in industrial consulting activities and joint projects pertaining to industrial problems. Not only are business school faculty members engaged in such activities, but so is a wide range of other educators, including in part engineers, theoretical economists, behavioral and physical scientists, logicians, mathematicians, and lawyers. Hundreds of American companies have programs which employ professors during the summer in their particular areas of interest, and numerous universities and colleges offer a wide range of special training programs for business managers and other types of business specialists. All of this cooperative activity undoubtedly does much to improve managerial effectiveness and productive efficiency in industry.

### Cooperation within Industry

The extent of voluntary cooperation among industrial firms and their respective staffs, either directly or through various associations, can have a significant impact on managerial effectiveness. If the managements and other personnel of industrial enterprises tend to exchange and disseminate information and ideas of common interest—even if they maintain a competitive spirit—all may gain in terms of greater productive efficiency. Such exchanges may take place through various professional or occupational societies, trade associations, employee federations, chambers of commerce, and so forth. Managerial effectiveness and productive efficiency may also be increased substantially where economies of scale are derived through joint cooperative ventures by industrial firms, particularly smaller enterprises. For example, such economies may be derived through joint export promotion and/or training programs, common repair facilities, joint procurement and/or research and development activities, and so on. Subcontracting relationships among enterprises may also increase productivity through greater specialization.

In the large majority of underdeveloped and newly developing countries industrial firms and their staffs tend to be very reluctant to exchange or disseminate information and ideas on common problems or to undertake joint cooperative ventures with other enterprises.[51] This situation is probably due to lack of trust, ignorance about the mutual benefits that may be derived from such cooperation, and/or sheer lack of interest in improving operations. Such attitudes also hinder cooperation within industry in several of the relatively advanced nations of western Europe, but perhaps to a lesser degree than in most underdeveloped countries.

In the United States cooperation within industry and among industrial

---

[51] See sources cited in Footnote 47 above and "Some Problems of Industrial Management Reported by Technical Assistance Experts," *Industrialization and Productivity*, No. 2, 1959, pp. 53–57.

personnel, regarding the dissemination and exchange of information and ideas, is rather pervasive, in spite of an essentially competitive environment. There are several national management associations—for example, the American Management Association—which serve this purpose. There are a large number of societies and organizations composed of a wide range of industrial specialists—marketing, finance, procurement, personnel management, engineering, and operations research associations, to name just a few. Many of these bodies organize seminars, conduct conferences, and publish journals with the aim of keeping their members informed of new information, ideas, and techniques in their respective occupational fields. There are also many other types of organizations which serve U.S. industry in a similar manner; for example, branches of industry and trade associations, chambers of commerce, and so forth. While many of the activities of the above associations, societies, and organizations are essentially social in nature, they also often contribute to greater managerial effectiveness and productive efficiency in U.S. industry.

Japan also ranks very high on cooperation within industry, probably higher than the U.S. if we also consider direct, joint cooperative ventures and subcontracting relationships among industrial enterprises.[52] In Japan the government actively encourages and does much to aid smaller firms to incorporate into cooperative associations. From such associations numerous firms derive substantial economies of scale in operations by establishing joint facilities for marketing, shipping, production, procurement, maintenance, research and development, obtaining capital, and various other activities. There are some 300 such cooperative associations in about thirty-four branches of industry. This cooperative structure is further strengthened in many instances through national federations of cooperative associations. This gives member firms considerable countervailing power in their dealings with large corporations. In many of the cooperatives individual firms maintain their identity as entrepreneurs; in others the association as a whole undertakes most entrepreneurial functions.

In a very real sense, many of the cooperative associations are legally sanctioned cartels. Large firms in Japan also operate like cartels in connection with major price, output, and investment decisions, since there is often considerable cooperation, consultation, and collusion—usually quite overt—among firms on such decisions. While cartels generally restrict competition and frequently tend to reduce productive efficiency, the Japanese government has adopted the position that this type of cooperative arrangement in Japanese industry has in fact been conducive to greater efficiency and productivity, because of the great scarcity of natural resources in Japan. The Japanese are evidently convinced that by pooling knowledge and resources in industry, and by collaborating on major economic deci-

---

[52] See sources cited in Footnote 50 above.

sions, more efficient and effective use is made of available resources, while the volume of Japan's exports in competitive world markets is also greatly enhanced. It may well be that thus far the absence of competition in favor of cooperation and joint action in several areas of Japanese private industry has been beneficial in terms of managerial effectiveness and productive efficiency.[53] Moreover, what has been lost—in terms of efficiency—by the lack of competition has probably been more than offset by industry's dedication and strong commitment to economic progress and by the apparently high achievement drive of Japan's industrial managers and workers.

Without such a cooperative spirit in Japanese industry, given the great scarcity of national natural resources, a much more destructive and inefficient sellers' market probably would have emerged. In numerous countries, critical supply shortages, in conjunction with a strong tendency on the part of enterprises in their roles as suppliers not to cooperate with customer firms, have been and still are serious barriers to managerial effectiveness and productive efficiency. This is most notable in the Soviet Union, other extensively planned economies, and poorer countries, although sellers' markets result in rather ineffective cooperation between firms in some advanced, essentially capitalistic countries as well. More will be said about this problem in the chapter on economic constraints. In general, the economic framework—and often the legal system—of a particular country tends to have a very important bearing on the degree to which productive enterprises cooperate with one another in the achievement of their respective plans and objectives. In turn, this has considerable impact on managerial performance and general economic progress.

One other aspect of cooperation warrants brief further discussion in this section, and that is the relationship between cooperation and trust in industry. If fair impersonal dealings and general trust of strangers in industrial endeavors are the norm in a particular country, this tends to be conducive to more effective cooperation and greater managerial effectiveness. On the other hand if there is typically distrust and lack of cooperation unless the parties involved are relatives or good friends, then it is likely that prices, supply relationships, financial dealings, and other business transactions would frequently be rather inefficient; for in such cases the economics of the situation would usually not be considered of major importance. One scientific study reveals that there is substantially greater trust of strangers among business managers in the U.S. than in Turkey, Italy, or Poland.[54] As will be indicated in later chapters, the degree of trust and resulting coopera-

---

[53] For an interesting related discussion on the lack of competition within Japanese industry see: D. Miller, "The Honorable Picnic: Doing Business in Japan," *Harvard Business Review*, November-December, 1961, pp. 79–86, and, J. Tokuyama, letter in response to Miller's article in *Harvard Business Review*, March-April, 1962, pp. 24–28.

[54] D. McClelland, *op. cit.*, Table 7.8, p. 288, and p. 291.

tion in business dealings is often closely interconnected with the politico-legal, and in some cases the economic, framework of a particular country.

Other sociological-cultural factors that tend to have a significant bearing on managerial performance are discussed and analyzed in the following chapter.

# Chapter 8

# Sociological-Cultural Constraints:
# External

In this chapter consideration is given to a number of sociological-cultural constraints which are closely interrelated in reality. The most important of these appears to be the dominant attitude toward achievement and work which exists in a given society, and this constraint is discussed first.

## VIEW OF ACHIEVEMENT AND WORK

Cultures vary widely in their views of productive achievement and work. Often those persons most admired are those who have risen far and achieved much. Work for the sake of work and the will to succeed rank highly in such situations. The American society is one example of such a culture, and our Horatio Alger legends, the Calvinist ethic, and several centuries of achievement-oriented tradition encourage such behavior.

Not all societies show this general attitude toward productive achievement and work. In many cultures work and achievement not directly associated with economic progress are regarded as the ultimate status symbol for an admired man. Leisure is a particularly desired status position in many cultures: a wealthy man is an idle man. In other cases, *work* to the wealthy implies labor at artistic, cultural, religious, military, or governmental positions, but rarely business. A wealthy man's sons are typically instilled with their father's values.

The focus of this study is on achievement in the economic sense. It is clear that other types of artistic or institutional labor may be quite important in the formulation of the total culture; but however important such noneconomic activities may be, they are not directly relevant to our analysis. It should be noted that if a given culture is concerned only with things which are unrelated to production, it will be a poor society, regardless of other virtues it may have. It also will be relatively unable to pursue its noneconomic goals, if these require economic resources such as high skill, high talent, manpower, and capital. A country like the United States can easily build more places of worship per capita than India, simply because more resources are available for such purposes.

The attitude toward achievement and work in many societies tends to be a significant constraint related to managerial performance and productive efficiency, and it may prove vital to raise achievement aspirations in the culture if the pace of economic progress and growth is to be quickened. Precisely how this can be done is beyond the scope of this study;[1] our primary concern here is that of analyzing critical sociological-cultural attitudes and resulting behavioral patterns which bear directly on managerial performance and economic progress.

### View of Achievement and Work, Managerial Performance, and Economic Progress

The importance of a country's view of achievement and work as a vital determinant of managerial performance and productive efficiency must not be understated. Indeed it may be the most critical determinant of all. One outstanding scientific study on achievement motivation and economic development, based on substantial empirical and experimental evidence, has this to say about the subject:

A concern for achievement as expressed in imaginative literature—folk tales and stories for children—is associated in modern times with a more rapid rate of economic development. The generalization is confirmed not only for Western, free-enterprise democracies like England and the United States but also for Communist countries like Russia, Bulgaria or Hungary, or primitive tribes that are just beginning to make contact with modern technological society. It holds in the main whether a country is developed or undeveloped, poor or rich, industrial or agricultural, free or totalitarian. In other words there is a strong suggestion here that men with high achievement motives will find a way to economic achievement given fairly wide variations in opportunity and social structure. What people want, they somehow manage to get, in the main and on the average, though . . . other factors can modify the speed with which they get it.[2]

This study—unlike many behavioral and economic studies—does emphasize the importance of management and entrepreneurship in economic progress. It is clearly not enough to merely have a population with a high achievement drive, such human resources must be effectively combined and coordinated through able management, if substantial economic progress is to be forthcoming. Also, both industrial managers and those they manage must, in sizable numbers, have a favorable view of achievement and work.

It is not essential that an individual be solely concerned with self-

---

[1] A comprehensive analysis of how the achievement drive of the population can be raised in order to accelerate economic growth is presented in *ibid.*, chap. x. See also G. Elder, Jr., "Family Structure and Educational Attainment," *American Sociological Review*, February, 1965, pp. 94–96.

[2] D. McClelland, *The Achieving Society* (New York: D. Van Nostrand Co., Inc., 1961), p. 105.

interest and his own personal achievement for him to work hard, although in extensively Calvinistic countries individual achievement is highly valued. In some countries the individual's identification with some notion of collective or even national achievement may result in hard work. For example: in the U.S. the primary emphasis is generally on individual achievement; in Japan it is on group and company achievement, although national achievement may play a more critical role than in the U.S.; in the Soviet Union emphasis on hard work and both individual and national achievement have been largely responsible for this particular country's economic progress in the past several decades.

If a given country succeeds in raising the achievement drive of the population generally, this may improve managerial effectiveness and productive efficiency; for people with a high need for achievement tend to be more favorably disposed toward hard work and doing a job well—particularly nonroutine jobs—than low achievement people. Equally important, however, is the allocation and distribution of high achievement human resources in different jobs and occupations throughout the society. It is critical that there be sizable numbers of industrial managers (including entrepreneurs) and workers who have a high achievement drive.

In general, in a country where much of the population has a relatively high achievement drive and views work associated with business and industry favorably, managerial effectiveness and productive efficiency would usually be much greater than if the reverse were true. Industrial managers with a high achievement drive would be inclined to desire and strive to accomplish fairly challenging—but realistic—enterprise plans and objectives. Such objectives would typically pertain to some notion of greater output, productivity, efficiency, and/or profitability. Such managers would also be more likely to take calculated rational risks, to innovate, and to be quite favorably disposed to change in the direction of greater economic progress,[3] as long as the attainment of their priority operational goals is not threatened.[4]

In an achievement and work oriented society it will usually be easier for

---

[3] *Ibid.*, chap. vi, and the sources cited therein; McClelland, "Business Drive and National Achievement," *Harvard Business Review*, July-August, 1962, pp. 103–106; J. Atkinson, J. Bastion, R. Earl, and G. Litwin, "The Achievement Motive, Goal Setting, and Probability Preference," *Journal of Abnormal Social Psychology*, LX (1960), 27–36; E. Shils, "The Concentration and Dispersion of Charisma: Their Bearing on Economic Policy in Underdeveloped Countries," *World Politics*, No. 11, 1958, pp. 1 ff; F. Sulton, S. Harris, C. Kaysen, and J. Tobin, *The American Business Creed* (Cambridge, Mass.: Harvard University Press, 1956), pp. 327 ff; H. Green, and R. Knapp, "Time Judgment, Aesthetic Preference, and the Need for Achievement," *Journal of Abnormal Social Psychology*, LVIII (1959), 140–142; J. Atkinson, "Motivational Determinants of Risk-Taking Behavior," *Psychology Review*, LXIV (1957), 359 ff; F. Redlich, "Business Leadership: Diverse Origins and Variant Forms," *Economic Development and Cultural Change*, VI (1958), 177–190.

[4] This qualification has been added because even managers having a high achievement drive may resist innovation and change if they are evaluated and rewarded on the basis of short term performance and results which are in conflict with innovation. Cf. B. Richman, "Managerial Opposition to Product Innovation in Soviet Union Industry," *California Management Review*, winter, 1963, pp. 11–26.

industry to recruit personnel who are willing to work reasonably hard and efficiently. It is true that in any society competent management may raise productive efficiency by establishing a proper work environment through clear goal setting, careful planning, effective direction and training, and sound organization; however, where the culture is not achievement oriented in the economically productive sense, even highly competent industrial managers and effective leaders may well have greater difficulty in motivating personnel to work hard and efficiently than will less able leader-managers in an achievement oriented country. Moreover, in a culture where achievement is highly valued both managers and workers would tend to put considerable effort into self-development and improving their qualifications, in order to become more successful in the future.

Evidence strongly suggests that able persons with a high achievement drive are likely to make the best managers of the entrepreneurial type.[5] Studies of industrial managers in the U.S., Poland, and Italy also suggest that a high achievement drive tends to contribute to managerial success—as measured by income or job responsibilities;[6] but, as will be discussed shortly, it does not necessarily follow that persons having a high need for achievement pursue business and managerial careers. Managers of this type are crucial, however, if business firms are to grow, and particularly if new ones are to be created; therefore, in less developed countries in particular, it is vital that many competent persons having a high achievement drive pursue careers in business and industrial management if economic progress is a key social goal.

A study based on some 800 tests administered to business and industrial managers in four countries—the U.S., Italy, Turkey, and Poland—reveals a fairly close correlation between the average achievement drive of the managers in each country and the relative levels of economic development of the four countries.[7] The American managers had the highest achievement score, followed by the Polish, then the Italian, and finally the Turkish managers. With the exception of Poland, which suffered much more extensive war damage than any of the other countries and which has a slightly lower real per capita income than Italy, the achievement scores correlated very closely and directly with the level of economic development of the countries; however, if the economic growth rates achieved during the late 1940's and the 1950's by the four countries were to be taken into account by weighting this factor by, say, 20 percent, then there would be a direct correlation right down the line.

## Cultural and Religious Values and Achievement Motivation

Prevailing religious beliefs and cultural values, in conjunction with parental behavior, child-rearing practices, and the formal system of educa-

---

[5] See the sources cited in Footnotes 3 and 4 above.

[6] McClelland, *The Achieving Society*, pp. 267–271.

[7] *Ibid.*, pp. 260–266.

tion in a particular country, usually have a direct and very significant bearing on the dominant view toward work and achievement. As early as 1904, the eminent German sociologist Max Weber discussed in convincing detail how the Protestant Reformation and Calvinism produced a new character type which infused a more vigorous spirit into the attitudes of both workers and managers and which ultimately resulted in the development of modern industrial capitalism.[8]

There is a close correlation of countries in terms of how deeply the Calvinist spirit has penetrated their economic and social behavior with real per capita income and level of economic development. Thus, in 1958, all fifteen countries of the world with per capita incomes of over $700 per year were those which had followed the Calvinist ethic extensively; and, with the possible exceptions of France and Belgium, all were quite extensively Protestant in religion. No country where the Calvinist ethic had deeply penetrated was not included in this list of most wealthy countries, while none of the extensively non-Calvinist nations had yet achieved such economic success.[9]

Calvin saw in each man a basic imperfection which could be partially ameliorated by prayer, thrift, piety, and work. The work notion was extremely significant; the argument here is that each man should attempt to achieve grace by being not only a God-fearing, pious man but also a man who would work for work's sake. It was not enough merely to earn one's bread; work should continue constantly through life, even if the individual was already very wealthy. Luxurious idleness was a certain prelude to sin.[10]

In the United States the familiar theme of the businessman returning home after his ten hour day with a full briefcase is one vivid representation of this attitude. This attitude is not only shared by men born to poverty. The familiar American pattern of the working millionaire, who has an option of luxurious leisure and idleness, is common. Many a third generation president of a large family firm could easily retire to his country estate but prefers to remain and work. In this culture, it is expected that they will try to push their sons to even greater achievements. Higher level jobs, including management positions, are eagerly sought, as they imply successful pursuit of the goal of personal achievement. Such attitudes pervade the American society from top to bottom, forming an important part of the

---

[8] Weber, *The Protestant Ethic and the Spirit of Capitalism*, translated by Talcott Parsons (New York: Charles Scribner's Sons, 1948).

[9] See: R. Farmer, "The Ethical Dilemma of American Capitalism," *California Management Review*, summer, 1964, p. 56, and footnote 32; P. Alpert, *Economic Development* (New York: Free Press of Glencoe, Inc., 1963), pp. 7–8. See also the pertinent data relating to Protestantism and levels of economic development in McClelland, *The Achieving Society*, chap. iii.

[10] Cf.: P. Tawney, *Religion and the Rise of Capitalism* (Gloucester, Mass.: Peter Smith, 1962), pp. 110 ff; A. Hyma, "The Economic Views of the Protestant Reformers," reprinted in *Protestantism and Capitalism*, (Boston: D. C. Heath & Company, 1959), pp. 94–106.

American scene. Schools, churches, and other social organizations also emphasize this attitude. The achievement drive among American business-men may be even higher than in most or all other Calvinistic societies.[11]

On the other hand, traditional Hinduism, Buddhism, Islam, and even Catholicism are not generally conducive to a high achievement drive in their orthodox followers. For example, orthodox Hinduism explicitly teaches that concern with earthly achievements is a snare and a delusion. In general, in the formal ritualistic ecclesiastical systems of these religions the individual is "safe" if he does exactly what he is supposed to do, performs correct rituals, says his prayers often enough, calls in the right priest at the right time, and so on.[12]

From the above discussion it is fallacious to conclude that one who considers himself a Protestant necessarily has a high achievement motiva-tion, or that a Hindu, Buddhist, Moslem, or Catholic automatically has a low achievement drive. It is true that the Protestant ethic and Calvinism make this religion particularly achievement and action oriented as against belief oriented involving dogma and ritual; but it is the values associated with Calvinistic Protestantism and their *implementation* that lead to a high achievement drive, not Protestantism per se. In the same vein, the achieve-ment drive of a member of one of the other great world religions is related to the extent to which he *behaves* in ways advocated by traditional religious doctrine and how he interprets such doctrine. If he adopts certain values associated with Calvinism he can have just as high, or even higher, an achievement drive as any Calvinistic Protestant.

There is evidence that where Catholics follow a course of modernistic (or liberal) as compared to traditional (or ultraconservative) Catholicism, they often encompass much of the Protestant or Calvinistic ethic regarding achievement and work. For example, studies dealing with Catholics in the U.S. and Germany reveal that traditional Catholics appear to have some of the values and attitudes that are associated with low achievement, while other groups of Catholics moved closer to the achievement ethic.[13] Catholic reform movements in such places as Monterrey, Mexico—and more re-

---

[11] Cf.: Lewis and Stewart, *op. cit.*, pp. 163ff; this source points out that British man-agers do not typically have as much drive as their American counterparts. It is part of American folklore that the U.S. businessman works extremely long hours and often ac-quires ulcers or a heart attack in the process. It appears that this is quite often the case in the real business world in America. Cf.: Editors of *Fortune, The Executive Life,* (Garden City, N.Y.: Doubleday & Company, Inc., 1956); Sutton *et al; op. cit.,* pp. 335 ff; Anne Roe, *The Psychology of Occupations* (New York: John Wiley & Sons, Inc., 1956), pp. 184 ff.

[12] McClelland, *The Achieving Society,* pp. 357 ff. See also the interesting and in-formative discussions in J. Goheen, M. Srinivas, D. Karve, and M. Singer, "India's Cul-tural Values and Economic Development," *Economic Development and Cultural Change,* VII (October, 1958), 1–12; K. Sundaram, "Social and Human Problems in Introducing Technological Change," *Proceedings* (CIOS), 1963, pp. 497–498.

[13] McClelland, *The Achieving Society,* pp. 359–362; D. Miller, and G. Swanson, *The Changing American Parent* (New York: John Wiley & Sons, Inc., 1958); Elder, *op. cit.,* pp. 89–91.

cently in Quebec Province in Canada[14] have done much to raise the achievement level of the population in general and to create a more favorable attitude toward careers in business and industry. One of the authors is from Montreal, in Quebec Province, and has experienced firsthand how a trend in the direction of modernistic Catholicism, in conjunction with French Canadian nationalism and feelings of oppression, has lead to a higher achievement drive, particularly among the Catholic youth, and is attracting many more of them into business and industry.

In general, scientific research in recent years has studied the core religious and ideological values associated with a high achievement drive much more closely than a superficial comparison of such vast religious bodies as Protestantism and Catholicism permits. There clearly are substitutes for Protestantism with regard to high achievement drive and hard work. One study indicates that in the Soviet Union between 1925 and 1950 the achievement drive of the population rose substantially.[15] Communist ideology and the vast amount of publicity aimed at national, and to a lesser degree individual, achievement, as well as dedicated hard work, has undoubtedly done much to spur economic progress and raise managerial effectiveness in Russia and various other Marxist countries. In Japan the great cultural emphasis placed on group and collective achievement and on dedication to one's job has undoubtedly had a similar effect. One study based on questionnaires and interviews conducted in Japanese industry reveals that workers tend to consider their work life at least equal in importance to their personal life.[16]

Vigorous nationalism in newly developing countries may also do much to raise the achievement level of the population and to create a more favorable view toward industrial work; however, in numerous countries desiring rapid economic progress nationalism has unfortunately not yet produced this effect to a significant extent. Frequently, ambitious national economic plans cannot be implemented with much success because much, if not most, of the population lacks a desire to be mobilized for economic progress, lacks interest in achievement and getting ahead, and tends to view work negatively. There is typically little concern for the quality of work; schedules and delivery dates are frequently not met; and there is often much idleness, lateness and absenteeism, even where enterprise managers are well trained, competent men.[17] In such an environment managerial effectiveness and productive efficiency are obviously hampered greatly.

---

[14] McClelland, *The Achieving Society*, p. 412; P. Siekman, "The Revolt of French Canada," *Fortune*, February, 1965, pp. 156 ff.

[15] McClelland, *The Achieving Society*, p. 413. See also R. Bauer, "The Psychology of the Soviet Middle Elite: Two Case Histories," in C. Kluckhohn, H. Murray, and D. Schneider, *Personality in Nature, Society and Culture*, (New York: Alfred A. Knopf, Inc., 1955), pp. 633–650.

[16] Whitehill, *op. cit.*, pp. 11, 109 ff.

[17] Cf.: *Economic Bulletin for Africa*, 1962, pp. 44, 85 ff; Reksodihardjo, *op. cit.*, pp. 342 ff; *The World Social Situation*, p. 79 ff; J. Fayerweather, *The Executive Overseas* (Syracuse, N.Y.: Syracuse University Press, 1959), especially p. 73.

### Class Status, Occupational Choice, and Achievement Motivation

Studies dealing with management and entrepreneurship in a number of countries—including the U.S., Turkey, Italy, Mexico, and Poland—indicate that the best place to recruit business managers is from the middle and lower middle classes, because they are more apt to have a higher need for achievement than if they come from an upper or lower class background.[18] Moreover, available evidence derived through studies conducted in several countries suggests that people from the middle and lower middle classes with a high achievement drive are inclined to prefer and pursue business and managerial careers, since they feel in view of their self-image and aspiration level that they can succeed in this type of occupation.[19] In terms of economic progress, therefore, it is very significant that it is precisely this group of broadly middle class families that in general also produces the highest achievement drive in its sons in the United States, and evidently in many other countries as well.

Hence, as long as there is freedom and opportunity to enter business and industrial management in a particular society, there appears to be a built-in recruiting mechanism for attracting candidates of the middle and lower classes having a high achievement drive. A fairly sizable and growing middle and lower middle class may, therefore, be essential for a high level of managerial effectiveness and sustained economic development. For underdeveloped and newly developing countries, however, a vicious circle is involved; development is typically necessary to create a substantial pool of middle class managerial and entrepreneurial talent which in turn makes rapid development possible.

There is also convincing evidence that in most countries upper class persons with high achievement drive are not inclined to pursue business and industrial careers. They generally prefer the traditional high prestige professions such as medicine, politics, law, or scientific research. Studies conducted in several countries—including the U.S., Japan, India, and Brazil—indicate that upper class boys interested in business careers tend to be highly conservative, not very high in achievement drive, and probably more often than not ill suited for a business or industrial management career.[20] They may often pursue business and managerial careers because they feel that they cannot succeed in the traditional, high prestige professions as a result of a poor school record or lack of confidence and ability, or family pressures may force them into such careers.

---

[18] See the studies and findings presented in McClelland, *op. cit.*, pp. 252–266, 276–280.

[19] *Ibid.*; see also C. Mahone, "Fear of Failure and Unrealistic Vocational Aspiration," *Journal of Abnormal Psychology*, No. 60, 1960, pp. 253 ff.

[20] McClelland, *The Achieving Society*, pp. 255–256. S. Lipset, and R. Bendix, *Social Mobility in Industrial Society* (Berkeley and Los Angeles: University of California Press, 1959), pp. 134 ff; J. Kahl, "Three Types of Mexican Industrial Workers," *Economic Development and Cultural Change*, VIII (1960), pp. 164–173.

Such a picture as that painted above helps to explain further the vicious circle that many less developed countries are caught in. Because they are typically faced with a critical shortage of high achievement human resources and because there is usually not a sizable middle and lower middle class, they do not have a steady flow of entrepreneurial and managerial talent upward from this class which creates new business enterprises or vigorously expands existing ones. Hence, business and industrial leaders in such countries must be recruited primarily from the upper classes where the capital and opportunity to go into business exist; but such persons very often have a low achievement drive. They also tend to have an ultraconservative ideology, believing strongly in family solidarity, so that family firms are established into which their sons are expected to go whether or not they have the talent or motivation for business and managerial activity. Thus opportunity to rise in the business and industrial world is often denied even to the small flow of people with a high achievement drive from the middle and lower classes. Such countries not only have a critically short supply of entrepreneurial and managerial talent, they frequently fail to even recruit or utilize efficiently the supply they have.[21]

## Class Mobility, Individual Opportunity, and the Achievement Drive

Class and individual mobility is the subject of a later section, but a brief discussion is in order here since this topic is closely related to achievement motivation. Class mobility and opportunities for individual advancement often have a direct and vital bearing on the view toward achievement in a given society. Where much of the population is explicitly excluded—because of class, racial, or religious prejudice, or other forms of discrimination—from getting ahead regardless of personal ability, it is not likely that a high achievement drive will persist among those groups acutely and constantly discriminated against.

On the other hand, members of minority groups who have a positive self-image, and have some leeway and means to get ahead if they have the ability, are likely to have a high achievement drive and often make excellent managers of the entrepreneurial type.[22] The Chinese in Indonesia, the Armenians in the Middle East, the Lebanese in Africa and elsewhere, and the Jews in various relatively underdeveloped (as well as advanced) countries are examples of minority groups with a high achievement drive which

---

[21] This is one of the central themes running through much of Harbison and Myers, *Management in the Industrial World.* See also: Kahl, *op. cit.*; Fayerweather, *op. cit.*, p. 100.

[22] See the outstanding comprehensive study by E. Hagen, *On the Theory of Social Change* (Homewood, Ill.: Dorsey Press, 1962). See also N. Jacobs, *The Bahai'i of Iran and Pariah Entrepreneurship* (mimeographed paper, International Development Research Center, Indiana University, April, 1964). Another interesting study is one that deals with the Antioquians of Columbia; see C. Savage, *Social Reorganization in a Factory in the Andes* (Monograph Number 7, [Ithaca, N.Y.: Cornell University, The Society for Applied Anthropology, 1964]).

perform crucial entrepreneurial and managerial roles in societies where much or most of the population is low in achievement motivation. While Judaism has in common most of the values pertaining to achievement and work associated with Calvinism, the traditional religions of the other minority groups cited above do not.

In general, societies which generate lower class or minority group high achievers and then block them off from important positions in the society often create a potentially explosive social situation. Such individuals, finding legitimate business, artistic, bureaucratic, military, and religious prestige posts impossible to achieve, often turn to revolutionary ferment to gain their personal ends. The result may be social ferment, class bitterness and strife, and unproductive unrest almost everywhere. The more driving and capable the outcasts are, the more dangerous such a situation is. Trotsky and even Lenin could hardly expect to achieve great heights in czarist Russia, however capable they might have been. Nehru, as an Indian in imperial India, was quite effectively cut off from any of the high positions he coveted. Such political examples are easy to find, particularly in cultural situations where business has not been highly regarded as a profession. The United States also has had some difficulties in this regard. Much of the rapid trade union development in the depressed 1930's was led by very capable men who, because of economic depression and some class bias, were unable to achieve status and success in business. Many an active Negro in the present civil rights movement would probably prove to be an extremely competent business leader—if his skin were not black.

A fairly common attitude in any society held by those in superior class positions is that the lower classes should behave; however, if, as in the United States, a strong pressure for individual achievement is also inculcated in individuals at an early age, the society will eventually pay the price (which may prove to be quite high) for such class blockage. If very competent and aggressive persons of what is deemed inferior status cannot even succeed in business, they may well turn their attention to revolutionary pursuits which eventually can lead to social change and, in extreme cases, a new social order.

### Public vs. Private Enterprise and Achievement Motivation

Contrary to a commonly held belief, it is not necessarily true that managers of public or state owned firms tend to have a lower achievement drive than those in private firms. Evidence available strongly suggests that there is nothing intrinsic in public enterprise which universally lowers the achievement motivation of personnel or tends to select those with a low achievement drive. All industrial enterprises are state owned in Russia and other Communist countries, yet several of these countries including the U.S.S.R. have experienced considerable economic progress in the past few decades. Yugoslavia, under a system of public ownership of industry, has achieved one of the highest average annual economic growth rates in the world during the past fifteen years.

One scientific research study dealing with management in the U.S., Italy, Turkey, and Poland presents some interesting findings regarding achievement motivation in public as compared to private enterprise.[23] While in Italy and Turkey the public managers apparently had, on the average, a lower achievement drive than the private managers under study, there was no significant difference between the two classes of managers studied in the U.S. The Polish public enterprise managers scored significantly higher than either the Turkish or Italian private enterprise managers.

## The Relationship between Achievement Motivation and the Need for Affiliation

There is evidence available which indicates that there tends to be a negative correlation between high achievement drive in managers and their need for affiliation, affiliation being defined as concern for establishing, maintaining, or restoring a positive affective relationship with another person or organization. In other words, where managers have a high achievement drive they tend to have little need for affiliation. This situation is generally more conducive to a high level of managerial effectiveness and productive efficiency than the reverse, since behavior associated with a high need for affiliation is often in conflict with productive achievement and efficiency.

The study dealing with management in the U.S., Poland, Turkey, and Italy reveals that the American and Polish managers have not only a higher achievement drive than the Turkish and Italian managers but also a lower need for affiliation.[24] Another study reveals that executives in countries like Italy and Mexico often seem more concerned with adjusting the relationships among people than with solving a problem more efficiently, whatever the cost in human relations.[25] For example, an American executive working for a U.S. subsidiary in Mexico tried to get his Mexican purchasing agent to do something about the poor quality of some supplies and the erratic way in which they were delivered. Both problems were costing the company money, and the situation was further aggravated because the production manager insisted on keeping a high inventory of supplies against a rainy day. The difficulty did not seem great to the American; it was a simple matter of getting tough with the supplier or finding a new one. To the Mexican, however, it was more complicated, because he was more concerned about the personal relationships involved. He wanted to please the American manager, and he understood the efficiency problem; but he also

---

[23] McClelland, *The Achieving Society*, pp. 292–230.

[24] *Ibid.*, pp. 287–290.

[25] Fayerweather, *op. cit.*, pp. 1–3, 73 ff.

felt that the American did not understand how loyal and helpful the supplier had been in the past and how much the production department just wanted a high inventory to feel better. The main point to be stressed here is that a high need for affiliation tends to be associated with a low achievement drive and, hence, with a lower level of managerial effectiveness and productive efficiency.

A lack of affiliation also means that high achievers are typically willing to move—and mobility, particularly in large countries like the United States, is often an extremely important factor in executive success. Not all men are willing to move their homes 2,000 or 3,000 miles to a different city, exposing their families to different local conditions, schools, and friends; but millions of families make such moves each year. A persistent American legend is that of the young man moving to the city to seek his fortune, while a more modern legend is that of the new junior executive in the modest suburb, who knows that this stop is just one way station in his career.[26]

### Effects of Education and Training on Achievement Motivation

A country's system of formal education undoubtedly has an impact on the achievement level of the population. Public education usually corresponds quite closely to religious and ideological values prevailing in the culture.

In many less developed countries much attention is being given to the expansion of management training programs, and they are enthusiastically recommended by various experts as a means of professionalizing management and generating high-level managerial resources. Since such programs are usually oriented toward improving the ability of managers to perform more efficiently and solve their problems successfully, it might be supposed that they would increase the achievement drive of participants, or at least change value attitudes in the direction of those held by managers in the most developed countries; however, there is little if any available evidence indicating that these programs definitely achieve their intended effect, particularly regarding achievement motivation.

In general, it is questionable whether most educational and training programs aimed at improving the qualifications of managerial or nonmanagerial personnel employed in industry serve to raise significantly the achievement drive of participants. Psychological studies and tests indicate that the crucial period for acquiring a high achievement drive typically lies somewhere between the ages of five and ten.[27]

---

[26] Cf.: W. Whyte, *The Organization Man* (New York: Simon and Shuster, Inc., 1956), Part VII.

[27] See the studies and evidence cited in McClelland, *op. cit.*, pp. 340–356, 415. See also: M. Winterbollom, "The Relation of Childhood Training in Independence to Achievement Motivation," in J. Atkinson, ed., *Motives in Fantasy, Action and Society* (Princeton, N.J.: D. Van Nostrand Co., Inc., 1958), pp. 453–478; B. Rosen and R. D'Androde, "The Psychological Origins of Achievement Motivation," *Sociometry*, XXII, (1959), 185–218.

A Harvard doctoral dissertation in the field of psychology presents evidence that Turkish middle managers attending the management training program at the University of Istanbul did not change in their attitudes in the direction predicted.[28] Moreover, the researcher found no difference in the achievement drive of participants when the achievement test was given before training to one group and after training to another comparable group. If the training had any marked effect, one would have expected the latter scores to be higher. The result is not conclusive, but it is not encouraging either.

Hence, the importance of creating new motives and values in management training programs—as well as other types of adult industrial training programs—in less developed countries needs also to be stressed if the achievement drive of participants is to be significantly increased. Otherwise, they may learn new techniques and concepts but not be motivated to apply them in practice. They may also fail to acquire a higher achievement drive or a desire to work harder and more efficiently. Character education may be needed for this purpose, and the study on Turkish managers suggests that ordinary management training courses do not attempt to develop character or change basic values.

## CLASS STRUCTURE AND INDIVIDUAL MOBILITY

### Social Barriers to Managerial Effectiveness and Economic Progress

If a given country deliberately or unconsciously prevents a substantial number of citizens from entering the ranks of management or other responsible industrial jobs, there is likely to be a negative impact on managerial effectiveness in many if not most industrial enterprises. Where certain large religious groups, races, or castes are excluded from various industrial occupations, including management, the constraint on the staffing function is clear. The same is true where people are extensively discriminated against or favored for certain jobs not on the basis of personal ability but solely for reasons of family connections, personal background, educational institution attended, political affiliation, age, or sex.

No matter how well qualified or potentially able an Indian Moslem or a member of the former "untouchable" caste might be, for example, he might prove unsuitable for training for higher management. A Pakistani Hindu might find himself in a similar situation in that country. In some countries, women managers or skilled women technicians might be tolerated or even highly regarded, as is often the case in Russia—in a traditional Moslem culture, the selection of women even for relatively menial positions in industry might be considered an abomination.

In such situations it may be possible to bend local custom to some

---

[28] N. Bradburn, *The Managerial Role in Turkey: A Psychological Study* (unpublished doctoral dissertation, Cambridge, Mass., Harvard University, 1960); also cited in McClelland, *op. cit.*, p. 415.

extent, but gross violations may in the short run prove very risky and costly; they may lead to considerable instability, insecurity, friction, and general unrest among enterprise personnel accustomed to a certain status or class hierarchy with regard to various occupations. This would be even more likely in a poor society where there is considerable unemployment and relatively few opportunities for advancement. Disregard for the prevailing traditional class structure in staffing various positions, selecting persons for promotion, or even in connection with compensation policies pursued, could also result in a destructive informal organization.

Any culture has some class mobility, and the history of almost any country contains the stories of at least a few capable persons from various classes or minority groups acutely discriminated against who managed to rise dramatically in business, politics, or other careers; but if the barriers are extensive, quite firm, and hard to surmount, the result will be to eliminate the potential capabilities of numerous citizens long before they have a chance even to try for success or advancement in business or other productive endeavors. Such an environment would tend to reduce sharply the potential efficiency of the productive system.

In general, if the society contains many barriers to class and individual mobility, the result is likely to be that responsible jobs in productive enterprises are staffed with only a small percentage of available persons. Other, perhaps more competent, people are excluded for social rather than economic reasons. The smaller the pool of acceptable candidates for managerial and other key posts in industrial firms as a percentage of the total population, the greater the constraint on managerial effectiveness throughout industry. If the pool of acceptable candidates is not only small but also consists on many persons not having suitable education or training and/or a fairly high achievement drive, managerial effectiveness will suffer even more substantially.

In countries where individual mobility and advancement are based in large part on educational achievement and where access to formal education at all levels is open to the large majority of qualified candidates regardless of their family background, this would tend to break down class barriers and increase individual mobility. This has already happened extensively in many Communist countries such as the Soviet Union and in advanced capitalistic nations such as the United States, where a growing number of families of all classes are often able to get their qualified sons and daughters into even the top universities and colleges. The trend is also in this direction in many newly developing countries which are rapidly expanding their public educational facilities; but here considerable progress in breaking down class barriers and prejudices through education will still take many years.

Individual mobility of the horizontal type may also have a significant bearing on managerial effectiveness and economic progress. If cultural values and tradition prevent most individuals in a given country from relocating to other communities and enterprises when opportunities exist to use their talents more fully and effectively in another job, this can hamper managerial effectiveness in industry over time. This appears to be the case currently, for example, in Japanese industry under the lifetime employment system. In traditional rural cultures, such as those found in Africa, there tends to be little or no individual mobility. Here urbanization in the economy does increase class and individual mobility, but this typically takes considerable time.

The ideal staffing situation, in terms of managerial effectiveness and economic progress, would be one in which responsible jobs are filled by individuals who, on the basis of objective evaluation, appear to have the abilities, skills, and motivation necessary to do the job well. Each individual would be chosen with little or no weight being given to his general class standing, and each would be quite free to relocate when he could obtain a job that would use his talents and energies more fully and effectively. For such a staffing philosophy to be adhered to extensively in industry—leaving aside the important problems involved in accurately appraising the abilities of job candidates—it would be necessary for the majority of the working population to support or at least accept it. There is obviously no society in the real world where this ideal situation exists to a truly high degree; however, the degree and extent of discrimination in staffing that does exist in industry varies enormously among countries.

The rigid power of organized religion and/or ruling dictatorships in various African, Asian, and Latin American nations, and even in countries like Spain, has preserved hierarchical social relations and greatly hindered economic progress. In countries characterized by political instability and corruption, appointments to important managerial posts in public enterprises and even in major private firms are frequently based on political pressure, loyalty, or affiliation, with no regard for individual competence. Often high school or college graduates whose political loyalties are questionable must settle for inferior jobs far beneath their talents or abilities. In countries characterized by a system of patrimonial business enterprises whose managements strive for personal security and family solidarity, nepotism in staffing important positions tends to be very extensive. Unless the sons and relatives who assume such positions have a fairly high achievement drive and proper training—and this is typically not the case in many countries—managerial effectiveness and economic progress suffer accordingly.

In most countries that were formerly under colonial rule—such as Indonesia under the Dutch, India under the British, Vietnam under the French, and the Congo under the Belgians—nationals were typically prevented from advancing up the managerial hierarchy in business and industry regardless of their potential ability. When such countries obtained their independence they were faced with extremely critical shortages of local high talent manpower resources because of discrimination under colonial rule. In some of these countries their governments have attempted to break down class barriers in society at large and in industry. While some progress has been made, nepotism, connections, and politics rather than competence still tend to be the major criteria used in staffing important posts in probably the large majority of cases.

### Examples in Various Countries[29]

In general, it seems that in probably the large majority of countries in the world today the class structure and barriers to individual mobility still serve as significant constraints with regard to managerial effectiveness and economic progress—but the problem is usually more serious in less developed as compared to advanced countries. In Pakistan, for example, managerial personnel for industrial firms are, with very few exceptions, recruited from the same family, clan, tribe, or community, rather than on the basis of ability. Often relatives of powerful government officials are appointed to key industrial positions in order to get special favors or treatment from the government.[30]

In Indonesia there is still much emphasis on class and social standing in industrial staffing. Nepotism is pervasive, political pressure leads to the creation of unneeded positions which are frequently staffed by incompetent individuals, and educated and talented people are often blocked from attaining positions more suited to their talents.[31] Competent persons blocked from career advancement in this manner tend to become frustrated and probably less efficient in their work over time. Their achievement drive is likely to be lowered as well, if they are consistently confronted with this type of situation.

In India, nepotism, religion, caste, and business community connections are still typically the major criteria used in staffing major positions in industry, although gradually more higher management positions—particularly in public enterprises—are being filled on the basis of individual competence. Recent empirical studies indicate that the caste system still plays a significant, albeit slowly declining, role in shaping the occupational structure in the Indian economy—but apparently its roll is somewhat less in

---

[29] Harbison and Myers, *Management in the Industrial World*, contains much relevant data on the impact of class structure on management staffing and entrepreneurship in twelve countries. While the book is now several years old, the findings presented appear to be generally applicable today in view of our recent research. It often takes many years, or even decades, to change substantially staffing and entrepreneurial patterns in industry, although some countries are moving much more rapidly in the direction of more efficient industrial staffing than others. Considerable use has also been made in this section of the findings and sources referred to in Berleson and Steiner, *op. cit.*, chap. xi, and Hagan, *op. cit.*

[30] Raza, *op. cit.*

[31] Reksodihardjo, *op. cit.*, chap. iv and pp. 333 ff.

urban as compared to rural areas.[32] One source sums up the nature and consequences of this situation aptly:

The recruitment policy pursued within the private sector of the economy is said to follow caste lines especially as far as the higher and middle administrative conditions are concerned. Thus personnel belonging to the same caste or region as the founder of the concern may be "imported" from places hundreds of miles away from the seat of the company. Employment policies may thus degenerate into a form of caste and kinship charity which is liable to cause serious undercurrents of resentment among those aspirants who do not belong to the "right caste," quite apart from the fact that positions are not filled by the most competent persons available.[33]

Nepotism, favoritism, and other social factors in staffing in Indian industry also significantly hinder managerial effectiveness. This situation is reflected in a recent statement made by a prominent Indian authority in the field of administration: "Heredity, status, nepotism and favoritism play an uncomfortably large part in the selection and employment of management personnel, and the system of recruitment on the basis of potential ability, competence and skill has not yet taken firm root."[34] It is true that the lack of job opportunities in the Indian economy due to the present stage of industrialization is a major reason why social factors of the types noted above play a major role in staffing decisions. Nevertheless, inefficient staffing practices greatly hinder managerial effectiveness and economic progress.

Nepotism and family ties still serve as key factors in staffing decisions throughout much of Latin America, even in the large private firms. A candid statement made recently by a Brazilian business executive reveals some of the reasons and consequences of nepotism in industry in that country.

The family idea here is strong, you get a young fellow with ability and he works hard expecting to get ahead and then along comes the 20-year old son of the owner and he's the boss. It discourages people who are not relatives. Of course, it's pretty important to have close family control at the top because you need absolute loyalty. No one in Brazil considers it dishonest to cheat the government. But to cheat, you need close family type management and control.

---

[32] E. Driver, "Caste and Occupational Structure in Central India," *Journal of Social Forces*, October, 1962, pp. 26 ff; U. Pareek and T. Moulik, "Sociometric Study of a North Indian Village," *International Journal of Sociometrics*, III (1963), 7 ff; G. Ghurye, *Caste and Class in India* (Bombay: Popular Book Depot, 1957); R. Lambert, *Workers, Factories and Social Change in India* (Princeton, N.J.: Princeton University Press, 1963), chap. v.

[33] W. Kapp, *Hindu Economic Development and Economic Planning* (New York: Asia Publishing House, 1963), p. 47; See also, C. Vakil, "Business Leadership in Under-developed Countries," *Industrialization and Productivity*, No. 2, 1959, pp. 46–51.

[34] A. Agarwala, "Management of Big Business in India," *The Indian Journal of Public Administration*, April-June, 1962, p. 178.

You can not afford to let outsiders in. You have to keep management in the family.[35]

Even in relatively advanced western European countries such as France, Italy, and Germany, appointments to responsible posts are frequently and extensively based on nepotism, although more emphasis is gradually being given to the individual's competence as the need for professional management is recognized, particularly in large companies.[36] As was pointed out earlier, nepotism in industry has not been as serious a constraint upon managerial effectiveness in Germany as compared to other countries characterized by an extensive system of patrimonial firms, since the sons and relatives appointed to key posts in Germany often have received a good higher education and effective training.

Nepotism and family ties are probably not as important in managerial staffing in Egyptian industry as compared to the countries discussed above. Emphasis on individual competence, education, and experience have grown increasingly more important as nationalization of industry and the establishment of new public enterprises have been extended. Managerial positions in the public sector are being filled in many cases by former civil service and government administrators, military officers and university graduates;[37] however, in recent interviews and discussions with graduate students from Egypt studying in America, and with businessmen from various Arab countries, it has been pointed out that in Egyptian industry many managerial jobs are filled by individuals who are politically loyal and completely "trustworthy" but are clearly deficient in the talents and abilities necessary to perform the job effectively and efficiently.

The class structure and barriers to individual mobility are somewhat more flexible in Saudi Arabia than most people might be inclined to think. A fairly sizable number of people of humble origins, including slaves (slavery was officially abolished only in 1962) have risen very far in vocational and class terms. The extreme shortage of literate and educated Saudis means that any Saudi who obtains virtually any kind of education that makes him literate is able to go about as far as his own abilities and ambitions will take him. Aramco has also helped greatly in this class mobility process. Starting around 1947, the company has consistently attempted to create a local entrepreneurial class able to own and manage supporting contracting and distributing facilities required by the oil company, and many Saudis have had an unparalleled opportunity to rise very rapidly in the past generation. At least a handful of millionaires have been created from rather humble origins, and hundreds of others have achieved more modest, but still impressive, success. The careers of such men are well known, and typically approved of, in Arabia.

---

[35] Oberg, *op. cit.*, p. 133.

[36] Harbison and Myers, *Management in the Industrial World*, chaps. xi, xii, and xiv; Granick, *op. cit.*, Parts II and VI.

[37] Harbison and Myers, *Management in the Industrial World*, chap. viii.

In Japanese industry the class structure and barriers to individual mobility are causing growing concern in that country, although changes in the system will probably only evolve very gradually.[38] The employee classification system has traditionally been based on formal education and length of service. Under this system education determines which industrial class or occupational sphere one belongs in when hired. Length of service determines location within the class. For example, it is generally impossible to enter the ranks of management if one has only obtained a junior high school education, and a production worker typically cannot even become foreman. At the top echelons of management, nepotism and/or the "right" prestige university, in conjunction with length of service, are still major determinants in staffing decisions. In this connection, favoritism and "old school ties" are particularly important in top management cliques who decide on major promotions. Yet, even under this system, Japanese industry has achieved a higher degree of professional management than most other countries, and even the son of a peasant may achieve considerable upward mobility if he graduates from a good university.

The problems inherent in the Japanese system are reflected in the following quotations from a study published a few years ago; since that time the situation has not changed significantly:

Even where the (top management) cliques do not exist, the imperviousness of the class to entry from the lower ranks or even from the lower-status universities makes Japanese professional management one of the tightest and most class conscious in the modern world . . . There are indications that by modern standards, today's Japanese management has some shortcomings. Being so sharply differentiated as a class it fails to communicate effectively with its workers. And in basing entry solely on formal education, it stifles upward mobility from the lower ranks. Its insistence on uniformity and its rigid adherence to age as the principal factor in advancement often lead to stagnation and resistance to fundamentally new concepts. The complete absence of horizontal mobility between firms tends to divide the managerial class into airtight compartments.[39]

In British industry, the criteria typically used in making managerial appointments at the top levels, particularly in large corporations, have been under increasing attack in recent years by the British press, journals, and various economic development and government agencies, as well as the British Institute of Management. The British social system, although much more flexible than it was a few decades ago, still carries over a strong feeling of the virtue of "aristocratic" values and gives a high mark to the "right" background in a man being considered for a high level job in industry—more so than in the U.S. or even Sweden.[40]

---

[38] Cf.: Whitehill, *op. cit.*, pp. 19, 54 ff; *Business Week*, October 17, 1964, pp. 45–46.

[39] Harbison and Myers, *Management in the Industrial World*, pp. 260, 263.

[40] *Ibid.*, chaps. xv, xvi, and xviii.

The right type of public school (for example, Eton), the right university background (Oxford or Cambridge) and membership in the proper upper class private clubs continue to be often very important in reaching the top.[41] The so-called Old Boy Network at the top rungs of corporate management persists; and a recent survey reveals that the average age of 100 top British business executives was recently given as sixty-one—older than either bishops or members of the Cabinet.[42] One prominent British publishing executive has recently stated: "The standard of management in business in this country is abysmally low. Too many old men cling on long past their ability to contribute anything. Too many jobs are given to school friends or relations";[43] however, at lower management levels in large British firms, at all levels in smaller firms, and in industries of lower social standing, such as those producing various types of consumer goods, managerial positions are being filled increasingly by persons from the middle and lower classes. In such cases personal competence is often the determining factor in staffing, and it is likely that many individuals from these classes have a high achievement drive. In general, it seems that British industry is moving farther in the direction of professional management.

There does, however, still seem to be considerable antagonism between the blue collar working class and management in many enterprises. This situation is reflected in a statement made recently by an American executive of a U.S. subsidiary firm in Britain:

> A problem that we have encountered in England is that of class feeling. It has been most difficult for us to promote workers into supervision. We have had several capable workers who were promoted to supervisors but were so ostracized by the others in supervision that they asked to be transferred back to work on the bench.[44]

Cultural barriers to horizontal mobility are also hindering economic progress. Many Britons feel that moving from one area to another, for example from Wales to Yorkshire, in order to obtain more favorable employment in industry, is about the same as emigrating. Hence, there exists a great deal of reluctance to move, particularly in established families, which contributes to territorial distinctions and tends to serve as a constraint on potential productive efficiency.[45]

Even the United States—which is commonly regarded as a rather open society in class terms—has many class barriers and constraints on individual mobility. High level management in many major business firms

---

[41] Granick, *op. cit.*, especially pp. 49 ff and chap. vii. Lewis and Stewart, *op. cit.*, pp. 96 ff. "Shaking the Old Boy Network," *Time* magazine, May 22, 1964, pp. 96–97.

[42] "Britain—The Halfhearted Economy," *ibid.*, December 25, 1964, p. 61.

[43] *Ibid.*

[44] "American Business Looks at Britain," *The Manager*, July, 1964, pp. 27–28.

[45] National Economic Development Council (U.K.), *op. cit.*, pp. 11–13.

frequently excludes virtually all minority groups, including Negroes, orientals, Mexicans, and American Indians; most women; and probably most people with unusual physical characteristics, to say nothing of many Jews, Mormons, atheists, and even Catholics.[46] While such barriers have tended to slip gradually over many decades, it is still true that social barriers form a formidable obstacle to many competent persons who might otherwise be qualified.

There is an undoubted cost involved to U.S. society for this type of behavior. As indicated earlier, large, complex productive enterprises are voracious consumers of high grade manpower; and it seems clear that productive efficiency is somewhat less than it might be if such class barriers did not exist. These barriers are not simply those of the firms themselves—quite often many companies are quite willing to hire any acceptable candidate who is qualified; but because few Negroes in the United States are employed as managers, the educational system produces few trained for this job; because few women are engineers, few are encouraged to educate themselves in this demanding profession; and so on. The result can be a perpetuation of the existing system, at a loss to the entire society.

In spite of various social barriers to individual mobility, staffing in American industry is based on professional competence and objective criteria to a much higher degree than in most other countries. Educational qualifications and ability have become increasingly important to a managerial career, and persons of all backgrounds now have access to good schooling and training if they are qualified and have sufficient ambition. In smaller U.S. business firms where nepotism is still practiced quite extensively, sons and relatives who take over the business frequently have a good education, proper training, and/or a fairly high achievement drive. In larger firms where promotions to higher management positions are based largely on social factors, even here the individual selected often has had enough education and training to perform the job fairly adequately, even though someone else could perform it better.

There is considerable evidence that as the United States' economy has developed, business leaders have been drawn more widely from a less elite group.[47] A fairly recent study of the backgrounds of 158 executives attend-

---

[46] See, for example, the following sources which deal with discrimination and prejudice in American business and industry: "Invisible Persuader on Promotions," *Business Week*, December 12, 1964, pp. 154–158; R. Powell, "How Men Get Ahead," *Nation's Business*, March, 1964, pp. 56 ff; Powell, "Elements of Executive Promotion," *California Management Review*, winter, 1963, pp. 83–90. Powell has recently completed a comprehensive field study on prejudice in management staffing in the U.S., *The Executive Promotion Process*, to be published by McGraw-Hill.

[47] Cf.: Lipset and Bendix, *op. cit.*; W. Warner and J. Abegglen, *Occupational Mobility in American Business and Industry* (Minneapolis: University of Minnesota Press, 1955).

ing the Advanced Management Program at the Harvard Business School indicates that executives with lower, lower middle, middle and upper middle, and upper class backgrounds were roughly equal in proportion; the respective percentages being 22, 26, 32, and 20.[48] The results of similar surveys involving business executives in Turkey, Italy and Mexico are presented in Table 8–1.

The figures in Table 8–1 suggest two things. First, it is tempting to see a trend in these data indicating that increasing proportions of business managers are drawn from lower status groups as the country develops more. Secondly, it is possible that in a majority of countries having both public and private industrial sectors, there will be a greater proportion of managers from the lower classes in the public sector.

Surveys conducted with the same groups of American, Italian, and

## TABLE 8–1

|  | TURKEY | | ITALY | | MEXICO |
|---|---|---|---|---|---|
| Social Class | Private Sector N = 39 Percent | Public Sector N = 24 Percent | Private Sector N = 49 Percent | Public Sector N = 61 Percent | Private Sector N = 69 Percent |
| Lower | 0 | 4 | 2 | 8 | 12 |
| Lower Middle | 18 | 54 | 53 | 49 | 30 |
| Middle | 28 | 25 | 22 | 26 | 39 |
| Upper Middle and Upper | 54 | 17 | 22 | 16 | 19 |

Source:   McClelland, The Achieving Society, p. 277.

Turkish executives also reveal that the Americans believe to nearly the fullest possible extent that deserving workers should be promoted; the Italians believe this to a somewhat lesser extent; while among the Turks there was considerable doubt whether workers should be promoted, because if they are, "it would destroy the respect for authority which workers must have toward management." Similarly the U.S. managers reject seniority, education, and family upbringing as determinants of a man's standing more firmly than the Italians, who reject them more than the Turks.[49] These limited results suggest that belief among managers in a man's right to make his way in the world may be an accompaniment or result of economic development. Whether this type of belief is also a significant spur to economic development may be open to question, although we are inclined to feel that it generally is.

It is possible that in the Soviet Union—as well as in various other Communist countries such as Poland and Czechoslovakia—there is some-

---

[48] McClelland, *The Achieving Society*, pp. 277–278.
[49] *Ibid.*, pp. 290–291.

what greater class mobility in industry than in the U.S.[50] Educational background and professional competence have come to play an increasingly significant role in determining individual advancement up the managerial hierarchy. There is undoubtedly some discrimination on the basis of nationality, religion, personal background, and so on in both the educational and industrial systems; however, formal education at all levels is probably accessible to the large majority of those persons who have the required intellectual ability for entry. Upward individual mobility in industry has been greatly enhanced by the great expansion that has taken place in part time education in the last decade. Currently, more than half of all persons enrolled in higher educational degree programs are studying on a part time basis;[51] a majority of them are employed in industry. Successful completion of a part time higher educational program frequently leads to career advancement in industry.[52]

As a Soviet citizen moves up the managerial hierarchy, Communist party membership and particularly party approval become increasingly important. It is estimated that at least 90 percent of all enterprise directors are party members.[53] In earlier periods—particularly during the 1920's and 1930's—zealous party activity and support were essential for membership. In contemporary times, a high level of professional competence and leader-

---

[50] This statement is of course quite subjective and speculative. There is discrimination of various types in the Soviet Union, primarily on the bases of nationalities. For example, persons of Russian nationality may generally have a better chance of obtaining a higher education or key job—other things being roughly equal—than a member of an Asiatic or oriental nationality. There is also some evidence that quotas involving Jews exist in the Soviet educational system, although the per capita enrollment of Jews is well above the national average. In general, however, the Soviet Union probably has less discrimination on the basis of class, race, sex, nationality, and even religion (as long as one is not an ardent believer and a zealous practitioner of a religion other than atheism) than most other countries of the world, including *perhaps*, the U.S.

In addition to information contained in the two sources cited here, the above statement on class mobility in the Soviet Union is based on the observations and interviews of one of the authors of the present study with more than 100 industrial managers, workers, educators, economists, governmental, party and union officials in the Soviet Union, Poland, and Czechoslovakia. See also the discussions and data pertaining to class, nationality, education, and employment in the U.S.S.R. in: N. Dewitt, *Education and Professional Employment in the USSR* (sponsored by the National Science Foundation. [Washington, D.C.: U.S. Government Printing Office, 1961]), pp. 201–203, 354–360, 420, 530–533, 656–657, 769; D. Granick, *The Red Executive* (Garden City, N.Y.: Doubleday & Company, Inc., 1961), Part II.

[51] V. Stoletov, translated in *Current Digest of the Soviet Press*, Vol. XV, No. 21, 1963, p. 9. The Soviets anticipate that by 1965, 60 percent of all students enrolled in higher educational programs will be holding a regular job at the same time; see F. Kotov, *Voprosy Truda v Semiletnem Plane* (Moscow, 1960), p. 137.

[52] This was the case of several of the Soviet industrial managers interviewed by one of the authors. See also: V. Elyutin, *Higher Education in the USSR* (New York: International Arts and Science Press, 1959), pp. 34 ff; E. Brown, "The Soviet Labor Market," *Industrial and Labor Relations Review*, January, 1957, p. 186.

[53] Cf. R. Bauer, and Tschirwa, "The Illiberal Education of the Soviet Manager," *PROD*, July, 1958, p. 4.

ship ability are generally sufficient for party membership as long as loyalty to the regime is not in question. It is now probably more common to promote a highly competent industrial employee to a high level executive post and grant him party membership, rather than appointing a party member to such a post without regard for his ability to do the job.

In all cases of upward mobility to responsible managerial positions in industry the party comes directly into the picture. Not a great deal is known of the precise procedures by which party organs exercise their control over executive appointments; the whole question of how Soviet managers are appointed still remains somewhat of an enigma.

There have been frequent criticisms in the Soviet press that party agencies are often not very familiar with the capabilities of appointees and that personal friendship and favoritism are at times deciding factors in promotion. There have also been complaints that very capable young persons are often overlooked in the promotion process, although in 1959 the party launched a campaign to have responsible managerial jobs filled by competent young professionals.[54] There is also considerable evidence that managerial appraisal is often carried out in an arbitrary manner, with the candidate's bonus record, which depends on the fulfilment and overfulfil-ment of certain enterprise targets, serving as a key determinant in promotions, transfers and dismissals; however, this bonus record usually depends on many factors beyond the control of the individual manager; in many cases a large bonus is earned because the targets were easy, and not because of the manager's ability.[55]

In spite of the above shortcomings in the managerial selection, appraisal, and promotion process, there is probably a higher degree of class flexibility and upward individual mobility based on competence in Soviet industry than in most other countries. One of the authors—during two trips to the Soviet Union in the early 1960's—had the opportunity to interview dozens of Soviet industrial managers of all types. The social backgrounds of these managers were greatly varied, as were their ages. Moreover, many of these managers were women. In 1958 women constituted nearly half of all industrial enterprise personnel in the U.S.S.R. As of 1959, 32 percent of all professional engineers having a higher education were women, and 74 percent of all the professional economists were also women. As of 1957, 45 percent of all managers and staff specialists at Soviet industrial enterprises were women; however, at the highest managerial levels there is probably somewhat greater discrimination against women,

---

[54] For discussions and analyses of the managerial appraisal and promotion process in Soviet industry see: Dewitt, *op. cit.*, pp. 463–466; J. Haugh, *The Role of the Local Party Organization in Soviet Industrial Decision-Making* (unpublished doctoral dissertation, Cambridge, Mass., Harvard University, 1961); *Pravda*, March 20, 1959.

[55] See Richman, *Soviet Management*, chaps. vii and viii; J. Berliner, *Factory and Manager in the USSR* (Cambridge, Mass.: Harvard University Press, 1957), chaps. iii and iv.

since only 12 percent of the top management positions at all types of enterprises were not filled by males as of 1959.[56]

Voluntary horizontal mobility involving higher level managers in Soviet industry is greatly restricted. The party and appropriate superior economic authorities must approve all relocations and transfers involving higher level enterprise executives, and in fact such transfers are usually undertaken at the intitiative of these officials rather than at the request of the individual manager. Lower level managers and workers have much greater opportunities for voluntary horizontal mobility since 1956 when a "liberalization" edict repealed an earlier law tying personnel of this type to their jobs. They can now leave after giving relatively short notice. The situation has lead to somewhat greater staffing flexibility in Soviet industry and has probably been beneficial in terms of economic progress.

## VIEW OF WEALTH AND MATERIAL GAIN

The dominant view toward wealth and material gain in a given country tends to have a significant bearing on economic progress at three levels. First, the social attitude toward wealth and material gain in general and the views of wealth derived from different sources tend to influence the types, qualities, and numbers of individuals who pursue managerial and entrepreneurial careers in industry. Also relevant at the societal level is the view toward saving and the investment of accumulated funds in industrial pursuits. Secondly, the dominant attitude regarding wealth and material gain among the industrial managers themselves is likely to have a significant impact on the way that industrial enterprises are managed and operated. Finally, the way that industrial employees and workers typically view money and material gain tends to have an important bearing on their responses to material stimuli and on their motivation and behavior in general. All productive enterprises create wealth and material gain of some sort—typically taking the form of income, profits, and/or interest to owners, investors, and/or the state and material compensation to employees.

While most cultures are quite willing to utilize whatever income and wealth may be at hand at the moment, the general view toward wealth and material gain varies strikingly among peoples. On the one hand, to take individual examples, it is possible to find completely economic men, calculating every step of their lives in terms of the monetary gains or losses which might be entailed. Scrooge in Dickens' *Christmas Carol* was perhaps the perfect characterization of this type of man. On the other hand, one can find men in religious orders who have taken complete poverty vows, and who demonstrate absolutely no interest in any wealth whatsoever. Societies

---

[56] The data on the role of women in Soviet industry have been obtained from: Dewitt, *op. cit.*, pp. 492 ff, and *Staffing Procedures and Problems in the Soviet Union* (Washington: U.S. Government Printing Office, 1962), pp. 4–5.

peopled largely by each of these types of individuals clearly would be quite different from each other in terms of industrial managerial effectiveness and productive efficiency. One would expect in a world of economic men that every possible step would be taken to increase wealth as rapidly as possible; while in a world of men who had renounced worldly wealth, the society may forever be in danger of collapsing completely for lack of production of even the most basic necessities of food, clothing, and shelter.

One immediate interrelationship here is with general social goals. A society where wealth is not highly regarded is unlikely to be as interested in economic progress as one where people constantly pursue income and wealth. In a few cultures—for example, some primitive tribal and orthodox Hindu societies—any wealth has historically been regarded as immoral by much if not most of the population, and status as well as self-satisfaction have been derived by either remaining poor or destroying accumulated wealth. Such a general negative view toward wealth and material gain clearly has a petrifying impact on managerial effectiveness and economic progress.

There are few present day countries in which most of the population has such a general negative view toward wealth. There still are, however, some traditional societies in Africa, Asia, and Latin America which have their social organization built entirely around the family or community. All social, moral, and economic life is permeated by this community structure. Life is typified by a closed subsistence society operating on a barter system with no notion of saving and investment. There is virtually no attempt to accumulate wealth, assets, or goods that do not have immediate use.[57] The number of such closed, non-wealth conscious societies has been diminishing rapidly in recent decades through exposure to the outside world, and as this happens their members gradually adopt the economic motive and become more materialistic.

Throughout most of the world today wealth tends to be considered quite desirable and is even envied, although in most countries some, and frequently much, weight is given to how an individual obtains his wealth, income, and assets. If the rich are highly regarded in a given country, and if industrial management and entrepreneurship offers a respectable path to riches, the profession is likely to benefit.

Traditionally, however, a man who has earned his money as a merchant or manufacturer has been less highly regarded in most societies than one who has earned his income from the land in farming. In some societies there have been, and in a few cases still are, religious taboos placed on income derived from interest on capital and/or business profits.[58] Most desirable of all, throughout most of the world, including many early Euro-

---

[57] Cf.: *Economic Bulletin for Africa*, 1962, pp. 92 ff.

[58] In countries like India social and religious prejudices against interest still persist among much of the population, although such prejudices have been on the decline in recent years. See C. Vakil, *op. cit.*, pp. 50–51.

pean countries, has been the man who has had an unearned income through land rents or inheritance or because of his aristocratic or noble position. These attitudes grew in the period when most wealth was in land and/or acquired through inheritance or birthright, but they have persisted well into the modern era in many societies.

Connected with this view toward wealth is the view of business and industrial managers, since in such a culture a gentleman farmer has clearly been superior to a manufacturer, while a man with an unearned income has been superior to both. Where different kinds of wealth are regarded quite distinctly, but without much rancor, this type of problem remains trivial; but in many contemporary societies such attitudes are strong and serve as significant negative constraints upon efficient industrial staffing. The traditional prestige professions, such as the priesthood, law, the military, medicine, and the government bureaucracy, continue to drain off most of the capable, educated persons in the society; and industrial enterprise is left largely with the dregs.

This attitude is far from obsolete in many less developed countries where this general rank order of desirable occupations and types of income still persists. In such countries managerial effectiveness is likely to suffer greatly since there is typically a negligible source of fairly well educated managers from the small lower middle and middle classes, and industrial managers as well as capital must come largely from those families which are already wealthy. As was pointed out in the section on achievement, upper class persons who pursue industrial careers tend to be those having a relatively low achievement drive. Moreover, in many less developed countries the wealthy tend to view industrially created riches in a negative way; therefore, they are typically reluctant to invest their funds in industrial pursuits. This situation is aptly summed up by a prominent economist who states that in many underdeveloped nations, "the rich have always counted their assets in terms of gold, jewels, houses, and land and do not easily learn to count as wealth an ugly factory or printed stock certificates."[59]

Class mobility frequently is interrelated with the attitude toward wealth. A country in which land and inherited wealth are very highly regarded, while industry created wealth is viewed negatively, is likely to be a relatively inefficient traditional society; and such societies have rather strict class barriers in most cases. As a result, the outcases, in class terms, often are pushed into business and industry because other more desirable opportunities for wealth, material gain, and achievement are lacking. In the Western world, with the beginnings of the industrial revolution, with its opportunities for the amassing of sizable fortunes in industry, a number of capable men began to appear in every generation who made millions in previously despised occupations. Many a regal seventeenth century manor house in Europe is now owned by a latecoming industrialist, who took advantage of

---

[59] R. Heilbroner, *The Great Ascent* (New York: Harper & Row, 1963), p. 61.

industrial and business opportunities. The lesson typically has not been lost on younger generations, and capable recruits for the management profession have been increasingly easy to find in many advancing and advanced nations. Money is beginning to talk, even in various traditional countries; and, gradually, as the industrial movement continues in such countries, industrially created riches and the management occupation become increasingly desirable.

Some societies, however, have not yet made this type of transition. In many nonindustrial countries, the more common pattern is to revere traditional forms of wealth, in part because there is no successful industrial class to emulate and in part because in such countries the entrepreneurs and industrial managers who do exist are largely from "pariah" groups. The elite is typically not interested in entering business and industry; and in a tight class situation, not enough of the nonelite are well enough educated or have the capital to fulfill the critical industrial managerial or entrepreneurial role effectively. The few that are well educated typically tend to emulate, as rapidly as possible, the elite and demand high prestige jobs in government, law, religion, medicine, or the military. This type of situation is common in various countries in Asia, Africa, and Latin America. Education is seen as the road to prestige and possibly higher income through nonproduction, as it was in ancient China.

The combination of rigid class structure and predilection toward nonindustrial prestige positions and income often leaves a country with few qualified industrial management candidates. The poor, who might be very interested in obtaining greater wealth and better positions in industry, are typically uneducated and untrained, while the rich are typically uninterested in such positions or this kind of wealth. As was pointed out earlier, those scions of wealthy families who do enter business or industry are frequently those persons with a low achievement drive.

One of the authors encountered ample drive for wealth, material gain, and achievement among a number of individuals in various Middle Eastern countries. In reviewing application forms for positions such as office manager, accountant, and various middle level and front line technical management positions, he quickly learned to compare signatures on the standard job application forms with the way the remainder of the form was filled in. Semiliterates would hire scribes to fill in the forms, complete with glowing testimonials and long records of fictitious education and experience. These unqualified applicants were quite willing to take relatively large risks (including the investment of some extremely scarce cash) on the outside chance that they would be hired without detailed investigation. Unfortunately, these rather eager job entrepreneurs desiring higher incomes and greater wealth were totally unqualified for the positions they sought, because of their lack of education—and very few potentially qualified applicants were interested or available.

The countries in the best position in terms of managerial effectiveness and economic progress are those where wealth and material gain derived from industrial activity are viewed quite favorably and where society has developed relatively large groups of achievement oriented, bright young persons with reasonably good educations, who are unable or unwilling to enter traditional prestige occupations. One frequent side effect of education is to expose those educated to the "good life" of consumption in the Western style. If taking industrial positions offers the best or only path to this good life, these people will be willing to pursue careers in this direction.

Various Marxist countries have successfully propagandized for large movements of well educated and highly motivated young people into industry, by offering relatively high incomes and by arguing for the critical need for more production. In various Western countries, the Calvinist ethic has played a similar role; and in some newer countries, the nationalistic spirit and growing materialism may yet provide similar popular motivation.

The dominant attitude toward wealth and material gain among members of the industrial managerial class in a given country also has a significant bearing on managerial effectiveness and economic progress. Incomes and profits obtained from industrial and business activity may be desired by managers only for what they can buy outside of the business, or they may be viewed in large part as a symbol of achievement and success to be largely reinvested in order to expand the business further.

In the former case industry-created wealth would tend to be expended primarily on conspicious consumption items, material status symbols, and/or pursuits of higher social status than business activity. Managers of this type would tend to have a fairly low achievement drive and would be inclined to pursue an egocentric conservative and essentially noninnovating course in operating their enterprises, typically stressing immediate profits through rapid turnover of capital. Instead of using their incomes and profits to expand their business enterprises, such managers typically prefer to speculate and invest in purchases of land, goods, and stocks—often abroad in more advanced and stable countries.[60] This type of attitude among the industrial managerial class is common in many African, Asian, and Latin American countries; and this situation is vividly described as follows by one authoritative source:

The prevalent orientation toward money making is different in a typical Asian or African or Latin American nation from our own. The psychology of most businessmen is not that of the Western entrepreneur. It is more that of the bazaar merchant. Not large-scale production and long-term return, but fast trading and quick profit are the usual objectives. Nor is this surprising in an economic environment where much business tends to be petty and transient,

---

[60] See, for example, the discussions in: *Economic Bulletin for Africa*, 1962, pp. 85 ff; Reksodihardjo, *op. cit.*, pp. 352 ff; *Management of Industrial Enterprise in Underdeveloped Countries*, pp. 13 ff.

and in which even big business depends for its profits more on the vagaries of international commodity fluctuations than on the slow improvement of the domestic market.[61]

One of the authors has observed that Saudi Arabians typically respect wealth, however gained, and rich businessmen or managers have no trouble in this regard; however, wealth often implies waste and conspicuous consumption, which tend to dissipate scarce resources. It also is frequently held to mean passive wealth, in the form of lands or livestock owned, not the creation of new income streams. The consumption habits of Saudi potentates have for years been subject to much astonishment, criticism, and scorn both inside and outside of Arabia; and lesser figures in the country, including business managers, have on occasion tried to emulate their leaders. In recent years there has been some shift away from fantastic types of consumption to the merely conspicuous; but the tendency of the small class of relatively rich businessmen and other citizens to display assets, rather than to invest and work at creating a continuing larger income, undoubtedly inhibits managerial effectiveness and economic progress.

In societies where a large proportion of industrial managers view income and profit as measures of achievement and success, to be used in large part to expand business operations and generate even more wealth, managerial effectiveness and economic progress would be enhanced. Managers of this type are likely to have a fairly high achievement drive; energetically to pursue moderately ambitious organizational objectives; to take calculated rational risks; and to strive to improve enterprise performance and results, often through innovation. There is ample evidence that for managers having a high need for achievement, profit or material gain in the form of income (the personal profit motive) is pursued not primarily as an end in itself but because it represents a measure of achievement and personal competence.[62] In other words, money income or profit serves as concrete feedback indicating how well the manager is doing in running the firm or his department; hence, it also serves as a measure of success. An owner-manager of this type would also frequently be inclined to reinvest his own savings or even borrow capital in order to expand his firm and create even more income and wealth.

In general, this type of manager and a favorable view of industry created wealth have been much more common in extensively Calvinistic countries than in most other societies. Calvinism (or the Protestant ethic) stresses as supreme virtues not only individual achievement and hard work but also thriftiness. Expenditures of income on luxury items or conspicuous consumption should be discouraged, according to the Calvinist tradition.

---

[61] Heilbroner, *op. cit.*, p. 62.

[62] See the relevant discussions and findings presented in McClelland, *The Achieving Society*, chap. vi, especially pp. 233–237, and his article, "Business Drive and National Achievement," pp. 104–106. See also: Sutton *et al.*, *op. cit.*, pp. 328–332; J. Ross, "The Profit Motive and its Potential for New Economies," *Proceedings* (CIOS), 1963, pp. 425–426.

Funds that are saved should be invested, either in charitable works or business ventures. Children should be taught this virtue at the earliest possible age. On the economic level, this ethic has traditionally come to mean that an individual should be motivated largely by monetary stimuli.[63]

In past centuries, the Quakers and Dissenters in England were ardent and rather pure Calvinists in their business and personal lives. In modern times, the values set forth in the teachings of Calvinism may no longer be *rigidly* adhered to by much of the population even in extensively Protestant countries. For example, there is much evidence that monetary stimuli are no longer as potent a motivating force as in the past in the U.S. and various other advanced Western nations; and there is a great deal of conspicuous consumption in various Protestant societies. The majority of the citizens, however, including probably most industrial managers, are at least partially indoctrinated in, and behave in accordance with, the values associated with Calvinism. All of Western microeconomics has such values at its base; and the American Republican party, among others, is basically oriented toward this ethic. The usual result has been to make businessmen and various other citizens in the advanced extensively Protestant nations view wealth in a very particular kind of way which is alien to much of the rest of the world.

It is true that nonwesterners, as individuals, are in numerous cases willing to respond to monetary incentives and material gain, but their motivations and ethics in so doing may be somewhat different than those found in the West. This dichotomy tends to obscure both similarities and differences in views of wealth and material gain.

Even among the advanced Western nations the degree to which businessmen typically adhere to the values associated with Calvinism in running their firms tends to vary somewhat. It appears that the American businessman is inclined to be more of a Calvinist than his European counterpart, who often sees income derived from the firm as a means for embarking on other higher status nonbusiness pursuits, rather than as a means for expanding the business in order to generate even more wealth from this source.[64]

In some respects there has been a revival of certain Calvinist values pertaining to wealth, particularly in American industry. This is most evident in connection with community relations and uses of funds. In the not too distant past, American corporations were not expected to contribute much to charity or educational institutions, since their basic aim was to increase the wealth of stockholders. Now, firms increasingly are expected to regard their net income as a public trust, to be dispensed "altruistically" and

---

[63] See: Farmer, "The Ethical Dilemma of American Capitalism," pp. 48–49; Tawney, *op. cit.*, pp. 110–113.

[64] Cf.: Lewis and Stewart, *op. cit.*, pp. 165 ff, and chap. x. The prevalent view of wealth and material gain among businessmen in a European country like France may explain in part why the French economy is characterized primarily by small patrimonial business firms.

in good works, as well as to stockholders. In some cases the company may be motivated by tax considerations and other reasons which are not purely altruistic. Nevertheless, rare indeed is the large corporation which fails to make at least symbolic gestures in this direction of donations and charity, for it is expected of them. This change represents a fairly important shift in attitudes toward industrial wealth, how it is used, and who gets it. In the process, the general social view toward private business, particularly "big business," and its managers in the U.S. probably becomes more favorable.

In the Soviet Union, and various other Marxist countries, the state rather than the individual follows the "Calvinist" ethic by replacing private thrift and accumulation with state investment in order to expand industry and production; however, the individual Soviet industrial manager also tends to behave in accordance with some of the Calvinist values, such as those pertaining to hard work and achievement. He tends to be motivated largely by a quarterly monetary bonus, the size of which depends on the extent to which he fulfils and overfulfils certain key enterprise total production and cost of production targets. The bonus is eagerly sought by the Soviet manager not only for what it can buy but also because it serves as a measure of achievement and competence in running his enterprise or department. Moreover, the manager's bonus record often has a significant bearing on whether he achieves other personal goals such as promotions, status, prestige, and greater responsibilities and power.[65]

In many newly developing countries, the state is now also playing the major role in capital accumulation and investment for industrial expansion. A major problem remains, in most cases, at the industrial enterprise level where the managers often lack the achievement drive and view of wealth and material gain which are essential to a high level of managerial effectiveness and economic progress.

The way that the typical nonmanagerial industrial employee or worker tends to view money and material gain in a given culture can have a significant bearing on managerial effectiveness and productive efficiency. Here Maslow's famous theory of human motivation and the hierarchy of human needs is relevant.[66] Modern psychology reveals that new human needs take priority whenever former or lower level needs are reasonably satisfied. In other words, man is motivated more by what he is seeking than by what he already has. Human needs are generally recognized to be in some order, with physiological and economic security needs preceding social and ego (also referred to as psychic or self-expression) needs.[67] Wealth and

---

[65] Cf.: Richman, *Soviet Management*, chaps. vii and viii; Berliner, *op. cit.*, chaps. iii, iv, and xviii.

[66] H. Moslow, "A Theory of Human Motivation," *Psychological Review*, L (1943), 370–396, and *Motivation and Personality* (New York: Harper & Row, 1954).

[67] *Ibid.*; see also Berelson and Steiner, *op. cit.*, chap. vi. For a clear exposition of human needs with implications for business and industrial management see W. Newman and C. Summer, *The Process of Management* (Englewood Cliffs, N.J.: Prentice-Hall, Inc., 1961), chap. viii.

material gain relate directly to physiological or economic security needs. Paradoxically, as will be discussed below, money income and material gain tend to be less potent motivating forces for industrial workers in both affluent and highly primitive societies than in countries which fall somewhere in between these extremes.

Western behavioral studies of the past several decades—most notably the pioneer Western Electric Company studies of the late 1920's and the 1930's—have presented much evidence that in U.S. industry monetary incentives and material gain may not be the most potent motivating forces in many cases. Social and psychic needs often may be more important to individuals and work groups, and overemphasis on money incentives and material gain may be both wasteful and inefficient for the firm.[68]

These findings are probably now applicable in varying degrees to other advanced nations as well. For example, there is growing evidence that industrial personnel in the Soviet Union are gradually beginning to place more emphasis on social and ego needs, as compared to physiological needs. It seems that with rising living standards the attraction of monetary incentives and material gain is beginning to wear off in many cases, and Soviet industrial man cannot be thought of as merely "economic man." While many employees of Soviet enterprises still change jobs because they can obtain better pay and/or housing elsewhere, in many instances they now also relocate because they are unhappy with their jobs per se, their superiors, and/or the general "human" environment of their place of employment. Soviet industrial managers are now being increasingly criticized because they "don't know the needs and moods of the people."[69]

In general, as countries and their individual citizens become quite affluent they tend to lose some interest in extra income, although in most cases additional money or material gain probably never loses all of its charm in most cases—at least not in contemporary times. At the same time, in countries where much of the industrial labor force is recruited from highly traditional cultures or primitive rural areas, monetary incentives and material gain, even when linked to productivity performance by able and efficiency conscious managements, often fail to work effectively. This is the case in a number of African, Asian, and Latin American countries where employees lose their motivation to work once they have earned enough to

---

[68] Cf.: E. Mayo, *The Human Problems of an Industrial Organization* (New York: The Macmillan Company, 1933); F. Roethlisberger, and W. Dickinson, *Management and the Worker* (Cambridge, Mass.: Harvard University Press, 1939 and 1964); L. Sayles and G. Straus, *Personnel: The Human Problems of Management* (Englewood Cliffs, N.J.: Prentice-Hall, Inc., 1960); C. Barnard, *The Functions of the Executive* (Cambridge, Mass.: Harvard University Press, 1938 and 1962), especially chap. xi. For an excellent study dealing primarily with psychic or self-actualization needs in productive enterprise see C. Argyris, *Integrating the Individual and the Organization* (New York: John Wiley & Sons, Inc., 1964). See also the findings and sources presented in Berelson and Steiner, *op. cit.*, chaps. viii and ix.

[69] Cf.: Richman, *Soviet Management*, chap. x, especially p. 215; *Current Digest of the Soviet Press*, Vol. XIV, No. 50, 1962, pp. 18–19; *Pravda*, December 8, 1962, p. 2.

fulfil their own and possibly their families' basic subsistence needs.[70] The backward sloping supply curve of economic theory is based on this proposition. This type of situation is vividly described in one authoritative source as follows:

In the least developed areas the worker's attitude toward labor may entirely lack time perspective, let alone the concept of productive investment. For example, the day laborer in a rural area on his way to work, who finds a fish in the net he placed in the river the night before, is observed to return home, his needs being met. The worker in an urban area who receives an increase in pay works less and goes back to his native village so much the sooner.[71]

Through educative effort and training, the attitudes of such workers can be changed. They can be taught to desire more income and material things and hence to respond effectively to monetary incentives. One of the authors had considerable experience with this type of cultural change in Saudi Arabia. Old oil hands told of an earlier day (1940–55) when workers wandered casually off the job as soon as their most rudimentary needs were met; but by 1958, enough Saudis had learned to want more wealth to make it a quite acquisitive society. One of the best ways to increase productivity and output was to put crews on piecework, since even illiterates appeared quite capable of figuring out how much more they could earn in this way. Because of the low living standards in Saudi Arabia, monetary incentives of this type proved highly effective. Since physiological needs took priority over social and psychic needs in most cases, there were virtually no group social pressures on individuals to hold back their productivity, as is often the case in American and even Soviet industry.

It can, however, entail considerable time, effort and expense effectively to change highly traditional or primitive cultural attitudes regarding wealth and material gain. This has been the experience of both domestic enterprises and various international firms with subsidiaries in underdeveloped countries. One recent source cites the following actual case in this connection:

In South America, an international petroleum company employed about twenty natives in an oil well perforation team managed by a non-native executive. In spite of management efforts, each perforation job averaged nine days. Since a similar job with similar equipment was done in the United States in one and one-half days, management reasoned that—even considering the more primitive operating conditions in South America—the job could surely be done in six

---

[70] Cf., *Economic Bulletin for Africa*, 1962, pp. 85 ff. A common theme running through many business management cases dealing with less developed countries is that employees fail to respond effectively to monetary incentives. See, for example, *Joseph Kodjoe—Canning Machine Operator*, a case developed by the Business Administration Program of the University College of Ghana, available through the International Clearing House (ICH) at the Harvard Business School under No. 4G142. Several similar cases can also be obtained from this source.

[71] *Report on the World Social Situation*, p. 79.

days or less. Since the job did require genuine teamwork and the men worked in isolated locations less subject to direct supervision, management decided on a drastic step to break the cultural pattern. It offered nine days pay for each job regardless of actual work days. This dramatic incentive proved sufficient to alter long-standing cultural habits.

The employees attitudes changed gradually. Within four years, they had reduced perforation time to one and one-half days, the same as in other efficient countries. Team members readily offered suggestions to improve teamwork and adapt technology to the special conditions of that area. On two occasions, the team encouraged transfer of men who would not change their habits and were thus holding back the team.[72]

In probably the large majority of the less developed and semiadvanced nations, regardless of the stated goals of their elites, much if not most of their working populations are likely to be highly money conscious and materialistic—they have entered the material acquisition stage. In such countries, money and material rewards linked to productivity performance in industrial enterprise can prove very effective in terms of economic progress. A major obstacle here is that enterprise managements, in numerous cases, are ignorant of this fact and do not have the proper education or training to design and implement potentially effective employee incentive and compensation systems.[73]

The various views toward wealth and material gain discussed above have direct implications for the management of productive enterprise. Obvious examples relate to the staffing and direction functions. In a country where individuals tend to be highly responsive to money, an effective method to use in recruiting personnel might be simply to raise the price until enough qualified persons present themselves; but such direct methods may prove of limited value in a relatively affluent society such as the United States today, if young persons beginning their careers respond more to promises of on the job satisfaction, important responsibilties, opportunities for creativity and future advancement, high ethical appeal, or other nonmaterial stimuli. Levels of basic compensation may be very important in a highly money conscious culture; while in a culture less interested in income, other types of compensation and appeals may prove much more effective.

In a similar manner, the ways in which direction, leadership, and motivation are or "ought to be" practiced in an enterprise depends in large part on the ways in which employees tend to respond to monetary incen-

---

[72] K. Davis, "Managing Productivity in Developing Countries," *Management International*, Vol. IV, No. 2, 1964, p. 72.

[73] Cf. the empirical findings presented by managerial and technical consultants in United Nations, *Trade in Manufactures and Semi-Manufactures: India* (Report E/CONF. 46/76 [New York, March 9, 1964]), pp. 45 ff; see also: U.N., *India's Experience in Industrial Planning* (Report ST/ECLA/Conf.11/L.9 [New York, February 5, 1963]), pp. 44 ff; U.N., *Public Industrial Management in Asia and the Far East* (ST/TAO/M/15 [New York, 1960]), pp. 64 ff; *Management of Industrial Enterprise in Underdeveloped Countries*, pp. 59 ff.

tives. Such incentives are typically easier to apply than incentives related to complex social and psychic needs. The common measuring unit of money can be applied by able managements to many diverse situations in ways calculated to improve productivity and efficiency; but if employees fail to respond to monetary stimuli in the desired directions, the impact on managerial effectiveness and productive efficiency will be small, if not negative. In primitive societies workers must often be taught to respond in desired ways to monetary incentives if they are to work effectively. In affluent societies employees frequently cannot be "taught," persuaded, or coerced into responding effectively to monetary stimuli, since their social and psychic needs take precedence in their behavior.

The general view of wealth in a given society appears to affect the industrial firm and its management in various other guises. For example, such consumer goods as automobiles and clothes are sold or fail to sell depending on the way in which the population sees them in terms of its view of wealth and material gain. One could infer much about the American culture from its auto designs. The change from gaudy, flamboyant chariots of the 1950's to more sedate, angular vehicles of the 1960's may be a reflection of changing attitudes toward wealth, and perhaps one could write an interesting book about German attitudes toward wealth as exemplified by its Volkswagens, or of Italy exemplified by its Fiats, or of England by its various types of automobiles. Here product lines and sales promotion are directly influenced by the way a culture sees wealth. In various newly developing countries that have only recently become extensively money oriented economies, it is frequently extremely difficult for even able enterprise managements effectively to plan and market output and predict consumer demand for their products, because of constantly changing and often irrational consumption patterns.

To conclude, in any society where human wants seem to increase faster than incomes—this describes most present day countries—money incomes and material gain can spur productivity and economic progress, albeit with varying degrees of effectiveness, in many diverse kinds of cultures. The majority of Americans, Russians, Japanese, Europeans, Africans, Asians, and Latin Americans all appear to want as many consumer goods as they can get, up to rather considerable amounts. No country has ever managed to yield enough income per capita to give the vast majority of its citizens their expected due—not even in the U.S., since a minimal asset position in the United States in consumer durables is probably at least several thousand dollars.

At present levels of economic development and growth, however, there are some signs that at least a few countries will achieve a moderate saturation point within the next few decades, led by the United States. This may explain in part why wealth and material gain are apparently becoming less important in such countries. Until the family accumulates its one or more cars, washing machine, stereo, color T.V. set, a modern house or flat, etc., these items appear very important; but the novelty can wear off, and a new restlessness evolves. At this point occupation prestige and status as well as job satisfaction per se, rather than wealth or income, tend to become increasingly important (we both are pleased to note the rapidly climbing status of professors in the United States). Young men increasingly seek out jobs and careers for satisfactions other than money, granted that all occupations pay reasonably well. At this point, there may be a return to medieval standards of status based on position, not on money or wealth, and the view toward wealth may undergo considerable change. One of the authors predicts that this change is already taking place in the United States, most notably among the upper middle class young people, who, of course, can best afford it.

## VIEW OF SCIENTIFIC METHOD

*Scientific method* here refers to the methodology developed for the analysis of various problems in the physical and social sciences. Critical to this notion is the idea that events can be described, explained, and predicted. The thinking runs, "if we do A then B will occur," with the idea that this hypothesis can be verified by trying A to see if B in fact occurs. If it does not, a new hypothesis is proposed and tried. Another way of looking at this problem is to suggest that "Event x depends on factors y and z," and then to relate, mathematically if possible, the relationship between the variables. Once hypothesized, the prediction is verified by observation, experience, and/or experimentation—and again, if the hypothesis fails to work out in practice, a new hypothesis may be proposed and tested.

This kind of thinking is not ancient—it dates back essentially to seventeenth century England, most notably to the writings of Sir Francis Bacon.[74] Earlier societies used this sort of analysis in a rather crude way for certain kinds of problems, most notably agriculture (when the sun is at an angle z to the pyramid, the Nile will rise); but seldom if ever was such thinking applied to all sorts of problems.

All of the major technical and scientific gains in the past few centuries have been caused by application of such scientific methodology. More recently, the same methodology has been applied to the social and behavioral sciences, with considerably less meaningful results. Even here, however, considerable progress has been made, particularly in the Western world. The major difficulty is in trying to experiment in a situation where extraneous variables cannot be eliminated from the system, as in economics, psychology, sociology or management; but in any case, the notion of observing a system, proposing various hypothesis about the behavior within the system, and checking results is central to scientific methodology. This

---

[74] Bacon's major work dealing with scientific method is "Novum Organum," Book One, and it can be found in S. Commins, and R. Linscott, eds., *Man and the Universe: The Philosophers of Science* (New York: Random House, 1947), pp. 73–158.

type of thinking is so common in most advanced countries today that it is taken for granted in literally millions of simple situations. Machinists, electricians, salesmen, managers, in addition to persons working in hundreds of other types of occupations, apply this technique without even considering what methodology they are using.

Hence a skilled worker will plan his work, thinking intuitively: if A, then B. In fact, even relatively routine types of skilled work involve such thinking on a fairly complex level—which becomes apparent if one looks closely at the type of work such a person does. An electrician does not use Number 14 wire for 220-volt circuits as a matter of course—since to do so would be a failure to predict burn outs, short circuits, and fire hazards. A machinist sees to it that his equipment is oiled at regular intervals, lest it function improperly and eventually break down. A salesman keeps after his customers so that they will not switch to another company. Only when one has lived in a culture where such apparently trivial rules are violated does he realize the nature of such training in workmen and other personnel.

In management, the use of scientific methodology is even more pronounced. Managers spend a great deal of their time predicting what will happen, given certain conditions, and in trying to prevent undesirable results by effectively adapting to or changing the conditions. If we charge $x$ dollars per unit how will this relate to sales, profits, and costs? If we undertake project A how much financing will be required? If we spend $x$ dollars on this advertising program can we expect at least $y$ additional sales? If we introduce this new incentive system will productivity increase $x$ units? To fill job opening A effectively we need a man with qualifications $x$, $y$, and $z$. If we establish territorial divisions instead of our functional departmentation this would probably yield results A, B, and C.

The whole area of planning and decision making is basically this sort of activity, as is much of control, organization, staffing, and direction. In the functional business areas, a prime consideration is that the manager will be able to predict events and eventually control them as far as possible through his manipulation of and adaptation to his environment. Numerous American firms use highly sophisticated tools and techniques in their application of scientific methodology to various business and technical problems, including operations research, electronic computers, intensive marketing research, highly intricate forecasting, budgeting, personnel testing and appraisal techniques, and so forth.

The dominant view toward scientific method also has a direct and very significant bearing on the development and introduction of more productive technology in a given enterprise, and throughout industry in a particular country. For all but a handful of countries, technical research and development consists largely of applying technology borrowed (often in a modified form) from other countries. The initial development of complex, new technology requires a level of education and scientific method which is virtually absent in most of the world. Most countries find it is much more feasible to borrow and implement known technology developed in advanced countries than to develop their own unique types; however, the effective implementation of borrowed technology also requires considerable use of scientific methodology and thinking. Here industrial management is extremely relevant. Unless managers, be they technical or general, are able and willing to look closely at available technologies to determine what is feasible for increasing productivity in their own enterprises, and unless they have the interest, staff and knowhow to introduce potentially effective new technical processes, there will typically be relatively little technology utilized, and the country will remain technologically backward.

In general, relatively few countries have a very scientific view of the world—probably the great majority do not. The extent to which scientific method is effectively applied in industry in a given country is primarily a function of the overall religious, cultural, and educational environment.

Scientific method is basically a future oriented, revolutionary way of looking at one's environment—it implies that somehow one can alter this environment through conscious action. In many cultures, such an attitude would tend to be considered dangerous, heretical, and unsound. God, or some equivalent surrogate, is responsible for the future, not puny man. In this sense, managerial competence (as well as pure science and engineering) comes close to interference with established religious order. Few young persons in such a culture are trained to think scientifically—and results show up in the ways in which firms are managed and the economy functions. Without scientific methodology, the society runs out of control most of the time—in the economically productive sense—and business enterprise has no way of effectively planning for its future. There is a vicious circle operating here. Since few persons or enterprises make use of scientific method in planning, plans tend not to work out, pessimism becomes prevalent, and people become even more reluctant to try to plan for the future. On the other hand, where scientific methods and planning is a way of life—as is the case in the United States—coordination of activities tends to be quite effective among interdependent and interrelated business enterprises, plans tend to work out reasonably well, optimism tends to be quite prevalent, and all this reinforces the use of scientific methodology in planning and decision making.

Western countries which tend to have the most favorable attitudes toward scientific method are those which have traditionally been influenced strongly by the protestant Calvinist philosophy.[75] This blend of religious spirit and rational thinking in regard to things material has been particularly noticeable since the beginning of the nineteenth century in countries such as England, the Scandinavian countries, Germany, Benelux, and the United States.

In previous eras and societies, rational, scientific thought was not

---

[75] For an analysis of this religious movement and its impact on Christian thought and business behavior see K. Fullerton, "Calvinism and Capitalism: An Explanation of the Weber Thesis," reprinted in *Protestantism and Capitalism* (Boston: D. C. Heath & Company, 1959), pp. 11 ff.

regarded as a moral activity. Religion is basically charismatic, not rational, and the acceptance of purely scientific doctrine seemed dangerous to the established order; however, Calvinism itself, though starting from a mystical foundation, was evolved quite rationally from this base. Calvinist thinking and theology was directed to the rational development of the individual, given the basic premise of the philosophy. Hence a Calvinist could accept easily the idea that scientific development was an integral part of his personal life, and entrepreneurs and managers trained in this tradition were not afraid of the apparently mysterious forces which science was developing. Much of what is known as Yankee ingenuity and urge toward experimentation in business, economics, and industrial technology stems from the basic compatibility of science with Calvinistic religious philosophy. Having accepted the basic religious philosophy, there was no further conflict in accepting the rationalism of science as well.[76]

Countries with strong Catholic traditions, as Spain, Italy, Portugal, and much of Latin America, have had considerably more difficulty in accepting scientific method in their cultures as an operating force. Tradition, cultural pressures, and religious dogma have tended to make purely scientific applications to practical production problems much more difficult. The traditional Catholic view of man apparently tends to push managers and technicians away from the rational thought processes so necessary to modern efficient production of goods and services.

Extensively Moslem, Buddhist, and Hindu societies also have been much more reluctant to view scientific methodology as being compatible with their religions and cultures. Again the cultural and religious pressures tend to make scientific applications to productive problems much more difficult.

It should be pointed out that the above paragraphs would be violently objected to by many religious leaders and laymen as irrelevant. If a culture is interested in saving souls, productive efficiency is among the least important of human problems. One can object to the value judgment, but no rational resolution of ethical conflict is possible. If the major goal of a society is not productive efficiency, but the salvation of mankind in the hereafter, this entire book is totally irrelevant for such a society.

A frequent conflict emerges here, however. Societies want to preserve their traditional cultures, save souls (or proceed to whatever religious goals seem valid), *and* to gain maximum productive efficiency. The point here is that if the cultural values conflict sharply with the necessities of productive efficiency, some tortuous compromise must be made, often leading to unfortunate cultural and/or economic results.

It is fallacious to conclude that only extensively Calvinistic cultures *can* make extensive and effective use of scientific method in industry, although industrial progress throughout the world to date strongly suggests

---

[76] This point is more fully developed in Farmer, "The Ethical Dilemma." See particularly Footnotes 12, 13, and 17 of his article.

that such cultures *have* generally made much more effective use of such methodology. In recent years, however, many less developed, essentially non-Calvinistic countries have been slowly breaking down the barriers to scientific method and its uses through major changes in their educational systems.

It is also fallacious to conclude that all extensively Calvinistic countries apply scientific methodology with equal effectiveness to managerial and business problems. As compared to practices in the United States, in some of the advanced western European nations—for example, Great Britain—where management is not generally considered a profession based on its own body of theory or scientific underpinnings, less use tends to be made of scientific methodology in such areas as planning and decision making, budgeting and control, and personnel testing and appraisal, and greater reliance is placed on intuition. There is also less use made of staff specialists and various types of experts who make considerable use of scientific methodology in aiding management in solving a wide range of business problems.[77] This does not mean that such extensive use of "scientific methodology" and staff specialists in American industry is always worth the cost and effort involved—but the results to date suggest that more often than not it may well be. This appears to be true in spite of the emotionalism and informational biases that may often enter into organizational decision making.

Some non-Calvinistic countries have already made considerable and effective use of scientific methodology in industry. Japan has done so, except in certain areas of organization and staffing where cultural tradition has overruled the use of scientific methodology. The Soviet Union, and various other Communist nations, have also made effective use of such methodology, particularly in the physical sciences, engineering, and other purely technical fields; however, in the Soviet Union in particular, much less use has been made of it in the behavioral and social sciences, including economics and management. There has been a conflict between scientific method and dialectical materialism in these fields.[78] Only in current times have the Soviets come to realize that this situation has had and is still having a significantly negative effect on managerial effectiveness and productive efficiency.

In October, 1962, a two day meeting of the U.S.S.R. Academy of Sciences was held in Moscow under the title "The Building of Communism

---

[77] Cf., Granick, *The European Executive*, Part V.

[78] Cf.: R. Bauer, "Our Big Advantage: The Social Sciences," *Harvard Business Review*, May-June, 1958, pp. 125 ff; D. Bell, "Erosion of Ideology," *Survey*, April, 1963, pp. 64 ff; A. Broderson, "Soviet Social Sciences and Our Own," *Social Research*, autumn, 1957, pp. 253 ff; R. Meek, "The Teaching of Economics in the USSR and Poland," *Soviet Studies*, April, 1959, pp. 343 ff. For those who can read Russian a very important recent Soviet source in this connection is *Stroitelstva Kommunisma i Obshestvennie Naukii* (The Building of Communism and the Social Sciences) (Moscow: Publishing House of the USSR Academy of Sciences, 1962).

and the Social Sciences." The participants represented the "who's who" of the Soviet intelligentsia. The purpose of this gathering was to consider and adopt measures for the improvement and further development of scientific method, research, and education in all of the social sciences.[79] At the meetings Stalin was blamed more vigorously than ever before for existing shortcomings in the social sciences. Here are a few typical statements made by highly eminent Soviet authorities:

During the period of Stalin the social sciences were suffering the most because research was not based on statistics, facts and analysis, but on directives and slogans from higher up.[80]

The economic sciences, including planning and management, have suffered greatly under Stalin because of the separation of theory from its application.[81]

In the last few years there has been growing criticism in the Soviet press and scholarly journals regarding the lack of scientific methodology and a scientific foundation in the field of management. Here is a typical statement in this regard:

Effective management can only be performed on the basis of systematized, scientifically valid knowledge. So far we have neither a system for preparing managerial personnel that meets modern requirements, nor criteria for a comprehensive evaluation of the results of the manager's activity. Amateurism in the questions of management theory, underestimation of the modern means for rationalizing managerial work, and insufficient attention to the scientific working out of the problems of administration impedes the utilization of the enormous industrial possibilities inherent in our socialist system.[82]

At the extreme, there are still entire societies which operate, with relatively few exceptions, on a mystical, nonscientific basis, so that virtually no area of the society—except for those under foreign control—can apply scientific techniques effectively in any field. In such an environment we find a country which necessarily operates at a subsistence level; where there are very few locally owned rational productive enterprises; where governments have no meaningful plans, even for next year (a budget, after all, is a rational, forward looking plan of action); where virtually everything is attributed to the will of God, not of men. Such extreme cultures still exist, primarily in Africa and Asia, though few people would want to live in them. They are characterized by per capita incomes of around $50.00 per year.

Although perhaps not quite this extreme, a highly traditional society like Saudi Arabia has had very little to do with scientific method in any

---

[79] *Stroitelstva Kommunisma.*

[80] P. Fedoseev, paper entitled "To Perfect the Organization of Social Research," in *Stroitelstva Kommunisma.*

[81] A. Arzumanian, paper in *ibid.*

[82] D. Gvishiani, article entitled, "Administration Is Above All a Science," in *Izvestia*, May 19, 1963, p. 2; partially translated in *Current Digest of the Soviet Press*, Vol. XV, No. 20, 1963, pp. 25 ff. Similar translated statements by other prominent Soviet authorities can be found in N. Adfeldt, *CDSP*, Vol. XIV, No. 40, 1962, pp. 3–4, and K. Plotnikov, *Problems of Economics*, April, 1963, pp. 25–26.

sense. As one of the authors experienced for two years as a manager, one of the most difficult problems in this country is to try to get local managers and workers to work out causation problems. This can range from an apparently trivial but real life problem such as, "If tire pressures are not checked, tire damage is likely," to "If operational plans are not made, a firm may be unable to adjust to changing conditions." The former statement may seem trivial—until $3,000 worth of truck tires are ruined on a single forty mile trip—as happened on several occasions. The second problem may seem more important—yet virtually no local firms have any notion of the complex problems inherent in planning and controlling business activities. The result is too often bankruptcy and/or extreme avoidable inefficiency.

The basic difficulty seems to be great reliance on God not only as a creator, but as a causal factor in everything. *Inshallah* (God willing) those tires would not blow out—but they do. This fatalistic acceptance of whatever God may have in mind prevents thinking about how man might help God out in many kinds of problems, including the classic scientific one of identifying causal and dependent variables and working out predictive relationships. Since one of the major reasons for industrial managerial effectiveness is the successful application of scientific methodology to business, human, and technical problems, its lack of application in Arabia, and numerous other countries, leads only to confusion and great inefficiency.

One depressing symbol of modern industrailization in many developing countries is the gutted, cannibalized new truck—taken apart piece by piece for the parts to be used in other similar vehicles. The modern, subtle, and complex inventory problems inherent in the operation of such equipment are far too often beyond the grasp of managers whose basic cultural orientation is non-Western. At the other extreme, one can also find warehouses full of left front fenders for 1947 Chevrolets—all of which have long since disappeared in the country. Such reflections of inefficiency in inventory and maintenance planning reflect the inability of managers in such situations to analyze properly the complicated predictive problems inherent in the modern production process.

Foreign owned industrial firms operating in the Congo have great difficulty with local employees because of their complete lack of insight into scientific method due to their environment, culture, and lack of pretraining. In fact most of them have no perception of straight lines, and this is critical in even very simple, routine technical problems. As a result, "Native workers seldom rise above routine jobs, with all work and materials laid out. When a native runs out of materials, e.g., rivets or screws, he is unable even to recognize his problem, let alone solve it." One Belgian executive concludes that except for an occasionally and rare gifted Congolese, "There is little hope of making managers out of Africans for several generations."[83]

A recent doctoral dissertation by an Indonesian student on Indonesian

---

[83] *International Committee of Scientific Management*, 1960, *op. cit.*, Project Study on the Belgian Congo.

industrial management points out that because of the lack of education in scientific method in his country terms like *efficient, effective,* and *rational* have virtually no meaning, while emotional, traditional, and mystical attitudes are dominant in most situations. Fatalism and a day to day philosophy prevail in industry, and only today is important for most workers since there is barely enough income for survival. At the managerial level there is virtually no conception or awareness of the need for policies, procedures, cash planning, and the like, even in larger firms. Transactions typically only provide for one cycle of operations; for example, money is borrowed for one transaction, price is bargained for one shipment of goods, and longer term contracts are rarely negotiated.[84]

Throughout the underdeveloped world, a major barrier to economic progress and managerial effectiveness has been a rather unfavorable view of and ignorance about scientific method. As one comprehensive study of industrial management in underdeveloped countries points out: "In most underdeveloped countries the culture is traditionalist and contains virtually no elements of scientific and technological experience and consequently no habit of experimentation."[85]

Managers throughout the underdeveloped world typically fail to understand fairly simple relationships among demand, prices, and costs; among wages, performance standards, and productivity; between poorly led, discontented personnel and absenteeism and turnover; between poorly trained workers and spoilage; among maintenance, spare parts, and equipment breakdowns; between costs and benefits entailed in important decisions; and so on, ad infinitum.

Numerous problems and related serious inefficiencies due to inadequate or no use of scientific method are also prevalent in macromanagerial decisions in the newly developing "mixed" economies of Asia, Africa, and Latin America. In this regard there are frequently hasty, rather irrational, and very inefficient decisions made pertaining to foreign exchange and import needs, supplies and social overhead capital required for newly constructed factories to function, irrational investments, and so forth.[86] Such decisions have a very negative impact on managerial effectiveness and productive efficiency within numerous industrial enterprises.

Persons raised in a basically nonscientific culture, even when extremely

---

[84] Reksodihardjo, *op. cit.,* pp. 155 ff., 337 ff.

[85] *Management of Industrial Enterprise in Underdeveloped Countries,* p. 13.

[86] Numerous examples of this type can be found in the country and regional sources cited in Footnotes 68 and 71 above. See also, J. Delaplaine, "The Inter-American Development Bank and Industrial Development in Latin America," *Industrialization and Productivity* (United Nations), No. 7, 1964, pp. 54–55. Considerable factual evidence regarding the serious industrial inefficiences resulting in large part from the lack of scientific method in macromanagerial decision making in Burma since that country's independence is presented in Hogen, *op. cit.,* pp. 452–462. Similar examples on Egyptian industry are presented in R. Mosely, "Egypt in Deep Trouble as Industries Falter," *The Los Angeles Times,* February 7, 1965, Sect. A., p. 9.

intelligent, cannot be made into good managers or administrators in a short period of time. Their whole philosophy of life must usually be changed before they gain insight into what the industrial enterprise is trying to accomplish. Western firms operating in cultures of this sort have had considerable difficulty in attempting to obtain local managerial talent because of this factor. This situation has been vigorously acknowledged by several executives of U.S. multinational firms—including IBM, Merck, Union Carbide, Olin Matheison, Singer, Bank of America, Standard Oil, Aramco and Pepsi Cola—whom we know well and/or have interviewed. One escape from this problem is to send promising young men abroad to a Western country for their education, in the hope that they can be trained in scientific methodology before it is too late.

Before concluding this section, it should be noted that every country, including modern ones such as the United States and the Soviet Union, exhibit some dichotomy of feeling toward scientific method. The method, when used extensively, is unsettling, dynamic, and potentially dangerous to those presently in power or held in high esteem. In any culture the folklore, religious biases, and mores of society weigh heavily against productive efficiency. To take an extreme example, consider the American practice of giving tax exemptions to religious organizations. This tends to distort economic resource allocation, in that it leads to "excess" investment in religious buildings and activities. A case could be made, by a brave individual, that such expenditures actually make the country less wealthy in the material sense than it might be, since such expenditures could be used in more economically productive ways.

Here again the question of goals arise. No culture is really interested in the kind of pure productive efficiency assumed desirable in this book. It is likely that if such a culture did exist, it would be a rather sterile and horrible place to live. "Man does not live by bread alone," and many of the most interesting and fulfilling parts of human existence are the wealth of non-economic cultural attainments of any society. Some sort of trade-offs must necessarily be made between economic efficiency and other values. Our point is that if the trade-offs tend to interfere seriously with productive efficiency, the culture or country pays the price—which may be economic stagnation, inefficiency, famine, and a host of other undesirable characteristics associated with unproductive societies. Too often a country feels it can beat the game by remaining nonscientific and nonrational, while at the same time trying to create a productive enterprise system which is fundamentally founded on purely rational considerations. The results typically are abortive.

A paradoxical situation appears here which is quite closely connected to economic advance. Wealthy countries are able to engage in enormously more purely ethical, religious, and cultural activities than poor countries, simply because the income exists, in real terms, to finance such activities. The United States has more religious activities, more cultural pursuits, more art, and more charitable works now than it ever had—because the wealth exists to finance such activities easily. A primitive society, where nineteen peasants labor to create a small surplus for the twentieth man, a city dweller, is not in a position to divert many resources to such noneconomic pursuits. It cannot afford to allow many young men to become preachers, artists, or medical doctors for humane or artistic reasons; but the wealth is generated basically by highly scientific and rational processes—not by mysticism.

To be mystical and/or emotional in regard to many areas of human experience is probably a powerful force in most people. Mysticism in its various forms has the grand advantage of offering total and absolute truths to counteract many of life's most vexing problems; however, productivity, economic progress and managerial effectiveness all lie in the rational, scientific realm. No one ever built or ran a railroad, a steel mill, or a shoe factory with even a modicum of efficiency with prayers to the Almighty or emotion alone. For that matter, no enterprise ever solved a budgetary, marketing, production or engineering problem with prayers or emotion. This type of problem is solved effectively and efficiently only with consistent, sound applications of scientific methodology. Realization of this fact has caused a revolution resulting in vast economic progress in some of the traditionally oriented areas of the world. One of the more critical world problems at this point is the inexorable race between the more widespread use of scientific method and the reluctance of many members, if not the large majority of most populations to recognize and accept this methodology with all of its implications in all phases of human endeavor.

## VIEW OF RISK TAKING

Risk is an inherent part of any economic activity. Since productive operations are necessarily forward oriented in time and involve at least some degree of uncertainty, any industrial firm must assume some risks. The problem here is not to recognize that such risks are inevitable but to examine the dominant views and patterns of risk taking found in different societies. Substantial differences in dominant attitudes toward risk occur in various countries, and these views directly influence managerial effectiveness and productive efficiency within industry.

### Relevant Levels of Risk Taking

There are three levels of risk taking relevant here—national, firm, and individual. Our primary concern is with the dominant view of risk taking held by industrial enterprises and their managements in a given country. This pertains to the kinds of risks a firm might be willing to undertake and the ways in which firm management analyzes such risks before it proceeds. Examples would be a product innovation, such as a new petro-chemical or dress style; shifts into untried technological areas and production processes;

an aggressive sales promotion campaign undertaken to expand sales and market share substantially; a reorganization of the company or one of its major departments; or significant changes in various other operating policies or procedures. Here the managers of industrial enterprises must make decisions about the kinds of risks they are willing to undertake. Such a decision may not even be a conscious one. A chemical firm which never gets around to considering the expenditure of funds for research and development may be taking a major risk (of product and process obsolescence and eventual decline in earnings), even though management is not aware of this. Such a lack of awareness of the risks the firm and its management are undertaking can be considered a negative factor for the firm; it exists nonetheless.

Also relevant is the total social risk or the kinds of risks a country may collectively take which bear significantly on the industrial sector. Political leaders and governments made decisions with varying elements of risk; and as a result many, and at times all, productive enterprises may be affected. The kinds of national decisions involving risk that might have a direct impact on industrial firms are such things as the decision to go to war or seek peace; to expand output and investment in new and untried regions; to finance long term projects such as moon landings in 1970; to undertake major long term structural developments, such as a major dam project or the development of a steel or chemical industry virtually from scratch; or even to effect changes in governmental fiscal or monetary policies. National or collective decisions such as these frequently influence significantly the policies and productive and managerial functions, as well as the operating efficiency, of many or most industrial firms. The way in which a particular government or country handles such decisions involving risk usually shows up in various other environmental constraints—for example, political and economic stability.

The third level of risk taking relevant here is individual risk. Clearly in the cases noted above, individuals eventually make the risk taking decisions which influence countries and firms, and in the last analysis all risk tends to be largely a personal issue. As politicians and industrial managers, however, such individuals are playing roles for the society or the firm; the risks they take in such roles are focused directly on the future of the country or the firm; but this type of risk taking may also have direct influence on their individual careers and personal lives. In this individual category, the question is one of whether or not individuals are willing to take risks as individuals, in terms of the effect on themselves of the decisions they make.

Unwillingness to take personal risks may lead men, as managers, to be unwilling to take firm risks. Fearing loss of status and prestige if decisions prove wrong, managers may be unwilling to take any risk. Thus a firm may have a good chance to be the first to produce and sell detergents in its market to compete with traditional fat-based soaps; but to introduce this product may involve some risk. Technical contracts must be made with foreign firms, new plants have to be built, and marketing channels may have to be shifted. Changes of this sort may result in problems, and some risk is present even in favorable situations. If the manager's personal aversion to risk is high, the result may well be to avoid taking on the project at all. The firm stagnates, and if this attitude is widely held in the society, the entire country may stagnate as well. No one is willing to take even reasonable risks to take advantage of potential opportunities.

Individuals—both managers and nonmanagers—also gamble and take risks with themselves when they choose jobs and careers. In societies where the idea of personal risk taking is not widely held, it may prove difficult to find men who are willing to risk a bit in order to achieve much personally. This often shows up in educational aspirations. In many underdeveloped and newly developing countries the idea of taking a degree in engineering, science, or business may be seen (properly) as quite risky, since relatively few jobs are available at present in these occupations; but even where the relatively few qualified earn very good salaries, young men prefer to study law or medicine, being unwilling to risk anything in this critical career area. The staffing impact, where trained managers and technicians are needed, is clear. A firm may want qualified men and find that only legal clerks are available.

Everyone probably knows some persons who, because they were unwilling to take reasonable risks, have failed to achieve their maximum potential. The idea of a good safe job as compared to a more risky but potentially more profitable and satisfying occupation is relevant here. If potentially able management candidates are satisfied with minor, safe positions and are unwilling to take reasonable chances to improve themselves, and incidentally their enterprises, the productive efficiency of the firm and society at large will suffer.

Similarly, we probably know of persons who ruined their chances by taking risks that turned out to be too extreme. The small businessman who fails or the manager who proves unable to perform his high level job are examples. Where men are restlessly unwilling to endure the usual routines inherent in any job, and are always searching out new and riskier alternatives, the problem of productive efficiency will also exist.

The literature of many cultures is full of tales of both sorts of individuals. Here the literature of a particular country may reveal more than any economic or business statistic about the nature of risks taken or foregone and the dominant view toward risk taking existing in the country. In general, a balanced and rational view of personal risk taking is conducive to greater productive efficiency and economic progress. If much of the population in a given country tends to be either extreme or ultraconservative risk takers, productive efficiency is likely to suffer substantially.

At this point an analysis of the theoretical dimensions of risk taking is in order. Following this a further discussion and analysis, as well as some concrete examples of national and firm level risk taking, will be presented.

## Dimensions of Risk Taking

There are two dimensions of risk taking of interest here: (*a*) rationality and its boundaries and (*b*) degree of aggressiveness or conservatism. Let us first deal with the concept of rational risk taking and the boundaries of rationality. Rational risk taking in the truly optimum sense defies precise definition. Human beings and enterprises are typically at least somewhat limited in knowledge, information, foresight, skill, and time in arriving at decisions involving uncertainty and estimates of the future. Moreover, much of the human decision making and risk taking process often involves unconscious thought processes. It is essentially a matter of semantics whether the process of rational risk taking and decision making is a "satisficing" or "maximizing" process.

In spite of these problems it still makes sense to talk in terms of the degree and boundaries of rationality in risk taking and decision making. The degree to which risk taking is rational in a given situation is dependent on the degree and extent to which the following conditions are present:

1. The decision is based on the realities of the situation, including a well reasoned evaluation of the relevant facts which are available.
2. The decision is based on logical assumptions and carefully calculated courses of action with weighted estimates of the potential risks and probabilities of success involved. Such weighting may be unconscious or conscious, depending on the significance of the decision and related risks involved.

Hence, rational risk taking and the effectiveness of risk taking depends largely on knowledge, the availability and uses of strategic information, and the level of skill in applying scientific method. The boundaries of rational risk taking may be enlarged through more and better education which imparts knowledge, through the generation and provision of more relevant information that decision makers can draw upon, and by creating a more favorable attitude toward scientific method.

Many basically cautious and rational persons in various countries may, for example, expose themselves to typhoid fever by drinking impure water, because they are not aware that there is a connection between disease and water. Here the boundaries of rationality are clearly constrained by lack of knowledge. On the other hand an individual, because of mystical, religious, or other purely emotional forces, may behave irrationally and drink impure water even if he is aware that he may become ill.

In a similar manner, politicians or business enterprises and their managements in various societies take risks that seem highly irrational and strange to Americans. They may take such risks either because they are in fact irrational in their decisions, relying solely on mysticism and faith, or, more commonly, because they lack the knowledge, information, and/or skill necessary for adequate evaluation of the risks entailed. In the latter situation it is also likely that relevant information which may be available is not utilized because of lack of knowledge of its existence.

In general, the level of education and knowledge in any society will probably influence significantly the types of risks undertaken. The less known about various types of risks, the more likely that an individual, an enterprise, or a complete country will take risks that are long shots—in the sense that the possibilities of desired payoffs or winning the game are remote. Here the level of risk taking effectiveness, in terms of intended or desired results, would tend to be low. Where the decision makers are highly aware of the implications and uses of scientific methodology, including the relatively recent work on chance and probability, as well as the basic principles of decision making under uncertainty, it is likely that the types of major risks taken will reflect better probabilities of success than if these concepts are unknown.

In a society where risk taking bearing on industrial enterprise performance tends to be quite irrational, or where the boundaries of rationality are very narrow, managerial effectiveness and productive efficiency would tend to suffer greatly. One can expect to find much in the way of idle and underemployed resources, wasteful output, and considerable unproductive time and human effort in a relatively large proportion of industrial firms. Many if not most of the elements of the management process would probably be performed in a relatively inefficient manner. The planning function in particular is directly related to the degree to which risk taking is rational and effective.

The second dimension of risk taking pertains to degree of conservatism or aggressiveness. Here individual preferences toward risk taking under similar conditions and odds can be measured in order to determine degree of conservatism or aggressiveness in each individual case. In recent years there has been a growing number of research experiments and empirical studies of this type, mainly in the United States.[87] There is no conceptual reason why this type of research and experimentation cannot be done cross-culturally, on a fairly extensive scale, in order to determine dominant preference patterns of individual, firm, and/or even national risk taking in different countries.

Available evidence to date suggests that in terms of managerial effectiveness and economic progress, industrial managers, and other persons,

---

[87] Cf.: J. Marschak, "Actual Versus Consistent Decision Behavior," *Behavioral Science*, Vol. 9, No. 2, April, 1964, pp. 103–110; G. Becker, M. DeGroat, and J. Marschak, "Measuring Utility by a Single-Response Sequential Method," *Behavioral Science*, Vol. IX, No. 3, July, 1964, pp. 226–232; A. Scadel, P. Ratoosh, and J. Minas, "Some Personality Correlates of Decision Making Under Conditions of Risk," *Behavioral Science*, Vol. IV, No. 1, January, 1959, pp. 19–27. See also McClelland, *The Achieving Society*, pp. 210–225, and "Business Drive," pp. 104–106; Atkinson, Bastian, Earl, and Litwin, *op. cit.*; Atkinson, *op. cit.*; L. Littig, *The Effect of Motivation on Probability Preferences and Subjective Probability* (unpublished doctoral dissertation, Ann Arbor, Mich., University of Michigan, 1959).

possessing a relatively high achievement drive are the best risk takers. They tend to be neither highly conservative nor overly aggressive and speculative. As was pointed out earlier, they are inclined to undertake moderate, calculated risks—given their boundaries of rationality—which entail some challenge but at the same time a relatively good chance of payoff and success. Such persons also tend to prefer moderately ambitious operational objectives, and would also be inclined to innovate—assuming that other constraints do not substantially act against innovation—in order to improve performance and results.

The highly conservative or ultraconservative risk taker is likely to be an individual or manager with a low achievement drive, although in some cases such conservatism may be due to nonsociological factors, such as various economic or political-legal constraints, which are operating on him and/or his firm. The highly conservative risk taker would tend to oppose innovation, change, and even expansionary courses of action, and enterprises under this type of management would be likely to remain quite static.

It may be difficult at times to distinguish between an irrational risk taker and one who is very aggressive and bordering on extreme speculation. The irrational risk taker would not necessarily be aware that the chances of payoff are remote, while the highly aggressive risk taker would be willing to pursue his decision even in the light of relatively long odds. The latter type of risk taker may be behaving in a relatively rational manner, if he has considerable (and warranted) self-confidence in his ability to succeed even at long odds; however, the overly aggressive risk taker who borders on extreme speculation and irrationality may or may not have an abnormally high achievement drive, but in any event he is likely to be somewhat psychologically maladjusted. He would certainly be psychologically unfit in terms of effective management or political decision making. Even though political leaders or business managers who are overly aggressive or speculative risk takers may hit a big payoff from time to time, industrial enterprises operating in such an environment would tend to be in a constant state of flux, instability, and inefficiency, assuming that they did not completely collapse.

In general, if a substantial portion of the business and industrial managers in a given country are explicitly or implicitly willing to take long chances, it is likely that through time losses will outweigh gains, and their firms as well as society will be poorer and less efficient as a result. Conversely, if firms and their managements tend to be overly cautious and conservative, and hence unwilling to take virtually any kind of meaningful risk, the individual enterprise, and the country, will be unable to make the productive gains possible under such meaningful risk taking. The former situation will be revealed by excess and widespread business losses and possibly failures resulting in considerable waste and inefficiency, while the latter will emerge as a situation where firms fall behind their foreign rivals and fail to substantially expand useful outputs and increase productivity within the country. In both situations manageriai effectiveness and economic progress would suffer. A balance between conservative and aggressive risk taking within industry is essential for a high level of managerial effectiveness and productive efficiency, although such a balance is not subject to precise measurement.

Such a balance is also needed with regard to national risk taking. One would expect that a country which fails to take any overt risks at all would soon be in serious trouble in a dynamic world. Nothing stays constant for long, and efforts to keep the future away by doing as little as possible to change things are almost certainly doomed to failure. On the other hand, extreme risk taking, including irrational or improper evaluation of major national risks, can be equally disastrous in terms of managerial effectiveness and economic progress.

The ideal environment in terms of risk taking as it relates to managerial effectiveness and economic progress would be one in which there is an extensive and diverse system of high quality education at all levels; a favorable view toward scientific method, achievement, and change; and a high degree of interorganizational cooperation which permits the extensive generation, dissemination, and utilization of information and knowledge relevant to rational individual, firm, and national decision making.

## Some Examples of National Risk Taking

Some examples of various types of risk taking and their impact on industrial management and economic progress are in order at this point. Consider first a few examples of national risk taking. History is full of ultraconservative countries which have fallen behind economically because their governments and leaders have been unwilling to adjust to changing conditions largely because of the risks entailed and consequently have failed to provide an environment in which the industrial sector could function properly and expand. Spain, Afghanistan, Ethiopia, much of the Moslem Middle East, and various other African, Asian, and Latin American countries fall in this category.

Many countries, particularly some of the newly emerging countries seeking very rapid economic development and/or pursuing highly aggressive expansionary courses of action, tend to engage in very speculative and often irrational risk taking which has a very negative impact on industrial managerial effectiveness and productive efficiency. Such risks include both external and internal political and economic decisions. Highly speculative military ventures with little hope of success characterized many petty kingdoms in past centuries, and even in modern times some countries seem willing to gamble extensively on the hope of making relatively small gains. Such ventures, if they end in failure, can have extremely serious negative impacts on the productive efficiency of the country and its industrial enterprises. When one hears discussion of "irresponsible" political behavior of a particular country, what usually is meant is that the country is taking untoward political risks.

Japan's adventures in World War II is an example of country risk taking which was improperly evaluated, at great cost to the nation and much of its industrial sector. This unfortunate experience has obviously led to a more balanced and rational view of national risk taking in Japan.

Currently, Indonesia and several other countries have been engaging in very risky and rather irrational warlike activities which hinder industrial managerial effectiveness and economic progress greatly. Such activities typically cause severe foreign exchange crises, considerable economic and often political instability, and serve to drain critically scarce resources of all types from nondefense industries. In such an environment it is extremely difficult for industrial managers to plan effectively and firms—even those staffed with able managers—are frequently confronted with serious break-downs in operations which result in much idle plant, equipment, working capital, and manpower.

Internal politics and macroeconomic decision making also involve a good deal of risk taking. Major changes in policy or activity, such as the nationalization of an important economic sector, large investments in the establishment of new public industrial enterprises, major shifts in national resource allocation patterns, the implementation of a new fiscal or mone-tary policy, entering into a new customs treaty, or overthrowing the ruling political faction, all have risk implications which can have a major bearing on industrial management and economic progress. In many countries such decisions often tend to be made in an irrational manner. In some cases the political or macroeconomic decision makers do not even attempt to make a meaningful assessment of the important implications and risks entailed; they rely on mysticism or blind faith and hope or assume that their deci-sions will prove effective. In other instances, the boundaries of rationality may be so narrow because of the extreme dearth of knowledge and relevant information, thus making the outcome of the decision highly uncertain, speculative, and risky; yet the decision is still made.

In numerous instances, national decisions aimed at increasing indus-trial managerial effectiveness and economic progress have the opposite effect. Cuba's rapid shift to a Marxist state is a case in point. Real income has fallen substantially in this situation, reflecting various unwanted and unintended consequences of a major social and political change; and the gamble, in economic terms, has been lost, to date at least. The impact on productive enterprise has been quite the reverse of what was wanted, since managerial effectiveness and productive efficiency have declined at probably most enterprises.

Indonesia's drastic action in 1957 against Dutch interests and its extensive and rapid nationalizations of business and industry have led to a mass exodus of scarce managerial and technical manpower, as well as shipping services. This in turn has led to a very substantial drop in both industrial production and exports, which has not yet been reversed; and the situation has further aggravated Indonesia's foreign exchange and inflation crises, and general economic instability.[88]

Irrational and highly speculative macroeconomic decisions in many if not most newly developing countries are leading to considerable waste and inefficiency at the industrial enterprise level in both the public and private sectors.[89] Even well managed firms tend to have great difficulty in effectively planning future operations because of the great uncertainty resulting from macrodecisions which effect them. As a result their own potential risk taking efforts are severely handicapped and constrained. Numerous enterprises throughout much of the less developed world are operating at a fraction of fixed productive capacity and are faced with extreme shortages of capital, spare parts, materials, and skilled manpower, largely because macroeconomic and/or political decisions have been arrived at with little or no analysis of the risks or probabilities of success entailed. At the same time, enterprises operating in a highly inflationary environment, such as that in Brazil and Chile, typically prefer to build up large inventories in order to sell them at rising prices, rather than increase production and productivity.

Some countries appear to learn more quickly from their past irrational and ill conceived risk taking activities than others. The failure of Communist China's "Great Leap Forward" during the 1958–61 period—which resulted in considerable waste and inefficiency throughout the economy— has apparently led to somewhat more rational and less speculative macroeconomic decision making in that country.[90] In the Soviet Union, it seems that a major reason for Khrushchev's recent ouster was his tendency to make arbitrary and often irrational national decisions. A case in point was his "Virgin Lands" gamble in the 1950's, which deflected much in the way of scarce economic resources from the industrial sector as a whole, and which proved to be a failure; however, in recent years the Soviet Union, even under Khrushchev, has made increasing use of exprimentation, analysis of facts, the generation and utilization of relevant information, discussion, and debate in macroeconomic decision making. With Khrushchev's departure it is very likely that this trend will be greatly intensified, thus resulting in a higher degree and extended boundaries of rational national decision making. This will undoubtably enhance managerial effectiveness and productive efficiency in the future.

---

[88] Cf. United Nations, *Economic Survey of Asia and the Far East—1963* (New York, 1964), pp. 170 ff.

[89] See the evidence and examples presented in the sources cited in Footnotes 73 and 86 above.

[90] Cf.: H. Schurman, "Peking's Recognition of Crisis," *Problems of Communism*, September-October, 1961; E. Jones, "Peking's Economy: Upwards or Downwards," *Problems of Communism*, January-February, 1963; "Red China's Troubles Pile Up," *Business Week*, July 7, 1962; *The Economist*, January 7, September 29, and October 17, 1962.

The trend throughout much of the less developed world is probably in the direction of more rational and balanced national risk taking; however, mysticism, pure emotion, the lack of knowledge and information, and a relatively unfavorable view toward scientific method, will continue to serve as significant constraints on effective national risk taking, and hence industrial managerial effectiveness and economic progress, in many countries for some time to come. The emergence of a small core of highly intelligent, well educated, and rational political leaders and top level advisors can do much to promote more effective national risk taking in an underdeveloped or developing country. Unfortunately, such countries, more often than not, do not yet have such a core of able persons.

Advanced industrial nations are typically characterized by a relatively high degree of rational, balanced, and effective national risk taking and decision making, although the degrees and boundaries of rationality do vary somewhat among the advanced countries in comparable situations. There clearly are occasions where emotion outweighs rationality in national decision making and risk taking even in the developed countries. A case in point is the nationalization of the British steel industry under the Labor government following World War II. This decision involved considerable risk in terms of economic progress, yet it was based largely on ideological and emotional factors as opposed to rational economic considerations, even though the Labor party desired rapid economic progress for the nation. The result of this nationalization decision was lower productivity and greater inefficiency in this sector,[91] and subsequently when the Conservative party returned to power in the 1950's it denationalized the segments of the steel (and motor trucking) industry that had been nationalized. The Labor government came to power again in 1964 and is once again considering the nationalization of the steel industry primarily on emotional and ideological grounds.

The general trend, however, in advanced countries is to strive for greater rationality and effectiveness in connection with important national decisions involving significant risks. This is done by constantly generating and utilizing more and better knowledge and relevant information in macro-decision making and by applying scientific methodology more extensively and with greater skill.

The American tax cut in 1964 is an example of a carefully calculated and basically rational risk. In this case, the possible favorable impacts, such as increases in income, stimulation of demand, and the creation of an expansionist atmosphere, were balanced against the possibilities of unfavorable results, such as price inflation. A responsible and able government, when faced with these alternatives, plus as much knowledge and predictive information as could be accumulated, could make a rational decision about this important economic policy. To date, it appears that the decision ar-

---

[91] Cf. G. Gayder, *The Responsible Company* (Oxford, England: Basil Blackwell, 1961), especially chap. xviii.

rived at has had a favorable impact on industrial managerial effectiveness and economic progress in general.

## Risk Taking Patterns at the Enterprise Level

The kinds of risks that industrial enterprises are willing to take depend primarily on the view of risk taking held by high level management. While risk taking behavior among enterprises within the same country often varies greatly, there do seem to be dominant patterns of firm risk taking in different countries.

In the advanced nations of the West, risk taking at the firm level tends to be quite rational in probably the majority of cases, although the boundaries of rationality often vary substantially in specific situations. It is true that even in the United States there are businessmen, most typically owner-managers of relatively small firms, who either knowingly or unknowingly take risks that have little chance of paying off, and it is such business enterprises that account for the vast majority of failures and liquidations each year; however, in the majority of cases in the U.S. and advanced western European countries enterprise managements probably act quite rationally in arriving at important decisions that involve significant risks. At the same time there is a greater tendency in American industry than in European industry to enlarge the boundaries of rationality in risk taking and decision making by obtaining and analyzing more relevant information, by taking into account the knowledge and advice provided by a wide range of staff experts and specialists, and by applying scientific method to a wider range of business problems.[92] The difference in this connection may be greater between the U.S. and Britain or France as compared with Germany or Sweden.

A seemingly more significant difference between American industrial enterprise and its counterparts in western Europe regarding risk taking behavior pertains to the degree of aggressiveness vs. conservatism. With the possible exception of Germany, enterprise managements in the U.S. tend to be substantially more aggressive risk takers in general than their European counterparts, especially with regard to marketing and research and development activities.[93] It is not surprising that American firms tend to be more aggressive in the areas of marketing or research and development, since the American economy is still considerably more abundant and affluent than the economies of western Europe where a sellers' market mentality still lingers on in many instances. In addition, the competitive and entrepreneurial spirit tends to be a somewhat more potent force in the U.S., even though the shift from owner-managers to more security conscious professional managers throughout much of industry during this century has probably diluted this spirit to some extent.

---

[92] See the sources referred to in Footnotes 32 chapter 7, and 77 of this chapter.

[93] Cf.: Granick, *The European Executive*, especially Part III; Lewis and Stewart, *op. cit.*, especially chaps. vii, viii, and ix; Nowotny, *op. cit.*, pp. 101–108.

In Britain, France, possibly to a somewhat lesser degree in Belgium, and in various other European countries industrial managers tend to be rather conservative risk takers. The achievement drive of high level managers is probably an important factor here, as are various other sociological, cultural, and psychological factors.

A leading authority on European management has constructed vivid sociological prototypes of the kinds of persons typically occupying higher level managerial positions in British industry. Through this model he has analyzed why British managers tend to be highly conservative risk takers. This authority also explains why Belgium managers tend to be conservative risk takers with regard to marketing and product innovation activities, and why French managers, particularly owner-managers, have typically been conservative and highly security conscious in running their firms.[94] In the case of France, it is possible that in recent years *Le Plan*—the French National Economic Plan—and the provision of more relevant information for micromanagerial decision making in business are leading to a somewhat less conservative view toward risk taking and to a somewhat more expansionist business attitude. The German industrial manager tends to be the most aggressive risk taker in Europe. High level German managers frequently have a high achievement drive, considerable self-confidence, and are imbued with an expansionist ethic.[95] They are typically willing to take reasonable risks pertaining to all of the enterprise functions.

Also relevant with regard to risk taking is the common social attitude in Britain, and elsewhere in Europe, in connection with bankruptcy and even loss of position. A businessman involved in either situation is typically viewed as a disgrace and moral failure. In the U.S. the typical attitude is that this can happen to anybody, and the businessman who fails, even a number of times, and then strikes it big is a common success story in American folklore and reality.

Another important factor is that the British civil service often serves as the model for large industrial organizations in that country, and civil service administration sets the tone for much of industrial managerial behavior as well. Social responsibility is the keynote, not aggressive risk taking, which frequently claims both from company personnel and competitors. An aggressive risk taker victims whose activities do claim victims is likely to be subject to social blame by his peers at the private club.

David Granick, in his book, *The European Executive*, relates the

---

[94] Granick, *The European Executive*. Part III of this study deals with risk taking and managerial behavior in Britain, Belgium, France, and Germany. For a comprehensive discussion and analysis of *Le Plan* in France, see E. Learned, F. Aguilar, and R. Valtz, *European Problems in General Management* (Homewood, Ill.: Richard D. Irwin, Inc., 1963), pp. 277–316.

[95] In addition to Granick's discussion of German management, see "Krupp Forges a New German Economic Weapon," *Business Week*, February 6, 1965, pp. 92–94. This interesting article reflects the aggressive and expansionist philosophy held by a growing number of present day German industrial firms.

following firsthand experience which illustrates the commonly held conservative view toward risk taking and change, even among research and development executives, in British industry. The experience cited—which is typical in British industry in Granick's opinion and in the opinion of one of the authors of this study who has observed and interviewed a number of British managers—is taken from a food processing company. To quote Granick directly:

I talked to a company's chief chemist who had just returned from a four-week visit in an American plant of the same industry. He was full of the differences between his own factory—an important one in the industry—and the American plant.

There was little experimentation with the production process in Britain, he said, and the techniques remained essentially those employed half a century ago. The process was not chemically understood, and thus there was fear that any experiments might have a bad effect on product quality. In the American firm, however, there was considerable experimentation and even the use of a pilot plant. In fact, the American industry was converting into a chemical industry, with strict control over the process at all points.

After hearing all this, I asked this chief chemist if it would pay his firm to increase sharply its research and development—say, doubling it as a minimum. (The American firm employed ten times as many chemists for control and research as did the British company, although its total labor force was only 40 per cent greater.) The chemist was doubtful, feeling that the cost would be more than the research was worth. Imagine such a response, whether correct or not, from a control-and-development manager in the United States.[96]

There is growing concern in Britain about the ultraconservative view toward risk taking in industry, particularly in connection with the marketing and research and development functions. One recent source states:

While the advance of technology has produced professional managers elsewhere, many of Britain's 500,000 managers are arrogantly suspicious of the new breed of engineers and scientists and slow to spend money on research. . . . British managers also tend to look down their noses at the self-made man and the aggressive merchant. A tremendous amount of work has to be done, in the opinion of Sir George Briggs, deputy chairman of Hawker Siddeley Industries, to root out the prejudice that trade is non U.[97]

This source goes on to discuss the conservative philosophy of British firms regarding sales activities in export markets. A recent survey reveals that for every British salesman abroad there are 2.0 Germans, 2.3 Americans and 2.8 Japanese.

Another recent source points out that in various British industries, particularly metalworking, an ultraconservative philosophy regarding

---

[96] *Ibid.*, p. 253.
[97] "Britain—The Halfhearted Economy."

marketing, product design, and other research and development activities is leading to stagnant enterprises and poor results in many cases.[98]

A London newspaper, in an editorial commenting on Harold Wilson's book, *The Relevance of British Socialism*, has expressed concern over the effect that a Labor government, headed by Mr. Wilson, will have on risk taking in British business and industry:

> Mr. Wilson very justly deplores our present lack of industrial innovators and courageous enterpreneurs. Would there be more under his rule? Would there be any? He expects them to take big risks. What reward does he offer? If they fail, they fail: if they succeed, they become capitalists, objects of Mr. Wilson's loathing. They may be nationalized in any case. They may wish to give their children a better start than their own: again they will defend Mr. Wilson's egalitarian prejudices, his distaste for advantages conferred by wealth or inheritance. Play safe—if Mr. Wilson gets power—do as he did, and join the Civil Service.[99]

The dominant view toward risk taking in Japanese industry appears to be fairly rational and rather aggressive with regard to marketing, especially for export, production, product and technical process innovation, and other enterprise functions; however, Japanese management tends to be highly conservative and rigidly maintains the status quo with regard to the organizing, directing, and staffing functions. Because of various cultural factors it may well be risky to undertake changes in these areas; but the almost complete lack of experimentation, risk taking, and change regarding these managerial functions at most enterprises to date may be hindering managerial effectiveness and productive efficiency under present conditions.

At the enterprise level in Soviet industry there is less potential opportunity for entrepreneurship and risk taking than in private enterprise. This is also often the case in public industrial enterprise in other countries—both Communist and non-Communist—where the government and/or high level state planners make the most important financial, resource allocation, and other decisions. Here rational and balanced risk taking in the face of uncertainty does not lose its importance, but much of the risk function is shifted from the individual and the microlevel to a more impersonal macrolevel. Soviet enterprise management, however—as well as its counterparts in public enterprise in various other countries—still makes various decisions and undertakes activities involving risk and uncertainty.[100]

To the extent that the Soviet enterprise manager is a risk taker, he tends to be a relatively rational and fairly aggressive one. He also typically has a fairly high achievement drive. A large part of his risk taking decisions and activities involves the procurement function. Probably a substantial

---

[98] "Britain's Crisis in Efficiency," *Business Week*, December 26, 1964, pp. 82–84.

[99] "Wilson's Socialism," *The Daily Telegraph*, London, July 17, 1964.

[100] For a comprehensive discussion and analysis of risk taking and managerial behavior in Soviet industry, see Richman, *Soviet Management*, especially pp. 127–128 and chaps. viii and ix.

majority of Soviet enterprises are often confronted with considerable problems and uncertainty regarding the allocation and receipt of adequate
physical resources required to fulfil their operating plans. Since the managers are judged and rewarded according to the degree to which certain key
production and cost targets of their enterprise plan are fulfilled and over-
fulfilled, they frequently engage in risky ventures in order to obtain urgently
needed supplies. Such ventures typically include both semilegal and illegal
procurement practices—including in part "special favors," bribery, personal
influence, swapping commodities, and so forth.

This type of risk taking activity can have either functional or dysfunc-
tional consequences in terms of economic progress. Where resources ear-
marked for, and urgently needed by, other plants are deflected through
unofficial procurement practices, one enterprise is like to gain in efficiency
at the expense of another, thus leading to problems of subsystem optimization. In many instances the resources procured in this manner are not
needed by another enterprise and are standing idle. Here the overall productive system would tend to benefit from such entrepreneurial procurement
activity. Penalties are only infrequently imposed for unofficial or illegal
procurement activities in Soviet industry. Two speculative assumptions can
be drawn from this situation:

1. The Soviet managers engaging in illegal procurement activities are very
   shrewd and rational personal risk takers.
2. The state condones such activities because they aid the overall productive system more than they hinder it.

There is probably a great deal of truth in both of these assumptions.

Soviet enterprise managers also tend to pursue other potentially risky
decisions and activities. For example, they frequently produce goods not in
accordance with the product mix plan, of substandard quality, and/or
having improper specifications, in order to fulfil the aggregate targets by
which they are evaluated and rewarded. For the same reason, they falsify
records and results, conceal productive capacity, inflate prices and costs of
output, and so forth. More often than not they get away with such
activities, thus suggesting considerable risk taking skill, even if such risk
taking is often not conducive to productive efficiency. On the other hand,
Soviet enterprise managers are generally very reluctant to innovate in the
product or technical process sense, even though they are expected to do so.
They tend to oppose vigorously and avoid major innovational risks of this
type because of the systems of rewards, performance standards, and resource
allocation under which they must operate.

It should be pointed out here that American managers—as well as
managers in other countries—often skillfully engage in a variety of
unofficial, as well as undesirable, practices involving risks in order to perform well in terms of the key standards by which they are evaluated. At
times some American managers even engage in risky ventures that are

completely illegal in terms of the law of the land. A case in point is the price fixing scandal in the electrical industry in 1961. It is highly debatable whether such price fixing was conducive to a higher or lower degree of productive efficiency. On the one hand, the firms involved reduced uncertainty in their planning; on the other hand, higher prices were obtained for their products whether quality was improved or not.

The above examples of unofficial, undesirable, and illegal risk taking practices in Soviet and American industry have been presented to point out that rational managerial or firm risk taking is not always conducive to a high level of managerial effectiveness, from society's point of view.

In the underdeveloped and newly developing countries of the world rational and fairly aggressive risk taking at the enterprise level is generally critical for substantial economic progress; however, the view of risk taking held by enterprise managements, and their resulting risk taking behavior, throughout most of Africa, Asia, and Latin America tends to act as a significant constraint on managerial effectiveness and higher productive efficiency.

A major problem here is the extremely narrow boundaries of rationality within which even an able industrial manager is confined in decision making under uncertainty. The great dearth of information, statistics, and knowledge available to draw upon typically compels the rational decision maker to be highly cautious in most instances. It is frequently impossible to assign meaningful estimates of the risks and probabilities of success entailed in decisions involving a significant break from the status quo or tradition. Extreme uncertainty often looms as the major problem in such cases. Another serious problem in these parts of the world is that numerous industrial managers have little or no conception or knowledge of what rational decision making is. They often undertake highly speculative and irrational risks without even attempting to assess the critical implications involved in their decisions and risk taking activities. Achievement motivation also tends to serve as a constraint with respect to effective risk taking. As was pointed out earlier, high level industrial managers in less developed countries frequently have a low achievement drive.

In many less developed countries both ultraconservative and irrational patterns of risk taking are pervasive at industrial enterprises. Consider, for example, the building of a new plant under such risk taking conditions. A highly conservative management typically has a plant designed and constructed with just enough capacity to meet present demands, and potential growth in the future is greatly hampered. Irrational industrial managers often have plants constructed taking into account only optimum size in terms of production costs in relation to output, without considering the potential market for the enterprise's products. Both of these patterns of risk taking are quite common in many less developed countries of the world,[101]

---

[101] Cf. *Management of Industrial Enterprise in Underdeveloped Countries*, pp. 67 ff.

and we shall cite an actual detailed case of irrational risk taking in this regard shortly.

Conservative businessmen in many underdeveloped countries frequently prefer to invest their incomes and savings abroad rather than to expand their enterprises, since they feel that various unstable environmental conditions make local investment too risky. One underdeveloped country in Africa requested a loan of $25 million from the World Bank in the early 1960's for industrial development purposes. It was discovered that $75 million had been invested in New York by businessmen, government officials, and various other citizens of this country during the same year.[102]

In India many industrial enterprise managements, particularly most of those operating under the managing agency system, tend to be highly conservative risk takers. They stress quick profits and short run activities and are typically very reluctant to innovate or to break from traditional patterns of operation. Indian enterprise managements also tend to have a strong sellers' market mentality, assuming that whatever is produced will be sold. This is a potentially dangerous philosophy to adhere to as conditions change, and this is recognized by American executives of U.S. firms in India who have observed Indian industrial managers firsthand over the years. Those Indian firms willing to take major risks often do so in an irrational manner; and this typically leads to considerable losses, waste and inefficiency.[103]

Enterprise managements in Indonesia, Burma, Turkey, Egypt, Chile, and most other less developed countries tend to be highly conservative, overly speculative, or irrational risk takers.[104] The degrees of conservatism, speculativeness, and irrationality may vary somewhat from country to country; but probably only relatively few firm managements are both highly rational and fairly aggressive risk takers. The blame for this situation, however, must be attributed in large part to the environment and not merely to the enterprise managers themselves.

One of the authors had the opportunity to observe firsthand the risk taking behavior of a number of Saudi enterprise managers during the period 1959–61. This experience vividly illustrated to the observer the relationship among risk taking, scientific method, education, knowledge, and achievement motivation. Several of the Saudi managers appeared to have a high achievement drive and desired to expand their businesses as rapidly as possible; however, without some predictive methodology and very little

---

[102] United Nations, *Economic Bulletin for Africa—1962* (New York, 1963), p. 85.

[103] For discussions dealing with risk taking philosophy and behavior in Indian industry see: Sundaram, in *Proceedings* (CIOS), 1963, pp. 495–498; A. Negandhi, *An Evaluation of Foreign Investment Climate in India* (unpublished doctoral dissertation, East Lansing, Mich., Michigan State University, 1964), especially p. 88; Vakil, *op. cit.*, pp. 46–51.

[104] Cf. the sources cited in Footnotes 88, 101, and 102 above. See also: Reksodihardjo, *op. cit.*, chap. vii; United Nations, *The Development of Manufacturing Industry in Egypt, Israel and Turkey* (New York, 1959), pp. 82 ff.

relevant information to utilize, it proved extremely difficult and often impossible for them to decide which risks were rational and had a fairly good chance of paying off and which were wild speculations. Moreover, the Saudi managers observed all were rather limited in their knowledge about sophisticated business operations, and all had limited formal educations. None of them had more than a high school education. A few of them acquired most of their knowledge about business operations working in semiskilled or frontline supervisory jobs at Aramco. Where the Saudi managers decided to undertake major risks, with very few exceptions, inept choices were made, and considerable waste, inefficiency, and loss resulted in several cases. The other Saudi managers observed tended to be reluctant to undertake even minor risks or changes in operations.

It may prove interesting to relate in some detail an actual case of enterprise risk taking behavior in Lebanon observed by one of the authors a few years ago. It should be noted that in our opinion, risk taking behavior in Lebanese business firms tends to be sounder and more effective than in many other countries of the world, in spite of the problems and shortcomings to be presented below; this suggests how unsound and ineffective risk taking behavior probably is in many other countries. Our account of this case follows:

A fairly small and relatively prosperous Lebanese firm became interested in the prospects of processing and canning orange juice concentrate in that country. Since the country is a fairly large producer of oranges, and since at that time these were in surplus, the idea had a certain degree of plausibility. This firm's management, aware that they did not know much about such manufacturing processes, hired a consultant to plan the production processes involved. The production report was duly prepared and presented, showing that a plant could be built for approximately $150,000. It also explored the kinds of technical labor which would be required to operate properly this sort of plant.

To this point, the firm was behaving in a fairly rational and straightforward manner. Their production planning and contemplated production organization seemed sound. The managers, however, now convinced that this plant would be a sure profit maker, began to plan the purchase of necessary land for the site. In discussing this plan with the managers, the author found that they firmly believed that they were acting in a completely rational manner. Further questioning, however, revealed that the only marketing planning done to that point had been to assume that the entire output of the plant could be sold as it was produced. Moreover, no one had instructed the consultant to plan a factory of a given size. As an American, he had presented the most economically sized plant for the United States—which, after a bit of calculation on the back of an envelope, one could see would be large enough to utilize the entire Lebanese orange crop per year. Costs presented included only the basic machinery, not the building, utilities, storage facilities, or shipping docks. These additional items would cost far more than the basic machinery, although they had not been included in the cost calculation.

Financial planning to that point had included the costs of the machinery only. When it was pointed out that initial capital requirements for plant and equipment alone were almost three times the initial estimate, considerable revisions had to be made. A further factor overlooked was that no one in Lebanon at that time had the necessary cold storage vehicles to transport the finished product to market—which would add at least $100,000 to costs.

The entire physical distribution system for this product had not even been considered. Investigation revealed that only about seventy shops in the entire country had any cold space of the type needed for this product and that the total cubic capacity of these cold boxes would be less than one day's production of the proposed plant. Enormous additional investment in storage facilities would be needed even before the firm could begin to produce.

The cans used for this product have to be of a special type, and none were available in the country. To import them would cost, in transportation charges, more than the product could be sold for, since ocean freight charges are based on volume. Empty cans are extremely light per cubic foot, and the shipper in effect pays for the air he ships. An alternative would be to ship the cans flattened, but this would require additional special equipment to round the cans at destination, adding to the capital costs. Another alternative would be to approach the local can manufacturer and work out a plan for local manufacture of the cans, but no one had done this.

No marketing analysis had been done to this point. The projected sales figure was the total production capacity of the plant multiplied by the price per can. This worked out to about two cans of juice per person per day—in a country with a per capita annual income of about $400.

Discussions about management and personnel revealed that the firm expected to be able to hire local technicians to run the plant properly, in spite of the fact that no manufacturing of this sort had ever been done before. The local labor pool had not been investigated at all, since it was assumed that good foremen, mechanics, and cold storage technicians were available. A few were, as it turned out; but this was not immediately obvious.

The final crude planning pass at this project revealed that if the plant were built in the manner initially planned, and if the necessary auxiliary investment were also included, total costs would run over a million dollars. This did not include working capital and costs of training workers and managers for the new plant.

The follow-up analysis in this case was quite quick and rather rough, but it was enough to indicate that the expectations of the managers were wildly unrealistic. Yet, for industrialists in this country at this time, they had done a relatively good job of planning, and they saw themselves as preparing to take quite rational risks in this venture. Their definition of *rational* was clearly different from others'; but it does indicate how a group of managers, isolated from Western traditions of scientific methodology in business topics, conceived their problems. It is not surprising under such conditions that business failures, poorly planned enterprises, and inept management of defective production facilities are so common.

The direct impact of the educational and other sociological constraints was quite clear in this case. The managers in this case had not been trained in modern business practice, economics, or any other subject remotely relevant to their problems. They saw the use of scientific methodology rather well in production terms, having observed Western firms utilize it quite effectively in their country; but it never occurred to any of them that similar techniques might be useful in planning, control, marketing, or finance. Failure to see that this type of scientific thinking might prove useful in other business areas led to this view of "rational" risk taking, which proved to be irrational risk taking in this specific business situation.

## VIEW OF CHANGE

### The Process of Change

The initiation and implementation of change—whether it is technical, economic, social, cultural, political, legal, or managerial in nature—is essentially a human process. Changes, however large, that are desired by the people involved can usually be implemented quite effectively and assimilated with little social disruption. Changes that are not acceptable or desired, even quite small ones, can be put into effect only at considerable social, personal, and possibly economic cost.[105] As one anthropologist has pointed out:

We have learned the pleasing truth, that society talks back. Even the small-scale, technologically inferior peoples of the world have tremendous powers to resist changes they do not want, and to adhere, often at great cost, to their valued and distinct way of life. At the same time, we have learned that changes which people desire, radical or not, can be made swiftly, without great cost, and that a society may nearly redo itself—in a generation—if it wants to.[106]

Russia after 1917 and Japan following World War II are examples of the latter type of society, while various countries in Africa, Asia, and Latin America correspond to the former type.

While those holding political power, intellectuals, business entrepreneurs and managers of all types, and/or external forces may be the key

---

[105] Berelson and Steiner, *op. cit.*, pp. 613–614.

[106] M. Nash, "Applied and Action Anthropology in the Understanding of Man," *Anthropological Quarterly*, XXXII (1959), 79. See also M. Mead, *New Lives for Old* (New York: William Morrow & Co., Inc., 1956).

potential initiators of change in a given society, the effective implementation of change does, in the final analysis, depend on its acceptance by the people involved and affected. Hence, the rate and extent of actual change in the direction of greater managerial effectiveness and economic progress in a particular country depend not only on the presence of initiators of change who desire economic progress and increased managerial effectiveness but also on the acceptance of such change by the persons involved.

The more a given change threatens or appears to threaten the traditional values of the society (or group), the greater the resistance to that change and the greater its attendant cost in social and personal disorganization. As one authoritative anthropological source states:

In relation to ideological and value systems . . . the thesis seems inherent in recent work by a number of students that if, under conditions of change, the basic cultural rationale retains its validity, even extensive behavioral changes can take place without threat to group or individual integrity and morale . . . But if these basic elements are threatened or undermined the group or individual concerned is likely to lapse into states of disorganization, insecurity, anxiety, self-depreciation, and low morale, though usually accompanied by attempts to establish a new rationale . . . Several theorists have suggested that, so long as the basic value system stands reasonably firm, selective change can proceed with minimum strain and stress.[107]

The above quotation provides considerable insight into why Japan has been able effectively and successfully to undertake and contend with its dramatic economic, technological, and social revolution in recent decades.

In order to implement technical change successfully and with minimum disruption it is frequently necessary to employ some aspect of the old or traditional way of life in order to justify the desired change. A classic illustration of the effectiveness of this technique has been attributed to the first King Saud of Saudi Arabia. Religious elders are reputed to have objected to the introduction of telephones in Saudi Arabia on the premise that they were instruments of the devil because they were not mentioned in the Koran. It is said that King Saud had a passage of the Koran transmitted over the telephone line and won acceptance of the new technology with the argument that the devil would not permit an instrument of his to be employed for such a purpose.[108]

In general, religious teachings, cultural values, and the system of formal education in a society tend to be highly critical forces shaping the dominant attitude toward various types of change among the population. Flexibility and tolerance of change are not part of most religions. In many societies, religion encompasses much more than the spiritual and moral values of individual conscience. Religious authority may extend to areas

---

[107] F. Keesing, *Culture Change: An Analysis and Bibliography of Anthropological Sources to 1952* (Stanford, Calif.: Stanford University Press, 1953).

[108] Cited in T. Brannen and R. Hodgson, *Overseas Management* (New York: McGraw-Hill Book Company, 1965), p. 92.

such as personal relations, laws of succession, economic activity, education, and legal codes. Where religious institutions embrace man's overall social and political customs, flexibility and change in these areas may be prohibited as long as traditional religious values are adhered to. Yet many religious tenets devised in an earlier age are no longer applicable after the introduction of the industrial process. Much of religious dogma may be brought under question by the introduction of modern industry and technology. This extends pressure on the religion to change. As religious institutions change, the importance of certain functionaries, including at times the countries' rulers or political leaders, is threatened.[109]

The time required by the peoples of developing countries to assimilate values, attitudes, habits and motivations associated with the industrial way of life of the advanced nations can vary a great deal. Mysticism, superstition, emotionalism, fatalism, and low achievement motivation stubbornly persist as major barriers to all types of change, at all levels, in many present day underdeveloped and newly developing nations. Even among advanced nations cultural values and other forces serve as significant obstacles to various types of change in varying degrees.

In this section we are interested in view of change at the level of society as a whole, and particularly at the industrial enterprise level. At the enterprise level our concern is with management, particularly higher level managers, as initiators of change and with the attitudes of employees and workers as they relate to change and its effective implementation.

## The Firm Level

Of major interest here is the dominant attitude toward change held by industrial enterprise managements in a given society and the rate and extent of change taking place in the overall management process and operations of the typical firm because of managerial initiative and leadership. Changes initiated by management may be substantial in nature, involving such activities as major product, technological, or process innovations or an extensive company reorganization; or they may involve relatively minor changes in policies, operating procedures, methods, and processes—such as a new communication technique or incentive scheme, a change in material requisition forms, a new budgetary system, the adoption of a supervisory training program, and so forth.

As was indicated in the preceding section, attitudes toward change at this level frequently tend to be closely connected with management's view toward risk taking; however, managerial attitudes and behavior in connection with various types of change may not be shaped primarily by risk considerations in many instances. Management may not want to undertake a particular change, irrespective of the risks or potential gains entailed, because of certain values, beliefs or customs; here various cultural or religious reasons may restrict change. Or management may be willing to

---

[109] *Ibid.*, pp. 95 ff.

introduce changes and innovate in order to improve enterprise performance, but it may be ignorant of how to proceed; here educational constraints
and/or view of scientific method may be the key obstacles. Or management
may have the desire and/or ability to introduce a certain change, but union
resistance, extreme governmental red tape, legal restrictions, or the system
of economic incentives serve as critical discouraging or preventative obstacles; here interorganizational cooperation, political organization, relevant
legal rules, or general economic framework may be the actual underlying
constraints.

Also relevant here is the dominant attitude toward change among
enterprise employees and workers. Even where management is inclined to
initiate various changes in enterprise operations in the pursuit of greater
efficiency, it may be greatly hampered from successfully implementing
them if employees are either opposed to or unable to comply with these
changes. Here cultural, religious, or educational factors may be the key
obstacles to change. Employee attitudes and abilities regarding the implementation of changes or innovations initiated by higher management can
often be major constraints upon managerial effectiveness and productive
efficiency; and management may not have much control over the situation,
especially in the short run. Hence, firm managers should take into account
employee attitudes and abilities when assessing the major risks and implications entailed in effectively implementing a desired change in enterprise
operations.

A number of executives of multinational companies have told us that
the time, training, and overall costs entailed in successfully introducing a
similar change or innovation in U.S. operations and in various foreign
subsidiaries often vary greatly. It is generally easier to introduce comparable
changes in the U.S. as compared to most other countries, particularly less
developed nations where both cultural and educational factors may serve as
significant constraints. Often in less developed countries both local workers
and managers resist change for various cultural reasons, and frequently they
cannot cope with change because of educational and training deficiencies.
Not infrequently a desired change cannot be effectively introduced abroad
at all, or a sizable number of U.S. personnel must be sent to the foreign
based subsidiary firm in order to implement successfully a particular change
or innovation. There are also times when it is substantially easier to implement effectively similar changes in U.S. operations as compared to subsidiary enterprises in various advanced European countries, or even Canada.

There is, of course, often considerable resistance to innovation and
change even in U.S. industry at all levels. Regardless of basic cultural
differences, people employed in business and industrial firms throughout
the world often tend to resist managerial and technical changes that directly
affect them and their work for a variety of reasons including economic and
psychological insecurity, personal risk, uncertainty, and so forth. In general,
innovation in the direction of greater productive efficiency in American
industry is certainly not without its imperfections. Sheer complacency or

ultraconservatism in various quasimonopolistic or monopolistic companies, the lack of financial resources in small firms, commercial secrecy, the buying up of inventions, trade union resistance, and unemployment caused by change are all significant problems present in the American economy. Moreover, with a shift from owner-managers with a vigorous flare for entrepreneurship to more security minded professional managers, many American companies are currently confronted with managerial opposition to innovation and change.[110]

A division manager of a large decentralized American company points out why he and his division sometimes resist innovation and change:

When we drop a product or change a process which we have had for years, it invariably means getting rid of equipment, people, and at times, a complete installation. Emotionally, this is never an easy thing to do particularly when in exchange you must embark into areas which will require a greater amount of risk and hurt your profit picture for several years. Certainly a growing organization must trim its product line and move into new areas, but it would be contrary to human nature to expect those people who must suffer through the transition to welcome such a change.[111]

In spite of the above problems and obstacles regarding change and innovation, change is probably accepted as a way of life and viewed favorably to a greater extent in American industry than anywhere else in the world. Competitive forces, patent laws, high achievement motivation, and the pursuit of profits encourage and compel American enterprises to initiate changes in operations, and to innovate in both products and processes, in order to survive and grow. Numerous American industrial managers, both owners and nonowners, are instilled with a sense of mission to cause change. There is undoubtedly much truth in the report, referred to in the introduction of chapter 7, of sixty British businessmen who visited the United States for nine months. In their report the Britishers were highly impressed with the belief in change which pervades American industry, "a belief whereby a successful experiment is not allowed to crystallize into accepted custom, whereas an unsuccessful experiment is accepted as an occupational risk and is set against experience that has been gained."[112] In spite of frequent friction and opposition, change and innovation in the direction of greater economic progress are also probably more acceptable to American industrial personnel at all levels (and to labor unions) than to their counterparts in most other countries. The educational level of the industrial labor force (as well as cultural attitudes) is probably an important factor in this regard.

Let us present a few concrete figures which indicate that there is a

[110] Cf. G. Strauss and L. Sayles, *Personnel: The Human Problems of Management* (Englewood Cliffs, N.J.: Prentice-Hall, Inc., 1960), chap. xii. For substantial evidence of managerial resistance to innovation based on many interviews with American company executives, see K. Warren, *Long Range Planning in Decentralized Corporations* (unpublished doctoral dissertation, New York, Columbia University, 1961).

[111] Warren, *op. cit.*, pp. 103–104.

[112] See Footnote 2 in Chapter 7.

relatively favorable view of change in American industry. In 1959, private industry spent $9.6 billion on research and development activities;[113] in recent years the figures are probably substantially greater. In 1964 American manufacturers spent approximately $18.5 billion for new plant and equipment; about 20 percent of this went for automated equipment. In early 1965 there were some 4,000 numerically controlled automated machine tools in use. This type of equipment was first introduced about 1957. It is estimated that by 1969 50 percent of the machine tools sold will be of this variety. There are currently about thirty firms making computers, and in 1964 the leaders sold or leased some $2 billion worth of electronic computers. In early 1965 there were more than 20,000 general purpose computers in operation—a two-thirds increase in less than two years—and about 10,000 more were already on order.[114] The highly favorable impact of plant automation and electronic computers in U.S. industry on productivity, inventory control, economic and price stability, and general economic progress is well known. Also very significant in terms of managerial effectiveness and productive efficiency, but less spectacular, are the relatively minor changes and innovations that are constantly introduced in the operations of productive enterprises throughout the country.

The view of change, and hence the extent and rate of change, is substantially less favorable in British as compared to American industry. As discussed in the previous section, a more conservative view toward risk taking in Britain explains much of this difference regarding change; however, even where risk is not an important factor, British firms and their managements are generally less favorably disposed toward change than their American counterparts. Tradition, history, habit, custom, and a general desire to maintain the status quo all tend to play a bigger role in British industrial management thought and action.[115]

In 1957 Britain had seventy-five installed computers as compared to fifty-five for the entire European Common Market Community. Six years later Britain had only 550 installed computers, while the figure in the Common Market countries rose to 1,500.[116] Taking into account differences in population and national income, the number of computers per capita in Britain is strikingly below that of the United States.

While Britain does boast some of the world's most efficient and dynamic companies, notably a number of chemical and electrical equipment firms, plant and equipment throughout most of British industry is

---

[113] Harbison and Myers, *Education, Manpower and Economic Growth*, p. 166.

[114] "The Challenge of Automation," *Newsweek*, January 25, 1965, pp. 73 ff.

[115] For evidence and sources dealing with managerial resistance to change in British Industry see: J. Dunning and C. Thomas, *British Industry* (London: Hutchison and Co., Ltd., 1961), especially pp. 17 ff, 125 ff; Granick, *The European Executive*, chaps. ix and xviii; National Economic Development Council (U.K.), *op. cit.; The Growth of the Economy*; Lewis and Stewart, *op. cit.*, chaps. vii, viii, and ix; and the articles cited in Footnotes 97 and 98 of this chapter.

[116] "Britain—The Halfhearted Economy."

antiquated by American standards. Three out of every five machine tools, or a total population of 1,484,496, are more than ten years old, and more than 20 percent are more than twenty years old.[117] While union opposition and employee attitudes frequently stifle technical change, management's view toward change is also a major obstacle.

As a percent of GNP, British outlays for industrial research and capital investment are low compared to many other countries. In recent years much of British industry has been stagnant or falling behind in product design and development, production and marketing techniques, process innovation, and general management practices and techniques which have proved effective in the U.S. as well as in various other countries. Moreover, British industry has not yet given much enthusiastic support to formal management education. The chairman of the board of one large British corporation recently exclaimed, "What do we need most in this country? In a word: change, the acceptance of change."[118] Resistance to change in British industry, particularly at the higher managerial level, is undoubtedly hindering managerial effectiveness and productive efficiency under present conditions, even though the extent and rate of change and innovation are still greater than in many less developed countries.

Soviet industrial enterprise managers tend to resist vigorously and stifle changes and innovations that are seen as obstacles to the fulfilment and overfulfilment of the short run targets upon which they are evaluated and rewarded.[119] They typically resist product and technical process innovational activity, major adjustments in enterprise organization structure, the implementation of new management techniques and practices, and so on, even where the state encourages such change and innovation at the enterprise level. In cases were enterprise managers may desire to implement a change in operations that would lead to greater efficiency and productivity, the inflexibility of the economic system frequently prevents or discourages them from doing so. For example, if they want to introduce a new cost saving device, but the capital, materials, manpower, and/or other resources required are not provided for when the annual enterprise plan is drawn up and approved, it is generally extremely difficult if not impossible to obtain these resources once the plan is put into effect.

The general economic framework and political-legal system in which enterprise managers must operate serve as the major underlying barriers to innovation and change. More specifically, the system of resource allocation, the price structure, the managerial incentive system, and the absence of competitive forces and effective patent laws are all important negative

---

[117] *Ibid.*

[118] *Ibid.*

[119] The data and examples on Soviet industry to be presented in this section, as well as the original Soviet sources from which they have been obtained, are referred to in Richman, *Soviet Management*, chap. ix, and Richman, "Managerial Opposition to Product Innovation in Soviet Union Industry."

constraints regarding innovation and change in Soviet industry. While Soviet enterprise managers frequently do display considerable initiative and ingenuity when it comes to relatively minor changes that are beneficial to short run plan fulfilment, constant pressure from higher level planners and Communist party officials is typically required to compel them to undertake and implement changes and innovations that may endanger the fulfilment and overfulfilment of their quarterly success indicator targets.

Khrushchev, when he was still in power, frequently expressed great concern over managerial resistance to innovation and change, although he tended to ignore the environmental causes of this situation. On one occasion he exclaimed:

In our country some bureaucrats are so used to the old nag that they do not want to change over to a good race horse, for he might tear away on the turn and even spill them out of the sleigh! Therefore such people will hold on to the old nag's tail with both hands and teeth.

On another more recent occasion Khrushchev displayed surprising candor in discussing the effectiveness of competitive forces under capitalism as a potent spur to technological change:

In capitalist conditions the application of new technology in production is spurred by competition. Capitalist firms regularly renew their machine tool equipment in order that they may not go bankrupt. Some firms, for example, do not permit machine tools in their plants to remain in operation for more than ten years, since this equipment wears out and becomes obsolete. And the capitalists know that if they use old equipment they cannot survive in competition with firms that use improved equipment.

Data issued by the Central Statistical Administration of the U.S.S.R. in 1963 disclose that 25 percent of all metal-cutting machines and 27 percent of all forge-press equipment in use in the Soviet machine-building industry were more than twenty years old. About 8,000 metal-cutting machines and 3,000 forge-presses are more than forty years old. Khrushchev pointed out that such equipment is "more fit for museum display than for production."

One Soviet source discloses that the same type of turret lathe has been made by enterprises in one region since 1925 even though many improved lathes have been available to them. Another source reveals that a major equipment producer has manufactured the same product for many years despite the fact that similar equipment that is 50 percent more efficient has long been developed and can be produced at about the same cost. A Soviet enterprise manager made the following extensively applicable statement in *Pravda* "All plant personnel, without exception, are interested in having the plant produce the same machine for the longest possible time without any change whatsoever."

There are also constant and widespread complaints and examples cited in Soviet sources revealing that new consumer goods for which there is a significant demand are frequently withheld from production by enterprise managements. As a result, unsalable inventories of obsolete goods continue to pile up in warehouses and stores.

It is true that innovation and change at the enterprise level has historically not been a critical problem in the Soviet economy. Western technology, processes, and products could be copied directly or adapted to Soviet conditions without serious strain. In the formerly simple Soviet economy considerable progress could be made without recourse to very sophisticated innovative techniques. In the consumer goods sector the crudest forms of output served to satisfy the demands of an impoverished population.

In contemporary times, however, the problem of innovation and change has gained considerable importance in Soviet aims. Instead of there being surplus manpower and productive capacity, shortages of skilled labor have become increasingly critical and innovation and change in the form of increasing productivity is deemed essential. Soviet concern about managerial resistance to process innovation and technological change has come to the fore in connection with increased emphasis on automation and mechanization of plant production processes. In view of skilled manpower shortages and ambitious economic plans, the need for technical progress is presently more crucial than ever.

Rising living standards and somewhat greater consumer discrimination and choice are leading to mounting inventories of obsolete, poor quality, unsalable consumer goods valued at billions of rubles. Now that the consumer has at least one pair of fairly adequate shoes, he is not inclined to buy just any kind of shoes, and product innovation in the consumer goods sector becomes more important. Hence, it is no longer enough for the Soviets to undertake major changes and innovational activities only in a few high priority and strategic spheres of industrial activity such as missiles, armaments, and atomic power projects.

Japanese industry has effectively undergone a dramatic technical and economic revolution by preserving many traditional cultural values and sociological relationships. Japanese enterprise managements, as well as non-managerial personnel, tend to view change quite favorably; and changes in operations tend to be implemented quite effectively, except in areas involving cultural change. Paternalism, traditional superior-subordinate relationships, view toward authority and subordinates, the lifetime employment system, selection, compensation and promotion policies, and various other traditional cultural practices and patterns have been preserved to date. While the preservation of such cultural values has undoubtedly been conducive to greater managerial effectiveness and economic progress in the recent past, as was pointed out in earlier sections, resistance to cultural change is currently becoming a growing problem in Japanese industry.[120]

---

[120] See the sources on Japanese management cited in Footnote 25, Chapter 7.

Resistance to change by industrial enterprise managements in the newly developing countries, and even more in the stagnant underdeveloped countries, of Asia, Africa, and possibly to a somewhat lesser extent Latin America, is pervasive and strong.[121] In many less developed cultures conformity is considered a virtue while nonconformity is viewed with considerable suspicion, and this tends to make industrial managers very reluctant to initiate change or introduce innovation. In the private sector highly inefficient firms can frequently survive and reap easy profits with little or no change or improvement in operations over time, because of the sellers' markets and general protective environments in which they function. Subsistence level employee wages in numerous countries serve as a disincentive with regard to the introduction of modern and expensive equipment and technical processes.

Businessmen in such environments typically become psychologically and culturally adjusted to poverty, backwardness, economic stagnation, and the status quo. In larger firms authority tends to be highly centralized; and consequently there is frequently no flexibility or authority at lower levels which would permit the introduction of even minor changes in policies, procedures, and methods of operation.

In public industrial enterprise in underdeveloped and newly developing countries resistance to change by management is also pervasive. Ultra-conservatism, a civil service mentality of tradition, fear of responsibility, failure and blame, and overcentralization serve as significant barriers to change. Lack of knowledge and inadequate education and training tend to make industrial managers—both private and public—ignorant, insecure, and extremely cautious when it comes to initiating changes in enterprise operations, including management practices. The lack of desire and/or ability to use scientific methodology also greatly hinders the introduction of changes and innovations, particularly technological innovations, even where they can be borrowed from more advanced nations. This situation is vividly described by an astute top level executive of a relatively progressive Indian textile firm as follows:

One of the necessary attitudes for bringing about technological changes and implementing them is a spirit of inquiry. To ask oneself, "What," "Why" and "Why not" is a necessary condition of bringing about change. The entire industrial structure of Europe and America is based on the spirit of logical reasoning. Methodology of science, observation, experiment and deduction has been the basis of the industrial revolution and it has permeated Western thinking until technological innovations which were a mere trickle in the 18th century has now become a flood. In developing nations, societies have been used to doing things in a particular manner and they got used to doing it in

---

[121] For related discussions, analyses, and evidence see: the sources cited in Footnotes 88, 101, 102, and 103 of this chapter; Brannen and Hodgson, *op. cit.*, chaps. vi and xii; A. Rice, *Productivity and Social Organization: The Ahmedabad Experiment* (London: Tavistock Publ. Ltd., 1958).

that manner. They never question as to whether there is no better method. In a few cases this habit has been glorified as something sacred. Until such time as the habit of tradition and belief is replaced by a spirit of logical reasoning, a number of technological innovations cannot be expected from developing nations and implementations of such innovations will meet with considerably more resistance.[122]

Where managers in underdeveloped and newly developing countries have both the desire and potential know how to improve enterprise efficiency by introducing changes in operations, prevailing environmental conditions frequently discourage or prevent them from doing so. In many countries—for example, India and Egypt—overpopulation in conjunction with underemployment results in highly restrictive labor legislation which prohibits the dismissal of unneeded workers if more productive technology is introduced.[123] In the private sector in particular, firms frequently cannot obtain the capital required to implement potentially highly effective changes and innovations. Severe foreign exchange restrictions and extreme difficulties in importing or obtaining domestically needed supplies and equipment are also common obstacles to the implementation of changes and improvements in industrial enterprises in many less developed countries.

Probably the most serious obstacles in connection with the effective implementation of changes that are desired by higher level industrial managers in less developed countries pertain to the attitudes and abilities of the personnel involved and affected. Psychological insecurity, mysticism, and superstition arising out of cultural values, religious beliefs, and lack of knowledge are common personal traits among the labor force in numerous countries. These traits and attitudes are not compatible with change and innovation, especially technological change. While cultural and religious factors tend to hinder change in productive enterprise to the greatest degree in highly traditional underdeveloped countries, they are also potent negative forces in most newly developing countries as well. As the Indian industrial executive referred to above points out:

Another inhibiting factor in the adaptation of technological changes is the spirit of other worldliness that prevails in many countries of Asia. Almost all religions have glorified the simple life but this feeling has had a greater impetus in Asia than in Europe—particularly in India. The world is an illusion; what matters is not this life but the life hereafter. While this feeling has been a consolation in periods of stagnation and degeneration it is certainly not conducive to the adaptation of technological changes.[124]

---

[122] Sundaram, *op. cit.*, p. 497.

[123] For a discussion of restrictive labor practices and other common obstacles to change in less developed countries which affect foreign subsidiaries as well as domestic firms see A. Sherbini, "The Quandary of Foreign Manufacturing Affiliates in Less Developed Countries," *California Management Review*, spring, 1965, especially pp. 11–12.

[124] Sundaram, *op. cit.*, p. 497.

Even in newly developing countries that are consciously striving for industrial expansion and modernization, it can take several decades or longer to change substantially and extensively dominant negative attitudes toward change which prevail among the industrial population. While persons may be willing to seek employment in industry in order to fulfil their most basic needs, they do not change overnight the basic values, beliefs, habits and attitudes which they have acquired from their families and through religious and educational instruction. Hence the evolution of a sizable industrial subculture whose members are adaptable to change and innovation is usually a long run process. In Saudi Arabia, for example, a small industrial subculture of this type has slowly emerged with the extensive foreign oil company operations in that country; but even after several decades the number of Saudis who are adaptable to change in the Western sense is still only a minute fraction of the total population.

In cases where industrial managers in less developed countries attempt to introduce modern technology as well as other changes in enterprise operations they frequently try to implement such innovations in the same way that they have been adapted in the more advanced countries from which they are transplanted. The "borrowed" innovations are not stripped of the nonapplicable cultural characteristics, personal relationships, and techniques which are associated with them in the advanced countries. Cultural and social change are not minimized with the introduction of technical and managerial changes, even though cultural and social change may not be essential in terms of greater operating efficiency.

With change forced upon enterprise personnel in this manner, the result is too often considerable insecurity, uncertainty, unrest, frustration, low morale, low productivity, and at times much labor turnover. Technical change is commonly implemented in this ineffective manner in public enterprises in newly developing countries, often with the aid of foreign experts, and in U.S. subsidiary firms in foreign countries. In line with the above discussion it has been forcefully stated that:

Where specific technical practices are to be introduced into a culture or a part of society which has not hitherto used them, it is desirable to strip these technical practices of as many extraneous cultural accretions (from the lands of origin) as possible . . . Western professionals carry about with them an enormous amount of cultural baggage which could very well be discarded . . . Extraneous and culturally destructive effects can be avoided by stripping each scientific technique to the bone, to the absolute essentials which will make it possible for other people to learn to use it, and to handle it in a living, participating, creative way.[125]

Educational constraints also significantly retard the effective introduction of changes and innovations at industrial enterprises throughout the less

---

[125] M. Mead, ed., *Cultural Patterns and Technical Change* (New York: The New American Library of World Literature, Inc., 1955), pp. 293–294.

developed world. Because of serious educational and basic training deficiencies among enterprise personnel, management must often expend considerable time, effort, and expense in order to introduce successfully even minor changes in operations. Executives of several multinational U.S. companies have related many actual incidents to the authors which reveal, that because of such deficiencies, how difficult and costly it frequently is to implement desired changes in the operations of their subsidiaries or affiliates in various Asian, African, and Latin American countries, and even in Spain. There have been cases where, primarily because of educational constraints, it has taken several months to introduce successfully changes in management practices, operating procedures, and production processes abroad; while similar changes have been implemented effectively in U.S. operations in a matter of days. As was discussed earlier, in many such cases negative cultural attitudes toward change, as well as educational deficiencies, are major obstacles.

One of the authors in managing a Saudi business firm constantly encountered great difficulties in introducing relatively minor changes in operations, because of the cultural attitudes and inadequate educational backgrounds of employees. Even to get personnel to fill out a simple new form properly, to use a new hand tool effectively, or to load a truck with a new type of merchandise required considerable training, extremely patient direction and supervision, and very close control, often for several weeks. Getting subordinate managers to implement effectively new budgetary techniques, paper handling procedures, and inventory control policies presented much greater problems and frustrations.

Yet, even though Saudi Arabia is a relatively stagnant and highly traditional underdeveloped country, cultural resistance to change among enterprise personnel does not seem to be quite as strong there as in various other underdeveloped and even some newly developing countries. The author who was in Saudi Arabia also had an opportunity to observe the operations of some business firms in Syria and Egypt; and in these countries, particularly Syria, it is quite possible that resistance to change among personnel tends to be somewhat greater than in the typical Saudi firm. In spite of an inflexible religious system, the Saudis have proved to be surprisingly adaptable to change in several areas. Perhaps the most revolutionary development in millennia—the extensive substitution of motor vehicles for animals in the transportation system—was achieved in less than two decades without major social upheavals. Television, radio, air conditioning, and many other Western comforts and gadgets have been incorporated into the local society—albeit primarily among the relatively well to do—without major confusion. The typical Saudi may view all this as the mysterious ways of God, but the rapid, almost revolutionary changes wrought in the country have not yet torn it apart. At the same time, however, in other aspects Saudi Arabia is still a highly traditional country.

A major problem in many poor countries striving for economic progress is one of integrating their rural populations, with their traditional village and bare subsistence community values, into industrial employment. The change from their traditional way of life to an industrial way of life—even in rather primitive productive enterprises—typically leads to considerable insecurity, frustration, absenteeism and turnover.[126] Workers may be attracted by the income which industrial employment provides, but the change proves too great for them in numerous cases. Because of housing shortages, and other critical social overhead capital deficiencies, they must often leave their families behind in order to obtain work in industry. This situation makes their adjustment to an industrial way of life even more difficult, and enterprises which can afford it may be forced to provide housing and other facilities for them and their families. This is often done by U.S. subsidiaries and public enterprises in a number of African, Asian, and Latin American countries where it is necessary or desirable to recruit labor from highly traditional rural areas.

### Society at Large and Social Change[127]

Before concluding this section (and this chapter) the topic of change at the general societal level warrants further discussion. The dominant view of change which prevails at this level, particularly among the ruling or dominant elites, can have significant implications for industrial managerial effectiveness and economic progress over time. Thus far the various environmental constraints bearing on managerial effectiveness and economic progress have been treated largely as static conditions examined at a given point in time. In reality social change over time can do much to lessen substantially—or at times to increase—the negative impact of the various environmental constraints on industrial managerial effectiveness and productive efficiency; however, the rate and extent of effective social change in the direction of greater economic progress vary strikingly in different countries and cultures.

The problem of social change is most crucial in a stagnant and highly traditional underdeveloped country which has not yet emerged into a developing nation where industrialization and modernization is a goal consciously and eagerly sought by its elite and a substantial portion of the population. This class of country is typically characterized by a dynastic elite or rigid dictatorship, often of the military type, and a vast, bare subsistence level population whose members have neither the abilities nor

---

[126] Cf., *Economic Bulletin for Africa*, 1962, pp. 92 ff; *Management of Industrial Enterprise in Underdeveloped Countries*, pp. 53 ff; C. Wynne, *op. cit.*, pp. 42–45.

[127] The following sources have provided many data and have been very helpful and influential in shaping our ideas and analysis in the area of social change: Hogen, *op. cit.*; Jacobs, *op. cit.*; Harbison and Myers, *Education, Manpower and Economic Growth*; Kerr, Dunlop, Harbison, and Myers, *op. cit.*; Berelson and Steiner, *op. cit.*; Sundaram, *op. cit.*; M. Millikan and D. Bockmer, eds., *The Emerging Nations: Their Growth and United States Policy* (Boston: Little, Brown and Company, 1961).

opportunities to initiate change or reforms. There are also some countries in this class which have emerged only recently from colonial rule or are in the process of transition to independent status, but in which economic stagnation persists because no major effort has been made to embark on a course of development and modernization. Some of the countries that fall into this overall category are Afghanistan, Ethiopia, Liberia, Nepal, Yemen, Saudi Arabia, Haiti, Sudan, Niger, Tanganyika, Kenya, Uganda, and possibly Bolivia. The rigid power of organized religion and/or ultraconservative leaders and dominant elites in such societies tend to preserve the traditional class structure, as well as traditional cultural, social, and religious values.

In the traditional underdeveloped countries negative social attitudes toward scientific method, rational aggressive risk taking, achievement and work, industrially created wealth, business and its managers, and business and technical education persist through time and greatly hinder industrial managerial effectiveness and economic progress. Moreover, little or nothing is done consciously to change the political-legal structure or economic framework of the country in order to increase managerial effectiveness and productive efficiency. If large social changes entailing a major break from tradition come about rapidly in such a country it is likely to be through a major revolution, such as that in China in 1948.

If such changes emerge through an evolutionary rather than a revolutionary process the key human agents initiating change are unlikely to come from the group traditionally in control. They are more apt to come from deviant, marginal, disaffected groups—often minority groups who are discriminated against but who have the ability, achievement drive, and other means necessary to initiate the process of social change. The "pariah entrepreneur" or "innovational deviant" who engages in business and industrial pursuits is often an important agent of social change in the direction of economic progress.

Substantial economic progress is unlikely to come about, however, unless the newly emerging entrepreneurial class adapts a permanent personality that differs from dominant social values, beliefs, customs and motivations. If the pariah entrepreneurs tend to revert to traditional social customs and behavior once they acquire wealth, they and/or their heirs will be inclined to get out of business into land or other more prestigious occupations. Where this happens neither the business entrepreneurial class nor the industrial sector is likely to expand substantially through time. Hence, economic progress would tend to be facilitated where able and aggressive pariah entrepreneurs are locked into their entrepreneurial business managerial roles and are emulated and accepted through time by an increasing portion of society. In this type of environment a dynamic and expanding industrial subculture can emerge. If, however, substantial economic progress is to result it is also essential that a significant portion of the society's elite must want economic progress enough to give it priority over other desires and goals; for the dominant elites usually play the crucial role in shaping the educational system, political-legal structure, and macroeconomic framework of the society.

Since technological change and industrial modernization typically upset the rigid status structure in traditional societies, the dominant elites often do not wish to create a more favorable macromanagerial structure in which industrial firms could function more efficiently and effectively. For a highly traditional country to embark on the road to industrialization and modernization, the traditional culture often must undergo drastic alteration; and such alteration frequently threatens the position and status of the dominant elites. As one study points out:

It is thus of the very nature of the modernizing process that at every step of the way the impulses making for modernization are in active contention with powerful forces tending to retard and to frustrate the transformation of traditional society into full constructive modernity.

In some traditional, underdeveloped countries a major revolution may be seen by the discontented as the only path by which substantial economic progress can be forthcoming. A Communist revolution and takeover in a given country often leads to quite rapid and extensive social change, frequently at the cost of great human sacrifice and suffering. Individual desires tend to be subordinated to the interests of the state and its rulers, and individual freedom is greatly restricted. At the same time, however, a conscious and vigorous effort may be and typically is made to shape an educational system and sociological-cultural environment conducive to greater industrial managerial effectiveness and productive efficiency. If a substantial portion of the population desires economic progress and is willing to accept such drastic reform, considerable economic gains are likely to be made. In the reform process a more favorable view of technological change tends to emerge in the society, and a professional managerial class evolves. In the Soviet Union the government expends considerable funds and resources on research and development and on the pursuit of knowledge, chiefly in the physical sciences and engineering.

As the typical Communist state develops economically, the regime's view toward change with regard to economic and political-legal matters and the social and behavioral sciences tends to become a major constraint on managerial effectiveness and productive efficiency. Marxist-Leninist politico-economic doctrine is largely a matter of faith, and it is often extremely difficult to rationalize changes that are contrary to this doctrine and traditional Communist ideology. The Soviet Union, in particular, has found itself in this dilemma for several years, although changes in structure and policy which are contrary to dogma are gradually emerging. Various other Communist nations—for example, Poland, Czechoslovakia, Hungary, Rumania, and Yugoslavia, if this latter country can be labeled as Communist—have been and are implementing changes involving major breaks from tradition and ideology in their economic, political-legal, and social systems at an even faster and more extensive pace than the Soviet Union.[128]

The Communist world is learning that when theology in economics breaks down, much of the dogma has to be discarded, and new values, as well as painful changes, must be adapted. The stakes—in terms of demonstrating the productive superiority of the Communist system—are too high to allow for failure through blind adherence to faith. Ironically, many of the changes being introduced entail the use of more capitalistic techniques and practices, such as greater use of profit incentives, more product prices determined by market forces, more flexible customer-supplier relations, greater decentralization of authority, interest charges on capital, marketing research, sales promotion and advertising, and so forth.

The nationalistic leaders of many developing countries which are not essentially communistic desire rapid change in the direction of greater industrial managerial effectiveness and economic progress. This includes technological change; extensive educational reforms; changes in the values, beliefs, habits, and motivations of the population; and often changes in the political-legal and economic structure of the country. Where the country lacks a sizable class of able industrial entrepreneurs and managers, the government typically assumes a major entrepreneurial and business leadership role by establishing and operating a sizable number of state owned productive enterprises.

In spite of their good intentions and efforts, in many cases the leaders of developing nations are confronted with major problems and obstacles in their pursuit of effective change in the direction of greater managerial effectiveness and economic progress. A highly critical problem is typically one of implementing desired changes—apart from the capital that may be involved. As was pointed out earlier, it is extremely difficult, if not impossible, to implement changes successfully, even relatively minor ones, where the population involved does not desire or accept them. Many of the changes that the leaders of developing nations wish to implement are not compatible with the traditional values, beliefs, habits and motivations of much and often most of the population. This is frequently the case in numerous newly developing countries—for example, India, Egypt, Burma, Tunisia, Pakistan, Nigeria, Turkey—and even in various semiadvanced nations such as Chile and Colombia.

The Indian business leader referred to earlier forcefully points out that on a national scale sociological-cultural factors tend to be the major obstacles to technological change, as well as other changes, in developing countries:

Unlike other factors, social environment cannot be changed very quickly. Lack of capital resources can be made up to a certain extent by borrowing from out-

---

[128] Cf.: "The Iron Grip Falters," *Business Week*, November 28, 1964, pp. 74–88; Vickers, *op. cit.*; Grammp, *op. cit.*; Richman, *Soviet Management*, chap. xii and conclusion; M. Goldman, "Economic Controversy in the Soviet Union," *Foreign Affairs*, April, 1963.

side. Lack of technical knowledge can be overcome by importing large numbers of technicians from abroad. But social environment is something that is inherent and part of the social structure of a nation. It is made up of a sense of values that a community holds, the relationships between individuals and groups within the community, and habits, traditions and customs that are the results of history. These are internal to society and cannot be supplemented or changed by a wholesale import of ideas as may be done in the case of machines. In fact, any attempt to do so beyond a natural process of assimilation and absorption might result in the development of resistance to such a move and make any changes more difficult. Consequently, one of the major problems of the adaptation of technological changes in developing nations is the social environment in which such changes have to be brought about.[129]

He goes on to stress that social relationships and the social structure tend to persist as major obstacles to change even after a country has begun the transformation from a stagnant and traditional underdeveloped country to a developing nation:

The social relationships existing in the developing nations have also been inhibiting factors as far as the adaptation of technological changes is concerned. In these countries society is largely hierarchical and tradition continues to play a major role in human relationships. Men are not judged on the basis of merit but on the basis of status based on tradition. In such societies men with ambition have no opportunity to come to the top either by virtue of their performance or by virtue of some social prohibition. Conformity is a virtue and non-conformism has its dangers. The stratification of society has also resulted in creating pockets of economic vested interests which resist the adaptation of technological changes.[130]

Hence, it can and frequently does take considerable time and costs to implement effectively changes desired by the leaders and governments of developing countries. For example, it may take decades or even generations substantially to change dominant attitudes regarding education, modern technology, class structure and individual mobility, achievement and work, scientific method, risk taking, wealth, and so forth.

Another major problem is that the leaders and governments of many developing countries often do not have the knowledge or ability to design programs or plans of action which would lead to the effective implementation of desired changes—even where such changes would not meet with significant resistance from the population. They frequently attempt to introduce major changes too rapidly and without careful thought. This pertains to political-legal and economic change as well as educational, social, and technical change. Here attitude toward risk taking, the boundaries of rationality in risk taking, and view of scientific method are frequently the major obstacles to the effective implementation of changes potentially

---

[129] Sundaram, *op. cit.*, p. 497.
[130] *Ibid.*, pp. 497–498.

conducive to greater managerial effectiveness and productive efficiency. Where the governments of developing countries strive to implement change too rapidly, considerable social disorganization, unrest, frustration, and insecurity among the population often results, and this may hinder rather than promote greater managerial effectiveness and productive efficiency. The Indian business leader referred to above has this to say in this regard:

These [developing] nations, with their inexperience in the administration of their countries start experimenting and in their over enthusiasm for quick changes lose sight of these [social and cultural] factors and commit many a mistake which definitely calls for better management of affairs. Until such time as these factors can be overcome, the rate of adaptation of technological changes will be slow and progress will also be slow.[131]

Advanced industrial nations of the West tend to be under continuous pressure and compulsion to undergo changes, to innovate, and to make new discoveries in science, technology, management, public administration, politico-legal structure, economic policy, and social relations; for this is necessary in order to maintain a position of leadership and stature in the modern dynamic world, and most advanced countries desire to maintain such a position. They feel it necessary, or are forced, to spend increasing amounts on research and development; and this is no less true of governments than of private enterprises.

In 1962 the U.S. government spent nearly $15 billion on research and development. This was more than the government spent on research and development from the beginning of the nation up to and through the second world war.[132] During the 1955–64 period the country poured some $100 billion into research and development, and it is likely that double this amount will be spent in the next ten years.[133] Such expenditures reflect military budgets, space exploration, the search for new knowledge for its own sake, and research on new industrial processes and products. All are imperatives in the advanced nations, although the pressures are clearly greater in some than in others, and the general social view toward change is more conservative in some than in others.

Probably in no other country in the world is change in general accepted as a way of life by the population at large to a greater degree than in the United States. This cultural trait regarding change has a direct impact on the view of change at the industrial enterprise level.

In general, social change tends to be a constant, relatively stable, and evolutionary rather than revolutionary process in the advanced Western nations. This process of social change has taken many generations to emerge as such, while the leaders of various developing nations often desire to

---

[131] *Ibid.*, p. 498.

[132] Harbison and Myers, *Education, Manpower and Economic Growth*, p. 166.

[133] "The Challenge of Automation," *Newsweek*, January 25, 1965, p. 80.

implement extensive social changes almost overnight. The advanced Western countries are typically relatively heterogeneous and largely urban societies; and social change is much more likely to occur and evolve in this type of environment than in a relatively homogeneous and extensively rural society, which characterizes many less developed countries. There are more different points of view available in a heterogeneous society, more ideas, more conflicts of interest, more groups and organizations of different persuasions, plus greater secularism and tolerance that tend to promote change by opening more areas of life to decision rather than subjecting them to superior authority.[134]

The advanced Western nations are also typically democracies characterized by rising middle class elites who favor economic progress. Since economic progress is an important goal to the dominant elites, social change is probably more often than not in the direction of greater productive efficiency, in spite of the frictions which arise because of conflicting interests and pressure groups. Countervailing power serves as a compromising balance and stabilizing mechanism in society; however, friction, pressure groups, conflicting interests, and cultural values in the process of social change serve as greater constraints upon industrial managerial effectiveness and productive efficiency in some advanced countries than in others. For example, Britain seems to fare worse in this regard than the United States. This has been brought out in some earlier sections treating interorganizational cooperation, class structure and individual mobility, and attitude toward education.

## CONCLUDING REMARKS

The sociological-cultural constraints considered in this chapter have impacts on the management process and efficiency of industrial enterprises which are frequently subtle and difficult to work out in practice; however, the impact is clearly there and it tends to be highly significant. Persons visiting different countries and diverse cultures often comment on characteristics of a society which breed low industrial managerial effectiveness and low productive efficiency, although seldom has any major effort been made to work through in detail how a given general sociological-cultural characteristic or constraint might directly impede or aid managerial effectiveness and economic progress.

The problems entailed in research and analysis of this type are clearly extremely complex, and we have only scratched the surface in this book. It should be noted that sociological and cultural factors interrelate not only with each other but also with other types of constraints. The quality, type, and amount of education available in a given country, for example, will depend in large part on sociological and cultural factors. Legal, political,

---

[134] Berelson and Steiner, *op. cit.*, pp. 615–616; Keesing, *op. cit.*, pp. 83 ff.

and economic characteristics and constraints also will be strongly influenced by sociological-cultural factors.

Our difficulty in this study is in attempting to determine how each of these complex constraints or factors works out in practice in the management of productive enterprise and in economic progress. As yet, aside from focusing largely on the likely or implied impacts, we have not examined this problem in much depth. This remains to be accomplished through the work of others and through a future volume which will deal with comprehensive studies of specific countries.

# Chapter 9

# Environmental Constraints:

# Legal-Political

## INTRODUCTION

Productive enterprises must operate in some type of legal and political environment, like other types of social organizations. Laws must generally (but not always) be obeyed and political factors taken into account in formulating business decisions. Political science and law study the operations of these factors generally in the society. Still other disciplines, such as economics, business administration, and sociology, are concerned directly with the impact of such factors on various parts of the society. Not generally explored in depth, however, is the problem presented here. Our argument is that legal and political constraints directly affect the internal operations of productive industrial enterprises through their impact on the critical elements of the managerial process. A given law, or a political event, can cause firms to shift the way the critical elements of the management process are performed and, hence, directly affect the firms' efficiency.

Our concern here is to show in a general way, using various country and firm examples, how various legal and political rules, actions, and events can directly affect the managers and the critical elements of the management process in both positive and negative ways, leading to changes in managerial effectiveness.

## RELEVANT LEGAL RULES OF THE GAME

Any society has a legal code, written or traditional, which bears directly on the operations of productive enterprises. Included in relevant legal structures are such codes as general business law, tax law, labor law, and general law which may have some relevance to business.

General business law includes such items as rules governing property rights, the law of contract, and similar matters. Depending on the country considered, this law can range from simple traditional tribal or religious law generally defining the rights of parties to elaborate and complex legal codes covering all phases of these subjects exhaustively. The degree of codification generally follows other developments in a country, in the sense that as incomes and literacy rise, law tends to become more organized and more complex. The judicial process itself, in terms of organization of courts, systems of judicial appeal, qualifications of judges, and similar matters, tends to become equally complex as a society finds need for such organization.

## Business Law

General business law provides a framework within which productive firms must work. The results have a direct effect on the internal operations of firms. Hence, for example, the limiting of liability of corporations in a precise manner in a given country affects the basic organization of a firm. In the United States, corporations are chartered by states, and there are fifty state laws governing the manner in which a corporation may be formed. In many states, it is quite easy to form such a corporation, as the law is general, and any group which meets the basic requirements of the law is entitled to a charter. One result is that there are many limited liability corporations in the United States, and they are organized in many ways under relevant state legislation. Such issues as the number of members of the board of directors, the type of financial disclosure which must be made, and the duties and responsibilities of the officers and directors of the corporation are flexible and often vague. The effect on staffing and organization is quite different than it would be if the country had a uniform federal corporation code.

In Tunisia, many limited liability corporations must first obtain formal approval of the minister of planning and finance, while in Lebanon such a corporation's charter must be approved by the cabinet. In these cases, basic organization objectives may be altered to fit the needs of the state. Since the state is directly involved in the formulation of basic objectives of a firm from the very formulation of the first plans for the firm, the nature and extent of innovation and risk taking could well be altered. A proposed firm might be willing to take risks on new products for the local market, but the government planning ministry might force the firm to change such plans before a charter was granted.

In a similar manner, the law of contracts could directly influence planning. In Japan, a given contract has one set of implications, in terms of rights of parties, certainty of conditions, and similar issues. In the United States, a completely different set of implications may prevail for the same document. Thus, in Japan contractual relationships are by nature quite precarious and typically can not be sustained by recourse to the courts.[1] Contracts in Japan are not viewed as legally binding if changing conditions make their original provisions obsolete. A firm may make a long run supply

---

[1] A. Von Mehren, *Law in Japan: The Legal Order in a Changing Society* (Cambridge, Mass.: Harvard University Press, 1958), p. 47.

contract with one of its contractors to supply a given part for a set price. If conditions change enough to make the contract unprofitable to the supplier, he may be able to avoid legal penalty. The impact on production make or buy decisions and on the number and types of suppliers available is clear in this case. An identical contract between buyer and supplier in the United States or England would be enforceable even if conditions did change, and the constraint impact on the same production functions in these countries could be completely different.

In Saudi Arabia, firms are hampered by the fact that most law has not yet been formally codified, and legal rules are derived from *Sharia,* or Moslem religious law. Contracts of sorts which have direct religious implications, such as family rules, rules concerning thefts, and similar matters, are dealt with rather consistently by the religious courts; but a contract dispute involving violations of quality control provisions in a complex technical contract might be resolved in almost any way, depending on how the religiously trained judges drew analogies from the Koran. An immediate result of this condition is considerable uncertainty for firms which need to make such agreements with suppliers. In almost any legal problem in the modern industrial world, this lack of written, codified law makes many kinds of business agreements subject to much more uncertainty than one would encounter in countries where legal traditions trend to written precedents based on statutory law.

Law pertaining to trademarks, patents, and similar critical business factors also have direct implications for planning. They may also have direct influence on such productive functions as marketing, particularly on product line and sales promotion functions. In the United States, it is typically true that a trademark cannot be infringed directly by competitors, and legal enforcement of this trademark protection is relatively consistent. Hence, firms can make major marketing investments in brand names with little fear of direct copying; but in other countries such protection may be much less, and investment in marketing names may well be much more risky. Behavior of similar firms, or even the same firm operating in several countries, may therefore differ.

Hence, Goodyear Rubber can use its brandnames in Europe or the United States without fear that competitors will pirate them; however, in many less developed countries, exact copies of this company's (and many others') products, manufactured by outside firms in obscure places, can be bought for a fraction of the price of genuine articles. The usual quality of the pirated items is also a fraction of the quality of the original as well. One of the authors saw many examples of this type of piracy in Kuwait and Saudi Arabia, with the rumored source of supply being Hong Kong and Japan. The pirates are capitalizing on the reputation of the major company, and a considerable amount of the major firm's marketing effort in such cases is to educate its clientele to discover the value of the original and genuine items. Here failure to protect a common property right leads to changes in sales promotion and sales appeals.

Some countries (notably the Soviet Union) do not observe copyrights granted in Western countries. One result of this legal quirk is that the Russians steal various published materials from the West without compensation to the copyright holder (have fun with *this* book!). At times, Western publishing houses do the same with Russian writings. In this case, a copyright is not even considered a property right and hence has no value to the holder. It is clear that marketing strategy for a publishing company would be quite different in this international market than in one where this particular property right is respected.

Similar situations could be noted for patent laws. Some countries observe patents granted in other countries, while others do not. Some countries have specific time limitations for patents (in the United States, seventeen years), while in other countries the time span is different or indeterminate. A firm interested in marketing a patented product could be expected to have completely different marketing strategies in separate countries, depending upon the degree of protection available to the firm in each.

Such patent and copyright laws have sharp impacts on the planning and research and development functions of any firm. A company with short run (seventeen year) patent protection must necessarily look to the day when such patents expire and competitors can directly compete, if the firm expects to survive in the long run. The Du Pont Company in the United States had such protection for some years for nylon, for example; but if this firm had not foreseen the need to do further research and development during the patent life of nylon, it might have drifted into serious competitive trouble. In a similar manner, the American Polaroid Company now has exclusive patent rights to cameras which develop pictures immediately, though this protection will not last forever. When such rights expire, pricing policies and product promotion policies will change sharply. At present it is certain that this particular group of patents held by the company has directly influenced both research and long run planning.

## General Law

Law not directly intended to influence productive enterprise also can have significant effects on the internal operations of firms, although in this case the impact often is not general. Such laws as those governing smoke or smog control, for example, can affect the internal organization of firms that produce smoke or smog as a byproduct of their operations. Instead of leaving control up to a general production group, such a law might require the establishment of a special unit to make sure that the company is operating legally. Here organization would be directly affected. A further example of such relationships is that a speed limit on a highway can have far reaching effects on the organization of a trucking company. If this causes the firm to cover less distance per eight hour shift than it otherwise might, the result could be to require branch terminal operations at distant points, including driver rest facilities, which otherwise would not be required. Here changes would occur in communications, employee services, compensation, scheduling, and organization.

Many kinds of laws relating to health, welfare, and safety have direct business implications, occasionally by design. Thus, in Britain petroleum companies have considerably higher distribution costs than they might have elsewhere, because of severe restrictions on the size of tank trucks and the way in which they are operated. Certain tunnels cannot be used, storage must be done in a prescribed manner, and so on. While the need for safety in handling of inflammable materials is clear, unduly restrictive regulations can raise costs and help competitors.

Pharmaceutical manufacturers in the United States operate under quite different safety rules than do companies in Europe. In the recent thalidomide scandal, few defective American babies were born, because the drug had not yet cleared the Department of Health, Education, and Welfare, which has the responsibility, and the authority, to clear new drugs for sale. Manufacturers in this case were angry at the department for procrastination and delay, since in several European countries the drug (which was a quite profitable item) was already widely sold. The result of extensive sales in Europe was many births of defective children in countries such as West Germany, as well as a new and more stringent drug control law in the United States. In this type of case, the impact on the affected firm's research and development and marketing is clear. Considerable direct impact also is seen in such cases on the firms' public and external relations. Some types of firms, particularly those which sell food and drugs, rely heavily on government for protection from poisoning their own customers. The United States and most other developed nations have rather extensive pure food and drug laws, as well as many agricultural and chemical inspectors stationed in industrial plants to assure that products will not be dangerous.

In recent years, the cranberry growers and processors and the tuna fish canners have been hard hit by food poisoning cases in the United States. When customers were poisoned by defective products, the immediate reaction was a sharp drop in sales and a large decrease in public confidence in these industries. The effect here on marketing and public and external relations was quite large, caused in part by legal and technical failure in an area only peripherally related to economic issues.

A final point on general law is that the enforcement and interpretation of existing law are very important to firms. Clear law and uniform enforcement have the effect of reducing legal uncertainties and making the planning process easier for firms. Uncertain or unclear law and erratic, unsound, or dishonest enforcement lead to greater uncertainty, more risk, and less efficiency in productive enterprises. Thus, it is sometimes argued in the United States that the manner in which some law is written and enforced is so obscure that in many cases a firm is not aware of what the law might be in a given case. The result is considerable uncertainty, the risk of being taken to court for violations, and inability to plan carefully for future actions.

## Laws Affecting Prices

Governments have tinkered with price legislation since Biblical times. Prices are crucial matters to firms and consumers alike, and most individuals and firms find that some prices appear too low or too high. Inevitably pressures arise to adjust matters in a more rational way, and laws are passed setting "fair" prices for many kinds of goods and services.

This price setting law has been used by virtually every country in the world, with almost universally poor results. The reason is not hard to find. Prices are usually too high or too low because supply and demand conditions are what they are at the time the law is passed. If a legal price is too high, a surplus then accumulates; if it is too low, a shortage occurs. Where firms are organized as tight oligopolies or monopolies, high prices lead to idle capacity and unemployment. Where the prices are too low, the result is excess demand and shortages. Service prices set too high also lead to excess capacity, since the services cannot be stockpiled.

The usual sign of a price set too low is a queue. Where price is too high, it is warehouses full of something which can not be sold. In spite of these evidences of the difficulty of setting prices by law instead of through markets, lawyers throughout the world, not being economists, continue to pass laws regulating prices. The usual results for business firms are less efficient operations.

One major type of price fixing is in the area of foreign exchange prices and tariffs, which will be treated below under foreign policy. Another concerns the price of money (interest), which will be covered in Chapter 10 on economic constraints. Both of these price controls have quite significant effects on all sorts of critical elements of the managerial process.

Many kinds of business regulations apply to pricing and price policy. In the United States, resale price maintenance is a common practice in many states, while the Robinson-Patman Act bans certain types of price discrimination. Such restrictions on price policy have direct implications for marketing strategies, since some potentially profitable strategies for given companies are illegal. It is common to find in Western countries a variety of confused policies in regard to firms' pricing, all of which affect marketing and market organization. Hence, in the United States, some prices (in agriculture, motor trucking, railroading, milk sales, liquor, etc.) are held up, while others (rents in some cities, pharmaceuticals, etc.) are held down. The rationale for any given policy may differ drastically from that for a second policy. Business firms producing the good or service under control are directly affected by such controls. They also are frequently affected by laws or regulations influencing supply of the commodity, as in the case of agricultural acreage limitations or the case of restrictions on the number of establishments, such as liquor stores.

In most economies industrial goods prices are controlled much less often than other kinds of prices, reflecting perhaps the recognition by lawmakers of the dynamics of the production process; however, many other types of price controls have direct influence on manufacturers. Thus, for many decades, England has had a retail price maintenance law. In 1964, this price fixing act was drastically modified, allowing price competition at retail in many kinds of manufactured goods for the first time. Until 1964, English manufacturing firms marketed their products at fixed prices under force of law. Discounters were subject to legal prosecution. The system was sedate, inefficient, and comfortable for many types of consumer goods manufacturers and retailers. One result of the law over the years was to create much excess capacity in retailing, since smaller shops had no price competition from larger outlets.[2]

After 1964, however, firms had to consider major revisions in their channels of distribution, sales promotion, and price policies. Firms trying to operate in the old way found that aggressive retail discounters, taking advantage of their new found legal freedom to cut previously substantial markups, were able to expand volume sharply at the expense of the smaller shops. Consequently, marketing plans had to be changed.

This sort of price fixing also has considerable impact on public and external relations. In New York State, price control legislation was changed in 1964 to allow for considerably more flexible price policies at retail for liquor than previously had been allowed. One major retailer, Macy's, immediately started cutting prices on various brands of whiskeys. The manufacturers were upset, though unwilling to take full advantage of their legal rights. If they did, the full blast of newspaper publicity about the case might prejudice their eventual customers. If they pressed legal charges, the manufacturers might be seen by the public as firms which took advantage of a law to exploit customers by holding up prices. Macy's, quite content to be seen in the press as the champion of lower prices, publicly taunted the companies whose alcohol they were selling. This whole situation revolved around a rather detailed and complex change in price legislation which had been made in this state.[3]

This type of price fixing has effects on firm management often not thought of when the law was passed. Thus, a state may have a law governing the price of milk and milk products. The usual intent of such a law is to protect the income of dairy farmers, who often are quite powerful politi-

---

[2] R. S. Edwards and Harry Townsend, *Business Enterprise: Its Growth and Organization* (London: Macmillan, 1958), p. 285.

[3] "Cuts in Liquor Prices by Macy's Trigger War with Big Distiller," *The Wall Street Journal*, February 5, 1965, p. 1.

cally; but if butter is eighty cents a pound, the real gainers here may be the margarine producers, whose marketing policy is shaped by the law governing its major competitor. Pricing and sales promotion of margarine become in part directly connected to price controls on butter, and even the makers of synthetic ice cream prosper in such an environment. A major change in pricing laws governing butter would cause major changes in such factors as planning, types of financing, research and development, pricing, and sales promotion for margarine manufacturers, since these activities are keyed to the fact that butter will continue to be an overpriced commodity.

Resale price maintenance laws usually are intended to help small retailers; but if a manufacturer utilizes the legal protection to which he is entitled, he may find that large retailers simply refuse to push the price regulated brands and move to private brands instead. Instead of selling Sunbeam mixers, they may find an independent manufacturer and have a similar product manufactured under their own brand name, to sell at a lower price. The major impacts on managerial elements in such cases are on choice of suppliers, marketing channels, and price policies of manufacturers.

Poorer countries often have price controls at retail on types of commodities which are essential to the masses, such as basic grains, bread, matches, tea, and milk. The Indian government has the authority to control prices in this manner, while the Saudi government controls such prices as those for rice and canned milk. Such controls can have some effect on industrial costs, particularly if the controlled item is also used as an industrial material. Higher grain prices, for example, can affect costs for manufacturers of industrial alcohol.

### Antitrust and Cartel Legislation

Many countries have laws regulating competition and formation of business combinations in restraint of trade. Included in such legislation would be public utility legislation regulating both publicly and privately owned firms in areas such as electric power, banking, transportation, insurance, water supply, communications, and occasional other industries affecting the public interest.

Since laws are usually passed at various times in response to various political pressures, they are rarely completely consistent. Hence, in the United States, some types of firms can form legal cartels (agricultural cooperatives, railroads, firms engaged in foreign trade),[4] while others would be prosecuted under the antitrust laws for the same behavior; but if the result of a well constructed, well administered law is to increase competition in a meaningful fashion, producing lower prices, pressures for cost reduction in firms, and substantial product improvements through the competitive

---

[4] See R. L. Kramer, *International Marketing* (2d ed.; Cincinnati: South-Western Publishing Company, 1964), pp. 324–334, for provisions of legal cartels in U.S. export trade under the Webb-Pomerene Act.

process, such a law would be highly positive in its effects on managerial effectiveness. If the law were framed and administered in such a way as to give firms advance notice of the proposed action, benefit would also come from increased business certainty about public policy, in that business planning could be more precise; but if such a law resulted in erratic and inept prosecution of firms for almost any act, resulting in considerable uncertainty, or if the law were enforced only against those in political disfavor, or if the courts constantly changed their minds about rulings under the law, more harm than good would come from the legislation. Business and managerial efficiency could be decreased by such legislation.

A few American examples may illustrate this point. The well known electric conspiracy case in 1961[5] showed that various American electrical manufacturing firms were conspiring to fix prices and allocate bids for various types of heavy electrical equipment. This type of price conspiracy had the effect of making the conspiring firms' planning and production more efficient, at a much higher cost to purchasing firms. Prompt prosecution of the conspirators, once discovered, had an immediate effect on competitive relationships, prices, and planning in this industry.

When, however, the Chrysler Corporation and the White Motor Company were planning a merger in 1964, little was said by government officials until the last possible moment. Then it was announced that this merger would be attacked legally if consummated. The two firms, facing the possibility of a lengthy and expensive court fight, agreed to call off the merger. The impact created by delayed government reaction had major effects, particularly in the planning area, for both firms.[6]

In the first case above, antitrust prosecution probably had beneficial managerial effects. In the second, the price paid in terms of uncertainty and necessary changes of plans prepared at considerable cost was too high, because the applicability of the law was not spelled out in detail soon enough. There is fairly constant criticism among American businessmen on this point, since they note that one major problem they have is trying to find out in detail what the antitrust law is, so that they can obey it. The law is so complicated as to place many situations in doubt, which leads to considerable negative effects on long run planning.

In Europe, fairly extensive changes are being made in antitrust type legislation which could have major effect on the planning, marketing, and production policies of firms. The EEC has included strong anticartel provisions in its basic treaty,[7] while in England a new series of laws designed to

---

[5] R. A. Smith, "The Incredible Electric Conspiracy," *Fortune*, Vol. LXIII, No. 4, April, 1961, p. 132.

[6] See Milton Handler and Stanley D. Robinson, "The Supreme Court vs. Corporate Mergers," *Fortune*, Vol. LXXI, No. 1, January, 1965, p. 164, for a discussion of American law pertaining to mergers.

[7] Isaiah Frank, *The European Common Market* (New York: Frederick A. Praeger, Inc., 1961), pp. 194–150. See also J. R. Crowley, ed., *The Antitrust Structure of the Common Market* (New York: Fordham University Press, 1963), 179 pp.

promote more competition has been placed in effect in the past few years.[8] Firms which have been able to set policy based on one concept of competition now must revise their thinking to reflect striking changes in their legal environment. The extensive comment in general magazines, specialized trade journals, and financial papers about such changes clearly suggests how important such changes are expected to be on firm operations in the future.

A frequent legal dichotomy appears in this legal sector. Very small enterprises are encouraged to merge, since it is felt that they are inefficient (usually on incomplete technical and economic evidence). At the same time, larger firms are viewed with suspicion and made subject to antitrust legislation. In Japan, the 1952 Stabilization Law (directed toward small enterprises) provided for the amalgamation into cartels of small firms. The cartel could regulate investment, output, deliveries, and prices. Since 1947, however, large Japanese firms have been subject to an antitrust act inspired by the American occupation. The trend in Japan seems more toward cartelization than trust-busting, however, since most thinking of economists and industrialists in Japan since the beginning of the industrial era has been that only through extensive cartelization can firms become more efficient and compete in world markets. This view, like the one on inefficient smaller enterprises, has not really been tested scientifically; but the fact that it is widely believed by influential industrialists and political figures means that antitrust activity in Japan has been very small, in spite of the laws on the books.[9]

Public utility legislation, with its typical close government control over prices and entry of new firms, also has direct bearing on managerial effectiveness. A firm desiring to establish a new operation may not even be able to begin operations, since the governing commission may disallow entry. Such policies are typically established to improve efficiency (at least in theory), as it is argued that it would be extremely inefficient technically to allow, for example, two competing telephone companies the right to operate in a single area. Those long suffering Mexican businessmen who struggled for years with two unintegrated phone companies would agree with this efficiency argument. In some utility sectors not subject to substantial economies of scale, however, restriction of entry could lead to higher, not lower, operating costs.

The usual effect of most public utility legislation on manufacturing companies is through impacts on prices and services. These public utilities form a large segment of the social overhead capital of any country, and their services are utilized by every manufacturing firm. In many countries, most public utility firms are government owned and operated, and the relevant

---

[8] *Tax and Trade Guide, United Kingdom* (New York: Arthur Anderson & Co., 1964), pp. 185–192.

[9] G. Allen, *Japan's Economic Recovery* (Oxford: Oxford University Press, 1958), p. 142.

legislation is that which determines what organization and operation the government firm will have. A badly framed basic law can easily lead to poor services, inept organization of firms, and higher costs of operation for manufacturing firms and other users of the basic utility service.

Some problems in this area can be illustrated by considering American trucking legislation. Law in this sector is complex, since some trucks are not controlled, while others are controlled by the federal government, and still others by state governments; but the complex of laws regulating prices and entry in the controlled common carrier sector have resulted in prices in this part of the industry being at times twice as high as prices for similar services in the uncontrolled portion of the industry.[10] Here industry pressure to get legal sanction for cartel type ratemaking and entry controls has had major impacts on pricing and product line marketing problems for the carriers. Industrial firms using trucking services have higher costs in some cases than they otherwise might have. This causes changes in the firms' physical distribution practices, and these result in changes in channels of distribution and types and locations of customers and the way they are served. Such cost changes may also affect production functions, including locations of suppliers and inventory levels.

In places as diverse as Lebanon and New York City, the legal restrictions of entry of taxicabs into given markets has raised prices significantly and, not inconsequentially, given owners of existing licenses a valuable and scarce property right in the form of a license to operate.[11] This type of law not only has direct impact on pricemaking but also influences such factors as the types of financing done. Taxi firms in Lebanon have little trouble in obtaining loans from banks for new equipment, since they put up their licenses as collateral. Since the license is worth more than the vehicle, the risk to lenders is small. An apparently minor change in law here could have major effects on both prices and financial practices.

Defective law in this sector, leading to poor management of public utilities, can have quite severe effects on productive enterprises. Thus, in Brazil:

The big problem in this state is transportation. We've neglected our river and coastal shipping, which is the cheapest possible kind of transport, and built expensive roads that run alongside the rivers. Social laws have killed river traffic by requiring so many employees.

.   .   .   .   .   .   .   .   .   .   .   .   .   .   .   .

We can ship even by truck to Rio cheaper than by boat. This is completely foolish: the main reason is that when you ship by boat you have to go through customs twice.[12]

---

[10] R. N. Farmer, "The Case for Unregulated Truck Transportation," *Journal of Farm Economics*, Vol. VII, No. 3, July, 1959, pp. 199–205.

[11] Farmer, "Motor Vehicle Transport Pricing in Lebanon," *The Journal of Industrial Economics*, Vol. VII, No. 3, July, 1959, pp. 199–205.

[12] Winston Oberg, "Cross-Cultural Perspectives on Management Principles," *Journal of the Academy of Management*, VI (June, 1963), 136.

Such legal restrictions and policies cause changes in firm production and marketing policies which result in higher costs than otherwise might be incurred.

## Labor Law

Labor law in most countries is now extremely complex, and many of its provisions have quite direct impacts on firm and managerial functions.[13] Among other important restraints, labor legislation applies to hours and conditions of work, control of working conditions for women and miners, unemployment compensation schemes, tenure and job security requirements, forced use of nationals, employer responsibility for health and welfare of employees, and similar provisions. Such restrictions have considerable impact on the staffing functions in many kinds of companies. The familiar requirement in many less developed countries that a certain percentage of employees be nationals has caused firms to seek out actively local citizens qualified to perform various jobs, often at premium wages. Training also is affected, since many countries require local manpower training by law. Such constraints may in the short run make firms less efficient, since they are required to use less skilled labor. The longer run effects are much less certain and depend in part on how well given firms utilize and train local labor. If the end result is to develop a skilled, efficient local work force, the effect on efficiency may well be positive; but in any case the direct impact of the law is on staffing and direction within the firm.

Such laws as govern unemployment compensation or insurance may have far reaching effects on firm management. One common provision in such laws is that firms with the most erratic employment levels pay the highest taxes for the program; therefore, many firms have been encouraged to study their operations with a view to stabilizing their work force levels. This has had beneficial effects not only on the firms but on society in general. Similarly, effective workman's compensation laws governing payments for industrial injuries have had a beneficial effect in that they have focused managerial attention on safety and accident control. These laws have the effect of forcing many kinds of general social costs onto firms, forcing them to include in their planning process provisions for such costs and preventative programs to avoid still higher penalties.

Since the usual effect is to raise firm costs to some extent, it is possible that overzealous use of such legislation has the effect of forcing productive enterprises to use less labor and more of the other productive factors. In an economy where labor is extremely plentiful, this effect may not be positive.

Many examples are available to illustrate the direct effect of such

---

[13] See Dale Yoder, *Personnel Principles and Policies (Second Edition)* (Englewood Cliffs, N.J.: Prentice-Hall, Inc., 1959), pp. 153–175, for a discussion of American public policy in this area.

legislation on firm and managerial functions.[14] Thus, in Egypt the use of overtime and part time labor is severely limited. This legislation is designed to increase employment; but its practical result is to affect directly firms' recruiting, selection, and compensation policies. It also affects production factors, since the shortage of a few key high skill workers cannot be made up easily through overtime or moonlighting.

In Brazil, companies are required to pay indemnities to employees who are discharged, and only in cases of serious misconduct are companies able to avoid this cost. The indemnity paid rises as the workers' service time increases. The result is to tie up company capital, create rapid turnover of new workers, and generally increase labor costs. Lebanon has a similar indemnity law, as do many other countries; and they experience similar results.

In many poorer countries, the supply of ill trained, unskilled labor far exceeds demand; and many countries have tried to protect workers through such devices as indemnity pay and tenure requirements. The laws tend to be self-defeating, however, since they provide an incentive for firms to avoid long term employees as much as possible. Getting caught in an economic downturn with such labor can wreck the firm. Since few firms in such countries have ever calculated the cost of labor turnover, this method of avoiding legal requirements is not seen as expensive—but it is.

Developed and semideveloped countries often have extensive social benefit schemes for labor financed in part by employees. The increases in costs incurred have direct effects on firm production decisions, particularly in the choice of capital as compared to labor. In some European countries, these social benefit payroll taxes are quite large. In France, they amount to 44.5 percent of payrolls, while in Italy the average is 47.8 percent; but the cost in Germany is only 10 percent, while in the United States it is less than 5 percent.[15]

Saudi Arabia, like many other underdeveloped countries, has labor legislation designed to protect citizens and expand employment. Thus a given percent of any firm's work force must consist of nationals, while discharges are governed by a complex code which discriminates against foreigners. A firm wishing to discharge a foreigner for any cause can easily do so, but to discharge a national requires formal cause as interpreted in the law. The labor office has the power to insist that local citizens be employed and foreigners discharged, if the national has "equivalent" skills. The direct impact of this policy on production efficiency, combinations of factor inputs, recruiting, selection of employees, and training policies of firms is extensive. Often the firm is pressured to hire less qualified nationals when it

---

[14] See John Fayerweather, *Management of International Operations* (New York: McGraw-Hill Book Company, 1960), pp. 278–356, for many examples and cases in this area.

[15] "Taxes: Where is the Bite Bigger—U.S. or Western Europe," in *Special Report on Major Business Problems* (Business Week: 1963).

might prefer to obtain foreigners who are more highly skilled. In some categories of jobs (such as truckdriving), foreigners can not be used at all. Rules of this type tend to raise cost and create various operational problems for the firm.

Minimum wage legislation, which is common all over the world, is typically intended to force firms to pay workers a minimum living wage, according to local ethical views on this matter. The typical result of such legislation, however, is to cause firms to shift their combination of factor inputs by using less labor and more capital. Automation and mechanization is enhanced by such legislation. A quite common problem throughout the world (with the single exception of western Europe at present) is the relative abundance of unskilled labor and the relative scarcity of highly skilled personnel. Minimum wage legislation, by placing a higher price on the less skilled manpower, makes more highly skilled labor still more scarce (since this type of personnel is required in more heavily capitalized plants), while it makes the less skilled type of worker even more abundant. This particular problem demonstrates the interdependence, in terms of total productivity and firm efficiency, of education and law. Countries which have failed to invest enough in worker education and training attempt to make up for this deficiency by passing minimum wage laws and other acts designed to improve the lot of the unskilled, without conspicuous success;[16] but the effect on productive enterprise is considerable, nonetheless.

Where firms cannot fire workers without clear cause, the impact on staffing and direction is obvious. Most countries also have rather elaborate laws covering such problems as the activities of labor unions, the form of collective bargaining agreements, means of paying workers, and similar matters. The difference between personnel policies and strategies in the United States, where collective bargaining is encouraged and unions are very common, and Saudi Arabia, where all labor organizations are banned by law, is quite clear. The organization of a personnel department in the United States is focused on dealing with unions in bargaining questions; while in Arabia, where firms are also typically much smaller, a personnel manager spends much more of his time on legal problems pertaining to job rights, pay grievances, and individual complaints to the Saudi Labor Office. Workers do have written legal rights in Arabia, but they are on an individual basis. Collective handling of labor problems is much more common in the United States, as in other countries where trade unions are strong. Personnel functions in these countries are organized and managed to reflect this difference.

Direction within the firm may be affected by legislation. Employee discipline, in terms of the type of discipline possible, may also be regulated

---

[16] For comments about this situation in Africa, see Wilbert S. Moore, "The Adaptation of African Labor Systems to Social Change," in M. J. Herskovits and M. Harwitz, eds., *Economic Transition in Africa* (Evanston, Ill.: Northwestern University Press, 1964), pp. 294–297.

by law. In some countries, workers might be legally allowed to take time off from work for political purposes (as in Bolivia), and the employer cannot object. In others (Saudi Arabia), such behavior might require immediate dismissal. As in other aspects of the analysis of the legal framework and its effect on managerial effectiveness, this type of legal constraint cannot be generally evaluated, and detailed analysis of given laws in given countries must be made.

In Saudi Arabia and some other Moslem countries, employers must give Moslem employees time off for prayers, while firms in the United States may have to allow some of their employees time during working hours for union shop steward duties. During the month of Ramadan in some Moslem countries, employers are sharply restricted as to the types of work they can compel their workers to do, since the men are fasting during the daylight hours. One of the authors, who spent several Ramadans in Arab countries, noted that techniques of direction changed completely during this month. Discipline techniques and employee motivation methods which worked well during the other eleven lunar months had to be quite drastically changed during this special religious month. While the month was mainly dedicated to religious responses, these had force of law in several Moselm countries.

Staffing is also directly affected when certain kinds of labor are regulated or prohibited by law. Many states in the United States have child labor laws, which ban the use of young people under a given age (commonly sixteen) in various industries.

Labor law is one of the more complex kinds of legislation which directly affect most productive enterprises. Since working conditions, job security, and pay are items which directly affect a large proportion of the population of any country, legislators everywhere have paid much attention to law in this field, and no summary analysis can hope to cover even a fraction of the maze of detailed law in the area; but this area is critical to the performance of many of the major elements of the management process, since labor plays a key role in most activities. Since each country is willing and able to legislate separately in this area, it is one in which the diversity of comparative management, with its sometimes widely different environmental constraints, can be truly appreciated.

## Tax Law

Tax laws also influence industrial efficiency and managerial effectiveness in a major way. All countries have some form of tax structure, although any complete list of business taxes would fill volumes.

The key impact on internal firm operations in this case lies in the way in which taxes, or absence of taxes, force firms into different types of behavior than they otherwise would take. Hence, the present structure of American income tax law encourages corporations and discourages proprietorships and partnerships; this produces forms of organization which are considerably different than they might be if tax law were constructed differently. This follows from the fact that American corporate income taxes average around 50 percent and personal income taxes need be paid only when corporate income is paid out as dividends. Personal income taxes have ranged up to 90 percent until 1964. Since legally a proprietor or partner is an individual, a firm organized as a proprietorship or partnership could have a much higher tax liability than a corporation.

In other countries, such as Lebanon, the situation is reversed. Here corporations pay higher taxes (in some cases) than individuals, and it may be advantageous to remain a proprietorship until the firm becomes quite large. In this case the external legal constraint acts directly on the form of organization of the productive enterprise.

Possibilities of tax evasion, either legal or illegal, also are relevant here. A large public corporation, particularly a foreign one, is not usually able to evade its taxes; while a large private local proprietorship may evade taxes successfully in some countries. Such possibilities, combined with the ethical attitudes of firm owners, can have considerable impact on such factors as the types of financing used, the distribution of earnings, and the way in which the firm is organized and controlled.

This process is seen in extreme form in the oil rich countries of the Middle East. The foreign owned oil companies pay taxes negotiated specially in their concession agreements, and many of these taxes and special payments will be unique to the oil company. Small proprietorships and partnerships in the same countries rarely pay any income taxes at all, although the rate on the oil companies exceeds 50 percent in most cases.

There may also be administrative discrimination in favor of local companies, in terms of concessions granted by the tax authorities. Foreigners rarely get any breaks, unless these are negotiated in advance; but local companies often can avoid many kinds of taxes in this manner.

Most countries tend to encourage various types of selected firms through tax benefits and to penalize others through excess taxation. The depletion allowance in mineral and oil production in the United States has led to more investment, and more firms, in this sector than would be found if they were taxed as other firms are taxed. Accelerated depreciation allowances may lead firms not only to gain tax advantage from fast writeoffs on equipment, but also to change their investment policy. Such taxes can lead to more rapid change in capital equipment, which can lead to increased firm efficiency over time. In another direction, high excise taxes on such "luxuries" as jewelry, furs, and automobiles have tended to reduce consumption of these items and affect the operations of the companies involved in their manufacture. High luxury taxes on given products make prices higher than they otherwise would be, reduce sales potential, and hence influence directly marketing factors and such production factors as the size of production runs. A seemingly minor point such as whether taxes are levied on a product such as whiskey at the time of production or at the time of sale can have major impacts on inventory policies and financial arrangements made by firms. Fairly small changes in depreciation rules in American tax policy in 1962 have led to large changes in rates of investments in various American industrial sectors since that time, as these changes have changed the profitability, after taxes, of many kinds of investments. The list of how such tax law changes business decisions in virtually every economic sector is very long. Indeed, many books have treated this subject alone.[17]

The rapid increases in taxes and the increasing complexity of tax legislation in advanced countries have led to major structural organizational changes in top management in many cases. Historically the office of comptroller was essentially that of an internal auditor and record keeper; but with tax questions becoming increasingly more important, comptrollers have gained considerable decision making power from their ability to analyze the potential tax impacts of critical managerial decisions. Instead of being passive onlookers in the managerial process, such highly skilled men now have a very active part in this process. The effect of such considerations on planning also is clear. A major investment decision of a large firm would not be made in the United States today without careful analysis and consideration of the tax impact on the profit position of the firm, and often tax angles are a key consideration in the final decision.

Governments are quite aware of the impact of their tax policies on firms, and often a critical consideration of a new tax measure is the impact it will have on companies. Often a tax law is specifically tailored to achieve a desired effect, such as to stimulate some firms or cause others to diminish their activities.[18] Since money paid in taxes is quite visible and directly out of pocket for firms, they also spend considerable time in analyzing proposed measures and encouraging or discouraging various proposals.

One area of taxation of firms which tends to be critical is the kinds of business expenses which can be taken legitimately. Particularly important where corporate income taxes are relatively high are noncash expenses such as depreciation. Each country has its own rules on this matter, and each rule affects net profits directly, which in turn affects planning, finance, and control, among other critical elements. Thus, in the United States, firms can now recover up to 41 per cent of the cost of a new asset in depreciation in the first three years; while in France, up to 58 percent of the cost can be recovered. In the United Kingdom, the figure is up to 66 percent, depending on the industry; while in Sweden it can range up to 65.7 percent.[19] Such differentials can mean a difference of millions of dollars in net cash flow to a

---

[17] See, for example: *Federal Tax Handbook, 1964* (Englewood Cliffs, N.J.: Prentice-Hall, Inc., 1964), 598 pp., for empirical work; or R. A. Musgrave and C. S. Shoup, eds., *Readings in the Economics of Taxation* (Homewood, Ill.: Richard D. Irwin, Inc., 1959), 581 pp., for more theoretical considerations.

[18] For American examples, see John F. Fennelly, "International Trade and the Common Market," *California Management Review*, Vol. V, No. 3, spring, 1963, pp. 31–37.

[19] *Special Report on Major Business Problems*, op. cit.

large corporation; and they can dramatically affect total new investment, profit payouts to stockholders, types of financing, major uses of capital, and other critical elements.

Taxes are often used to prod firms into actions which they may not want to take or to discourage them from activities which they may wish to engage in. Thus one American tax levies very high rates on the sale of slot machines used in gambling to discourage this activity, while many countries offer tax concessions and rebates to manufacturing firms willing to start operations in their country. Puerto Rico has used this tax holiday device on new manufacturing firms for many years with good success.

The impact of legal structure on productive enterprises is considerable, but it cannot be generalized for all countries at all times. This constraint requires a great deal of detailed analysis, often down to the individual firm level, to determine whether this constraint has a positive or negative effect on business efficiency. Since many countries have local taxing units, such as cities, school districts, provinces, states, and counties, tax law must also be studied down to the local level to determine all relevant impacts. The impact of law generally must be considered in the context of the entire society. No law is perfect, and in any system it is possible to find laws which adversely affect managerial efficiency; but the evaluation desired is that of the economy taken as a whole.

In general, it can be argued that if the law pushes in the direction of creating a climate of more certainty in productive activities, while at the same time prohibiting such antisocial activities as might be detrimental to efficiency, the country is in a better position than one where the above is not true. If law becomes a cynical process for milking the public, competitors, foreigners, or any other group at the expense of a small number of insiders who use the law as an exploitative tool, this constraint will generally work against managerial effectiveness and productive efficiency.

## DEFENSE POLICY AND NATIONAL SECURITY

All countries have some defense posture, ranging from such massive military establishments as are found in the United States and the Soviet Union to countries such as Monaco, where a small ceremonial guard forms the major defense force. The major impact of such policies is in the area of international politics and the world cold war, but the defense strategy adopted by any country can have a considerable impact on the internal management of industrial enterprises.

In a country such as the United States, where tens of billions of dollars are spent annually by the Defense Department for military supplies and research and development work, the interest of firms in such contracts is obvious. The fact that for many companies the military is the only large customer also has its impact. In aerospace, for example, firms tend to be organized in a manner suitable to their major customer, regardless of the propriety of this in efficiency terms. Virtually all planning for a company of this type will revolve around the actions and plans of the Defense Department.[20]

Such dependence upon military contracts leads to considerable concern by Defense Department officials about the manner in which these firms function. Management audits, examinations and evaluations of key executives, and concern over productive facilities and research and development capability characterize Defense Department activity in this field. The way in which the customer places his orders also can have a significant impact on firm efficiency. A cost plus purchase contract, where costs are not seriously examined, can lead to much poorer results than a contract which is structured to reward efficient management. Since many of these defense oriented firms are also sellers in other nondefense markets, the inefficiencies or efficiencies determined here may well spill over into civilian markets with marked results on firm effectiveness. The American Boeing company was able to sell passenger jet aircraft very successfully after 1957, capitalizing on many years of experience in manufacturing such equipment for the United States Air Force. In this industry much concern is expressed in Europe because the firms (particularly in Britain) do not have the large development contracts for defense work enjoyed by various American firms. Without such defense related support, the multi-billion dollar research efforts necessary to develop economic passenger aircraft for sale in world markets are extremely difficult.[21] In this case, the direct impact of defense policies on research and development and production policies in firms is important.

A second result of extensive defense expenditures is in the area of staffing. Military business tends to be quite sophisticated, in the technical sense; and many high skill scientists and engineers, as well as managers, are drained away from the civilian sector to create new and better defense items. Recruitment of key personnel in lower priority industries may be difficult or impossible, and this can produce poorer results in this area of industry.

This forced allocation of manpower and other resources is particularly noticeable in Marxist countries, where such allocations can be easily accomplished from the center by planners. Russian spacecraft were the most advanced in the world in 1964, reflecting the quality of the manpower and materials put into this program; but the Soviet textile and refrigerator industries are composed of inefficient firms using relatively low quality manpower and managers, producing inferior products. Rarely does a country have enough superior resources to meet all needs. Some American

---

[20] For a discussion of the general impact of American defense policy, see Marshall E. Dimock, *Business and Government* (4th ed.; New York: Holt, Rinehart & Winston, Inc., 1961), pp. 312–329.

[21] "Aircraft are too Expensive," *The Economist*, Vol. CCXIV, No. 6534, January 16, 1965, p. 231.

thinkers are concerned on this point also, since the demands of highly sophisticated military programs syphon off many of the best American managers and technicians into defense work. It is alleged that some American industries (such as coal mining, textiles, and homebuilding) are quite inefficient, mainly because the best brains are elsewhere. The major impact here is on production and research and development, as well as staffing and organization.

Defense policy also includes such economic factors as permission to export to potential enemies, where exports could be damaging in the future. Hence, some countries (including the United States) carefully regulate the export of such items as advanced computers to Communist countries. At the extreme of such policy, all trade is banned, as in the case of United States restrictions against Red China and Cuba or those of the Arab countries against Israel. Such policies have considerable effect on the export organization of private firms, since in some cases they cannot conduct the type of trade they might prefer. In some cases, third parties become involved; and foreign policies of foreign states affect foreign operations. Hence, the Arab states blacklist the products of any foreign firm which manufactures items in Israel. An American automotive firm may have the choice of either assembling cars and trucks in an Arab country, and gaining this market, or doing it in Israel and losing the Arab market. A restriction of this sort will in part determine much of the international production and marketing organization of an international company.

Military policy may also determine whether or not some firms exist at all. If critical production is relatively high in cost yet determined to be vital for national defense, subsidies and/or tariffs can be arranged to provide for production at home. The American shipbuilding industry is of this type. American vessels cost much more than similar vessels built in foreign yards; so the federal government, using the defense rationale, pays large subsidies to ship purchasers if they buy the vessels in the United States. Similar programs can be found in some European countries. The effect here is to make the industry much larger than it otherwise would be and, ultimately, to allow it to exist. A second example of this policy is in American oil import quota restrictions. The amount of foreign oil which can be imported (at prices considerably lower than the domestic price) is strictly limited by quota, so that higher cost domestic producers can survive. The result is higher energy costs for consumers and the survival of many marginal firms in the industry.[22] Again, many similar policies can be found all over the world, often focused on the protection of a domestic production of high cost coal as compared to lower cost foreign supplies of oil or coal. West European countries, such as West Germany and France, follow such energy policies in part dictated by strategic military considerations.

Tariffs and other trade barriers often have this defense rationale for

---

[22] Fennelly, *op. cit.*, pp. 35–37.

justification. It should be noted, however, that there is an interrelationship here among defense problems; the political power of various pressure groups in the country, such as labor, firm owners, and managers; and such non-defense related policies as the desire to develop industry in the country. Even ethics are relevant here. The Americans, for example, have chosen (politically) to give higher incomes to local oil producers at the expense of consumers through its oil import quota system.

While such military policies do not directly affect all firms, they do often significantly influence many companies. Consider the American oil quota case noted above. Here a refiner will find that his entire production policy will shift, since the type of crude oil he might buy in the absence of such regulations will be unobtainable. The crude oil he can buy will also be considerably more expensive than that he can not buy. His production runs will probably be of different size, inventory levels will change, and the number and types of suppliers will shift. His product line will be different (since local crude may be of different quality, as well as cost), and pricing policies will change.

Buyers of the products will also experience major changes. An electric company producing power may well use coal instead of fuel oil, thus changing the types of suppliers. His combination of factor inputs will shift, since his energy costs, no matter what his energy decision, will be higher than they otherwise would be. Still farther down the production channel, users of electricity will find that the cost of this product is higher in coal and/or oil deficit regions than it otherwise would be. While this may be relatively unimportant in some cases, firms with major electrical demands now may shift locations of plants to lower cost sources. Manufacturers of aluminum and steelmakers using electrical reduction processes are examples of this type of user. Their research and development programs may now be refocused in the direction of finding out how to use less power and more of other, relatively lower cost inputs, thus changing combinations of factor inputs over time. Possible relocations of newer factories mean changes in marketing; shifts in channels of distribution, possible price policy changes, and sales promotion shifts. If the firm spreads out because of this factor, the nature of the firm's organization will also change, as will staffing techniques. The chain of shifts occasioned by such a relatively simple change as an oil import quota could be expanded indefinitely, as one traces the successive changes in managerial and firm functions brought about by the initial change.

Such changes are not restricted entirely to manufacturing companies directly affected by changes in military policy. When a major defense plant or military installation is opened or closed, many smaller service industries serving as subcontractors or as supporters of employees—such as laundries, groceries, and other retail establishments—are directly affected. The multiplier effect on income can clearly be seen when the closing of a major plant is announced. Firm managers in these subsidiary sectors are keenly aware of this impact on their planning and organizing.

Many countries are not concerned with major military expenditures. Germany and Japan have been sharply restricted in the period since 1945 as to the types of weapons and troops that they can have, and one major reason for these countries' successes in achieving rapid postwar growth has been that they have had relatively small defense burdens to carry. Their manpower is free to work creatively in the civilian sector, and firms and individuals do not have large tax burdens to finance military establishments.

Another potential impact of defense expenditures is linked closely to sociological views about the desirability of the various professions and class mobility. Latin American countries have been noted for maintaining large defense forces far in excess of any reasonable need for them. It is not uncommon to find than half a Latin American country's budget goes to the military, although the nation may not have had a war for fifty years. Here the pressures of military men to build up their prestige, in comparison with nearby countries, is evident. Also relevant is the notion that only a military career is desirable for sons of the elite class. If Brazil obtains an aircraft carrier, Argentina must also have one, for prestige reasons which are quite obscure to outsiders. This type of behavior can lead to major drains of quite scarce high talent manpower into completely useless activities.

One encouraging sign that perhaps the futility of such activities is being recognized is taking place in countries like Colombia, which is beginning to use the armed forces as a development group rather than a parasitical force. Troops are sent to the interior to build roads and bridges, and literate officers and noncoms attempt to develop local educational programs. Since in many less developed countries the military has a relatively large number of skilled managers and workers, such efforts often can be extremely productive, in relation to efforts of other segments of the population.

A final point here is that the nature of war, and defense, appears to be changing very rapidly; and few countries or persons yet see the total implications of the shift. The new trend to atomic weapons, plus the paradoxical trend to guerrilla type warfare, has forced many changes on armies and countries and has made much pre-1945 thinking obsolete. Americans, for example, still subsidize their merchant marine, with major effects on production, research and development, and marketing in this industry. The reason for the subsidy is defense, although it appears quite improbable that the merchant marine will play the same massive role in the next war as it did in World War II. Yet the subsidies attempt to maintain the same type of industry as was needed in World War II. The results, in terms of impacts on maritime firms and suppliers, still exist; but they may be completely obsolete.[23] One can predict with confidence that considerable change is likely to occur in this sector in the next few decades, although few

---

[23] Allen R. Ferguson, *The Economic Value of the American Merchant Marine* (Evanston, Ill.: The Transportation Center, 1961), 544 pp.

would venture to predict the precise shape of new policies, let alone how productive enterprises might be affected.

## FOREIGN POLICY

In its relationships with other countries, a nation will be faced with various political, economic, and social decisions affecting the welfare of all its citizens. Such decisions also have direct impact on the internal activities of business enterprises. An immediate example might be a nation's policy toward tourism. If the policy is to encourage visitors from abroad, one can predict with confidence that government policy toward hotels, passenger transportation firms, and similar establishments will be expansive and encouraging. Firms in these sectors can expect to receive various forms of encouragement, ranging up to cash subsidies; however, if the country is uninterested in this source of income, as in East Germany or eastern Saudi Arabia, such enterprises will languish.

Tariffs and quotas have already been mentioned under defense policy, but they are also relevant in terms of foreign policy. The reasons for various types of import restrictions often are basically connected with the country's foreign relations, rather than with defense, and hence need further exploration here. Thus, two or more countries may agree to reduce tariffs on stated items with the basic objective being some effect on trade and relations, rather than on defense. The kinds of results stemming from such policies will be similar to those noted in the defense section above.

A country which decides to join a customs union, such as the present European Common Market, will experience a variety of direct impacts on enterprise and managerial functions. In this case, the goal is to reduce internal duties (within the union) to zero, while adjusting all external tariffs of the member to the same level. Further aims are to achieve freer mobility of capital and labor within the market.[24] Thus, labor, previously unable to move freely from France to Germany, is now able to do so.

Foreign policy changes of the magnitude of the EEC have major impacts on firm and enterprise function, and it is possible to illustrate only a few examples here. The general effect of reducing tariffs to zero within the market has the effect upon any firm inside the system of creating a completely new system of competition and competitive relationships. Firms previously noncompetitive are now able to sell in direct competition in other member countries, with major impact on all of the marketing functions of the firm. Policies on product lines, channels of distribution and types of customers, pricing, and sales promotion shift as firms now find both new competition and new markets available to them.[25] When the agree-

---

[24] Max J. Wasserman, C. W. Hultman, and R. F. Moore, *The Common Market* (New York: Simmons-Boardman Publishing Corp., 1964), pp. 1–29.

[25] See Bela Belassa, *The Theory of Economic Integration* (Homewood, Ill.: Richard D. Irwin, Inc., 1961) for an excellent study of economic changes which may occur in such situations.

ment began to be worked out in practice after 1958, the immediate effect upon many European firms was to expand the market of various local companies significantly, since they now could sell with much less restrictions in five additional wealthy countries; but the price paid was much more intensive competition at home, since previously excluded foreign competitors now could compete equally vigorously in the home country. Firms which had paid little attention to marketing opportunities in foreign countries now began to develop much more elaborate selling organizations; staffing problems arose as the need for salesmen and sale managers who were familiar with different cultures and languages arose; production staffing needs shifted as the more intense competition caused new demands for redesigned, lower cost products; and the planning horizons of top managements shifted overnight as dazzling vistas of new, untapped markets suddenly emerged. Previously protected firms whose management techniques had not changed significantly in centuries suddenly were forced to make drastic changes in these techniques, in order to achieve efficiency levels necessary for survival. This common market agreement has the effect of rearranging the basic political-legal structure under which firms had operated in Europe for centuries, and the direct impact on companies is profound. In this case, the overall result has been to create more efficient internal managements, mainly through the pressures applied and opportunities created by changing the external constraints.

The new tariff reductions within the market shift prices of components and raw materials used by enterprises, causing changes in make or buy decisions, procurement policies, size of production runs (also influenced by marketing changes), inventory levels, combinations of factor inputs, and so on. The general attempt to make the EEC financially integrated has had significant impact on financial policies in many cases, as firms in one of the countries now find it possible to obtain funds in others. Plans of firms, both for the short and long run, shift as the new external constraints begin to operate; and reorganizations occur to take advantage of new production and marketing conditions. The increased mobility of labor within the Common Market has had wide impact on staffing policies, as Italians work in Germany, Belgians go to France, and Frenchmen go to the Netherlands. Personnel policies must change, since one goal of the EEC is to bring various social benefits of the various countries to equality over time.

The keen interest in the EEC shown by other powers suggests the general realization that such a market will result in far reaching changes in business practices and efficiency, typically for the better. The various attempts to follow the same course, as with the formation of the Latin American Free Trade Association, the Central American Common Market, and the European Free Trade Association, suggest that many governments view such changes as a chance to make major shifts toward increased productive efficiency by shifting many external constraints in a way which will enhance firm efficiency.

Any country, no matter how large or small, has a tremendous potential for creating a business environment internally through its trade policies with other countries; and few nations have resisted the temptation to shift policy in a manner calculated to enrich some firms, destroy others, and generally manipulate the environment to meet real or imagined national goals. Business firms are quite aware of this potential, and most firms make their needs known in the political capital. A real difficulty here is that the protection of a local firm need not necessarily lead to a more efficient productive system or managements. It is quite likely that the reverse will be the case. Protected managements, not fearing what competition will do if they make mistakes, are likely to become more sloppy in their internal operations in such a case.

For most countries, the major impact of such policies is in their impact on the competitive position of the enterprises in the economy. If trade is sharply restricted in many areas, the local firm now has potentially fewer competitors than it would have if foreign firms could compete vigorously. A company might suddenly shift from intense monopolistic competition to tight oligopoly or monopoly as a result. Such market shifts would have quite significant impacts on elements such as organization. A competitive firm would need an aggressive, widespread marketing organization, spread effectively over its marketing area; but if the same firm were granted a near monopoly by restricting imports, the type of organization needed or wanted in marketing would change dramatically. Staffing would also be affected in this case, since the kinds of managers effective in a highly competitive situation might not be the same types of men needed under a more sedate competitive situation.

As an example of how import competition affects firms and industries, Americans might ponder what would have happened in the American automobile industry in the past decade if importation of autos had been banned entirely. Such foreigh competition, while not exactly appreciated by business managers, has the effect of forcing local firms to keep up with the best in the world in order to survive. The impact of such foreign competition on American automobile manufacturers has been quite notable in terms of sales promotion, product lines (particularly in the introduction of American compact vehicles in 1959–61), and planning.

Highly protected local enterprise, from California to Leningrad to Sao Paulo, are more noted for high prices, inept management, and inferior workmanship than they are for their contribution to national welfare. Here a real conflict often arises, as individuals and governments are torn between their desire to obtain the best at the lowest prices and their desire to protect jobs, prestige, and welfare at home.

Many countries, particularly those developing rapidly, have exchange controls in effect which require firms to obtain licenses for imports. The usual pattern in such cases is that the firm has to apply for licenses for a wide range of items which are needed by the firm. After review of the application, the exchange authority issues permits or rejects the application.[26]

The complexities of the industrial process often lead to difficulty here. Production managers know exactly why they may need a carborundum cutting wheel of a certain size or grade, but this need is not immediately obvious to the nontechnician. Any manufacturing plant needs an incredible variety of bits and pieces of specialized items, the absence of any one of which may cause the factory to shut down. While these items are not typically expensive individually, in the aggregate they may represent a fairly large exchange drain; and planners in exchange control departments are likely to take a dim view of unrestricted imports. The result is likely to be a great deal of supply uncertainty on critical items which lead to costly plant down time, changes in production plans, and attempted use of high cost, local substitutes.[27]

Similar problems occur in spare parts and components. Foreign firms in less developed countries have had great difficulty convincing exchange control authorities that various items cannot be produced locally and must be imported to be included in the total product, most of which is manufactured locally. A frequent sight in many parts of the world is a new plant totally or partially shut down because some key component is not on hand to allow assembly work to continue.

This area is one in which petty corruption also tends to be apparent. Even a small country must have a large bureaucracy to approve the thousands of import licenses needed, and ill paid officials are under constant pressure from harassed firms to allow licenses for needed items. Foreign and local firms all over the world complain constantly about this point. The more corruption here, the less respect for law generally, which typically does not improve firm effectiveness.

This exchange control problem is not restricted entirely to less developed countries. A major American manufacturer built a plant in Scotland before 1958, when English exchange controls were still in effect. Virtually all of the necessary components for their diesel engines could be, and were, manufactured in England; but a few key fuel pump parts could not be manufactured there. These parts looked like little lumps of metal to the layman, but actually they were specially honed to .0001 inch tolerance and were made of special steel which could be purchased only in the United States. Moreover, the machine tools to cut the parts, as well as the skilled labor to make them, existed only in the United States. This company, justly proud of its quality control record, refused to use English parts of poorer

---

[26] See P. T. Ellworth, *The International Economy* (New York: The Macmillan Company, 1958), pp. 332–349, for a general discussion of exchange controls.

[27] A detailed examination of modern exchange restrictions is found in International Monetary Fund, *Fourteenth Annual Report: Exchange Restrictions* (Washington, D.C., 1963, 430 pp.

quality, while the English exchange control authority refused to allow import licenses for the components. The impasse was resolved only when the company succeeded, after spending much time and money, in convincing English authorities that this part could not be manufactured locally.

The enormous and highly varied requirements for spare parts for industrial enterprises is very imperfectly understood by laymen, and obtaining exchange licenses for parts in countries such as India and Egypt is often difficult. At times, it has proved easier to import new machines rather than parts to keep old ones running. The cost falls on production, although this type of regulation has a percolation effect through the entire firm. One cannot market what has not been manufactured.

In one small African country, the spare parts problems for autos and trucks became so acute that a minority political party ran for office on a one point program. They demanded that the country pass a law restricting imports of vehicles to one European manufacturer only—to reduce the spare parts problem to manageable proportions, so that *something* would run. The party ran far behind the leaders, but not through lack of enthusiastic support of merchants, truck operators, and manufacturers.

## POLITICAL STABILITY

This constraint usually affects planning more than any other critical element of the managerial process. The complex and often tenuous interconnections between government and business are difficult enough to maintain in a stable environment, where firms have a clear picture of policies, personalities, and actions on the government side. Even slow and evolutionary developments, such as the routine changes in policies toward corporate registrations, can be unsettling to firms on occasion. The most stable governments are rarely completely static, as close examination of any modern, stable state will demonstrate. Change is necessary, but it creates a variety of problems for firms.

Where political change is violent, abrupt, and disruptive, however, firms are often placed at a serious disadvantage in terms of productivity. A revolution of the Cuban type has such a dramatic effect on planning, staffing, control, and organization of productive enterprises that they almost invariably show declines in productivity in such a situation. Countries wracked by frequent and violent revolutions, rapid changes of governments and policy, and similarly disruptive forces seldom are noted for their progressive, efficient, productive enterprises. The proper organization of any firm involves, among other things, long term arrangements with labor, suppliers, customers, and governments; and any factors which tend to disrupt such arrangements typically lead to low efficiency. Any effective long term planning is difficult or impossible in such circumstances.

The usual change of regime in a two party system seldom has this disruptive effect, since neither party is interested in overturning major policies established by its predecessors. Where the situation does become a problem is when revolutionary regimes, from right or left, gain power with the avowed purpose of making massive changes, only to be followed by counterrevolutions of violently opposed parties. The first party may nationalize all transportation companies, which leads to major changes in staffing, long run objectives of the firms, and internal organization, as well as in relations with customers and governments. The second party may try to seize power to return these enterprises to private control, and succeed. The problems of management under such conditions are so difficult that all that can be done is to operate from day to day, hoping that the firm will somehow survive.[28] Managers, uncertain of their tenure, are able only to make minimal decisions, while larger problems to be worked out over longer periods are ignored. Such an environment also encourages political, rather than professional, management. Only the right people politically are trusted to operate economic enterprises, and their managerial abilities may be irrelevant. The usual impact on managerial effectiveness is bad.

This point is important enough so that it is difficult to discover any historical situation where a politically disturbed country was able to progress economically at all, although there are ample examples of situations where the reverse occurred. Periods of political strife are typically periods of economic deterioration, when managerial effectiveness tends to decline steadily.

The case of Cuba since 1958 illustrates this sort of problem. By 1964, income per capita in Cuba had not yet quite recovered to 1958 levels, although several hundred thousand Cubans had left the country for political reasons. Many of the exiles were professionals and managers; and, quite apart from their political feelings, they had been instrumental in managing various sorts of Cuban enterprises. As they left, staffing became extremely difficult, since equally skilled men were impossible to find. Managers in the early Castro era were undoubtedly less competent than their immediate predecessors. There is a normal tendency in any revolutionary situation to appoint only "loyal" men as key industrial figures, which tends to cause further deterioration in managerial effectiveness. Political loyalty and managerial competence have no particular relationship to each other.

As management of various enterprises deteriorated, production also fell. The problem was complicated by the inability of the new regime to arrange for purchases of critical spare parts from the United States, where most industrial and agricultural machinery had originally been purchased; but income continued to decline for some time in Cuba, in large part because management also had much to relearn about productive processes.

---

[28] Even in quite stable countries, sudden changes such as new nationalizations can force many competent managers to leave. For an English example during the 1947–51 period, when many firms were being nationalized, see E. Golob, *The Isms: A History and Evaluation.* (New York: Harper & Row, 1954), pp. 293–296.

Algeria presents another case of extreme political instability affecting managerial effectiveness. Starting in 1958, the French Algerians began to leave that country because of the political troubles there. As they left, purchasing power began to decline, creating new marketing problems for Algerian firms. The early leavers typically were not industrialists or managers but small farmers, proprietors, and shopkeepers; so the initial impact on firms was not direct. As revolutionary turmoil increased, however, more French left, including, by 1962, many managers and industrialists. Left behind were factories without management; and the Algerians, like the Cubans, had to recruit a new managerial class from relatively untrained personnel. By 1964, over 90 percent of the French had left Algeria, representing over 40 percent of total prerevolutionary purchasing power. The replacement group of Algerian managers could not, in the short run, restore production to prerevolution levels; and deterioration of the total economy was continuing in 1965.

In both of these cases, extreme political change resulted in the virtual elimination of the entire professional management class, as well as many professionals, technicians, and factory owners. The results were production declines and loss of income for the country. Here the constraint impact was on the total productive effectiveness of the enterprises, since total managements were wiped out. No critical element of the firm was left untouched, because new managers had to deal with all of the critical elements of the management process, and they often did not have the knowledge and skill of their predecessors to do so efficiently.

More moderate political uncertainties also can have considerable effect on managerial effectiveness. The return to power of the British Labor party in 1964 with the avowed goal of renationalizing the British steel industry certainly had very direct impact on steel companies' planning, particularly on the time horizon and types of plans. In this case, where the industry must necessarily have quite long run plans to remain efficient, even the uncertainty of a possible government takeover, no matter how remote, can have significant long run effects on managerial effectiveness.[29]

## POLITICAL ORGANIZATION

The general political rules under which a country operates have considerable impact on internal firm and managerial effectiveness. Consider the United States, which has a federal system, with various political powers divided between the several states and the federal government. In this case, a corporation can be chartered by any state, subject to the laws and regulations applying in that state. One predictable result is that many large, national corporations are charted in states like New Jersey and Delaware, where legal requirements of corporations for disclosure, operating and

---

[29] "Figuring out British Steel," *The Economist*, Vol. CCXIII, No. 6326, November 21, 1964, pp. 889–891.

organizational rules, and similar matters are considerably more lenient than they are in other states. The internal organization of the company is directly affected by such rules. In other countries with federal political organizations, such corporate chartering could be the province of the federal government; and this difference would result in substantially different internal organizations of many firms. One state may spell out in detail the legal duties of certain key officers in a corporation, such as the treasurer and secretary, while another state may have no such rules. In the latter case, the duties and responsibilities of officers might be quite different. Also, taxation of corporations may differ for firms incorporated in one state and for firms incorporated in another, and this may have some effect on financial planning and on sources and uses of funds.

Similarly, the commerce clause of the United States Constitution divides the regulation of commerce in the United States between the states and the federal government. A firm operating in only one state is subject to state law only, while a firm operating in several states is subject to federal control. Such legal differences can directly affect the planning and organization of the companies.

Some countries, such as France, are noted for high degrees of centralization in government. The central government directly controls various local functions, such as the school system, appointment of provincial officials, and similar activities. Most tax funds flow to the central government for redistribution to local areas. Other countries, such as Australia, are equally noted for extreme decentralization. The states or provinces collect the bulk of taxes, and many more governmental functions are carried out at the local level. Such differences have direct effects on enterprises. Markets in a centralized country might be quite different than in a decentralized one, particularly if the provinces have the ability to levy tariffs or otherwise prevent the free flow of goods. In the United States, considerable interest is shown by business firms in local educational systems, which are controlled and directed by state or local governments, since the availability of skilled labor and managerial candidates will in part depend on how well educated local citizens are. The substantial differences in local educational standards and quality mean that the staffing function will be closely related to this variable, and localities anxious to attract firms have an option of improving schools as one method of attracting firms. Note that this attraction in itself implies that firms have the privilege of seeking locations in any area they choose, which in itself is not a right held universally in all countries. In the United States, local governments are quite free to try to attract companies; while in England the central government, through its control of key taxes and its ability to plan, attempts to encourage industrial location in areas deemed useful by the central government.[30]

---

[30] P. D. Henderson, "Government and Industry," in G. D. N. Woswick and P. H. Ady, eds., *The British Economy in the Nineteen Fifties* (Oxford: Clarendon Press, 1962), pp. 337–345.

Governments at all levels are major buyers of industrial supplies, such as fuel, school supplies, cement, and many other items; and this purchasing function will be organized according to how the powers of government are distributed. This organization has a direct effect on marketing organization within industrial firms, since their sales forces must be in a position to influence customers as much as possible. A firm manufacturing school desks in the United States may have tens of thousands of local school boards as potential customers, and be organized accordingly; but in a highly centralized country, a similar firm might have just one customer, the minister of education. Organization of the marketing function in this case would be quite different from the former example.

Any government, however dictatorial or democratic, is subject to pressure from various vested interests, such as labor, landlords, consumers, and businessmen. Pressures of this sort vary dramatically in intensity, depending on such factors as who has the votes or the power to force political change. Where any privileged group gains disproportionate power, the likely result is a diminution of productive efficiency, since this group will take rights away from others.

One example of this is the American agricultural policy (similar examples are found in Brazil, France, West Germany, England, and other countries) toward cotton prices. In order to protect farm income, the price of raw cotton domestically is set above the world market price (ranging from five to ten cents per pound higher in recent years); but in order to allow American growers to compete in world markets, international sales are made at world price levels, with the federal government taking the loss instead of the farmers. American cotton users thus had a five to ten cent price disadvantage in their raw materials costs, and frequent objections to this disadvantage by textile producers went unheeded until 1964.[31] It was common for a Japanese or Hong Kong producer to buy American raw cotton, spin it into yarn or cloth, and export it to the United States to be sold at low prices. American cotton producers complained bitterly for years about this system, but to no avail. In this case, the strongest pressure group succeeded in placing another pressure group at a severe disadvantage; and this resulted in quite marked impacts on marketing and price policy. American cotton growers were able, with considerable government export subsidy support, to sell more cotton in the Far East and less to American spinners. American textile firms, having to pay more for their raw materials, had higher prices and smaller markets than otherwise would have been the case. Their product lines, price policies, and sales promotion were therefore different. Some American import firms found that new textile lines could be expanded in the United States, again at the expense of American textile producers. Here major impact was felt on channels of distribution and sales promotion for these companies. Any foreign policy which has the effect of

---

[31] "Will it Last?" *Forbes*, November 1, 1964, p. 52.

shifting prices of either inputs or outputs for various firms will have this sort of chain effect, penalizing some companies and rewarding others, often doing so in ways not entirely anticipated by the proponents of the legislation. The usual result is lower productive efficiency within the economy.

Similar undesirable efficiency results are obtained when labor groups succeed in pressuring governments into overprotective attitudes. In some countries, it is virtually impossible for large firms to fire labor for any but drastic causes. Labor cost then becomes a fixed cost, work standards tend to become sloppy, and unit production costs typically rise. Firms are unable to correct the situation, lacking the ability to revise government rules, regulations, and laws governing such behavior.[32]

Not all such favoritism runs counter to business interests. In Europe, particularly before 1940, business firms succeeded in pressuring government into enforcing powerful cartel agreements between firms. Such agreements often included specific quotas of output for firms, price fixing at extremely high levels, and shares-of-market agreements between firms. The purpose was to protect powerful business interests from the winds of competition, either domestically or internationally.[33]

While such agreements were quite popular with most businessmen, since they made management much easier, the results, in efficiency terms, were usually bad. Lacking any incentive to become more efficient, firms did not do so; and countries which really enforced such potent cartel rules eventually found themselves slipping badly behind the more competitive and aggressive rivals. What is best for productive efficiency is not necessarily what firm managers think is best. Far too often such men are more interested in making their own jobs easier (like the rest of us) than in trying to make the productive system work better.

The nature and organization of political parties can have considerable impact on the operation of business firms. Many countries have at least one major party which is avowedly Marxist; and its power at the polls may have considerable effect on the future of business, and hence on planning. The existence of such a party may also have considerable effect on how a firm performs its staffing and direction functions, since to alienate a large number of citizens by inept policies in these sectors may lead to even more disastrous results in the next election. A significant effect of the pronounced improvement in productivity and efficiency in western Europe in the past fifteen years (accomplished in large part by private enterprises) has been the steady decline of the success of very left wing Marxist parties in elections. Another significant problem in party organization is the number of parties. Countries like Mexico and Egypt have, in effect, one official party, and pressures and requests from firms and others work through the party machinery. Countries like the United States and England have basi-

---

[32] For a Brazilian example, see Oberg, *op. cit.*, p. 135.
[33] See Ellsworth, *op. cit.*, pp. 130–137, for examples and discussion of this point.

cally two party systems, and managers, like other citizens, have the option of supporting either. Countries like France and Italy have multi-party systems, with various coalitions making up the government. One party or two party systems are typically more stable than multiparty governments, which again leads to better planning possibilities for firms. The existence of a large number of parties usually means that at least one of them will be violently antibusiness, which may lead to considerable uncertainty about courses of action to take, since these are subject to public debate. Plant closures, reductions of staffs, new plant sites, key price changes, and similar business decisions might not be questioned seriously in a one party or two party state, but may become the focal point of disapproval for a minority party. As is common for all these political constraints, only a close study of actual situations could determine whether such a condition would have a positive or negative effect on productive efficiency. It is clear only that such factors are not neutral in this regard.

## FLEXIBILITY OF LAW AND LEGAL CHANGES

The rapid political, economic, and social changes of the period since 1850 in industrializing countries have had a revolutionary impact on law and politics. Change is the keynote here. As countries shift from agrarian, subsistence level economies to urban oriented, factory based systems, the necessity for rapid change in law and political institutions proceeds endlessly. Law tends to be conservative, seeking precedents for action; and this tendency conflicts with the necessity of being able to keep pace with the rapid changes demanded in a modern industrial state.

Ultimately, resistance to necessary change prevents change of all kinds. Consider a situation in which railroads are being built and no right of emninent domain is presently in law. Unless the law can be modified, it will probably prove impossible to build the railroads, since the problems of negotiating purchases of land rights of way from thousands of individual landholders will be impossible. Unless legal strictures can be removed, no development will take place, and the productive enterprise will not even be able to commence operations. Similarly, it may turn out that a country badly needs a modern corporation law (with limited liability and immortality for firms) in order to allow for the framework necessary to the creation of large companies. In the absence of changes in law, the large firms will never come into being, and the development process may well be aborted at the outset.

The law books of any country are full of anachronistic rules which presently serve no purpose, or even retard desirable trends. Failure to come to grips with rapid change can only mean inefficiency and less progress than otherwise might be possible. As pressures build to change the law, various undesirable sorts of behavior arise which may do more harm than good.

One example would be the present trend in the United States for large cities to turn to the federal government for aid in finance and rebuilding. Changes in core cities have major impacts on productive enterprises, determining in extreme cases, whether firms can even survive or not. The impact of urban land use; social overhead capital, transportation facilities; and amenities on staffing, planning, and organization of many firms is large; and this can be influenced by what steps a local urban government takes to change its shape and economy. It is argued that cities with problems should turn to local and state governments for aid in these matters; however, many of these local governments were established in their present form when the country was still agricultural and rural, and their organization is such that they are dominated by rural interests who have little interest in urban problems. Similarly, the available tax sources have been usurped by other governmental units, and the cities literally have no place to turn. The bypassing of state and county governments by cities (often led by prominent businessmen) reflects the failure of government to adjust rapidly enough to needs seen by citizens in cities. The waste created by such situations, in terms of excess governmental costs and inadequate fire, police, and other civic protection, is borne by productive enterprises, and can be a drain on their resources. All management functions are affected by such difficulties in obtaining needed political and legal reform.

A final point here is the question of certainty of law enforcement. Any prosecutor has options about how the law will be enforced, and only if the enforcement process is fair and equal will efficiency be maximized. Thus, in the United States, the man who is attorney general has considerable discretion in determining which types of antitrust cases will be prosecuted, and under what sections of the law. One official might press cases based on allegedly illegal mergers; another might push price fixing cases. Quite legitimate differences of opinion on what is important in such situations, in terms of the public interest, could have very different results on various industrial firms, with corresponding impact on firm and managerial functions. The planning process in firms is directly affected by such problems, since, in laying out long term policies on such key issues as firm expansion and the ways in which it will expand, knowledge of legality of the plans is crucial. If a company wishes to expand through merger and finds that mergers are unfavorably regarded and subject to antitrust proceedings, the firm will have to change its plans, with corresponding changes in managerial effectiveness. A change in enforcement activity or focus can have extensive impacts on the company.

In many countries, prosecution of law violators may depend more on who is influential than on the law. Prosecutors may be very willing, for example, to attack foreign owned firms for antitrust violations, or labor code transgressions. Local firms doing the same things may escape notice. Special interest groups, such as farmers, may enjoy more favorable legal attitudes than industrialists using the same kinds of labor. The law may be the same, but enforcement among various groups may not be. This sort of discrimination can lead to lower overall firm efficiency, since some firms are forced to obey laws while others are not.[34]

Legal discrimination was seen clearly in Saudi Arabia in the attitude toward enforcement of existing legal codes when the oil companies, instead of local firms, were involved. In many situations, the law was the same for both; but the large, foreign, and powerful oil companies were required by the government to observe carefully every aspect of law relevant to their operations. Labor law in particular was usually observed to the letter; and the oil companies could not fire employees, discipline them, or change their work in violation of the labor code without being hailed into court. Local firms, on the other hand, sometimes observed the law and sometimes violated it, depending in part on how their workers protested and how efficient the Labor Office was in any given case. The overall level of enforcement was much lower among Saudis than between Saudis and foreigners. As a result, the kinds of problems which oil company personnel managers had to deal with tended to be considerably different from those faced by managers in locally owned firms.

On the other hand, some countries offer equal treatment, to an unprecedented degree, to both foreign and local firms. One industrialist commented about England in this way:

Government committees of one sort or another are always changing, and every new committee tends to get on the backs of industry . . . Let me reiterate my original statement, however, that Britain is one of our best operations. We feel it is one of the few places in the world where we can go to government officials and get a straight answer. In many cases, we may not like the answers we get—but at any rate we know what the rules are. This is probably one of the few countries in the world where this happens, and I include the United States.[35]

England also has many problems of inflexibility, however, one of the more important being the rigid industrial location rules which are intended to force firms to move away, or stay away, from highly congested urban industrial complexes. The approved areas may be more costly than available urban sites, and a firm may have higher expenses as a result of being unable to convince officials that in its case rigid rules on location should be relaxed somewhat.

---

[34] See Richard D. Robinson, *International Business Policy* (New York: Holt, Rinehart & Winston, Inc., 1964), pp. 45–98, for a detailed discussion of this point. In many cases, law pertaining to foreign firms may be different than law pertaining to local companies.

[35] "American Business Looks at Britain," *The Manager*, Vol. XXXII, No. 7, July, 1964, p. 28.

## CONCLUSION

These political and legal characteristics of a society interact with the internal process of management to a considerable extent. As in the case of sociological constraints, there is considerable difficulty in determining exactly how these interrelationships work out in practice, and it is necessary to examine carefully actual situations and examples to evaluate this impact properly. In this chapter we have considered the more general effects, rather than precise situations which one will encounter in actual situations. As we turn to detailed evaluations of different countries and cultures, such impacts will be worked out in more detail. The critical point to consider here is that much of what is commonly regarded as the province of the firm manager may in fact be quite beyond his control, formed instead by the interactions of management with environment.

# Chapter 10

# Environmental Constraints:

# Economic

## INTRODUCTION

The various economic constraints will affect managerial effectiveness through their impact on the critical elements of the management process. In this chapter, such impacts will be explored for each of the economic constraints. These constraints are not single variables but complex sets of interrelated economic phenomena. Our problem is to generalize for the economy as a whole, in terms of how the various economic constraints the management of a firm faces influence its effectiveness. This type of analysis is quite old and honored; economists as early as 1750 were concerned with how economic structures and constraints affected production. A large amount of literature now exists discussing virtually every aspect of this economic question.[1]

Economists have, however, usually analyzed this type of problem in terms of the economy as a whole, or in terms of firms which are assumed to be managed efficiently. Thus an economic change might lead to some price change, and it is assumed that business managers will adjust properly to this price shift. If they do, results can be analyzed. Economic analysis has tended to stress the price-output results of given economic changes, which in our analysis of enterprise and managerial functions would be largely included among production and marketing issues. Our purpose here is to extend the economic analysis, where it is applicable, to other relevant firm and managerial functions, to determine how such economic constraints would work out in practice in their impact on various individual productive enterprises.

---

[1] John F. Bell, A *History of Economic Thought* (New York: The Ronald Press Company, 1953), particularly the numerous references, shows how extensive this economic work has been.

## GENERAL ECONOMIC FRAMEWORK

**Basic Issues.** Every society has to develop some form of economic organization to answer the fundamental economic questions: How much of each good or service is going to be produced? For whom are these goods and services to be produced? What kinds of goods and services are to be produced? This essentially is the problem of resource allocation. No society is wealthy enough to give every citizen all of every good or service he may want. Given this fundamental constraint, some form of rationing of scarce resources must be developed.

Such rationing will take place in two areas: first, productive enterprises will be unable to use all the resources they might demand to produce the goods and services they are capable of producing; and second, some method of allocation of the necessarily scarce final products and services must be devised. The system necessarily becomes interrelated with ethical decisions which the society collectively must make, since some of the scarce goods, such as food, are absolutely necessary to human survival. Some goods are physiologically more valuable than others as well, since at least some men cannot survive without them. Quite apart from any price rationing scheme, a rationing system which does not give needed drugs to the critically ill would be regarded in most societies as ethically unsound.

The system of resource allocation used in any society will have direct impact on the productive firms in that society. In extreme cases, the survival of firms is at stake. For example, suppose that in one country, the manufacture or sale of alcoholic beverages is prohibited; here the rationing system of both inputs and outputs prevents a firm from operating at all in this sector. In another country, such production may be permitted, but only under close supervision by means of restrictions upon quantity of inputs and outputs. Again, the direct impact of the allocation system on the firm's marketing and production policies is clear.

**Basic Economic Systems.** The most common modern economic system is capitalistic. In practice, most capitalist countries are actually mixed economies, as we shall see later; but it is useful at the outset to consider a pure capitalist state, at one extreme of economic organization, in order to grasp the essential features of such an economy. The basic features of a purely capitalist system are as follows:[2]

1. Private property is legal. Individuals or firms can hold any form of asset in whatever quantity they choose.
2. The measuring rod for all economic transactions is money. Money is a scarce commodity, in the sense that its supply is restricted, and no one has as much as he might prefer. Scarcity is determined either by the in-

---

[2] Taken from George N. Halm, *Economic Systems* (New York: Holt, Rinehart & Winston, Inc., 1961), p. 22.

herent nature of the medium of exchange (such as gold or silver) or by a government process of money creation which assures relative scarcity. This means that money also has value.

3. Persons obtain money incomes by selling services (inputs to firms). Services consist of labor, land, management, or capital. Owners of assets (including the asset of labor service) get incomes based on the value of their assets to productive enterprises.

4. Anyone is free to sell or withhold either his services or his goods in any market.

5. There are no government controls over the economic system. No goods or services are restricted, in the sense that they are not subject to rationing, price controls, or any other controls. Governments' main function is to insure law and order and guarantee the sanctity of contracts.

In such a system, the total allocation of resources would be through the price mechanism. Firms would produce goods and services which consumers demanded—and these demands would be based on the prices of goods and income and tastes of individuals. Inputs to firms would consist of the purchase of various services from individuals, either in the form of labor or managerial services or as rents and interest on assets owned by individuals. Wherever a firm saw a chance to make a profit, it would do so. Such opportunities would arise whenever the cost of inputs was less than the price of outputs. The residual amount, profits, would accrue to the owners of the productive enterprise and would form their incomes.

In this theoretical situation, the allocation of resources would be accomplished without any control whatsoever. If some good was produced in excess of demand, its price would fall. As price fell, firms would produce less of it, since profits would be falling. The restriction of supply would cause price eventually to stablize at some level which would allow just enough to be produced to cover necessary costs of production, including necessary profits for producers. Shortages of goods or services would result in higher prices, higher profits, and more goods being produced, as firms were attracted to production by the prospect of higher profits.[3]

While such a society might seem the best of all possible worlds, serious practical difficulties have prevented pure capitalist systems from surviving for very long. Flexible prices in theory are fine; but in practice, few persons are pleased to find that their wage rate is declining, or that their commodity price has fallen greatly, since this means lower incomes for them. The usual result is some stickiness of prices downward, which in practice means unemployment or excess production.[4] This in turn leads to government action to correct the situation, which in turn usually means that other prices are made less flexible.

---

[3] A complete analysis of this complex point is found in John F. Due and Robert W. Clower, *Intermediate Economic Analysis*, Fourth Edition (Homewood, Ill.: Richard D. Irwin, Inc. 1961), pp. 3–292.

[4] For a basic (and excellent) treatment of this subject, see Paul A. Samuelson, *Economics* (6th ed.; New York: McGraw-Hill Book Company, 1964), pp. 328–345, particularly p. 340.

In time of war, no country has ever been willing to tax enough to raise revenues to pay soldiers what would be required in a free market. Hence, one finds extensive interference with the system in terms of labor service pricing. Governments also hesitate to tax enough to bid away needed resources from the private sector, and rationing schemes apart from the price system are applied.[5] Managers are reluctant, for perfectly good practical reasons, to pay superior workers much more than average ones; and for ethical reasons few persons are willing to let some persons' incomes drop so low (because their services are so relatively useless) that they might starve to death.

In a perfect capitalist state, the question of input allocation also would be solved perfectly. Labor would go to the firms offering the best pay, as would capital and management.

This system would offer managers in productive enterprises the maximum flexibility for their actions, and it is no accident that most competent managers in most countries prefer extreme freedom of pricing.[6] The system would mean that the managerial job could be done more easily than if managers were faced with complex physical controls, elaborate governmental directives, and similar direct controls. Less competent managers often prefer a more leisurely life under some kind of direct control system, however, since this pure capitalist system rewards only the competent.[7] If someone isn't very capable, his income drops.

An often overlooked advantage of this economic system is that of rapid information feedback to producing companies. If a product does not meet the needs of the market, the resulting poor sales, income losses, and necessary withdrawal of the firm leads to rapid correction of errors. While in practice no country has a pure system, the existence of this kind of feedback to some extent in some industries in all capitalist countries means that the problems of planning resource allocation are minimal. One rarely hears of a milk shortage in New York City, a vegetable shortage in London, or a shortage of Size 34 suits in Brussels. Such defects do not occur because shortages and surpluses are easily and automatically handled by the price system.

One does hear, however, of unemployment in Pennsylvania, surplus coffee in Brazil, and unsalable butter in Wisconsin. In these cases, interference with the price mechanism has led to disequilibria in these markets, reflecting the common problem facing most capitalist states. For a variety of good and bad reasons, they have elected to interfere with the pricing process at key points, thus creating disequilibria.

**Pure Marxism.** Until 1917, no Marxist state existed; and the Soviet

---

[5] Albert G. Hart and Peter B. Kenen, *Money, Debt and Economic Activity, Third Edition* (Englewood Cliffs, N.J.: Prentice-Hall, Inc., 1961), pp. 418–429.

[6] For American examples of managerial ideologies, see R. J. Monson, Jr., *Modern American Capitalism* (Boston: Houghton Mifflin Company, 1963), 142 pp.

[7] A good example of this reasoning is shown in James R. McIlroy, "The Case for Tariffs," reprinted in H. Madheim, E. M. Mazze, and C. S. Stein, eds. *International Business* (New York: Holt, Rinehart & Winston, Inc., 1963), pp. 219–228.

Union is not conceptually, even today, a purely Marxist country. Such a theoretical system can, however, be conceived, although, like the pure capitalist state, it is difficult to imagine how it might operate in practice.[8] In such a system, all means of production would belong to the state, and all allocation decisions would be made according to state plan. An immediate difficulty here is that one key means of production is labor, and—unless one cares to imagine a slave state where all workers and managers literally belong to the state—some element of voluntary allocation of labor resources enters the picture. Perhaps the most reasonable theoretical system is one in which workers and managers are paid wages, and these wages will vary according to plan. Where more workers are needed, wages will be relatively higher. The other inputs to productive firms, capital and land, do belong to the state and are allocated according to plan.

A second major problem emerges at this point. Workers will have money incomes, and they will demand various consumer goods. The Marxist planners must decide how to meet this demand. If they choose to ignore it, in the sense of producing what they feel is "good" for workers, rather than what is wanted, some goods will be in short supply while others will be in surplus. This can be handled by setting prices reflecting relative scarcities; but in all but the simplest societies, the amount of demand analysis necessary to set correctly millions of consumer goods prices will usually mean that shortages and surpluses will be a perpetual problem.

If the planners decide to let private demand determine the goods to be produced, there is little to plan, since the mix of goods and services produced will most easily be determined by doing what the capitalist states do—namely, letting the price system determine resource allocation. The major problem in such a case would be to devise some allocation system for nationalized resources (capital and land) which would properly reflect consumer demand.[9]

The question of proper allocation of land, and more importantly, capital, has plagued Communist planners since this type of system began operating. Marx believed in the labor theory of value, which meant that all value is embodied in labor. Following this philosophy, land and capital are free, and should have no price; but free goods are to be used without limit, which is clearly impossible in any productive system. If an enterprise manager is given the instructions to produce a given good, and he is told that labor has some price (the wage rate), while capital is free, the inevitable tendency is to maximize the use of capital. This leads to the need for some capital rationing, which merely changes the mechanism of allocation, not the need.

The direct impact of this system on managerial performance comes basically from the need for an extensive planning mechanism to allocate

---

[8] System description taken from Halm, *op. cit.*, pp. 159–201.
[9] *Ibid.*, pp. 162–164.

scarce resources properly. Managers cannot be allowed to decide what they need—they must be told by the planners; but the planners cannot possibly know all of the needs and problems of each firm, so the firm managers must present plans for approval. Here begins a complex bargaining-negotiation situation affecting virtually every managerial and firm function.[10] Production policies must wait for the planners to decide what is to be produced, and with what resources. Marketing channels of distribution will be those laid down by planners from above, not by firm managers. Finance takes a secondary role in such a system, as the necessary financing of payroll, materials, investment, and so on will follow naturally from production plans. The process of management becomes considerably different in this type of system from that in capitalist systems.

**Workability of Systems.** Our problem here is not to evaluate the various types of theoretical systems but to try to determine under which kind of system managers are more likely to perform effectively. In the real world, there are no perfect Marxist or capitalist systems, only a continuum of possibilities ranging perhaps from such countries as Albania, Red China, and the Soviet Union on the Marxist side to the United States, Lebanon, and Switzerland on the capitalist side, with countries like Yugoslavia and India somewhere in the middle. In all cases, one can find some capitalist as well as some Marxist influence. The capitalist states plan agriculture, fixing prices and outputs, while the Communist states allow considerable freedom in pricing and private enterprise in such sectors as vegetable growing and selling.

It would appear that industrial enterprise management is in a position to be more effective the more capitalistic the society is. This stems from the basic nature of resource allocation. If a country is interested in efficiency, it wants its resources placed in the most valuable places, and the price system does this more efficiently than any planner conceivably could. The usual attacks on capitalism are not really focused on the allocation problem in this sense, but rather on the ethical aspects of the system. In a country where prices and incomes are free to go as high or as low as the market might take them, it is typically true that there will be extremes of wealth and grinding poverty in the country. Accepting demand as it is may mean that millionaires throw hundred thousand dollar parties while unfortunates starve outside. Volatile shifts in demand may destroy both wealthy and poor alike. The numerous historic efforts to modify the rigors of a truly capitalist system typically revolve around such considerations.

A second kind of modification which businessmen hesitate to discuss is that involving the protection of business firms and managers. Price supports, subsidies, entry controls, and similar measures are often intended to

---

[10] B. M. Richman and R. N. Farmer, "The Red Profit Motive: Soviet Industry in Transition," *Business Horizons*, Vol. VI, No. 2, summer, 1963, pp. 21–28, particularly n. 5., B. Richman, *Soviet Management* (Englewood Cliffs, N.J.: Prentice-Hall, Inc., 1965), chaps. 5, 8 and 11.

control competition to the benefit of the firms now in business. The Lebanese pride themselves on being quite capitalistic, but a Lebanese businessman cannot compete legally in motor trucking[11] or in pharmacies—these fields are restricted to the present (and rather incompetent) firms. A Swiss or an American also would have trouble entering various types of enterprise because of present government controls. It is often easier to get one's government to hold up prices than to devise other means of sales promotion, and incompetent businessmen and managers seek protection from the rigors of the market as avidly as do other "unfortunate" groups in the society.

In a capitalist state, however, in so far as it is capitalist, managers are pressured to become more efficient. Since errors are penalized by loss of profits and, in extreme cases, business failure, the market weeds out incompetents vigorously. A firm is unable, in this sort of dynamic situation, to rest on its laurels, since any competitor is free to change any firm or managerial policy at any time. If the traditional means of financing in an industry is through short term bank credit, and an innovating firm finds that long term insurance company financing leads to lower costs and better results, the laggard firms will be dragged along or suffer the inevitable losses. If some new method of sales promotion proves successful, or if a new concept of employee training lowers costs, competitors must try to match the best performance or suffer the consequences. The general effect of competition, combined with a flexible and responsive price system, is to force firms to perform their managerial and firm functions in the most efficient manner possible. The rapid feedback of information from the market tends to correct quickly any laggard performance.

A key point in restricting competition is the restriction of this feedback of performance. An irate letter from a captive customer of an electric power monopoly can be ignored, since the customer may have no alternatives. The excess production of a firm with a guaranteed market at a given price piles up as unwanted inventory. The fact that a given service of a monopoly railroad has long since failed to cover even direct costs of operating it may not be discovered for decades, since total revenues may be large enough to hide this fact.[12] The world is full of incompetent managers who to date have been able to hide their incompetence from the world, since the world lacks the information to discover what really is going on.

A similar problem arises in an economy characterized by hidden or overt price inflation and excess demand for goods and services. In this type of sellers' market, inept firms can often prosper because all outputs are so badly needed. If costs are high, demand pushes prices still higher. Many Marxist countries have experienced this problem in consumer goods indus-

---

[11] Farmer, "Motor Vehicle Transport Pricing in Lebanon," *The Journal of Industrial Economics*, Vol. VII, No. 3, July, 1959, pp. 199–205.

[12] For one extreme example, see British Railways Board, *The Reshaping of British Railways* (London: Her Majesty's Stationery Office, 1963), 148 pp.

tries, where perpetual shortages of almost all kinds of goods have enabled very incompetent firms to survive unnoticed for decades. Developing economies with inflationary problems, such as Brazil and Argentina, have also experienced similar problems for many years.

No presently utilized control system in productive management has yet proved as effective as the simple mechanism of competition. This problem has bothered firms ranging from oligopolists in capitalist countries through state owned public utilities in nominally capitalist countries to Marxist planners in monolithic economies. A firm manager or a state planner may make a critical error, such as failing to include enough production of steel of a given size and grade to cover all requirements in the plan. The error need not be so blatant—the steel production may be planned—but far back in the planning process a clerk may have failed to include, say, the needed brick to make the new coke ovens to make the steel. As production for the planned period gets under way, this shortage of steel begins to appear. Managers, unable to get needed inputs, fail to make necessary deliveries to other firms, who in turn fail to produce up to plan. The information necessary to make corrections may take months or years to accumulate, given the complexities both of the total productive process and of the planning system.[13] In the meantime, firm managers are performing badly, and no system exists to prevent them from doing otherwise.

More dramatic errors arise when capital resources are put in the wrong place. Plenty of mistakes are made in capital investment in any system, given the usual uncertainties and lack of necessary knowledge; but in the planned system, errors are perpetuated through lack of any mechanism to call a halt at the proper time. State railroads are constructed at a cost of millions of dollars, and operated at large losses, but they are rarely abandoned, while similar private systems, perhaps erroneously planned, are closed quickly.[14]

Virtually any combination of free price competition and state planning will work, in the sense that a country can produce enough to feed, clothe, and house its population at some minimal level. Moreover, there are wealthy capitalist and relatively wealthy Marxist countries, just as very poor countries in each category exist. While it may be true that a system allowing maximum managerial flexibility may be *potentially* more efficient than a totally planned system, the efficiency problems of any society are very important here. Questions of knowledge, subsystem optimization, measurement, uncertainty, and goals determine in large part whether or not a given system will function better than another. A totally planned system, with rigid controls on managerial behavior, which has a highly educated, well motivated population seeking relatively simple and straightforward eco-

---

[13] See Richman, *Soviet Management, op. cit.,* chaps. 1, 6, 8, and 12, for a more detailed discussion of this point.

[14] See James N. Sites, *Quest for Crisis* (New York: Simmons-Boardman Publishing Corp., 1963), particularly pp. 69–76, 164–174.

nomic goals, will probably be more efficient than a totally capitalistic country populated by largely illiterate workers and managers. The question of which economic organization a country has *is* important, but it is far from the only relevant question.

**Evaluation Techniques.** One can usually describe fairly accurately the kind of economic system a country has. Interrelated with this system is the legal-political complex of constraints which attempts to give practical substance to the philosophy embedded in economic practice. Once such a system is described, the problem is to determine how it affects the internal management of productive enterprises. As a general rule, any general system feature which forces managers to perform their jobs more effectively is desirable, while any pressure which enables managers to perform badly in an undetected fashion is considered undesirable. A few of the key points which lead to more effective managerial performance are as follows:

1. *Input Controls.* A country which for any reason attempts to force input uses into patterns which are uneconomic is potentially in trouble in its managerial behavior and effectiveness. Capital rationing, through plans, special laws, or tradition, has the effect of putting this productive factor into the wrong places, with direct effects on production, finance, and marketing functions of the firm. Some firms will have too much capital and will tend to waste it (in the economic sense), while others will be capital starved.

Rent controls, traditional utilization of land, and other forms of land rationing will have the same effect. Laws governing working conditions and wages which force wages either up or down will also tend to distort resource allocation and make firms less efficient than they might otherwise be. Special discriminatory taxes on particular inputs (such as high property taxes, social security taxes, or excises or tariffs on capital equipment) also will tend to misallocate resources.

It should be emphasized that there is no particular ethical content in the above points. A nation may feel strongly that workers should be protected from dangerous jobs and be paid a minimum rate which is above the economic equilibrium. This type of legislation would have the effect of making labor more expensive, and firms would tend to use less of this factor than of the others. If the extra cost of labor is quite high, the usual result is unemployment. If the country prefers (ethically) some unemployment to "exploitation" of labor, there is no quarrel with the ethics involved—the point here is that in such a case resources will be poorly allocated, and productive enterprises will be somewhat less efficient than they otherwise would be. Here is a problem of trade-off between social justice and economic efficiency, which every country must face.

Given the typical lack of knowledge and uncertainty about production, it is usually true that some interference with input prices often has little economic effect. If the "true" value of labor is $1.15 per hour, and minimum wage legislation sets the rate at $1.25, little damage would be done in most instances; but if the "true" price of capital is 12 percent, while legislation or rule sets the maximum at 2 percent, considerable damage is likely to occur. The problem is always one of degree. Perhaps most countries tend, for social reasons, to overprice labor somewhat[15] and underprice capital,[16] resulting in considerable overt or hidden unemployment in productive enterprises—which again is a trade-off for social, as compared to economic efficiency.

**2. *Output Controls.*** The more distorted the pattern of outputs is in a society, the less likely it is that the economy will be efficient. In this case, such controls as those over prices of goods and services, either making such items more or less expensive than they otherwise might be, tend to distort firms' output patterns and make them relatively less efficient. Legal restrictions governing size of output also have similar effects, since the typical result is to have too little of some items and too much of others. Here, again, values are important—a country may well decide that it *wants* too much milk and too little whiskey.

**3. *Firm and Personal Entry Controls.*** Most governments have some control over the entry of firms into given industries and of individuals into given jobs or professions.[17] The result of such controls is to create shortages of either competitors or outputs in some sectors, as well as to make some kinds of labor more expensive that it otherwise would be.

Such restrictions have direct and important effects on management. The marketing policies of an American airline which because of legal restrictions need not fear new, direct competition is considerably different than it would be otherwise. Pricing and sales promotion tend to be quite different than they might be if potential new competition were a serious threat. Personnel and staffing policies are directly affected by various laws and regulations governing the supply of such workers as medical doctors, plumbers, mechanics, electricians, accountants, and many others. The need to pay higher prices for such skilled men results in changes in combinations of factor inputs, compensation, training, and other factors.

**4. *Planning Efficiency.*** In countries where the government takes a substantial direct role in the economy, it is possible to have quite efficient firm operations, if the planning efficiency of the central planners is high. If feedback mechanisms designed to show discrepancies from efficient opera-

---

[15] Hence, social legislation of all sorts tends to make labor costs rise. See Eugene Staley, *The Future of Underdeveloped Countries* (rev. ed.; New York: Frederick A. Praeger, Inc., 1961), pp. 245–246. See also Dudley Seers, "The Mechanism of an Open Price Economy" (Paper No. 47, Yale University Economic Growth Center, 1964).

[16] Capital underpricing is also notable in such international lending institutions as the World Bank and the International Finance Corporation, as well as in international loans by individual governments. Interest rates here rarely rise above 6 percent, although on a purely economic and commercial basis they should be much higher. See Murray D. Bryce, *Industrial Development* (New York: McGraw-Hill Book Company, 1960), pp. 173–212.

[17] For examples of such controls and their economic impact see R. N. Farmer and H. H. Kassarjian, "The Right to Compete," *California Management Review*, Vol. VI, No. 1, fall, 1963, pp. 61–68.

tions are well planned and executed, if controls are adequate to inform planners about deviations, and if both planners and managers are skilled and conscientious, then the economy will function better than if control and direction are absent. Note that this is related directly to the various educational constraints, since such planning efficiency depends quite directly on how good the various personnel trying to run the economic system are.[18]

**5. *Other Rules and Traditions Affecting the Economy.*** In some countries, workers rarely move from the place where they were born; in others, they easily and quickly move thousands of miles to take new jobs. Some countries have intricate traditional land use and tenure patterns,[19] while others treat land much like any other kind of asset. Every country has its traditional "sacred cows," which tend to use up resources and to make the economy less efficient, by making managers of productive enterprises less able to utilize the inputs available in the most effective manner possible. In some countries, such sacred cows are trivial, in that they have relatively little effect on productive efficiency; in others, they are key constraints. One can evaluate such constraints at least in a general manner, though seldom as precisely as might be desired.

**General Comments on Economic Systems.** This constraint is interrelated to a substantial extent with the other economic, legal-political, educational, and sociological constraints. In the illustrations noted above, it is easy to see how these other constraints in part determine the kind of general economic framework a country may have; but the framework itself tends to influence directly all of the managerial and firm functions, making the firms more or less efficient than they otherwise might be.

A key problem here is subsystem optimization. Most individuals in a society see the society in terms of their own welfare and well-being. "If I am prosperous, the country must be prosperous," is a quite common line of reasoning. Hence, one feels that while restrictions on labor inputs generally are bad, restriction of his own kind of inputs is generally good. (We are, of course, convinced that one needs a Ph.D. degree to teach properly in a university; but the various trade union restrictions on plumbers' supply and output are terrible—an obvious waste of economic resources!) Similarly, firm managers are convinced that restrictions designed to lessen *their* competitive problems are sound, preventing destructive competition and chaotic markets.

The usual result of such attitudes is a morass of restrictions, even in economies which proudly proclaim their competitive virtues (such as the United States). Certain favored firms and individuals are protected, with the usual result of relative managerial ineffectiveness. Every country, how-

---

[18] Richman, *op. cit.*, pp. 94–107.

[19] See, for example, Thomas F. Carroll, "The Land Reform Issue in Latin America," in Albert O. Hirshman, ed., *Latin American Issues* (New York: The Twentieth Century Fund, 1961), pp. 161–201.

ever, has its own set of restrictions; and their relative impact can be evaluated independently. Such evaluation is important; hence, this particular discussion of the problems of economic systems in general is important.

Countries all over the world are perpetually tinkering with their economic systems to try to make them work more efficiently. Underlying this experimentation is the notion that if the general economic framework can be set up properly, managers of productive enterprises will be able to manage their firms more effectively, producing higher levels of real income per capita.

The economic systems of Marxist states in particular are going through a major crisis of change. The structure of traditional Marxist economies has long been that of a centrally planned state where all resources were government owned and where managers received their key instructions from planners above them. As long as the product mix of these societies was relatively simple, this sort of direct planned economy worked reasonably well. The Soviet Union also was in a good position to try such an experiment because of its size and resulting minimal interaction with the rest of the world. If the local Marxist economy is closely interlocked with events beyond its borders, planning is made much more difficult.

In recent years, as the more developed Marxist countries have grown and become more complex, the problem of detailed planning for the entire economy has become so complicated as to threaten to swamp the planners. Several consecutive plans in the Soviet Union have had to be canceled because the economy could not meet the demands placed on it. When there are only a few grades of steel to produce, the central planners can possibly lay out intelligible and practical plans; but when the product types expand to the thousands, or even millions, planning errors become so huge as to make the plan unworkable. Consequently, the Soviets are experimenting with a profitability system which will permit profits to be used as a feedback information system to managers. It is hoped that this will enable the managers in consumption goods industries the opportunity to produce for demand, not according to plan. Within the Soviet Union the program has been subject to many attacks as a return to degenerate capitalistic ways, but there appears to be no alternative to some form of reform of the classic and far too rigid Marxist system.[20]

Developing economies also have experimented widely with various kinds of mixed economies. Thus, in India, the state is responsible for many sectors, such as public utilities and most transportation, while private firms have various industrial sectors staked out for them. In intensive capital industries such as steel, there is a combination of mixed and private ownership of enterprises. To date, such systems have not worked very well. In part, this is because it is not yet clear how the public firms are to be

---

[20] Richman, *op. cit.*, pp. 228–252.

controlled, in the sense of rationing to them only necessary inputs. A firm which can turn to government to cover every deficit is in an enviable position from the firm's point of view but may prove quite wasteful and inefficient from society's point of view. Indian public industry has not performed even as well as similar private firms to date, and it remains unproven whether the experiment is the best of all possible worlds.

There is a general tendency to impute too much to any economic system. Implicit assumptions about a system (such as rights of private property) lead to violent condemnation or support, without much reasoned analysis of actual possibilities. Thus, it is common in the United States to find criticism of Marxist states on the rather irrational grounds that no Communist country can possibly produce anything efficiently. Similarly, Marxists cannot see anything useful about any capitalist country, simply because it is a capitalist country. Persons in countries like India expect economic miracles to occur through economic reorganization, since they originally saw economic organization as being the most important problem the country faced. Other underdeveloped countries have also felt that once key industries were brought under local control, incomes would necessarily jump dramatically.

In reality, major economic changes rarely improve productive efficiency in the short run, and not very often in the long run. The reason is that income streams are generated not from abstract economic organization but from actual production of goods and services at the plant and firm level. A good economic organization can make a manager's job easier, and it can help him become more efficient in the long run; but economic organization cannot substitute for management. Other factors, including all of the constraints discussed in this book, are also important.

Thus, the result of rapid economic organizational change is often disillusionment, since relatively little changes immediately. The century-long dialog between Marxists and capitalistic supporters has often assumed that the ideal system would somehow give ideal results, but this ignores all of the other factors which help create maximum managerial effectiveness.

## CENTRAL BANKING SYSTEM AND MONETARY POLICY

One of the most important problems in efficient management is that of providing credit (i.e., liquid capital) to industrial enterprises. The capital must be provided in the correct amounts to the right people and firms. Everyone is sure that he could use more money; the problem is rationing out scarce resources, expressed in money terms, to the people who will use this asset most efficiently. A second related problem is to control the supply of money in an economy so that there is neither too little nor too much on hand at any time. Too much money will lead to price inflation, as excess money chases scarce goods and services; too little may well lead to deflation and depression, with correspondingly poor overall results.

The basic organizer of the money stream in most economies is the central banking system. Some few countries manage without central banks, but they still have some institution in the economy that performs traditionally accepted central banking functions.[21]

A major central banking task is to control the supply of money in the economy. The central bank has various tools to accomplish this task, typically including the right to rediscount commercial bank paper, to set reserve requirements for commercial banks, to create money or destroy it, and to set interest rates.[22] Often other agencies may have some of these functions to perform, but in any economy they must be performed by some one. Only in the most primitive barter economies can the problem of monetary control be ignored.

The manner in which the central bank (or similar institution) performs its duties has a direct bearing on the way in which management is performed in industrial enterprises. Poor planning about the available supply of money can lead to unnecessary crises and depressions, causing firms literally to be destroyed or to operate vastly below potential plant capacity. The history of the U.S. before 1913 is full of such events. Economic panics were caused in part by the inability of the monetary system to perform efficiently in the sense of expanding or contracting the money supply when required.[23] The Federal Reserve Act of 1913 alleviated this trouble in part,[24] although the question of timing monetary expansions and contractions remains. It is significant that the 1913 act, together with various modifications since that time, have been widely debated by business leaders, bankers, and economists, since it is clearly realized that the manner in which the central banking system does its job has a very direct bearing on the general health of the economy.

It is easy to find examples of impacts on management effectiveness by operations of the central banking system. Suppose that, for reasons connected with an international trade deficit, the central bank decides to contract the money supply.[25] It can do this in several ways: interest rates can

---

[21] For a general review of American central banking, see Harold Barger, *Money, Banking and Public Policy* (Chicago: Rand McNally & Co., 1962), pp. 142–197. For foreign central bank operations, see Peter G. Fousek, *Foreign Central Banking: The Instruments of Monetary Policy* (New York: Federal Reserve Bank of New York, 1957), 116 pp.

[22] Hart and Kenen, *op. cit.*, pp. 86–106.

[23] C. W. Wright, *Economic History of the United States* (New York: McGraw-Hill Book Company, 1941), pp. 446–483, 817–883.

[24] Barger, *op. cit.*, pp. 149–158.

[25] The complex rationale underlying this action is covered in Charles P. Kindleberger, *International Economics* (3d ed.; Homewood, Ill.: Richard D. Irwin, Inc., 1963), pp. 333–382, 501–537.

be raised (i.e., the rediscount rate is raised by central bank fiat); open market operations can be performed (i.e., government bonds are sold in the open market to investors, and the proceeds are allowed to stagnate in the central bank vault); or the reserve requirements of commercial banks can be raised so that their loan potential is curbed. The decrease of money in circulation will mean that less is available for loans to business, which will have a very direct effect on business planning, organization, and staffing. It may also lead to less demand for consumer and capital goods, with direct effects on marketing and production policies. More than one sales manager has been fired and his department reorganized because the central bank was busily contracting demand for labor and this resulted in direct impacts on staffing policies.[26] As aggregate demand shrinks in recessions, sales strategies, product lines, production runs, inventory policies, and similar functions must change to reflect these external changes beyond the control of internal management.

The usual general aim of central bank policy is to try to stabilize the economy by avoiding either excess demand, boom, and eventual collapse, on the one hand, or, on the other hand, recession through deficient demand. International stability and full use of the country's resources may also be major goals of central bank policy. The banks will try to maintain the value of the country's currency in international markets by the use of appropriate policies at home and the proper manipulation of gold stocks and exchange reserves in international markets.[27] This latter goal may be inconsistent with the former. A country may be enjoying such a boom at home that its firms tend to import too much and export too little, and this can lead to a foreign exchange crisis.[28]

The central bank may have to make some agonizing decisions about decreasing the boom at home and conserving reserves, at the cost of causing a decline in aggregate demand domestically. Failure to do so could result in gold and foreign exchange outflows, leading to currency devaluation. Whatever a central bank may do in such a case will directly and drastically affect productive enterprises. Decreasing demand could cause a firm to become less efficient by restricting the market size; or it could make it more efficient by causing the price of labor, raw materials, or components to decline. Actual results will depend on the export position of firms in a given situation.

In many countries heavily involved in international trade, the central bank authorities may also be constrained in their actions by obligations to

---

[26] See the *Economic Report of the President* (Washington, D.C.: U.S. Government Printing Office, 1960), pp. 9–23, for an indication of how income declines in 1957–58 and increases in 1958–59 influenced total demand for labor and goods.

[27] Kindleberger, *op. cit.*, pp. 597–617.

[28] The United Kingdom in 1964 entered a classic crisis of this sort. Evaluation of the crisis and its direct impact on English business operations was covered closely in *The Economist*, in its issues from October 1964 onwards. See particularly "The Economic Inheritance," *The Economist*, Vol. CCXII, No. 6322, October 24, 1964, pp. 407–410.

other governments (through treaty agreements) or to international institutions. Thus, members of the International Monetary Fund (IMF) or the General Agreement on Trade and Tariffs (GATT) may not be able to follow domestic policies which seem proper and might result in less harm to firms within the country. Currency devaluations, discriminatory exchange rates, and exchange controls can be used only in accordance with the terms of previously agreed commitments to such international bodies governing their use. In a similar manner, member states of such common market organizations as the European Economic Community may be constrained by their commitments to these organizations.[29]

Thus, in late 1964 the United Kingdom faced serious balance of payments difficulties with the rest of the world. Actions taken to alleviate this situation—including a temporary 15 percent duty on all imports, the preparation of drawing rights from the IMF for over $1 billion of foreign currency, the preparation of a borrowing pool from other countries' central banks, and the raising of the central bank discount rate from 5 percent to 7 percent—were selected from other alternatives on the basis of what would be possible, given U.K. international obligations, and what would have favorable (or the least unfavorable) effects on British firms.[30] Such actions affected British firms directly. The temporary duty increase made almost all imports more expensive than domestic products, thus shifting pricing policies and marketing tactics for both domestic and foreign firms. The increase of interest rates tended to make capital more expensive than other inputs, changing production factor input patterns. Here international financial necessities and internal firm policies and problems are directly interlocked. Some central banks or monetary authorities also have the power to control consumer credit directly. Hence, in a period of excess demand, the bank can raise down payment requirements for autos, refrigerators, and similar high cost consumer items.[31] The impact of such credit restrictions on firms' marketing policies and organizations is clear. Since the legislation giving central banks their powers is a domestic matter, there are as many types of central banks as there are countries; however, the general types of monetary and commercial bank controls utilized tend to be roughly the same from country to country.

Perhaps more important than any legislative details is the quality of central bank personnel which determines the quality of money management in the country. The goals of central banking are typically agreed on and clear, but such goals must be accomplished within given institutional

[29] E. Strauss, *Common Sense About the Common Market* (New York: Rinehart and Company, 1958), pp. 92–127.

[30] "Labor Faces its First Major Money Crisis," *Business Week*, November 28, 1964, pp. 29–30.

[31] Peter G. Fousek, *op. cit.*, pp. 69–81. Other types of selective credit controls apply in some countries to different types of productive investments. Thus, in France, export commercial paper has at times had a preferential rate over domestic paper covering similar items.

frameworks by men who must necessarily have a keen appreciation of and ability to forecast often subtle economic events well in advance of their occurrence. Poor timing, moves in the wrong direction, or simple incompetence can cause an economy to fluctuate wildly, bring on heavy depressions or severe inflations, produce periodic foreign exchange crises, and generally create an atmosphere of uncertainty for productive enterprise managers.[32] Questions of timing here can be critical, and the central bank may do all the right things at the wrong times. In the long and sometimes tumultuous history of central banking, virtually every country has had the misfortune to have key decisions made erroneously. The results have ranged from crushing depressions to hyperinflations, with each extreme causing tremendous problems for enterprise managers.

Courage is a real virtue in central banking management also. Many central bank decisions are highly unpopular with business managers. Who wants to end a period of booming prosperity, with demand for one's product rising spectacularly, just because the country happens to be running a relatively small (it seems) foreign trade deficit? Successful central bankers seldom win popularity contests, and they must have internal fortitude in amounts seldom required for more prosaic management positions.

Central banking in purely Marxist countries has a lesser role to play than in capitalistic societies. Capitalistic states typically use a system which will allow close economic control by means of aggregate monetary decisions, leaving most other business decisions to micromanagers; but Marxist states typically are involved in extensive central planning concerning the allocation of resources to productive firms, excluding managers from major policy decisions.[33] Hence, some of the central banks' major powers in a capitalist state become relatively unimportant in a Marxist country.

Even Marxist countries, however, use money and bank accounts extensively; and central banks are required to control this function. The national plan could be well conceived and the country's resource allocation sound; but too much or too little currency available to handle the necessary purchase of goods, services, and labor could result in annoying confusion, waste, and delay in the system—with corresponding impact on firm managerial effectiveness. A well conceived banking system in such an economy acts as an effective control system on firms, which may be piling up cash (or losing it) in great amounts. Too much cash may prove tempting, since *something* can be purchased with it; effective controls here may prove very useful. Conversely, poor controls can lead to enterprise problems in planning, control, and organization.[34] A major part of the central bank's activi-

---

[32] Among other advanced countries, the United States has been severely criticized on this point. See M. Friedman and A. J. Schwartz, *A Monetary History of the United States* (Princeton, N.J.: Princeton University Press, 1963), pp. 676–700.

[33] Alec Nove, *The Soviet Economy* (New York: Frederick A. Praeger, Inc., 1961), pp. 97–114.

[34] Richman, *op. cit.*, pp. 226–227.

ties in such a society involves the careful control and audit of the activities of commercial banks in the country.

Evaluation of central banking in terms of business efficiency is relatively easy. If the country has experienced relatively little price level fluctuation, if the currency holds its value on international markets, if business recessions and booms are relatively mild, if economic growth continues steadily, if productive firms that deserve capital and can use it efficiently can get it, it can be inferred that the central bank is doing an effective job. Not all of these factors are completely under the control of a central bank, as we shall see later; but if such economic stability and efficiency is to occur, it is necessary that the central bank perform efficiently.

This area is one where institutional changes can be made with relative ease. The nature of modern society, with its extreme dependence on money and prices, means that small changes in the legal framework of central banking can often have large impacts on the economy generally. A central bank may not have the power to control the level of commercial bank reserves; giving it this power, which requires only a change in law, can have dramatic effects on the availability of credit in the economy.[35] Since commercial banks usually are few in number and usually subject to intensive and frequent audit, such legislation is easy to enforce, unlike many new business laws. In a Marxist country, a reform in the type and frequency of audits of commercial banks in regard to enterprise accounts could have an equally strong impact on managerial planning and control in the firm, if such audits corrected such discrepancies as the piling up of liquid assets which might have considerable impact on demand for key goods and services.

## FISCAL POLICY

Governments usually account for from 5 percent to 80 percent of all expenditures in an economy. In underdeveloped countries, with poorly developed systems of public administration and management, government expenditures range typically from 5 percent to 15 percent of all expenditures,[36] while in the more developed capitalist and mixed economies the government share ranges from 20 percent to 35 percent.[37] In Marxist countries, where most or all of productive effort is in the government sector, this percentage can run much higher.

---

[35] Arthur I. Bloomfield, "Central Banking in Underdeveloped Countries," In L. S. Ritter, ed., *Money and Economic Activity* (Boston: Houghton Mifflin Company, 1961), pp. 452–453.

[36] Paul Alpert, *Economic Development* (London: Collier-Macmillan, 1963), pp. 143–153.

[37] See Morris A. Copeland, *Trends in Government Financing* (Princeton, N.J.: Princeton University Press, 1961) 210 pp. See also A. T. Peacock and Jack Wiseman, *The Growth of Public Expenditures in the United Kingdom* (Princeton, N.J.: Princeton University Press, 1961), 213 pp., particularly pp. 164–165.

In any case, the government expenditures, both local and national, will commonly be the single largest item of outpayments in the economy. The magnitude of the sum alone has some impact on business effectiveness. A country with a social goal of producing more religious monuments (churches, mosques, and so on) at public expense may divert funds from other types of expenditures into this sector, with corresponding effects on marketing policies and industrial enterprise organization.

If a country has more government expenditures, it is likely that firms producing buildings and materials, armaments, school books and supplies, and similar items will experience more demand than they would in less government oriented economies. Firms producing consumer goods may well experience less total demand, as tax revenues are taken from the private sector to finance these government expenditures. Thus, in the United States, the publishing of school textbooks is regarded as an important growth industry, since local governments are willing to obtain tax money and spend it in this sector. Marketing and production plans of such publishing companies are quite different than they would be if these government expenditures were not made. Massive highway and other public works programs in many countries, financed from tax revenues, have led to large growth in sales for contractors, firms manufacturing tractors and other earthmoving equipment, and cement companies, at the expense of consumer goods manufacturers. Construction equipment firms pay special attention to government contracts under consideration in planning their marketing efforts, since a significant portion of their sales depends on this factor.

Stability in expenditures is also relevant. In countries whose public budget is stable and consists largely of customary items which vary little from year to year firms are affected quite differently than they are in a country where the budget fluctuates widely and is spent on different items from year to year. Examples of both situations exist in the United States. The defense budget has varied remarkably in the past two decades for compelling reasons of national defense, ranging from a high of almost 50 percent of GNP in the war years 1943–44 to less than 5 percent of GNP in 1949. Moreover, even when the amount spent was stable, the items purchased were not. The cutting of large expenditures on certain weapons produced in a single city has had extremely powerful effects on the city's economy, affecting many firms not even directly associated with the defense spending.[38] Conversely, other cities, benefiting from the same shift in that they serve as locations for the new factories producing the new items, have boomed at the same time, with equally powerful effects on firms directly and indirectly involved. Many a small businessman, producing a service used by plant workers, has been literally wiped out by such shifts, while

---

[38] Richard R. Nelson, "The Impact of Arms Reduction on Research and Development," *American Economic Review*, Vol. LII, No. 2, May 1963, pp. 435–446.

others have prospered. Such shifts have major effects on firm planning and organization.

Expenditures by local governments in the United States for education, on the other hand, have remained quite stable, rising as the number of students rose.[39] Firms serving this market (such as sellers of textbooks, school classroom equipment, and similar products) have had much more certainty in their market than those firms specializing in defense items. Hence, the planning process of a firm in this educational sector tends to be markedly different from that of one in the defense area.

A second factor in fiscal policy is who spends the money. If the country is highly centralized politically, most of the public funds will be spent by the central government, and those firms selling goods and services to government will be affected by this fact. Their marketing organization will vary significantly from that in a country where a decentralized government allows local government units to control the expenditures of the bulk of the money.

The effect of such fiscal policies can be seen by examining the market organization of firms selling products mainly to local government units, such as school boards, in the United States. Here, the company has literally thousands of customers, often with strikingly different preferences. The products, as well as the selling organization, must be tailored accordingly. On the other hand, a firm specializing in defense products has one customer—the Defense Department—and its selling organization is built accordingly. The situation would be far different in France, where the central government exercises much greater control over schools than in the United States. It would be even more different in a country where most education was not even in the public sphere but, rather, was handled by various private agencies, such as charitable bodies and religious organizations.

Governments, or their closely controlled or owned central banks, have the power to create money simply by expanding bank deposits, selling bonds to their central bank, or printing banknotes.[40] They also have the option of raising money by taxation or selling government bonds to the public. The manner in which they obtain the funds they spend has a direct and immediate impact on the economy and, through various tax policies utilized, on business firms.[41] Tax law and its effects were analyzed more thoroughly in Chapter 8, on government and legal factors; but it is to be noted that the manner in which taxes are levied will have a direct and

---

[39] Per capita expenditures have also risen in recent decades. See T. W. Schultz, *The Economic Value of Education* (New York: Columbia University Press, 1963), pp. 20–37.

[40] See R. L. Heilbroner and Peter L. Bernstein, *A Primer on Government Spending* (New York: Random House, Inc., 1963) for a lucid discussion of this point.

[41] A discussion of this problem in the United States in 1964 is found in Edmund K. Faltermayer, "The Next Turn in Taxes," *Fortune*, Vol. LXX, No. 6, December, 1964, p. 105.

important impact on internal firm management. A high tax on corporate net profits, for example, will tend to make firms aware that marginal expenditures are paid for in part by the government and will cause them to alter budgets and planning. Thus, if a tax is set at 50 percent of net income, any extra dollar of legitimate expense incurred by the firm will in effect be half paid by the government. Under such conditions, an extra advertising campaign, or an additional entertainment allowance for executives, will be more easily permitted than in a situation where taxes are levied on other items.

Tax policy will also have the effect of altering resource allocation in an economy, with corresponding direct impact on various firms. Hence, a high tax on watches will reduce their sales and will cause firms in this business to be smaller than they otherwise might be. Tax policy in any country will reflect in part the values of the culture: high excises on whiskey, tobacco, and similar items in part reflect the desire for revenue; but they reflect also the feeling that consumption of such goods should be discouraged. Producers of such goods suffer accordingly.

Almost any tax levied on anyone or anything in the economy will have some effects of this sort, with corresponding impacts on productive enterprises. In general, a country which heavily taxes consumption (through sales taxes, excises, and import duties) will tend to encourage investment, whereas a country taxing potential investment heavily (through corporate income taxes, taxes on savings, and taxes on capital) will achieve the reverse effect. The impact on various firms in the economy is obvious, although, given the complexities of a modern economy, the actual impact of a given tax may be hard to trace. Economists have frequently debated the effect of a given tax, often without clear results.[42]

If a country obtains its money through money creation, the impact on the economy will be substantially different than if it had financed its expenditures through taxation or through selling bonds to citizens. A balanced budget (where revenues equal expenditures) will alter demand in the sense noted above, but it will not create additional purchasing power. A surplus budget, where the surpluses are held by the government, will have the effect of reducing aggregate demand in the economy, to the detriment of businessmen. Money which might have been spent on goods and services by someone in the economy is now taxed away and not spent at all. Given the fact that any economy may be having some excess demand at any time, such a dampening effect is sometimes desirable; however, in a period of depression, when excess resources are available for employment by productive firms, such a policy may reduce demand still further, causing considerable distress for companies.[43]

---

[42] E. R. A. Seligman, "Introduction to the Shifting and Incidence of Taxation," in *Readings in the Economics of Taxation* (Homewood, Ill.: Richard D. Irwin, Inc., 1959), pp. 202–213.

[43] Heilbroner and Bernstein, *op. cit.*, pp. 33–54.

A more common government policy in the modern world is for the government to spend more than it receives in taxes.[44] The deficit can be covered by the creation of government demand deposits or by simply printing banknotes. Deficits of this type compete for goods and services along with other types of money, possibly leading to excess demand and price inflation. The government can always win in this game, since it alone can create more money; and a depressingly familiar pattern observable in many countries in the past thirty years has been rapid price inflation caused by such excess government purchases of goods and services.[45] Note that the role of the central bank is critical here as well. Government deficits can be offset by appropriate central bank deflationary policies if the central bank is strong and independent. If it is an appendage to the finance minister's office, it may be unable to stem the tide. Here personalities, managerial abilities, and institutional structures of both government spending units and central banks are critical.

The interwoven complex of central bank activities and policy and those of the governmental spending units thus forms a critical part of the general control of price levels, recessions, and booms in the economy. The effects on enterprise managers, in the form of price changes for raw materials, labor, and other needed goods, as well as the demand for their products and services, is considerable; and such changes have critical impacts on the internal operations of the firm. An enterprise struggling to survive in a depression, with inadequate demand for its products, excessive competition from rivals, and depressed profits, is operated in a quite different manner from a firm operating in an economic environment characterized by strong and rising demand, stable prices, and less destructive competition. The way in which monetary and fiscal policy is controlled (or ignored) by the central bank and the government has tremendous effects on internal firm management.

A point often ignored by business managers is that monetary and fiscal policy can be managed. The range of possibilities open to government and banking officials in an economy is greater than generally realized by many managers, preoccupied with their own internal managerial problems. A common attitude of managers who have successfully managed in the given environment is that the government should do nothing in this sector, but they forget that to do nothing is as much policy as some positive (or negative) action.[46]

---

[44] Thus, both local and national governments in the United States operate at chronic deficits. See Copeland, *op. cit.*, pp. 19–63.

[45] For American experience during recent times, see Friedman and Schwartz, *op. cit.*, pp. 546–638. For Italian experience, as one foreign example, see Shepard B. Clough, *The Economic History of Modern Italy* (New York: Columbia University Press, 1964), pp. 280–297.

[46] Some managers are activists in this sense, however. American organizations such as the C.E. D. frequently advocate positive government action to alleviate existing problems. See Monson, *op. cit.*, pp. 25–29.

No society is perfect, however, and every country has economic problems from time to time. Economists, concerned with problems of price stability, income fluctuations, booms, and recessions, have long studied such problems; and they are capable of giving quite good advice to finance ministers and central bankers about such questions.[47] Traditionally conservative businessmen thus find themselves on the outside looking in when serious monetary and fiscal problems face the nation; but just as war is too important to be left to the generals, fiscal and monetary policy is too important to be left to the politicians and economists, since the results of any policy (including doing absolutely nothing) have tremendous impacts on internal firm management. Exploring the complexities of modern economic analysis is well worth the effort, if for no other reason than to learn to analyze the effect of such policies on the managers' own firm.[48]

The very complexity of fiscal policy makes evaluation in business terms difficult, and even skilled economists differ sharply in their views about the impact of given policies; however, if the net result of a country's fiscal policy is to create a situation which is stable, which does not distort resource allocation unduly, and which helps create an economic environment in which firms can plan with reasonable accuracy, the policy can be judged relatively successful. If, on the other hand, the country is characterized by extreme resource allocation problems caused by government spending, if prices rise or fall erratically, if government spending enhances booms and deepens depressions, this factor may prove to have a large negative effect on efficient firm management.

Marxist countries have a somewhat different kind of problem in monetary and fiscal policy than capitalistic countries. The government makes, by plan, virtually all of the investment expenditures, and the private sector uses only consumer goods. Hence, much of the complicated incentives and disincentives necessary to get desired investment in a capitalist state are unnecessary; but the problem is far from easy, since the state must somehow extract from consumers the sum equal to the amount invested each year.

Consider a situation where the total value of output is 200 billion units of money, 80 billion of which represents investment and 120 billion of which represents consumption. The figures noted are obtained from the economic plan, which states in physical units what is desired. This list of units is then converted to money figures. The reason it is worth 200 billion units of money is that its cost (in labor) is this much, which means that if each worker were paid what he is worth, the total wage bill would be 200 billion units of money. Only 120 billion is intended for consumption,

---

[47] This advisory relationship is formalized in the United States by the Council of Economic Advisors, which was set up in 1946 with the specific intention (among others) of giving the President professional economic advice.

[48] Recognition of this point by American businessmen has led to the hiring of substantially greater numbers of professional economists by private enterprise. At present, over 10 percent of all new professional economists are hired by such firms, as compared to many fewer in earlier years. See Francis M. Boddy, "The Demand for Economists," *American Economic Review*, Vol. LII, No. 2, May 1962, pp. 503–508.

however; and unless 80 billion is taxed away from consumers in some way, the result will be either price inflation or shortages of consumer goods. The state could always create enough new money through its central bank to buy its share of the output, but to create an additional 80 billion units of money again would mean price inflation.

The usual way that Marxist states drain off this excess purchasing power is through turnover taxes. In effect, prices of goods are raised above cost, and the excess is put in the treasury, to be used to purchase investment goods. To do this properly, the state would have to know a great deal about demand for every possible consumer good, in order to place exactly the right tax on each item. If the tax were too high, too little would be sold, and surpluses would accumulate (remember that consumption goods are produced not according to market demand but according to plan). If the tax were too low, demand would be too high, and shortages would occur. The Soviet Union and other Marxist countries have never been able in practice to sop up all excess purchasing power the way it is done in theory, and Marxist countries have had inflations quite similar to those in capitalist countries.[49]

Another important factor in Marxist countries is that monetary restraint rarely prevents production. Productive enterprises have budgets approved in the plan, and the central bank makes funds available to the firms to finance purchases; but if the firm overruns its budget, it rarely is forced to curtail production. New funds are usually obtained. The result is further inflationary pressure, since, if this process is widespread, the effect is large creation of new money. In societies where production is valued more than anything else, monetary restraints are likely to prove relatively ineffective, except fortuitously.

The same kind of inflation can occur in state firms in mixed economies. Cost estimates are overrun, and the firm appeals to the state bank for more funds. To deny funds to the firm might hinder critical production, and they usually are granted. Again, the result is to create more money and lead potentially to price inflation.

## ECONOMIC STABILITY

### Price Stability

An economic system may be said to have price stability when various indices of price changes (such as consumer goods prices, wholesale prices, agricultural prices, etc.) tend to remain stable over long periods of time.[50] Perfect stability is not necessary here; small positive or negative movements

---

[49] Robert W. Campbell, *Soviet Economic Power* (Boston: Houghton Mifflin Company, 1960), pp. 148–152, gives a description of this process.

[50] Stability in price indices is a very relative concept, and warnings are in order about the looseness with which modern price series (such as the U.S. BLS index of consumer prices) are used. See Frederick A. Ekeblad, *The Statistical Method in Business* (New York: John Wiley & Sons, Inc., 1962), pp. 692–730.

of up to 1 percent or 2 percent per year are regarded as reasonably normal, given the complex price making procedures in a modern economy. In most industrialized countries, price indices of this type have varied historically, even in stable periods, as much as 3 percent per year for short periods and have had average movements of as much as 2 percent per year over decades.[51]

Table 10–1 indicates the price stability in selected countries in recent years. No country in the group has had declining prices. The last major deflationary movement in the world occurred in the early 1930's, and the allied economic misadventures of that era suggest that it will probably be the last.

TABLE 10–1

INDICES OF MONEY VALUE IN SELECTED COUNTRIES, 1952–62

| Country | Money Value (1952 = 100) | | Annual Average Depreciation |
|---|---|---|---|
| | 1952 | 1962 | |
| Ceylon............ | 100 | 94 | 0.6% |
| Venezuela........ | 100 | 93 | 0.7 |
| Canada.......... | 100 | 90 | 1.1 |
| U.S.A............ | 100 | 88 | 1.3 |
| India............ | 100 | 79 | 2.3 |
| Netherlands...... | 100 | 78 | 2.4 |
| U.K............. | 100 | 75 | 2.9 |
| Japan........... | 100 | 72 | 3.2 |
| Mexico.......... | 100 | 62 | 4.7 |
| Israel........... | 100 | 46 | 7.5 |
| Brazil........... | 100 | 9 | 21.5 |
| Bolivia.......... | 100 | 1 | 35.2 |

Source: "Currency Values Around the World Continues to Drop," *International Management*, November, 1963, p. 27.

It is fairly common in the modern era for industrial firms to anticipate price increases annually over long periods of time and to adjust their planning accordingly. One example of this is the fairly common price escalation clause in contracts covering long term, complicated projects. Firms constructing dams, power plants, factories, mills, or other projects which will take years to complete may insist on increased payments if price increases at a later date cause their costs to rise. Another common adjustment to inflation is the wage contract which calls for increase in wage rates according to specified changes in the cost of living price index. A firm laying out long term plans for any industrial project in the modern world now virtually has to take into account some price changes upwards.

Price indices are weighted averages of many kinds of commodities, and it is not true that all prices increase. Firms cannot assume that every

---

[51] See Wright, *op. cit.*, pp. 218–223, 473, 547, 968–969, 1003–1004, for historical American examples of price fluctuations.

possible item they buy will be more expensive in the following year. One area in which prices have not increased to any extent in the United States in recent years is agriculture. An industrial firm using major agricultural inputs may actually find its prices lower now than fifteen years ago. Some raw materials and metals also have not increased much in price since the Korean War (1950–53), and many are still below peaks reached at that time. In fact, the American wholesale price index has advanced less than 1 percent in the period 1958–65.

It is also true that price level changes can be quite difficult to measure. Conceptual difficulties in measurement are particularly difficult in periods when quality changes are occurring at a rapid pace, or when the pattern of purchases is shifting. One can be sure that a 1965 Ford costs more than a 1915 model; but it is not clear that even the same product is being compared, given the qualitative differences in the two autos. Similarly, if the price of coal rises rapidly, but consumers have shifted to the use of natural gas, it is not clear how to measure the true price change.

Price stability in an economy depends largely on the monetary and fiscal policies being followed by governments. In the modern world, where government deficits and printing press money are common, the general trend of prices, if anything, is up; and considerable concern is expressed in most economies most of the time about such inflationary pressures. Proper monetary and fiscal policies can go far to minimize this impact.

There are, however, other factors causing prices to shift radically. Open economies typically export a substantial portion of their output, and changes in demand overseas can cause major price changes. Underdeveloped economies with one or two crop economies are particularly vulnerable to such changes.[52] Hence, in 1964, Malaysia boomed because the price of tin was extremely high. This price is determined externally, and the Malaysian economy must simply adjust to this fact. Colombia in 1960 suffered because the price of coffee was low, but in 1964 it boomed because the price was high. Such external fluctuations in key prices have significant effects on local incomes, changing demand drastically and causing other prices to shift. In a similar manner, changes in prices of key imports can cause price indices to change sharply.

Prices and price indices can change for a variety of reasons only loosely connected with monetary and fiscal policy. Crop failures, strikes, natural catastrophes—such as fires, floods, and earthquakes—and wars have often caused supply shortages and rising prices in the past.[53] Extraordinarily good weather conditions have led to bumper crops and price collapses as well.

---

[52] Benjamin Higgins, *Economic Development* (New York: W. W. Norton & Company, Inc., 1959), pp. 345–383.

[53] One classic example of this type of price behavior occurred in 1956, immediately after the closing of the Suez Canal. Tanker charter rates increased sixfold in three months. R. S. Nielsen, *Oil Tanker Economics* (Bremen: Weltschiffahrts-Archiv, 1959), pp. 124–125.

This type of price change normally affects only a few prices, but the effects percolate over to other prices as well. In an agricultural country whose major crop is largely exported, a key crop failure may reduce income to growers, causing declining demand for imports and domestic production of both capital and consumer goods. Industries dependent on raw materials such as soybeans or cotton clearly have direct interest in the prices of these commodities, and sharp increases or decreases in them will lead to changes in textile or margarine prices as well.

In spite of careful monetary policy, most countries have relatively large stocks of money on hand at all times, in the form of bank deposits, banknotes, and coins in the hands of the public. Sudden changes in attitudes, such as that caused by threat of war, can cause rapid dishoardings of cash, resulting in increased aggregate demand and higher prices. Expectations of price declines can lead to increased hoarding of cash, declining aggregate demand, and falling prices. No country can manage its affairs so well as to eliminate such psychological effects, but sound policy can probably alleviate the worst of such situations.

Business managers generally prefer stable prices to fluctuating ones, since stability here removes one major uncertainty of management. In cases where prices do fluctuate, business risks are greater, and the firm must adjust to this fact. Some firms using raw materials the prices of which do fluctuate wildly have to set up special purchasing sections to engage in hedging and arbitrage activities to alleviate the price fluctuation risk.[54] Here the impact on organization is clear. Planning in a situation of price uncertainty is, or may be, completely different from planning with price stability.

Large industrial firms are accustomed to performing long run planning in many phases of their operations. The more unstable prices may be over the long term, the more difficult such planning becomes. Consider an integrated oil company with a 50 million barrel reserve within the United States. At present prices, this reserve may be worth $150 million; but if prices may rise or fall sharply, how can this firm plan efficient utilization of its reserves? If it expected the price to be $10.00 a barrel in five years, one plan would be feasible; if the price were to be $2.00, a completely different plan would be relevant. In this case, the entire future of the firm might depend on a price (or prices) which has to be estimated some years in advance. The more certain the firm could be that some price pattern would prevail the more easily and more efficiently it could plan.

*Price stability* normally refers to prices of goods and services, but other kinds of prices are relevant to the firm. Labor costs are one kind of price of considerable relevance to the firm—as are prices for money and foreign exchange. Rapid, erratic changes in the foreign exchange rate or in interest rates can lead to substantial impacts on the firm's financial planning, while

---

[54] See Gerald Gold, *Modern Commodity Futures Trading* (New York: Commodity Research Bureau, 1959), pp. 6–11, 112–149.

shifting labor costs have staffing implications. The continuous rise in the price of new college graduates in the United States has led to extensive changes in staffing policies of many companies. Whereas a firm historically could waste such labor because it was relatively cheap, changes must now be made to insure more effective utilization of an expensive resource.[55]

The most disturbing impact on firms stems from extreme price inflation or deflation in the economy. When prices rise by over 10 percent per year, the company is faced with the problem that at any future date inputs will cost more than they now do. Moreover, inventories of finished goods will be more valuable than they now are. Hence, the inventory policies of firms tend to change sharply in such a position, which directly influences the planning function. Enterprises will buy large inventories of inputs when this is possible, and they will produce for finished goods inventory as well. In effect, they will try to stay away from cash (the depreciating asset) in order to hold things (the appreciating assets). Where capital goods prices are also rising rapidly, they will tend to overinvest in assets as well, since failure to do so will raise the cost of investment later. Such scrambles for things, instead of money, by many firms will cause still more pressure on prices, encourage speculation, and increase risks for the firm. The impact of such a situation on internal management can be profound.

This problem is particularly acute in smaller countries where many items must be imported. As inflation proceeds, the value of the country's currency in relation to other currencies begins to decline, raising the price of imports rapidly. Speculators, seeing the decline, can force the currency still lower, while capital flight may also begin to present a problem.

A furniture manufacturer in Brazil in the recent inflationary period thus tried to build up his inventories as much as he could by borrowing from banks. As might be expected, in this kind of situation credit is extremely expensive, ranging in this case to over 30 percent per year; but the rate of inflation in some years was greater than this, leading to inventory appreciation gains in spite of high credit costs. This firm also expanded its finished goods inventory rapidly and profited from higher prices at a later date when the items were finally sold. The firm delayed payments of bills as much as possible, since paying later meant paying less in real terms. As time passed, this firm's management spent more time speculating with price fluctuations than in performing more valid managerial work; but the rate of return continued to rise as the inflation continued.

In such cases, the end of inflation can be very painful. Even a slowing of the rate of inflation can cause illiquidity in many firms as their anticipated capital gains are not realized. Countries trying to taper off their inflation rates in recent years have found that the cost includes many bankruptcies, the writing off of many dubious inventory assets, and similar

---

[55] New college graduates at Indiana University with a B.S. in Business received an average of $514 per month in 1964. Average income of factory workers in the United States at that time was $104 per week.

problems. The variation in rates of inflation can actually increase management uncertainty in planning. If prices are increasing 10 percent a year in a relatively steady manner, this can be taken into account; but if they increase 10 percent this year, 1 percent the next, and 40 percent the following year, the firm may find it almost impossible to lay out long run plans for part of its operations.

Sharp deflation, while rarer in the modern world, can be equally disastrous. Here, the reverse of price inflation occurs; firms scramble to get out of things and into cash. Excess firm liquidity, bare minimum inventories, and enhanced speculation about the further decline in prices occur, with equally bad impacts on internal management. This type of behavior was much more common before 1935, when governments began to use fiscal and monetary policies which eliminated such price deflations; but they still might occur, particularly in open economies when export prices decline drastically.

As a general rule, relatively stable prices will result in greater firm efficiency than will unstable prices. The risks of the productive enterprises are reduced, and they can organize internally in a more efficient manner than they could if prices changed radically through time. Mere price controls to maintain stability will not create this optimum situation, however, since the result of such controls is shortage of the item of which the price is artificially reduced, and such situations may be as disrupting to the firms as actual price changes.[56] In such situations, the enterprise has to organize cadres of expediters, "5 percenters," and similar types to obtain its share of the item in short supply. In Marxist states, where prices are often set arbitrarily, such concealed inflations often occur, and the overall effect on industrial enterprise is disruptive.

### General Economic Stability

Economic stability may be defined as a condition of full utilization of productive factors. That is, there is no unemployment, either of men or of inanimate factors such as capital and land. Clearly, such stability is a relative matter since no economy ever fully utilized every possible factor of production all the time. An unemployment rate of 2 percent or 3 percent is commonly considered an indication of full employment,[57] while most countries have at any time some idle plant capacity and land as well.[58] If, however, a country suffers long periods of substantial unemployment of

---

[56] For a Turkish example, see C. Wickham Skinner, "A Test Case in Turkey," *California Management Review*, Vol. VI, No. 3, spring, 1964, pp. 53–66.

[57] In the United States an unemployment rate as low as 3 percent has not been achieved since 1955. In the United Kingdom, even at the very peak of the 1964 boom, the unemployment rate was 1.5 percent. *The Economist*, Vol. CCXIII, No. 6322, October 24, 1964, p. 418.

[58] After four years of increasing economic activity, the United States in 1964 was utilizing about 88 percent of its manufacturing plant capacity. "Stable Prices," *Wall Street Journal*, November 30, 1964, p. 1.

resources, followed by periods of overutilization of the same resources, it is unstable.

Stability usually implies some consistent growth rate as well. Population and work forces grow, real capital is added, and reclamation projects add to land stocks. A country which has the same per capita income year after year may be stable, but not very desirably so, given possibilities for improvement in incomes through progressively improving management, labor quality, additional capital, and technological developments. Absolute income growth rates have been as high as 8 percent to 10 percent per year for sustained periods in countries such as the Soviet Union, Japan, West Germany, Rumania, and others,[59] while up to 5 percent gains have been achieved by many countries over even longer periods of time.[60] Per capita growth rates depend on birth rates, but gains of from 1 percent to 6 percent are well within the realm of feasibility for most countries.

One important part of economic stability is the occurrence of boom and recession. Usually, but not always, price fluctuations follow such income changes, rising in booms and falling in depressed periods. The same kinds of instabilities discussed in the preceding section on price stability hence have impact here. By the same token, monetary and fiscal policy has much to do with the economic stability of a country. Proper policies well timed can alleviate the bulk of both price and income fluctuation in a country, and all of these factors are closely interrelated.

Economic instability has drastic effects on firms. Recessions lead to unemployment; and firm managers, as the major employees in most economies, bear their share of implied blame for such events. Political actions following major depressions often focus on the firm as the culprit, rightly or wrongly; and the enterprises pay a high price for such instability. Workers are discharged because markets collapse, not because it is desirable to get rid of them; but managers still take the blame in the popular mind.

The effect on staffing and personnel policies of major shifts in demand for products is easy to see. Today the firm may have 3,000 workers; tomorrow, 300. The problems of discharging and restaffing plants is expensive and time consuming, as well as inefficient; and, as noted above, the firm may be

---

[59] The Soviet Union had a growth rate in GNP of from 7 percent to 10 percent per year from 1959 to 1964. See A. Nove, "Prospects for Economic Growth in the Soviet Union," *American Economic Review*, Vol. LIII, No. 2, May 1963, pp. 541–554. Rumania's industrial growth was around 25 percent per year from 1948 to 1952, and 13 percent per year from 1955 to 1960. See J. M. Montias, "Unbalanced Growth in Rumania," *American Economic Review, ibid.*, p. 562. Japan has managed to obtain a GNP growth of 9.1 percent from 1951 to 1960, which topped its 7.4 percent rate from 1931 to 1938. See K. Ohkawa, "Recent Japanese Growth in Historical Prospective," *ibid.*, pp. 578–580.

[60] American growth in GNP for many years has averaged a bit over 3 percent. See E. F. Denison, "How to Raise the High-Employment Growth Rate by One Percentage Point," *ibid.*, Vol. LII, No. 2, May 1962, pp. 67–86. See also American Bankers Association, *Proceedings of a Symposium on Economic Growth* (New York, 1963), 139 pp., and Chase Manhattan Bank, *The European Markets* (New York, 1964), p. 21.

held responsible for a condition over which it has little or no control. Problems of planning and organization in such a situation make efficient management difficult.

Overutilization of resources may be equally inefficient. Excess demand for given types of workers and technicians leads to staff shortages which can be overcome only by expedients such as inflating wage rates or doing without certain personnel.[61]

In any complex society, there will typically be some imbalance between supply and demand for various types of workers; but if the discrepancies are relatively small, little harm is done. When excessive shortages of a given factor persist, however, the effect may be to make firms less efficient than they otherwise would be. A further result might be to cause unemployment of associated factors.[62] For example, a serious shortage of doctors could lead to unemployment for medical technicians, nurses, orderlies, and janitors.

Marxist countries tend to have different kinds of stability problems than capitalist states. These countries usually keep productive factors employed, even though the need for the item produced is small or nonexistent. The problem is not only keeping men and machines at work but also keeping them engaged in the production of *useful* goods and services. Whereas capitalist states allow unemployment rather than production of useless items, the Marxist countries typically do the reverse.

A problem facing many Marxist countries at present is that past plans have focused too many resources in industries which are now overexpanded in relation to demand, while putting too few resources in others. Khrushchev used to refer sardonically to the "steeleaters" in the Soviet Union, who perpetually insisted on more and still more resources for this industry, at the expense of other sectors. The 1964 agricultural crisis in the Soviet Union brought abrupt attention to the pressing need for more fertilizer capacity; but to increase supply in this sector involved many major shifts of resources out of other sectors, and the complex technology involved in petrochemicals also meant that such transfers could not be made easily. If they are to be made, the Soviets face difficult problems of maintaining production (or, more precisely, planned rates of growth), elsewhere, while rapidly building up the new sector. The likely outlook is for considerable idle resources as this major transfer is made.

Other Communist states have had similar transfer problems of this sort. China's "Great Leap Forward" of 1958–60 was an attempt to transfer resources in a major way from agriculture to industry, and the result was

---

[61] This problem in the Common Market is discussed in A. Lamfalussy, "Europe's Progress: Due to the Common Market?" in L. B. Krause, ed., *The Common Market* (Englewood Cliffs, N.J.: Prentice-Hall, Inc., 1964), pp. 104–107.

[62] Frederick Harbison and Charles A. Myers, *Education, Manpower, and Economic Growth* (New York: McGraw-Hill Book Company, 1964), pp. 115–129.

disastrous for that country. The usual result of such major resource shifts is extreme economic instability, but the outward manifestations of such shifts are not the same as are seen in capitalist countries when similar shifts occur.

As with prices, the best stability situation for managers is as much stability, coupled with reasonably attainable growth, as possible. No country is perfect in this regard, since even in the best run economies some anomalies persist; however, countries do differ widely in stability, and the most stable are those most conducive to effective internal firm management.

## ORGANIZATION OF CAPITAL MARKETS

Liquid capital is the lifeblood of any business enterprise operating in the modern world. Lack of access to needed money capital can force a firm out of existence, or at least cause it considerable harm. A key problem for enterprises thus becomes one of obtaining supplies of capital in the economy in which they function.

A second major consideration of industrial firms is the cost of capital. In theory, capital markets in capitalist countries are competitive, and interest rates indicate supply and demand conditions; but in practice many market imperfections, including the critical one of lack of knowledge, operate to raise prices of capital for some users to very high levels. Capital costs in the context of the economic system as a whole also reflect the way in which capital should be allocated in order to obtain most efficient production. If markets are structured so that valid capital users must pay excessive prices for money, the result will be some misallocation of resources. Some productive firms may not obtain funds for productive use.

Both of these problems are emotion laden for managers of productive enterprises, because the manager of any firm is usually convinced that he can use capital more effectively than the (suspicious) money market feels he can. Money is always too expensive, in the view of the borrower; and much folklore about usurious interest rates exists in every country with any sort of free money market. Since potential borrowers almost always outnumber potential lenders, the loudest criticisms typically come from the borrowing side.

One major source of capital in most countries is commercial banks. Here the organization of commercial banking is relevant, since the way in which such banks allocate their limited funds to productive firms may determine in part the managerial effectiveness of these firms.[63] It may also determine in part the general efficiency of the economy. If the only firms to obtain funds are those favored by family relations with commercial bank

---

[63] Barger, *op. cit.*, pp. 214–232, 255–296.

managers, industrial enterprise results will be far different than if funds are allocated, after careful analysis, to companies most able to use them profitably.

In most countries, commercial banks are controlled or influenced by the central bank through controls on discount rates, reserve requirements, open market operations, and various forms of audit and direct credit control. By controlling commercial banks, governments have an indirect control over firm credit in this sector. The implications for productive enterprise financial planning is clear. A firm dependent on bank credit must take into account, at least indirectly, the total government plan concerning credit supplies, even if, as is typically the case with smaller firms, the managers have little idea what such policy may be. They find out quite quickly when they visit their local banker.[64] The possibilities of expansion, diversification, entry into new markets, and many similar factors are thus influenced by general monetary policy worked out through commercial banks.

The importance of bank sources of funds for many firms can influence such firm functions as staffing as well. Banks have options of refusing to do business with individuals for any reason they see as valid; a person high in management who is regarded unfavorably by the firm's bankers will not be a manager for long. In many countries, the bankers will be found on boards of directors of many sorts of firms, and it is common for the banks themselves to take an active part in determining firm policy.[65]

The United States legally requires the separation of commercial and investment banking.[66] This rule stems from the often noted fear that if bankers can act as long term investors, firms will end by being completely dominated by their bankers. In countries where such restrictions are not in force, as in West Germany, it is common to find bankers acting as managers of important enterprises. In still other countries, such as Egypt, commercial banks have been nationalized, or placed under extremely close government control, including control over the flow of lendable funds. This type of control leads directly to control over the types of investments made in the country. If the government decides that certain types of industries are desirable, funds will flow in these directions, while "nonessential" enterprises are starved for cash. Financial planning and policies of all firms are directly affected in such cases.

The critical importance of credit to firms has led to the image of the banker as a man of tremendous power and prestige. Radicals attack bankers as if the fall of existing bankers could drastically reform the economic

---

[64] "Free Reserves of Banks Rose to $101 Million," *The Wall Street Journal*, November 30, 1964, p. 8; also "Atlanta Bank Raises Prime Rate," *ibid.*, p. 3.

[65] Barger, *op. cit.*, pp. 282–283. In Germany, Switzerland, and Japan, this is particularly true, while France and England follow the separatist pattern similar to that in the United States.

[66] *Ibid.*, p. 260. This law has been in effect since 1933 in the United States.

system overnight; conservatives react violently to such implications, suggesting that the importance of bankers and banking is not overestimated. Most countries with relatively free presses have produced unending streams of books, articles, and pamphlets over the past century condemning banks and bankers for every real or imagined sin possible; and every university and college in almost every country has a series of courses on money and banking, analyzing the problems of this activity. Much of the emphasis on the importance of banking is pure mystique—after all, bankers have what we all want, namely money. Those not able to get it are obviously unhappy, and it is easy to move from disappointment to a position that after all "they" are in a position to destroy the economy.

Completely planned economies, such as the Communist states, also have monetary problems, although of a somewhat different sort. Money still is used in such countries, and firms must have credits to meet their major obligations; but the plan generally tells the firms what they must produce, and in what quantities.[67] Hence, state banks serve a passive role, providing what funds are necessary to meet plan requirements. They do serve a real function of control, however, in that firms cannot utilize endless amounts of credit to achieve their plan goals. An inept industrial manager who cannot meet his plan quota without recourse to excess amounts of cash finds that his control function is influenced by his bank. Poorly audited firm accounts, or incompetent planning and control by the commercial bank, in this situation can lead to serious monetary problems, particularly inflation. If the excess cash gets into individuals' hands through wage payments, excess demand generated can cause serious price problems in the economy. Most Communist states at one time or another have had serious problems of this sort. The plan provides for too few consumer goods (at going prices) for the money put in circulation by the enterprises hiring labor. With fixed prices, the result is that people queue up at stores waiting to get their share of the scarce goods. Enterprise direction can be influenced here, since if personnel are more concerned with obtaining goods than with working, or if they feel that it is useless to work because the money they earn cannot be used, the enterprise can suffer seriously.

There are other types of nonbank credit institutions in many countries which also provide capital to industrial enterprises. Some of the more common are as follows: mutual savings banks, savings and loan companies, life insurance companies, pension funds, credit cooperatives, installment finance companies, and government development or loan companies.[68]

All of these institutions perform the same general financial functions: they accumulate funds from some sources in the economy and lend it to productive firms, among other recipients. Savings and loan associations and installment finance companies deal largely with consumers, lending money

---

[67] Nove, *op. cit.*, pp. 61–96.
[68] Hart and Kenen, *op. cit.*, pp. 107–129.

for housing and consumer purchases; but they do occasionally lend money to firms.[69] Credit cooperatives (as credit unions in the United States) also usually deal with consumer finance; but in some cases such cooperatives are formed by producers, such as farm groups, to make loans for productive purposes.[70]

Mutual savings banks perform many of the functions of commercial banks, but they are typically restricted as to the types of funds they accumulate. They normally do not have the familiar business accounts and checking account business associated with commercial banking.[71] The life insurance companies and pension funds typically accumulate large amounts of money through their operations in other areas, and they are primarily concerned with maintaining cash to pay claims against them; however, in countries where such institutions are well established, these institutions may have very large sums of money available for investment. Thus, in recent years in the United States, insurance companies have had available for loans funds greater than half the total available from commercial banks.[72] The nonbank credit institutions combined have sums available that are about the same size as those available through the commercial banking system. The implications for credit availability for productive enterprises are considerable.

However adequate a country's private sources of capital may be, they are usually considered inadequate politically. There are always productive enterprises in any unplanned economy which are unable, for various reasons, to obtain capital from any source. Hence, one modern development in many areas has been the government finance agency, which typically is charged with lending money to enterprises unable to obtain it from other sources.[73] In nonindustrial countries, such lending has typically been concentrated in this sector; in developed countries such as the United States, such lending has been focused on smaller enterprises, which traditionally have had considerable trouble obtaining capital from private institutions.[74] The more developed and variegated the supplies of capital in an economy may be, the easier a productive enterprise's financial planning becomes. Strategies perfectly logical in the United States, where all of the above institutions are well developed and organized, become impossible in countries where such financial institutions are rudimentarily developed or nonexistent. A productive enterprise which is able to pick and choose its

[69] Commission on Money and Credit, *Money and Credit* (Englewood Cliffs, N.J.: Prentice-Hall, Inc., 1961), pp. 154–164.

[70] *Ibid.*, p. 192.

[71] Hart and Kenen, *op. cit.*, pp. 107–108.

[72] *Ibid.*, p. 110.

[73] For American practice, see Commission on Money and Credit, *op. cit.*, pp. 181–201. One famous early example of government credit was Mexico's *Nacional Financiera*, established in 1933. See H. F. Cline, *Mexico: Revolution to Evolution* (New York: Oxford University Press, 1963), pp. 244–250.

[74] Barger, *op. cit.*, pp. 270–273.

source of funds has considerably more bargaining power and flexibility in financial planning than one which is tied irrevocably to a single source.

Another important financial institution which directly influences the internal management of firms is an organized stock and bond market. The most familiar example of such a market is the New York Stock Exchange, which actually is one of a series of interrelated stock and bond markets dealing both in public and private stocks and bonds. The major activity of this market is dealing with "used" securities, which have been issued in the past by various firms; but it also handles the underwriting of new financial issues for reputable firms.[75] Other countries, particularly those which are advanced industrially and have large numbers of joint stock corporations, also have similar securities markets. Such markets also handle bonds and notes of public institutions. While many of these issues are for nonproductive (in our sense) activities, even in the United States some public enterprise exists and can obtain funds in this manner. Toll highways, bridges, and public transit facilities in cities are examples of such operations.

These securities markets in effect evaluate the firm for outside investors from day to day and in a sense act as an outside auditor of the firm's management. The exchanges themselves usually require some financial disclosure on a periodic basis, which also influences the activities of insiders. Hence, the firm whose stocks are listed must typically file with the exchange at periodic intervals a profit and loss statement and an income statement, subject to public inspection.[76] The necessity of doing so acts in itself as a spur to efficient management, since poor financial results can only have a negative impact on the managers themselves. For example, financial disclosure means that firms will be more reluctant to engage in unsound risks. Losses become public quickly, the firm's stocks decline on the market, and the managers are placed in an awkward, and sometimes disastrous position. The fact that other, similar firms are also disclosing financial information may deter unsound practices as well. Financial analysts are quick to compare items of expenditure such as research budgets, the percentage of revenues spent on overheads, and similar information, in addition to the usual rates of return on capital and sales. A firm far from the average is again placed in an awkward position. If it is noted that one firm in a given industry makes 10 percent on its capital and has 5 percent of its expenses in overheads, while the second comparable firm makes 2 percent and has 20 percent in overheads, the market will respond quickly enough, and management changes in the second firm are highly probable. In a country like the United States, a highly developed information system operated by

---

[75] See Gilbert W. Cooke, *The Stock Markets* (New York: Simmons-Boardman Publishing Corp., 1964), 540 pp., for a complete description of American institutions and practices.

[76] Birl E. Shuly, *The Securities Market—And How it Works* (New York: Harper & Row, 1957), pp. 320–331.

persons interested in investments and speculations has evolved, and it is difficult for any large public firm to practice really poor management over long periods of time. When a firm does much better than the average, it is subject to intensive analysis by brokers, stockholders, and competitors to find out why; and again the result is considerable pressure to improve other firms up to the known potential in the industry.

As one example of the way in which a capital market evaluates performance, the case of Republic Steel Corporation is instructive. This company ranks eighth of the eight largest steel producers in terms of operating profit margin, although it is the third largest producer. In the period 1962–64, it spent less per share in modernization and expansion than the other large producers. This information is, of course, public knowledge, since this is a large public corporation, with its shares traded on all major stock exchanges in the United States. Republic's management argues publicly that it has a long term strategy which will eventually move it upwards in earnings and sales; however, the market views the situation much more dubiously. The price/earnings ratio of its common stock was among the lowest of the steel producers in 1964 (10), while the selling price of the stock was only 53 percent of its 1959 high.[77] The fact that management of this company is literally forced to defend itself indicates the nature of such market pressures when an informed group of sophisticated investors and investment advisors observe critically the activities of the various firms whose stocks are sold publicly.

European markets typically are not as open as the American, and information about public companies is much harder to obtain; but examination of almost any issue of such magazines as the English *Economist* suggests that really poor performance would be noted quite quickly, and laggards in any industry or almost any country would be forced to improve if they expected to maintain the value of their shares on the European bourses, as well as their other credit sources.

In some countries, as in Lebanon in the late 1950's, stock exchanges may be more akin to gambling casinos than financial markets, given the possibilities for insider manipulation of data, prices, and similar underhanded tactics. In the limit, such an exchange can be as much a hindrance as a help to good business management. But, in any case, the existence of such an exchange has some significant effect on the internal financial operations of business enterprises.

Other economic factors that tend to have a significant bearing on managerial performance are discussed and analyzed in the following chapter.

---

[77] "The Waiting Game," *Forbes*, December 15, 1964, pp. 24–25. *Forbes* is one of many American journals specializing in analysis of companies whose stocks are publicly traded.

# Chapter 11

# Economic Constraints:

# External

T his chapter examines three critical economic constraints not yet discussed: factor endowment, market size, and social overhead capital.

## FACTOR ENDOWMENT

In economics, the term *factor* means an item of production necessary
to create useful goods and services. The usual division of factors is in
the form of land (including natural resources), labor, and capital, and
management or entrepreneurship.[1] This latter factor is the key item in our
analysis, since we are arguing that the effectiveness of management in fact
determines how well a country does economically. Without management,
nothing is produced. Regardless of the supplies and qualities of other
factors of production, no useful goods and services would emerge without
the managing of the combination of these factors. This is as true in a
primitive agricultural village as in a complex, modern industrial economy.
The major difference between two such economies is in the nature and
quality of management.

The relative supply of the other factors of production is relevant,
however, since it is clear that it is easier to manage a system in which the
other factors are in abundant supply of all factors. It is hard to imagine any
production taking place without any labor at all, for example; and some
land is required for any type of output. The problem here lies in the term
*relative supplies*. Shortages of key factors can lead to higher production
costs and greater management problems for industrial enterprises.

### Land

The land factor can be defined as all that nature supplies, external to
man. Thus, land would include all agricultural land, all mineral resources,

---

[1] This division of inputs follows traditional economic analysis. J. Due and R. Clower,
*Intermediate Economic Analysis*, Fourth Edition (Homewood, Ill.: Richard D. Irwin,
Inc., 1961), pp. 6–7.

all resources found in the oceans, all urban housing plots, and so on. The relative supply of such resources per person in a culture could be determined by evaluating such supplies against population.

While the supply of land is relatively fixed, changes can be made, both for the better and for the worse. Farm lands can be exhausted by poor farming practices, and range lands can be overgrazed into deserts. Reclamation and irrigation projects can expand the supply of arable land, and dredging can create land from the sea. Knowledge is also a key factor in determining supplies, particularly in the area of mineral deposits. Oil has existed in Oklahoma for millions of years, but its value was nil until the petroleum was found by people. Minerals now considered valueless may in time prove quite useful, if technological changes make their use feasible in industry or agriculture.

The supplies of land in this general sense definitely influence the managerial effectiveness of firms. Thus, if one country has very large supplies of low cost, easy to mine coal, one result will be relatively low fuel costs for industries using this mineral. Production costs will be lower than those in another country not so fortunately endowed. Production planning gains increasing flexibility when this factor is in abundant supply.

Where minerals are hard to get and scarce, cost problems exist for mining operations. If coal is close to the surface and consists of high quality grades, mining costs are low and the firms appear efficient. If, on the other hand, the firms have to engage in extensive underground tunneling to reach their supplies of this mineral, costs will be higher because of more complex production techniques needed. Such a situation will also influence such managerial functions as staffing, organization, and direction. An open surface coal mine, from which coal is dug by large power shovels operated by a few men, has a completely different organization than one in which many men dig by hand or smaller machines hundreds or thousands of feet below the surface. In the latter case, the direction problem is made more complicated by the need to supervise the work of many men working in numerous locations to which access is difficult. In the former case, on the other hand, a different kind of skill, utilized by many fewer men, leads to much easier direction techniques and problems.

In general, the more accessible and cheaper the natural resources are, the easier and simpler enterprise operations will be. The problems noted above in coal mining suggest why this would be the case. If the resource is so easy to get or use that even the least trained men can obtain it with little effort, managers have few problems caused by this factor, but difficult or hard to get resources imply that considerable ingenuity must be used by management to obtain consistently efficient production from this factor.

One example of how this problem can lead to the need for better and more efficient management is shown in iron ore mining in the American Messabi Range in Minnesota. Until the 1950's, the available iron ore in this area could be mined in open pit operations which, while complicated, were a relatively straightforward operation, both technologically and managerially; but the exhaustion of standard ores meant that steel companies had to switch to the use of taconite ores in the 1950's. This special ore required a whole new mining technology; and the shift from older, more easily worked ores caused shifts in production techniques from the mines through the mills which used them. This change could not have been accomplished successfully without the proper application of first-rate management in a wide variety of ways in this industry.

Problems of land use are typically interrelated with other external constraints. A common interconnection here is with legal requirements affecting factor use. This may be illustrated by the petroleum case, where firms are engaged in drilling oil wells and pumping petroleum as their major output. In the United States, subsoil rights generally belong to the owners of the land above the subsoil minerals, and any man owning a small plot of ground has access to the oil below. The fact that the oil pool may extend for hundreds of miles below is irrelevant in law. Hence, upon discovery of an oil pool, American firms may be forced to drill literally hundreds of high cost wells to get their share, since in most cases the land above is owned by hundreds of different persons. If an owner wants his share, he must drill on his land. The result is overinvestment in wells and storage facilities, plus possible wasteful exploitation of the total pool, as all owners try to get their share before someone else pumps it out from under the surface land.

In the Middle East, subsoil rights belong to the rulers or governments of the countries concerned, not to the owners of the surface lands. Hence, oil companies must make agreements with governments about oil exploitation, not with local surface landowners. The usual result is that exploitation of this resource is much more efficient, since the number of wells drilled becomes a problem in petroleum technology, rather than property rights. The entire field can be considered as a unit, and production plans can be made accordingly. There are more oil wells in single small fields in Oklahoma or California than there are in a single Middle Eastern country producing a thousand times as much petroleum per day. The wasted investment and resultant inefficiency of firms in this business in the United States has nothing to do with the caliber of internal management of these firms—it is directly a result of the way in which such resources must be exploited under American law. The interrelationships which follow in this situation affect many sectors of the economy. Oil from the Middle East may cost around $1.50 per barrel delivered in the United States, while local oil costs $2.50 to $3.00 per barrel; but for foreign policy and defense reasons, the American government has decided to refuse entry of more than a stated amount of foreign crude oil. Hence, American firms using petroleum or petroleum based products have to pay higher prices than competitors in other countries, which in turn affects their relative efficiencies. Firm managers (aside from the local petroleum producers), may not like this policy but they have no choice in the matter.

Nations are endowed historically and at times accidentally with natural resources and land. In the rapid development of technology since 1800, resources once considered critical (i.e., indigo, natural rubber) have lost their importance or faded completely from the scene, while other resources, such as uranium and petroleum, have become extremely important. Countries once regarded as hopelessly poor (such as Kuwait) are now wealthy, and countries once regarded as very rich (such as Indonesia and the various spice islands) are relatively poor. Also relevant here is the ability to make poor resources more useful through human skill and management; many countries now produce abundantly on lands once regarded as infertile deserts. Even these same infertile deserts occasionally prove to be rich sources of nitrates and other critical chemical products needed in modern industry.

A critical problem for any country is the amount of available resources per capita. Indonesia has excellent resources; but it also has a very large population, and the resource base is not large enough (given presently known extractive techniques) to yield more than a miserable low level of living to Indonesians. Australia and Canada, on the other hand, have very large amounts of resources per person, which would tend to make their populations wealthier, other things being equal. A common problem of all of the poorer countries is that they do not have enough easily extractable resources per capita to allow for more than a poverty stricken standard of living for most of their people.

Favored countries which do have more resources per capita will have less complex industrial management problems than those with fewer resources, given the same levels of managerial competence. Firms in the better endowed countries will tend to have superior managerial effectiveness from this constraint alone.

## Labor

This factor consists of the potential available man hours per period of time available in a society. Clearly, few countries ever use all potential man hours, since many persons do not work up to the physiological maximum. Still others prefer not to work in the formal sense at all; such persons are housewives, rentiérs, older persons, young people under sixteen, and so on. A country may have involuntary unemployment also, in the sense that persons want to work and cannot find employment.[3]

In quantitative terms, the maximum number of labor hours available in any culture is determinate and finite; and production dependent on labor is also finite as a result. The total population of any country determines

---

[2] M. A. Adelman, "Efficiency of Resource Use in Crude Petroleum—Abstract," *American Economic Review*, Vol. LIV, No. 3, May, 1964, pp. 219–220.

[3] This problem is explored in some detail in American Bankers Association, *Proceedings of a Symposium on Employment* (New York, 1964), 128 pp.

maximum production; and the more available labor there is in a society, the larger the potential maximum production will be.

Qualitative evaluation of labor is more complex. Historically, labor was lumped into a single homogeneous blob, since most work was unskilled, and most workers were good substitutes for any other laborer.[4] Even here, difficulties arise, since a well fed, healthy manual laborer is probably a better worker than a poorly fed, sickly peon; and when skill levels are considered, the issue is still more complex. A modern industrial economy may have as many as 15,000 different jobs and occupations; and while many of these are virtually interchangeable, large numbers are not. A welder is not directly interchangeable with a clerk-typist, for example. Many sorts of jobs are interchangeable only in one direction. Engineers can serve as machine operators, and many have at various times in the past; but few machine operators can work satisfactorily as engineers.

One entire constraint section, that on education, dealt with a major problem in all labor forces. The manner in which the work force is educated, in terms of their literacy, specialized training, and so on, as covered in Chapter 6, determines in large part the level of managerial effectiveness a society will have. Our argument here is that virtually all of the production and management problems in any society can be solved effectively by a well trained group of managers and workers. A badly educated society is almost definitionally an inefficient society, and the level of managerial effectiveness in such a situation is bound to be quite low.

Another dimension of the labor factor is the general health and well being of the labor force. In poorer countries, it is typical that most workers are at least a little sick most of the time. Parasitic infections, venereal diseases, and other debilitating maladies affect a major portion of the work force in many countries. The usual result is low levels of worker performance; extensive absenteeism; high labor turnover; and, if the firm is required to pay some of the necessary medical expenses, higher operating expenses through need to provide clinics, doctors, and nurses.

The general level of health in the labor force depends in part on the educational and income levels of the workers. It also depends in part on the very important social overhead capital facilities such as hospitals, doctors, public health programs, sewer systems, clean water supplies, and similar investments which directly affect the health of the population. Housing conditions also are important, since very poor housing can lead to rapid spread of infectious diseases, respiratory infections, and a host of diseases spread by living under unsanitary conditions.

In more developed countries, worker health is typically higher, resulting in lower operating costs for productive enterprises. The firm does not have to replace men as frequently, with attendant training costs. It may not have to maintain as large a health service within the organization as it

[4] See B. Higgins, Economic Development, (New York, W. W. Norton and Company Inc., 1959), pp. 85–198, for expositions of some earlier economic theories showing this tendency.

would if workers were less healthy. Plant safety may prove easier to improve if alert, healthy workers are being used. Production costs in particular can be reduced, not only because of the above factors but also because healthy men can produce more and have more stamina than those ill or badly nourished.

Nutritional standards also vary widely between countries, ranging from around 1,200 calories per day in poorer Asiatic countries to 3,000 and more in modern industrial states. One result is that better-fed workers have much more stamina; another is that the poorly fed men are much more susceptible to disease. One author found that Saudi Arabian workers could not be expected to do more than half the manual labor which a European or an American could reasonably be expected to perform in a working day. The Saudi men were quite willing to work, but the nutritional standards in the country were such that they simply could not do more work; therefore, about two to three times as many men would be assigned to a task such as unloading a truck as would be used in better-fed countries. The result was a direct decline in productivity per man and a lowering of firm efficiency.

Most of the less developed countries in the world today have a surplus of labor, in the sense that they cannot effectively utilize all manpower available with existing capital equipment, land, and labor. The usual result is overt or concealed unemployment. One author had the experience in Egypt of having nine waiters serve one simple meal. The men were employed, but not, one suspects, in a very productive fashion. Hidden unemployment in peasant agriculture is a very common phenomenon in many countries. Men may work for a month or so at harvest time, but they remain idle for most of the remaining part of the year. The effect of this type of unemployment on system efficiency is large.

A related problem is that the cost of labor in the economic sense may be close to zero, but wage rates are somewhat above this minimum. There is virtually an unlimited supply of untrained, unskilled labor available for work; but the price of labor is such as to keep it from being used completely. Until much more of the necessary related factors, such as capital and management, have been expanded in supply, the problem remains. On the other hand, developed countries, particularly in western Europe in the 1960's, have been bothered by labor shortages. Rapid economic expansion in many countries has caused the demand for many kinds of labor, including unskilled labor, to be greater than supply.

The problem in both cases is that the price of labor, which rarely is set by a perfect market in any country, is in disequilibrium. In Europe, much higher wages would be required to end labor shortages, while in the labor surplus countries, still lower wages might (if institutional rigidities such as lack of mobility could be overcome) result in more employment. The difficulty here is that the oversupply is so large that even a zero wage rate in some cases would not put all men to work.

A further difficulty is that labor markets are not homogeneous. Skilled labor usually is in short supply in all countries at going wage rates, even in such labor surplus countries as India, while unskilled labor typically is abundant.[5] Generalization is difficult here, since a modern country may have perhaps 10,000 to 15,000 separate occupational categories, with limited interchangeability between them, and some types of labor always are abundant, while others are scarce. The discussion in Chapter 6 of educational match with requirements attempts to evaluate this problem for industrial firms; but the problem of relative scarcities and shortages of labor of various types is basically both an educational and economic problem, and the two constraints are interrelated to a considerable extent. Sociological constraints also play a role here, since the relative supply of various types of labor may depend in part on prestige elements of various occupations.

The factors of land and labor may also be interrelated. A good endowment of land may in part offset a poor endowment of the labor resource, in the sense that less skill is required to get good production from such good land. If the land factor is scarce or of poor quality, the labor skills of the population may in part offset this disadvantage.

## Capital

The meaning of *capital* here is goods used in future production, not money capital. Money can be printed when needed in the modern world; but real capital must be manufactured laboriously by previously existing capital, management, land, and labor. With modern technology, it is often true that the most efficient processes use capital intensively—that is, the more capital applied in production, the lower unit costs will be.[6] The whole development of automation, with its profound implications, is basically a development of this type. The notion here is that capital goods can be used to produce either more capital or more consumption goods efficiently. Labor and land are required, but in lesser amounts than before.

A second point is that some types of production are almost impossible without considerable capital investment. It is hard to see how electric power could be generated without extensive investments in generators, power transformers, electric lines, and similar equipment. There is almost no second best alternative in such a situation, and an economy short of capital becomes inefficient for this reason alone. Until it can accumulate the necessary capital equipment, it cannot be managed effectively.

In other cases, options between the use of other factors and capital are abundant, and choices of the precise factor mixes to be applied in firms in capitalist countries lie with management. They will usually depend on the costs of the various factors. This type of choice is seldom clearcut, however. An industrial firm might use much capital to mold plastic radio cabinets

---

[5] "Skilled Labor Shortage Holds Down the Gains," *Business Week*, February 6, 1965, p. 84.

[6] For a theoretical discussion and some empirical transportation examples of these cost characteristics, see John R. Meyer, Merton J. Peck, John Stenason, and Charles Zwick, *The Economics of Competition in the Transportation Industries* (Cambridge, Mass.: Harvard University Press, 1960), pp. 18–144, particularly pp. 126–128.

(using less labor), or it might use much more labor to make them by hand out of wood; but such labor is not unskilled, and the choice might turn on whether or not it is believed by management that such skilled labor is available, or can be trained for less cost than the necessary capital investment.[7] Not only could the production technique vary here, but also the actual quality of the product could differ. In some cases, *handmade* denotes a quality item; in others, it implies a crude, inefficient product. What is thought may in itself be a part of managerial efficiency, since the way in which the various products are marketed can influence their value in such a case. Given the complex of potential situations and strategies here, the proper managerial action is not self-evident.

It is generally true that the countries with the highest amount of capital per worker are the wealthiest, and one result of this observation has been a scramble among less developed nations to obtain capital in any way possible; however, implicit in the concept of having large relative amounts of capital is the notion that the country also has the necessary human resources and management to use it intelligently and efficiently. A familiar and depressing sight in many underdeveloped countries is the new plant unused because of lack of demand, or because the management failed to see the need for spare parts to maintain expensive machinery. Managers who know how to use capital equipment intelligently and profitably can usually obtain the necessary financing for it. Knowing how to finance capital acquisitions is a key part of managerial knowledge and skill; but the piling up of capital assets in a country without adequate management, simply because it is believed that somehow these assets will generate wealth, is a fraud. Nothing happens, because management is not competent. Conversely, a good manager with inadequate capital also is less effective than a man whose capital equipment is adequate.

Again the interrelationship between economic and educational constraints is clearly seen. Capital by itself is passive. It requires the combination of skilled technicians and management to make it usable in any way, and failure to consider this point carefully has proved very expensive for many firms and countries.

Capital equipment supply is also closely related to capital market organization and efficiency in an economy. A firm may be competent and willing to obtain new equipment; but if it is unable to obtain money capital, it cannot finance the necessary real capital. There is a close connection here also between managerial competence and sources of capital. A firm that does not have a capable financial planner, who can convince banks, stockbrokers, or insurance companies that his firm can efficiently utilize new capital, is not well managed.

In general, the relative supply and quality of all factors have a direct bearing on the quality and effectiveness of internal management. Countries

---

[7] Yale Brozen, "Invention, Innovation, and Imitation," *American Economic Review*, Vol. XLI, No. 2, May, 1951, p. 256.

where labor is skilled, healthy, and diligent; where natural resources are abundant; and where supplies of real capital are adequate will have a much simpler managerial problem than countries where these conditions do not hold. Analysis here tends to reveal a chicken and egg problem, in the sense that an absolute shortage of any factor will cause serious difficulties. It does not prove very useful to debate what might happen if additions of one factor are made. Ample supply and good quality of each factor tend to reinforce development of another. Thus, more development of skilled labor tends to make possible the efficient use of larger amounts of more complicated capital equipment, while extensive and efficient development of natural resources may well depend on more development of certain types of skilled labor, plus more capital. Attempts to force the question by overrapid development of one factor may prove less useful than an integrated approach which takes into account the simultaneous development of all factors.

## MARKET SIZE

It has long been noted in economics, and in practical business as well, that in many lines of business a firm's costs will decline as production increases. In cases such as automobile manufacture, the minimum efficient size of plant may be huge, requiring the production of perhaps as many as 500,000 vehicles per year. In others, the minimum efficient size of plant may be smaller, as in motor trucking, where a one truck firm might prove as efficient as a larger operation. Even in this case, however, the market must be large enough to utilize the equipment a substantial portion of the time.

Also relevant here are market economies. A firm manufacturing a consumer good capable of being differentiated will often find that the minimum efficient plant is too small for effective marketing organization. Here, it is difficult to organize a sales force to cover very small markets, or warehouses are too small in a given market to be efficient, or advertising cannot be placed in purely provincial outlets. Too many small and relatively inefficient middlemen may be required to serve a scattered population, or one with relatively low purchasing power. Such firms may be characterized by numbers of plants strategically located within the total market. In the United States, firms manufacturing soap, toothpaste, and cigarettes are among enterprises of this type.[8]

Many countries are too small to support the optimum size plant, from the technical or marketing point of view, in the country. Even one firm may be too many in this case. Such situations can be alleviated by exporting in some cases; but many products, because of national policies, transfer costs, or communications problems, are not normally exported in large quantities.

[8] Joes S. Bain, *Industrial Organization* (New York: John Wiley & Sons, Inc., 1959), pp. 210–265.

Services such as internal transportation and communication cannot be exported, nor can such products as buildings. In these cases, the firm is constrained by market size.

One example might be a telephone company in a country like Costa Rica. Even if every possible subscriber had a phone and used it regularly, the efficiency of the company might be less than that of the Bell system in the United States, because the firm could not possibly become large enough to achieve maximum economies of scale. In this case, no matter how effective the Costa Rican managers were, they would be less efficient than their colleagues in larger countries. In a similar manner, railroads, contractors, and manufacturing companies may be trapped by their market size. The problem is often intensified by the desire of countries to have certain key manufacturing industries located within the country. Hence, a steel mill may be built, even though the internal market is too small to allow its managers to become efficient. As a result, the mill enjoys protections from imports, in the form of high duties or tariffs. The small market means high cost steel, which in turn means that the manufacturers can not export. Many countries have deliberately created this sort of problem, and the management of such enterprises is consequently inefficient.[9] No amount of internal managerial improvement, however, can offset the initial disadvantage.

In these cases, the organization within the firm may be directly influenced. One would not expect a small Chilean steel mill to have an organization analogous to that of United States Steel, or for that matter, even of a Russian steel mill. The absence of scale economies causes a restructuring of the internal organization of the firm. The production function will be equally affected, particularly in terms of less work specialization, since the way in which underutilized plants are organized for production may differ considerably from the organizational procedure of a more efficiently utilized factory.

A further problem arises in many countries where markets are too small to support more than one or two firms. In a large country, considerable competition is possible between firms in many sectors because of the large market size. There is room for enough firms to make competition reasonably effective; but if the natural tendency in a small market is toward monopoly, the competitive results will clearly be different, and the firm effectiveness may also be different. A competitive firm has a much different outlook on its market and its customers than a monopolistic one. In the former case, pricing policies merit close examination at all times, service to customers becomes critical, sales promotion is carefully planned and executed, and the organization of the marketing function is oriented to gaining

---

[9] One excellent detailed study of this type of problem is Lee C. Nehrt, A *Pre-Investment Study of the Flat Glass Industry* (Washington, D.C.: International Bank for Reconstruction and Development, 1964), 98 pp.

at the expense of rivals. Since customers have extensive alternatives, the productive enterprise must make sure that it is performing as efficiently as possible.

The monopolist, on the other hand, need not fear competition. Customers who are dissatisfied have no alternatives, nor can they play one firm against another. Carelessness in handling a customer's complaints can be tolerated, since they have no options. Inefficiencies within the firm can be glossed over, since prices can be raised as costs increase. This type of phenomenon is not restricted to private monopolies only—some of the worst examples of firm efficiency in the world are publicly owned monopolies in various countries. A monopolist's organization will differ considerably from a firm with competitors, particularly in the marketing area. The monopolist's attitude is too often, "If you want it, we'll be nice to you and get it for you—for a price." Selling effort consists of taking orders, and sending men into the field is seldom attempted. Customer complaints are handled perfunctorily, if at all. The customer is forced to seek out the seller, rather than vice versa. The marketing organization of a firm in the same business in competition is typically just the reverse, and marketing strategy and organization tend to be critical. If the firm fails here, it goes bankrupt quickly.

Monopolies may be created for reasons other than market size, as in the Marxist countries, where, for political reasons, virtually every branch of industry is organized in this way. The results, incidentally, are all too often similar to those described above, and the consumer is damned; but often overlooked are the large number of smaller countries where many industries are of such a size that natural monopolies or duopolies (with colluding companies) are the rule rather than the exception. Some relief can be obtained by allowing imports of competitive goods; but often, again for political or social reasons, such imports are banned. The impact on managerial effectiveness seldom is good.

## SOCIAL OVERHEAD CAPITAL

Social overhead capital generally is defined as the supply and quality of public utility type services available to consumers and firms. Such services are: the transportation systems, including airports, harbors, highways, railroads, inland waterways, and similar facilities, plus the necessary capital equipment needed to operate on them; the telephone and telegraph systems, including the number of phones, miles of lines, quality of interconnections, and similar factors; the development and extent of electric and gas transmission systems; postal facilities, including the extent of parcel post operations, post offices, and so on; worker housing; and such factors as the quality and availability of public warehousing. Equally important would be the cost of these services to the firm.

Firms in countries which have poorly developed social overhead capital facilities are more difficult to manage than those in countries with good facilities. A manufacturing firm in Brazil may have problems of erratic electric power supply, poor telephone service, and inadequate sewers around the plant. If the firm is a major user of electricity, stoppages of power will mean unexpected shutdowns of production from time to time, raising costs as workers wait idly for power to be restored. It is common to find that electric companies cannot provide industrial power at times of peak demand, and the firm may not be able to operate at all at certain times of the day when it wishes to. The alternative open to the firm here would be to build its own power plant, but this also would raise costs to a considerable extent. Production planning is difficult in this case, because the firm cannot be sure that schedules can be met. Failure to meet delivery schedules will also have some impact on marketing and finance.

Lack of good telephone communications means that much time is wasted and money spent sending messages in other ways. It is difficult to communicate with customers, suppliers, and other branches of the firm, and misunderstandings are common. Sales are lost because customers may find it difficult to get in touch with the firm's marketing personnel. Also important is time wasted because outsiders visit officials rather than call them.

Sewer defects can create health problems, even if the company is not a heavy user of such facilities. If the firm has large amounts of industrial waste to dispose of, lack on good sewer systems can result in production delays, as production must occasionally stop to clear the factory area of noxious wastes by hand.

Such social overhead capital constraints tend to restrict the locational possibilities of the firm within the country. Firms can locate only where these facilities are available, or face expensive problems of building their own facilities. This might lead to overcrowding in the few cities in the country where these facilities are available, and the result for the firm would be higher costs because of congestion.

In a similar manner, the absence of key facilities alters the internal operations of a firm. A country with poor railroad service may force the firm to get into the trucking business in order to get its goods to market. Inadequate and erratic transportation may cause the firm to carry larger inventories than it otherwise might, in order to cover possible shortages of key components or to avoid being out of stock at the retail level. Poor communications facilities can lead to lost executive time through the need to travel to branch plants or other organizations, rather than merely call them by phone or send them a telegram. Such factors are accepted as obvious in an economy where they are available, but the lack of such facilities is quickly felt in countries where they are not. Firms may be required to make major investments in such facilities, hence restricting investment elsewhere. It is not uncommon for manufacturing firms in many countries to have to invest in standby electric power facilities because the local public system is too unreliable for dependence. The capital tied up in this way cannot be used elsewhere.

In the limit, absence of such facilities restricts firms absolutely. A mail order catalog activity such as Sears, Roebuck depends entirely upon parcel post and other transportation facilities for small packages. Such an operation could not exist in a country where such facilities were unavailable. Lack of electric power deters or bans such firms as those producing frozen foods, since retail freezers require a steady, dependable supply of electric power if the product is not to be ruined. Note in this case how a food processing firm is constrained in its marketing organization. Regardless of the desirability of such a product in the market, it cannot be produced and sold successfully if the electric power is not widely available. Hence, a food processing firm in such a country will have a different product mix and a different organization than a similar firm in a country where the social overhead capital is available.

Equally important is the quality of management of the social overhead facilities themselves. In many countries, such facilities are largely owned by governments, since many of them are of monopoly nature. Thus, the United States is one of the very few countries of the world where telephones, telegraphs, power companies, and railroads are not owned and operated by some form of government corporation. Bad management of these facilities means poor service to customers, which in turn directly affects the internal operations of such firms. Good and effective management is not restricted only to private enterprise, even in countries where most manufacturing and retailing is done by privately owned enterprises. Even in the United States, the efficient operation of the post office and numerous public power companies is a matter of considerable concern for private managements.

Even very wealthy countries typically have major shortfalls of available social overhead capital. Thus, it is estimated that in the United States, $100 billion per year could be spent for the next ten years on cities alone, for development of housing, public buildings, streets, sewers, and similar facilities, just to bring these items up to generally accepted standards.[10] Given potential requirements, projected on the basis of what could be constructed with present skills and to meet existing demands for these services, demand is virtually unlimited for more and better facilities. Every country is short of social overhead capital in some absolute sense, and its productive firms must necessarily make do with what is available; but this leads to costs which cannot be avoided by industrial firms.

Here again it is often argued that more applications of capital can improve the country's situation: more transformers, power generating equipment, and power lines are needed to improve social overhead capital. While this is often true, equally needed is effective management of this

---

[10] "America's Cities," *The Economist*, Vol. CLXIV, No. 6337, February 6, 1965, p. 542.

capital when put in place. Many countries suffer as much from inept management of such enterprises as they do from absolute lack of capital.

## CONCLUSION

For well over a century, economists and businessmen have been keenly aware of the interrelationship between economic problems and business performance. The nature of such interrelationships has been the foundation of much of economic analysis during this period. Economists, with their professional interest in international trade, resource allocation, pricing problems, competitive relationships, money and banking, economic growth, comparative economic systems, and similar matters, have long debated the effect of various economic shifts and changes on productive enterprises.

Business managers have been somewhat slower to realize the economic strait jacket they necessarily are in. Concerned with complex managerial problems, and dimly aware that economic theory, while important, yields only partial insights into their internal management problems, they have tended to accept the economic environment they are in as given, subject only to occasional attacks or plaudits depending on their political and ethical viewpoints.

A major difficulty here is that economic insights yield only partial results in many cases for business managers. The problem of sales promotion does depend in part on economics—but it also is a problem in applied psychology, sociology, political science, and, one suspects, astrology as well. Economists, assuming that businessmen are efficient, fail to come to grips with the involved internal managerial problems of the firm, creating still more misunderstanding. This chapter has attempted to bridge the gap between these disciplines, noting the direct relevance of economic constraints not only to obvious external firm behavior but also to the way in which internal firm operations and management are pressured by economic factors.

# Chapter 12

# Comparative Management Matrix:
# Country and Firm Ratings

## INTRODUCTION

It is desirable to measure more precisely the educational, sociological-cultural, legal-political, and economic external constraints discussed in earlier chapters. Mere identification of the external factors determining managerial effectiveness is useful; but to know more exactly which of these is most important, and by how much, would be still a better guide for analysis and policy decisions. Is, for example, general literacy more important than political stability; or is educational match more critical than a society's view toward managers? If such questions could be answered accurately, considerable insights into firm and country economic performance could be made.

If all external constraints could be rated quantitatively, it would also be possible to pinpoint weaknesses in a given country. Thus, economic growth might be slow, but what should be done about it? If the various weaknesses were known and could be evaluated relative to other constraints, policy implications would be clear. A country might have serious educational match problems, as well as negative views of managers. If it could be determined that the match problem was far more critical than the negative view, the necessary policy questions have been asked.

Industrial managers themselves could also utilize such quantification of the external constraints. Knowing that the country was weak in educational match, it could organize its own training programs where necessary to cover critical gaps. If only lawyers are available, and accountants and engineers are needed, a well conceived internal training program could cover at least some of the lack.

Even if the quantification is somewhat imprecise, the actual statement of what is important can lead to debate about the necessary corrective measures. One might point out that educational match is poor and cite (always incomplete) evidence such as the noted demand for scarce accountants. A second observer might note that the demand for accountants stems largely from improper use of this type of personnel in firms. Since quality control specialists are in short supply, accountants are pressed into these positions. Who is right in such a debate is relatively unimportant. What is important is that the problem is recognized, evidence is gathered to support various conclusions, and key questions about the performance of the educational system and the labor markets are debated. Out of such debate will emerge insights into the true nature of problems affecting the productivity of enterprises in the economy.

Another major use of such quantification would be the comparison of various countries. Comparisons of gross national product per capita is one existing measure of how well a country does economically compared to others, but this measure does not explain why one country is superior to others. England has a higher GNP per capita than Japan, but why? If the various external constraints in fact determine the efficiency of productive enterprise in the country, and if GNP in effect measures this total flow of production, then evaluation of the external constraints item by item should throw light on why one country is economically superior to another. Is England wealthier than Japan because it has superior resources, better overhead capital facilities, a more efficient legal system, or what? If each constraint could be quantified, one could point to specific points of superiority or inferiority for each country. In the aggregate, one would expect England to be superior; but it is possible that in terms of some constraints Japan is better.

Again the policy implications emerge here. If it can be shown that Japan has certain key legal constraints which adversely affect productivity, changes can be made. Also, firms operating in Japan can make whatever internal corrections are possible to overcome unfavorable environment, as can those in England.

## QUANTIFICATION PROBLEMS

The advantages listed above seem to make some effort at quantification worthwhile; however, the difficulties of precisely measuring such aggregative variables must not be underestimated. Clear analysis of these difficulties is necessary if any quantification effort is to succeed.

All of the constraint variables are highly aggregative, and hence subject to various loss of detail when applied to specific situations. It may be true that a given country has a poor view of managers, but it is also possible that various subcultures in this country do not have this negative attitude. The notion of the "pariah entrepreneur"[1] suggests that often a minority group can hold significantly different attitudes towards management and business than the general population, with significant impact on the economy. Not

---

[1] Norman Jacobs, *"The Bahai'i of Iran and Pariah Entrepreneurship"* (mimeographed paper circulated by the International Development Research Center of Indiana University, Bloomington, 1964). The IDRC, under the direction of Professor Fred Riggs, is actively doing research in this general area.

everyone needs to be a manager, and at times even a small minority opinion may be enough to carry the country forward economically. The general economic system may be poorly organized, but some subsectors may have excellent organization favorable to good managerial performance.

In many countries, two or three major social blocs may exist. There may be a modern sector, consisting of those in major cities involved in modern production and distribution techniques; a traditional peasant sector, whose sociological attitudes may be completely different; and a third sector consisting of interaction between the first two. Any sociological scores will be wrong, since the average score lies somewhere between the two major sectors. Such difficulties of aggregating complex constraints in any country cannot be overestimated. Which scores are relevant for the United States: Those for New York or Mississippi? Firms in either state face local problems, not average ones.

A second problem is that some constraints are quite difficult to quantify. It is relatively easy to measure illiteracy (although the statistical problem here should not be underestimated), but how does one evaluate the constraint for the total economic system? To do this properly would take volumes—and has, without any author convincing the others that his case is impeccable. The sociological constraints generally offer the most difficulties in this regard, although considerable progress has been made in recent years in terms of measuring extremely complex sociological and psychological attitudes. In many cases, the problem is not in getting some general consensus at the extremes but rather in evaluating finer gradations. A country which has had a decades-long history of revolution, intrigue, assassination, and political turmoil is an obvious case; but how should the shift from a Conservative to Labor government in Britain be evaluated in relation to a slight turn to the left in an Italian election? It is usually easy to distinguish a completely inept economy—characterized by price inflation, depression, extensive private monopolies, inept central banking practices, mass unemployment, and similar factors—but how can the difference between the Netherlands and West Germany be scored? Even rank ordering in such cases can be difficult.

It is never clear what a perfect score on any constraint might be, given the difficulties of evaluating such complex material. Presumably any country could make some improvement in almost any external constraint, regardless of how well the country was doing at present. Thus, no one seriously argues that the most advanced countries could not do still better, for example, in reforming their legal structures. A country like England may have a very excellent legal system in terms of its favorable impact on productive firms; but further reform is still possible, and the constraint score could still be raised, if the country were willing to spend the necessary time, high skill man hours, and money on this problem.

For these reasons, the constraint scores are generally open ended. Some improvement is always possible, and no country is regarded as perfect.

Some of the constraints are relatively passive and static, while others are quite dynamic and subject to rapid change. Still others tend to change rather steadily, if unspectacularly, through time. A country's evaluation thus changes at different rates. A politically stable country can become unstable in weeks if a long hidden revolutionary movement suddenly seizes power; or an inept central bank can become competent quite rapidly if a brilliant new central bank official is appointed (this particular change can of course work in reverse as well). The general literacy rating tends to change in many countries rather slowly but steadily toward more literacy, and while year to year changes seldom appear spectacular, over decades major changes can occur. Legal constraints can at times be changed in a matter of months as critical new laws are passed or old ones are changed.

Virtually all constraints are subject to change, although the difficulty of making changes differs. Here again, careful evaluation of how difficult change is, or how dynamic the constraints are, can serve as policy guides. If a country has both an educational and legal problem, it may prove useful to allocate resources for change along the lines of relative resistance to major shifts in the constraint values. A million dollars spent on legal studies can be evaluated against a million spent on elementary schools. Both would be helpful, but the cost of change might prove relevant in making the allocation decision.

All of the external constraints are interrelated to some extent. Hence, a change in one starts a series of changes which ultimately affects them all. The kind of legal system a country has, for example, depends in part on the educational, sociological, and economic factors in the economy, and vice versa. The educational system and its performance depends also, among other things, on economic factors and the various sociological constraints. The proper mathematical statement of the constraints is

$$X = f(C_1 \cdot C_2 \cdot C_3 \cdot C_4), \quad \text{not } X = f(C_1 + C_2 + C_3 + C_4)$$

where X represents managerial effectiveness.

Such changes are extremely difficult to quantify, since it would be necessary to write a formal set of quantified and interrelated equations to evaluate properly the changes resulting from one given change. The problem is made still more difficult by the fact that in any society changes occur simultaneously. We do not find a given law being changed, then a shift in educational standards, and later a shift in sociological attitudes. All of these things occur at once, making it very difficult to find out which variable depends on what others, and to what extent. This is, of course, the curse borne by all social scientists—since they live in the dynamic model they are studying, they often cannot isolate individual variables for detailed analysis.

Many of the individual constraint variables have been studied individually without any effort to integrate all of them into a single system. Many scholars, as well as men of affairs, are quite familiar with many sections of the matrix; and not a few students of society can claim considerable (nonquantified) familiarity with the entire system. Hence, we already possess significant insights into how the total constraint matrix operates in practice. With this start, it is possible, in spite of all difficulties, to attempt some quantification of the matrix. The most usable method is the Delphi Technique, developed by the Rand Corporation; and to this method we now turn.

## THE DELPHI TECHNIQUE[2]

The Delphi Technique is a method for obtaining a consensus of opinion about a matter not subject to precise quantification. It was developed to handle problems of the sort presented here, where interactions of variables, difficult aggregations, and difficulties of quantification make it impossible to apply more common methodologies. The technique can be used to weigh relative values of a set of interrelated variables, or to indicate which variables are critically important for future events. The Delphi Technique is intended not to provide precise, totally accurate information about problems but rather yield key insights into the nature of crucial information in the problem. It can also be used to identify the major contingencies upon which future developments will depend, which makes it particularly valuable for the type of dynamic applications of the external constraint matrix which may prove most useful.

The basic application of the Delphi Technique is as follows:[3]

First, experts are identified to consider the problem at hand. These experts would be men, who by general agreement, are the best suited to meaningfully discuss the issues. In our case, experts would be those persons capable of evaluating (to the best of their expertise) the constraints which do directly influence internal firm management in a given country. Such men might be development economists, political scientists, businessmen who have demonstrated competence in social affairs outside their firms, sociologists, public officials dealing with major national problems, and similar persons.

Second, the selected experts are asked, independently, to evaluate the problem and to give answers to the selected key questions. In this study, the first problem would be to identify the key external constraints. Hence,

---

[2] This technique is explained in: Olaf Helmer and Nicholas Rescher, "On the Epistemology of the Inexact Sciences," *Management Science*, Vol. VI, No. 1, October, 1959; Norman Dalkey and Olaf Helmer, "An Experimental Application of the Delphi Method to the Use of Experts," *ibid.*, Vol. IX, No. 3, April, 1963; and T. J. Gordon and Olaf Helmer, *Report on a Long-Range Forecasting Study* (Santa Monica, Calif.: The Rand Corporation, 1964), 65 pp. and appendix.

[3] We are indebted to Mr. David Hitchen, University of California, Los Angeles, for his assistance in preparing this section. Mr. Hitchen also prepared Figures 12–1, 12–2, and 12–4.

experts would be given the initial tentative constraints and asked if these are the ones most relevant in affecting industrial management effectiveness. For clarity, it would be necessary for the experts to have read the statement of the problem, as given in Chapters 4 and 5.

Third, the various answers are collected by the investigator, read and evaluated, and compiled. Note that to this point no expert is aware of what the other experts have decided. A key part of this technique is to avoid direct face to face contact of the various experts, as in this way personality dominance is avoided. The experts are not identified to each other in any way. If agreement is more or less general, the experiment ends; however, it is typical in this type of situation for some dispersion of answers to occur. One expert may feel that economic variables are critical, and go on to expound still further variables in this sector at some length; another may feel that the sociological factors are critical; and so on. The relevant points of disagreement are tabulated, concise statements of differences are made by the investigators, and these statements are sent back to the experts, with a request for re-evaluation. The experts respond again, commenting if they choose to on the new evidence, and changing their opinion if their initial statements deserve modification in light of new evidence.

The new responses are then tabulated as before, and changes are noted. In this type of problem, it is typical to find that the experts begin to converge in their opinions. On the first pass at the problem, the expert often tends to overvalue his own special field of competence; and in first looking at the constraint and constraint-behavior matrices developed in Chapters 3 and 4, some misinterpretations are common. As the additional evidence is fed back to capable men, they tend to see the problem in roughly the same way. Key points previously overlooked are noted, and changes are made; additional evidence focuses attention on critical items not originally thought of.

At first glance, this technique appears to be merely a compilation of opinion, lacking any scientific validity; however, as Olaf Helmer of Rand points out, the technique actually is quite objective.[4] The expert opinions gathered are referred to as personal probabilities, which are then used as estimates of the objective probability statement. Moreover, the experts, if selected properly, are chosen according to objective criteria. The experts are not those who happen to agree with the researchers; but rather they are those men who, in the opinion of serious students of the field under investigation, are the most highly qualified to give correct opinions and evaluations of the problem under consideration. The expert's past performance is also taken into account, and his reputation as an expert in the field is considered.

A further factor leading to objective judgment is that the experts tend

---

[4] Helmer and Rescher, *op. cit.*, pp. 47–48.

to agree independently. If no consensus is achieved in developing the external constraints matrix presented here, this would be serious evidence that the total approach was defective and that completely different avenues of research should be explored. The contributions of the experts actually supplement the theory and are subject to the same safeguards of objectivity used in other scientific investigations.

We actually used this technique to help formulate the external constraints discussed and developed in this book. Some modification of the procedure was necessary because of lack of funds and time, but the general methodology was followed as far as possible. The external constraints shown in Table 3–1 in fact have been subjected to considerable modification from experts—they are rather far indeed from the original list prepared. A similar technique was used in getting the proper B's in Table 2–1. The development of the initial question and hypothesis, combined with frequent feedback from independent experts, allowed us to develop a consensus matrix which reflects more accurately the items seen as important by persons competent in this field.

Figure 12–1 shows the detailed steps taken in applying the Delphi Technique to any problem. This general format was followed in all uses of this technique in connection with this book. The first use of the technique was to identify variables which were the external constraints. The second problem attacked, using the same method, was to determine how important, relative to the other sectors, each area was. The method used was to ask the experts to weight each area, then to rank each constraint within each area, using a 250 point scale in each case. Note that this is not precisely correct, since the implication is that the constraint areas are additive, when, because of their interrelationships, they are probably multiplicative; however, the complexities of the interrelationships and the difficulty of evaluating interrelationships made this first step necessary. Figure 12–2 indicates the way in which this problem was set up. In most cases in which we experimented, the experts' answers tended to converge quite quickly, suggesting that the basic approach was probably sound. Each sector was rated about the same by all experts (in Part 3a of Figure 12–2), so 250 points per area were assigned in the final quantified matrix. The various evaluations for subareas also tended to converge, though more slowly. Lack of time prevented following through with the complete Delphi method to obtain complete convergence. Scores in each subarea were converted numerically to add to 250 for each major sector.

The final quantified matrix is shown in Figure 12–3. This general matrix is now ready for tentative application to any given country, or to any specific region or branch of industry within a given country. As noted earlier, it may prove wise to rate California independently of New York, or the steel industry independently of the textile industry, if it seems that aggregative ratings will not focus on key questions.

## FIGURE 12-1

*Steps to be Taken in Applying
the Technique*

*Step 1.* Define the *Problem to be Solved*
—make the answer quantifiable wherever possible.

*Step 2.* Determine *Areas of Expertise* which bear on the problem
—these can concern the total problem or sectors of it.

*Step 3.* *Select Experts* to be used in solving the problem (5–10)
—must have requisite knowledge and be able to apply it to the problem.
—must have good performance record in their areas.
—must be rational, objective and impartial.
—must be available over a period of time (2–4 months).
—must be willing to participate in the study.

*Step 4.* *Contact Experts* being considered
—this can be done in person or by letter: explain:
  (*a*) the total study being undertaken.
  (*b*) the central problem under consideration.
  (*c*) the role they will be expected to play in solving the problem (responding to questionnaires and analyzing data between questionnaires).

*Step 5.* Prepare the *First Questionnaire*
—restate the problem under consideration inspecific terms; i.e., request a numerical estimate of rating at this time.
—also include questions which bring out:
  (*a*) the respondent's *reasoning*.
  (*b*) the *factors* which he considers relevant.
  (*c*) *information* as to the kind of data he feels would enable him to arrive at a better appraisal of these factors and thereby at a more confident answer to the primary question.

*Step 6.* Distribute the first questionnaire.

*Step 7.* Analyze the results from this questionnaire.

*Step 8.* Prepare the information which is asked for and examine the factors which are being considered.

*Step 9.* Initial *Feedback*
—feedback information that was either requested by some one of the experts or which deals with factors and considerations which are considered relevant.
—care must be taken to conceal opinions of the other experts.
—correct misconceptions about empirical factors or theoretical assumptions underlying those factors.

*Step 10.* Prepare the *Second Questionnaire*
—included here is a statement of how the questions appear to have been broken down, i.e., list items which are taken into consideration and what these lead to.
—ask questions about their agreement or disagreement with the basic considerations listed; ask them to revise this list.
—ask for a revised estimate of the answer to the basic question.

.　.　.　.　.　.　.　.　.　.　.　.　.　.　.

This procedure of distributing questionnaires and controlled feedback between them is continued until the consensus is considered accurate enough to be used as an estimate for the answer to the problem.

*Step 11.* *Correct Final Responses*
—this can take the form of replacing some of the individual component estimates with a consensus of estimates.
—the median of the responses can be used.
—some weighted average taking into account the relative expertise of the participants can be used.
—unsatisfactory participants can be ignored.

*Step 12.* *Apply Final Consensus* to the original problem (in whole or in part).

*Step 13.* *Acknowledge Assistance*
—in publications allow respondents to review the final answer.
—acknowledge their assistance and identify the possible shortcomings of the method.

FIGURE 12-2

*Rating the Matrix*

1. *Statement of the Problem.*
   In an attempt to measure the importance of external constraints (economic, legal, educational, etc.) on internal management effectiveness, a *numerical value* must be placed *on each of the external constraints* in order to suggest its relative importance.

2. *Letter to the Experts.*
   Include the following:
      *a.* Description of overall study
      *b.* The problem under consideration
      *c.* Their role in answering the questions and solving the problem
         —5–10 questionnaires over a period of 5–8 months
         —analysis of data between questionnaires
         —need for independent answers
   Who qualifies?
         —a person familiar with international business operations
         —a development economist
         —an international management specialist

3. *Questionnaire #1.*
   Attached is a suggested list of external constraints. Read through the entire list and then answer the following questions:
   (Note: The lower the assigned score, the greater the impediment to efficient internal management. Higher scores suggest a favorable impact.)
      *a.* Weigh the *four major areas* (total = 1000)
         i Educational.....................................——
         ii Sociological....................................——
         iii Political & Legal...............................——
         iv Economic.......................................——
      *b. Educational.* Using your above score for this area as a total value, weigh the five subfactors listed below.
         *C.*1.1 Literacy Level.............................——
         *C.*1.2 Higher Education..........................——
         *C.*1.3 Specialized Technical Training..............——
         *C.*1.4 Attitude toward Education..................——
         *C.*1.5 Educational Match with Requirement.........——
   It is permissible to eliminate items from this list and to add others which you consider important.
   Give a brief listing of *relevant factors* in this area.
   What *information* about these factors would you feel would enable you to arrive at a better appraisal of these factors and thereby at a more confident weighing of the subfactors?
      *c. Sociological.* Repeat above.
      *d. Political & Legal.* Repeat above.
      *e. Economic.* Repeat above.

   Questionnaires are completed, tabulated, and revised according to the instructions of Figure 12–1 above.

The experts who proved most useful to us were sociologists and social psychologists, industrial executives, macroeconomists and developmental economists, and bankers. This latter group appears most useful because of its general business orientation. Being interested in many kinds of businesses and situations, they are accustomed to dealing with evaluations of external situations, including the environment of the firm. Operating (in the United States) in a complex and controlled legal environment, they tend to be quite aware of legal restrictions and their effects on productive

FIGURE 12–3

*Final Quantified Matrix*

| Constraint Educational | Total Value |
|---|---|
| C1.1 | 100 |
| 1.2 | 25 |
| 1.3 | 50 |
| 1.4 | 25 |
| 1.5 | 25 |
| 1.6 | 25 |
| Total C1 | 250 |
| *Sociological-Cultural* | |
| C2.1 | 30 |
| 2.2 | 10 |
| 2.3 | 20 |
| 2.4 | 70 |
| 2.5 | 20 |
| 2.6 | 10 |
| 2.7 | 50 |
| 2.8 | 20 |
| 2.9 | 20 |
| Total C2 | 250 |
| *Legal-Political* | |
| C3.1 | 80 |
| 3.2 | 20 |
| 3.3 | 25 |
| 3.4 | 80 |
| 3.5 | 25 |
| 3.6 | 20 |
| Total C3 | 250 |
| *Economic* | |
| C4.1 | 40 |
| 4.2 | 20 |
| 4.3 | 20 |
| 4.4 | 40 |
| 4.5 | 30 |
| 4.6 | 40 |
| 4.7 | 25 |
| 4.8 | 35 |
| Total C4 | 250 |
| Total C | 1,000 |

firms. Experts typically are where you find them, and the more competent they are the better the Delphi results will be; but some good experts for this type of evaluation exist in almost every country of the world—if they can be persuaded to cooperate.

## Country Evaluation Matrix

Once the total quantified general matrix is obtained to everyone's satisfaction, it is possible to evaluate individual countries. The selected countries can be rated according to the general matrix by experts for those countries. If the initial hypothesis is correct it is to be expected that the additive matrix scores, or managerial effectiveness index, will correlate with gross national product per capita, since the matrix is in effect also indirectly evaluating system efficiency.

Several discrepancies may lead to lack of correlation here. Since the constraint ratings evaluate industrial enterprises in large part, there may be a discrepancy between the constraint ratings and GNP per capita, since this latter figure measures all production. If agriculture or service activities account for a large proportion of GNP, some deviation is to be expected. This type of deviation would be particularly large if there is a large, traditional economic sector operating alongside a modern industrial sector. Economic, sociological, and educational constraints may vary sharply between sectors; and the bigger the deviations of this sort, the less useful the GNP per capita cross check may be. Where agricultural and trading sectors are relatively modern, however, as in Canada, England, and the United States, relatively little deviation would occur.

Another type of discrepancy would occur in small, less developed countries where a modern foreign concern accounted for most of the wealth and income through some exploitative type of activity. The foreign concern would probably operate as nearly as possible in the manner of the home country, and its activities would be much more progressive than the local economy. Kuwait, Saudi Arabia, and Liberia are cases of this sort. Income generated in the foreign owned sector may be as much as 95 percent of total income, yet the constraint ratings are those for the local economy.

Another reason for large differences between the C ratings and GNP could occur if one of the C factors had importance all out of proportion to its general value in most countries. The usual reason for this is in factor endowment, where a country may face critical problems through almost total lack of proper factors, or in the reverse case where a major resource endowment is so huge as to overwhelm all other difficulties. Some of the oil rich sheikdoms and countries in the Middle East present examples of this latter situation, while a few of the new African states may have the former problem. A country like Libya was considered to be a hopeless factor endowment case until 1958, when oil discoveries pushed it into the enormously wealthy resource category, suggesting that even this type of factor endowment problem can change rapidly if new resources are discovered.

Additive, rather than multiplicative, use of the matrix may lead to inaccuracies and potential distortions. The argument for using the matrix in this way is that to date no better way of determining how the environment interacts with productive firms has yet been found. Future development and evaluation of the matrix still is quite desirable. Figure 12–4 indicates the nature of the Delphi questionnaires used for this purpose. The countries evaluated here were the United States, the Soviet Union, Great Britain, Egypt, India, Japan, Brazil, Mexico, the Netherlands, and Saudi Arabia. Experts were relatively easy to find for all countries but Saudi Arabia; the

## FIGURE 12-4

*Rating a Country*

1. *Statement of the Problem.*
   In an attempt to measure the importance of external constraints (economic, legal, educational, etc.) on the internal managerial effectiveness of a particular country, a *numerical value*, has been placed *on each of the external constraints* to suggest its relative importance. We now wish to *rate a particular country* according to this scale.

2. *Letter to the Experts.*
   Include the following:
   *a.* Description of overall study.
   *b.* The problem under consideration.
   *c.* Their role in answering the questions and solving the problem:т
   —5–10 questionnaires over a period of 5–8 months.
   —analysis of data between questionnaires.
   —need for independent answers.
   Who qualifies?
   —a person familiar with the general cultural, economic, business and political environment of the particular country.

3. Attached is a weighted list of external constraints (Figure 12–3 above). Read through the entire list to determine the relative rankings and then answer the following questions:
   (Note: The lower the assigned score, the greater the impediment to efficient internal management. Higher scores suggest a favorable impact.)
   *a.* *Educational.* Using your above score for this area as a total value, weigh the five subfactors listed below.
   C.1.1 Literacy Level. . . . . . . . . . . . . . . . . . . . . . . . . . . . . . . . . . . . . . . . . . ——
   C.1.2 Higher Education. . . . . . . . . . . . . . . . . . . . . . . . . . . . . . . . . . . . . . . . ——
   C.1.3 Specialized Technical Training. . . . . . . . . . . . . . . . . . . . . . . . . . . ——
   C.1.4 Attitude Toward Education. . . . . . . . . . . . . . . . . . . . . . . . . . . . . . . ——
   C.1.5 Educational Match with Requirements. . . . . . . . . . . . . . . . . . . . . ——
   It is permissible to eliminate items from this list and to add others which you consider important. Give a brief listing of *relevant factors* in this area.

   What *information* about these factors would you feel would enable you to arrive at a better appraisal of these factors and thereby at a more confident weighing of the subfactors?
   *b.* *Sociological-Cultural.* Repeat above.
   *c.* *Political & Legal.* Repeat above.
   *d.* *Economic.* Repeat above.

author who managed a Saudi firm for several years did most of the "expert" work for this country.[5]

Table 12–1 indicates the actual rankings of the countries, and also compares GNP per capita. The managerial effectiveness index correlates relatively well with the present GNPs per capita for the countries ranked. It is fairly easy to obtain significant differences between countries such as the United States and Egypt, given the large absolute differences in income and

---

[5] It should be noted that lack of time and funds prevented a complete Delphi evaluation for the formulation of the C's, the C values, and the country evaluations. Initial experiments done by us, however, showed significant convergence, particularly in education and economics—even, in many cases, on the first pass. Tentative Delphi experiments were carried out with bankers, the U.C.L.A. Executive Program students (who are executives), a few international business firms, faculty members, foreign doctoral graduate students in business, and European executives. The composition of the list of critical elements of the business process (Table 2–1) was developed through a more complete use of the Delphi Technique with members of the business faculty of U.C.L.A. Again, convergence tended to occur rather rapidly.

the various constraints in these two countries; however, comparisons between Egypt and India are much more subtle, and minor errors of rating could change the relative positions, in terms of both income and the matrix. In such cases, more detailed cross checks, such as growth in GNP per capita and utilization rates of inputs, as developed in Chapter 5, could help in refining the actual measures. This will be done in more detail in the second volume of this study, when individual countries are studied.

Saudi Arabia's score illustrates the difficulty of ranking a country which has major subsectors which differ strikingly from the social mainstream. Here the matrix score is very low, but GNP per capita exceeds that of Egypt and India. The major reason for this discrepancy is that the oil production in Arabia is performed by American firms, whose mode of operations and business techniques are taken from the American, rather than the Saudi, evnironment. The oil companies are influenced to a considerable extent by the local environment, particularly in the educational and legal-political sectors; but they are in a position to overcome most of these disadvantages by extensive training programs, importation of foreigh high skill personnel, and direct bargaining and negotiation with the Saudi government. If the constraint matrix were rated in Arabia for the oil companies as a subsector, the scores would be fairly close to (but not as high as) the American. Since over two-thirds (and possibly as high as 90 percent) of Saudi GNP is derived directly and indirectly from oil production, the GNP figure is a poor measure of the performance of the local economy. Here is a classic bimodal situation. The Arabian GNP figure reflects oil income divided by the total number of Saudis, while the constraint matrix evaluates only the local sector. The resulting average is directly between either of the two major sectors of the economy, leading to potentially erroneous interpretations.

One notable fact about this quantified matrix is that the rater does not necessarily have to be completely right to make the matrix useful. The act of rating a country forces the rater to consider all of the constraint variables and how they affect internal firm management. If he is not completely knowledgeable about all constraints, as is typical of most experts, he may guess at a given score. Another expert, more sensitive to this area, gives, say, a lower score. In the Delphi feedback, this area then becomes a point of debate, and the experts must reconcile their differences. Forcing a trained economist to focus on legal, pedagogical, or sociological problems in this matter can be both educational and useful, particularly if the matrix rankings are to be used for policy analysis of the country in question.

Another use of errors results when a specialist in one of the areas is shown the ratings of general experts. A sociologist who disclaims expertise in all other areas may note the sociological ratings and disagree; but the act of disagreement implies he is able to argue his case, and he may be able to point to problems, data, or subvariables not considered by generalists. Again, the ratings can be changed to reflect this sort of insight. In working out constraint ratings, we have often had this type of experience, resulting

## TABLE 12-1

### EXTERNAL CONSTRAINT EVALUATION

| Constraints | U.S. | Nether-lands | U.K. | Japan | U.S.S.R. | Mexico | Brazil | Egypt | India | Saudi Arabia |
|---|---|---|---|---|---|---|---|---|---|---|
| **Educational** | | | | | | | | | | |
| $C_{1.1}$ 100.. | 95 | 95 | 95 | 95 | 90 | 40 | 35 | 25 | 25 | 15 |
| 1.2  25.. | 20 | 15 | 19 | 17 | 23 | 8 | 7 | 8 | 5 | 2 |
| 1.3  50.. | 42 | 25 | 22 | 21 | 32 | 8 | 7 | 9 | 7 | 2 |
| 1.4  25.. | 24 | 11 | 13 | 19 | 17 | 7 | 6 | 6 | 6 | 1 |
| 1.5  25.. | 23 | 20 | 19 | 22 | 24 | 13 | 12 | 10 | 10 | 11 |
| 1.6  25.. | 23 | 19 | 17 | 19 | 18 | 8 | 7 | 11 | 7 | 2 |
| Total $C_1$  250.. | 227 | 185 | 185 | 193 | 204 | 84 | 74 | 69 | 60 | 33 |
| **Sociological** | | | | | | | | | | |
| $C_{2.1}$  30.. | 24 | 24 | 18 | 26 | 27 | 17 | 18 | 17 | 15 | 19 |
| 2.2  10.. | 8 | 7 | 6 | 9 | 8 | 4 | 4 | 3 | 3 | 3 |
| 2.3  20.. | 16 | 16 | 12 | 18 | 12 | 14 | 13 | 7 | 4 | 13 |
| 2.4  70.. | 64 | 62 | 54 | 67 | 66 | 30 | 28 | 30 | 23 | 18 |
| 2.5  20.. | 17 | 14 | 12 | 12 | 18 | 12 | 11 | 13 | 6 | 10 |
| 2.6  10.. | 8 | 7 | 6 | 7 | 9 | 6 | 6 | 4 | 4 | 7 |
| 2.7  50.. | 42 | 37 | 35 | 30 | 31 | 23 | 22 | 15 | 14 | 5 |
| 2.8  20.. | 17 | 13 | 12 | 13 | 14 | 11 | 10 | 7 | 8 | 5 |
| 2.9  20.. | 18 | 15 | 12 | 15 | 12 | 12 | 11 | 6 | 5 | 10 |
| Total $C_2$  250.. | 214 | 195 | 167 | 197 | 197 | 129 | 123 | 112 | 82 | 90 |
| **Legal-Political** | | | | | | | | | | |
| $C_{3.1}$  80.. | 66 | 69 | 68 | 48 | 40 | 30 | 30 | 25 | 30 | 20 |
| 3.2  20.. | 15 | 15 | 16 | 19 | 8 | 13 | 10 | 3 | 13 | 10 |
| 3.3  25.. | 15 | 22 | 18 | 20 | 10 | 13 | 12 | 5 | 8 | 10 |
| 3.4  80.. | 75 | 72 | 68 | 61 | 70 | 55 | 25 | 47 | 50 | 50 |
| 3.5  25.. | 19 | 21 | 21 | 18 | 10 | 14 | 8 | 8 | 9 | 8 |
| 3.6  20.. | 15 | 10 | 17 | 14 | 10 | 10 | 10 | 6 | 9 | 5 |
| Total $C_3$  250.. | 205 | 209 | 208 | 180 | 148 | 135 | 95 | 94 | 119 | 103 |
| **Economic** | | | | | | | | | | |
| $C_{4.1}$  40.. | 33 | 35 | 28 | 24 | 19 | 22 | 22 | 13 | 16 | 28 |
| 4.2  20.. | 16 | 17 | 17 | 15 | 13 | 8 | 6 | 7 | 7 | 8 |
| 4.3  20.. | 16 | 17 | 14 | 13 | 12 | 10 | 2 | 7 | 7 | 4 |
| 4.4  40.. | 30 | 35 | 28 | 25 | 24 | 20 | 10 | 15 | 16 | 20 |
| 4.5  30.. | 29 | 19 | 27 | 22 | 16 | 10 | 10 | 10 | 10 | 4 |
| 4.6  40.. | 37 | 6 | 18 | 9 | 24 | 8 | 26 | 5 | 10 | 34 |
| 4.7  25.. | 23 | 18 | 19 | 16 | 14 | 6 | 8 | 6 | 9 | 4 |
| 4.8  35.. | 33 | 33 | 27 | 21 | 18 | 14 | 11 | 7 | 5 | 7 |
| Total $C_4$  250.. | 216 | 180 | 178 | 145 | 140 | 98 | 95 | 70 | 80 | 109 |
| GRAND TOTAL 1,000 | 863 | 769 | 738 | 715 | 689 | 446 | 387 | 345 | 341 | 335 |
| GNP/cap. (est.) 1965 | $3,366 | $1,431 | $1,527 | $798 | $900 | $414 | $305 | $170 | $66 | $200 |

in extended debate about a given constraint, which in turn leads to more knowledge of how one constraint subvariable affects the total picture.

The rankings in Table 12-1 immediately suggest policy emphasis for the countries in question. Some constraints are poor, but others are worse. The problem of how to get additional growth in income can be focused on in terms of which variables are easy to change, or as quick to change as others; and evaluation of weaknesses in constraints can suggest at least a meaningful debate on priorities. Japan can do little about its relative lack of resources (except search for more in a systematic fashion); but the country might be able to do a great deal, in a relatively short period of time, about educational matches, legal changes, and economic shifts.

Business managers also can use the matrix, in spite of its imperfections. A firm about to launch an enterprise in India could note the relatively low constraint scores and take necessary steps, within the limits of its resources and talents, to improve these for its own internal operations. The low $C$ scores, when evaluated with the $B$ scores discussed in Chapters 2 and 4, will indicate which business and management functions will suffer as a result of poor external constraint conditions. Again, even error can be useful here, since the firm can observe the constraint scores, evaluate its own internal operations which are likely to be directly affected by such factors, and determine whether or not the conditions indicated by these low scores will in fact be a hindrance to the firm. The matrix is a useful tool for asking the right questions—although it hardly gives the correct answers at this stage.

## GROWTH PROBLEMS AND CONSTRAINT RATINGS

The constraint ratings in Table 12–1 are static, representing a country at a given moment in time; but the ratings will change over time—indeed, one of the major reasons for evaluating a country in this way is to assist planners and policy makers to change key constraints as rapidly as possible. Thus scores obtained today will be obsolete tomorrow, and continuous checks must be made on countries to observe the rate of change.

A method of evaluating constraints over time would be to plot the matrix from decade to decade. There is no necessary reason why a country must improve, although most do. Education improves, as do law and legal systems; social overhead capital is increased, and monetary and fiscal policy makers often improve their general performance as more is learned about complex economic problems. Such changes can be measured and shifts noted, for individual $C$ values as well as for the entire matrix.

Figure 12–5 indicates what has probably happened in some of the countries rated in Table 12–1 over the past thirty years. All countries show improvement, although at differing rates. These rates, incidentally, should compare closely with GNP per capita gains, as they are measuring the flow of production. An advantage here is that individual constraint rankings can also be compared in detail, to determine which factors are changing the most and which are changing little, if at all. Thus, in Figure 12–5 the Soviet curve rises rapidly in the 1930's, reflecting rapid improvements in education, social overhead capital, legal structures, view of achievement, possibly changes in view toward scientific method, and so on. Egypt changes hardly at all in this period, reflecting the stagnation of the country during that decade. The U.S.S.R. then passes through the war years, where rapidly improving sociological constraints are offset by absolute declines in education and social capital, then begins again to improve in the 1950's. Saudi Arabia, the usual exception, improves steadily, reflecting again the average between very rapid oil company gains and relatively slow improvements in the nonoil sector.

Projections of changes in the future can be made by experts familiar with the country, and modifications may emerge as a result of insights gained by using the matrix. Thus, Egypt has grandiose plans for industrial expansion, but unless such plans are accompanied by more concrete gains in education and sociological constraints, plans are likely to exceed reality. The Soviets can plot massive economic gains; but unless economic and legal-political weaknesses are corrected, growth will probably fall short of expectations.

Advanced countries will have more difficulty in improving the external constraints quantitatively than will the less developed. Egypt, India, and Saudi Arabia are in a position to improve the educational constraints quite rapidly, since they all are beginning from a relatively low base. In a decade, for example, the literacy constraint could move up more than ten points if this area were actively worked upon. The developed group already has over 90 percent literacy in its population, and for this group a similar rate of gain

FIGURE 12–5

MATRIX CHANGES OVER TIME

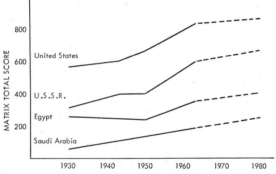

is impossible to achieve and not very important in terms of managerial effectiveness.

This point suggests that one thing the external constraint scores do not measure very precisely is the quality of the constraints. No one seriously argues that the United States and England could not improve the quality of their education, with considerable benefits for productive firms. It is possible to evaluate educational and sociological constraints in a qualitative, as well as quantitative manner; and experts do tend to do this as they explore the ratings. Lacking concrete evidence, however, indicating the overall quality of basic education, for example, the tendency is to take statistical measures wherever available. This may tend to overstate scores in various countries where such data typically are available.

Similarly, new developments in government fiscal policy, in central banking, in communications technology, and in many other areas may make rapid advance possible for the more developed countries. Such changes cannot be easily handled by the constraint scoring system utilized here. The fact that the United States scores 840/1000 or 84 percent of the maximum, does not mean that this country is 84 percent efficient, given this quality evaluation problem. The score reflects the fact that given known possibilities and the relative positions of other societies, the United States ranks somewhat higher than the others. Even this sort of rank order evaluation can prove most useful for a variety of purposes.

In Chapter 5, it was noted that GNP per capita was one measure of country efficiency; this figure is used in Table 12–1 as a cross-check on the constraint scores. However, another useful measure of efficiency is rate of growth of GNP per capita over the past decade. Countries improving their income rapidly are probably more efficient than those with lower growth rates. If rank order comparisons with an index of GNP per capita plus growth rates were made, it is possible that a more precise comparison of the value of the constraint scores could be made as well.

Table 12–2 indicates how this might be done. Columns 2 and 3 are taken from Table 12–1, and indicate the constraint scores and estimated GNP per capita for the various countries considered. Columns 1 and 4 give the rank orders of the countries based on these figures. Note that several countries are out of line. The Netherlands ranks second on the constraint scoring, but third in GNP per capita terms. One possibility here is that the Netherlands will grow faster than the United Kingdom because its external constraints are better, and in fact this has been happening for the past decade. Column 5 of Table 12–2 indicates estimated growth rates for the various countries. The Netherlands has been growing at about 6 percent, while the United Kingdom has been growing at about 2 percent. If this discrepancy in growth rates is considered, the rank order will change.

Column 6 of Table 12–2 is a composite index of growth and GNP, with the weighting of 0.9 for GNP and 0.1 for growth of GNP in the past decade being applied. The choice of a 90-to-10 weighting for these two factors is arbitrary—if an 80-to-20 system were used, the rankings would again change. The authors feel that some weight should be given to growth, but how much is perhaps more of a value judgment than a rational choice. Growth implies saving today in order to consume tomorrow, and how this is valued is more ethical than economic.

Column 7 of Table 12–2 indicates the rank order of the GNP-growth index. Every country is in the same rank order as in Column 1, with the usual exception of Saudi Arabia, for the same reasons noted earlier.

A complex and probably useless numbers game can be played with these figures. The constraint ratings are somewhat arbitrary, as determined by experts. Another set of experts would probably produce slightly different scores. GNP per capita figures are estimates, subject to wide margins of error. GNP growth per capita estimates are also subject to considerable error. To take three very shaky numbers and combine them to get precise figures is ridiculous, and readers are warned that the figures presented are to be taken as illustrative examples, not the last word in precision. To take one example, the Soviet growth rate of 5 percent represents the authors' (subjective) evaluation of estimates ranging from about 2 to 10 percent, depending on which experts are quoted. If the rate used is 6 percent, the Soviet score in Column 6 of Table 12–2 rises to 31.8 and the rank order in Column 7 changes. We could "prove" the value of the constraint ratings by shifting growth rates (i.e., taking the estimates by experts which yield the scores desired) and picking GNP estimates which would yield perfect rank orderings. Such tinkering with the data is hardly worthwhile, given the large potential errors in all of the figures used.

TABLE 12–2

CONSTRAINT SCORES, GNP, AND GNP PER CAPITA

| Country | 1 Con-straint Rank Order | 2 Constraint Score | 3 GNP per Capita | 4 GNP Rank Order | 5 Growth Rate 1955–64 | 6 GNP-Growth Index | 7 GNP-Growth Rank Order |
|---|---|---|---|---|---|---|---|
| U.S.............. | 1 | 863 | 3366 | 1 | 3.0% | 93.8 | 1 |
| Netherlands......... | 2 | 769 | 1431 | 3 | 6.0 | 47.1 | 2 |
| U.K............... | 3 | 738 | 1527 | 2 | 2.0 | 43.0 | 3 |
| Japan.............. | 4 | 715 | 798 | 5 | 8.0 | 31.6 | 4 |
| U.S.S.R........... | 5 | 689 | 900 | 4 | 5.0 | 30.6 | 5 |
| Mexico............. | 6 | 446 | 414 | 6 | 2.7 | 14.4 | 6 |
| Brazil............. | 7 | 387 | 305 | 7 | 3.5 | 9.4 | 8 |
| Egypt............. | 8 | 345 | 170 | 9 | 2.0 | 7.0 | 9 |
| India.............. | 9 | 341 | 66 | 10 | 1.0 | 3.1 | 10 |
| Saudi Arabia......... | 10 | 335 | 200 | 8 | 4.0 | 10.4 | 7 |

## CONSTAINT RATINGS AND THE MANAGEMENT PROCESS

A further refinement of the analysis of the internal firm management process and its relationship to given external constraints could be effected by the Delphi method. In Chapter 4, the impact of the external constraints on internal management was discussed. It was pointed out there that the number of interrelationships between the various C and B values was both complex and large; however, it would be possible to use the Delphi Technique both to evaluate the relevant impact of C values on given e's and to determine just what this impact might be.

In Table 4–1, the evaluation would be that of placing the x's in the proper matrix squares. That is, the Delphi experts would be asked to indicate which critical elements of the management process would be related directly to the various external constraints. The experts here are typically businessmen who have had extensive top managerial experience, preferably in several countries. Again, bankers can be useful experts, as can economists with business experience.

This initial step serves to indicate what is important, but it does not indicate how important each of these constraints may be in determining the performance of this marketing policy within the firm. The next step, which also might be done initially with the Delphi Technique, is to determine how each of these external constraints affects product line performance and planning, and to what extent. Is general literacy more important than social overhead capital, and if so, why? What kinds of social overhead capital are critical in this sector, and why? Questions of this sort would quickly become extremely complex, and considerable time would be required to obtain meaningful answers for any firm or any society; but such research would be necessary if full use of the constraint evaluations were to be made. In short, there is a need to quantify the critical C-B relationships to identify the critical relationships in a given country. Interrelationships again cause difficulties. The product line problem interacts with the various production, staffing, and organization functions, to indicate a few; however, the manageable method of analysis is probably to take the elements of the management process one at a time, in an effort to determine which external constraints are most relevant.

This more detailed analysis of managerial and enterprise functions and their relationship to external constraints can be most useful to firm managers, particularly those managers who deal with several countries. One major reason for relative lack of interest in external variables in management theory has been that most of the theorizing has taken place in the United States, where the constraints, while changing through time, are relatively constant for most firms; but when the firm moves to a new environment, these previous constants become variables, and the firm is forced to consider how they differ and what impact these differences have on the internal operations of the firm in different countries. Failure to realize the variability of the environment can lead to waste, costs higher than expected, and general inefficiency. Again, the effort here is focused on asking the right questions—the answers in any specific case depend largely on detailed analysis of the case under consideration. Full quantification here, given the complexity of the problem, would be a major task which to date has not yet been accomplished for any country. Conceptually, however, there appears to be no reason why quantification could not be accomplished, given enough time, skilled manpower, and funds.

## Quantification of the Critical Elements of the Management Process for a Single Enterprise.

While the total quantification of the C-B matrix (Table 4–1) is presently impossible, another type of quantification which may prove quite useful to individual firms can be made. Each firm in a given environment may have quite different evaluations of the relative importance of the critical elements listed in Table 4-1. For some companies, research and development may be relatively insignificant, since the firm does not actively engage in such activity, nor does it have to do so to survive. For others, such as a major chemical firm in a developed country, this firm function may be the most important of all policy questions. An electric power company with a statutory monopoly will have quite different emphasis on marketing variables than a manufacturer of toys.

These differences suggest that firms could improve their analytical ability by exploring some rough quantification of their policy variables to determine which are most important to them. Given the relationships between business policies and the external constraints, it would then be possible to focus attention on the external factors which have the most effect on the critical elements of the management process ($B$'s) which happen to be critical to this firm. If particularly critical elements are identified, then exploration of the external constraints which have a direct impact on these becomes more relevant for the firm. Thus a research oriented firm, whose R&D function was critical, could quickly note the direct relevance of the educational variables to this factor and could begin to question its policies in terms of the scores obtained on these constraints.

This sort of quantification of the business and managerial functions would differ for each firm, even for those within the same general economic sector. The major reason for this is that each firm has its own history, personnel, minor technological modifications, size, location, and accidents. Consider two trucking firms of roughly similar size in California, for example. One might determine that financial factors were of overwhelming importance, since its history contained various misadventures in financial planning, excessive dividend payouts, and similar factors. The second might see marketing problems as critical, since its history of obtaining legally granted routes differed from that of the first. The first may have been astute or lucky in obtaining routes with a high volume of traffic, making their marketing problem easier. The second may have missed this opportunity, thus creating major problems for current managers.

This sort of firm differential would mean that the initial quantification of the $B$ values in Table 2-1 would probably apply only to one firm; yet the quantification, however tentative, could also lead a firm to focus on problems critical to itself in the given environment, and this process could assist any firm in asking the key questions necessary to effective management.

Quantification of this sort could easily be accomplished by use of the Delphi Technique. The experts in this case would be top level executives of the firm; members of the board of directors who have detailed knowledge of the firm's activities; and possibly outside consultants, lawyers, or other experts who have examined the firm's position in detail. The technique could be refined to some extent by using relative weights for each of the major elements of the management process. Thus marketing could be given a weight of .20, production a weight of .10, and so on. When multiplied by the values given to each major element, these weights would give an overall weighting of the importance of the functional problem to the firm.[6]

Delphi questioning here could be kept relatively open ended, since the potential variation in importance of given firm or managerial functions might be extreme. Experts would be asked to give their evaluation of the various *B* factors for their firm, giving values from 0 to 100 (or even higher if necessary) for each *B*. It might be supposed that after requestioning per the Delphi technique some general consensus of values for each major *B* category could be determined. The second Delphi questionnaire would deal with assigning values for the sub-*B* variables within each category. Figure 12–6 reproduces a rating of this type made by one of the authors for an American food canning company. In this particular case, the management saw finance as its most important problem by far. As in the more general ratings used earlier, the interrelationships here are not stated; and this can lead to error. That is, the apparent problem is finance, but marketing or production failures could be the root cause of this particular problem; but for this firm at a given point in time, the managers saw their key problems in this way.

There is also the problem of double counting in using this sort of quantification. Managers in the above case see financial factors as most relevant; however, the reason they do is that the external constraints in this case are what they are—that is, in this system, the financial constraints operate on the firm in a way which makes internal financial problems appear most serious. The countering argument is that this type of double counting is beneficial, since the firm management is thus forced to focus only on its major internal problems, and this necessarily involves evaluation and study of the key external constraints connected with this problem. There is a reinforcement effect here on critical problems which probably does more good than harm.

A further argument for use of this sort of internal firm ranking is that it forces managers, as an expert group, to decide collectively what is important for them. Quite apart from the external constraint index, this sort of thinking may be quite helpful in focusing attention within the firm on key factors which can conceivably be improved through collective managerial action.

A firm moving into an alien environment, such as an American company beginning an operation in a foreign country, can utilize this sort of dual quantification to focus on new difficulties. Here, evaluations could differ even for the same firm. A large, integrated oil company might be

---

[6] See B. Richman, "A Rating Scale for Product Innovation," *Business Horizons*, Vol. V, No. 2, summer, 1962, pp. 37–44, for an example of this weighting technique applied to a single firm.

considering entering one new country as a marketer of refined products and another as a producer of crude. When the internal question of relevance is asked about the managerial and firm functions, different evaluations will be forthcoming for each case. Once the critically important internal variables have been quantified, examination of the external constraints closely influencing these particular internal factors can be accomplished. This effort of B factor quantification may help the firm in deciding which of the various external constraints are of most relevance in determining the course of development of the new project.

This project can be illustrated by considering the company B ratings considered in Figure 12.6. Since finance is seen as the key issue, reading across Table 4–1 shows that none of the educational constraints is particularly relevant for this factor. The cannery can thus concentrate on more valid external factors, which in the finance cases are largely legal and economic; however, an oil company entering crude production might find that personnel and staffing problems are critical, in which case Table 4–1 indicates that educational and sociological constraints are very important. The canning company can ignore much of the educational constraints without difficulty, while the oil company ignores these factors to its own loss.

## CONCLUSION

It is useful to attempt to quantify the external constraints and the interactions of the constraints and firm and managerial functions, in spite of the rather extensive conceptual and practical difficulties involved in such attempts. The Delphi Technique, developed at the Rand Corporation, offers a relatively clearcut and simple way to accomplish this goal. The use of experts in developing values for the various constraint variables offers a means of quickly deducing values for the various constraints.

The problems involved in this quantification, particularly the problems of measurement and interrelationship of the variables, suggests why various managerial, economic, and development problems have proved so intractable to analysis in the past. The number of variables is large, and no easy answers can be expected. From the point of view of the productive enterprise, the large number of factors, both internal and external, which directly influence its performance is so big as to make careful analysis almost impossible. At best, the firm can barely recognize what is relevant, let alone manipulate or analyze the variables. As the firm moves into more than one general environment, as firms do when they become international operations, the complexities tend to increase even more rapidly. From the point of view of a national planner, concerned with improving GNP per capita, the complexities are equally depressing. Interactions between constraints are often subtle and unforeseen. Pressures applied in the economic sector may reappear unfavorably in the sociological sector. General economic

FIGURE 12–6

*Ratings of the Critical Elements of the Management Process*

| Total B | Sub-B | | |
|---|---|---|---|
| 35 | | $B_1$: | *Planning and Innovation* |
| | 3 | | 1.1 Basic organizational objectives pursued and the form of their operational expression. |
| | 2 | | 1.2 Types of plans utilized. |
| | 2 | | 1.3 Time horizon of plans and planning. |
| | 2 | | 1.4 Degree and extent to which enterprise operations are spelled out in plans (i.e., preprogrammed). |
| | 2 | | 1.5 Flexibility of plans. |
| | 2 | | 1.6 Methodologies, techniques and tools used in planning and decision making. |
| | 2 | | 1.7 Extent and effectiveness of employee participation in planning. |
| | 2 | | 1.8 Managerial behavior in the planning process. |
| | 4 | | 1.9 Degree and extent of information distortion in planning. |
| | 2 | | 1.10 Degree and extent to which scientific method is effectively applied by enterprise personnel—both managers and nonmanagers—in dealing with causation and futurity problems. |
| | 10 | | 1.11 Nature, extent, and rate of innovation and risk taking in enterprise operations over a given period of time. |
| | 2 | | 1.12 Ease or difficulty of introducing changes and innovations in enterprise operations. |
| 33 | | $B_2$: | *Control* |
| | 15 | | 2.1 Types of strategic performance and control standards used in different areas; e.g., production, marketing, finance, personnel. |
| | 5 | | 2.2 Types of control techniques used. |
| | 5 | | 2.3 Nature and structure of information feedback systems used for control purposes. |
| | 2 | | 2.4 Timing and procedures for corrective action. |
| | 2 | | 2.5 Degree of looseness or tightness of control over personnel. |
| | 2 | | 2.6 Extent and nature of unintended effects resulting from the overall control system employed. |
| | 2 | | 2.7 Effectiveness of the control system in compelling events to conform to plans. |
| 28 | | $B_3$: | *Organization* |
| | 2 | | 3.1 Size of representative enterprise and its major subunits. |
| | 2 | | 3.2 Degree of centralization or decentralization of authority. |
| | 3 | | 3.3 Degree of work specialization (division of labor). |
| | 3 | | 3.4 Spans of control. |
| | 5 | | 3.5 Basic departmentation and grouping of activities. Extent and uses of service departments. |
| | 2 | | 3.6 Extent and uses of staff generalists and specialists. |
| | 2 | | 3.7 Extent and uses of functional authority. |
| | 2 | | 3.8 Extent and degree of organizational confusion and friction regarding authority and responsibility relationships. |
| | 2 | | 3.9 Extent and uses of committee and group decision making. |
| | 3 | | 3.10 Nature, extent, and uses of the informal organization. |
| | 2 | | 3.11 Degree and extent to which the organization structure (i.e., the formal organization) is mechanical or flexible with regard to causing and/or adapting to changing conditions. |
| 31 | | $B_4$: | *Staffing* |
| | 2 | | 4.1 Methods used in recruiting personnel. |
| | 2 | | 4.2 Criteria used in selecting and promoting personnel. |
| | 2 | | 4.3 Techniques and criteria used in appraising personnel. |
| | 1 | | 4.4 Nature and uses of job descriptions. |
| | 3 | | 4 5 Levels of compensation. |

FIGURE 12-6—*Continued*

*Total B*   *Sub-B*

| | | |
|---|---|---|
| | 2 | 4.6 Nature, extent, and time absorbed in enterprise training programs and activities. |
| | 2 | 4.7 Extent of informal individual development. |
| | 10 | 4.8 Policies and procedures regarding the layoff and dismissal of personnel. |
| | 2 | 4.9 Ease or difficulty in dismissing personnel no longer required or desired. |
| | 5 | 4.10 Ease or difficulty of obtaining and maintaining personnel of all types with desired skills and abilities. |

49   $B_5$:   *Direction, Leadership, and Motivation*

| | | |
|---|---|---|
| | 2 | 5.1 Degree and extent of authoritarian vs. participative management. (This relates to autocrats vs. consultative direction.) |
| | 2 | 5.2 Techniques and methods used for motivating managerial personnel. |
| | 4 | 5.3 Techniques and methods used for motivating nonmanagerial personnel. |
| | 5 | 5.4 Supervisory techniques used. |
| | 3 | 5.5 Communication structure and techniques. |
| | 6 | 5.6 Degree and extent to which communication is ineffective among personnel of all types. |
| | 5 | 5.7 Ease or difficulty of motivating personnel to perform efficiently, and to improve their performance and abilities over time (irrespective of the types of incentives that may be utilized for this purpose). |
| | 4 | 5.8 Degree and extent of identification that exists between the interests and objectives of individuals, work groups, departments, and the enterprise as a whole. |
| | 4 | 5.9 Degree and extent of trust and cooperation or conflict and distrust among personnel of all types. |
| | 5 | 5.10 Degree and extent of frustration, absenteeism, and turnover among personnel. |
| | 10 | 5.11 Degree and extent of wasteful time and effort resulting from restrictive work practices, unproductive bargaining, conflicts, etc. |

62   $B_6$:   *Marketing (Policies Pursued)*

| | | |
|---|---|---|
| | 30 | 6.1 Product line (degree of diversification as specialization, rate of change, product quality). |
| | 20 | 6.2 Channels of distribution and types and location of customers. |
| | 10 | 6.3 Pricing (for key items, in relation to costs, profit margins, quantity and trade discount structure). |
| | 2 | 6.4 Sales promotion and key sales appeals (types used and degree of aggressiveness in sales promotion). |

79   $B_7$:   *Production and Procurement*

| | | |
|---|---|---|
| | 5 | 7.1 Make or buy (components, supplies, facilities, services, extent to which subcontracting is used, etc.). |
| | 20 | 7.2 Number, types and locations of major suppliers. |
| | 20 | 7.3 Timing of procurement of major supplies. |
| | 10 | 7.4 Average Inventory levels (major supplies, goods in process, completed output). |
| | 5 | 7.5 Minimum, maximum and average size of production runs. |
| | 10 | 7.6 Degree to which production operations are stabilized. |
| | 2 | 7.7 Combination of factor inputs used in major products produced. |
| | 2 | 7.8 Basic production processes used. |

FIGURE 12-6—*Continued*

| Total B | Sub B | | | |
|---|---|---|---|---|
| | 5 | | 7.9 | Extent of automation and mechanization in enterprise operations. |
| 10 | | $B_8$: | *Research and Development* | |
| | 10 | | 8.1 | Nature and extent of R & D activity (e.g., product development and improvement, new material usages, new production processes and technology). |
| 300 | | $B_9$: | *Finance* | |
| | 80 | | 9.1 | Types of financing (e.g., equity, debt, short term, long term). |
| | | | 9.2 | |
| | 100 | | 9.3 | Sources of capital. |
| | 50 | | 9.4 | Major uses of capital. |
| | 50 | | 9.5 | Protection of capital. |
| | 20 | | 9.6 | Distribution of Earnings. |
| 34 | | $B_{10}$: | *Public and External Relations* (The Relationships, attitudes and policies of enterprise management regarding major types of external agents and organizations.) | |
| | 10 | | 10.1 | Customers and consumer relations (E.g., does firm management regard consumer loyalty and satisfaction as being important, or is it chiefly interested in short run results, quick profits?). |
| | 5 | | 10.2 | Supplier relations. |
| | 5 | | 10.3 | Investor and creditor relations. |
| | 10 | | 10.4 | Union relations. |
| | 2 | | 10.5 | Government relations. |
| | 2 | | 10.6 | Community relations (e.g., educational institutions, chamber of commerce, business and professional associations, community welfare activities). |

changes may lead to impacts on productive enterprise which are negative, thus worsening rather than improving the situation.

It appears that any efforts toward systematic evaluation of critical factors affecting productivity and growth would at least help ease these problems for both of the above groups. Hence, this effort to quantify, while imperfect, may represent some achievement in this regard. It presents a useful checklist at worst, and at best it may yield insights into what is really important for both firms and countries.

The point that being wrong quantitatively may be useful should also be emphasized. In developing this analysis, we have frequently been challenged, particularly in quantification, by experts who argued for different values being placed on particular variables. In some cases, the expert won his case—but not before extended debate had provided a considerable education for both the expert and us. Many people have learned to rely on numbers, however inaccurate—and if the basic approach is sound, the numbers can always be changed.

# Chapter 13

# The Firm in Islandia

## INTRODUCTION

Previous chapters have developed a view of what might be the ideal environment for economically productive enterprises. In no country is the environment perfect; and more is likely to be wrong than right in any given country, in terms of the actual environment which firms face. In some countries, however, some environmental conditions are excellent; and it is possible to imagine a situation where the best conditions of all countries are joined to make an ideal environment for ideal firms and their managements.

The general theory presented here is that if the external constraints are the best possible in a world populated with somewhat imperfect men, productive enterprises will have maximum managerial effectiveness, which will lead to maximum firm and system efficiency. This system efficiency can be measured by GNP per capita, rate of growth of per capita GNP, and the other measures developed in Chapter 5. Hence, the utopia we shall create here is one in which focus is on the external constraints of the ideal society. If these are ideal, one will have created the most productive society imaginable.

Utopia creation is an ancient art. Such ideal societies are commonly organized around some philosophical idea of the "good life." In our case, little is said about the quality of life; we merely present a picture of a society in which managerial and productive functions can proceed with a minimum of interference. Our Utopia is a model of what a society might be if intelligent, farsighted citizens really had as a major goal the optimization of production, in terms of the largest possible output of goods and services. Perhaps such a country will never exist, since in the last analysis, productive efficiency is not really the ultimate goal of man's existence; but it is useful to see what such a model country might look like, if only to debate the potential trade-offs between more cherished noneconomic goals and economic efficiency. Like any model, this one is incomplete and sketchy, and the imaginative reader can fill in his own details of the kind of life which would exist in such a system. Hence we move to an examination of the Republic of Islandia, a country that never was, and never will be.

## THE ISLANDIAN EXTERNAL CONSTRAINT SCORE

Table 13–1 shows the constraint score for Islandia, compared to scores for a few other major countries. No score is perfect, since men are hardly perfect, even in Islandia. Islandian scores are higher than any for existing countries, however, reflecting potential improvements in external constraints which might be achieved with current arts, knowledge, and skills.

It should be noted that only two of the external constraints are beyond the control of the population of the country being rated. These are factor endowment ($C_{4.6}$) and (domestic) market size ($C_{4.7}$). Even in these cases it is possible to alter the constraints to some extent. Resources are more likely to be discovered by a population trained to look, and marginal resources can be most effectively exploited by a productive firm which is well managed. Markets can be expanded domestically by creating more income for purchasing power and internationally by producing goods and services of quality and price acceptable to other countries, but the remainder of the constraints are within the power of the population of the country to alter to their own advantage. In a world where technology and management are far more important than the natural endowment which a country happens to possess, the society is really what its citizens choose to make of it. Islandians prefer to create the most efficient economic system possible.

In order to see how the external constraints might be made as effective as possible, it is useful to review the constraints. To this problem we now turn.

## EDUCATIONAL CONSTRAINTS

Islandia scores as high as possible in a world not populated entirely by geniuses. Over 98 percent of the population can read and write, and has completed at least eight years of education. The result is that virtually the entire labor force is literate. Any firm can confidently write up job specifications, work rules, work instructions, pay rules, and similar matters and expect that the entire work force will be able to read and understand them. When jobs change in nature, new instructions can be prepared to tell workers what is now expected and how it can be done. Work goes smoothly in outlying locations—on delivery trucks, for example, drivers are able to read addresses, follow instructions for keeping equipment in order, and prepare reports to superiors. In places like the United States, Japan, and western Europe, where universal literacy is a fact, such problems seem too trivial even to mention; but the implications of trying to work with an illiterate work force might be pondered. This act of reading has profound consequences, all of them favorable, for Islandian firms.

In Islandia, over 60 percent of the present eighteen-year-olds are enrolled in some form of higher education beyond high school. Some training

## TABLE 13-1

### Islandian External Constraint Evaluation

| Constraints | | U.S. | U.K. | U.S.S.R. | Islandia |
|---|---|---|---|---|---|
| *Educational* | | | | | |
| $C_{1.1}$ | 100. . . . . . . . . . . . . . . . . . . . . . | 95 | 95 | 90 | 98 |
| 1.2 | 25. . . . . . . . . . . . . . . . . . . . . | 20 | 19 | 23 | 24 |
| 1.3 | 50. . . . . . . . . . . . . . . . . . . . . | 42 | 22 | 32 | 48 |
| 1.4 | 25. . . . . . . . . . . . . . . . . . . . . | 24 | 13 | 17 | 24 |
| 1.5 | 25. . . . . . . . . . . . . . . . . . . . . | 24 | 19 | 24 | 24 |
| 1.6 | 25. . . . . . . . . . . . . . . . . . . . . | 23 | 17 | 18 | 24 |
| Total $C_1$ | 250. . . . . . . . . . . . . . . . . . . | 227 | 185 | 204 | 242 |
| *Sociological-Cultural* | | | | | |
| $C_{2.1}$ | 30. . . . . . . . . . . . . . . . . . . . . | 24 | 18 | 27 | 29 |
| 2.2 | 10. . . . . . . . . . . . . . . . . . . . . | 8 | 6 | 8 | 9 |
| 2.3 | 20. . . . . . . . . . . . . . . . . . . . . | 16 | 12 | 12 | 18 |
| 2.4 | 70. . . . . . . . . . . . . . . . . . . . . | 64 | 54 | 66 | 66 |
| 2.5 | 20. . . . . . . . . . . . . . . . . . . . . | 17 | 12 | 18 | 19 |
| 2.6 | 10. . . . . . . . . . . . . . . . . . . . . | 8 | 6 | 9 | 9 |
| 2.7 | 50. . . . . . . . . . . . . . . . . . . . . | 42 | 35 | 31 | 48 |
| 2.8 | 20. . . . . . . . . . . . . . . . . . . . . | 17 | 12 | 14 | 19 |
| 2.9 | 20. . . . . . . . . . . . . . . . . . . . . | 18 | 12 | 12 | 19 |
| Total $C_2$ | 250. . . . . . . . . . . . . . . . . . . | 214 | 167 | 197 | 236 |
| *Legal-Political* | | | | | |
| $C_{3.1}$ | 80. . . . . . . . . . . . . . . . . . . . . | 66 | 68 | 40 | 78 |
| 3.2 | 20. . . . . . . . . . . . . . . . . . . . . | 15 | 16 | 8 | 19 |
| 3.3 | 25. . . . . . . . . . . . . . . . . . . . . | 15 | 18 | 10 | 23 |
| 3.4 | 80. . . . . . . . . . . . . . . . . . . . . | 75 | 68 | 70 | 79 |
| 3.5 | 25. . . . . . . . . . . . . . . . . . . . . | 19 | 21 | 10 | 24 |
| 3.6 | 20. . . . . . . . . . . . . . . . . . . . . | 15 | 17 | 10 | 19 |
| Total $C_3$ | 250. . . . . . . . . . . . . . . . . . . | 205 | 208 | 148 | 242 |
| *Economic* | | | | | |
| $C_{4.1}$ | 40. . . . . . . . . . . . . . . . . . . . . | 33 | 28 | 19 | 38 |
| 4.2 | 20. . . . . . . . . . . . . . . . . . . . . | 16 | 17 | 13 | 19 |
| 4.3 | 20. . . . . . . . . . . . . . . . . . . . . | 16 | 14 | 12 | 19 |
| 4.4 | 40. . . . . . . . . . . . . . . . . . . . . | 30 | 28 | 24 | 39 |
| 4.5 | 30. . . . . . . . . . . . . . . . . . . . . | 29 | 27 | 16 | 29 |
| 4.6 | 40. . . . . . . . . . . . . . . . . . . . . | 37 | 18 | 24 | 30 |
| 5.7 | 25. . . . . . . . . . . . . . . . . . . . . | 23 | 19 | 14 | 20 |
| 4.8 | 35. . . . . . . . . . . . . . . . . . . . . | 33 | 27 | 18 | 34 |
| Total $C_4$ | 250. . . . . . . . . . . . . . . . . . . | 216 | 178 | 140 | 228 |
| GRAND TOTAL | 1,000. . . . . . . . . . . . . . . . . . . | 863 | 738 | 689 | 948 |
| GNP/cap. | . . . . . . . . . . . . . . . . . . . . . . . . . . . | $3,200 | $1,400 | $1,000 | $4,500 |

is purely technical and short term, such as learning how to be a dental technician, a welder, an electronics technician, or a hairdresser, in a two year or shorter junior college type of program. Many other young people attend four year colleges, learning in every possible field from astronomy to zoology. Thousands of others attend professional graduate schools in law, education, business administration, dentistry, medicine, the natural sciences, and so on. There are numerous colleges and universities, public and private; and while all are not of the first rank, enough are to guarantee that most competent young persons will obtain a first rate education. Even the lesser schools tend to specialize in areas in which they can do a good job, and a completely poor higher education is rare.

In addition to the formal types of education noted above, our country has a bewildering variety of informal educational programs, designed to assist anyone in the culture who wants to learn anything to do so as easily as possible. Public schools and colleges support extensive adult education programs, ranging from studies of the classics to body and fender repair courses. Many types of firms also underwrite programs in areas of interest to themselves—real estate practices, hotel management, accounting, and many others. Trade unions cooperate with employers to develop and improve apprentice programs for various types of skilled craftsmen such as machinists, plumbers, bakers, and electricians. City employees can take courses in public administration; executives have a wide choice of executive training programs run by foundations, schools, and universities. There are ways of obtaining virtually any type of knowledge desired in some way or other; and when new ideas come along, many people are willing to organize new courses to train those interested.

Education is an interesting topic in Islandia. There is persistent fear that the system is not doing a good job of educating young or old, and frequent articles in leading papers and magazines view with alarm the low level of achievement of Islandia's young people in critical skills. There is also concern that not enough people are getting enough education, either formally or informally; and the school dropout rate is cause for extended debate in parliament. The people support education heavily, being willing to tax themselves extensively for better facilities. Educators are respected for their wisdom and achievements on the one hand and damned for their relative incompetence on the other. All seems ferment, confusion, and extended and vitriolic debate. Because education is regarded as a good way to get ahead, both in terms of status and income, and because this is increasingly recognized by large numbers of citizens, the number of years of schooling completed by the average citizen is steadily rising, as more young people stay in school longer; but the improvement is too slow and too uncertain to satisfy many Islandians, and they complain bitterly about the type of education they are getting—while at the same time taking extraordinary advantage of what is offered at the moment. One thing is sure: next year will see still better opportunities and still more citizens taking advantage of them.

Islandians are rather pragmatic about their education, seeing in learning a chance to improve their economic status. Hence, there is an informational system run by the various schools which informs those interested about potential future careers. One result is that occupations now oversupplied with trained persons do not attract many new entrants, while those jobs which offer expanding possibilities do. If engineers are plentiful, while accountants are scarce, college enrollments will shortly correct discrepancies. The wide publicity given to such studies of the labor market has the effect of guiding education along the lines of economic needs.

In the elite group of managers, bureaucrats, and administrators who actually make the critical decisions in the total economy, there is perpetual soul searching about the quality of education for top positions; and colleges are forever modifying their curricula to meet real or imagined deficiencies. Given the complexities of management in a complex industrial economy, the recruits into top managerial positions are never well enough educated. Their educations are always deficient, and academicians and practical men are forever debating the types of training which will have maximum impact.

The result of such an educational environment is that firms are usually able to obtain the types of manpower they need to operate their business efficiently. Since there is not a large pool of unemployed individuals, this does not mean that any position can immediately be filled with a perfectly qualified individual; but it does mean that if an electronics technician is desired, a man (or woman) can be found who has had the necessary academic or apprentice training and who is capable of rapidly being assimilated into the work force. If an engineer is needed, a visit to the universities will normally produce a qualified young candidate. The staffing problem is more to train a basically qualified person to fill his role in the firm than to make do as well as possible with a person who is trained as a bookkeeper but who now must become a machinist. Nor do firms have to take a man with a third grade education and put him to work at a job which needs a college graduate's skills to be performed properly.

Islandian education is expensive, draining off a significant portion of GNP each year, but the Islandians are willing to spend the money. They have learned a simple secret which is obvious enough to be completely overlooked in many societies. A country is only as good, in economic terms, as the quality of persons in it; and investment in human capital has a higher rate of return than investment in any other kind of asset. Almost any country can invest more in education, and most can invest in what they now do more wisely. Failure to do so is costly in terms of lost opportunities and lost production.

## SOCIOLOGICAL-CULTURAL CONSTRAINTS

A society's view of man and itself is formed over centuries. Obscure religious writers and thinkers, half forgotten philosophers, and long dead political leaders, among others, help create the kinds of present sociological attitudes relevant for production efficiency today. Such sociological attitudes also tend to change over time; and they can be bent, but seldom forced completely, into desired patterns. Islandians are perhaps luckier than most, since their sociological position is almost ideal for maximum productive efficiency. Anyone desiring to follow the same road might have patience, for the changing of long held beliefs does not occur in days, years, or even decades in most cases; but changes do occur, for better or for worse.

Managers are respected in Islandia. This does not mean that they are believed blindly, or that they take on the aspect of oracles; but in debates on issues concerning business problems, their opinions are treated with respect. Since the profession is respected, competition for top jobs in productive enterprises, public and private, is keen; and the man who reaches top level management is usually worthy of the respect he can get. Managerial ability includes an ethical position analogous to similar positions in law and medicine, and it is expected that managers will live up to their own code of ethics. While there may be a dishonest businessman on occasion, just as there are quack doctors and ambulance chasing lawyers, cases of chicanery in management are viewed with grave concern. Management in Islandia is a position of trust, and managers are expected to live up to their role. Since managers are respected, the marginal fringe of con men, phonies, and fast-buck artists is of minimal size. There is an instinct of craftsmanship here in management—managers are proud of the job they do, and they are recognized as doing an adequate job. Pride in work leads to better work, as does the respect for good work well done.

People generally respect each other in Islandia. The reasons are complex, depending in part on the relatively high educational achievement of the population, generally held ethical views about the way man should regard his fellow man, and the relative absence of class barriers; but the result is that Islandians respect each other and their views. Managers and persons in authority typically have earned their right to be where they are, and it is not difficult to get Islandians to observe industrial discipline. The discipline is not harsh, given the Islandian propensity for enjoying work. Since the society is quite advanced technically, it is rare to find harsh discipline being tried, simply because it produces poor results when applied to intelligent workers who must think on the job. One can be tough with essentially homogeneous mass-production workers, but trying to force technicians to obey silly rules and regulations merely results in less work being done. One usually finds in Islandia a quite decentralized pattern of management, because it is more effective with the type of work to be done and the workers on hand than any other possible organizational pattern.

Islandians generally cooperate with each other. The competitive economy forces suppliers to cooperate with their buyers, if they expect repeat business; and the social complex in Islandia strongly urges social cooperation rather than strife. Unions exist, and bargain hard, but they seldom form a dead-handed barrier to progress, particularly when full employment is the rule rather than the exception and when rapid changes in individual jobs are offset by official action to assure that no worker is left unemployed for long. A few simple national rules help here. Pension rights are transferable and standardized in all cases. Hence, a railway worker forced out by modernization to another job does not lose whatever rights he has gained in the years he toiled for the railroad. A national employment service tries to match available persons to jobs anywhere in the country, and moving expenses are financed out of the unemployment insurance fund. Such aids tend to minimize blind resistance to change and encourage cooperation between persons. Government officials are trained to consider sympathetically the problems of businessmen, while managers are willing to cooperate with the relatively mild types of controls applied by government against business. National productivity gains are the entire nation's business, and all groups seem willing to do their part, provided, of course, that everyone else does his.

As might be expected from other attitudes mentioned above, Islandians have a high regard for personal achievement. Persons gaining fame in any field, including management, are highly regarded, and well paid. It is commonly felt that any man can achieve much, if he only sets his sights high enough; and children are encouraged to plan their lives with maximum, rather than minimum, achievement in mind. The culture backs this feeling with large investments in education for all, making it possible for even humble persons to gain much; and in every generation there are many examples of high achievers who started from the very bottom of the social structure. Achievement is not unrealistic, however; persons with limited capabilities are not encouraged to seek more than they can reasonably gain. An unskilled worker is encouraged to learn a skill, however, so that he can move up the income and prestige ladder, while the skilled are encouraged to acquire still more professional skills to move still higher.

No one in Islandia is imprisoned in his class or sex. Black or white, male or female, poor or rich, all are encouraged to try to move upward in the class structure. The barriers to mobility, particularly in income and environmental terms, are real enough; but the culture is wise enough to realize that the maximum potential of every citizen is needed to assist in the improving performance of a complex industrial economy. No person, however humble his origin, is excluded from the race. This feeling is backed by the cradle to the grave educational system, plus a lack of negative feeling about race or sex which has taken centuries to achieve. Educational authorities are always alert for the occasional genius which may appear in any social class, and such a person will not lack for opportunity. The use of official or unofficial quotas on the employment of various types of persons is alien to Islandian thinking, since it is clear that such a system is inherently inefficient. The tendency is to evaluate persons on their performance, not on where they came from or what their class or racial background might be.

It is not considered improper to be wealthy in Islandia, as long as wealth is used wisely. Islandians tend to be somewhat Calvinistic in their attitudes toward money. Managers, among other important and productive persons in the society, are quite well paid, but the concept of the idle rich is alien. A wealthy man is regarded as having opportunities for public and private service which poorer men may not have, and he is expected to act accordingly. In the status pecking order, earned income is considered better than unearned riches; and one result of this view is that favored heirs scramble quite energetically for key jobs along with poorer qualified applicants. Surplus wealth, moreover, is expected to be invested in productive enterprise, along with the owner's managerial talents, if need be.

Since Islandians have no intention of creating a small class of extremely wealthy individuals, income and estate taxes are high in the upper brackets, and a wealthy man has to be quite ingenious to pass on his wealth to his heirs. Even if one does obtain wealth in this way, it is difficult to become a playboy and still maintain status in this curious culture.

The folklore of management is at a minimum in Islandia. While managers are aware of the significance of their jobs, they are not convinced that management is the end result of all human activity. Managers are made, not born, in Islandia; and it is realized clearly that a good manager is more than an instinctively adept person who intuitively forecasts the general trend of his business and adjusts accordingly. In short, the use of predictive scientific methodology is widespread. Managers know that they are dealing with extremely complex behavioral-technical situations which are exceedingly difficult to forecast accurately; but they are willing to try, bringing to bear on their problems all of the powerful tools of modern scientific methodology. If the critical variables in a situation can be identified and related, the prediction problem becomes manageable. Hence, we see widespread use of scientific forecasting techniques used in business for all types of problems involving critical elements of the management process. There are no crystal balls in Islandia, nor astrologers, nor fortune tellers—at least, not in executive suites. Wishful thinking about management problems is done only off the job. What is done is to apply the major tools of the scientific revolution to management. Like other countries, Islandia is barely beginning to tackle some of the difficult problems of prediction, including those involving human behavior; but at least most companies are trying.

The application of scientific methodology is not restricted in Islandia to business only. The schools stress the internal logic of relationships, and subjects from economics to ecology are taught with this basic methodology in mind. One result of this approach is that actions in many fields, such as politics, economics, engineering, business, and public administration, are characterized by a rationality which is rare in this emotional world. It is widely recognized that complex social problems are only partially amenable to such logical analysis, but decision makers try to apply what they can of scientific methodology.

Islandians are quite willing to take reasonable risks in business, politics, war, and society. Experimentation with new products, processes, or changes in the social structure are considered promising, and they are made consistently. Since risk is regarded favorably, it is recognized by occasional large rewards, which further encourages risk taking; however, the Islandians have little regard for countries or firms which take wild risks without reasoned analysis of the consequences. If the payoff to a risk appears good, however, and if the costs of failure can be borne successfully, they will attempt it.

Islandians rather enjoy change. They are wise enough to know that this century necessarily is the era where nothing will stay as it is for long, and they are confident enough to know that they can probably force changes for the better for themselves. In material terms, their world has been steadily improving for a hundred years, and they see no reason why it should not continue to improve for an indefinite time in the future. There may be some nostalgia for a simpler, easier past; but it does not take the form of blind resistance to change.

Sociologically, Islandians have learned to live with the industrial age, which is perhaps more than can be said about any other culture. This age came far too quickly for easy adjustment, and the managerial problems created by the unleashing of enormous energy resources have presented still more unsolved questions for societies to struggle with. No society knows all the answers; but in observing the way in which various countries have met the demands of the modern age, one can gain some insight into how best such problems might be solved. The Islandians have simply put this knowledge together in their sociological system in a somewhat better way than anyone else, to date, has managed to do.

## LEGAL-POLITICAL CONSTRAINTS

A major factor in the relevant legal structure of Islandia is its certainty for businessmen. This is not to say that managers have unusual rights as compared to other parties at law. What is true is that a man can be sure whether he is violating the law, given existing statutes and legal precedents. If a contract is written and agreed on by the parties involved, violation will be certainly penalized. In any complex society, such relative certainty is hard to come by, and the Islandians have to work at their law constantly to achieve this result. Dynamic changes are always appearing to upset old precedents, and changes must constantly be made to keep law up to date and make sure that justice is granted to all parties.

A second major feature of the Islandian legal system is that it is just. Persons are equal in law, and violators are punished impartially. Since lawyers, like managers, are well respected citizens, they feel a strong obligation to guarantee a continuance of justice in their perpetual reform of the law; and citizens feel strongly that if they are brought to justice they will pay the same price for error as any other citizen.

Tax laws are designed to yield necessary revenues, not to give favored loopholes to insiders in specific enterprise. If given types of business are to be encouraged for social reasons, they are encouraged openly, not by means of some obscure paragraph in a complex tax bill. Such situations as excess depletion allowances and accelerated depreciation are unknown in Islandia, and the idea of having such a grossly unfair treatment of different types of firms or citizens is regarded as unsound. Taxes are rarely designed as punitive factors, brought to bear on social classes for social reasons. There are other ways of punishing or rewarding citizens, and the misuse of the revenue gathering power of the state is not one of them.

Labor law likewise is fair, firm, and consistent. There are no privileged businesses which gain advantage by being exempt from critical segments of law governing working conditions, wages, and hours; and trade union activity is regulated in a consistent manner. The effect of consistency is to remove an element of uncertainty which interferes with normal business planning and decision making. A firm's lawyer can inform management with little delay about the legality of any proposed action. Not only is the law consistent, but it is enforced consistently. Violators can expect to be punished, and erratic law enforcement is unknown. Dead-letter law is removed from the statute books, not held in abeyance to be used as a weapon against unfortunates at some later date.

Islandia tries to maintain reasonably consistent foreign relations with important nations with which it trades. Tariffs are levied for specific and detailed purposes, not just as a sop to high cost internal producers. Islandia really believes in comparative advantage, and its government rarely levies duties to protect the incompetent. Firms in Islandia are faced with the prospect of import competition at all times, which makes the rest of the world a competitor in many industrial activities. One result of this condition is that goods tend to be cheaper in Islandia than in most countries, since if Islandia cannot make something for less, it will be imported. Islandia naturally enough favors lower import duties for its products in foreign countries, and its government works diligently toward this end in negotiations with other powers. Since there are few impediments to low cost production in Islandia in regard to obtaining raw materials, energy, or capital from other nations, Islandia production costs tend to be low—aided also by the high skill work force and managements which the country has developed. Hence, exports are not difficult in many lines. One effect of this policy is that the effective market size of many of Islandian manufacturing and agricultural sectors is worldwide, rather than local. A second effect is that many of Islandia's firms are import agents for products from other countries and Islandia's market is of more than passing interest to many other economies, with beneficial further effects in the political sphere.

The Islandians, like others in an unstable world, need some defense force, but they are careful to limit their expenditures here to the minimum required, rather than the maximum possible. Hence, there is a minimal effect on the economy of high skill manpower and capital being drained from the productive sector into defense activities. Islandia is not so large as to dream of conquering the world, although it is important enough to be interesting to the major powers. Hence, it can maneuver to obtain maximum advantage from political and defense pacts rather than from working alone to maximize its military potential. Since Islandia has no real enemies, it has no problems in trading with whichever countries seem to offer maximum economic advantage. It also has little need to develop high cost, strategic industrial sectors to provide needed defense items. In the modern world, where atomic wars may wipe out whole continents in moments, it is not terribly important to have large standing armies or massive conventional armaments available—or so the Islandians believe.

The country has an extremely stable political system, evolved over centuries of experimentation and debate. The last revolution occurred centuries ago; and while political parties change in power from time to time, there are no massive changes of a revolutionary character occurring. Again, the effect is certainly within wide ranges. Change will constantly occur, but it will be evolutionary rather than revolutionary. Managers do not fear that tomorrow the political system will be radically different from today's, although it will be different in some ways.

Islandia centralizes the political functions which need to be centralized and decentralizes those of primarily local importance. This is easier said than done, but considerable effort is devoted to dividing the political power between central and provincial governments. Hence, the various details of a major water conservation project will be decided locally, while the major, overall planning will be done centrally. In a world rapidly growing smaller, the Islandians manage to avoid such anomolies as provincial truck speed, weight, and size restrictions, while preserving legitimate local functions. Good management extends to government bureaucracies as well as to private and public production enterprise; and there is no deadweight, overcentralized decision making in government, nor are there hoards of petty local officials interfering with national goals and policies.

Political parties tend to stick to crucial issues rather than wander down irrelevant byways, and election campaigns are based on significant problems facing the society. A highly educated electorate helps insure that the important problems with significantly different solutions are debated intelligently and properly. The capital is full of lobbyists for all factions; but their actual influence is limited to presenting the facts for their employers, and there is little chance for any group to apply excess pressure. Above all, Islandian politics and administration are flexible, without being erratic. The dead hand of the past weighs heavily on all societies, particularly in periods of rapid change; and there is a real danger that ancient interests may prevent necessary change and reform. The Islandians recognize this danger, realizing at the same time that a nation's heritage is indeed precious; and they make a conscious effort to maintain a balance between what is old and valid and what is new and useful.

To an outsider, Islandian politics might seem quite dull. There are no violent issues or men; debates are subdued, and critical issues are discussed in an air of calm deliberation. If the country has its angry young men, they are not in politics, at least in the portion of political life which bears heavily on business efficiency. What does happen is that business managers have some notion that changes, when made, will not completely upset established orders and that the degree of legal certainty of their actions is considerably greater than in any other country. The result is that a great deal of planning is ruled out, and managers are free to devote considerably more time to other phases of their complex operations.

## ECONOMIC CONSTRAINTS

Islandia is primarily a free enterprise, private property country. In part this is because it was such a state historically and, like many Western countries, has never had a major Marxist revolution or coup; but there is a further reason why Islandians favor private enterprise—efficiency. The system works extremely well as a resource allocation mechanism, with a minimum of necessary government interference, planning, or cost. The use of profits as a feedback mechanism allowing the proper allocation of resources by a society has been realized for over a century; but this valuable asset of such a system has long been obscured by cyclical fluctuations, resulting in occasional mass unemployment, wartime hyperinflations, and similar catastrophes. Islandians have been perceptive enough to realize that, from an efficiency point of view, a free enterprise system is superior to any other known form of economic organization.

Free enterprise also is most effective when the basic value judgment of the society is that most men know best themselves what they want. Islandians believe this, and they are quite willing to let buyers in the market determine the types of consumer goods which are produced. Since they live in a political democracy, Islandians are able to tax themselves as they see fit to obtain necessary collective goods, such as defense, education, parks, police protection, and similar items, which the society sees as necessary. Incentives for investment by private firms are left to the marketplace, aided by laws governing such key items as taxation of assets, depreciation tax policy, and similar levers for raising or lowering the rate of investment.

Perhaps the major economic problem facing firms in free enterprise economies is drastic changes in demand caused by hyperbooms or, more critically, deep depressions. The Islandians are good macroeconomists; and over the years they have developed the necessary fiscal discipline to prevent excess government expenditure and price inflation, as well as deficiences in aggregate demand, leading to depression, collapse of markets, and business failures.

The Islandian central bank is a centralized system which works closely with the chancellor of the exchequer. The basic aim here is to provide a monetary policy which will be neither too expansive nor too contractive over time. By means of open market operations, control over commercial bank reserves, and direct credit controls, the central bank has been able to keep the supply of money rising about as fast as economic growth. Since Islandia is a fairly large country, with a big internal market, the balance of payments problems it has are relatively easy to handle with conventional central banking tools, and the central bank is seldom forced to contract the domestic economy to prevent a foreign exchange crisis.

The Islandian government also cooperates in creating economic stability with its management of fiscal policy. Government deficits are seldom large, unless aggregate demand is too small; and in periods of prosperity and boom the government manages to run a surplus in its budget. When unemployment rises and income growth tends to fall, the central government does not hesitate to run a deficit large enough to balance off declines in expenditures in the private sector. Unlike most governments, the central government of Islandia encourages provincial governments to expand expenditures in periods of general contraction and cut them in periods of expansion, as much as is feasible. The economic sectors which have a big stake in both public and private spending, such as construction, thus are assured of a much more stable aggregate demand through time than in most countries. As in many European countries, Islandia's budgets are prepared annually and passed by the parliament; and the Islandian finance minister spends much time doing long range forecasting and planning about the state of the economy (in cooperation with the central bank) and setting levels of expenditure and taxation accordingly.

As a result of coordinated monetary and fiscal policies, Islandia's economy is remarkably stable, tending to grow at a rate of from 4 percent to 6 percent per year, with occasional drops in the rate of growth to below 2 percent. Absolute declines are extremely rare, since with the kinds of monetary and fiscal tools available to the central authorities, there is no need to have less growth unless planning and execution is done badly. Years of slow growth are almost always years when the foreign balance of payments situation is difficult, for in these years purely domestic controls are difficult to apply successfully; however, such years are quite rare, since the other countries of the world have a high regard for Islandia's internal progress. There seldom is any sign of lack of confidence in Islandia's eventual success in economic matters. A more common problem facing Islandia is the excess flow of foreign capital into the country, leading to overinvestment and overemployment. The country has been able to handle this type of problem by revaluing its currency internationally on several occasions, as well as by direct controls over foreign capital flows by the central bank.

Competent businessmen have little difficulty in obtaining capital in Islandia. There is a commercial banking system which is extremely well organized to provide routine types of commercial credit to businessmen. The central bank has various audit and control powers over commercial banks which insure that unsound loans and banking practice will rarely be attempted, and deposit insurance protects depositors in cases of crisis and fraud. As noted earlier, Islandia appears to be an island of security in an uncertain world; and the country in recent years has had more problems with excess supplies of capital rather than shortages.

Other financial institutions also are well organized and carefully regulated to protect against frauds. The Islandian stock exchange has a SEC type of regulation which insures that the obviously phony promotions will not be allowed to be active on the exchange, and persons with even a casual connection with the market can buy or sell securities with reasonable confidence. Other sources of capital include savings and loan associations, mutual savings banks, and insurance companies, all of which are carefully regulated and capable of providing long term and medium term capital to qualified businessmen.

As might be expected in a country which strongly emphasizes education, the labor force in Islandia is highly skilled and quite capable. Seldom does a manager have to cancel a project for lack of either skilled labor or management deficiencies. Islandia also, luckily, has a reasonable supply of key raw materials, such as iron ore, coal, petroleum, copper, sulphur, and zinc, within its borders, which allows for effective exploitation of these key industrial components. Agricultural land is available in amounts which allow for a majority of foodstuffs to be produced domestically. Given the high level of organization of Islandian industrial production together with its very well educated population, it is not surprising that agriculture also has a very high level of production per farmer and that Islandia ranks close to the top of the most efficient agricultural countries in the world.

Islandia is a fairly large country with a very high per capita GNP. One result is a large internal market for its production, resulting in potential economies of scale for many types of productive enterprise. The large internal market plus the potential import competition prevent many firms from being natural monopolies, and most businessmen complain bitterly about the tough competition in the country most of the time. Since Islandian firms also export extensively, even the sectors characterized by large firms with enormous economies of scale are able to produce at minimal costs of production if they choose.

The Islandian enterprises have a relatively certain legal and political environment, together with the prospects of a fairly stable economy, without extremes of price inflation or deflation, or major hyperbooms or deep depressions. While such an environment may appear utopian, it is well within the reach of most advanced countries today.

One area where the government does nothing to insure safety and stability is in the various markets. One sure way to get inefficiency is to guarantee to businessmen that they will always be protected and that the harsh winds of competition will never chill them. No one is guaranteed a sure deal, or a high income. These things must be worked for; they are not granted as a matter of right.

The Islandian government does not directly interfere with the market mechanisms except in extremely unusual situations. If farmers have low incomes, and additional support is judged necessary, the Islandians would directly subsidize those persons needing more income, rather than try to raise prices by means of price supports. If a critical defense industry needs protection from foreign competition, a direct subsidy is paid, rather than raising duties to make the price higher for all consumers. Since direct subsidies are subject to the close scrutiny of all members of parliament, they tend to be extremely rare. Pressure groups and special industrial interests trying to make it easy for themselves at the expense of the general public have a hard time in Islandia, but the Islandians have been practicing their economics this way for many years. The basic idea here is to make the market determine what is demanded and supplied, except in cases involving national survival, where stronger measures can be taken.

Prices are typically flexible enough to allow for changes in demand to show response in the market. Hence, if the demand for electric fans increases sharply, prices will rise, and existing firms or new entrant firms will expand supply because it has become profitable for them to do so. Similarly, if electricians are needed badly, their wage will rise, and it will become profitable for other citizens to enter this business. The reverse is also probably true. Declining demands mean lower prices, and this leads to eventual withdrawal of firms from the area. While wage rates are probably sticky downward, the decline in demand for a given skill will result in unemployment in this area, leading to discouragement of new entrants and the probably shift of present workers into other, more promising fields.

The existence of competition implies competitors, and Islandia is a large enough country to have a number of firms competing in most productive areas. The number of competitors in most sectors is sufficient to have some sort of workable competition in most areas; and where the competitors are few, foreign competition helps keep the competitors honest. Forming a monopoly in Islandia is extremely difficult because of the country's antitrust laws, which make formal and informal collusion a crime.

In areas where natural monopoly is inevitable, as in telephones, telegraphs, electric power, and similar public utility sectors, there is extensive public utility control, in the form of government commissions, whose members have more than a passing knowledge of both law and economics, to say nothing of management. Some of the utilities are publicly owned, and a perpetual debate rages as to which type of system is preferable. Since public and private managers nervously try to outdo each other in providing service at lower cost in their own geographic areas, both groups perform far better than they might if all were either public or private.

The Islandian government attempts to protect persons and firms from uncertainties of rapid sectoral shifts in demand by protecting, for a limited period, those unfortunate enough to be trapped in a declining industry or region. Enterprises caught in declining industries are given tax credits against losses incurred; and an advisory service, jointly sponsored by government, labor, and business, attempts to provide guidance for such firms into new and more promising lines. Lump sum subsidies are paid to firms and persons who are forced to move for real economic hardship reasons.

In line with preventing supply uncertainties, the Islandian government has long attempted to promote the maximum development of social overhead capital facilities. This policy also has the advantage of preventing poorer areas of the country from drifting into backwardness and apathy.

Like most other advanced countries in the world, Islandia has been undergoing a transportation and communications revolution in the past few decades. Unlike many, it has not tried to protect the obsolete agencies by supressing the more modern techniques, and the country is presently expanding and modernizing its roads as rapidly as possible. It also has a pipeline system for petroleum products, as well as an extensive network of railways, which, as is common these days, is somewhat larger than necessary in the new highway age; however, the railway is busily trying to hold its position through new low commodity rates, containerization, and TOFC operations, while at the same time lopping off unprofitable branch lines built before the motor trucking era. Motor trucks, for their part, pay enough in taxes to cover all their costs of using the extensive highway network.

The Islandians are not concerned with the dead hand of the past, and their controls in this sector are minimal. Competition is the rule rather than the exception, and the transportation carriers complain constantly about the terribly rough competition between companies. The competition is tough; and prices do tend to drop, with the result that Islandian manufacturers have some of the lowest cost internal transportation in the world. Ports and airports, largely owned by the local governments, also scramble to compete by providing the most modern facilities possible, with resulting low costs for export and import traffic.

The post office, the cables, and the telephone system are also complete, complex, and available at low cost to Islandian firms. Similarly, a nationwide power grid guarantees low cost power to firms anywhere they choose to locate. Industrial location in Islandia therefore shows relatively little regional variation, since there are few underdeveloped areas without adequate transport, power, and communication facilities. The construction of such social overhead capital facilities has taken a century, but the Islandians feel that it was most decidedly worthwhile.

The Islandian economy functions relatively well, although it is not exactly an easy place to work for managers of productive enterprises. Islandians are too wise to listen very closely to managers when they plead for special privilege to make their industry or firm easier to operate. The easiest way to satisfy a manager is to give him a perfect monopoly, where all his errors will pass unnoticed, to be paid for by unprotected consumers, but this typically produces not added social efficiency but subsystem optimization of the worst sort. Business interests in all capitalist countries tend to assume, far too readily, that what is good for them, in terms of making their job easier, is good for the country. This may be true when a country expands aggregate demand or trains more young people better, but it is not true when the overall effect is to raise costs or prices for consumers or other firms.

Islandians are generally too wise to fall into this subsystem optimization trap. While there are plenty of pressure groups and lobbyists to present the points of view of various vested interests, legislation, particularly of the protective kind, is analyzed with the total system in mind. The proper question asked is, "How does this measure benefit the total country?" not, "How does this measure benefit the woolgrowers?" A type of cost-benefit analysis is used to analyze various measures proposed; and if the costs outweigh the benefits, the proposal seldom is put into practice.

Politically, this type of analysis is perhaps most difficult; but in Islandia one can assume a wisdom amongst the population not found in more mundane environments. It is assumed here that the voting public is aware of the advantages of total system optimization—an assumption which requires more economic sophistication and perhaps less self-interest than is found in any political unit in the world today.

## THE ISLANDIAN ECONOMY OPERATES

As might be expected from the above description, the Islandian economy performs quite efficiently. GNP per capita is high relative to that in other nations, boosted by a combination of large capital per worker built up over many decades; a high investment per worker in the critical area of education; a good macromanagerial structure, well administered by high caliber, well trained civil servants; and a competitive economic system which has the effect of allocating scarce resources into their most productive pursuits.

The growth rate in GNP per capita is also high. Islandians have a high rate of public investment in education; knowledge accumulation about their economy; and social overhead capital facilities such as roads, water supplies, and power facilities. Given this investment, plus an elite group of high skill management personnel and a proper fiscal-monetary economic macroenvironment which tends to move money incomes steadily up, firms are quite willing to make necessary investments in economic sectors which appear promising for growth. The minimization of uncertainty and the efforts to spread relevant economic knowledge help also, since firms can be reasonably sure that major and drastic shifts in public and economic policies will not occur.

Islandia may be lucky in that it also has an adequate supply of natural resources, including good agricultural land, critical industrial raw materials, and similar factors; but Islandia makes its own luck in large part by investing heavily in two improvable factors of production, labor and management. Even without other types of good natural resources, the country would be relatively well off, since it would be able to utilize its acquired skills to gain more income and wealth. The Islandians would have little trouble with unusable outputs. One major virtue of competition is that the market clears supplies offered at *some* price. As noted earlier, the Islandians are quite willing to subsidize unfortunates whose industry is in trouble due to excess production or declining demand; but these subsidies would not take the form of holding prices above equilibrium levels. The common Western problem of agricultural surpluses, or the Marxist problem of unsalable industrial materials produced in excess of plan or usable amounts, would be alien in Islandia.

One would also expect relatively little unemployment of resources in the country. The combination of rapidly improving worker and management skills, plus a fiscal-monetary policy which provides for relatively steady growths in income and aggregate demand, would tend to make overemployment more of a problem than underemployment. A really effective system of disseminating economic information would tend to minimize the problem of excessive investments in plant and equipment, as would effective management of firms by men aware of the need to use macroeconomic data to plan for expansions within the firm.

The competitive nature of the Islandian state would be supported by import, competition, the use of government "yardstick" operations in the public utility sector, an effective antitrust law, and extensive knowledge about the economy. While no modern country can expect to approach economic models of pure competition, it is possible to have quite workable and perhaps violent industrial competition within the framework of a modern industrial economy. It is doubtful that businessmen and entrepreneurs enjoy this particular feature of the Islandian economy, since the more competitive the economy is, the more efficient and hard working managers must be to perform adequately. An efficient economy is definitely not the kind of economy most managers would prefer to have—it is too tough on the managers themselves! This system is set up not to enrich professional manaement but to enrich the nation.

Beyond the planning for increasing GNP as steadily as possible through proper monetary and fiscal matters, the Islandian government would not find it necessary to do extensive planning in the economic sector. In this sense, Islandia resembles one of the smaller advanced countries, whose military potential is not large enough to allow it to become a major power. This can be a real advantage economically, since it forestalls heavy investments in military power. Implicit in this statement is the value judgment that citizens themselves are most able to choose the goods and services they prefer. A government does not have to do it for them. Whatever social services are performed are done as far as possible outside the economic system, financed by taxes on all citizens and firms, not by special groups. This kind of planning could be as extensive or as minimal as the taxpayers and voters prefer.

In this general environment, the Islandian firm attempts to do its business. Note that the above factors give no clue as to whether or not Islandia is a pleasant place to live. Nor does it give any indication whether it is socially refined or crude, significant or insignificant in the noneconomic affairs that are important to men. It is not necessarily a place in which businessmen would enjoy doing business, since the prime test of good management is not whether businessmen enjoy their work or not, or whether they get rich or not, or whether they are major power centers or not. These factors are basically peripheral to the central issue, which is whether or not businesses and managers are efficient. One might expect that an efficient manager is a happy man; but it does not follow that this is true, although this need not concern us here.

## OF TIME AND MEN

A critical point to be noted here is that the construction of Islandias takes time. It is not usually possible to transform human institutions or men themselves overnight, by passing a few laws or making a few speeches. Thus, universities can be created in a few years, but Harvards or Oxfords take centuries to construct. Antitrust laws can be passed by parliaments in hours; but it takes decades to develop a workable, meaningful system of enforcement and general consensus about such laws. Men do not change their lifetime habits and patterns because a government changes, or because such a change might, in some grandiosely aggregate way, influence productivity for the better.

Every modern country which has achieved some degree of efficiency higher than the subsistence level has been working on the problem consciously or unconsciously, for decades, or even centuries. Thus, England began its tortured development process centuries ago, in a halting and uncertain manner. Included in the process were such diverse developments as enclosure acts, educational reforms, religious changes, and a host of other disconnected events which eventually led to the nineteenth century burst of progress. Such diverse countries as the Soviet Union and Mexico, both of which were latecomers to the development process, spent decades (and quite bloody ones at that) in restructuring their societies so that productive efficiency could be improved. For decades, in both countries, very little overtly happened. Men had to be educated, institutions had to be restructured, and human attitudes centuries old had to be pressured into new channels. None of this comes easily to any nation or any people.

There is a new sense of urgency in this type of task. Nations far behind desire to catch up as rapidly as possible, and certainly it is possible to hasten the slow process as followed by presently developed countries; but some time dimension still remains, and no country has succeeded in advancing from inefficiency and total poverty to even moderate affluence in less than forty or fifty years.

## PERFORMANCE OF THE CRITICAL ELEMENTS OF THE MANAGEMENT PROCESS

Typical industrial firms operating in Islandia would have considerable advantages over many of their foreign counterparts in terms of the efficiency with which they could perform the critical elements of the managerial process. All of the external constraints in Islandia are more favorable to managerial effectiveness than in any other country, yet all are achievable in terms of what is presently known.

The planning function of Islandian industrial firms will be easier than in most countries, because many things that are uncertain elsewhere are certain in Islandia. National income and employment will continue to rise, the only question being at what rate. The large number of statistics collected by government are available to the firm for planning purposes; and such marketing factors as the number of households with electric power, their location, the income of households, and numerous similar items of information, are available at nominal cost to the firm. Few legal problems which cannot be easily foreseen will plague Islandian firms in the future, given the relative certainty of business law. The generally stable economic environment prevents the kind of uncertainty caused by sickening declines in income and employment. One major effect of the Islandian social structure is the limiting of uncertainties to factors beyond the control of man. Those uncertainties which can be controlled without serious trade-offs in inefficiency *are* controlled.

Staffing problems for Islandian firms are equally easy. The major problem is that of any expanding economy, where most capable men are already employed, and where no pool of unemployed skilled workers and managers exists; however, the strong educational system continuously generates a good potential talent pool of trained men, who need only experience and seasoning to be capable employees. Moreover, the strong competitive nature of the Islandian economy implies that some sectors will be declining from time to time, and available manpower is generated in this way. The strong urge for achievement among individual Islandians helps firms find men who are seriously interested in advancing themselves.

The firm is able to organize itself in any way necessary to achieve its goals, since no external constraints exist to cause problems in this area. A good system of transportation and communication, plus good personnel, means that a decentralized organizational structure is feasible, whereas the respect for managers and management makes possible a highly centralized structure if such is necessary. The way in which the firm will be organized will depend entirely on the type of goals management has in mind and on the managers' competence and skill. In the Islandian environment it is likely that managers will be quite skilled in performing the critical elements of the management process. Certainly the society will have done its best to generate this type of manager.

Direction can again be anything the firm wants it to be, subject to the overall goals of the firm. An autocratic system might work well, given the nature of Islandians and their individual attitudes. More permissive managerial techniques could also succeed well, as the Islandians are quite able to work on their own if necessary. The point here is that there are, again, no external constraints against the firm's performing its direction in the manner for which it is best suited for internal reasons. How direction might most efficiently be accomplished depends on the internal problems of the firm, not on the external environment, which tends to be neutral in this area.

A similar analysis could be used for control purposes. Controls are in large part effective to the extent to which skilled managerial personnel are able to devise effective control techniques. They also are dependent on the types of persons subject to control and on their reactions to the controls. With a skilled competent management and work force, well educated in a forward looking, scientific methodology, it is unlikely that few Islandian firms would run out of control for long. Proper controls involve planning for the future and setting standards in various work areas, and Islandians would be able to handle this kind of problem without serious difficulty.

As one examines the critical elements of the management process in Table 2–1 and considers the way in which the environment of productive enterprises affects the efficiency with which they are performed, the reason for the particular construction of the Islandian constraints might be seen. In effect, the question asked in every case was: how might the firm's environment be adjusted so that there would be a minimum of interference from such factors on the firm's internal efficiency? Given the complex interaction of the various constraints, this is hardly an easy task, but already many advanced countries have shown remarkable insight (or luck) in structuring their environments to yield excellent internal firm results. It is not hard to push known constraints in favored countries a bit farther to see how they might help firms become even more efficient through their impact on the critical elements of the management process and on the managers themselves.

It could be pointed out that in the last analysis the way in which firms operate depends on the managers themselves. No environment, however favorable, could directly create a proper plant layout for an automatic washing machine assembly line, or create the proper marketing channel for textbooks in comparative management. Such performance of the critical elements of the management process must always be done by the managers themselves, combined with the various skilled and unskilled workers, professionals, and technicians working with them; but the key point of this entire book is that the "proper" external environment definitionally is that type which will create such managers, properly motivated, at the right time and right place. The educational and sociological constraints play a major role in operating directly on managers in this way, in addition to their direct impact on the critical elements. Our Islandia, if it were the kind of productive utopia it is intended to be, would have to have the kinds of external constraints which would lead to this result.

The general effect of the external environment on Islandian firms is to set up a system which provides the maximum amount of needed resources, particularly human resources, which are needed to manipulate the other available resources. The system also tries to develop certainty as far as possible in an uncertain world, mainly by reducing unnecessary uncertainty in the business system. Still further, Islandia tries to isolate such critical factors as problems of social welfare and unemployment from the business context. This does not mean that the country does not try to solve such problems. It merely makes sure that they are treated as general social problems within the general social context, rather than as special problems for which businessmen must pay. By the same token, special problems which affect productive enterprises, such as subsidies for needed public services, special defense production, and agricultural price supports, are not buried in the business system in the form of special indirect subsidies via tax policy or tariff favors to privileged groups. One result of this policy is that the Islandians are not forever debating the probable effects of complex indirect benefits and their probable impact on other economic sectors. Another result is that managers in diverse sectors have a fairly uniform problem of internal management, uncomplicated by special favors or disadvantages levied against their area.

## CONCLUSION

Islandia would be a strange and lopsided economy. Like most other utopias created to explain the proper way in which man should deal with man, our version presents only a small portion, and perhaps the least important portion, of a nation's life.

Businessmen and managers, absorbed in their interesting jobs, and aware that the world badly needs the goods and services that only productive enterprises can create, too often tend to assume that their occupation is the most critical in the society. In their view, a business or production oriented society is the ideal state of affairs. A result of this view in the past several decades has been the rather meaningless propaganda race between capitalists and Marxists about who can produce the most, as if the maximum production bestowed the maximum desirability on the society.

This focus on production is necessary in a society which has difficulty in providing the minimal supplies of food, shelter, and clothing for its population. Any underdeveloped nation does have the crucial problem of production to solve; and, properly, these nations should ponder the implications of the kind of Utopia for management noted above. Moreover, there is no country on earth so rich and so well managed that it can conscientiously ignore the vital problems of creating at least a decent minimum standard of living for all its population.

Such production requires management, and the purpose of the above discussion was to focus on the kinds of social factors which would hopefully lead to really effective management; but effective management leads to increased productivity, and this leads to greater wealth per capita. At some point, the society is rich—and at this point, problems of management and production become secondary to more closely held values which the culture may have, such as religion, art, literature, or whatever. Managers and management can do little here to aid a country's progress, except to recognize that production is just the way in which most other things are made possible.

# Chapter 14

# Implications for International
# Management

## INTRODUCTION

To this point, this book has focused on managerial problems and domestic industrial firms within countries. We have compared external constraints in various countries, indicating how these constraints directly affect firms operating entirely within the local environment.

The problems of an international enterprise have not been handled, except peripherally. These firms may operate in two or more countries linked by various international trade, law, and cultural patterns. In this case, the firm has several environments to consider, and failure to evaluate the different patterns in its relevant countries can prove disastrous. International firms are usually more sensitive to environmental differences than purely local firms, because the major differentials between environments are so obvious. A firm in New York, which operates only in the United States, may not have to worry very much about its environment, since it changes slowly and all the firm's local competitors are faced with the same general problems. The degree to which such a firm is environment bound may not make very much difference in the firm's day to day operations; but a firm in New York with a branch factory in India very quickly becomes aware of differences in its Indian environment, since proper evaluation of these differences is essential to survival.

The question explored in this chapter is how the methodology developed to this point might be applied to such international business problems. It seems clear that such a firm will operate in a much more complex environment than that of a purely local firm, and we now turn to more detailed analysis of this international environment.

## INTERNATIONAL BUSINESS IMPLICATIONS

When a firm begins to operate in two or more countries, it finds that the external constraints are now variables, in the sense that obviously constant factors at home are now different abroad. Labor laws, which rarely change rapidly, now are new and complex; dominant cultural attitudes so ingrained as to be taken for granted now are strangely different; and so on. As the firm operates in an alien environment, the problems of how this environment can be handled grow, and the kind of constraint analysis offered in earlier chapters may prove useful. In effect, the firm has internal comparative management problems.

Three sets of external constraints become relevant in such a situation. First, the local external constraints (C's) of the home country still determine in large part many operations which may have overseas implications, such as staffing, production problems, and financial planning. A firm may operate in Pakistan but do its financing in New York, subject to laws, custom, and economic constraints in that city. Second, the external constraints of the foreign environment become relevant. The firm with a plant in Pakistan has to observe Pakistani law; sell in a market constrained economically, legally, and socially by Pakistani events; and handle labor problems in accord with its local, rather than home, environment. Finally, the firm may face various international constraints, which may differ from those in either country. Thus, Pakistan may have one type of legal structure dealing with expropriations, the Americans another, and various international conventions still a third. All may be relevant if the question of a government takeover becomes important.

The relevant local environmental constraints of any country could be handled in much the same manner as they have been earlier in this book. The country can be evaluated and the constraints scored by the Delphi Technique. The scores achieved might indicate that different policies were proper in this country as compared to the home country.

The usual flow of investment is from a more developed to a less developed country, which implies that the local external constraints in the international company's home country are probably better than those in the country in which the firm is investing. This is normally true for American international investment, for example, even when the funds flow to relatively developed countries in western Europe. At worst, the country in which investment is taking place is usually no better than the country from which the investment is coming. Much intra-European investment may be of this type.

This suggests that almost any international firm will be better off, in productivity terms, if it could export its relevant local constraints as far as possible, particularly in areas where the local external constraints are particularly weak. Thus, for example, an American oil company operating in the Middle East would note the obviously low educational levels and the total lack of personnel skilled in the oil production business in its host country. It would then attempt to import necessary managerial and technical personnel to perform the production job properly.

A vital question for international business management is to what extent such exports of local abilities can be made effectively to countries in which they operate. The usual answer is that almost anything can be transferred, if the firm is willing to pay the necessary cost to achieve successful transfer. In some cases, such as the export of pure technology embodied in a given machine tool, transfer is quite easy and straightforward; but in other cases, such as the "export" of most of the sociological factors relevant to effective management, transfer may be extremely expensive and take many years. Firms necessarily have to operate, at least in part, within the framework of local external constraints; and avoiding them can only be done at some cost.

This point is often ignored by firms just entering the international arena. It is tacitly assumed by management that if the die casting plant in Chicago is organized and operated in a given way, there is no reason to suspect that a similar plant in Argentina should not be operated in precisely the same manner. This ignores, of course, the entire *C-B* matrix for Argentina, and even a cursory examination of Table 4–1 indicates that even production functions are directly related to the environment. Such naive international operations are certain to encounter serious difficulties, which will result in less managerial effectiveness than otherwise might be obtainable.

Another mistake often made by new firms in international operations is to copy older, successful international companies operating in the same host country. Overlooked here is the fact that the established international firm has already incurred the necessary costs of making constraint transfers and has learned which adaptations are necessary to its particular operation. For example, if an American competitor of Colgate-Palmolive decides to set up a firm in India, it may be dangerous initially to pattern its management process closely after Colgate's, since this company has been operating in India for a long time and has probably adjusted its management process rather slowly, and at substantial costs in many cases, because of various Indian cultural constraints.

Although all constraint areas are potential trouble spots for the international firm, the usual major difficulty here is in the sociological sector. The problem of dealing with people oriented to strange customs and values always presents problems. In so far as the entire work force cannot be imported, this type of problem is also reflected in the differences in the various educational constraints; and our examples of problems are drawn largely from these two areas.

As an example of this type of problem, consider an international firm which has successfully decentralized its domestic operations in the United States. Since this type of direction and organization is superior at home, the company may wish to use it abroad; but if local personnel tend to prefer and perform better under a system of highly authoritarian, centralized management, the newly established foreign based firms may be wise to adjust their practices accordingly. If, for some reason, the company wanted to move in the direction of greater participative management or greater decentralization of authority involving local personnel, it would be prudent for the company to estimate carefully the overall costs, benefits, and time required to implement such a change successfully.

For example, it may be much more costly, time consuming, and risky to introduce substantially greater participative management effectively in Saudi Arabia, Peru, or even Germany, than in the United States, Canada, or Yugoslavia. Empirical research studies based on interviews and questionnaire surveys conducted in business firms in the United States and Peru strongly suggest that authoritarian management tends to be more acceptable and effective in Peru than in the United States. If participative management were to be applied in a fairly short period of time in a firm in Peru, it is likely that productivity would decline and employees would tend to lose respect for their superiors.[1] In countries where cultural conditions cause employees to perform better under a system of highly paternalistic management, it may be costly and possibly dangerous for the international firm to deviate substantially from such a pattern of management.

If the international firm decides to engage in fairly extensive operations in a country where high achievement human resources are critically scarce, it may prove extremely difficult to motivate many locally recruited personnel to perform their jobs effectively, even where the firm's managers are competent and able leaders. In such a situation it may be better for the firm to undertake training programs that emphasize changing basic attitudes and values than to focus only on the improvement of skills or new techniques which may not be utilized effectively because of lack of proper motivation.[2]

There are also some indications that the achievement drive among members of minority groups of subcultures isolated from the dominant cultural mainstream in various countries is often significantly higher than that of the general population. The Chinese in Indonesia, the Armenians in the Middle East, and the Lebanese in various African countries appear to fall into this category. The international company may recruit such men if these subgroups can be identified through research.

One other aspect of achievement is worth noting here. In countries such as Japan it may be wise for the firm to emphasize group or collective achievement, rather than stress individual achievement as is typically done in American industry and business.

The dominant view toward change in a particular country may have

---

[1] W. Whyte and L. Williams, "Supervisory Leadership—An International Comparison," *Proceedings of the International Management Congress* (CIOS), September 16–20, 1963, New York City (New York: Council for International Progress in Management (USA), Inc., 1963), pp. 101–104.

[2] Cf. a relevant study indicating the ineffectiveness of management training programs in Turkey: N. Bradburn, *The Managerial Role in Turkey: A Psychological Study* (unpublished doctoral dissertation, Harvard University, 1960). Also see David McClelland, *The Achieving Society*. Princeton, N.J.: D. Van Nostrand Co., Inc., 1961), p. 415.

considerable relevance for international business management. Where research reveals that locally recruited personnel in a given country are generally inclined to resist vigorously changes and innovations in enterprise operations, and where cultural conditions are largely responsible for such behavior, then management would be in a much better position to anticipate and overcome this problem. It is true that people employed in business firms throughout the world often tend to resist managerial and technical changes that directly affect them and their work, for a variety of economic and personal reasons; however, there are some indications strongly suggesting that purely cultural factors tend to result in significantly greater opposition to change in some countries than in others. For example, it is likely that human resistance to change in India tends to be greater than in the United States, largely for cultural reasons.[3]

The degree to which resistance to change is the result of certain cultural constraints might be ascertained by comparing the time, costs and training entailed in introducing a similar change in the American based firm and in different foreign subsidiaries. If a large number of personnel must be recruited from outside a particular country in order to implement an innovation or change in operations successfully, this may suggest a high degree of cultural resistance to change.

The dominant attitude toward scientific method varies substantially in different cultures and countries, even among individuals having considerable formal education. The values associated with Calvinism, if adhered to in practice, tend to be associated with a favorable view toward scientific method.[4] Where the international firm must recruit local personnel who have little pretraining in scientific method, basic training in this area may be required in order to reduce waste and inefficiencies in company operations.

It appears that the overall educational system in any country affects virtually every important aspect of managerial and business life. It tends to have bearing on the entire staffing function and goal setting and decision making process; the size of firms and their overall organization structure, including degrees of centralization and decentralization, degree of work specialization, departmentation and grouping of activities; the specific types of operations, techniques, and technology employed; costs of production; and managerial effectiveness and the overall productivity of firms.

There are large discrepancies in the number, types, and quality of personnel employed in similar types of industrial firms, producing a given level of output, between advanced and less developed countries. These differences are evident not only among unskilled workers but also through

---

[3] Cf. K. Sundaram (Managing Partner, the Coimbatore Cotton Mills Ltd., India), "Social and Human Problems in Introducing Technical Change," in *Proceedings of the International Management Congress*, pp. 495–498. Also see A. Rice, *Productivity and Social Organization: The Ahmedabad Experiment* (London: Tavistock, 1958).

[4] McClelland, *op. cit.*, chaps. ix–x.

the entire vertical skill and occupational structure. Such discrepancies are often due to differences in the overall educational systems found in different countries.[5]

In countries where formal educational and training systems are not properly geared to the needs of modern industry, the number of personnel required to produce a given level of output, even with the same basic technology, tends to be substantially greater than in an advanced economy. From three to ten times as many employees are required in a less developed economy than in an advanced economy. In numerous cases more productive technology can not be employed and many positions remain unfilled because of lack of suitable manpower.

Even among the developed countries there are often significant differences in the organization structures and staffing effectiveness in similar types of firms which are caused by differences in educational systems. For example, a few years ago a large company in Great Britain tried to recruit a person with a background in both economics and psychology to head its recently established marketing research department. In the United States, highly talented people of this type can usually be found if the firm is willing to pay the price, but this English company could not recruit such a person in Britain even after a costly and extensive search. A less qualified man was finally selected, and top management is convinced that the job is not being performed nearly as efficiently as it could be.

Executives of several multinational firms interviewed by one of the authors have asserted that educational constraints, particularly in less developed countries, often have a substantial negative impact on managerial effectiveness and firm operations. In many cases the educational system of a particular country has been the major limiting factor with regard to establishing a subsidiary operation in a particular country. It is possible for the foreign based firm to import manpower from other countries to staff its operations, or to send promising nationals abroad for study; but there are usually limits to how far a company will go in this direction. In the final analysis, the local educational system usually plays the major role in determining the types and quality of human resources available to the international firm.

The stress here on sociological and educational constraints should not be taken to imply that the legal-political and economic factors are unimportant when a company goes abroad. Table 4–1 suggests the large number of interactions between the firm and the local economy, and the ratings for various countries in Table 12–1 suggest the extent to which these con-

---

[5] Cf. the pertinent data presented in *Training of National Technical Personnel for Accelerated Industrialization of Developing Countries* (E/3901 [New York: United Nations Economic and Social Council, June 3, 1964], Parts II and III, Add. 1 and 2. See also P. Kuin (Director of Unilever Company, Netherlands), "Meeting Economic and Social Needs in a Variety of Countries," *Proceedings of the International Management Congress*, p. 436.

straints can differ between countries. Detailed analysis of the total nature of the international company's problems in an alien environment will have to wait for another study, however. Here the intention is merely to note that the relatively fixed environmental constraints at home are variable abroad and that the international firm should be sensitized to the nature of the impact of the foreign environmental constraints on their overseas operations. Failure to realize the nature of this problem results in losses, confusion, and inefficiency.

## INTERNATIONAL CONSTRAINTS

The firm operating in two or more countries has two local constraint matrices to consider, as noted above; however, there is also an interaction between countries which is relevant to its international operations and which must be considered in the course of operating effectively.

### FIGURE 14–1

TOTAL ENVIRONMENTAL CONSTRAINT SITUATION FOR AN INTERNATIONAL FIRM

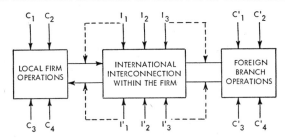

Figure 14–1 indicates the total nature of the constraints on an international firm. The local firm operations are partially determined by the local constraints ($C$'s), as discussed above. Similarly, the foreign branch operations are affected by the foreign local constraints ($C_1$, $C_2$, and so on, in Figure 14–1). These sets of constraints interact to some extent.

There is, however, a third set of constraints which is still different from the two sets of $C$'s. These $I$'s in Figure 12–1 refer to the various types of international regulations which any given country may have and which may be quite different from many of the local constraints. Table 14–1 suggests some of the relevant problems which would arise in this sector. Some of these are in effect partially covered domestically, as in the case of import restrictions (foreign policy). In this case, local policy directly interlocks with what is happening abroad. A country may have high protective duties on selected products to protect local manufacturers, but this same duty is a relevant factor in the consideration of a foreign firm planning construction of new plants abroad. Given the tariff protection within the country, the

## TABLE 14–1

### INTERNATIONAL CONSTRAINTS

$I_1$: *Sociological Constraints*

$I_{1.1}$: National ideology: The general collective ideology of a nation, as exemplified by their writing, speaking, and other manifestations of a national point of view.

$I_{1.2}$: View toward foreigners: The general attitude toward nonnationals, as evidenced by overt behavior.

$I_{1.3}$: Nature and extent of nationalism: The manifestation of the collective nationalist feelings within the country, as evidenced by actions, writings, and behavior.

$I_2$: *Legal-Political Constraints*

$I_{2.1}$: Political ideology: The political viewpoints of existing governments, as demonstrated by the prevailing pattern of rule, philosophy of leading political parties, and similar factors.

$I_{2.2}$: Relevant legal rules for foreign business: The special rules of the game applied only to foreign owned firms, including special discriminatory labor and tax legislation.

$I_{2.3}$: International organization and treaty obligations: Formal obligations of the country in terms of military responsibilities; political obligations; copyright, postal, and patent obligations; and similar matters.

$I_{2.4}$: Power or economic bloc grouping: Membership in formal and informal political, military, and economic blocs, such as Communist Marxist, or neutralist groups; explicit and implicit obligations of such blocs.

$I_{2.5}$: Import-export restrictions: Formal legal rules controlling exports and imports, including tariffs, quotas, export duties, export restrictions, and similar matters.

$I_{2.6}$: International investment restrictions: Formal legal and administrative restrictions on investments by foreigners within the country.

$I_{2.7}$: Profit remission restrictions: Formal legal and administrative restrictions on remittance of profits of local operations to foreign countries.

$I_{2.8}$: Exchange control restrictions: Formal legal and administrative controls on the conversion of the local currency to any or all foreign currencies or gold.

$I_3$: *Economic Constraints*

$I_{3.1}$: General balance of payments position: The general state of the balance of payments, including deficits or surpluses on current account; the flows of capital, both long and short term; new term international financial obligations; and tendencies for chronic deficits or surpluses in the balance of payments.

$I_{3.2}$: International trade patterns: The usual flows of exports and imports to and from the country. Patterns of commodities and services traded, by countries and regions.

$I_{3.3}$: Membership and obligations in international financial organizations: Obligations and responsibilities of the country toward international organizations such as the World Bank and the IMF; rights of the country as a member of such organizations.

firm might find it profitable to invest in manufacturing within the country, assuming that it is otherwise legal to do so.

The international constraints listed in Table 14–1 are for a single country as seen by a foreign country or firm. Thus, one might rate the United States in terms of its international constraints as seen by a firm in West Germany. Note that these international constraints are not replacements for the internal environmental constraints of the country in question; rather, they are supplements to them. The multinational firm, once it is established in the host country, is constrained by these internal factors in much the same way as local firms are; however, the international firm has the advantage, particularly if it is from an advanced country, of being able to overcome some of the local constraints by importation, as was discussed earlier in this chapter. Such importations are also subject to the international constraints. A firm might wish to import skilled labor, but legal rules are such as to preclude this ($I_{2.2}$ in Table 14–1).

Perhaps the biggest advantage an international company has in its operations in foreign countries is its cosmopolitan viewpoint, created necessarily by the operations in various cultures. Factors which appear fixed and immutable to local firms are seen as local obstacles which can be overcome—and often they are. This attitude tends to interact with local firms as well, as they observe the operations of the international companies. Saudi Arabian local companies, for example, found out a great deal about finance and methods of capital accumulation and borrowing by observing how the American oil companies and other non-Saudi firms conducted their operations. Whereas very few such firms obtained loans from foreign sources before World War II, many now obtain credit from banks in Lebanon and New York.

In examining the international constraints the focus is on the effect of such constraints on the efficiency of international business operations. Americans normally consider such operations in the private sector, as virtually all American firms operating internationally are privately owned and controlled (but don't forget the government owned Panama Canal Company and Railroad). This is also true for most international firms based in other countries; however, some publicly owned companies conduct international operations, and the same constraints would apply to them as well. Some of the best known examples are international airlines, such as BOAC, Air France, and Air Italia, among others, which are owned and controlled by their respective governments; but to date the international business sector is more dominated by private firms than are the domestic economies, where entire nations, as in the Marxist states, have almost no private enterprise.[6] The effect, for practical purposes, is to focus more closely, in the international constraint matrix, on operations of private as compared to public enterprise.

Another relevant point here is that the flow of international direct investment is usually from the more developed, high income countries to the less developed, low income nations. Few Iranian firms are particularly concerned about American international business constraints, although many American companies do worry about the Iranian constraints. Wealthy countries therefore rarely have extensive differences in rules governing the use of foreign, as compared to domestic, capital. The problem typically is not especially important. Less developed countries, highly conscious of alleged managerial superiority, greater capital resources, and general managerial effectiveness of foreign firms, are more likely to have special restrictions on foreign firms' operations within their borders.[7]

---

[6] The Marxist countries do occasionally operate profit making firms abroad. Thus, the Soviet Union owns and operates a profitable bank in London.

[7] Benjamin Higgins, *Economic Development* (New York: W. W. Norton & Company, Inc., 1959), pp. 569–594, particularly pp. 583–586.

A final point is that absolute restrictions exist in many countries for many kinds of foreign operations. Communist countries will import from other nations, and they will occasionally buy process licenses or patent rights, or order turnkey projects from capitalist firms; but they do not normally allow any direct investment within their countries. Some socialist countries, such as Egypt, have equally severe restrictions, while others have formally restricted certain economic areas, typically public utility type enterprises, from foreign penetration.[8] This type of restriction is included in the international constraint matrix in the category of legal-political rules.

It is useful to explore the various business implications of the international constraint matrix to determine how these constraints operate on internal business operations. The general orientation and logic of the matrix is similar to the domestic matrix.

## Sociological Constraints

Nationalism has proved to be a potent force in the modern world, and typically countries present fairly well structured postures to the rest of the world. Thus India is seen as a neutralist democratic nation, a compromiser and peacemaker; Burma as a socialist (but not Communist) nation; Greece as a rapidly developing nation with strong maritime activities and a glorious past; and so on. Such postures can influence business activities of foreign firms. The ultranationalistic attitude of Algeria, characterized by belligerent statements from its leaders, tends to make foreign investors dubious about possibilities in this country, even though the other structural constraints may not be particularly poor. Here the risk of foreign investment is evaluated differently because of the country's posture. Many examples of this type of ideological pressure on risk evaluation, and hence on firm planning, are evident in the less developed, newly independent nations. On the other hand, the national image of welcome to foreign investors in Lebanon, backed up only in part by favorable international constraints in other sectors, tends to lead to undervaluation of risk by foreign investors. Switzerland has long had the image of a haven for foreign funds. The major internal firm effects of this constraint are on planning and finance.

The attitude toward foreigners varies widely throughout the world. At one extreme, foreigners are almost completely excluded, as used to occur in Tibet. At the other extreme, virtually no difference is seen in most foreign visitors, as probably is true in countries such as Switzerland and the United States. If the foreign worker or visitor is different, racially, linguistically, or otherwise, many countries regard him with sympathetic curiosity—while in others, police guards are required to protect him from bodily harm. Such attitudes have direct effects on firm staffing, recruiting, and planning. A

---

[8] See Planning Commission, Government of India, *The New India* (New York: The Macmillan Company, 1958), pp. 244–262, for one example of this type of restriction.

manager visiting a foreign country to consider investment will typically adjust his plans, in part as a result of the reception he gets. Even if foreign technicians are legal, they may not be employed if the area is dangerous for foreigners. This was true in the Congo in 1965. At the other extreme a very hospitable country may find its foreign firms tend to use foreigners even for jobs for which nationals are qualified. This variable is often interlocked with various legal rules about the operations of foreign firms and activities of individual representatives of such firms in the country. The usual kinds of legislation discriminating against foreigners stem largely from such sociological attitudes.

The nature and extent of nationalism vary widely throughout the world, and national feeling takes many different forms. These range from hypersensitivity and convictions of superiority in some countries through barely discernible national feelings in many new states which cut across ancient tribal boundaries. Strong feelings of national identity and purpose may make a country resentful or contemptuous of foreigners and may result in various types of discriminatory legislation. Paradoxically, a country with quite weak nationalistic sentiment may also react strongly against foreign firms, feeling that national cohesion can be achieved only if systematic discrimination against outsiders is practiced.

## Legal-Political Constraints

These constraints are more numerous, and perhaps more important, than those in the other categories. This is because international firms may be subject to special rules, which typically must be observed and which have major impacts on the possibility of doing business, the way in which it is accomplished, and the costs of operations.

Political ideology is one variable which may determine ultimate feasibility of an international operation. As noted above, Marxist countries typically do not allow international investment by private companies, and many capitalist and socialist states have prohibited private foreign investment in such sectors as transportation and public utilities. This type of restriction is found not only in less developed countries. A foreign firm attempting to invest in American motor trucking or airline operations would find entry very difficult.[9] This international constraint interlocks often with various other legal constraints such as profit remission restrictions and exchange controls. The usual direct effect on foreign firms is in the area of planning, since this constraint may determine whether or not the firm can operate at all. For firms already established in a country, ideological changes may prove extremely important, as American firms in Cuba learned to their sorrow.

---

[9] *Any* firm, American or foreign, would find entry in transportation difficult in the United States, given existing entry controls. See Dudley F. Pegrum, *Transportation: Economics and Public Policy* (Homewood, Ill.: Richard D. Irwin, Inc., 1963), pp. 341–345.

The discussion below of specific legal constraints focuses on critical problems in crucial areas; however, many kinds of legal rules may apply in some special manner to international concerns. A company may be required to hire a certain percentage of local labor, special taxes may be levied on foreign firms, or even different accounting requirements may be demanded. Such special rules have effects on firm effectiveness in such areas as staffing, personnel, marketing, finance, and planning. The requirement that 80 percent of the work force must be local citizens, when applied to a foreign oil company in a less developed area, can lead to extensive shifts in recruiting and training for the firm. Such policies may also lead to higher costs, affecting marketing and production plans. Special taxation can lead to extensive changes in financial activities. If a country has a special profits tax, some effort might be made to shift some items from profit to expense, perhaps by changing depreciation accounting. Each country must of course be examined for each type of business to determine how such special legal rules apply.

Most countries are not islands unto themselves. They usually belong to international organizations such as the United Nations, and they may also belong to regional groups such as the Organization of American States. Numerous economic, political, and military organizations also exist throughout the world. In many cases, such memberships imply international obligations which the sovereign states have agreed to comply with; and some of these obligations may have business implications. Countries may also have treaties with major capital exporting nations guaranteeing certain kinds of treatment for resident foreigners and foreign firms. Such obligations and guarantees may have direct effects on multinational business firms. A country with a treaty guaranteeing certain procedures in expropriation cases, for example, might be more favorably regarded than one which did not have this sort of guarantee. A country with which the investing country has had long and observed military ties might be more favorable to foreign investment than one which had been historically hostile.

Countries usually belong to various economic or political blocs, such as NATO, SEATO, the EEC, the EFTA, and so on. Such bloc relationships also have direct effects on international firms, particularly if special economic rules apply to block countries.[10] For example, tariff eliminations internally in the EEC between all members have had the effect of expanding markets for foreign firms operating within any of the member countries, thus directly affecting the various marketing functions. Agreements which have mainly military implications can also influence such firm functions research and development, if the military research plans and procedures are altered by such an agreement. Thus, as one country may concentrate on small weapon development, while another might tend to do research on new trucks and tanks. Both local and international firms might be affected by such agreements in all countries covered by the agreement.

Each country in the world has the power to control its foreign trade as it sees fit, through tariffs and quantitative controls.[11] These controls can be changed at any time for any purpose. Thus, in late 1964 England suddenly raised the majority of its import duties by 15 percent because of serious strains on its balance of payments.[12] This meant relative increases in prices of imports, to the benefit not only of local English firms but also of foreign companies with plants in Britain. It also meant that foreign and local firms in other countries faced the problem of selling at higher prices in England. The direct impact on price policy for all firms is clear.

It is common for countries interested in certain types of development to adjust tariffs so that some foreign investment will take place. Mexico, for example, has adjusted duties and quantitative controls on automobiles and parts to make auto assembly relatively cheap and importation of finished cars quite difficult and expensive. In this case, foreign auto manufacturers had to decide whether to make a direct investment in Mexico or lose their market. For those that opted for investment, a later rule provided that certain kinds of components previously imported now had to be manufactured in Mexico, thus requiring additional investment in facilities. Firms not willing to make such investments were not allowed to import. The impact of such rules on planning and production within the firm is obvious. Actually, some firms had options of making components themselves or buying them from existing or new Mexican suppliers. Here the production make or buy decision was changed as a result of the change in an international external constraint.

Some countries also have export restrictions on selected items for military, political, or economic reasons. American manufacturers of advanced computers may find that they cannot export this equipment to the Communist countries. A firm unable to sell in foreign markets may thus decide to develop overseas manufacturing facilities, or its marketing patterns may shift. In 1964, an American diesel engine manufacturer with a plant in England had to decide whether to sell his profitable engines to an English firm exporting buses to Cuba, when it was illegal to do so from the United States. Such international rules may cause notable shifts in marketing policies in international companies.

Many companies, particularly those with serious development and monetary problems, have some form of profit remissions control over foreign firms. Such restrictions may change rapidly, depending on the foreign exchange balances and political climate of the country in question.

---

[11] P. T. Ellsworth, *The International Economy* (New York: The Macmillan Company, 1958), pp. 193–209, pp. 332–349; see also pp. 156–192, 358–392 for historical coverage of this point.

[12] "To Stop the Bleeding," *The Economist*, Vol. CCXIII, No. 6323, October 31, 1964, pp. 467–468.

A foreign firm which makes money but is unable to export it or convert it to its own currency may have serious thoughts about new international investment or expansion of existing facilities. Most international companies will investigate this aspect of foreign investment quite closely before making commitments, and here the effect on planning is strong. Firms with unremittable profits may have to make financial adjustments in the home country to cover the loss of existing but unobtainable funds on hand. This can even affect make or buy decisions. A firm with a quantity of unneeded, inconvertible foreign currency may decide to spend it locally, hoping to get some good out of the funds; thus, the firm's pattern of procurement is affected.

Before 1958, when most European currencies became fully convertible, the Arabian American Oil Company steadily piled up large amounts of inconvertible European balances. Rather than let this money stand idle, the company launched a major "buy European" campaign among its many purchasing units, even to the extent of encouraging European firms to manufacture many items not previously produced. Fairly important shifts of suppliers between countries resulted, and the company eased its currency convertibility problem in this way. Critical elements of the firm's operation directly affected by this problem were make or buy activities, procurement timing, inventory levels, number and types of suppliers, types of financing, sources and uses of funds, and the nature and extent of research and development activity. Apparently small changes in these international rules can make major differences within a large international company operating in many countries.

Exchange control restrictions also apply in a general way to convertibility of a country's currency. The same kinds of problems noted above for profit remission arise in this case, except that such exchange controls may be much more pervasive, applying to all sorts of money transfers between countries, rather than just profits.[13] A firm may wish to import some key component for its product and be unable to do so. The result will be fairly substantial changes in the firm's production functions.

These constraints also interrelate with the domestic constraints to a considerable extent. The various exchange controls and restrictions discussed above have similar impacts on local firms; this particular subject was covered in our discussion of the domestic political-legal constraint of foreign policy.[14] The difference here is that the impact being measured is on foreign firms operating in a country, not the locally owned operations. Often the effects will be similar, but the strategies and policies open to the multinational firms may be quite different, and possibly much more flexible and extensive, than those open to domestic enterprises.

Another difference here is that local firms have operated in most

---

[13] Ellsworth, *op. cit.*, pp. 332–349.
[14] See Chapter 8 above, pp. 153–237.

countries for centuries, while international business operations of major economic magnitude are relatively recent.[15] While the local firms may have changed ownership, management, and products over the years, a continuity of productive effort by such firms has often existed for a long time. The multinational firm, on the other hand, is just beginning to have major economic impact in the Western world. Hence, the international constraints tend to be more interesting from the standpoint of planning. A firm in France, operating locally, can do little about its external constraints; but an American firm contemplating new investment in France is in a position to examine carefully, as a part of its general planning process, both French local and international constraints. If these constraints offer serious problems, other countries can be examined. Similarly, an American firm expanding internally typically worries little about American internal constraints, since they will generally be the same throughout the country; but an international firm considering expansion has some 150 sets of internal and international constraints to ponder, and the constraint constants in one country become variables for the firm. This ability to explore international alternatives again focuses greater attention on constraint impact on planning than in the local case.

## Economic Constraints

The most important economic constraint here is the balance of payments position.[16] The balance of payments always balances; but the key balancing factor may be a large current account payable, which puts pressure on the country to earn more abroad or to spend less. In the international economic framework, each country is in effect analogous to an individual within a country. It can only spend abroad as much as it can earn or borrow. A balance of payments crisis usually means the country has spent (in imports, tourism, capital exports, gifts abroad, and so on) more than it earns or can borrow in the long term. The usual result is pressure on the country to bring its foreign spending into line, which gets translated in practice into exchange controls, capital remissions controls, import quotas, higher tariffs, increases in internal interest rates, and other deflationary actions to bring demand into line with available resources.[17]

The balance of payments in itself simply is an international statement of the country's position. It is not a variable operating directly on foreign firms; however, the general position of the country vis-à-vis the rest of the

---

[15] See Richard D. Robinson, *International Business Policy* (New York: Holt, Rinehart & Winston, Inc., 1964), pp. 1–44, for a historical survey of the development of international business. Such enterprises have existed for centuries, but only in the past few decades has their development been extremely rapid.

[16] See Charles P. Kindleberger, *International Economics* (3d ed.; Homewood, Ill.: Richard D. Irwin, Inc., 1963), pp. 17–45, for a full discussion of the balance of payments concept.

[17] Ellsworth, *op. cit.*, pp. 300–331.

world is critical, in that the actions to correct unfavorable balance of payments situations do have direct impacts on foreign firms. The underlying reasons for many of the legal constraints noted above is the balance of payments position of the country in question. Here again is the common interrelationship of the constraints. This particular international constraint also interrelates closely with such local constraints as foreign policy, economic stability, and monetary and fiscal policy, since many of the steps necessary to correct a balance of payments problem revolve around either expanding exports or dampening internal demand, including demand for imports.[18]

The general international trade patterns of a country may also influence strongly its attitudes and actions toward international firms, with corresponding direct impacts on internal management actions. Many countries have a pattern of one or two key exports, typically raw materials, which earn most of foreign exchange.[19] Imports consist of various types of manufactured goods. Many of the less developed countries have trade patterns of this type. This pattern affects the balance of payments, particularly when sharp price declines or increases change earning power abroad. Imports may be less sensitive to such shifts, and this may result in large balance of payments deficits or surpluses on current account.[20] Results are again transmitted to firms through legal restrictions, with direct impact on international and local firms. An American factory in such a country may find it difficult to get enough foreign exchange to obtain necessary components; this can lead to production changes in make or buy decisions, length of production runs, and similar factors. These changes may in turn affect marketing product lines, prices, and sales promotions.

Underlying trade policies also are a part of this constraint. Some countries may want to produce all of their key foodstuffs or industrial raw materials, even if imports could be obtained more cheaply.[21] The result may be business opportunities for both local and foreign firms in sectors not precisely economic. If West Germany wants to produce wheat at almost any cost, fertilizer and farm implements manufacturers may benefit. Here again, the legal manifestations of policy would appear as import controls, high tariffs, and other restrictions noted in the legal international constraint discussion above.

Most countries belong to various international financial organizations which have some impact on their foreign policies and economic reactions to changes in their international positions. A member of the International

[18] Kindleberger, *op. cit.*, pp. 597–617.

[19] Paul Alpert, *Economic Development* (New York: Free Press of Glencoe, Inc., 1963), pp. 40–44.

[20] See Higgins, *op. cit.*, pp. 345–383, for an analysis of such situations, particularly Prebish's argument.

[21] Alpert, *op. cit.*, pp. 173–183.

Monetary Fund (IMF)[22] or the General Agreement of Trade and Tariffs (GATT)[23] has agreed to comply with the rules of these organizations in return for certain privileges of membership. Thus if an IMF country has a balance of payments problem, it can draw on the IMF for foreign currency within the limits of the rules of the organization. A GATT member agrees to certain stipulations about tariffs and exchange controls, in order to gain lower tariffs in other countries for its exports. Such rules can affect foreign and local firms directly. It may prove impossible for the country, without violating its international agreements, to devalue its currency, raise key duties, or impose exchange controls. International firms operating in the country thus may have more certainty and less risk of unpleasant controls of the sort discussed in the legal constraint section above.

### The Structure of International Constraints

These international constraints could conceivably be included within the local constraints as a subset of factors applicable mainly to internationally oriented firms. All countries have some international dealings, and some portion of the local constraints do have international content. If the international constraints are evaluated closely, it can be seen that by expansion of some of the internal constraints it would be possible to handle all of them within the general constraint matrix.

They have been presented separately here, however, on the grounds that to talk about both local and international management simultaneously would unduly complicate the study of comparative management. The management process, as related to the external environment, is complex enough when seen as a single country process; and it is useful to concentrate first on the local context, then move to the international scene after insight has been gained in one country. The probable process of analysis for a multinational firm interested in expanding into other countries would be to examine the international constraints first, seeking veto factors. Such factors would be those which would prohibit the activity within the country in the first instance, as is true of Communist countries. Study of the Communist internal constraints might prove interesting for a variety of reasons, but determining possibilities for international firm investment is not one of them.

If there are no absolute vetoes in the international constraint list, the firm could move directly to the local constraint matrix to examine factors which may directly influence the managerial effectiveness of the firm. The international constraints would be returned to for proper evaluation of costs and extra risks involved in operating internationally. The problem is that

---

[22] See Ellsworth, *op. cit.*, pp. 421–444, for a description of the role and functions of the IMF.

[23] *Ibid.*, pp. 445–460.

## TABLE 14–2

### INTERNATIONAL-LOCAL CONSTRAINT INTERRELATIONSHIPS

| International Constraints (I) | Educational 1 2 3 4 5 6 | Sociological 1 2 3 4 5 6 7 8 9 | Political-Legal 1 2 3 4 5 6 | Economic 1 2 3 4 5 6 7 8 |
|---|---|---|---|---|
| 1 | X X X   X | X X   X X X X X X | X   X X | X |
| 2 | X X X   X X | X X   X X X X X X | X   X X | X |
| 3 | X   X | X X   X X X X X X | X   X X | X |
| 1 | X   X   X | X   X X X X X X | X   X X X X | X |
| 2 |  | X X X X X X X   X | X X X X X X | X |
| 3 |  | X   X   X X | X X   X X | X |
| 4 |  | X X | X X X   X | X |
| 5 |  |  | X X X   X | X X X X X X X X |
| 6 |  | X   X | X X X | X X X X X |
| 7 |  | X   X | X X X | X X X X X |
| 8 |  |  | X X X | X X X X X X X |
| 9 |  | X   X | X X X | X X X X X X |
| 1 |  |  | X X X X X X | X X X X X X X X |
| 2 |  |  | X X X | X X X X X X X X |
| 3 |  |  | X X X | X |

For definitions of *C*'s, see Table 3–1.
For definitions of *I*'s, see Table 12–1.

when a firm leaves its home, it encounters a series of problems which would not normally be considered significant in the home country; and the international matrix is a method of checking off which of these might prove critical to the firm.

This international matrix could be evaluated and quantified by use of the Delphi Technique in the same manner that the local matrix was in Chapter 10. The same kind of conceptual difficulties would be present, although the task would probably be more time consuming than intellectually demanding.

The interrelationships between the international and local constraints can be shown by a matrix as in Table 14–2. Here the local constraints are listed across the top of the page, as in Table 4–1. The international constraints are listed vertically. The *x*'s in Table 14–2 indicate the probable interconnections between the international and local constraints. As might be expected, the sociological international constraints are typically interlocked in most cases with the educational and sociological local constraints. Political-legal international constraints are directly connected with local economic and political-legal constraints. The major reason for the economic interconnections is that many of the international variables which appear as laws to international firms are based on economic conditions within the given country. A nation will seldom have tight exchange controls, for example, unless total demand for foreign exchange is greater than supply, creating a balance of payments problem.

This matrix could be refined by use of the Delphi Technique. New variables we have not seen might be added, while others might be changed. The interrelationships could be explored and possibly changed in view of better evidence about them.

## Evaluation of Foreign Environments

One use for the international and local constraint matrix for an international firm working in several foreign countries would be for evaluation of management effectiveness in different settings. Companies now exist which operate in eighty or more countries, and one major problem facing top management is to determine which managers are performing best in the various operations around the world. To use a single performance standard, such as profitability, for managers faced with strikingly different external constraints would not be especially explanatory, since poor local or international external constraints could make a good manager look bad. Actions which seemed irrational from the vantage point of the United States might be quite reasonable from the viewpoint of the local manager faced with his local problems.[24] Thus, in a country like Brazil, where inflation frequently occurs at the rate of 30 percent per year, inventory policies might be completely different than in the price stable United States. Such inflation also would result in serious balance of payments problems, leading to changes in the international legal constraints of exchange control, profit remissions control, and import restrictions. A manager in such an environment who behaved like his counterpart in the United States, holding minimal inventories to minimize losses from interest charges, storage costs, and deterioration and obsolescence, would actually be acting irrationally in Brazil. Here the good manager would hoard inventories, since price increases would yield large returns while idle cash would not. He would probably also import far in advance whatever critical components he might need from hard currency areas, if such inflation portended new import restrictions, exchange controls, or rapid declines in the value of Brazilian currency.

Firms whose major operations are in the United States often fail to realize that these external constraints make management behave quite differently abroad than at home, and a frequent complaint of branch managers is that their own bosses don't understand them. It is hoped that utilization of this matrix—when combined with the business and managerial function interrelationships with the local constraints, covered in Chapter 4—would enable top management to make more valid and reasonable evaluations of their own key local managers in foreign countries.

Introduction of international constraints complicates our analysis considerably, but we hope it also casts new light on a complex subject. A major problem of business management theory is that to date it has largely been a product of a few developed countries, whose external constraints could be

---

[24] For examples of this in manufacturing, see Robinson, *op. cit.*, pp. 177–191.

ignored in observation of the single firm within the environment. While international firms have existed for centuries, and while international trade goes back to Biblical times, the phenomenon of the international corporation in its modern form is just getting under way. Management and management theorists have to date focused, properly, on internal problems in single environment situations; but further progress in this critical area may well rest on how well these external firm factors are integrated into general management theory.

## CONCLUSION

When a firm begins to operate in several countries, new environmental dimensions become quite relevant. The local domestic constraints, the international constraints for given countries, and the local foreign country constraints all operate on the company's managerial performance. The critical elements of the management process are directly affected by the four sets of constraints (the fourth set being the not often relevant international constraints from the investing country).

If our initial hypothesis is true, it is clear that any efficient international firm would have to come to grips with the constraint problems as soon as it becomes an international company. This chapter has attempted to sketch the way in which a foreign firm might adjust to such local and international constraints. Clearly a complete analysis of even a relatively simple, two country international firm would involve detailed analysis far beyond that attempted here; but it is hoped that this structure will be of some assistance in analyzing international company problems of this type.

# Chapter 15

# Convergence of Industrial Firms and Countries

## INTRODUCTION

It was noted in Chapter 13 that the various local external constraints tend to change over time at varying rates. If anything, the international constraints may change even faster, as countries appear more willing to make a major change which will largely affect other peoples than their own. Thus countries often shift exchange controls or import duties, feeling that these adjustments might solve other local problems without seriously affecting the local society. The changes in both local and international constraints generally tend to have a more favorable impact on the management of firms, although the case is less strong for international changes. The usual reason for this is that countries typically do want *more*, in terms of obtaining a greater gross national product per capita. This goal is often modified by desires to obtain more equitable distribution of income, to seek religious or other noneconomic goals, and occasionally to provide more income or privilege for special groups; but the usual minimal economic goal is some gain in income per capita over time. A country might trade off 10 percent per year growth for 5 percent and some social welfare or religious objectives, but few countries have traded off income for noneconomic objectives when the result would be actual declines in living standards or per capita incomes.[1]

It is thus possible to take as a working rule that all countries want some economic growth, which can be translated, in our terms, to meaning more effective management of productive enterprises. If everyone wants eco-

---

[1] Dr. Lee C. Nehrt, of Indiana University, has pointed out to us that in the Algerian case, leaders may be willing to endure a short run decline in production and income in order to rid their country of all colonial influences; but even here, the long run goal is greater income for Algerians.

nomic growth, what can be said about the possible future changes in the various external constraints for the 180 countries of the world? Our problem in this section is to consider the direction in which changes in the constraints might be predicted to move.

Our basic contention here is that in the long run the result will be a convergence of cultures, as well as applicable management principles and practices, throughout the industrial world;[2] however, this type of universal convergence is likely to take decades, generations, and even centuries in some extreme cases. In the interim it seems apparent that the external constraints will continue to have varying and often major impacts on managerial performance, and deviations will often seem quite extensive. To develop this argument of convergence, it is useful to re-examine the basic environmental constraints to determine how they might move closer together over time.

## SCIENTIFIC CONVERGENCE

In technology, the West is supreme, in the sense that the only known way to create a modern, energy oriented civilization is to use the basic science and technology developed in the West over the past 400 years. No other civilization or mode of thought is able to create the scientific, energy oriented mass production and consumption cultures now existing in many parts of the world. Traditional cultures have always used animal power (including manpower), and the available energy in such a system has never been large enough to allow substantial incomes for more than a few favored citizens.

In the process of creating a modern industrial society, it is clear that in the scientific realm all nations are constrained by natural laws. Water freezes at the same temperature in Moscow as in New York or London, and atomic physicists follow the same methodology and science wherever they may be. There are certain chemical problems relating to steel production which are immutable for all firms, regardless of location or ownership, or even how they are managed. If one wishes to obtain some end product, he must usually follow rigorously the scientific laws relating to this production. Production basically is the transformation of inputs, including products of the land itself, into usable outputs; and technological constraints force firms everywhere to follow the same general production patterns. This in turn forces production managers to be somewhat similar regardless of other

---

    [2] For similar views, see R. Likert, "Trends Toward a World Wide Theory of Management," *Proceedings of the International Management Congress*, September 16–20, 1963, New York City (New York: Council for International Progress in Management (USA), Inc., 1963), pp. 110–114. See also B. Richman and R. Farmer, "Ownership and Management: The Real Issues," *Management International*, Vol. V, No. 1, 1965.

differences in firms.[3] Such managers may use more or less labor than others, build bigger or smaller furnaces, use coal or electricity for fuel; but the logic of production sharply limits the range of choice in this sector of management.

Our argument here, which runs throughout this book, is that there may be a roughly similar process going on in other management sectors, and as countries and societies become more aware of what is workable, in terms of creating conditions favorable for effective management, the external constraints of a wide variety of countries will tend to move in the same direction, for the same reasons. Within fairly narrow limits, there are only a few "right" ways to structure an economy, the overall enterprise environment, and the macromanagerial framework to meet the managerial requirements of a modern society. As these "right" ways are discovered, either fortuitously or by rigorous scientific analysis of the managerial problem, other countries will tend to follow the trend set by more successful countries. Over time, one can expect considerable convergence of various countries toward some optimum which will tend to provide the necessary framework for a really effective micromanagerial performance.

## EDUCATIONAL CONVERGENCE

This tendency can already be seen quite clearly in the educational sector. Correlations of educational achievements and output per capita suggest that one major way to achieve high incomes is to improve the education of all peoples.[4] Countries all over the world, of every shade of political opinion, are frantically attempting to provide the types and varieties of educational experiences required by their people for economic development to proceed rapidly. While the types of education may vary strikingly between countries, particularly in areas dealing with religious training and national mythology, certain key requirements are already clear. Young people must be taught the elements of scientific methodology if they are to staff the complex production facilities of tomorrow as technicians, skilled workers, professionals, or managers. The educational system must make an effort to match its output to requirements from industry, agriculture, government and trade. In short, the country must attempt to improve the various educational constraints discussed at length in Chapter 6 above. Already, most of the world's countries aware of the industrialization process

---

[3] Rarely does one find a course in international production management in the United States; but courses in international economics, management, marketing, and finance are common. This may reflect the fact that production, in the technical sense at least, is not that different from these other subjects. See Stefan H. Robock and Lee C. Nehrt, *Education in International Business* (Bloomington: Graduate School of Business, Indiana University, 1964), pp. 165–175.

[4] Frederick Harbison and Charles A. Myers, *Education, Manpower, and Economic Growth* (New York: McGraw-Hill Book Company, 1964), 229 pp.

are rapidly moving in this direction. Developed countries with match problems are opening new technical institutes and business schools,[5] while less developed countries are endeavoring to develop primary and secondary schools along the patterns found most effective in more developed countries. It is already true that in some disciplines, such as mathematics, the natural sciences, medicine, and even psychology, a keen student can get in any one of a dozen countries an education which will be equally acceptable in any other. The same could not be said for economics or business or public administration, but already the trend toward convergence is visible. In these fields, substantial amounts of value judgment, resulting from hypotheses untested in the field, lead to distortions between countries with different political ideologies. Even here, however, the Soviet Union is now interested in a Harvard-like business school; Leontieff's input-output analysis is used by ministers of economy all over the world;[6] and in the United States the growing number of publicly owned and operated firms in the areas of public utilities and urban transportation has led to demands for public administrators with a business orientation.

The trend is clear in education. The constraint scores for many countries will tend to move closer together, as the less developed countries try to achieve what already has been achieved in more developed nations. While various local traditions may linger for many years, the parts of education which deal with the natural sciences, most professional training, and the parts of the social sciences which can be taught in a systematic, scientifically oriented manner, will tend increasingly to converge in nations all over the world.

## SOCIOLOGICAL-CULTURAL CONVERGENCE

Our analysis of the sociological environmental constraints has focused on the parts of sociology which bear directly on the efficient operation of the productive enterprise. Thus, the view of managers is relevant, but not necessarily the view toward people generally; class mobility is relevant if this structure cuts off potentially able business managers; and so on. It seems clear that a society in which widely held views toward wealth, management, and achievement are such as to inhibit good management will have to change in the direction of providing a more effective sociological environment in which productive firms can work. Failure to make changes of this sort can lead to inefficiencies which cannot be tolerated if the society really wants to develop into an efficient modern state.

---

[5] See "Business Back to School." *The Economist*, Vol. CCXII, No. 6323, October 3 1964, pp. 501–502, for one British example.

[6] See C. E. Ferguson and Juanita Kreps, *Principles of Economics* (New York: Holt, Rinehart & Winston, Inc., 1962), pp. 158–170, for a descritpion of this analysis. Its applicability to all types of economic systems is clear.

The United States and the northern European nations created the proper climate for economic achievement through use of the Protestant ethic[7]—and modern Soviet propaganda directed to its own workers and managers sounds suspiciously like nineteenth century English and American church sermons on these subjects, devoid, of course, of the religious content. The necessary exhortations to work hard, try to achieve much, respect one's superiors, and save one's money sound the same, however, in Japan, the Communist countries, and the Western developed nations, in spite of the local cultural mystique which surrounds this sort of educational propaganda.

Of particular importance here is the need to have a proper view of scientific method. Unless enough persons in the culture appreciate the need for predictive methodology, the economic growth of the country will be aborted at a very early stage. There is no substitute for this attitude, which of course interlocks with virtually every one of the other external constraints.[8]

In the sociological sector, the usual tendency is to emphasize differences, not similarities; and it seems quite clear that many types of cultural differences will remain for a long time to come. As long as these do not directly interfere with the managerial effectiveness in the country, they really do not matter. What is important is whether a country has deeply held sociological attitudes which, directly or indirectly, affect managerial effectiveness adversely. It is surprising how clearly leaders in such diverse countries as Japan, the Soviet Union, Red China, the United States, and West Germany have sensed this point and made efforts to create the proper sociological attitudes for effective management. Other nations will do likewise as the necessity for change in this sector becomes clear.

## LEGAL CONVERGENCE

There is no particular reason why countries will converge directly in their legal systems, since only the part of law pertaining directly to the effective management of productive enterprises is relevant here. A given country may continue to have a legal system based on civil law, English common law, or religious tradition, but the critical result must be to raise the relevant legal constraints which determine the effectiveness of manage-

---

[7] Kemper Fullerton, "Calvinism and Capitalism: and Explanation of the Weber Thesis," reprinted in *Protestantism and Capitalism* (Boston: D. C. Heath & Company, 1959), p. 11.

[8] It might be noted that the Western world almost won the cold war without even struggling on this point. The Soviets seemed about to impart to pure science a Marxian mystique during the Lysenko controversy in genetics. If science had had to conform to such dogma, the inevitable result would have been eventual deterioration of all Soviet science, and the West would only have had to wait for eventual total victory in the present ideological struggle. Unfortunately, Lysenko was overruled, and Soviet science remains on a logical course.

ment. Critical here is the need to create an atmosphere of stability, certainty, and reasonable flexibility to adjust to rapidly changing industrial conditions. While the legal ways of achieving these goals are diverse, the end result must be the same, and countries have tended to converge in much of their law dealing directly or indirectly with productive enterprises.

Legal systems need not converge in philosophical or ethical terms, but if law or legal systems do interfere directly with the management process they will tend to change over time. No country can afford, for any legal reason, to be inhibited in this manner. Given the rich diversity of legal systems and legal philosophies, total convergence will probably never occur; but the ultimate results of good law, whatever its base, will tend increasingly to be the same, and the constraint scores in most countries in this sector will steadily move closer together.

Political systems can range from pure democracies to one party dictatorships to monolithic totalitarian states; but any system which improves the constraints is workable. The most important political necessities are stability and flexibility, in terms of allowing productive enterprises to operate with maximum effectiveness. Almost equally bad are the unstable states presently common in many less developed areas and the monolithic, unyielding dictatorships found at times in various parts of the world. The former tend to create an atmosphere of political uncertainty, which leads to extensive productive inefficiency, while the latter tend to be too inflexible to adjust to the requirements of modern industrial production, with its frequent dynamic changes. Totalitarian states also have a depressing tendency to suppress for political reasons the kinds of scientific knowledge which is badly needed in modern economies. They also often fail to educate their populations properly, since knowledge is dangerous in such a state. The usual result is less productive efficiency.

One point worth emphasizing is that more modern and developed countries, with highly trained populations engaged in complex tasks which are virtually impossible to police, are more likely to have representative democracies than primitive states where one illiterate workman is a perfectly good substitute for the next, and where such workers are always in plentiful supply. The kind of dictatorship which Stalin operated in Russia in the past is probably impossible to restore for this reason.

## ECONOMIC CONVERGENCE

Economic constraints present the most diffuse pattern in the world today, together with relevant law dealing with such critical factors as property rights. Marxism seems incompatible with capitalism, and many countries are found in both economic camps; however, even here some convergence is noticeable. Capitalist countries have moved steadily toward the welfare state, with the rich being taxed to provide benefits for the poor.

Dismaying cyclical fluctuations in capitalist economies, once regarded as certain as death and taxes, have been modified tremendously through the proper application of Keynsian macroeconomics. Few capitalist states now hesitate to nationalize key economic sectors, such as public utilities, if this is seen to be in the public interest. On the Marxist side, there is growing interest in the use of the profit motive and the price system as an allocation tool, since classical Marxism, when applied in a complex, developed economy producing literally millions of separate goods and services, has no meaningful answer to questions of allocation of resources. All types of countries can suffer (and have suffered) from price inflation, and the corrective tools in any economist's kit are the same. Factor endowments and market size cannot be changed quickly; but countries in the same general position in these cases, regardless of ideology, tend to operate in roughly the same way. All kinds of countries attempt to build up the same general social overhead capital structures, differing only in details as to the precise types of technologies used. Capital markets still are far from converging, however, in large part because the kind of capital markets a country has will be closely connected to its concept of property rights. Central banking also differs sharply between the Marxist and capitalist countries, in part for the same reason.

Increasingly there is a trend to use whatever seems to work empirically in a given country. It is unlikely that we shall see again in the West the kind of mass unemployment or depression of the 1939's, caused by the failure of leaders even to consider alternative courses of action, nor shall we see advanced Communist countries suffer their equivalent of depression (actually the increasing production of useless and unneeded output) because leaders must follow the Marxist dogma. Economic convergence may be closer than we realize, if we search for it.

The nations of 1984 or 2000 may look much more alike than one would expect today, as a result of this need to develop a society in which managerial effectiveness is optimized. Presently poor countries are becoming increasingly aware of their needs, in terms of improving the external constraints. Marxist countries are experimenting to determine how improvements can be made without destroying the basic dogma. Capitalist states seem willing to take the necessary steps to alter their systems in the direction of improving their constraint structures. All may end in the same position.

## INTERNATIONAL CONSTRAINT CONVERGENCE

In regard to the international constraints, it is likely that more regional cooperation will emerge before major breakthroughs occur on a world basis. Already the several customs unions—such as the EFTA, COMECOM, the EEC, the Latin American Common Market, the Central American Common Market, and the Arab Common Market—are struggling with the problems of integrating economic systems along regional lines. The general effect of these groups, if successful, will be to present a relatively uniform set of international external constraints for the member countries to the outside world.[9] Already this has begun to happen on a major scale in the EEC, in spite of many difficult integrative problems. Most of the other unions are in their formative stages, as bickering individual states appear unwilling to yield many of their nationalistic privileges; but the remarkable success of the EEC in raising growth rates, improving economic performance, and allowing all members to share in the gains has acted as a powerful example for others to follow, if they can. Twenty more years may see more moves in this direction, together with some expansion of existing trade groups and possible merger of several.

## CONCLUSION

The general shift towards convergence of the various external constraints in countries all over the world is a part of the same general trend toward bigger productive units spanning larger geographic areas, cutting across time honored national boundaries which steadily tend to become more tenuous and obsolescent. Our grandfathers' horizon was the county line or the next village—our grandchildren's may be some distant star. The technological explosion, well explored and recognized, has been partially responsible for the expansion of man's horizons. Less well observed have been the tremendous changes in administration and management of these technological possibilities.

We began this book by observing differences in management between nations; we can conclude, perhaps, by speculating on potential similarities. As the general similarity of men everywhere is recognized, and as managerial and technological necessity presses all types of cultures toward a common road, nations everywhere become more similar. Not all countries will arrive at the end of the trip at the same time, and a few may never really get started; but those who make the journey may, to their own surprise, discover that the road of others was not so different after all. Studies in comparative management at that time will be largely obsolete, a victim of its own success. Instead of differences, we shall find similarities, because the logic of technology and management will lead all to the same general position.

This conclusion is far from final. Far more remains to be done than has been done to date. Perhaps, in some distant future time, we shall all be better organized; but in the meantime, our problem is to grope for more efficient methods of reaching this goal.

---

[9] See Morgan Guarantee Trust Company, *Market Europe* (New York, 1961), pp. 1–72, for a discussion of how the EEC and EFTA are shifting international constraints in this way for countries in these organizations.

# Chapter 16

# Conclusion

The main purpose of this book has been to present a method of analyzing complex managerial and efficiency problems. We began by asking the question: why are some economies and firms apparently much less efficient than others? This question led to consideration of the management of productive enterprise as the key link in the productive (and hence efficiency) process. This in turn led to detailed considerations of both what the major elements of the managerial process are and what environmental constraints directly affect the performance of these elements by firm managers. The complex interrelationships of the elements themselves, of the elements with the external constraints, of the external constraints with one another, and of the managers and their effectiveness with the external constraints were explored.

In effect, this volume has set up a hypothesis. We have found this working hypothesis most useful as a question asking device. Following the reasoning that if the proper question can be asked, the answer can probably be found, we have discovered that this approach does yield a set of relevant questions to a variety of business and economic problems; but verification of this hypothesis will require much detailed empirical work, which will have to wait for another volume. This work will consist of detailed analysis of a number of countries, using the methodology developed here, to determine whether this comparative management approach does yield valuable insights into the nature of business operations and into growth problems in diverse economies.

The work involved in putting this book together demonstrated one major fact—business and industry, when considered as a part of the more complex productive society, is extremely complicated. It is not surprising that relatively little has been done in research in comparative management, given the inherent complexity of the subject matter; nor is it surprising that all societies to date have performed, in varying degrees, rather inefficiently. The tremendous number of interrelationships between the internal firm and the external environment demonstrates the difficulty of reaching quick and easy answers to any growth or firm productivity problem.

Existing theories of the firm, as well as those connected with environ-mental problems, such as economic growth, have tended to be quite simple in the past. One must begin somewhere, and rather remarkable insights into the nature of firm and environmental problems have been made with somewhat meager kits of tools. Theory usually starts with a very limited concept, usually of a two variable nature. One hypothesizes that event A depends on factor B, and proceeds to demonstrate how this relationship can lead to further insights into the problem under consideration. Typically this type of analysis does turn out to be too simple for any kind of complicated social science question, and additional relationships and variables are intro-duced, usually in a nonmathematical fashion. Thus, event A is hypothe-sized to depend on events B, C, D, and E. Precise formulation is avoided, since data are hard to get and good quantifiable equations are even harder to develop. As analysis and discussion continue, even more variables are introduced, and the event considered is seen to be extremely complicated—particularly if it is some key factor such as economic growth. Writers, both theoretical and empirical, add bits and pieces to the original problem, not-ing other factors which have proved important in given situations. Even-tually, the entire problem may be set up formally as a multivariable, inter-dependent problem which is susceptible to detailed, systematic analysis. If the new theory is useful, it will prove predictive, in the sense that knowl-edge of the key variables will allow prediction of the desired event.

In this work, we have tried to enumerate systematically the relevant variables in the problem. We have been enormously aided by many earlier students of both economic growth and management problems, who have set out in various ways the elements of the total model. Simply to list what appears to be significantly relevant and to explain why it is relevant has taken one book; it remains for others to quantify the total system, develop the necessary precise mathematical relationships, eliminate what proves to be of secondary importance, and to determine whether the system really is valid.

If this schema does prove useful, it will be in two different ways. *The first is as a tool for individual firms.* Every productive enterprise has internal problems of managerial effectiveness and firm efficiency in working toward its goals. If the firm becomes aware of the external constraints which directly affect its internal performance, it is in a better position to lessen the effect of those constraints which can be partially overcome. Thus, if educa-tional constraints indicate that obtaining well trained men and managers will be a problem, the firm can begin to plan training programs, special scholarships for promising men, or whatever other remedies it may be in the firm's power to accomplish. While a firm can do little about political stability, it can recognize how this operates to influence internal firm actions and can take steps to minimize the impact. This type of analysis may help firm management in doing a better job, since it is clear that much of the firm management's effectiveness does depend on its environment, and awareness of the environment can be very helpful.

Another micromanagerial use of this schema is in evaluating local constraints in a foreign country in which the firm operates or is contemplating operations. If the firm's internal effectiveness depends on the external environment, the firm can evaluate an alien environment in terms of how it affects this company in this country. Unlike many locally oriented firms, an international firm may be able to overcome local environmental constraints through importing needed factors, such as skilled technicians or managers, or by performing difficult tasks abroad. If local money markets are badly organized, for example, money can be raised at home. Many types of internal firm problems can be minimized if total awareness of the external constraint impact on the firm is achieved.

A final micromanagerial use of this schema is for an international firm to recognize the international environmental factors relevant to its operations in given countries. As with the local internal factors, clear awareness of the international constraint effects can avoid serious problems by allowing the firm to adjust in advance to the type of problems it will face.

*The second major potential use of the material stems from its possibilities as a macromanagerial planning tool.* Our argument has been that if a country is interested in economic growth, it must necessarily begin with the productive enterprises which generate this wealth. If they can be made more efficient, the society can become more productive as well; but unlike the single firm in a given country, the policy makers in that country *can* change external constraints. If education is a problem, resources can be diverted to improving this sector and hence the relevant educational constraints. If laws are defective, new laws can be passed. If the economic constraints yield poor productive results, they can usually be changed. The total constraint matrix, if accurately evaluated, indicates how important the various changeable environmental factors in a country are to encouraging economic growth. It is increasingly realized that economic development and growth is a very complicated process which cannot be explained by a few incantations about some economic variables (or, for that matter, political, legal, educational, or sociological variables). It is hoped that the schema presented here is complex enough to explain at least what is important in growth problems. What has not yet been explained is exactly how each constraint can be shifted in the direction of maximum beneficial change. This problem also awaits further research. The analysis to date may be good for directing one to ask the proper questions, but not for answering them in any precise way.

The potential uses described above have already been tried by us in a tentative manner. The analysis does seem to offer a method of attacking quite involved problems of firms and countries, although to date the question has been one of working out the problems rather than of getting exact solutions. A complete, detailed analysis of the total local environmental-international environmental-business element complex would take years to accomplish. To date, more is promised than produced.

The world seems to becoming increasingly organized. In every kind of country, with every conceivable kind of economic doctrine, sociological system, and political organization, the trend appears to be one of increasing bureaucratization of life. In the long run, we shall all be organized, since organization in the sense discussed in this book is the only way known to increase incomes and wealth per capita. In a real sense, there is no meaningful alternative choice. Men practice death control, through the organization of medicine and public health; and they face population explosions. The rather sloppy organizations of economic life and productive firm activity known historically cannot serve to support, even at subsistence levels, the billions of humans now occupying this planet—to say nothing of the increasing billions yet to come. To return to easier, earlier ways of production would involve giving up parts of the modern technology and society to an extent that no man can bring himself to advocate. We know of no one who really supports, for example, the reduction of world population by several billions, in order that earlier ways of organization and management can be meaningfully applied.

Not everyone sees in this increasing organization of human life a better future. Most artists and writers appear to view this development with horror, seeing it in the total degradation of man by man. Productive efficiency becomes, for the common man, a sort of maniac production line of the type portrayed in Chaplin's *Modern Times*, where stultified workers labor in unending monotony to produce more trash for other stunted, soulless men to consume mechanically without enjoyment or fulfilment. Increasing government participation in policy making becomes a Kafka-esque nightmare, where faceless bureaucrats impersonally manipulate the millions without meaning or reason. The more modern and progressive a society is, the more gloomy its poets, writers, and artists seemingly become. Newly awakened countries worship tractors rather unabashedly, as innumerable hack Russian writers have demonstrated; but artists in the more advanced U.S.A. are prophets of gloom, doom, and despair. For them, all is lost in a nightmare of mechanistic horror, where no man can be free.

Perhaps few persons who view the world this way will ever read this book, and certainly none will ever get this far; but we still wish to say that it is our basic value judgment that this particular view of the world is erroneous. At no time in man's long history has there been enough real output of goods and services for all men to be able to reach their full potential as men. Certainly even today, when we are further along this particular economic road than at any time in the past, this lack of production stunts the growth potential of two-thirds of the world's population at least. This book has been about organization and management, and how to get organized more efficiently so that *more* can be produced. If this problem can be solved, perhaps at some distant future time men can have the economic freedom to be men. Art, music, literature, reflective thought—these more valuable things in life have for millennia been the almost exclusive possessions of the elite, simply because no society could afford to do more. Some day, we all may be able to move beyond the material to something infinitely more desirable—but before this can be accomplished, more mundane problems have to be solved. We hope that this has been one way to approach this problem efficiently.

# A Day in the Life of an American Manager of a Saudi Business Enterprise

The incidents to be presented are taken from the actual experiences of one of the authors who served as general manager of a Saudi owned trucking firm in Saudi Arabia during the period 1959–61. The enterprise also engages in various small scale manufacturing and marketing operations.

It may be interesting to note that during the 1959–61 period, productivity rose sharply and enterprise costs dropped from about eighteen cents per ton kilometer to nine cents. Prior to 1959 the firm was run by a Saudi business or industrial manager. The major reason for this sharp decline in costs was the American general manager's greater awareness of the rational performance of internal firm and management functions, as well as his keen appreciation of how such rational management was tied (through the constraint-behavior relationships per Table 4–1) to the nearly unique environment in which the firm operated. This case indicates how severe educational and sociological constraints over managerial effectiveness and firm efficiency can be substantially overcome in an underdeveloped country by merely changing the top operating manager. Compared to the previous general manager, the American replacement was extremely well educated in fields directly related to business management and transportation, and he also had previous business experience in a number of progressive American firms. Moreover, in terms of managerial effectiveness, the American probably rated substantially higher than the previous Saudi manager on a number of sociological factors including view of scientific method, risk taking, change, wealth, and possibly achievement.

Let us now get a glimpse of a (harassed) day in the life of a manager of a Saudi business firm, as he recorded it. Footnotes are keyed to Table 2–1, and Table 3–1. The external constraints relevant in these incidents are far from inclusive, and no attempt has been made to consider all of the elements of the management process. Also no attempt is made to determine the relative impact of different constraints acting on a given element of the management process.

7:30 A.M.: I looked over the proposal drawn up by the maintenance supervisor and myself for the proposed production of a new line of plumbing fixtures. The problem was not primarily production, since available machine tools, labor, and sand casting facilities were on hand. Rather, marketing turned out to be the key issue. The present government's fiscal policy seemingly led to rapid shifts in demand in the building sector, and quite a few merchants who had imported fixtures were often stuck with large inventories in the slumps. I couldn't be sure that the present building boom would last—the balance of payments appeared shaky, and the rapid cutbacks of government expenditure might lead to disaster in this investment. Finance was another problem, as the money available would come from one of the local banks, which was traditionally suspicious of such manufacturing enterprises. Our firm was relatively strong, but there was no other source of external funds available.

Getting raw materials would be a problem, too—we could use scrap metal for most of the production, but any key small parts would have to be imported. Only the fuel was available easily in the area, and even this would prove expensive. Ten kilometers away, natural gas was flared for lack of distribution facilities. If only a small pipeline led to our city . . .

The market for such products was also too small to offer a good risk. Production runs would have to be short, and cost high as a result. Exports, given the impossible roads (or total lack of them) out of the area, plus the often congested port facilities and relatively high shipping costs out of Arabia, were out of the question.

We could gain a bit by the tariff protection offered almost all manufactured goods, which ranged around 30 percent. This duty was not for protection but for revenue, but it might just be possible, given high tariffs and high shipping costs, to compete on price with imports.

I pended this proposal for a while. The risks were too great, given the expected returns, to allow for investment in this sort of dubious activity. Also relevant to this decision was the rather negative attitude toward change among many of the enterprise employees. They tended to resist changes in operations, because they found it psychologically and culturally difficult to adjust to changes or to comprehend the reasons for them. Given the low level of education and literacy among enterprise personnel, it was usually necessary to spend considerable time on training direction and control in order to implement successfully even relatively minor changes in operations.[1]

---

[1] Product line ($B_{6.1}$) depends on foreign policy ($C_{3.3}$), fiscal policy ($C_{4.3}$), economic stability ($C_{4.5}$), factor endowment ($C_{4.6}$), market size ($C_{4.7}$), and organization of Capital

8:10:   I went over our new purchases for inventory with our warehouse supervisor. We saw that our inventories were already quite high; but the fact that we were over three months from key supplies of tires, batteries, ignition parts—in fact, any manufactured item—meant that we had to maintain stocks far above levels considered normal in the United States. We also suffered from errors made in the past—what can one do with forty-seven left front fenders for 1946 Chevrolets, valued at $57.50 each? Our historical method of ordering was to get ten of everything, and our order clerk's view of what might happen in the future consisted of a prayer and a long order blank. Parts shortages always resulted in much confusion and down time; and clerks, not willing to take the risk of being responsible for anything, tended to overorder everything.

Since our business fluctuated rather wildly because the local economy gyrated frequently, it was quite difficult to predict parts usage. It didn't help us to have to pay 8 percent interest on borrowed funds for excess inventories, but this was the best rate we could get from the local bank on our overdrafts. Still, carrying our own heavy inventories was better than paying the prices asked by local merchants for parts. They suffered from their own purchasing errors similar to ours, and someone had to pay the cost. The erratic nature of demand in this complex market meant a lot of waste.

We were trying to get more precise predictive work in our orders, but our lack of good parts men able to analyze usage rates for several thousand items made this extremely difficult. We were working on closer control of the key parts in most intensive use, and we finally agreed on the next order.[2]

9:05:   I spent some time with the comptroller trying to figure out how to get our overdraft down. I would have liked to utilize somewhat different credit sources, but none were available in the country. Our local banks were mainly foreign owned, mercantile oriented firms. Other capital markets simply didn't exist, although a few of the bigger local companies were able to get some credit from foreign banks in Beirut or New York. We didn't get very far with this problem.[3]

9:45:   The local Saudi Labor Office representative called to chide me for not hiring more Saudis to replace our skilled foreigners, who came mainly from the more developed Arab countries. I argued, as usual, that if he could send me some literate boys, we would start to train them as mechanics. He argued that mechanics did not have to be literate, so we went down to the shop again. I tried to explain to him that the boy

---

markets ($C_{4.8}$).

Ease or difficulty of introducing changes and innovations in enterprise operations ($B_{1.12}$) depends on literacy level ($C_{1.1}$), educational match with requirements ($C_{1.6}$), view of achievement ($C_{2.4}$), view of scientific method ($C_{2.7}$), view of change ($C_{2.9}$).

[2] Inventory levels ($B_{7.4}$) depends on view of scientific method ($C_{2.7}$), view of risk taking ($C_{2.8}$), foreign policy ($C_{3.3}$), economic stability ($C_{4.4}$), organization of capital markets ($C_{4.5}$), and social overhead capital ($C_{4.8}$).

[3] Types of financing ($B_{9.1}$) depend on organization of capital markets ($C_{4.5}$).

operating the crankshaft grinder had a few years of high school education and a couple of years of training, and even then he was not especially good. He stated that it was obvious that the man did not have to read—after all, he just stood there and watched the machine. I called in one of the Saudi helpers, who was illiterate, and asked him to mike the crankshaft—it was pathetic to see his confusion. He noted that he had a few boys with classical Arabic educations—but they would not work in the shop, since this was dirty, degrading labor. They wanted jobs as clerks or legal representatives. Since my legal boys were Saudis, I asked whether they could type—in English or Arabic. They could not and would not. One of the boys might be persuaded to learn enough English to fill out reports (we used English extensively in our work because much of it was done for the oil company). I promised to talk to him.

We went over to the grease rack, where our illiterate Saudi greaseman was puzzling over an oil filter level. He was working on one of our new pickup trucks, and he was not sure how much to put in. He finally slopped some oil in, using about half as much as required. This meant that if the engine was left alone, the odds were good that it would burn out its bearings in a week or so, as sand was sucked through the filter to the cylinders. I called over the maintenance supervisor, who found the instruction manual (in English). He called his clerk, and they puzzled over the instructions. They both left without checking the greaseman, who started to move the truck to the ready line. We called him back and got the oil level up to par—only to find that he had used the wrong kind of oil. Why not? He could not read the labels. The boys started to drain off the oil and replace it as we wandered off.

The labor representative (who was an Egyptian—the Saudis had no qualified man for the post) then started again on the percentage of Saudis we had to have. I again asked for some literate boys, and we went around for a while. Finally I promised to talk to some fellows who were supposed to be good mechanics. He had already sent us a dozen of these boys, and he and I both knew what would happen; but it was all part of the game. Since none of them could read, they all automatically flunked our quick mechanics test—which consisted of asking the boy to check the out of round on a cylinder of a dismantled engine. None of them had ever heard of an out of round engine, let alone learned how to use inside micrometers.[4]

12:15 P.M.: I had lunch with my operations superintendent. We tried to figure out what was bothering the Saudi drivers. Unions were illegal in Arabia, so there was no formal grievance mechanism for complaints being transmitted to the top. We knew that they were disturbed, but so far

---

[4] Ease or difficulty of obtaining personnel with desired skills and abilities ($B_{4.10}$) and methods used in recruiting personnel ($B_{4.1}$) depend on literacy level ($C_{1.1}$), specialized vocational and technical training and secondary education ($C_{1.2}$), attitude toward education ($C_{1.5}$), educational match ($C_{1.6}$), view of scientific method ($C_{2.7}$), relevant legal rules ($C_{3.1}$), and flexibility of law and legal changes ($C_{3.6}$).

we had not figured out what the trouble was. All of them were illiterate, and they could not even write us a petition. One of the dispatchers joined us later, and he suggested that the trouble might be the interpretation of the driver bonus system. We had changed it a month or so earlier, thinking that it might improve incentive. The boys apparently thought that it did not, and they were upset. They showed their anger by a mild slowdown on run times. The dispatcher had heard this from the shop clerk, who had heard it from our greaseman, who got it from his cousin, who was an uncle of one of our drivers. When I asked our dispatcher why he did not just ask his drivers, who after all worked for him, he replied that it would be undignified to beg his men for information. He was a Syrian, too—whatever this implied. We kicked it around some more and decided to change the system a bit to see if we could ease the problem.[5]

1:45:    I went back to the comptroller's office to work on our three year cash flow projection. As far as I knew, we were the only firm in the country which bothered with this sort of financial planning; and I'm not sure that we should have bothered. The uncertainties of both where the funds were coming from and where they were likely to go were so great as to defy analysis over this period of time. My comptroller was sure that it was a waste of time, but I was working to make him see the light. Our one month forecasts were pretty accurate now, after a year of experimentation; and we even hit our quarterly forecasts within 20 percent—but three years or even one year . . .[6]

3:00:    We held a meeting of all the supervisors to consider the purchase of three heavy trucks. These Kenworths cost around $40,000 each delivered. Their earning power was tremendous when they were working, but when they were idle it was horrible. They had a seven year life. My operations superintendent felt that we should get them right away, since he could forecast perhaps six months of steady work for them. I asked him about the other six and a half years, and he replied that God would provide. The comptroller, who already was worried about our cash position, counseled prudence, while my maintenance supervisor wanted to know how we were going to cover the new trucks with key spare parts. He had a point—the past year we had a new truck down for four months within a few weeks because some minor thing broke—it was our driver's fault, not the manufacturer's. This was little consolation, since the truck was earning $500 per day,

---

[5] Nature, extent, and uses of informal organization ($B_{3.10}$), communication structure and techniques ($B_{5.5}$), and degree and extent to which communication is ineffective among personnel ($B_{5.6}$) depend on literacy level ($C_{1.1}$), view of industrial managers and management ($C_{2.1}$), view of authority and subordinates ($C_{2.2}$), and relevant legal rules ($C_{3.1}$).

[6] Time horizon of plans ($B_{1.3}$) depends on view of scientific method ($C_{2.7}$), view of risk taking ($C_{2.8}$), and economic stability ($C_{4.4}$).

Types of plans utilized ($B_{1.2}$) depend on higher education ($C_{1.3}$), special management development programs ($C_{1.4}$), view of achievement ($C_{2.4}$), view of scientific method ($C_{2.7}$), and view of risk taking ($C_{2.8}$).

and business was heavy at that time. Our warehouse supervisor noted that he could not guarantee anything, since he was not sure that this new model would be the same as the old, or that he could predict parts use accurately.

We finally decided to postpone the purchase for three months and review the question again, not that this mattered—it was strictly a coin tossing decision out here.[7]

4:15: I worked with our maintenance and operations superintendents on the control system for reporting and correcting road breakdowns. Our diesel engines were giving us a lot of starting troubles on the road, but we had no records on why this was so. Feedback of difficulties was very hard to maintain, since our drivers were illiterate and could not communicate properly about difficulties. Often our mechanic would drive a hundred miles expecting to find battery trouble, only to discover that the starter motor coils were burned out. He would have to turn around, drive back to get the parts, and return. We were losing much time and money on this problem. We worked out a tentative form, which would be filled in by the dispatcher in the area where the trouble occurred. It was a stopgap measure at best, but there was not much we could do.[8]

5:20: Talked to our straw boss who supervised the loading and unloading crews we occasionally used at the port. On some trips, we needed as many as fifty unskilled laborers for this job. The one foreman could not possibly handle that many men, although he was a very aggressive and capable fellow. Just filling out the time slips and getting the men paid on a daily basis took most of his time. He and I both knew that we were not getting as much work as we should out of the men, and he wanted me to get an additional foreman, a Saudi. Most Saudis who could read did not like to work on this type of job; and, given the shortage of literate men, they usually did not have to.[9]

7:30: After dinner I looked at some applications from potential new middle managers. We were going to need a new operations supervisor soon, as our present man was being transferred to Kuwait. All were foreign, mostly from other Arab countries. None of them had the necessary experience, which was common; and few had the desired education. All were middle class or upper class fellows, which probably meant some trouble in

---

[7] Nature, extent, and rate of innovation and risk taking in enterprise operations ($B_{1.11}$) depend on educational match ($C_{1.6}$), view of scientific method ($C_{2.7}$), view of risk taking ($C_{2.8}$), and economic stability ($C_{4.4}$).

[8] Types of control techniques used ($B_{2.2}$), information feedback systems used for control purposes ($B_{2.3}$), and effectiveness of control system ($B_{2.7}$) depend on literacy level ($C_{1.1}$), specialized vocational and technical training and general secondardy education ($C_{2.2}$), educational match ($C_{2.6}$), view of scientific method ($C_{2.7}$), and view of risk taking ($C_{2.8}$).

[9] Spans of control ($B_{3.4}$) depend on literacy level ($C_{1.1}$), specialized vocational and technical training and general secondary education ($C_{1.2}$), educational match ($C_{1.6}$), view of achievement and work ($C_{2.4}$), and relevant legal rules ($C_{3.1}$).

the field as they worked with our men. A few wanted more money than they possibly could be worth, and a few others pointedly noted that they did not want to work in isolated desert areas. Well, we were better off than most local firms. We had placed some ads in the Beirut papers; and I had written a friend at the American University of Beirut, asking for some candidates. We did have some choice. I picked a few of the more likely candidates to write to the following day.[10]

8:15:   I was called out by our maintenance supervisor to settle a fight. Our electrician was a Lebanese Christian, and he had gone out to repair a truck in the evening. The driver and he had words, and this was quite common. The result in this instance was that the driver took after the electrician with a tire iron. Fortunately, cooler heads prevailed, and no one was hurt. There was an awful lot of shouting, though. We tried to calm everybody down, but the religious implications of the fight were obvious. Our electrician considered himself superior to the local driver in every way, and this attitude was resented. I could see trouble coming in days ahead if this feud continued, so we made a date for tomorrow to settle the question in a meeting with the operations supervisor. Such common conflict could probably be ended by letting the electrician go; but it would be extremely difficult, if not impossible, to obtain an adequate replacement locally.[11]

9:40:   I tried to figure out how to communicate with and motivate my supervisors better. Most of them were relatively good men, given existing manpower conditions; but they all lacked formal education and they came from another culture. Our biggest problem was getting them to look at the future—their usual reaction to a crisis was to shrug their shoulders and clean up the mess as best they could in the short run. Until recently, the idea of a budget or any sort of plan was alien to their thinking. The notion that they could influence the future by planning today was quite foreign to them. Of course, with only one exception, none of them had previous training or experience in business or industry. In all cases their formal educational experience was oriented to becoming scholars, religious leaders, teachers or government clerks; and the rough and tumble business world sometimes proved too strong for them to take.

Constant training, recruitment problems, and the need for close supervision and control absorbed most of my efforts and energies; and this left relatively little time for planning ahead. It was still extremely risky to delegate much authority to my supervisors except in cases where relatively routine activities and problems were entailed. Fortunately the men all seemed to respect me, as they tend to respect all superior authoritarian

---

[10] Methods used in recruiting personnel ($B_{4.1}$), criteria used in selecting personnel ($B_{4.2}$), and ease or difficulty of obtaining personnel with desired skills and abilities ($B_{4.10}$) depend on all educational constraints ($C_{1.1}$ . . . $C_{1.6}$), view of managers ($C_{2.1}$), view of achievement and work ($C_{2.4}$), relevant legal rules ($C_{3.1}$), and foreign policy ($C_{3.3}$).

[11] Degree and extent of trust and cooperation or conflict and distrust aamong personnel ($B_{5.9}$) depend on class structure and individual mobility ($C_{2.5}$).

figures, including business managers. Moreover, a number of them seemed quite eager to get ahead and to acquire greater wealth in the process.[12]

10:05:   I went to bed, counting the days until my contract expired. It would be soon!

---

[12] Here the planning, control, staffing, and direction functions are influenced by almost all of the educational and sociological constraints.

# Efficiency Models

## INTRODUCTION

Chapter 5 on efficiency indicated that economists have been interested in economic efficiency models for many years. Beginning with Adam Smith in 1776, numerous economists have attempted to develop ideal systems which would be efficient in the economic sense. This effort has in large part been concentrated among economists in the Western developed countries, where private property, relatively free Competition, and free consumer choice were the usual rules of the game. At worst, such models are inept defenses of the status quo. Apologists for whatever political regime happened to be in power have written tracts claiming that this is the best of all possible worlds and that hence all reforms are meaningless.

At best, however, such efficiency analysis does focus on the question of how a society might become most efficient in economic terms. Welfare economists are concerned with the extent to which the working of the economic system leads to desirable goals. If one accepts the general proposition that most men and all societies are eager to expand the production of useful goods and services as much as possible, then economic efficiency becomes of prime importance. If an efficiency model can be developed to indicate how a society might become more efficient, this would represent a real gain in clarity and analysis of existing systems. If we know what is efficient, we can evaluate the real system in terms of the ideal and, it is hoped, take steps to move the real world closer to true economic efficiency.

Except for this welfare economic efficiency model, there is no other total system efficiency model in existence. Many partial models exist and have been usefully applied to various practical problems. One such model is that of labor productivity in an economic sector or firm. One might study the output per man hour of labor, compare it with other sectors, and reach useful conclusions about the relative efficiency of manpower in the two sectors. This type of model is widely used; yet it measures only output per man hour, not total system efficiency. A firm's labor productivity may be very high, but the total firm may be very inefficient because too much capital is used, given the relative costs of capital and labor. Nor does this kind of model answer the question of whether or not what the men are producing is desired. One can, for example, determine that an airline produces available ton miles on a given route with admirable efficiency relative to other routes and companies; but the planes may fly almost empty because few persons want to travel this route by air at prices asked.

Other efficiency models exist for such things as land use. Here, an investigator may study the efficiency with which land is utilized in a given city or geographic area; but, again, the perfectly efficient use of land may result in inefficient uses of other factors, the production of unneeded outputs, or similar economic distortions.

As noted in Chapter 5, many engineering efficiency models exist. Efficiencies of any input-output system can be calculated precisely if inputs and outputs are stated in (or can be converted to) the same energy units; but the fact that a new gasoline engine is 40 percent efficient, compared to 20 percent for previous models, tells one nothing about whether this improves or retards economic efficiency. Costs of enhanced efficiency may be so great as to make the total system actually less efficient after the engineering efficiency improvements have been made.

These partial efficiency models all have valuable uses, but they do not get at the basic question raised here. How does one know that the society is economically efficient? Until a model can be developed to answer this question, our entire book is useless. To see how welfare economists have answered this question, we now turn to their analyses of this problem.

## THE TOTAL EFFICIENCY MODEL

The first problem here is to define economic efficiency. Most welfare economic analysis deals with a static situation. If we can decide at one moment in time how efficient a system is, it should be possible to determine how to move forward to make it more efficient. One definition of static economic efficiency is a state in which it would be impossible to make any person better off (in the material sense) without making any other person worse off.[1] If it were possible in any economic situation to give any individual more goods and/or services than he now has without taking anything away from anyone else, the situation would be economically efficient.

Goods and services have to be produced, and consideration of how more of these could be given to any person leads immediately to detailed consideration of the production process. As indicated in Figure 5-1, firms are engaged in taking productive resources and converting them to usable goods and services. The definition of economic efficiency above suggests that the productive enterprise could increase its outputs if the society were operating inefficiently. The basic question is how it might do this.

---

[1] Tibor Scitovsky, *Welfare and Competition* (Homewood, Ill.: Richard D. Irwin, Inc., 1951), p. 55.

Another key question is: how does one know what outputs and inputs are, since what is being measured here is variegated inputs and outputs? If we note that Mr. A. loses a shirt, while Mr. B. gains a coat, is the society better off or worse off? If a firm produces now with 100 man hours and ten machine hours per week, how do we know whether it is operating better or worse than a similar firm using fifty man hours and forty machine hours of inputs?

## The Values of Outputs and Inputs

To answer the above questions, it is necessary to obtain a common denominator of value; this is money. All inputs and outputs can be valued in dollars. If shirts are worth $4.00 and coats $10.00, some conclusion to the

### FIGURE A2-1

PRICE-OUTPUT DETERMINATION FOR AN INDUSTRY

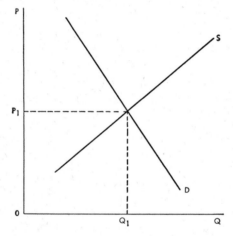

question of who loses or gains the most can be obtained. If machine hours of a certain type are worth $20.00, while man hours are worth $4.00, a firm can calculate its inputs in value, rather than real, terms. Knowing the price of its outputs, it can then maximize money profits by selecting a product mix and an input mix which will accomplish this goal.

Not any price for an output or input will do. The prices must reflect true economic value of the factor or output if prices are to be used in allocating resources to produce various types of goods. This observation leads directly to economic price theory, which is concerned with determining the value of any item which can be priced. The usual simplified explanation of price determination in any market is shown in Figure A2-1. Here, supply and demand are graphically illustrated. Where supply equals demand, a just price is determined.[2]

---

[2] See John F. Due and Robert W. Clower, *Intermediate Economic Analysis* (4th ed.; Homewood, Ill.: Richard D. Irwin, Inc., 1961), pp. 65–217, for a complete exposition of this point.

### The Consumer King

The demand function in Figure A2–1 is derived from the total demand by all consumers for the commodity or service in question, if this is a consumer good. This demand derivation is developed through the use of ordinal utility, or indifference analysis.[3] The key point is the acceptance of the notion that what the consumer wants, he gets, subject to his income or wealth constraints. If one accepts this notion for any given society, he also tacitly accepts income and wealth distribution, no matter what it may be. Millionaires may pamper their pets with canned foods, while paupers starve in the streets, if income distributions, and the demands derived from them, indicate these results.

Here is the basic ethical problem in the efficiency model. At least three basic positions can be held by analysts: first, that the consumer should be king, with given income; second, that he should be king but that incomes should be redistributed in some way, usually by means of progressive taxation; and third, that the consumer doesn't deserve to be king, and someone else should make the decisions about consumption for him. The someone else would presumably be some planning elite who know better than individuals what is good for them.

All three points of view have their rabid adherents. Soviet countries and many countries trying to develop rapidly tend to follow the third alternative, while most modern industrial states, including the United States, tend to follow the second. Relatively few societies are tolerant enough to allow anyone to consume anything he wants, subject only to his purchasing power. In the United States, for example, high taxes are placed on some commodities, such as tobacco and liquors, to discourage consumption; some commodities are banned, such as habit forming drugs; and some income redistribution is accomplished through progressive taxation and transfer payments.

The difficulty is not in deciding what a society does, but in deciding whether or not it is right. Here, economics yields to ethics. If a society decides that some pattern of consumption is proper, an economist can tell leaders how to get it—but he cannot, as an economist, make value judgments about what is right.[4] On this point welfare economics and the question of what is efficient flounders. If one country decides to consume little and invest much for future generations, while another prefers to live for today and let persons not yet born solve their problems for themselves, the production mix of the first society will be radically different than the second, yet no one can determine which mix is more efficient. Both are efficient, given the different goals. This relativity explains our confusion in

---

[3] George Stigler, *The Theory of Price* (New York: The Macmillan Company, 1949), pp. 63–99.

[4] See Paul Samuelson, *Economics* (6th ed.; New York: McGraw-Hill Book Company, 1964), p. 625, for a comment on this key ethical point. See also Stigler, *op. cit.*, pp. 15–16.

Chapter 5 on what is efficiency in an economy. Unless the goals of the society are spelled out and translated into production mixes desired, little can be said about the relative efficiencies of different countries.

### Firm Efficiency

It can be demonstrated that a firm is operating most efficiently when its marginal cost equals its marginal revenue.[5] The situations would appear as in Figure A2–2a or b. In the competitive case (Figure A2–4a), the price is given to the firm by the market. Here it would correspond to price $OP_1$ in Figure A2–1. Price = marginal cost = marginal revenue. In the imperfect market case, the firm has some pricing power, as indicated by the sloping demand function $(DD')$ for the firm. If it raises price, it sells less; if it lowers price, it sells more. It can be shown that in such a case the optimum

FIGURE A2–2

FIRM IN PURE COMPETITION

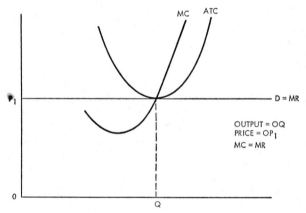

production for the firm, in terms of profit maximization, occurs when marginal cost equals marginal revenue.[6]

The effect of imperfect competition is to restrict output and raise price, as shown in Figure A2–3. It also tends to keep price above marginal cost. The firm able to do this makes an extra profit of $P_1 P_2$ per unit of output, as shown in Figure A2–3. This kind of output restriction can be shown to reduce welfare, as defined above. If firms are able to do this, the result will be that prices will not reflect true value in markets. Being priced too high, goods sold in imperfect markets will not be produced in quantities large enough to satisfy consumer wants (or producers' demands in markets for such goods). Fewer resources will be allocated to production of these goods than efficiency would demand.[7] In effect, a society with this problem could

---

[5] Due and Clower, *op. cit.*, p. 202.

[6] *Ibid.*, pp. 242–245.

[7] Scitovsky, *op. cit.*, pp. 423–443.

improve efficiency simply by making the markets more competitive—which, among other things, becomes an economic rationale for antitrust legislation. This also is one major reason for the problem of subsystem optimization discussed in Chapter 5. Note that from the firm's point of view the output restriction-price increase is desirable, since it makes higher profits this way; but from the society's point of view this behavior results in less total efficiency.[8] Since pure competition yields excellent efficiency results, it is useful to consider the kinds of conditions necessary to yield this type of market structure. The key conditions can be summarized as follows:[9]

1. There must be enough firms and buyers in every market so that no one buyer or seller is able to influence the market.
2. All buyers and sellers must possess enough information about the market and products to make rational decisions about purchases and sales. Relevant information includes complete knowledge of prices, production cost information, knowledge of quality differentials in different grades of output, and similar matters. Firm managers must know enough to be efficient. That is, managers must possess enough business knowledge and data about costs, prices, technology, and so on to organize production within the firm in the most efficient manner.
3. There must be reasonable factor mobility. This in practice would mean easy entry and exit of firms in the market. If losses were incurred, firms would be able to withdraw from a market; if excess profits were made, new firms would find it easy to enter.
4. Outputs must be homogeneous between firms. There can be no product differentiation, since this can lead to design monopolies and violation of Conditions 1 and 3.
5. Buyers and sellers must try to maximize individual advantage, in the economic sense. That is, they must try to gain the highest profits, the lowest buying prices, and the largest incomes they possibly can.

Further conditions of the static model are that technology is constant and that the economy is fully employed, in the sense that all inputs are being used for some purpose.

It is clear that there never was an economy which met all of these conditions, and that there never will be; however, the intention of this model is not to describe reality but to build a conceptual model of an idealized system which can be used for comparative purposes. If the model shows pure efficiency, it is analogous to a perfectly efficient machine in engineering, which also will never exist. Both concepts, however, can be quite useful.

### Input Costs

Firms buy inputs at prices asked in the market. In the perfect efficiency model, such prices also must represent true value. The means of getting

[8] Joe Bain, *Pricing, Distribution, and Employment* (New York: Henry Holt and Company, 1948), pp. 147–157.

[9] Scitovsky, *op. cit.*, pp. 16–19.

relevant prices here is to equate supply and demand for inputs. The price determination diagram would be similar to Figure A2–1 above.

One major difference in demand exists. Demand for consumer goods or intermediate goods used by producers is derived from the wants of these buyers. Demand for inputs of land, labor, capital, and management depends on their value to the firm. It can be demonstrated that the demand function for any input is equivalent to the marginal revenue product (MRP) of the factor.[10] MRP is defined as the value of the last small unit of input used, or

$$MRP = \frac{TP}{Q}$$

where TP = a small change in total product value and $Q$ = a small change in output.

If a firm is faced with a set of input prices and MRPs of different factors, it will tend (if it is trying to operate efficiently) to utilize inputs so that the price of each input relative to other inputs is proportional to the MRP of each factor,[11] or

$$\frac{P_1}{P_2} = \frac{MRP_1}{MRP_2}$$

This simply indicates that a rational firm would tend to use each input to the point where its value to the firm equalled the contribution of the factor to production. Thus, if the last laborer hired cost $2.00 per hour and his contribution to the firm's output value was $2.05, it would be logical to put him on the payroll. If his contribution was $1.95, however, he would be fired. Note that each firm would cut off hirings of labor at some different point, depending upon the contribution the last worker made. Also, under competitive input market conditions, every firm would pay the same wage to the same type of labor. The same logic would apply to all inputs, and similar demand functions could be constructed for each factor used by the firm.

### Perfect Efficiency

This model would have perfect markets for all inputs and all outputs. Thus, consumers would demand various goods and services. If a price was too low relative to demand, the price would be bid up by buyers who could not obtain their desired share. This price increase would appear as an increase in the $D = MR$ line (see Figure A2–4). At price $OP_2$ firms, being rational, would equate marginal costs and revenues, producing $OQ_2$; but this results in profits of CD per unit (Figure A2–4). These excess profits would attract new firms, which would enter the market and expand supply.

---

[10] Due and Clower, *op. cit.*, pp. 295–315.
[11] Scitovsky, pp. 351–356.

As supplies of the commodity increased, the supply curve of the industry (which is the sum of all marginal cost curves of producers) would move to the left, as shown in Figure A2–5. As this curve shifted, the equilibrium price would drop, until all firms were making only normal profits (included in the ATC curve as a necessary cost of doing business). Price would drop back close to $OP_1$, and now more firms would be creating an expanded supply at a price somewhat above the original price.

On the input side, the new entrants would need more labor, land, capital, and management. In a full employment economy, they would have to bid these inputs away from alternative uses. Thus, the price of inputs would rise as demand increased for specific types, and costs would go up

### FIGURE A2-3

#### FIRM IN IMPERFECT COMPETITION

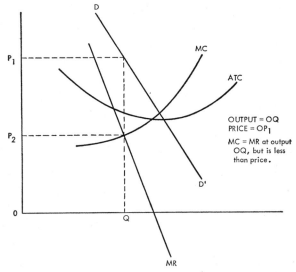

OUTPUT = OQ
PRICE = $OP_1$

MC = MR at output OQ, but is less than price.

slightly; but the effect of this would be to allocate scarce economic resources to exactly the areas where wants were to be filled. If resources were mobile, there is no reason why such shifts could not be constantly taking place as consumers shifted their demands from one commodity to another.

Violation of the competitive conditions noted above leads to misallocation of resources. Suppose that a monopoly, when faced with increased demand, raises price and does not increase output. Here, the profitability of the firm is enhanced, but consumers are less satisfied. Or a minimum wage law may be in effect, which keeps a labor price from falling. If demand for this type of labor falls, the price does not. The result will be unemployment, resulting in less output and less efficiency. This is shown in Figure A2–6. If $OW_1$ were set as the minimum wage, and demand shifted to $D_L'' D_L'''$, wages should fall to $OW_2$. Fewer men would be employed; but the supply curve indicates that fewer men would want to be employed at this lower wage. At price $OW_1$, $OQ_1$ represents the amount of employment desired—which is more than $OQ_2$, the amount demanded by employers. The result is unemployment of amount $Q_1 Q_2$. Given the large number of institutional and legal rules on prices in every economy, this sort of problem is invariably present to some extent.

The basic conditions for total system efficiency can be summarized as follows:

1. All markets must be purely competitive as described above.
2. Price will equal marginal cost for every product or service.
3. Firms in equilibrium will be producing at the lowest possible cost (see Figures A2–2 and A2–4).
4. Each factor price will equal its marginal revenue product.
5. Factor prices will be proportional to respective marginal revenue products.

FIGURE A2–4

ADJUSTMENTS TO EQUILIBRIUM

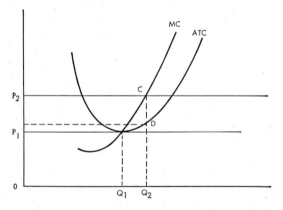

In this static case, the system would be perfectly efficient. It should be emphasized that no society is likely ever to achieve this sort of perfection!

## Socialist Efficiency Models

The preceding model was built on the assumption that the factors of production (capital and labor) were privately owned. Since they were privately owned, their owners, seeking maximum monetary gain, would tend to sell their inputs in sectors offering the highest prices; and this would lead to the maximum efficiencies noted. A democratic socialist state, however, can theoretically get the same results. Consider a situation where all factors except management and labor are owned by the state. Here, the immediate problem is to develop some allocative mechanism to put these collectively owned resources to the most efficient uses. A bureaucracy might attempt this task in some intuitive manner; but, given the millions of allocation decisions to be made even in a small economy each year, there is little likelihood that this would be successful. If the socialist state does hold the general view that consumers should get what they want, how can they build a system which will be most efficient?[12]

The answer lies in the nature of structuring capital and land markets in order to ration these scarce items to most efficient uses. Capital and land are not free; and any attempt to make them so merely results in overuse of the factor, followed by some administrative rationing device. If, however, the socialist state organizes its public firms into smaller units and sets rational prices (interest and rent) for capital and land, it can then instruct firms to maximize profits in exactly the same way that capitalist firms do. Firms, accepting these prices as given, would behave exactly as their free enterprise counterparts, assuming equal business competence. The results would be the same as in a purely competitive economy, *if* the socialist planners could somehow manage to get the right prices for all capital and land. This would not be an easy task, but at least it is conceptually feasible.[13]

The usual difference between capitalist and Marxist states is not as simple as this, however. Their basic ethical propositions about economic goals are different. Most socialist states are quite willing to do allocating for the consumer. Big Brother, in effect, watches the consumers and tells them, through fixed pricing of consumers' commodities, what is good for them. If there are shortages of goods, prices can be raised, with the profits going to the state, to finance (typically) more investment goods.[14] If prices are not raised, there are shortages and queues. Indeed, one dismal sign of any planned economy in the real world is the long lines of buyers outside shops. Few bureaucrats are sufficiently adept at pricing the thousands of consumer goods available to avoid this particular problem. In more developed Marxist states, where basic production problems have been partially solved, more recent phenomena are the enormous inventories of unsalable consumer goods.[15] They are unsalable only at current prices, and if prices were reduced they would move; but price flexibility in this sort of planned economy is difficult to achieve.

Capitalist states, while occasionally directing consumer demand through taxes of various sorts, are usually much more willing to give the consumer his way. This leads immediately to the measurement problems noted in Chapter 5. If two different countries are trying to achieve quite different goals, how can one determine which country is doing better? Failure to realize this has led to error. Americans point out that Russian

---

[12] See George N. Holm, *Economic Systems* (New York: Holt, Rinehart & Winston, Inc., 1960), pp. 159–182, for a discussion of the debate on this question and analysis of underlying issues.

[13] Samuelson, *op. cit.*, pp. 624–629.

[14] Holm, *op. cit.*, pp. 219–266.

[15] B. M. Richman, *Soviet Management: With Significant American Comparisons* (Englewood Cliffs, N.J.: Prentice-Hall, Inc., 1965), pp. 175–181.

consumers have a much lower living standard than Americans, not realizing that consumers' living standards are a quite low priority item in the Russian scale of values; but *any* comparative efforts are faced with similar difficulties, when goal differences are so extreme. The Soviets are in effect building for tomorrow in a major way, and the present consumers are paying the bill.

A more common Marxist technique is to plan the entire economy, beginning with the most aggregate types of decisions, such as what portion of output is to go to consumers, which to investment, which to the military, and so on. The plan then works down to microlevels, eventually giving detailed instructions to every producer for every type of output.

FIGURE A2–5

INDUSTRY

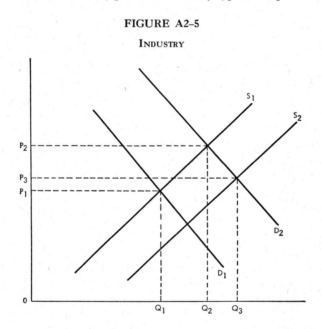

This type of planning presents the planners with the problem of not having enough information about the economy and the firm to select rational and efficient production plans. Whereas in capitalist countries the only instruction to be given to firm managers is to maximize profits, in a Marxist country, complete and detailed knowledge about all phases of demand and production for every firm in the country must be known. The problem of obtaining adequate information tends to become much more difficult in such a system than in a typical capitalist state.

This type of problem is illustrated in Figure A2–7. Here the planners might want to tell the firm to produce the amount $OQ'$ at price $OP_1$. They would also have to know enough about the firm's production function [16] to assign exactly the proper amount and quality of each input so that the firm

---

[16] See Scitovsky, *op. cit.*, pp. 113–121, for a definition and discussion of this function.

could operate on the *ATC* curve shown. Knowing enough detail about any firm to select these proper alternatives is uncommon even for mangers close to the production situation, let alone distant bureaucrats; and a more likely result would be, for example, to tell the firm to produce amount $OQ$ at price $OP_1$. This would be inefficient, since at this level of output marginal cost is $OP_3$, which is greater than marginal revenue. In this case, costs would exceed revenues, and the firm would also have to obtain a subsidy. It would also be operating inefficiently in the economic sense.

Informational and data gathering difficulties in a complex Marxist system must not be underestimated. Soviet writers have estimated that if present trends toward planning and industrial complexity continue, every worker in the Soviet Union will be engaged in planning by 1980.[17] Even

### FIGURE A2-6

#### PRICE FIXING AND EFFICIENCY

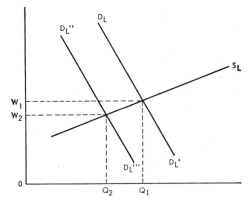

computers cannot help enough—the amount of computer capacity necessary to process the required data is so large as to be almost beyond belief.

A point worth stressing is that *efficiency* is a highly relative term. The bushman who uses stone tools to produce weapons is clearly extraordinarily inefficient when compared to even a badly run modern weapons plant. That is, even a very inefficient (in the economic sense) modern system appears to be quite efficient when compared to historic types of nonmechanical systems. The point is not that a poorly organized, badly run Marxist or capitalist country is hopelessly inefficient—it is that such a country could be substantially *more* efficient if it followed the economic precepts noted above.

The image of the manager as a key figure in firm efficiency emerges strongly in the preceding discussion. Firms do not somehow automatically become efficient. It is firm managers who organize their operations; plan their future activities, collect the necessary information; and set up control

[17] Richman, *op. cit.*, p. 241.

systems to give feedback about deviations, in order that the proper decisions about firm operations can be made. Such men do not necessarily appear automatically in the industrialization process, as some countries have learned to their dismay. Nor do existing managers automatically become drawn to more efficient ways of doing things—such a process results from the development of a group of men who are motivated to achieve still better results within the framework in which they operate. It is possible to define, at least conceptually, what a perfectly efficient manager might be. The fact that such men rarely exist does not negate the efficiency model which can be logically constructed to demostrate what a manager would do, given the necessary tools.

The problems of measurement, uncertainty, knowledge, and goals

## FIGURE A2–7

### Marxist Firm Production

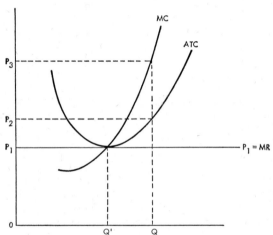

Firm is instructed to produce OQ at price OP₁ -- which is inefficient.

present formidable obstacles to achievement of efficiency in the real world. It is clear that even very advanced countries have moved only a fraction of the way toward adequate levels of efficiency in their productive firms; however, the fact that they have moved at all is suggestive. In 1800, the idea of becoming more efficient was an alien concept, and firms operated largely the way they had operated for millennia; but since the early nineteenth century there has existed an intuitive notion that production could be made more efficient by applying better managerial techniques and technology, and managers do typically try to improve their performance over time. This pace in the advanced countries seems to be accelerating, largely because of the superior type of subordinates (both managerial and technical) who are now available for firm service.

The efficiency model suggested above is one guide to the measurement of economic efficiency. It suggests that if profit maximization is taken as a goal of firms, the most efficient firms will be those which make the largest rate of return on their invested capital. While the model is certainly subject to many practical and theoretical imperfections, it is the only meaningful efficiency model known. Rejection of the model leads to chaos—because without any idea of what the goals of management may be, there is no way to determine how well they are performing their managerial function. It is possible to construct other models using other types of nonquantifiable goals (such as happiness or worker satisfaction) as the target, but such models tend to break down operationally because no one is able to evaluate performance in such a system. The lack of precise desiderata leads to no control at all.

There has never been built a total Marxist efficiency model like the capitalist one discussed above. The Marxist states use the same kinds of partial efficiency models as capitalist countries and firms, but the usual suboptimization problems plague the planners constantly. Avowed Marxists really don't know what they are doing conceptually, although they clearly have a good pragmatic view of goals and methods.

### Problems in Efficiency Models

The obvious point that the efficiency model discussed above fails to reflect reality has led to considerable effort to adjust the conditions of the model to reflect reality more closely. Such problems as capital indivisibilities, resource flexibility, external economies, social costs not reflected in producers' cost functions, and economies of scale have been considered and integrated into the model.[18] The result, however, is about the same. Distortions of these types generally reflect a move away from "perfect" efficiency to something close to it. In most cases, appropriate public policy can be suggested to alleviate most of the problems created by real world deviations from the model. Thus, if firms pollute streams with industrial wastes because no one firm is responsible for the total stream (a case of social costs not being reflected in the firms' cost functions), it is suggested that a tax collectively equal to the extra social cost be levied on producers. If economies of scale lead to monopoly, oligopoly, or imperfect competition, antitrust legislation or public utility type controls can be suggested to require firms to behave as if they were in competition.

These various distortions of the perfect efficiency model served as the basis for the various pragmatic efficiency difficulties explored in detail in Chapter 5. They exist to some extent in every economy. Since the efficiency model necessarily is tied to technical, social, and economic problems in the real world, it can serve only as a guide, not as a realistic appraisal of what is possible.

---

[18] These problems are covered in A. C. Pigou, *The Economics of Welfare* (4th ed.; London: Macmillan and Company, Ltd., 1952), 876 pp. This is one of the major works in welfare economics, and it is required reading for anyone seriously interested in welfare and efficiency problems.

## Dynamics and Efficiency

The model discussed above is a static model, indicating what perfect efficiency would be in a world where there would be no time dimension, and particularly where there would be no technical progress. Many of the external constraints, including all educational, legal-political, and sociological ones, are assumed constant in the model. When a more realistic dynamic model is considered, changes in the external constraints must also be studied. A time dimension has to be added to the model.

Efforts to dynamize the welfare model discussed above have not been very successful, since the assumptions needed are too far removed from reality to make them even remotely useful as a pragmatic tool of analysis.[19] Conceptual problems here become quite difficult; however, the various growth models in economics should be mentioned, because many of them deal with the problem of increasing income generally over time. Some deal with problems of maintaining income, in terms of avoiding depressions in advanced economies.[20] Worth mentioning are the theories of Keynes, Malthus, Marx, Shumpeter, and Harrod and Hansen. Most of these writers (even Marx) accept generally the static pure competition model for their microeconomic base and proceed to analyze the problems of total income growth and/or fluctuation. Since they attack the problem of getting more income per capita over time, they do imply some welfare gains. If per capita income does improve, someone will be better off, although it is not clear in these dynamic macrotheories who would be.

This is the basic difficulty of macrodynamic models. "Invest and grow" might be a simple-minded generalization of most theories, but none of these theories offers any insight into what to invest in. In this sense, they return to the static model discussed above for guides to investment decisions.

The result of adding dynamic change to the model is total confusion. Risk and uncertainty, caused both by technical change and external factors such as war, now have to be included. The notion that everyone is doing rather badly in efficiency terms suggests that something can be done over some future time span to better the situation, which may involve economic, social, and political pressures of some magnitude and may mean trading satisfaction today for more satisfaction tomorrow.

The major difficulty here is that no one knows over what time span efficiency should be optimized. Should a society plan to gain the most in one year, ten, or a thousand? If neighbors are aggressive, will diversion of resources now to military systems result in increased satisfaction for people yet unborn? There is no easy answer to this kind of question, and societies

---

[19] See Bela Belassa, "The Dynamic Efficiency of the Soviet Union," *American Economic Review*, Vol. LIV, No. 3, May, 1964, pp. 490–495, for a discussion of this point.

[20] These growth models are analyzed in Benjamin Higgins, *Economic Development* (New York: W. W. Norton & Company, Inc., 1959), pp. 85–213.

have answered it in a variety of ways. As with the other ethical dimensions of economic efficiency, however, no one can say for sure which solution is optimal.

The fact that societies now differ tremendously in productive efficiency has placed new emphasis on this kind of question. Less developed countries can observe results in western Europe, the United States, or the Soviet Union and see how far they might go if the necessary resources are diverted now to building up assets to be used for future production. There is also a very real reason for wanting to proceed in this direction as rapidly as possible. It is unlikely that a nation can remain viable for very long if it stagnates at some very low level of income per capita. Neighbors are likely to develop and absorb less effective states, which will not have the economic resources to resist aggression.

All modern nations are haunted by the ruins of antiquity. There were mighty states, possibly even efficient states, which, for a variety of reasons, proved in the long run to be unviable. No major culture has lasted much more than a millennium, and possibly the present Western society (which really has been in existence only since about 1750) will also collapse in some massive *Gotterdammerung*. However efficient such a state may have been, even for centuries, it may all prove to be irrelevant in the end. No efficiency model or theory has ever tackled this sort of time dimension successfully—and it is quite likely that none ever will.

## CONCLUSION

The model of economic efficiency discussed above, however inadequate, is the only complete model ever developed in this field. At worst, it represents the fanciful dreams of ivory tower theorists; at best, it can serve as a useful guide for practical decision making in questions of economic action.

Practical men are inclined to scoff at this sort of theorizing; yet without the model, there simply is no way of knowing what to do. One must have guides, however imperfect, of actions which will lead to the most rapid achievement of economic goals. Chapter 5 attempted to move this efficiency model, however imperfectly, into the realm of empirical practicality. The basic argument is that some guide is necessary, however crude. The reader may decide if this effort was even partially successful.

# Index

431

*This book has been set on the Linotype in 10 and 9 point Electra, leaded 2 points. Chapter numbers and titles are in 18 and 24 point Caslon Old Style #337. The size of the type page is 27 by 46½ picas.*